Modern
Latin America

Modern Latin America

SEVENTH EDITION

Thomas E. Skidmore
Professor Emeritus, Brown University

Peter H. Smith
University of California, San Diego

James N. Green
Brown University

New York   Oxford
OXFORD UNIVERSITY PRESS
2010

Oxford University Press, Inc., publishes works that further Oxford University's
objective of excellence in research, scholarship, and education.

Oxford   New York
Auckland   Cape Town   Dar es Salaam   Hong Kong   Karachi
Kuala Lumpur   Madrid   Melbourne   Mexico City   Nairobi
New Delhi   Shanghai   Taipei   Toronto

With offices in
Argentina   Austria   Brazil   Chile   Czech Republic   France   Greece
Guatemala   Hungary   Italy   Japan   Poland   Portugal   Singapore
South Korea   Switzerland   Thailand   Turkey   Ukraine   Vietnam

Published by Oxford University Press, Inc.
198 Madison Avenue, New York, New York 10016

http: //www.oup.com

Oxford is a registered trademark of Oxford University Press

Library of Congress Cataloging-in-Publication Data

Skidmore, Thomas E.
   Modern Latin America/Thomas E. Skidmore, Peter H. Smith,
James N. Green.—7th ed.
      p.   cm.
   Includes bibliographical references and index.
   ISBN 978-0-19-537570-1 (pbk.: acid-free paper)
   1. Latin America—History.   I. Smith, Peter H.   II. Green, James
Naylor, 1951–   III. Title.
   F1413.S55 2010
   980—dc22

                                                    2009039609

Printing number: 9 8 7 6 5 4 3 2

Printed in the United States of America
on acid-free paper

For
David, James, Robert
and
Jonathan, Peter, Sasha, Amanda
and
Sonya

CONTENTS

PREFACE

This seventh edition took much more work than we ever imagined. Early on, we not only decided to bring the contents up-to-date, but also determined to make the book more accessible and teachable. We discussed pedagogical issues, traded notes on classroom experiences, and tried to imagine anew the kind of book that would best meet the needs of colleagues and students.

As our conversations progressed, we realized that this challenge would require wholesale rewriting and restructuring of *Modern Latin America*. Toward this end, we have

- composed four entirely new chapters—on the central Andes (Chapter 6), Venezuela (Chapter 8), economic strategies (Chapter 12), and culture and society (Chapter 14);
- created two additional new chapters by recombining old ones—on Central America and the Caribbean (Chapter 4) and on political transitions in comparative perspective (Chapter 13); and
- developed a website for practical use by students, instructors, and the general reading public.

Throughout the text we have added maps and illustrations, reorganized the presentation, and done everything within our powers to enhance clarity and parsimony of expression. This is a new and different book.

As in the past, Latin America is now going through a period of great uncertainty. Over the last quarter century, the region has dispensed with dictatorship in favor of democracy; it has also embraced far-reaching economic reforms. But poverty and inequality nonetheless persist, and widespread popular protest has emerged—not in the shape of armed uprisings, but in the form of electoral support for opposition candidates and parties. Democracy has thus been doing what it should. And just as economic conditions in Latin America were starting to improve, the global financial crisis of 2008–9 took a terrible toll on countries of the region. What will happen in the future is anyone's guess.

For work on this seventh edition, we are pleased to acknowledge the very capable assistance of Matthew C. Kearney, Caroline Landau, and Tarso Luis Ramos. We thank Michael Shifter and Douglas Cope, professional colleagues whose sage advice rescued us from several unseemly errors. And we wish to recognize the special role of Felicity Skidmore, whose editorial guidance, logistical expertise, and moral encouragement made it possible for us to finish the job.

Lastly, we extend our gratitude and admiration to the peoples of Latin America. This is their story. As foreign scholars, we can only hope to have done it justice.

T. E. S.
P. H. S.
J. N. G.

PART ONE

Questions and Contexts

1

Why Latin America?

"The U.S. will do anything for Latin America, except read about it." So wrote the late James Reston, for many years the legendary dean of U.S. political journalists. Are there reasons why we should try to prove him wrong?

There are several. First, our nation's economic interests are deeply involved in the region. Latin America is one of our major trading partners. It is the site of much U.S. investment and a source for oil and other critical raw materials. An acceleration of growth in key countries—such as Mexico and Brazil—may soon produce significant new powers on the world scene.

We have close political links. Revolutionary upheavals and anti-American movements in Latin America have posed significant challenges for U.S. foreign policy. They have raised serious questions about how best to define, protect, and promote our national interests. U.S. presidents of both political parties have consistently acknowledged the importance of the region. President George H. W. Bush, a Republican, sought a special relationship with Mexico and in 1990 proposed a free trade agreement that would tighten economic bonds between all of Latin America and the United States. Bill Clinton, a Democrat, followed up in 1994 by hosting a hemispheric "Summit of the Americas." George W. Bush, Republican, selected Mexico as the site for his first foreign visit in 2001. And as president-elect, Barack Obama, Democrat, held a private meeting with Mexico's chief executive before taking office in 2009.

There is another consideration here at home. Large sections of our country have become Latinized by the influence of migrants from Mexico, Puerto Rico, Central America, the Caribbean, and even Brazil. This is in addition to the Hispanic descendants of the original Spanish-speaking population of what was once part of Mexico. Migration, both historical and recent, has brought peoples and customs from Latin America to the American Southwest (from Texas to California), Florida, and New York. Many major U.S. cities now have more children from Spanish-speaking families than from any other group. Bilingualism has become a political issue forcing us to rethink the meaning of Spanish-speaking America, both within our borders and beyond.

3

Most U.S. citizens (or "North Americans," as we are commonly called in Latin America) know little about our neighboring societies to the south. Many believe that the United States can impose its will on the region through "big-stick" diplomacy or military might. Others do not even care. Still others entertain obsolete stereotypes about the peoples of the region: the "Latin lover," the "Frito Bandito," the soulful Che Guevara, the Brazilian mulatta carnival queens—these are the images that often first come to mind.

When we move beyond these caricatures, we find Latin America to be a complex region. It is not an easy place to understand. Geographically, it includes the land mass extending from the Rio Grande (between Texas and Mexico) to the southern tip of South America, plus a number of Caribbean islands: a total area two and one-half times the size of the United States. Physical features present sharp differences: from the Andean mountain range, stretching the full length of western South America, to the tropical forest of the Amazon basin, from the arid deserts of northern Mexico to the fertile grasslands of the Argentine pampa.

It is a land of great ethnic and demographic diversity. The people of Latin America contain elements and mixtures of varied racial groups—native Indians,

---

U.S. Stereotypes of Latin America

Some time ago, a prominent agency for public opinion research conducted a nationwide poll in which respondents were given a card with nineteen words on it and asked to indicate which words best described the people of Central and South America. The results were as follows:

Dark-skinned	80%	Imaginative	23%
Quick-tempered	49%	Shrewd	16%
Emotional	47%	Intelligent	15%
Religious	45%	Honest	13%
Backward	44%	Brave	12%
Lazy	41%	Generous	12%
Ignorant	34%	Progressive	11%
Suspicious	32%	Efficient	5%
Friendly	30%	No answer	4%
Dirty	28%	No opinion	0%
Proud	26%		

Since respondents were asked to pick as many descriptive terms as they liked, percentages add to considerably more than 100.

From John J. Johnson, *Latin America in Caricature* (Austin: University of Texas Press, 1980), p. 18.

white Europeans, black Africans, Chinese, Japanese, and immigrants from all over the world. Nations differ importantly in population size (Brazil being nearly five times larger than Argentina, for instance, and more than ten times larger than Chile). By 2007 the total population of Latin America came to more than 550 million, compared with 300 million in the United States.

As an expression of this cultural mosaic, languages abound. Spanish is spoken almost everywhere, one might think—except in Brazil (Portuguese), part of the Andes (Quechua, Aymara, and other indigenous languages), the Caribbean (French, English, and Dutch), Mexico (scattered pockets of indigenous languages), and Guatemala (over twenty Indian languages).

Furthermore, Latin American society displays startling contrasts—between rich and poor, between city and country, between learned and illiterate, between the powerful lord of the hacienda and the deferential peasant, between wealthy entrepreneurs and desperate street urchins. Politically, Latin America includes twenty nations, large and small, whose recent experience ranges from military dictatorship to electoral democracy to a socialist regime.* Economically, Latin America belongs to the "developing" world, beset by historical and contemporary obstacles to rapid economic growth, but here too there is diversity—from the one-crop dependency of tiny Honduras to the industrial promise of dynamic Brazil.

Throughout their modern history Latin Americans have sought, with greater or lesser zeal, to achieve political and economic independence from colonial, imperial, and neo-imperial powers. Thus, it is bitterly ironic that the phrase *Latin America* was popularized by mid-nineteenth-century French, who thought that since their culture, like that of Spanish and Portuguese America, was "Latin" (i.e., Romance language–speaking), France could claim imperial leadership throughout the continent.

CONTRAST AND PARADOX

As these observations suggest, Latin America resists facile categorization. It is a region rich in paradox. This insight yields a number of instructive clues.

First, Latin America is both young and old. Beginning in 1492, its conquest by the Spanish and Portuguese created a totally new social order based on domination, hierarchy, and the intermingling of European, African, and indigenous elements. The European intrusion profoundly and ineradicably altered indigenous communities. Compared with the ancient civilizations of Africa and Asia, these Latin American societies are relatively young. On the other hand, most nations of Latin America obtained political independence—from Spain and Portugal—in the early nineteenth century, more than 100 years before successful anticolonial

---

*This is a conservative count. It does not include Belize, French Guiana, Suriname, Guadeloupe, Martinique, English-speaking islands of the Caribbean, or the commonwealth of Puerto Rico. The official tally of all entities in Latin America and the Caribbean comes to 41.

Map 1 Contemporary Latin America

movements in other developing areas. By the standard of nationhood, therefore, Latin America is relatively old.

Second, Latin America has throughout its history been both tumultuous and stable. The Conquest began a tradition of political violence that has erupted in coups, assassinations, armed movements, military interventions, and (more rarely) social revolutions. Ideological encounters between liberalism, positivism, corporatism, anarchism, socialism, communism, fascism, and religious teachings of every doctrinal hue have sharpened the intensity of struggle. Despite the differing forms of political conflict, old social and economic structures have persisted. Even where modern revolutions have struck, as in Mexico

(1910), Bolivia (1952), and Cuba (1959), many aspects of traditional society survive. While the advent of political democracy in recent years might look like an abrupt departure from the past, underlying continuities nonetheless persist. The pull of history continues to be strong.

Third, Latin America has been both independent and dependent, autonomous and subordinate. The achievement of nationhood by 1830 in all but parts of the Caribbean basin represented an assertion of sovereignty rooted in Enlightenment thought. Yet a new form of penetration by external powers—first Britain and France, then the United States—jeopardized this nationhood. Economic and political weakness vis-à-vis Europe and North America has frequently limited the choices available to Latin American policymakers. Within Latin America, power is ironically ambiguous: it is the supreme commodity, but it has only a limited effect.

Fourth, Latin America is both prosperous and poor. Ever since the Conquest, the region has been described as a fabulous treasure house of natural resources. First came the European lust for silver and gold. Today the urge may be for petroleum, gas, copper, iron ore, coffee, sugar, soybeans, or for expanded trade in general, but the image of endless wealth remains. In startling contrast, there is also the picture of poverty: peasants without tools, workers without jobs, children without food, mothers without hope. An aphorism oft repeated in Latin America summarizes this scene: "Latin America is a beggar atop a mountain of gold."

One can easily think of additional contrasts, but these should illustrate the difficulty—and fascination—in trying to come to grips with such complex and contradictory realities. To understand Latin American history and society requires a flexible, broad-gauge approach, and this is what we offer in this book. We draw on the work of many scholars, presenting our own interpretation, but also acquainting the reader with alternative views.

Interpretations of Latin America

For generations most analysts of modern Latin America stressed the area's political instability, marked frequently by dictatorship. North American and European observers were especially fascinated by three questions: Why dictatorships? Why not democracy? Why so much disorder? In 1930, a prominent American social scientist observed, "The years roll on and there arise the anxieties and disappointments of an ill-equipped people attempting to establish true republican forms of government." A British scholar also noted that "the political history of the republics has been a record of alternating periods of liberty and despotism." Implicitly assuming or explicitly asserting that their style of democracy is superior to all other models of political organization, foreign writers frequently asked what was "wrong" with Latin America. Or with Latin Americans themselves.

What passed for answers was for many years a jumble of racist epithets, psychological simplifications, geographical platitudes, and cultural distortions.

According to such views, Latin America could not achieve democracy because dark-skinned peoples (Indians and blacks) were unsuited for it; because passionate Latin tempers would not stand it; because tropical climates somehow prevented it; or because Roman Catholic doctrines inhibited it.

Each charge had its refutation: dictatorial rule flourished in predominantly white countries, such as Argentina, as well as among mixed-blood societies, such as Mexico; it appeared in temperate climes, such as Chile, not only in the tropics, such as Cuba; it gained support from non-Catholics and nonpracticing Catholics, while many fervent worshippers fought for liberty; and, as shown by authoritarian regimes outside Latin America, such as Hitler's Germany or Stalin's Soviet Union, dictatorship is not restricted to any single temperament. Such explanations did not merely prove to be inadequate. When carried to extremes, they helped justify rapidly increasing U.S. and European penetration—financial, cultural, military—of the "backward" republics to the south.

The scholarly scene improved in the late 1950s and early 1960s, when North American social scientists formulated "modernization theory." As applied to Latin America, this approach held that economic growth would generate the social change that would in turn make possible more "developed" politics. The transition from a rural to an urban society would bring a change in values. People would begin to relate to and participate in the voluntary organizations that authentic democracy requires. Most important, a middle class would emerge—to play both a progressive and moderating role. Latin America and its citizenries were not so inherently "different" from Europe and North America. Instead they were simply "behind."

Modernization adepts thought the historical record showed this process was well under way in Latin America. One optimistic U.S. scholar maintained in the 1950s that the "middle sectors" had "become stabilizers and harmonizers and in the process have learned the dangers of dealing in absolute postulates." Similarly, the author of a late 1970s history textbook saw "Latin American history since independence . . . as modernization growing slowly against the resistance of old institutions and attitudes."

Reality, however, proved harsher. Instead of spreading general prosperity, economic growth in the 1960s and 1970s generally made income distribution more unequal. The gap in living standards between city and countryside grew. The middle strata, relatively privileged, forged a sense of "class consciousness" which, in critical moments of decision, led them to join the ruling classes in opposition to the popular masses. Politics took an authoritarian turn, producing military governments. And in stark contradiction of modernization theory, these patterns emerged in the most developed—and most rapidly developing—countries of the continent. What had gone wrong?

Two sets of answers came forth. One group of scholars focused on the cultural traditions of Latin America and their Spanish and Portuguese origins. These analysts argued, in effect, that antidemocratic politics was a product of a Roman Catholic and Mediterranean worldview that stressed the need for harmony, order, and the elimination of conflict. Latin America's constitutions were never as democratic as they appeared, party politics was not as representative as it might have looked. The North American and European academic community, afflicted by its own myopia and biases, had simply misread the social facts.

A second group of scholars accepted modernization theory's linking of socio-economic causes with political outcomes but turned the answer upside down: Latin America's economic development was qualitatively different from that of North America and West Europe, and therefore it produced different political results. Specifically, these scholars argued, Latin America's experience was determined by the pervasive fact of its economic dependence. "By dependency," as one exponent of this viewpoint has explained,

> we mean a situation in which the economy of certain countries is conditioned by the development and expansion of another economy to which the former is subjected. The relation of interdependence between two or more economies, and between these and world trade, assumes the form of dependence when some countries (the dominant ones) can expand and be self-sustaining, while other countries (the dependent ones) can do this only as a reflection of that expansion, which can have either a positive or a negative effect on their immediate development.

By its intrinsic character, "dependent development" generated social inequities, allocating benefits to sectors participating in the global economy and denying them to other groups. In a country with abundant land, for example, the upper-class elite might reap large profits from agricultural exports while workers and peasants would gain little or nothing at all. Because of their interest in maintaining the status quo, landowners would have little reason to invest in diversification of the local economy—thus creating a situation characterized as "growth without development." When growth occurred, moreover, it would be vulnerable to substantial risk: if overseas markets contracted or prices declined, the entire economy would suffer. In other words, prosperity was dependent on factors and decisions well beyond the control of national authorities.

The proponents of "*dependencia* theory," as it quickly came to be known, maintained that economic dependency led to political authoritarianism. According to this view, the "dependent" location of Latin America's economics placed inherent limitations on the region's capacity for growth, especially in industry. The surest sign of this economic trouble was a crisis in the foreign accounts—the country's ability to pay for needed imports. Exports lagged behind imports, and the difference could only be made up by capital inflow. But the foreign creditors—firms, banks, international agencies such as the World Bank—denied the necessary extra financing because they believed the government could not impose the necessary "sacrifices." Political strategy fell hostage to the need to convince the foreign creditors.

The most frequent solution in the 1960s and 1970s was a military coup. The resulting dictatorship could then take its "hard" decisions, usually highly unpopular anti-inflation measures. Hardest hit were the lower classes. Implementation of such policies therefore required a heavy hand over the popular sectors. Thus, the coups and repressive authoritarian regimes that emerged in Brazil, Argentina, and Chile came about not in spite of Latin America's economic development, but because of it.

Within this overall context, the still-ongoing cycle of democratization throughout the region caught many observers—and experienced scholars—by surprise. Starting in the late 1970s, country after country replaced authoritarian regimes with civilian leaders and elected governments. Explanations for this trend took many forms. Once thought to be dominant and monolithic, authoritarian regimes came to display a good deal of incoherence and fragility. Everyday citizens rose up in protest movements, formed civic organizations, and demanded popular elections. Confronted by severe economic crisis, people from Argentina and Chile to Central America sought to express their political rights. Whether or not these new electoral regimes were fully "democratic," a point that led to much debate, they represented considerable improvement over the blatantly dictatorial patterns of previous eras.

Scholars approached these developments with intellectual caution. Instead of launching grand theories, such as modernization or dependency, political analysts stressed the role of beliefs, ideas, and human conviction. Some interpreted the turn toward democracy in Latin America and elsewhere as a global triumph of U.S. values, especially in light of the collapse of the Soviet Union (and the discrediting of Marxist ideology). Others emphasized the importance of leadership and tactical maneuvers at the elite level. Still others stressed the emergence of "civil society," especially the networks of grassroots organizations that gave shape and coherence to anti-authoritarian sentiments. And it was noted, too, that ideological traditions had ever since the 1820s enshrined the ideal of democracy as a widespread *aspiration* throughout Latin America, even if it had been systematically denied for decades on end.

Economic prospects brightened as well. Under pressure from international creditors throughout the 1980s, Latin American leaders imposed far-reaching measures designed to "liberalize" their national economies—reducing tariffs and other barriers to trade, selling state-supported companies to private investors, and curtailing deficit spending. Inflation declined and foreign investment increased. As a result, average growth in Latin America rose from a scant 1.5 percent per year in 1985–89 to 3.2 percent in the 1990s. But the unexpected onset of financial crisis in Mexico in late 1994 and in Brazil in early 1999, and Argentina's disastrous economic collapse in 2001, led to disenchantment and confusion. Hopes for economic development picked up from 2004 through 2007, when overall growth rates exceeded 5 percent, but the global economic crisis of 2008–09 brought this positive phase to a sharp and sudden end. Once again, the economic outlook for Latin America was plagued by uncertainty and doubt.

Within the economic realm, some experts regarded the growth spurt of the early 1990s as vindication for pro-capitalist, free-market policy reforms. Others noted that the surge tended to reflect the ebb and flow of international investments, and that capital promptly vanished in the face of crisis—leaving Latin

America just as "dependent" as before. Of continuing concern, for many, was the problematic relationship between economic and political transformation. Does economic liberalization lead to political democracy? Or might it be the other way around? Recent developments in Latin America thus raise new questions and pose continuing intellectual challenges.

Analytical Themes in This Book

This book is a survey of Latin American history, not a formulation of social theory, but we cannot escape the need for a conceptual framework in approaching our material. From modernization theory we borrow two central ideas:

- the causal premise that economic transformations induce social changes which, in turn, lead to political consequences; and
- the related idea that shifting alliances among social class groups give shape to changing patterns of political conflict over time.

For these reasons, each of our case study chapters includes an overview section on "economic growth and social change" that precedes the discussion of politics.*

While the original *dependencia* approach has long since disappeared from academic fashion, we still regard its basic framework as a useful heuristic device. Accordingly, we adopt the notions that:

- a country's place in the international division of labor defines the shape of available paths to economic growth;
- functional location on the "periphery" of the world system, as distinct from the commercial-industrial "center," and development at a stage when the North Atlantic system was already far advanced, meant that economic transformations in Latin America would be different from patterns traversed earlier in Europe and North America;
- these differences in economic processes would produce different forms of social change—with respect, for example, to the nature of the "middle classes," the urban and rural working classes, and the relationship among these classes;
- this combination of social and economic forces would define the options available to political leaders and help explain the alteration of democratic and authoritarian regimes;
- within these constraints, some Latin American countries did much better than others in exploiting their own resources (especially agricultural) for economic development.

---

* Our sole exception is Mexico (Chapter 3), where the Revolution of 1910 exerted such a strong influence on the nation's development that we chose to employ a different format.

In this context, it is essential to acknowledge the great variations in resources, capacities, and circumstances of nations in the region. Those with large populations and diversified natural resources (Mexico and Brazil) were eventually able to undertake substantial programs of industrialization. Those with essential raw materials, such as petroleum (Venezuela) and natural gas (Bolivia), managed at times to benefit from rising prices on world markets. Elsewhere, the presence of copper and other industrial metals (Chile and Peru) led foreign companies to establish large-scale mining operations. And in tropical and semitropical areas, conditions of climate and soil encouraged the cultivation of sugar (especially in the Caribbean) that gave rise to what we refer to as "plantation societies." A key challenge for all countries of the region has been how to transform the earnings from commodity exports into processes of economic diversification and self-sustaining development.

In other words, we intend to examine the relationship between society, culture, economics, and politics within an international context. We believe that this approach can be applied to the entire modern era. We shall be looking for such connections throughout the book.

We acknowledge limitations in this (or any) approach. We believe that historical transformations are complex processes, and to understand them we need to adopt a multicausal approach. Ideas and ideology, for example, are not merely adornments or superstructures; they have important effects on the perceptions, attitudes, and actions of the people who make history. Anyone who has ever tried to compare the political traditions of Argentina and Brazil can vouch for this truth. Demographic factors, such as rapid population growth, also have far-ranging social and political effects. In our portrait of Latin American society, we hope to integrate an "international political economy" approach with consideration of cultural and other noneconomic forces.

Our narrative begins by describing first the Conquest and the colonial period, 1492–1825, when Latin America entered the periphery of the capitalist world-system through subordination to Spain and Portugal. We then describe how the disruption of this connection led to independence, followed by a phase of economic and political consolidation between 1830 and 1880.

The core of the book presents in-depth case studies of long-term transitions from the nineteenth century to the present. We have deliberately adopted a longitudinal focus on individual nations (or clusters of nations) in order to facilitate the detection and analysis of historical change over time. In addition, the material in this section provides empirical evidence for testing, evaluating, and creating broad conceptual frameworks (any theoretical framework, we insist, not only the ones that we employ here). Chapters appear in the following order:

- Mexico, a close neighbor to the United States, the scene of a major popular upheaval in 1910;

- Central America and the Caribbean, areas characterized by plantation economies and American domination (such geographical units are properly regarded as "subregions," since we often refer to all of Latin America as a "region");
- Cuba, an island so dependent on sugar and so close to the Florida shore, the one Latin American society that has undergone a full-fledged socialist revolution;
- The central Andes (Bolivia, Peru, Ecuador), a subregion with strong indigenous traditions and uncertain steps toward stability and nationhood;
- Colombia, a nation where political democracy coexists with extensive drug trafficking in an atmosphere of systemic violence;
- Venezuela, a world-class producer of oil with a formerly stable two-party democracy that has given way to authoritarian rule;
- Argentina, a country blessed by fertile and productive pampas, wracked by internal strife and military intervention before the recent resumption of democracy;
- Chile, a leading source of nitrates and copper and the site of an abortive socialist experiment; and
- Brazil, an expansive nation so well known for its traditional emphasis on coffee and, more recently, its rapid industrial growth amid a democratic political transition.

We give full consideration to social and political themes in every one of the case studies, and each chapter can be read independently.

A subsequent section offers analytical syntheses and summaries. One chapter reviews economic strategies and policies; another locates patterns of political transformation within comparative perspective; the third and final essay concludes the book with an examination of national cultures, intellectual trends, and forms of artistic expression.

This book offers a picture of Latin American society, not a definitive catalog of facts. Our goal is to trace patterns and trends that help us to understand the complexities and variations in Latin America's paths to the present. We hope our presentation will stimulate discussion and debate, and we expect that students and colleagues will disagree with many of our interpretations. Above all, we want to introduce our readers to the excitement and fascination of the history of an area that is intriguing in its own right and has a vital role to play on the world stage.

2

The Colonial Foundations

Historical realities of conquest and colonization have cast ever-lengthening shadows over modern Latin America. Three centuries of imperial rule inflicted deep and painful wounds on cultures of the region, imposing hierarchical relationships of subordination and dependency. The power of external authority—initially Europe, later the United States—came to be accepted and rejected, admired and feared, an ambivalent object of fascination and concern. At the same time, heroic episodes of resistance to injustice and rebellion against oppression bequeathed persisting legacies of popular identity, personal pride, and collective self-empowerment. Amid tragedy and triumph, processes of mutual adjustment and accommodation made it possible for European colonizers, indigenous peoples, and imported African slaves to forge complex societies with hybrid traditions, enormous energy, and limitless capacity for change. Although independent nations would later traverse separate paths, they all reveal the lingering effects of this colonial experience. As the story of Latin America unfolds, we encounter endless tales of creative adaptation to inauspicious circumstance, enduring and uplifting testaments to human fortitude and ingenuity.

PRELUDE TO CONQUEST

When Europeans reached present-day Latin America, they found three important civilizations: Mayan, Aztec, and Incan. That we should still call the native peoples of this hemisphere "Indians" perpetuates the error of sixteenth-century Spaniards who wanted to believe they had reached the spice-rich Indies.

The Mayan people, who occupied the Yucatán Peninsula, southern Mexico, and most of present-day Guatemala, began to build their civilization around 500 B.C.E. The most famous achievements of this group were cultural—not only the building of exquisite temples but also pioneering accomplishments in architecture, sculpture, painting, hieroglyphic writing, mathematics, astronomy, and chronology (including the invention of calendars). Normally organized into a series of independent city-states, some with populations of 200,000 or more, the Mayans developed a complex social order. For reasons unknown, classic Mayan society collapsed, falling victim to domination (972–1200) and then absorption (1200–1540) by Toltec invaders from the central Mexican highlands. Yet, the direct descendants of the Mayans have survived in southern Mexico and Guatemala down to our own day.

Mexico's spacious central valley eventually became the seat of the Aztec empire. One of the Chichimec tribes that came from the north to subdue the Toltecs in the twelfth and thirteenth centuries, the Aztecs engaged in constant war with their neighbors, finally constructing the city of Tenochtitlán around 1325 (on the site of contemporary Mexico City). After gaining control of the entire valley of Mexico, they created a major empire—one that was just reaching its peak as Columbus touched shore in the Caribbean.

Aztecs were noted for their military organization and prowess at ceremonial city-building. Their art, except for their haunting poetry, was inferior in subtlety and craftsmanship to that of many other ancient Mexican civilizations.

In its final form, Aztec society was rigidly stratified. At the bottom were slaves and at the top was a hereditary nobility. Education, marriage, and labor were meticulously programmed. Land was owned individually by both commoners and nobles, but communities also shared the fruits of land held communally. Hereditary rulers, such as Moctezuma II, exercised immense political power. Despite centralization of authority, however, conquered states in neighboring areas were not incorporated into the empire. They were treated as tribute-paying vassals. Some—notably nearby Tlaxcala—retained their independence but kept up a perpetual state of war with Tenochtitlán. One reason for this warfare was that the Aztec religion required human sacrifice, and prisoners of war could be served up for bloody rituals.

Incas adopted a very different pattern of organization. Their empire stretched for 3000 miles along the Andes, from northern Ecuador through Peru to southern Chile, and into the interior as well. After consolidating their hold in the Cuzco Valley in Peru, the Incas began expanding their empire in the early 1400s and continued until the Spanish Conquest in 1532. (The term *Inca* means ruler or king and also refers to the people of Cuzco.) Once defeated, groups became integral parts of the empire. To strengthen support for the emperor, or Inca, local nobles from conquered areas were brought to Cuzco and treated as royal guests, while resistant elements in recently conquered zones were transferred to areas controlled by loyal followers. Political power belonged to a tightly organized, highly disciplined bureaucracy, with teams of local officials on the bottom and a single supreme ruler at the top. Incas were thereby able to command effective authority over most of the Andes.

Incas were master engineers, building a vast road system (for human and animal transit, since they did not use the wheel), an intricate irrigation system, and impressive terraced agriculture on mountainsides. They maintained vast granaries that supported their armies, as well as local populations in times of failed harvests.

The Incas also excelled in textile design and in treating head injuries, the latter made possible by extraordinary skills at trepanning the human skull.

Aside from the Mayans, Aztecs, and Incas, there were many other native cultures. In the area of modern-day Mexico alone, there were over 200 different linguistic groups. Estimates of the size of Latin America's indigenous population have varied widely. One scholar has set the figure at 90 to 112 million, with 30 million each in central Mexico and Peru. Though this calculation may be too high, it is clear that by European standards of the late fifteenth century, indigenous societies had grown very large. Then the Spaniards arrived.

The European Context

Europe's "discovery" of America (the Indians presumably knew where they were) was part of the remarkable European expansion in the fifteenth century. Europe was coming to know the rest of the world, as its navigators and explorers pushed back the frontiers of then-current knowledge of the globe. By the early 1600s they had woven a network of communications all the way around the earth, and had established the economic dominance that would shape the modern world.

This burst of European expansion was made possible by a combination of factors. One was technical skill. Pilotage and navigation were notable examples, as was the ability to adapt coastal ships to the challenges of the open ocean. Another example was weaponry, which was to fortify the Europeans against the occasionally well-armed native peoples, as in Mexico.

A second factor was the economic base, which furnished capital for the maritime and military enterprise. Technology alone was not enough. Vikings had shown the technical ability to reach America but lacked the resources to carry out settlement and colonization, which required men and money. In short, the New World was not to be had by speculators of small resources or limited purpose.

Third, there had to be a European power interested in more than technical expertise and profit. It had to be ready to pursue the unknown with exceptional determination. Spain and Portugal fit this description. These Catholic monarchies, with their crusading ideal of converting heathen masses to the true religion, had a unique motivation. Spain in particular had come late to the consolidation of its territory against the Muslims who had ruled the Iberian Peninsula since the eighth century. Portugal, although earlier rid of Muslim rule, was equally committed to the militant spread of the Christian faith. Their boldness set a precedent for European intruders into Latin America over the next four centuries. However much Latin America struggled, it was to remain an extension, at times a contradiction, of the Europe that had sailed west in the fifteenth century.

COLONIAL SPANISH AMERICA

It was no coincidence that Columbus reached America in the same year that the Spaniards liquidated the last Moorish stronghold in Spain. The reconquest down the Iberian Peninsula saw the warring Christian nobles acquiring land and the crown strengthening its political control. The result by 1492 was a nobility and would-be nobility anxious for more conquests, and a crown ready to direct these subjects overseas.

Spaniards therefore reached the New World in a conquest spirit already well developed at home. Spain had presented moderate opportunity for upward social mobility, and there is considerable evidence to suggest that the New World conquerors—Hernán Cortés, Francisco Pizarro, and their followers—came to America in order to win social status as well as wealth. Spanish motivation was no doubt complex. Ferdinand and Isabella and successive monarchs thought the wealth of the New World could strengthen their hand in Europe. Many dedicated missionaries hoped to save the souls of heathen Indians. The conquerors had multiple purposes in mind: as one conquistador said, "We came here to serve God and the King, and also to get rich." But their central motive appears to have been the achievement of noble rank and wealth. (About one-third of the conquerors of Peru came from the lesser or "common" nobility; two-thirds were of plebeian origin. These were people with status to gain.) Thus driven, they set out for they knew not what. In a few short years they had toppled the mighty empires of the Aztecs and the Incas.

How did they do it? When Cortés set out from Cuba toward Mexico in 1519, he had only 550 men and 16 horses. Within two and a half years, he and his battered Spanish contingent (bolstered by several hundred reinforcements) reduced to rubble the magnificent Aztec capital of Tenochtitlán, forced the capitulation of the disheartened and bewildered god-king, Moctezuma, and crushed the final resistance of forces led by the courageous Cuauhtémoc. One explanation for their feat was the superiority of Spanish equipment and technology—gunpowder (for muskets and cannons), horses, organization, and the confidence to stay constantly on the attack.* Important also was the role of non-Aztec peoples, such as the Tlaxcalans, who resisted and resented Aztec domination and who supplied the Spaniards with troops and advice on appropriate military tactics. Finally, and perhaps most important, an outbreak of smallpox, previously unknown in the Americas, ravaged a native population lacking natural immunity. By 1521, two years after the start of the Cortés campaign and less than thirty years after Columbus's first voyage, the Aztec empire had fallen under Spanish control. Cortés lost no time in asserting his authority. He extracted pledges of allegiance from neighboring chieftains and directed a vigorous reconstruction effort.

Some factors that favored the Spaniards in Mexico operated also in Peru, but Pizarro's task was simplified by the civil war then wracking the Incan empire: the Inca Atahualpa, preoccupied by the local conflict, never took Pizarro as seriously as warranted. The small Spanish band accomplished the takeover by 1533. They carted off as their booty a hoard of gold and silver large enough to fill a $12' \times 17'$ room to the height of a man's extended arm. The dream of El Dorado had come true in the Andes.

---

* It was traditionally thought that Aztec resistance was weakened by a belief that the invading Spaniards were divine beings and that Cortés personified the god Quetzalcoatl. Recent scholarship has sharply challenged this idea.

It did not take long for Spaniards to recreate many aspects of their own society in the Americas. They laid out typically Spanish designs for cities and created richly complex societies. Coopers, bakers, scribes—people from all walks of life in Spain—came, under tight immigration control, to make their way in the New World.

Men dominated this diaspora. According to a study on Peru, for instance, white males outnumbered white females by at least seven to one. This not only created intense competition for the hands of Spanish women; it also led Spaniards to take Indian women as their consorts. Their mixed-blood children, often illegitimate, came to be known as *mestizos*. In time, the *mestizo* race would become the dominant ethnic component of much of Spanish America, including Mexico, Central America, and the Andean countries.

The Spanish crown soon realized it had a conflict of interest with the independent-minded conquerors and promptly created an elaborate bureaucracy, designed to keep the New World economy and society under firm control. In Spain the key institution for New World affairs was the Council of the Indies. Overseas the main unit of organization was the viceroyalty, headed by a viceroy ("vice-king") appointed by the king. The first viceroyalty was established in Mexico (then known as New Spain) in 1535, the second in Peru in 1544; two others were set up in the eighteenth century. The church had parallel structures, led by the archbishop and by the officials of the Inquisition.

In practice, this bureaucracy led to intense conflict over matters of jurisdiction, but the genius of the system was that stalemates, once they developed, could always be transmitted to a higher authority, such as the viceroy or the Council of the Indies. This meant that the various institutions would serve as watchdogs over each other (aside from periodic reviews and investigations of performance in office). Another feature of the system was, surprisingly, its flexibility. Virtually all groups had some measure of access to the bureaucracy. And though the crown retained ultimate authority, local officials possessed considerable autonomy, as shown by their occasional responses to royal decrees—*obedezco pero no cumplo* (roughly, "I accept your authority but will not execute this law"). Despite its seeming idiosyncrasies, the Spanish bureaucracy operated rather well in the New World, keeping the colonies under royal rule for nearly 300 years.

Underpinning this political structure was a set of values and assumptions that legitimized monarchical, elitist rule. They stemmed from the fundamental Roman Catholic premise, most clearly articulated by Thomas Aquinas, that there were three kinds of law: divine law, that is, God's own heavenly will; natural law, a perfect reflection or embodiment of divine law in the world of nature; and human law, man's thoroughly imperfect attempt to approximate God's will within society. Born in original sin, humanity was fallible by definition, and it was only by the grace of God that some people were less fallible than others. The goal of political organization, therefore, was to elevate the less fallible to power so they could interpret and execute God's will in a superior way. And the ruler, once in power, was responsible to his or her own conscience and to God—not to the will of the people.

This rationale provided convincing justification for the supremacy of the Spanish monarch. Its theological origin revealed and fortified close links between church and state. Resuscitated in the postcolonial era, as it has often been, the code also furnished, as we shall see, a devastating critique of democratic theory. In time, political rulers would thus legitimize their power through residual aspects of traditional Roman Catholic doctrine.

The empire's economic structure reflected the prevailing mercantilist theory that economic activity should enhance the power and prestige of the state, measured on the basis of gold or silver bullion. The good mercantilist was supposed to run a favorable balance of trade, thus acquiring species or bullion in payment. Following this logic, Spain attempted to monopolize the access to wealth discovered in the New World. The first target was mining, first of gold and then mainly of silver. Another goal was to maintain complete control over commerce. Agriculture, by contrast, received little initial attention from crown officials (except for export products), and manufacturing, when later considered, was actively discouraged.

The central foundation for this economy was Indian labor, obtained from the natives by one form of coercion or another. They paid tribute to the crown and its appointed emissaries. Since cheap labor was so critical, the Spanish crown, colonists, and clerics fought bitterly for control of the Indians. In 1542, seeking to curtail the colonists, the king decreed the "New Laws," aimed at protecting the natives by removing them from direct tutelage of the conquistadores and bringing them under the direct jurisdiction of the crown. By 1600 the crown had largely succeeded in this task, at least in legal terms. In reality, however, these changes altered only the legal form of oppression; the fact of oppression persisted.

For the Indians, the Conquest meant above all a drastic fall in population. Scholars have argued long and hard about the size of the indigenous population when the Spaniards arrived. The most reliable studies of central Mexico place the pre-Conquest populations, as of 1519, at 16 to 18 million; for 1580 the figure is just 1.9 million, and for 1605 it is 1 million—a total decline of 95 percent! Data on Peru are less complete, but they also show continuing decline, from 1.3 million in 1570 (forty years after the Conquest) to less than 600,000 in 1620, a drop of more than 50 percent. However uncertain the exact magnitudes, the Conquest clearly resulted in demographic calamity, largely attributable to diseases such as smallpox, measles, and influenza.

The Indian survivors saw their social order undermined and distorted. Forced to give their labor and tributes to the Spaniards, the natives struggled to maintain their traditional social networks. Most of them lived in their own villages, governed by indigenous elites; in Mexico, these communities sometimes kept extensive written records, ranging from annals to real estate transactions to wills, which have been a vital source for modern historians. The most fertile land was seized by the conquerors— who, in many cases, converted the land to raising livestock. Indians saw the symbols of their old religion destroyed, and they clung to such syncretistic practices as they could

The fortress-like construction of this sixteenth-century Dominican monastery in south-central Mexico aptly illustrates the alliance of church and crown in the conquest of New Spain. (Courtesy of the Library of Congress.)

devise. Diseases took a heavier toll on men than on women, and the resulting gender imbalance further disrupted marriage patterns and family structure.

To offset the decline in Indian population, especially in tropical lowland regions, Spaniards began importing black slaves from Africa—a practice already familiar in Spain and Portugal and their Atlantic islands. Between 1518 and 1870, Spanish America imported more than 1.5 million slaves—over 16 percent of the entire Atlantic slave trade—mostly through Cuba and the northern tip of South America, destined for labor in the lowland coastal areas. Brazil, with its extensive sugar plantations, brought in about 3.7 million.

As we shall see later, Latin America produced largely multiracial societies, in contrast to the highly polarized biracial society that developed in North America.

The three ethnic components of colonial Spanish American population— Indians, Europeans, Africans—fit together in a social structure that divided itself along lines of race and function. The white sector, which included less than 2 percent of the sixteenth-century population, was the most powerful and prestigious. In the same period the mixed bloods included free blacks, *mestizos,* and mulattoes—all told, less than 3 percent of the total. Indigenous peoples, over 95 percent of the population, were placed in a unique position carefully limited and protected by a battery of royal laws.

In the first years after the Conquest, disputes arose between the original conquerors and their descendants, on the one hand, and, on the other, people of noble birth who arrived later and claimed special privileges. Careers in the church and the army, or occupations such as merchant, miner, and sheep farmer, also determined one's social rank. Overlapping social categories produced a complex system in which social status was the major prize. The continuous waves of Spanish newcomers often sought alliances through marriage with local families in order to integrate themselves into the social and economic fabric. In the eighteenth century, distinctions and rivalries developed between people of European descent born in the New World (*criollos* or creoles) and recently arrived people from Spain *(peninsulares)*. These conflicts and resentments would eventually shape the struggles that led to independence from European rule.

Interaction between the racial groupings was less tension-filled, but still tenuous. Though interracial concubinage was widespread, interracial marriage was probably rare, and even then it followed gradations—whites might marry *mestizos,* and *mestizos* might marry Indians, but whites seldom married Indians. Since civil and religious consecration was extended to interracial liaisons, especially those involving whites, they tended to blur social boundaries, legitimize aspirations for mobility, and foment uncertainty about the system of stratification. Movement definitely existed, both socially and geographically, and individuals could experience considerable change during their lifetimes.

Marriage and family customs generally assumed male domination of females. The cult of masculine superiority (*machismo*) appeared early in Latin America, within a broad range of social and ethnic strata, and many women led restricted lives. But contrary to the stereotypical image, the standard family was not always headed by a male patriarch presiding over a large brood of children. More often than not, families consisted of married couples reasonably close in age with two to four children.

But not all women married, and those who did often did not remain married for life. Data on the sixteenth century are sparse, but by 1811, according to census results, only 44 percent of the adult females in Mexico City were married. Many women were widows, and approximately one-third of the households in Mexico City were headed by single women. This was due in part to the lower life expectancy for men. For whatever reason, many Mexican women spent much of their lives as single women.

Spanish American colonies underwent profound changes by the early seventeenth century. The first impetus came from Europe, where Spain began to lose the power it once had in the late fifteenth and sixteenth centuries. After the defeat of the armada by the English in 1588, the royal treasury repeatedly went bankrupt, the nobles challenged the crown, Catalonia erupted in revolt, and in 1640 Portugal—since 1580 governed by the Spanish monarch—successfully reasserted its independence. At the same time, Spain and Portugal began losing their monopolies on the New World. The English, Dutch, and French established settlements in North America and also gained footholds in the Caribbean.

Elite Women and Economic Power

The predominant gender image from Latin America is one of violent men, cloistered women, and a strictly patriarchal society. It is often summed up in the word *machismo*. Yet there was a category of women which contradicted this image:

> Widows from the propertied sectors of colonial society enjoyed the greatest freedom of action and participated most extensively in the colonial economy. In Spanish America, a widow enjoyed full control over her dowry and the arras, if provided by the husband; in addition, she received half of all wealth acquired during the marriage. As a widow she usually also administered her children's inheritances while they were minors. One of the most remarkable of these women was Doña Jerónima de Peñalosa, widow of a wealthy and powerful lawyer who in the sixteenth century served as a judge and adviser to the viceroy of Peru. Once widowed, Doña Jerónima managed the family's vast economic holdings that included real estate, orchards, farms, mines, and a sugar mill in addition to property in Spain. She never remarried, choosing to manage, even expand, the family's wealth. When she died her eldest son inherited an entailed estate and her other children were provided for, with three sons sent to Spain for a university education and another put in the Church; her daughter was provided with a rich dowry of 35,000 pesos.

From Mark A. Burkholder and Lyman L. Johnson, *Colonial Latin America*, 5th ed. (New York: Oxford University Press, 2004), pp. 229–30.

With Spain's decline, the rest of seventeenth-century Europe sought to counterbalance France, now the leading power. The New World became a vital element in the European power equation. This became clear in the War of the Spanish Succession (1700–1713), which installed the Bourbons on the Spanish throne and gave the British the contract (*asiento*) for the slave trade to the Spanish colonies.

Far-reaching changes were also taking place within the colonies. The ethnic composition of society underwent profound transition. Continued immigration and natural increase turned the whites, mainly creoles, into a sizable segment of the population, perhaps 20 percent by 1825. Much more dramatic was the relative growth of the *mestizo* and mixed-blood category, from less than 3 percent around 1570 to approximately 28 percent by 1825. The shift in the Indian population was even greater, despite a slight recovery in absolute terms—down from over 95 percent to barely 42 percent. In the meantime, blacks had come to account for 12 percent of the Spanish American population.

The creoles began to assume active roles in key sectors of the economy, such as mining and commerce. Especially striking was their increasing ownership of land (something the early Spanish monarchs had discouraged) and, in some areas, the appearance of great landed estates, or haciendas. Typified by vast territorial holdings and debt peonage, the haciendas often became virtually autonomous rural communities governed by the owners or their foreman. Land titles were hereditary, and most were held by creoles. By the mid-eighteenth century, the crown was confronting a proud New World nobility.

The political role of the creoles was less obvious. In the late seventeenth and early eighteenth centuries, they held many important political posts, mainly on the local or regional level, such as in town councils or *audiencias* (courts). Upper-level positions were still reserved for *peninsulares*. With the decline of Spain as an imperial power, however, political institutions ceased to function as before.

PORTUGUESE AMERICA: A DIFFERENT WORLD?

The history of Portuguese America contrasts with the story of colonial Spanish America. Under the royal House of Aviz, Portugal had established a far-flung empire with outposts in Africa, India, China, and some Atlantic islands. In fact, Portugal had become the European leader in exploration by shrewd use of its superior technical skills in cartography and navigation. In 1494 the Treaty of Tordesillas between Spain and Portugal granted Spain all lands 370 leagues to the west of the Cape Verde Islands off the coast of Africa. Portugal received all the lands east of that dividing line. In 1500 Pedro Alvares Cabral, a Portuguese sea captain, landed along the coast of what is today Brazil and claimed that vast territory for his monarch.

This New World incursion differed from Spain's in two fundamental respects. First, there was no native civilization in Brazil comparable to the Aztecs or the Incas. The Tupí-Guaraní, the largest language group, lived along the coast from what is now Venezuela into southern Brazil and Paraguay, and Tapuias inhabited the interior. Some Indians were cannibalistic, and most were seminomadic— which meant that Brazil would have to be settled gradually, rather than taken at a single blow. More important, it meant that the Portuguese, unlike the Spanish, did not face a highly organized, settled indigenous civilization.

Furthermore, there was no trace of silver or gold, and consequently no easy path to fabulous wealth. The first important economic activity was the export of brazilwood (hence the country's current name), prized in Europe for its qualities as a source of dye. And in time, contrasting sharply with most of colonial Spanish America, agriculture, especially cane sugar cultivation, predominated in the Brazilian colonial economy.

The scarcity (compared to Spain) of human and mineral resources forced the Portuguese crown to resort to unusual means in trying to persuade or entice its subjects to occupy the New World holdings. In the 1530s the kings started making massive grants of effective power over (almost totally unexplored) land, usually to military men with prior experience in India or Africa or to handpicked personal favorites, and in either instance to men "of gentle blood." The land donations were huge, averaging about 130 miles along the coastline and running all the way west (as much as 500 miles or more) to the imaginary Line of Demarcation that divided Portuguese from Spanish America.

Not until 1549 did the crown begin to establish an effective imperial bureaucracy—but the purpose was to protect the area from French and British intrusions and not, as in the case of Spanish America, to reconquer the possessions

Map 2 Colonial Latin America: Political Organization

from the conquerors. On the contrary, it was the lack of a Portuguese presence that forced Lisbon to act.

Partly because in its first century Brazil received a lower priority than Portugal's other overseas dominions (which were more profitable), monarchical control started out much looser than in Spanish America. Even when the Portuguese crown tightened up after 1549, the royal institutions were largely limited to the Atlantic coast, where the taxes on exports could be easily collected. Power on the local level rested with the landowners and the town councils. Even the church was weak in sixteenth-century Brazil, compared to Mexico and Peru.

During the late sixteenth and early seventeenth centuries, landowners developed a lucrative sugar industry in the Brazilian Northeast. Having earlier made technological breakthroughs in sugar processing in their Atlantic islands, such as the Madeiras, the Portuguese had come to rely on the Dutch to retail the product in Europe. To grow sugar in America, however, required abundant labor. The Portuguese landowners first turned to the Brazilian Indians. As in Mexico and Peru, however, the natives soon fell victim to devastating European diseases. The survivors often fled into the interior. Although the Portuguese continued to exploit the Indians until well into the eighteenth century, they had to look elsewhere for a satisfactory labor supply.

The obvious source was Africa. By the early 1500s the Spanish and Portuguese already had a half century of experience with African slave labor, both at home and in their Atlantic islands, such as the Canaries (Spanish) and the Madeiras (Portuguese). It was not until the 1580s that the Portuguese saw enough potential profit to warrant importing African slaves. By 1650, however, northeastern Brazil had become the world's greatest source of cane sugar, produced predominantly with African slave labor. Sugar exports were estimated at £2.5 million a year, which made Brazil's coastal Northeast probably the richest single region in the entire Americas.

Other European powers wanted in on the sugar boom. The Dutch invaded Brazil itself in 1624 and controlled the sugar-rich Northeast until an alliance of Portuguese planters, merchants, and mixed-blood troops pushed them back into the ocean in 1654. The Dutch then moved to the Caribbean with new technology; in the late seventeenth and eighteenth centuries, sugar cultivation would transform this region, making it the center of the Atlantic trading system. The Portuguese were never again to duplicate the near monopoly on New World sugar production they had enjoyed earlier in the century.

In the central and southern regions of Brazil, the economy first centered on cattle raising and, more importantly, on slave raids against the Indians (who were often shipped to the Northeast). Carried out by the *bandeirantes,* whose legendary status in national history resembles a mixture of the California gold prospectors and the American backwoodsmen, these forays extended Portuguese control over the Brazilian interior. Furthermore, they led to the discovery of mineral wealth, which had so long eluded the Portuguese. In the 1690s gold was found in Minas Gerais ("General Mines"), and people flocked to the area. Diamonds were located in 1729. Mining reached its peak in 1750, with a yearly output of £3.6 million, although the low level of technological expertise contributed to a decline in mining near the late

1700s. The era also brought a brief export boom in cotton, but Brazil would have to await the nineteenth-century coffee boom before regaining much prosperity.

Brazil's colonial economy had been created for export. The resulting social structure reflected the investment the Portuguese crown had made. The most important single human consequence was the pervasive presence of African slaves. Over 2.5 million Africans had been brought to Brazil by 1810, nearly one-third of the Atlantic slave trade in that era. Blacks were a major component of Portuguese American society, in contrast to most areas of Spanish America.

As shown in Table 1–1, blacks amounted to nearly one-half of Brazil's total population around 1825, compared with 12 percent in Spanish America, and the mixed-blood group, mainly mulattoes, added another 18 percent. All in all, perhaps as much as two-thirds of the entire Brazilian population in the early nineteenth century were of partial or total African ancestry.

The multiracial colonial Brazilian society was highly stratified. Racial inter-marriage was rare, accounting for no more than 10 percent of all marriages, and, as in Spanish America, it followed lines of gradation—whites might marry mulattoes, but they almost never married blacks. Concubinage and common-law relation-ships were more frequent among blacks than whites. As in Mexico City, about one-third of the family units in a sample of colonial Brazilian communities were headed by single women.

A second major facet of the social structure was internal division within the white ruling stratum, particularly between Brazilian-born landowners and Portuguese-born merchants. This difference resembled the creole-*peninsular* con-flict in Spanish America, and it had the potential for leading to an independence

Table 1.1 Racial Composition of Early Latin American Population

	SPANISH AMERICA		PORTUGUESE AMERICA	
	1570 (%)	1825 (%)	1570 (%)	1825 (%)
Whites (legally defined or by social convention)	1.3	18.2	2.4	23.4
Mixed-bloods (*mestizo* or mulatto)	2.5	28.3	3.5	17.8
Blacks	(included with mixed-bloods)	11.9	(included with mixed-bloods)	49.8
Indigenous	96.3	41.7	94.1	9.1
Total	100.1	100.1	100.0	100.1

SOURCE: Adapted from Richard M. Morse, "The Heritage of Latin America," in Louis Hartz, ed., *The Founding of New Societies* (New York: Harcourt, Brace & World, 1964), p. 138.
NOTE: Some columns may not add up to 100 because of rounding.

movement. As it turned out, European politics cut the process short. In any case, the looser crown control of Brazil had generated less resentment among the colonists than in most of Spanish America.

Portuguese America's integration into the Western economy as a peripheral area resembled that of Spanish America, but with notable differences: first, for two centuries Brazil lacked the gold and silver that obsessed the Spaniards in Mexico and Peru; second, Brazil's main contribution until the eighteenth century was agriculture, not mining; third, and perhaps most important, Portugal had developed a simpler system for ensuring revenues from its prize colony. Unlike Spain, Portugal did not develop a vast bureaucratic network aimed at taxing and controlling the domestic market. Instead, it concentrated almost entirely on taxing Brazil's exports. As a result, Brazil offered less potential than Spanish America for breeding a powerful alliance of colonial interests which might rebel against the political authority of the mother country.

INDEPENDENCE FOR LATIN AMERICA

The independence movements that led to the creation of most of present-day Latin America's nation-states owed their origins to events in Europe. Most were not radical, and none brought cataclysmic changes in the social order. Much of the impetus proved to be conservative, thereby shaping the direction of the young republics in the early nineteenth century. Our story begins back in Europe.

The Bourbon monarchs of Spain, whose family had succeeded to the crown in 1713, had sought to reverse Spain's decline, both in Europe and America. Hoping to shore up New World defenses against rival European powers while also increasing revenues for the crown, the Bourbon kings imposed far-reaching administrative and political reforms, known as the Bourbon reforms. One was to create new viceroyalties—one at New Granada (first in 1717, then again in 1739) in northern South America, corresponding mainly to modern Panama, Colombia, Ecuador, and Venezuela, and another at Buenos Aires (1776), called the Viceroyalty of the Río de la Plata, corresponding to modern-day Bolivia, Paraguay, Uruguay, and Argentina.

In addition, Charles III (1759–88) replaced the complex administrative arrangement of the Hapsburgs with the intendancy system. In effect, this led to the replacement of the hated *corregidores* (local administrative and judicial officials) in Spanish America with "intendants"—local governors directly responsible to the crown, not to the viceroy. Almost all the intendants were Spanish-born *peninsulares,* rather than American creoles, presumably thereby assuring loyalty to the monarch. The intendants greatly strengthened crown control over government, but also collided with prosperous creoles, many of whom had taken advantage of the relaxed administration.

This trend could be seen in the administration of local courts. Desperately needing funds, the late seventeenth-century Hapsburg monarchs put court appointments up for sale, as had Philip IV earlier in the century. It was creoles who bought, and by 1750, fifty-one out of ninety-three judges were American born. The Bourbon monarchs reversed this trend, and by 1807 only twelve out of ninety-nine judges were creoles. Ultimately, creoles would decide to look elsewhere for positions of authority and prestige.

One place they looked was to the town councils, or *cabildos,* which were barely functioning by the early eighteenth century. *Cabildo* offices did not always find eager buyers. With the arrival of the intendants, however, more efficient taxation gave the *cabildos* increased revenues—and they reasserted their role as local councils. The *cabildos* thus became institutional bases of creole authority.

Charles III also sought to increase royal power by tightening crown control of the church. The most dramatic step was the expulsion of the Jesuit order from all of Spanish America in 1767. Charles saw the Jesuits as a state within a state, a rival source of power and wealth. The best properties of the Jesuits were auctioned off, and the proceeds, of course, went to the crown.

The military was another power source. To ward off outside threats and to crush any potential rebellion, the king decreed the establishment of colonial militias, an excellent source of prestige for status-hungry creoles. But it also altered the military balance. By 1800, for instance, there were only 6000 members of the regular Spanish army in the viceroyalty of New Spain—compared to 23,000 American-born members of the colonial militia. This was the foundation of the patriot army that would later fight for independence.

The Spanish Bourbons wanted especially to promote colonial economic development in order to strengthen their hand in Europe. In 1778 Charles III

Celibacy and Anticlericalism

Parish priests in colonial Peru were enjoined by their superiors to take good care of their flocks. Such care also had its dangers. One was intimacy with their female parishioners. As sons of the Roman Catholic Church, the priests were bound by the pledge of celibacy, on which they were often sorely tested. In response to a wave of reports about priests having entire families, the crown in 1727 ordered church authorities in Peru to crack down. They ruled that any servant of a priest be more than forty and have a perfect reputation. Their advice: "The best way to overcome the temptations of the flesh is to flee them; he who courts danger will perish in it." By the end of the colonial era in both Spanish and Portuguese America, more than a few priests had succumbed. The ensuing scandals did much to undermine public support for the church and feed the anticlericalism that was to dominate nineteenth-century Spanish American politics.

Quotation from William B. Taylor, *Magistrates of the Sacred: Priests and Parishioners in Eighteenth-Century Mexico* (Stanford, Calif.: Stanford University Press, 1996), p. 621.

promulgated a Decree of Free Trade, which meant that the twenty-four ports of Spanish America could now trade directly with any port in Spain or with each other (but *not* with any port outside the Spanish realm). Commerce would no longer be restricted to four colonial ports (Veracruz, Cartagena, Lima/Callao, and Panama) or tied to the Cádiz monopoly in Spain. Buenos Aires immediately began to profit from the measure. In fact, contraband trade had long flourished on these formerly forbidden routes. But the crown increased its customs receipts, since it could now place taxes on the goods that were once smuggled.

Partly for this reason, many aspects of the colonial economy flourished under the Bourbons. The port of Buenos Aires, a small and lackluster town in 1776, grew to a city of 50,000 by the year 1800. Mexico was minting three times as much silver and gold in the 1790s as it had been in the 1740s. Commerce was thriving by the turn of the century.

The Bourbon policies appeared to be a success. Administration became more efficient, defenses improved, commerce swelled, and governmental revenues increased. But creoles were upset by many of these changes, which threatened (and often managed) to reduce their status and influence. It was the challenge to creole status, more than the influence of Enlightenment thought or the example of British colonies in North America, that ultimately prompted the Spanish American dominions to opt for independence.

There had been colonial resistance, to Spanish rule to be sure. In 1780 Túpac Amaru II, claiming to be a lineal descendant of the Inca rulers, led an Indian revolt with an army of nearly 80,000 men. It took nearly two years of brutal fighting to stamp out the insurrections that swept over southern Peru and Bolivia. In 1781 the citizens of Socorro, in New Granada, violently protested against a tax increase, and the disruption spread through much of the viceroyalty. Although patriotic Latin American historians have often described these events as "precursors" to the creole-led independence movements of the nineteenth century, this was not the case. As for Túpac Amaru II, some strands in that insurrection pointed toward independence, but on terms of Indian leadership that would never gain solid creole support. In the 1781 rebellion in New Granada, the protestors did not seek independence from the Spanish crown. They were protesting within the system, not against it.

Then how did independence come? Once again Latin America's fate was determined by dynastic politics in the Old World. After having tried and failed to help the French Bourbons save their crown during the French Revolution, Spain forged an alliance with France in 1796, a pact that led directly to the annihilation of the Spanish navy at the Battle of Trafalgar (1805). Meanwhile, Napoleon Bonaparte, now France's dictator, in 1807 ordered his troops to occupy Portugal, England's longtime ally. Napoleon's armies reached the hills above the capital city of Lisbon just as the English royal navy was whisking the Portuguese royal house of Braganza and its court off to Brazil. Napoleon's forces then turned to Spain. In 1808 they occupied Madrid, planting Napoleon's brother, Joseph, on the Spanish throne. This was the act that prompted the colonies to revolt.

There was Spanish resistance to Joseph, as supporters of Ferdinand VII held captive by Napoleon rallied to the cause. A junta was set up in Seville to rule in Ferdinand's name. In 1810 there followed a parliament, or *cortes,* dominated by Spanish liberals who had moved into the vacuum created by the monarch's absence. In 1812 it proclaimed a new constitution that asserted the authority of parliament, abolished the Inquisition, and restricted the role of the king.

The Colonial Response

When Napoleon put his brother on the Spanish throne, the creoles rejected him as an imposter, just as most Spaniards had done. Since Spain no longer had a government, the colonists argued, sovereignty reverted to the people. Could this logic be extended to an argument for independence?

Yet there was nothing inevitable about the train of events that overtook Spanish America. Neither the European Enlightenment nor the example of the American Revolution alone would have fomented rebellions in Spanish America. Without Napoleon's intervention, the Spanish American colonies might all have remained Spanish until well into the nineteenth century, as did Cuba.

One of the focal points of resistance to Napoleon was Buenos Aires, the seat of the newest viceroyalty, whose *cabildo* had already acquired remarkable authority. In 1806 an English squadron occupied the city of Buenos Aires, sending the viceroy fleeing to the interior city of Córdoba. A citizen's army drove the British out, and in 1807 it made short shrift of a second British attack. So it was the creoles, not the viceregal authorities, who successfully defended Buenos Aires from invasion. This demonstrated both the weakness of the crown and the capacity of the local citizenry.

Another lingering issue in the Río de la Plata region was free trade. The proclamation of 1778 had partially opened up trade for Buenos Aires, which could now ship goods directly to Spain—rather than along the long, tortuous route overland to Panama and finally across the Atlantic. But it was England, not Spain, that offered the most promising market for hides and salted beef. A contra-band trade therefore flourished, and Argentine desire for open commerce with other European countries intensified.

In 1809, after Napoleon had ousted Spanish King Ferdinand VII, a young lawyer named Mariano Moreno from Buenos Aires called for a two-year experiment with totally free trade. Moreno argued that such a step would strengthen loyalties to the Spanish crown and provide increased revenues—since duties could be charged on legal trade, but not on contraband traffic. Late in the year the viceroy granted Buenos Aires limited freedom of trade with nations allied to Spain or neutral in the Napoleonic wars. Once again, the elite of Buenos Aires tasted political success.

When Napoleon's forces seized the centers of Bourbon resistance in Spain in 1810, leading citizens met and decided to create a "provisional junta of the Provinces of the Río de la Plata, governing for Ferdinand VII." Although it was not until 1816 that a congress formally declared independence, the pattern had been set.

In 1810 a similar movement emerged in Caracas, where the municipal *cabildo* deposed the Spanish captain-general and organized a junta to govern in the name of Ferdinand VII. As in Buenos Aires, the insurgent group consisted mainly of wealthy creoles. Its leaders had more decisive views. The most famous, Simón Bolívar, from the beginning wanted independence for America.

Born into a wealthy creole family in Caracas in 1783, Bolívar was orphaned at the age of nine. He was then sent to Spain to complete his education, and after three years he returned to Caracas with a young Spanish bride, who within months died of yellow fever. Bolívar was devastated and never remarried. (He did not deprive himself of female companionship, however.) With his magnetic, charming, persuasive personality, he inspired loyalty and confidence among his followers. Familiar with the ideas of the Enlightenment, he vowed in 1805 to free his homeland from Spanish rule. In July 1811 the congress that convened to govern Venezuela responded to his vision by declaring independence.

But the pro-Ferdinand regency in Seville proved more resilient than had been expected, sending troops to crush this upstart rebellion. Together first with blacks, then with *llaneros* (cowboys) of the Venezuelan interior plains, Spanish forces defeated colonial troops under Francisco de Miranda. Bolívar himself managed to escape to New Granada. In 1813 he returned to Venezuela and won a series of startling military victories.

Events in Europe again intruded. In 1814, after Napoleon's defeat, Ferdinand VII returned to the Spanish throne, annulled the liberal constitution of 1812, and restored himself in an absolute monarchy. Many creoles concluded that since the king was back, there was no reason to continue their mobilization.

Brimming with self-confidence, Simón Bolívar assumed military command of pro-independence forces around the precocious age of thirty. (Courtesy of the Library of Congress.)

Bolívar now saw his men and munitions dwindle. After a series of defeats, he was obliged in 1814 to flee again to New Granada and then to the English island of Jamaica. He hoped that Spanish America might become a single nation, but knew the odds were low. Here he was much influenced by the recent failures to establish republican government in Venezuela. His advice was concise: "Do not adopt the best system of government, but the one which is most likely to succeed."

In New Spain, events took a different course. In a preemptive strike against creole patriots, *peninsulares* ousted the viceroy José de Iturrigaray in 1808 and promptly recognized the regency in Seville. Mexico City was firmly in royalist hands until 1821.

The provinces of New Spain, particularly north of the capital, were another story. By 1810 a group of prominent creoles, including a priest named Miguel Hidalgo y Costilla, were planning to seize authority in Ferdinand's name. When the plot was discovered, Hidalgo decided to act. On September 16, 1810, in the little town of Dolores, he gave an impassioned call to arms. And, curiously, it was not the local notables who rallied, but rather the long-suffering mixed-bloods and Indians. They flocked to the banner of the Virgin of Guadalupe, whom they had long ago appropriated as their own. This "colored plebe" now formed a massive, angry, undisciplined army—"a horde," in the eyes of the startled creole elite.

Hidalgo's men stormed into the city of Guanajuato, where they massacred 500 Spanish soldiers and civilians, including the intendant, in an all-out assault on the municipal granary. After looting freely, they headed toward Mexico City. Hidalgo struggled to maintain control.

By November 1810, Hidalgo was on the outskirts of Mexico City with about 50,000 men in arms. In a decision that has prompted debate and speculation ever since, he then pulled back from the city. Surely he could have taken the capital. Why did he withdraw? Was he afraid of his own following? Instead Hidalgo moved north. After a defeat near Guadalajara in early 1811, he went on to Coahuila where he was captured and subsequently executed by a firing squad at Chihuahua.

Leadership of the ramshackle insurgency now passed to José María Morelos, another priest. Like Hidalgo, Morelos supported the abolition of Indian tribute and slavery and even proposed agrarian reform. The latter was an explosive issue among the colonial elite. He insisted, too, that citizens had the right to choose their own form of government. Ultimately, Morelos envisioned "a new government, by which all inhabitants, except *peninsulares,* would no longer be designated as Indians, mulattoes, or *mestizos,* but all would be known as Americans." Thus Morelos combined nationalism with a commitment to social and racial equality.

In 1813 the Congress of Chilpancingo declared Mexico's independence from Spain (although it is September 16, the anniversary of Hidalgo's speech, that is celebrated as the country's independence day). The congress also decreed that slavery should be abolished and that Roman Catholicism should be the state religion. The constitution, adopted the following year, affirmed the ideal of popular sovereignty, created a system of indirect elections, and designed a powerful legislature alongside a weak three-person executive.

Meanwhile the Spaniards were winning military victories. One of the Spanish commanders was the young Agustín de Iturbide, later to play a central role in Mexican independence. In 1815 Morelos was captured, tried (by the Inquisition as well as by secular authorities), and executed. Others continued to fight for the cause, but Spaniards now held the upper hand.

Thus ended the first phase of the Spanish American independence movements. New Spain's Morelos and Hidalgo were both dead. Bolívar languished in exile in Jamaica. The junta in the Río de la Plata struggled to maintain unity and had yet to call for independence. By 1815, with Ferdinand back on the throne, the Spanish crown appeared to have snuffed out its colonial rebellion.

Achieving Independence

The Spanish military advantage in South America did not last long. In 1816 Bolívar returned to Venezuela and began duplicating his earlier victories. But now he had allied with José Antonio Páez, the brilliant leader of the fearless *llaneros,* who had earlier fought for the royalists. Now Páez was fighting for independence from Spain. Bolívar's cause was further bolstered by the arrival of reinforcements from England, which by 1819 numbered over 4000. Thus strengthened, Bolívar established firm control of Venezuela by early 1819.

After defeating Spanish forces in New Granada, Bolívar attempted in 1821 to create a new state of Gran Colombia, uniting Venezuela, New Granada, and Ecuador. It gained little support, so Bolívar marched southward, hunting for more royalists and Spaniards to defeat.

Meanwhile, José de San Martín was conducting an extraordinary military campaign in the south. The son of a Spanish officer, born on the northern frontier of present-day Argentina, he began a military career at the age of eleven. In 1812 he offered his services to the junta in Buenos Aires, having decided in favor of independence for the colonies. A soldier by training and outlook, he did not have the political acumen of Bolívar or the social commitment of Morelos, but he was a skillful military strategist.

As commander of the rebel forces, San Martín was ready by early 1817 to attempt one of the most daring exploits of this era: leading an army of 5000 across the Andes for a surprise attack on royalist troops in Chile. He caught the Spaniards completely off guard, won a major victory in the battle of Chacabuco, and triumphantly entered the city of Santiago. San Martín now prepared for the next step in his campaign, the liberation of Peru.

By 1820 San Martín reached the Peruvian coast. Lima was even more monarchist than Mexico City. Although the elevation of Buenos Aires to a viceroyalty in the Bourbon era had hurt Lima economically, its monarchist sentiment was still strong. Creoles and *peninsulares* both tended to favor the continuation of Ferdinand VII's rule. San Martín withheld his attack, noting: "I do not seek military glory, nor am I ambitious for the title of conqueror of Peru: I only wish to free it from oppression. What good would Lima do me if its inhabitants were hostile politically?"

Here, too, radical change in Spain catalyzed events. When Ferdinand VII succumbed to political pressure and suddenly endorsed the liberal constitution of 1812, the turnabout stunned his Lima supporters. They were especially distressed over the abolition of the Inquisition and the challenge to the dignity of priests. Many could accept limitations on monarchical authority, but not on the role and power of the church.

This turn of events in Spain drastically altered the climate of opinion in Mexico City and Lima. Independence from Spain was no longer a radical or even a liberal cause. Now it was a *conservative* goal, a means of upholding traditional values and social codes. As if acknowledging this fact, the *cabildo* of Lima invited San Martín to enter the city in mid-1821. On July 28 he formally proclaimed the independence of Peru.

After further skirmishes with royalist troops, San Martín went to Ecuador for a historic meeting with Simón Bolívar. Exactly what happened there has never been established. Bolívar may have set the tone when he offered a toast to the two greatest men in America, General San Martín and himself. Apparently Bolívar rejected San Martín's proposal for a monarchy in Peru, insisted on the union of Gran Colombia, and declined San Martín's offer to serve under his command. In any case, San Martín then resigned all his offices and soon went to Europe, where he died in 1850.

In late 1823 Bolívar moved to Peru, where the Spaniards still maintained an imposing force. In 1824 the royalists were decisively defeated by colonial troops in the battle of Ayacucho. In 1825 Bolívar entered Upper Peru (present-day Bolivia) in the hope that Peru and Upper Peru might form a single nation, but he was too late. The regional leaders of Upper Peru were set on creating their own republic. They promptly did so, naming it for Bolívar and making him president for life.

After returning to Lima, Bolívar went on to Gran Colombia, hoping to patch up the failing union. By now he had grown bitter and vindictive, upset that his dreams had failed to materialize. In 1830 both Venezuela and Ecuador withdrew from Gran Colombia. Suffering from tuberculosis, Bolívar looked back in despair. "America," he said, "is ungovernable. Those who have served the revolution have plowed the sea." On December 17, at the age of only forty-seven, the Liberator passed away.

In Mexico the defeat of Morelos in 1815 stalled the independence movement—until Ferdinand VII declared submission to the constitution of 1812, thus pushing prosperous and prominent creoles to the side of independence. The cause was led by the same Agustín de Iturbide who had led the royalists against Morelos. Ironically, the independence movement acquired a conservative tinge.

The opportunistic Iturbide persuaded the viceroy to give him command of royalist forces in the south. He then marched against a rebel leader with whom he immediately struck an alliance—for the sake of independence. In 1821 he issued a call for three "guarantees": of religion (the Catholic faith to be the official creed), of independence (presumably under a monarchy), and union (fair treatment for creoles and *peninsulares* alike). Iturbide took Mexico City and established an empire—with himself, of course, as emperor. It lasted only two years.

In Central America, the landed creole class became as worried about liberal dominance in Spain as had been their counterparts in Mexico. In 1822 the Central American landowners decided to cast their lot with Iturbide's empire and announced their annexation to royalist Mexico. When Iturbide abdicated in 1823, the modern-day Central American states, from Guatemala to Costa Rica (excluding Panama), became the independent United Provinces of Central America. By the 1830s, Spain's holdings in the New World were reduced to Cuba and Puerto Rico.

The Brazilian Path

Independence came to Brazil in a manner very different from that of Spanish America. That was partly due to the fact that Brazil was by 1800 far more populous and prosperous than the tiny mother country. By contrast, no single Spanish colonial territory equaled metropolitan Spain in economic or political power. When the colonials proclaimed independence, Spain fought back doggedly, and Spanish Americans grew to hate the crown. The Portuguese, on the other hand, did not even have the military power to stop the Brazilians' move toward political autonomy.

The context of Brazilian independence pointed up another important difference. When the Napoleonic army invaded Iberia in November 1807, the entire Portuguese court was able to flee to Brazil, thanks to the British royal navy.

During the colonial period, Portugal had not allowed its most important possession to establish universities, operate printing presses, or trade with other nations. The newly arrived prince regent and later monarch Dom João VI promptly decreed the end of Portugal's commercial monopoly by opening Brazil's ports. His logic was obvious. Since Napoleon now controlled Portugal, the exiled Portuguese monarch could continue to benefit from Brazil's foreign trade only if the formerly exclusive link with Lisbon was severed. The prime beneficiaries were the British, who had, after all, brought the Braganza family and its retinue to Brazil.

Britain gained privileged access to Brazil in 1810 by official, fifteen-year agreements which (1) gave Britain the lowest tariff (even lower than Portugal!) on goods entering Brazil; (2) committed the Portuguese crown to the gradual abolition of the African slave trade; and (3) guaranteed British subjects in Brazil the right of trial by British-named judges. These treaties soon caused deep resentment among the Brazilian elite.

The exiled Portuguese monarch now set about creating new institutions, such as a national library, a national museum, and a botanical garden, all in Rio de Janeiro. Dom João VI invited a French artistic mission to speed professionalization in architecture, painting, and sculpture.

The crown also sought to attract foreign immigrants to Brazil. It had very limited success, and large-scale European immigration was not to begin until the late 1880s. There was a push to promote textile manufacture, including repeal of the 1785 royal decree that banned all industry. But such measures could not get at the deeper causes of Brazil's economic backwardness: the lack of capital, technology, skilled labor, a significant domestic market, and a reliance on slaves for all forms of manual work.

In 1814 French troops were driven from Portugal, but British forces that had joined the Portuguese in expelling the French remained. After they, too, left the country, an assembly (Cortes Gerais) was called to write a new constitution. The newly victorious Portuguese Liberals, interested in exploiting Brazil's wealth, pressed for the return of the royal court to Portugal. Dom João soon did return to Lisbon, leaving his son Dom Pedro behind in Brazil as the prince regent of the Combined Kingdoms.

Attention now focused on the Cortes Gerais, which approved measures that would have restored Lisbon's royal trade monopoly in Brazil. The Cortes also approved measures returning the individual Brazilian provinces to direct and separate rule from Lisbon, thereby undermining the central rule created in Rio de Janeiro after 1808. However "liberal" the Portuguese Liberals were in Portugal, they abhorred the move toward autonomy of their American "co-kingdom."

The landowners and urban professionals who constituted the Brazilian elite had been preparing to confront the Portuguese recolonizers. Their passionate rhetoric overflowed the fledgling Rio press. They wanted the prince regent, Dom Pedro, to remain in Brazil. The Cortes in Lisbon, however, demanded the prince regent's immediate return and took new steps to reverse Brazil's growing autonomy. The Brazilian plantation owners' pressure on Dom Pedro now paid off: on September 7, 1822, he defied the summons of the Cortes. "Independence or death!" he cried, giving birth to the only durable independent monarchy in modern Latin American history.

To win their independence, the Brazilians had to fight, but not on the scale of the Spanish Americans. The fiercest combat came in Bahia, on the northeastern coast, and Grão Pará, in the eastern Amazon valley. In Bahia a junta proclaimed loyalty to Portugal and fought off the local pro-independence rebels. In 1823 the rebels triumphed, aided by Admiral Cochrane, one of the English military officers hired to give the rebel governments experienced help in combat. Another mercenary, Admiral Grenfell, led the victory over a similar loyalist junta in Grão Pará. His forces then mopped up a local rebel wing that was demanding more radical social change. In Brazil, as in Mexico, the elite was alert to repress any fundamental challenge to the socioeconomic establishment.

Portugal's military weakness partly explains why Brazil's struggle for independence proved far less bloody than Spanish America's. Equally important, the Brazilian rebels did not split over the issue of republicanism because, with a few exceptions, the elite preferred a monarchy to a republic. Thanks to the exile of the court, the Brazilians could opt for an independent monarchy that legitimized centralized rule. Brazil thus entered independence with a unique legacy. Not least important, Brazilians did not associate independence with military prowess: no Brazilian Simón Bolívar or San Martín arose to dominate the patriotic imagination.

The Aftermath of Independence

The new Spanish American republics faced formidable problems as they embarked on independence in the 1820s. The physical violence of the wars wrought economic disaster. The destruction probably reached its highest point in Venezuela, where *guerra a muerte* ("war to the death") took a heavy toll on human life. The early phases of the Mexican wars, particularly during the campaigns of Hidalgo and Morelos, took a similar toll on people and property. Uruguay, where José Artigas led bands of gaucho rebels against well-entrenched Spanish troops, also suffered grave losses. During the second phase of the movement, the theater of operations shifted to other areas, especially Peru, where the fighting appears to have been less intensive than before—but the burden of supporting large armies was nevertheless heavy. The civilian labor force was decimated and, throughout the continent, capital was scarce.

The economies of the new nations were overwhelmingly based on agriculture and mining. This was equally true of most of the world outside West Europe. Yet Latin America differed from most of Africa, the Middle East, and Asia in that over the past two and a half centuries it had been partially brought into the world trading economy dominated by Europe. It was the exportable surplus from Latin American agricultural and mining production that linked it to the North Atlantic economy. With the creation of separate countries, this basic economic structure remained intact almost everywhere, slowly to be modified in succeeding decades.

Trade had come to an almost complete standstill between 1810 and 1826. Commerce with Spain had stopped, and trade among the former colonies was also greatly reduced. Northwest Argentina, for instance, suffered from the loss of trade with Peru. Guerrilla warfare in New Spain and other areas made transport difficult and dangerous. Communications systems within and between the former colonies, never much favored by the Spaniards, fell into near-total disuse.

There was also the factor of postindependence regional conflict within major areas of Spanish and Portuguese America. Mexico was wracked by battles which kept that country divided and without effective national direction before 1850. Brazil, at the same time, collapsed into a series of regionalist revolts after Pedro I abdicated the throne and returned to Europe, leaving his five-year old son and heir, Pedro II, under the guidance of a regency. This left the monarchy effectively neutralized until the 1840s. And in the Río de la Plata region, the fierce rivalry between the province of Buenos Aires and the rest of the country was temporarily resolved only by the dictatorship of Juan Manuel de Rosas (1829–52). Everywhere the move was to assert economic autonomy by locality or region. That meant fragmentation. In Spanish America it meant that Bolívar's dream would be buried under the advance of nationalism. One after another of the new republics claimed economic independence. They would soon find the world market a sobering test.

In many parts of Spanish America, the new governments had to deal with public debts even before they could attempt to rebuild their economies. To sustain the fighting, to equip the armies, the insurgent regimes frequently had to obtain or borrow funds. Tax collection, to put it mildly, was difficult. As a result, the national treasuries were empty, and government authorities had to turn elsewhere for funds. A prime source was Britain, where bankers supported the regimes with loans—particularly in Argentina, Chile, Peru, and Mexico. Thus the new governments immediately ran up debts to foreign lenders. Managing the foreign debt has remained, down to the present day, a major problem for Latin American governments.

Another area in which foreign capital invested was the African slave trade, which continued on a large scale to Brazil (until 1850) and Cuba (until 1865). Both had an export-oriented agriculture that made slave labor profitable during an era when it was being abolished elsewhere in the Western Hemisphere.

The years between 1830 and 1850 saw Latin America's exports to the North Atlantic economy increase. The following were key primary products: wheat and nitrates from Chile, tobacco from Colombia, hides, salted beef, and wool from Argentina, guano from Peru, sugar from Cuba, coffee from Brazil, and cacao from Venezuela. These same countries were heavily importing textiles and consumer goods, thereby often throwing local artisan producers out of work. It was the industrial producers in West Europe (especially Britain) competing against the small-scale Latin American producers who had survived from the colonial era. The result was a foregone conclusion.

This was all part of free trade, the dogma that had arrived in Latin America with Enlightenment philosophy and the postindependence commitment to the principles of liberalism. Applying this dogma was the most significant economic policy decision in nineteenth-century Latin America. Along with a rapid inflow of foreign (primarily European) imports came a small cadre of foreign merchants, especially British. They became key figures throughout Latin America in the import of goods and services, the latter including shipping, insurance, and financing.

Should we be surprised that manufactured goods from Europe steadily displaced domestic products? Wasn't it inevitable that Europe's greater technology and economies of scale would prevail? Transportation costs should have helped protect local producers, but the supposed (or genuine) superiority of foreign-made goods posed a serious dilemma soon after independence and has continued down to today. Latin American economies often failed to make their own industry truly competitive. Why? Lack of a sufficient market was certainly a factor. But equally important was the system of values and the social hierarchy which made it possible for the elite to perpetuate a society based on an agrarian-oriented economy.

The economic record of the 1830–50 period is therefore one of slow adaptation to the world economy. Latin America was on the fringes of the North Atlantic economy, which was to expand rapidly in the nineteenth century. Both research and data on the economic history of this era are distressingly scarce—but it appears, on the basis of evidence available, that Latin America's republics took a passive stance. The dynamism came from outside.

The creation and maintenance of large armies in most Latin American republics also crucially affected the social order because they created a channel for careers based on talent. As the fighting intensified and the stakes increased, creole rebel leaders had to recruit soldiers and commanders on ability, rather than on skin color or social status. Thus José Antonio Páez, a rough-hewn *mestizo*, became a valued military leader in Venezuela. In Mexico José María Morelos was *mestizo*. Other examples abound. Military prowess became a means by which members of marginal groups could gain social recognition. None of the newly independent governments retained legal disabilities for *mestizos* or others of mixed racial backgrounds, a fact which helped to blur once-rigid social lines.

But if the wars opened a social avenue for ambitious *mestizos* and others, mobility was limited. Economic resources, particularly land, remained in the hands of traditional creole families. Commerce was modest in the years right after the fighting, and many merchant families retained their control of trade. Industry barely existed. As a result, there was only one way for men of modest origin to get ahead: through the military, and from there into politics.

This social dynamic helps explain much of the political turbulence in Spanish America between the 1820s and 1850. The new republics finished the wars with large military establishments, often led by *mestizos* who had no alternative careers. To get ahead they had to stay in the army—or move into government. In the meantime, creole landowners, in many parts of the continent, did not compete for political power. They withdrew to their haciendas, which could function as self-sufficient units, and tried to increase their landholdings. In effect they left government to the soldiers and to the bosses known as *caudillos*, partly because political power did not seem worth the trouble. Later in the nineteenth century, when governmental authority became a valued commodity, *hacendados* and *estancieros* came off their lands and took over.

So governments were toppled and run by *caudillos*, often soldiers (or ex-soldiers) who took power by force. Once in the presidential office, they usually found that sparse treasuries offered little reward for their followers. Their bands then dispersed, and new *caudillos* would come forward with new bands of followers. The governments did not have strong finances and as a result were highly vulnerable to being overthrown. From the 1820s until midcentury, political authority in Spanish America was weak; the state, as a central institution, did not wield much autonomous strength.

During this era another current emerged, a move to consolidate and centralize power. It usually came out in attempted dictatorships, not popular consensus. The first two decades after independence thus saw the appearance of real or would-be "strong men," like Diego Portales in Chile and Juan Manuel de Rosas in Argentina, who sought to impose their will on their countries, thereby strengthening the role of the state. The struggle between locally based power and the centralizers—military or civilian—became a basic theme in the political life of the new nations.

If the Wars of Independence opened narrow channels for *mestizos* and middle-range groups in Spanish America, they did very little for the Indian masses. In general, natives played an ambiguous role in the struggle: though they sided with Hidalgo or stayed neutral in Mexico, they supported royalists in southern Chile, and in Peru and Colombia they fought on both sides. The leaders of the new republics therefore did not feel indebted to the Indians. More important, the Indians now lost the special protection of caste status they had enjoyed under Spanish colonial law. Whatever its drawbacks, that status had been an oft-used refuge for the Indians. They also lost their communal lands (which had been inalienable) and were theoretically forced into the competitive market so praised by nineteenth-century liberals. In fact, they became even more isolated and poverty-stricken.

Independence left a somewhat different social legacy for Brazil. Instead of *displacing* a ruling elite, as happened in Spanish America, Brazil *acquired* a ruling elite: the Portuguese crown and its attendants. Many of the Portuguese who arrived with the royal court quickly integrated into the local elite families, building close political, economic, and social ties with upper-class Brazilians. Brazil also acquired a monarchy that would last until 1889. But these political trends had little effect on the black slaves. In fact, the institution of slavery was not abolished at independence or by the 1850s, as in Spanish America (except for Cuba and Puerto Rico) and it would later become a central issue in Brazilian politics. In Brazil, as in other new nations, independence did not change life much for the poorest segments of the population.

THE PULL OF THE INTERNATIONAL ECONOMY

After 1850 Latin America moved from the postindependence consolidation phase to begin laying the foundations for its greater integration into the world economy. In political terms, this required governments ready to create the infrastructure needed to export key primary products, such as guano from Peru, coffee from Brazil, minerals from Mexico, and sugar from the Caribbean. As the era of the *caudillo* gave way to the era of the administrators, the prime task was national unification.

The independent republics moved to strengthen the use of two elements in their economies: land and labor. Most governments sought to put land into the hands of entrepreneurs to make it bear fruit. They also sought to reward political cronies, build tactical alliances, and strengthen ruling coalitions. In Brazil and Mexico that meant government pressure to sell off government (previously crown) land. Such strategies imposed devastating losses on Indian communities in Mexico and the Andes.

To provide labor, the Latin American elites in several countries hoped for immigration from Europe. Prominent intellectuals argued that European immigrants would improve the country's racial stock. These years saw repeated proposals to attract European immigrants, who would supposedly contribute to national development with little further investment. In fact, the elite—in countries like Argentina and Brazil—soon found that immigration was a sensitive issue, both at home and in the countries sending the migrants. Before 1880 immigration was nowhere a major factor in increasing the labor force. But the strong elite impulse to recruit migrants demonstrated their belief that their countries' economic and social salvation was to be found in Europe. As will become apparent, this reflected Latin American doubts about their countries' viability.

The mid-nineteenth century also saw an effort to improve Latin America's transportation network. What was needed were railroads, canals, docks, and roads. Since the sixteenth century, cargo (including people) had traveled by pack-mule or burro. In only a few areas did navigable rivers or lakes offer an alternative. By midcentury Latin America was the target for numerous proposals to build railroads. The capital usually came from foreigners, especially British and North American, while national governments provided the initiative.

The rhythm of economic activity quickened throughout Latin America after 1850. The stimulus came primarily from the dynamic economies of North America and West Europe, led by Britain. As Europe plunged ever more deeply into industrialization, it needed increasing imports of food, such as sugar, beef, and grain, as well as primary commodities, such as guano and nitrate fertilizers, wool, and industrial metals. These were the decades when economic ties—trade, investment, financing, technology transfer, migration—deepened between Europe and Mexico, Argentina, Peru, Chile, Brazil, and Cuba (even though still a Spanish colony). By 1880 the stage was set for even greater economic expansion.

The economic upturn after 1850 had important limitations. First, it resulted in very little growth of domestic industry. The rising Latin American need for metal tools, small machines, instruments, construction equipment, weapons, and similar light industrialized goods was primarily met from Europe, not from home-country shops or factories. The trend was hardly surprising. The British, French, or U.S. products were mostly of better quality than anything produced at home, although that advantage could have been narrowed if the domestic producers had had enough time and a sufficient market to upgrade quality. But that would have required government protection either through high tariffs or outright import prohibitions.

No Latin American government was prepared or able to take such a step at this time. Economic power groups, such as the landowners and cattlemen, were strongly committed to free trade, which their European customers preached as the only true road to prosperity; and merchants, strategically located in the largest cities, had an obvious stake in fighting protection. That motive was even greater when the merchant was a foreigner (usually British or French), as happened frequently by midcentury. Against this array of forces, the Latin American advocates of protectionism or state-aided industry could make little headway.

A second limitation was its reinforcement of the highly stratified socioeconomic structure inherited from the independence era: a thin elite at the top, a slightly wider middle group, and the other 80 to 90 percent at the bottom. The continued focus on agro-ranching and mining meant that most laborers would continue under working conditions and rates of pay that could never move them toward becoming the consumers that a "developed" economy both produces and needs.

Latin America was being pulled further into the international economy in a way that would strongly condition its subsequent development. The nature of that economic link has continued to provoke historical debate and will be a recurrent theme in the rest of this book.

PART TWO

Case Studies

Change over Time

3

MEXICO

The Taming of a Revolution

The history of Mexico offers a study in contrast. Rich in natural resources, the country has known both prosperity (if only for the elite) and poverty. For several decades after independence the nation's political life was a prototype of chronic instability. National governments came and went at gunpoint, threatening the new nation's territorial integrity. By the mid-nineteenth century, Mexico was embracing a political liberalism that would have greatly reduced church power and the corresponding burdens of its colonial legacy. Yet this thrust gave way to decades of dictatorship and then to the Mexican Revolution—the first of the world's great twentieth-century revolutions. Out of the Revolution came a political system which produced, for more than half a century, a political stability unmatched in Latin America. It also postponed Mexico's transition to electoral democracy, which would not occur until the year 2000.

Among all countries of Latin America, Mexico has had the most intense—and most complex—relationship with the United States. Symbolic of this situation is the 2000-mile land border shared by the two nations. This proximity has produced benefits and liabilities (according to a well-known adage, "Poor Mexico! So far from God, and so close to the United States!"). The countries have waged war with one other, joined together against common threats, and developed close and binding economic ties. Migrant workers from Mexico take low-paying jobs and remit billions of dollars to their home communities, while Mexican American voters form a sought-after bloc in U.S. politics. Cultural integration takes everyday form in popular music, cuisine, cinema, and sports. Like it or not, the destiny of Mexico has been unavoidably intertwined with the United States.

FROM COLONY TO NATIONHOOD

The Wars of Independence left Mexico in disorder and decay. Conditions were far worse in Mexico than in Argentina or Brazil because the actual fighting had been so much more widespread and protracted in Mexico. The economy was in

Map 3 Mexico

shambles. Spaniards had taken their capital out of the country. The gold and silver mines, once the pride of Spain's overseas empire, had fallen into disrepair. Insurgents and royalists had both made a point of killing technicians while thousands of miners had gone off to war; without sufficient supervision, the mines had flooded and machinery became utterly useless. Production plummeted to one-third its prewar level. Mining communities languished: Valenciana, for example, had 22,000 residents in 1810 and only 4000 in 1820. It would take another generation—and considerable sums of foreign investment—to restore the precious mines to full production.

The textile industry had also fallen on hard times. The scars of battle were visible throughout the country, especially the central valley. As one traveler recalled, there were "ruins everywhere—here a viceroy's palace serving as a tavern, where the mules stop to rest, and the drivers to drink pulque—there, a whole village crumbling to pieces; roofless houses, broken down walls and arches, an old church—the remains of a convent."

Roads had been neglected as well, so the country lacked a workable system of transportation and communication. Having ruled for 300 years, the Spaniards had managed to construct only three highways worthy of the name. Travel by stagecoach was difficult and hazardous, and transport—often by pack saddle—was costly and slow. This was a serious obstacle to economic integration.

Economic disorder meant very few jobs and much unemployment. According to one estimate, about 300,000 men, most of whom had fought in the wars, had no job or income when the battles came to an end. This represented 15 to 30 percent of the entire adult male population. They were eager, often angry, and usually armed. They posed not only an economic problem but a social threat as well.

Some of these veterans managed to find work. Others turned to crime (highway robbery being a particular favorite). Others stayed in the army. Still others drifted into unofficial, quasi-military units that provided support for local political bosses, generally known as *caudillos,* who were soon to play a dominant role in the Mexican political scene.

The wars also had a direct effect on Mexico's social structure. In the late 1820s the new government issued a decree expelling all Spaniards from Mexico. This ruling not only allowed the public to vent its hatred for the Spaniards, it also deprived the economy of an important source of capital. And it eliminated, at a single stroke, a leading segment of the nation's upper class or aristocracy. Now creole landowners, not Spanish born, formed the upper echelons of Mexican society.

Economic transformations dating back to the Bourbon era, together with gradual recovery in the 1830s and 1840s, had made it possible for new groups to acquire wealth and status. Centered mainly in Mexico City, these aspirants, like most nouveaux riches, were ostentatious, putting on elaborate displays. In sum, early nineteenth-century Mexico had a creole upper class with two parts: one consisted of old, traditional families who for the most part kept to their land; the other was new, drawn from commerce and the professions as well as land. And it was the new segment, the recently arrived, who became active in politics.

Poverty persisted among the vast majority of the population. Especially in the center and the south, Mexico had a classic peasantry—large masses of *campesinos,* or country people, who scratched out meager livings from the land. Largely of Indian origin, sometimes mixed-blood or *mestizo,* Mexico's peasants furnished labor for the agricultural sector. Many worked on haciendas, where they lived in virtual serfdom, and some went begging in the cities.

The existence of this underemployed peasantry also guaranteed Mexico a large surplus labor force. Partly for this reason and partly because of antiforeign sentiment, Mexican authorities did not encourage immigration from abroad. In contrast to Argentina (Chapter 9), Mexico never acquired a predominantly European-born working class. Nor did it undergo rapid population growth at any point in the nineteenth century. Starting with about 6 million residents in 1800, the country had about 7.6 million people in 1850; by 1900 the figure had climbed to 13.6 million, but even this represents a modest annual average growth rate of less than 1.2 percent over the fifty-year period. Mexico's population explosion would not come until the twentieth century.

There were two institutional bases of power in Mexico after independence—the church and the military. The church had come through the independence wars with most of its immense wealth intact. According to at least one observer, the

---

State Protocol and High Society

Outsiders can provide remarkable insight into social customs. Such was the case with Fanny Calderón de la Barca (1804–82), the Scottish-born wife of the Spanish minister to Mexico in the late 1830s and early 1840s. Her acute observations captured the fragility of a still-emerging social order, as in her description of reactions to her plan to wear a local dress from the state of Puebla to an upcoming "fancy ball":

> [On January 5, 1840] We had a concourse of Spaniards, all of whom seemed anxious to know whether or not I intended to wear a Poblana dress at the fancy ball, and seemed wonderfully taken up about it. Two indefinite looking young Poblana ladies . . . told me that every one was very much pleased at the idea of my going in a Poblana dress. I thought everyone had very little to do and was rather surprised that *every one* should trouble themselves about it.
>
> About twelve o'clock the president, in full uniform, attended by his aides-de-camp, paid me a visit, and sat pottering and talking for about half an hour, making himself very amiable as usual and as agreeable as he could. Shortly after came more Spaniards, and just as we were in hopes that our visiting was over, and were going to dinner, we were told that the secretary of state, the ministers of war, and of the interior, and others, were all in the drawing-room. In solemn array they came, and what do you think was the purport of their visit? To inform us that all Mexico was in a state of *shock* at the idea of my going in a Poblana dress, and to adjure me, by all that was most alarming, to discard the idea! They assured us that all Poblanas were *femmes de rien*—now this is what I call a sweeping clause on the part of the ministry—that they wore no stockings, and that *la ministra de España* should by no means wear, even for one evening, such a dress.

Ever the diplomat, Fanny "thanked the cabinet council for their warning" and managed to find a conventional gown.

Quotation from *Life in Mexico: The Letters of Fanny Calderón de la Barca*, ed. Howard T. and Marion Hall Fisher (Garden City, N.Y.: Doubleday, 1966), pp. 125 and 691 (note 1).

---

church may have controlled nearly one-half the nation's land. The church earned regular income from its vast real estate holdings and its investments, and it was by far the largest banking operation in all Mexico. Its generous loans to large land-owners not only guaranteed a steady income but also created a firm alliance with the upper echelons of Mexican society. Small wonder that the church and its economic holdings would eventually become a target of opposition, particularly among those who failed to benefit from ecclesiastical largesse.

The second power base was the military, which dominated national politics. During the forty-year period from 1821 to 1860, Mexico had at least fifty separate presidencies, each lasting for an average of less than one year; thirty-five of these ill-starred regimes were led by army officers. The basic means of winning presidential office was through a military coup. And looming throughout this period was the tragicomic figure of Antonio López de Santa Anna, who held the presidency on nine separate occasions and who installed figureheads at other times.

Santa Anna was the most famous of Mexico's *caudillos*. These strongmen assembled their armed followers—miniature armies—who were primarily seeking wealth. Once they fought their way into national power, however, they often found that the treasury was running out (usually from previous military spending). Eventually the reigning *caudillo* band would break up, and a new leader, with new followers, would seize power. The *caudillos* themselves did not bother with the arts of governance. That was left to a cadre of lawyers and professionals, many from Mexico City, who staffed the ministries (and in this, the same faces often reappeared: there were nearly 600 separate cabinet appointments between 1820 and 1860, but they went to only 207 individuals). Thus did *caudillo* politics entail continuity as well as change.

The North American Invasion

Crippled by the Wars of Independence, Mexico was a weak and vulnerable new nation. To the north lay another new nation, which had thrown off its English master fifty years earlier. Now the fledgling United States was rolling westward and southward, headed for the vast, virtually unpopulated northern domains of what was formerly the Viceroyalty of New Spain.

Spaniards had never found the resources to settle the north—the huge territories of California, the entire Colorado River valley, and Texas. The best they could do was to create a network of religious missions, manned above all by the resourceful and loyal Jesuits. These sprawling lands became an obvious magnet for the restless North Americans. In 1821 Stephen Austin and a group of settlers moved into Texas, then a part of Mexico. Eventually chafing under central rule from Mexico City, the Texans revolted in 1835 and declared independence the following year. Attempting to crush the rebellion, Santa Anna led Mexican troops against the Alamo, killing the Texan defenders to the last man, but he later suffered defeat at San Jacinto and Texas remained independent. In 1845 the U.S. Congress voted to annex Texas, whose leaders promptly agreed.

The Mexicans saw the annexation of Texas as equivalent to an act of war by the United States, and disputes over financial claims continued to complicate U.S.-Mexican relations. President James K. Polk sent American troops into a disputed border area, a step that the Mexicans saw as an invasion. When the Mexicans counterattacked, Polk called it war. By consent of Congress—but with the opposition of such prominent legislators as John C. Calhoun and Abraham Lincoln—Polk had the war he and his supporters sought.

It was a total mismatch. At first Santa Anna managed to resist American troops under Zachary Taylor, but in 1847 General Winfield Scott led his columns directly from Veracruz to Mexico City. Ordinary Mexicans joined the effort to fight off the U.S. army, and young military cadets—since remembered as the "boy heroes of Chapultepec"—chose death rather than to surrender their national flag. But it was to no avail. Mexico lost. The price it paid was heavy.

The treaty of Guadalupe Hidalgo brought a formal end to the war in February 1848. By the treaty, the United States paid Mexico a modest settlement of $15 million and took the entire expanse of territory from Texas to California— about half of Mexico's national domain. This was a galling defeat, and its painful memory has never died in Mexico. The official name of the dispute offers a clue to sensibilities. In the United States it is called the "Mexican-American War," but in Mexico they call it the "War of the North American Invasion."

Reform, Monarchy, and the Restored Republic

Military humiliation had long-lasting impacts on Mexico. One was to nurture a nationalistic sentiment that often took the form of a virulent Yankee-phobia, a deep-seated distrust and hostility toward the United States. An additional conse- quence was to solidify political division along partisan lines. As occurred elsewhere in nineteenth-century Latin America, Mexico developed two major parties: Conservatives, who upheld the notion of a strong central government in close alliance with the Catholic Church, and Liberals, who espoused limited government and the ending of clerical privilege. Each accused the other of causing the defeat. Led by Lucás Alemán, Conservatives maintained that Mexico had weakened itself by foolishly trying to adopt the values and institutions of Anglo-Saxons to the north. What the nation required, according to Conservatives, was a return to its Hispanic tradition. Specifically it needed to promote aristocratic ideals, protect the legal privileges of the military and the church, and create a constitutional mon- archy (perhaps by importing a European prince). In reply, Liberals argued that Mexico needed to embrace the cause of modernization, not tradition.

The standoff continued until the mid-1850s, when a desperate President Santa Anna sought to replenish the treasury (and his political fortunes) by selling off for $10 million the Mesilla Valley (today southern New Mexico and Arizona), which the United States wanted for building a railroad to newly acquired California. This decision was widely criticized as a betrayal of national resolve, and it prompted the opposition to oust Santa Anna from power in 1855.

This initiated a tumultuous period remembered in Mexico as *La Reforma* (the Reform). Civilian-led Liberal governments enacted a series of sweeping reforms aimed at building a new social order. One key measure abolished the military and ecclesiastical *fueros*, the special dispensations exempting soldiers and clerics from having to stand trial in civil courts. Another prohibited ecclesiastical and civil institutions from owning property not directly used in day-to-day operations: this meant that the church could keep its churches, monasteries, and seminaries, but would have to auction off the massive holdings that it had accumulated over the centuries. (This was not social revolution: the lands were sold to wealthy *hacendados*, not landless peons. In fact, this provision worked to the detriment of the poor, since it required the sale of properties held by *ejidos*, the communal landholdings of Indian villages.) A third initiative transferred the powers of registry from the church to the state: all births, marriages, adoptions, and deaths were henceforth to be registered by civil functionaries. In 1857 most of these provisions found their way into a new constitution, a liberal charter that granted Mexicans their first genuine bill of inalienable rights.

A Conservative reaction then resulted in the War of the Reform (1858–61), a struggle that was in many ways the culmination of the programmatic disputations, church-state controversies, and minor civil wars that had followed in the wake of independence. As military campaigns intensified, so did ideological disputes. Now under Benito Juárez, a self-made lawyer of humble Indian origin, a Liberal government-in-waiting issued a series of decrees extending the spirit of the Laws of Reform—establishing birth and marriage as civil ceremonies, nationalizing church assets and properties, limiting religious processions in the streets, and, most important, formally separating church and state. After years of bitter fighting Juárez made a triumphant entrance into Mexico City and was formally elected president in 1861.

Peace still proved elusive. As the country confronted bankruptcy, Juárez declared a two-year moratorium on Mexico's foreign debt—thus earning the wrath of European creditors. Seeking to expand its empire and influence, France, under Emperor Napoleon III, commenced a five-year war of occupation. (Mexican forces temporarily halted the French advance toward Mexico City in a battle at Puebla on May 5, 1862, a victory that continues to be commemorated in festive *Cinco de Mayo* celebrations.) With Juárez removed from office, Napoleon III installed the Austrian archduke, Ferdinand Maximilian von Hapsburg, as emperor of Mexico (thus enacting the Conservative prescription for national redemption). Arriving in May 1864, a naive Maximilian tried to ingratiate himself with his new subjects by touring the provinces, declaring freedom of the press, and proclaiming a broad amnesty for political prisoners. Juárez nonetheless resisted, and civil war ensued. Distracted by concerns in Europe, Napoleon eventually decided to withdraw French troops from Mexico. Hopelessly exposed by this betrayal, Maximilian surrendered in May 1867. An unforgiving Juárez ordered his execution the following month. Thus ended Mexico's experience with monarchy.

The resumption of power by Liberals ushered in what has come to be known as the "restored republic." Juárez and his republican cohorts earnestly attempted to set Mexico on the path of modernization. Reelected to a third term as president in July 1867, Juárez promoted extensive economic and educational reforms. Things went so well that he ran for a fourth time in 1871, in one of the most hotly contested elections of the nineteenth century. As Congress sealed Juárez's triumph, one of the losers, Porfirio Díaz, refused to accept the result and angrily proclaimed that indefinite reelection of the chief executive endangered the country's principles and institutions. The Díaz uprising was quickly put down, however, and Sebastián Lerdo de Tejada easily succeeded to the presidency after Juárez suddenly died of a heart attack in 1872.

Lerdo's term in office was relatively tranquil and constructive, but problems arose when the president announced plans to seek reelection in 1876.

A self-righteous Díaz once again revolted in the name of effective suffrage and no-reelection. After only one decisive military encounter, Díaz occupied Mexico City in November 1876. Directly or indirectly, he would dominate the country for decades to come.

The Díaz Era: Progress at a Price

For the thirty-five years from 1876 to 1911, Díaz proved himself to be a master of politics. He began with his military colleagues and followers and from there went on to create a broad coalition. He gave the regional *caudillos* room to maneuver, encouraging them to fight among themselves. As his presidency matured, he steadily built up the army. In order to maintain control of the countryside, where the vast majority of Mexicans lived, Díaz relied heavily on the feared *guardias rurales*, or rural police. In short, Díaz patiently built up the power of the federal government where it counted—in military and police power.

At first Díaz did not seem to represent anything new in politics. He was, after all, a product of the liberal movement. As time passed, it became clear that Díaz was a Liberal with a difference. He cultivated neutrality on the crucial question of the church, neither attacking it (like most Liberals) nor defending it. He conspicuously allowed his devoutly Catholic second wife to serve as a symbol of reconciliation toward the institution the Liberals had pilloried.

In other respects, Díaz stuck to liberal principles. In one of his most important and far-ranging measures, he ruled that the ban on corporate landholdings, a liberal measure of the 1850s aimed primarily at the church, should apply to Indian villages. This opened vast new areas to speculators, ranchers, and political favorites. In 1894 Díaz helped the landowners even more by decreeing that unused lands, or *terrenos baldíos*, could be taken over for private exploitation. The crucial source of new capital was to come from abroad. Díaz and his leading ministers sought out prospective foreign investors, especially U.S. and British, and offered them generous concessions. This overall strategy thus applied the principles of economic liberalism that had captured most Latin American elites in the closing decades of the nineteenth century. In Mexico the writers, technocrats, and intellectually inclined politicians who articulated these doctrines earned the label of the *científicos*, underlining their supposed link to positivist philosophy.

Díaz proved his command of politics in that most fundamental of ways: he stayed in power far longer than any would have dared to predict. For three and a half decades he held the presidency, with only one interruption (Manuel González: 1880–84). He believed that he was giving Mexico the precious gift of political stability, which he saw as indispensable for economic growth. If that required some repression, it was for a good cause. A shrewd politician, Díaz had the constitution amended, time and again, so that he could be reelected to the presidency—blithely contradicting his prior denunciations of self-perpetuation in office. Díaz knew how to appeal to the privileged sectors, how to make them loyal, how to orchestrate their support for the economic schemes that would raise their country to a "civilized" level.

Economic development was impressive. Railroads were a striking example. Díaz first tried to build them with public funds, but by late 1880 he began granting concessions to foreigners. In only four years the track in operation grew from 750 miles to 3600 miles. Mexico reached 12,000 miles of track by 1900. Originally foreign built, most railroads were taken over by the state in 1907.

As elsewhere in Latin America, foreign trade rocketed: ninefold between 1877 and 1910. The United States became Mexico's leading trade partner, as mineral exports expanded to copper and zinc, as well as silver and gold. Modest industrialization occurred, centered in textiles, cement, iron, and light consumer goods. Díaz set great store by the need to pursue economic policies that would maintain Mexico's creditworthiness in the United States and Europe. In 1895 the federal government produced a budget surplus, and for the rest of Díaz's regime all budgets were balanced. As celebrations for the independence centennial of 1910 approached, Díaz and his lieutenants could claim that they had realized in Mexico the widespread ideal of "order and progress."

Economic activity varied in character from region to region, and this led to differing social structures. The north was primarily a mining and ranching area, where the workers were hired laborers—miners, for instance, and cowboys. The central valley, by contrast, produced wheat and grain on medium- and large-sized farms. Sugar was raised in the south-central region, particularly in the state of Morelos, where traditional peasant lands were being seized for use by the mills. Vast henequen plantations prospered in the Yucatán, where local natives were compelled to work as peons.

Under Díaz, Mexico never developed a strong entrepreneurial class. Concessions and favors came from the state, and capital came from abroad— England, France, and, of course, the United States. The middle sectors were extremely weak as well.

These social factors bore deep political significance. Elsewhere in Latin America, middle-class professionals provided pressure and leadership for reformist movements, and on occasion they drew support from fledgling industrialists. Not so in Mexico. Turn-of-the-century Mexico had the social ingredients for a revolution, but relatively little material for reform.

The economic progress of the Díaz years also had its cost. While the wealthy prospered and duly copied the ways of the European aristocracy, the vast majority of Mexicans faced grinding poverty. Given its labor surplus, Mexico's wage rates remained very low. Indeed, one estimate (doubtless exaggerated) showed that the average purchasing power in 1910 was only one-quarter the 1810 level. Mexico exported agricultural products, while production of most Mexicans' dietary staples—corn and beans (frijoles)—barely kept up with population growth. Vital statistics were alarming. In 1900, 29 percent of all male babies died within their first year, and many of the survivors ended up working twelve hours a day in a sweatshop. Only a quarter of the population was literate.

This highly unequal economic "progress" drew repeated protests from workers, both urban and rural. There were strikes, sometimes fierce, especially where wage labor worked under industrial-type conditions. Between 1906 and 1908, for example, Mexican workers at the Cananea Copper Company repeatedly protested the higher wages given to U.S. laborers. Significant strikes occurred also among the railroad workers and at the Río Blanco textile mills. Labor protest was intensified by an international financial crisis in 1906–8. In the rural sector, peasants in the Morelos area bitterly resented losing their land to commercial cultivation of sugar and other market crops. In the north there was a similar reaction to the loss of land for railway construction.

Díaz and his advisers could pursue a consistent economic policy because they had created the most effectively centralized government that Mexico had seen since independence. Decision making was concentrated in Mexico City, at the expense of local or regional *caudillos*. Political office, especially at the federal level, was sought after by the higher level of society. Those who made it were envied, since economic gain so often required contact with the government. Pressure was mounting as frustration grew among the younger elite who were excluded from the Díaz coterie. Time was working against Díaz, but who could have predicted the result?

THE MEXICAN REVOLUTION

Few revolutions are precipitated by the oppressed. Far more often they begin with a split within the dominant elite. Disgruntled dissidents, frequently young, become angry enough to attack the system. So it was in Mexico in 1910.

One of the leading critics was Francisco I. Madero, scion of a family that had made a fortune in cattle and mining and that was linked to Díaz' political machine. Evaristo Madero, Francisco's grandfather, had been governor of the state of Coahuila from 1880 to 1884, and the Madero family had cultivated a close friendship with José Y. Limantour, Díaz' longtime finance minister. Francisco got the best of a foreign education, studying in Paris and at the University of California. He returned to apply his skills in commercial agriculture, especially on the family's cotton plantation. He was a strong liberal in economics, which fit the Díaz era, but also in politics, which did not. His belief in political democracy soon alienated him from the rigidities of the late Díaz regime. He became an outspoken opponent, arguing that Mexico was ready for electoral democracy and that if Díaz chose to run for reelection in 1910 (as everyone expected), then the vice presidential candidate must come from outside the presidential clique.

Díaz was by now the captive of his own success. Why should he take seriously the lamentations of an ambitious and spoiled young oligarch? When the dictator failed to heed his message, Madero did the unthinkable: he entered the 1910 presidential campaign as the candidate of the Anti-Reelectionist Party. Díaz now faced greater opposition than at any time in decades. His electoral machine produced another victory, but it was far from effortless. The police had to jail 5000 of the opposition, including Madero. The young rebel, now emboldened, refused to recognize the legitimacy of Díaz' reelection. Instead, he issued (while in jail—which

Emiliano Zapata gave determined leadership to the revolutionary peasant movement that began in the state of Morelos.

suggests that Díaz hardly had an iron grip) his famous *Plan de San Luis Potosí* and called for armed resistance. The rebel movement grew rapidly, as its troops took Ciudad Juárez (across the border from El Paso, Texas). In a surprising show of weakness, Díaz suddenly capitulated and left the country in May 1911. A new election was held, and Madero triumphed. In 1912, he became the nation's president before delirious crowds in Mexico City. Democracy, it seemed, was on its way.

Francisco Madero and his fellow dissidents may have started the Mexican Revolution, but they did not long control it. Other rebels had larger goals: Emiliano Zapata, for example, emerged as the rock-hard leader of landless peasants in the southwestern state of Morelos. They were the country dwellers who had seen their traditional land rights taken away by the smooth-talking lawyers and speculators using the new laws of "liberal" inspiration. These *zapatistas* (as they became known) saw the rebellion as a chance to restore justice. That meant regaining their lands. When Madero failed to support their cause, they dismissed him and declared their own revolution.

Madero was hardly a true revolutionary. He was a would-be parliamentarian who thought Díaz' abdication would open the way to true democracy. Madero

In the north Pancho Villa created a powerful military juggernaut, but his personal flamboyance earned him a dubious reputation in Mexico and the United States. (Courtesy of the Library of Congress.)

flinched at the thought—suggested to him by less squeamish rebels—that he should strike at his opposition before they struck at him. The mistake cost him his life in 1913. His killer was his own military chief of staff, Victoriano Huerta, a high-ranking general under Díaz. Huerta dragged the indiscreet U.S. ambassador Henry Lane Wilson into his plot, thereby ensuring that the United States would continue its notorious role in Mexican politics.

Huerta was a crude figure, who thought he could reestablish a version of the Porfirian regime. He tried to impose his authority across the aroused country, but soon met resistance. Many Mexicans who had been caught up in the revolt against Díaz now saw Huerta as the usurper. Opposition began to build, and as it gathered force it coalesced into the genuinely "revolutionary" phase of the Mexican Revolution. It also plunged the nation into a bloody civil war.

One of the most powerful centers of resistance to Huerta was the northern state of Chihuahua, where Pancho Villa gained control. Villa was a rough-hewn ex–cattle rustler who had mobilized a small army. Unlike Zapata, with whom he was often compared, he led no peasant rebellion. Villa's supporters, at least initially, were small ranchers, unemployed miners and workers, and cowboys: men who wanted jobs, not small plots of land. So it was not surprising that when Villa pronounced an agrarian reform, in December 1913, he called for confiscation of large haciendas, but not for their subdivision into plots. The state would administer the haciendas, and their commercial crops would help finance Villa's military machine.

Villa quickly put this idea into practice. Although it created administrative problems, it achieved its goal. Money was produced and supplies were obtained (mainly from the United States, which remained the great arms supplier for all Mexican revolutionaries). Villa's army was well fed and well equipped. Indeed, Villa's followers now had a sure source of employment in his army, which emerged as a well-paid professional mercenary outfit.

Another challenge to Huerta came from Madero's home state of Coahuila, where governor Venustiano Carranza mounted a strong resistance movement. Carranza, like Madero, was a dissident member of the elite, having risen to the level of senator during the regime of Díaz. A wealthy landowner, he had also been an interim governor. After some hesitation, he joined the "Anti-Reelectionist" movement during the campaign of 1910. Once the revolutionaries came to power, Carranza was designated as the governor of Coahuila.

Carranza contested Huerta's usurpation with little more than a counter-claim. Carranza's *Plan de Guadalupe* (March 1913) simply declared that Huerta held power illegitimately and that he, Carranza, should be recognized as "First Chief of the Constitutionalist Army." Once established, the new president would then convoke new elections. The plan included no attempt to discuss larger socioeconomic or ideological questions. The *carrancista* movement looked like another *caudillo*-type rumbling. Support was scattered, mostly rural, obviously limited to the north.

Eventually it was foreign intervention, not Mexican arms, that doomed Huerta. U.S. president Woodrow Wilson, determined not to recognize Huerta's government, had sent marines to occupy Veracruz after an incident involving the arrest of U.S. sailors. To counter the U.S. marines, Huerta had to deploy troops against the Americans—which weakened his position in the civil war. Soon his situation was hopeless. In early July 1914 he resigned, accusing the United States of having overthrown him.

By mid-1914, the social fissures in the Revolution were becoming painfully obvious. Villa, and especially Zapata, represented claims for radical social change. Carranza sensed that he would have to offer more than liberal rhetoric and began to edge leftward. He promised, without details, "legislation for the improvement of the condition of the rural peon, the worker, the miner, and in general the proletarian classes." Soon thereafter, he pronounced an agrarian reform, calling for the restoration or creation of agricultural communities *(ejidos)*, requesting procedures for restoring legal titles, and establishing a national agrarian commission. And then Carranza made his move toward labor: he got the anarcho-syndicalists—the best organized of the small urban labor movements—to agree that in return for favorable labor laws their Red Batallions would back the *carrancista* cause.

During 1915 the military tide turned in Carranza's favor. Álvaro Obregón, his brilliant army commander from the northern state of Sonora, decisively defeated Villa in a major battle. Villa retreated to the hills of Chihuahua to continue a guerrilla war, but no longer offered a national threat. The *zapatistas* could not mount a sustained challenge to Mexico City and withdrew into their native Morelos to hold out against federal incursions.

With his principal enemies safely at bay, Carranza could afford to call a constitutional convention in late 1916. In May 1917 he formally assumed the presidency. The stage was now set for the writing of the Mexican Constitution of 1917, a premier document of the Mexican Revolution.

Carranza himself had no radical ideas. He drafted a pale imitation of the Constitution of 1857, little more than a restatement of principles of classical liberalism. The convention delegates had other thoughts. They took control and wrote a charter that was startlingly radical for this pre-Bolshevik era. Article 27 empowered the government to redistribute land. Article 123 announced rights for labor that had certainly never been heard of in North America. Article 3 subjected the church to new restrictions, which imposed a virtual straightjacket. Socialist overtones permeated the constitution. Suddenly it became obvious that what had started as a mere revolt of dissident elitists against Díaz was threatening to become a social revolution, to change significantly the power and property relationships in Mexico. After 1917 every aspiring political leader had to adopt at least a rhetorical posture in favor of Mexico's workers and the peasants.

The agrarian rebels—Villa and Zapata—continued to maintain their strongholds and represent a possible threat to Carranza. Zapata was dispatched in 1919, murdered by *carrancista* troops in an ambush. The following year Carranza faced his own problem: he wanted to impose a little-known politician, Ignacio Bonillas, as his successor. In this Carranza was short-sighted. The "no-reelection" slogan of the 1910 campaign had been its most powerful rallying call, and it found explicit expression in the new constitution. Now Carranza was violating that rule in spirit by imposing a successor who would be his stooge. The Revolution reverted to its bloody practice: the valiant Obregón, the architect of victory over Villa, led an uprising. Carranza was forced to flee and, while on the run, was assassinated by one of his own guards, probably acting on behalf of Obregón. The succession problem, which had led to Díaz' fall, was still far from solved.

POLITICS AND POLICY: PATTERNS OF CHANGE

Obregón succeeded to the spoils of the presidency. His government launched an ambitious rural education campaign under the leadership of the noted intellectual José Vasconcelos. In the area of labor, the Obregón government bet heavily on the newly founded Confederación Regional Obrera Mexicana (CROM), which Obregón soon co-opted, while at the same time harassing the communist- and anarchist-led unions. On land distribution Obregón was cautious, fearing a loss of production. The last of the original popular rebels, Pancho Villa, succumbed to a fusillade of bullets in 1923, and the era of effective demands for fundamental social reform was over for the moment. Obregón did make two important contributions to the stability of the Revolution. First, he achieved an understanding with Washington—an agreement on how U.S. oil firms would be treated, in return for U.S. diplomatic recognition. Second, Obregón managed to transfer power peacefully to his successor, something no Mexican president had done since 1880.

The new president was another general from Sonora, Plutarco Elías Calles. This stolid officer-politician soon proved to be the man who would put the postrevolutionary political system on a strong footing. For Calles, however, the threat was from the right. Calling themselves the *cristeros* ("Christers"), Catholic militants mounted a broad-based ideological challenge to revolutionary ideals. The *cristeros* were by no means limited to the wealthy defenders of the old economic order; they included many simple folk who saw the Revolution as the work of the devil, to be stopped only by the sword. This pious belief was reinforced by reactionary clergy, especially in the state of Jalisco, where they desperately needed foot soldiers in their crusade against the anticlerical Revolution.

When the presidential term of Calles expired in 1928, Obregón, never politically reticent, presented himself for election anew. It was not a reelection, Obregón reassured Mexico, because he was not the incumbent. He won easily but did not live to enjoy his power play: before the inauguration, he was assassinated by a religious fanatic.

Into the vacuum stepped the lame-duck Calles. He got the political leaders to agree on a new election and on the creation of a new party, the Partido Nacional Revolucionario (PNR). During a succession of short-term presidencies, Calles continued to be the power behind the scenes.

Most observers expected Calles to continue that role in the presidency of Lázaro Cárdenas, elected in 1934. Cárdenas was a relatively obscure army officer and former governor from Michoacán who surprised everyone, promptly sending the stunned Calles into exile. It was the first of many moves proving that Cárdenas was going to be his own man.

Many peasants had grown cynical about the "revolutionary" goals of their rulers. Where was the land they had been so often promised? Cárdenas decided to make good on those promises. During his term (1934–40) he presided over the distribution of 44 million acres of land to landless Mexicans, almost twice as much as that distributed by all his predecessors combined. Cárdenas knew the dangers in simply distributing land without the necessary supporting services. All too often that led to subsistence agriculture, with the farmer able to feed his family but unable to produce a surplus for the market. That would create grave problems in the food supply to the cities, as well as for the export markets.

Cárdenas' solution was to rely heavily on the communal system of the *ejido*. It had the advantage of being genuinely Mexican, while being neither capitalist nor socialist. Land was formally distributed to the *ejido*, which became the collective owner, even if plots were subsequently apportioned for individual use. *Ejidos* could include hundreds, even thousands, of families. The plans called for schools, hospitals, and financing, which was to be provided by the newly founded Banco de Crédito Ejidal. Not all the land distribution was made to *ejidos*. Individual peasants and families got plots as well.

While the huge distribution created an initial euphoria, the longer-term results were rather mixed. Agricultural production for the market fell in many areas. The social and financial services promised by the government fell short of overall needs. The result was low productivity and disorganization on many communal units and an insufficient integration into the market for many smaller units. Notwithstanding these problems, Cárdenas became a hero to the peasantry. He had deeply reinforced the agrarian character of the Revolution.

Cárdenas also reorganized the party structure that he inherited from Calles. In 1938 Cárdenas rearranged the official party and renamed it the Partido de la Revolución Mexicana (PRM). It was now to be built around four functional groups: the agricultural (peasant) sector, the labor sector, the military sector, and the "popular" sector, which was a residual category including primarily the middle class. In applying this concept of functionalist representation, Cárdenas and his political advisers were borrowing from corporatism, the political doctrine then in vogue in Brazil and Mediterranean Europe, especially Italy, Spain, and Portugal.

In this fashion, Cárdenas devised a strategy for dealing with the lower classes: mobilize and organize *both* the workers and the peasants, but keep them apart from each other. Thus the creation of separate (and competing) sectors for each group within the official party. This way the government could maintain control of popular movements and prevent the possible appearance of a horizontal worker-peasant coalition.

Cárdenas also took a more radical line in relations with the United States. The toughest issue was oil. In the early twentieth century, Mexico possessed a significant percentage of the world's confirmed oil reserves. By the 1930s, foreign oil firms, mostly U.S. but some British, had huge investments in Mexico. The companies eventually got into a wage dispute with their Mexican employees; it was finally carried to the Mexican Supreme Court, which ruled in favor of the workers. The foreign companies disregarded the court decision, assuming that now, as before, there must be a way around such legal problems in backward Mexico. To everyone's surprise, the president intervened in 1938 and announced the expropriation of the companies. The precipitating factor cited by Cárdenas was the companies' refusal to obey the Supreme Court decision. The legal basis given for expropriation was Article 27 of the 1917 constitution, in turn based on the long-standing principle in Spanish law that all subsoil rights belong to the state (crown), not to the owner of the surface rights. The oil companies were infuriated. The American firms demanded that U.S. President Franklin Roosevelt intervene on their behalf. Right-wing propagandists in the United States had a field day at the expense of the "atheistic" Mexican revolutionaries who had first attacked religion and were now attacking property.

In Mexico the expropriation provoked an ecstatic response. Mexican nationalist sentiment, never far below the surface, poured forth; Cárdenas was now an authentic hero for standing up to the gringos.

At first Roosevelt issued some angry demands to the Mexicans, but cooler heads prevailed in Washington. After all, Roosevelt's much ballyhooed "Good Neighbor" policy meant, at a minimum, no more U.S. invasions of Latin America. In fact, the Mexican government had already said it would compensate the companies. Dispute then centered on the value of the expropriated properties.

The companies filed enormous claims, including the future value of all the oil in the ground they had owned, but they did not win their case. Subsequent negotiations eventually favored the Mexican government, whose support was badly needed by the United States on the eve of World War II.

The companies were paid, and the Mexicans created a state oil monopoly, Petróleos Mexicanos (PEMEX). For decades thereafter, it remained a high symbol of nationalism—above all, because its target had been the United States. The oil companies and their friends in the U.S. government did not forget either. For another thirty years they enforced a world boycott against all Mexican oil and effectively obstructed the development of PEMEX's refining operations by getting it blacklisted with all leading foreign equipment suppliers. One reason the companies and the U.S. government thought they had to punish the Mexicans for their nationalist boldness was to prevent other Latin American governments from attempting similar expropriations. Mexico paid a price for standing up to Uncle Sam.

In summary, the 1920s and 1930s witnessed the consolidation of Mexico's postrevolutionary political regime. It proved to be a complex and distinctive hybrid. While there were regular elections, it was clear from the outset that only the official party could actually win. Despite proclamations to the contrary, it was widely conceded that outgoing presidents would designate their successors through an informal process known as the *dedazo* (or "big finger"). (There were extensive consultations, to be sure, but the reigning president always had the last word.) Ambitious office seekers were obliged to declare fervent loyalty to revolutionary ideals, but there was no rigid ideology. And when faced by opposition, the regime's most frequent response was to bring its critics into the system—by offering a voice, a job, or a policy concession. As one observer summarized the dominant approach: two carrots, maybe even three or four, and then a stick if necessary. By embracing (and defusing) the opposition, the Mexican state managed to strengthen its support. These features would remain in practice until the 1990s, and, despite their undemocratic character, they would provide the basis for two of Mexico's distinct political achievements: civilian control over the military and more than a half century of political stability. In the wake of revolution, in other words, Mexico developed a relatively "soft" authoritarianism that bore little resemblance to the brutal military regimes that would dominate the Southern Cone from the 1960s to the 1980s.

Stability, Growth—and Rigidity

Cárdenas would have been a difficult act for any politician to follow. The choice of his successor followed a pattern repeated at the end of every six-year presidency to the 1990s: endless speculation, mostly ill-informed, over the likely nominee. In 1940 Cárdenas chose neither of the two much-discussed front-runners (one radical and one conservative) but turned instead to his little-known minister of war, General Manuel Ávila Camacho. Clearly there was a consensus within the political elite on steering the Revolution onto a moderate course.

In his campaign, Ávila Camacho made it clear that he was not anticlerical; he even declared himself a believer. And he actually faced an opponent: Juan Andreu Almazán, candidate of the Partido Acción Nacional (PAN), a fledging pro-clericalist party on the right. The official PRM candidate easily prevailed.

In several key policy areas Ávila Camacho soon proved more moderate than Cárdenas. One was land redistribution. While Cárdenas had endeared himself to the Mexican peasantry by his much-publicized land grants, Ávila Camacho targeted his distribution at individual families. And whereas Cárdenas had distributed 44 million acres, Ávila Camacho distributed only 11 million.

In the labor field, Ávila Camacho made another move away from the left. He replaced the official leader of the party's labor sector with Fidel Velázquez, who was openly hostile to the more militant union leaders and helped to make strikes more difficult. While autonomous union action was being discouraged, the government moved on another front: creating the Instituto Mexicano del Seguro Social (IMSS), a social security agency which provided workers with medical care through a network of clinics and hospitals. The coverage was limited to a few hundred thousand workers by the mid-1940s, but it was the precedent for a fringe benefit system which would be steadily extended to the best-organized elements of labor.

In addition, Ávila Camacho faced the challenge of World War II. Mexicans felt a strong sympathy for the Allied cause, but an almost equally strong suspicion of an automatic alliance with the United States. After Pearl Harbor the Mexican government broke off diplomatic relations with Japan, Germany, and Italy, but stopped short of declaring war. It was only the repeated sinking of Mexican ships by German U-boats that led the Ávila Camacho government to obtain a declaration of war from the national congress in May 1942. Mexico, along with Brazil, became one of the only two Latin American countries to supply combat forces to fight the Axis.

Another step would have grave importance for the future. After an explicit agreement between presidents Franklin Roosevelt and Ávila Camacho, Mexico began sending agricultural workers north to fill the gap left in the U.S. fields by the military draft. As the war continued, the Mexican laborers (known as *braceros*) began to fill nonagricultural jobs as well—a development that aroused the opposition of U.S. organized labor. The war ended with an important precedent established: the officially endorsed northward movement of Mexican workers to perform jobs for which no Americans could be found. By 1945, some 300,000 Mexicans had undergone the experience of working in the United States. Although many had encountered prejudice and discrimination, most had earned much higher wages than was possible in Mexico. The promise of a higher income across the border, however tarnished, remained a constant attraction to impoverished Mexicans for generations to come.

With the end of World War II, Mexico saw industrialization as a way out of persistent poverty. Chosen to lead the way was Miguel Alemán, the first civilian president since the Revolution. One of Alemán's first acts was to reorganize and rename the official party, now called the Partido Revolucionario Institucional

(PRI). Adding the word "institutional" signaled a turn toward pragmatism. The party was made up of three sectors: peasant, worker, and popular, the form it has since retained. It emerged as an utterly dominant official party, different from any other in Latin America.

The new president's hallmark was to be economic development. What Mexico most needed was infrastructure—roads, dams, communications, and port facilities. Alemán therefore launched an ambitious program of public works, stressing irrigation and hydroelectric projects. There was also highway and hotel construction to facilitate the tourist trade from the United States. This investment paid off, as tourism became an all-important source of foreign exchange for Mexico, although with cultural and social implications that Mexican nationalists found distasteful.

The Mexican economy showed significant growth. The foundations were laid by sharply increasing protection against imports. The short-run justification was to ease Mexico's severe balance-of-payments deficit, but the net effect was to provide a guaranteed market for domestic production. Domestic manufacturing responded with a spurt of growth, averaging 9.2 percent a year between 1948 and 1951. Agricultural production did even better in those years, averaging 10.4 percent. A slowdown in growth then cast a shadow over the end of Alemán's term, which was further tainted by mounting charges of corruption.

The bosses of the PRI knew, when it came time to choose a new successor in 1952, that they had to improve the government's image. Overriding Alemán's own preferences, they settled on a colorless *político* who provided at least a partial answer. Adolfo Ruiz Cortines had been governor of Veracruz and later secretary of the interior in the Alemán presidency, yet he had managed to earn a reputation for honesty. Once elected president, Ruiz Cortines made good on a campaign pledge to root out grafters by firing a series of suspect officials.

The most important policies of Ruiz Cortines came in the economic sphere. Since the war, Mexico had been experiencing an inflation rate which was high for Latin America. The Mexican economic managers made a crucial decision. They opted for a "hard-money," low-inflation strategy, which meant setting an exchange rate (peso/dollar) and then managing their economy (by conservative fiscal and monetary policy) so as to maintain that exchange rate. The first step was to devalue the overvalued peso from 8.65 pesos to the dollar to 12.5 pesos to the dollar in 1954. This devaluation gave an immediate stimulus to Mexican exports, now cheaper in U.S. dollars, and made Mexico cheaper for foreign tourists. Mexico quickly became known as a promising target for international investors.

When Ruiz Cortines left office at the age of sixty-seven, he and the king-makers chose a successor two decades younger. He was Adolfo López Mateos, the outgoing secretary of labor with a mildly leftist reputation. Somewhat cryptically, López Mateos himself declared that his administration would be "on the extreme left, within the constitution." Mexico was not highly unionized. The vast majority of lower-class citizens, especially the *campesinos,* had no independent means of protecting or promoting their own interests. The unions that did exist were closely tied to the regime itself.

Notwithstanding this pattern, López Mateos was quickly challenged by militant railworkers, who staged a major strike in 1959. Their leader, Demetrio Vallejo, was contesting the government-dominated structure of labor relations, and was demanding the right to genuinely independent union action. The workers followed the strike order and braced themselves for a long siege. López Mateos applied an old-fashioned remedy: he arrested the leaders and ordered the strikers back to work. The strike was broken and Vallejo remained in jail for years, an object lesson to other would-be militants.

López Mateos nonetheless sought to distance himself from his conservative predecessors. The obvious starting point was land. A chance to acquire land remained the greatest dream for Mexico's poorest rural dwellers. López Mateos ordered the distribution of approximately 30 million acres of land, giving him a land-reform record second only to Cárdenas. Furnishing basic services (and credit) for these new landowners was much more difficult and too seldom achieved. Nonetheless, revolutionary momentum had been resumed in a crucial realm.

In economic policy López Mateos continued the hard-money policies implicit in the 1954 devaluation. Investment remained high, and Mexico began raising capital abroad, above all in the New York bond market. The attraction was high interest rates, guaranteed convertibility (into dollars), and apparent political stability. The government succeeded in achieving extraordinarily low inflation, thereby making it possible to stick with its fixed exchange rate of 12.5 pesos to the dollar. Yet Mexico was by no means a completely open market economy. Indeed, state intervention in the economy increased in the years of López Mateos. U.S.- and Canadian-owned electric companies were nationalized, for example, as was the motion picture industry, which had been largely controlled by Hollywood.

The López Mateos administration brought some significant changes in foreign affairs. A 1964 formal agreement between López Mateos and U.S. president Lyndon Johnson gave Mexico sovereignty over a long-disputed riverbank territory in the area of El Paso. At the same time, López Mateos preserved independence on another issue: Fidel Castro's Cuba (see Chapter 5). After 1960 the United States was pushing incessantly for anti-Cuban votes in the Organization of American States. Mexico was the only Latin American country never to break relations with Cuba. It took pride in its refusal to bow to the U.S. demand for a uniform response from its Latin American allies.

The official candidate to succeed López Mateos in 1964 was Gustavo Díaz Ordaz, who many thought would swing the PRI back toward the right. He was from the state of Puebla, Mexico's Catholic stronghold. As the incumbent secretary of the interior, he had earlier ordered the arrest of certain "radicals," including the world-famous artist David Alfaro Siqueiros.

Díaz Ordaz countered this expectation by pledging to continue the policies of his predecessor. López Mateos had taken seriously the criticisms of the PRI's one-

The student movement of 1968 began as a limited protest with an eclectic ideology, as suggested by the declaration of solidarity with Che Guevara during this peaceful march along the Paseo de la Reforma in Mexico City. It eventually became a tragic crisis for the nation's political system. (United Press International.)

party system and pushed through a constitutional amendment that guaranteed opposition parties a minimum of congressional seats if they won a minimum national vote. Applying this principle in the 1964 elections, right-wing and left-wing opposition parties had won seats in Congress, although still overwhelmingly outweighed by the PRI representation.

Díaz Ordaz began by honoring this reformist thrust. But the entrenched PRI leaders soon made known their fury at the newly appointed secretary-general of the party, Carlos Madrazo, who was attempting to open up the nomination procedures—always the critical link in a one-party system. Responding to the party machine complaints, Díaz Ordaz fired Madrazo. The new hard line was further evident when the federal government annulled mayoral elections in two cities in the state of Baja California Norte which PAN candidates had won. The liberalization of the one-party system had overreached its limit.

Díaz Ordaz would have been lucky if mayoral elections had been his only political worry. But it was his fate to govern in the era of student protest that shook the Western world in the late 1960s. The precipitating factor was Mexico's hosting of the summer Olympic Games in 1968. The government went all out to "sell" Mexico to the world. The Mexican left, always strong among students, was upset at the idea that the government might succeed in gaining international respectability. There began a test of wills. A student protest in Mexico City in July 1968 was met by brutal force from the riot police. Protest spread to the national university in August, culminating in a strike. The government thought it was a "subversive conspiracy," bent on disrupting the Olympic Games. President Díaz Ordaz responded by sending army troops onto the campus, thereby violating its historic sanctuary status. The battle was joined. Could the student left stop the Olympic Games?

The tragic rhythm of confrontation between students and troops continued. On October 2, 1968, a rally of students in the Mexico City section of Tlatelolco drew an unusually heavy contingent of security forces. An order to disperse was allegedly not observed, and the police and paramilitary forces moved in. They began shooting and the crowd was caught in a murderous cross fire, as hundreds fell dead and many more wounded. The massacre at Tlatelolco sent a shudder through Mexico. There was no inquiry, no convincing explanation from the military or civilian authorities responsible for the slaughter. A chorus of critics said the massacre had proved the bankruptcy of the PRI monopoly on power. By the same token, the brutal show of force convinced virtually everyone that mass challenges to authority would only bring more wailing ambulances. The effect was chilling, and the Olympic Games took place on schedule.

Despite the turmoil on the political front, the Mexican economy continued to boom. The gross national product grew at 6 percent a year, although the distribution of income remained highly unequal. Between 1950 and 1969, the income share going to the poorest tenth of the population dropped from 2.4 percent to 2.0 percent. Meanwhile, the richest tenth increased its share from 49 percent to 51 percent. Mexico's "miraculous" growth had only increased the maldistribution of income.

When the time came for the presidential succession, Díaz Ordaz settled on Luis Echeverría, the secretary of the interior responsible for the security forces at Tlatelolco. It was hardly a choice likely to reunite embittered Mexicans. Echeverría tried to show a new face in his energetic campaign and, after the usual landslide victory, plunged into his new duties. The sphere in which the new president sought to make his greatest mark was the one where he was soon most criticized: management of the economy.

Echeverría and his advisers wanted economic growth, but also better distribution of its benefits. An obvious place to begin, as always in Mexico, was the rural sector. Effort centered on infrastructure, such as rural electrification and the road system. In order to pacify consumers in the cities, the Echeverría government tightened the existing price controls on basic foodstuffs. In effect, the federal government was committing itself to an escalating subsidy on food for the urban masses. This could be financed only by draining the federal treasury or by paying farmers below-cost prices for their goods. The latter would inevitably discourage production, and the former would tend to be inflationary. As Echeverría's term continued, he resorted increasingly to short-term measures that would channel resources (wages, land, social services) to the poor.

At the same time the state was increasing its general control over the economy. In addition to direct spending through federal departments and ministries, the government allocated a large share of the budget—well over half in many years—to dozens of special agencies and state-supported companies. The leading lending institutions, most conspicuously the Nacional Financiera, were operated by the government, and the manipulation of credit regulations endowed the state with considerable influence over the economy. As of 1970, for instance, the government controlled principal shares in nine of the country's top ten firms, in thirteen out of the top twenty-five, and in sixteen out of the top fifty.

While the Mexican state took an active part in the country's capitalist economy, it retained considerable independence from the private sector. Much of this autonomy stemmed from the fact that Mexico's public leaders were, for the most part, professional politicians. They did not come from wealthy families, and after finishing school or university, they moved directly into political careers. In contrast to the United States, there was very little crossover of personnel between private corporations and public office. Consequently the Mexican state was not captive to any social group or interest. It tended to collaborate with the private sector, to be sure, but this was not always the case—a situation that gave the government considerable freedom of action.

While this process continued, the Mexican government faced a new problem: a guerrilla movement. Mexican politicians had long reassured themselves that their country was "different" from the rest of Latin America, where guerrillas were rife. After all, Mexico had already had its revolution. But Mexico was not immune. Guerrillas called for violent action against the PRI and all its works. Beginning in 1971, they staged a series of bank robberies and high-profile kidnappings. In 1974 the father-in-law of the president was seized and held for ransom. In the state of Guerrero, an ex-schoolteacher, Lucio Cabañas, led a guerrilla army that began to strike at will. They kidnapped the official (PRI) candidate for governor and defied the army by direct attacks on isolated outposts. It took a 10,000-man army more than a year to hunt down and kill the rebels and their leader. Despite predictions on the left, Cabañas had no successor in Guerrero or elsewhere, so the guerrilla threat faded. Why? Was it the genius of the co-optive system of the PRI? Or was it the government's network of repression?

But Echeverría's major problem was not with the guerrillas. It was with the economy. The weak point in Mexico's economic strategy was inflation. In crude terms, Mexico could not expect to guarantee the peso's convertibility at a fixed rate unless its inflation was no higher than the U.S. level. By 1973 inflation was running at 20 percent and remained at that level in 1974. Mexico's goods, based on the 1954 exchange rate, were growing uncompetitive on the world market. Yet the government stuck with the fixed rate, which had been the bedrock of Mexican development and a powerful political symbol.

Why was inflation plaguing Mexico? Many Latin Americans might have reversed the question: How had Mexico avoided it for so long? The answer was that the Mexican government, trying to please so many constituencies, was running large deficits and financing them in an inflationary manner. There was also pressure from the balance of payments, which went into serious deficit by the middle of Echeverría's term of office. Mexico's continuing industrialization required heavy capital goods. But a relatively new import was even more worrisome: food. The economy's failure was in agriculture. Production had grown for selected foods (tomatoes, strawberries) for export, especially to the United States, but the output of basic foodstuffs, especially cereals, was falling short. Imports to meet this demand put an enormous burden on the balance of payments.

The reckoning came in Echeverría's last year as president. The drama centered on the greatly overvalued peso. With the government stubbornly maintaining its fixed rate of 12.5 to the dollar, every Mexican of means tried to convert pesos into U.S. currency. The government's ever more frequent denials of devaluation rang hollow. In September 1976, after capital flight had reached panic proportions, the government gave way. The peso was devalued by 60 percent. Government credibility was so low that another devaluation of 40 percent was needed to settle the market just one month later. Could this incompetently managed devaluation convince investors (including Mexicans) to make new commitments in pesos? Although Mexico at last had a realistic exchange rate, the Echeverría government failed to attack the rising public-sector deficit—an essential step if future balance of payments crises were to be prevented.

Echeverría ended his term in a flurry of histrionic gestures. Only eleven days before the end of his presidency, he expropriated rich farmlands in the north for redistribution to landless peasants. Panic spread among landowners. For the first time in years, Mexicans talked seriously about the possibility of a military coup. Despite widespread anxiety, his term ended peacefully and on schedule.

The new president was José López Portillo, the finance minister who had presided over an economy that seemed to be wildly out of control. Mexico had growing deficits, both in its federal budget and in its balance of payments. Annual inflation had reached 30 percent; though modest by Latin American standards, this was enough to erode confidence in the Mexican growth model. López Portillo therefore gave first priority to that eternal task of restoring foreign confidence in his economy. Within weeks after his inauguration in December 1976, the new Mexican president traveled to Washington for a highly publicized visit with outgoing president Gerald Ford and an address to a joint session of the U.S. Congress. It was a powerful reminder that the Mexican elite still saw its fate closely linked to U.S. opinion.

López Portillo's presidency came to be dominated by economic issues. Just as he took office, Mexico began discovering vast quantities of oil, and by 1980 López

Portillo could announce that the country possessed proven reserves of 70 billion barrels and potential reserves of more than 200 billion. In a world apparently beset by chronic shortages and soaring costs for energy, Mexico had suddenly acquired new international clout. Declared an ebullient López Portillo: "There are two kinds of countries in the world today—those that don't have oil and those that do. We have it."

Bolstered by these windfall profits, López Portillo asserted independence from the United States in foreign policy—especially in regard to Central America, a region soon to be engulfed in violence and civil war (to be described in Chapter 4). He expressed sympathy for a left-wing revolutionary movement that in 1979 toppled a longtime U.S. ally in Nicaragua. In 1980 he offered low-priced petroleum to poverty-stricken countries of Central America as a means of building influence throughout the isthmus. And in mid-1981, the Mexican government joined with France in a declaration that recognized leftist rebels in El Salvador as a "legitimate political force" and proposed to cut the "Gordian knot" of regional strife through mediation. As U.S. leaders frowned in disapproval, Mexican nationalists fervently applauded these assertive diplomatic gestures.

Yet problems persisted at home. Mexico was finding that the hard-money strategy which had worked so well between the mid-1950s and the late 1970s was no longer possible. By 1982, inflation shot up to almost 60 percent, an unprecedented rate for postwar Mexico. Another painful devaluation became inevitable in early 1982.

Mexico had hoped to avoid all this by cashing in on its huge oil reserves, but a world slump in oil prices after 1981 reduced dramatically the projected foreign exchange earnings. The López Portillo government was therefore driven to heavy foreign borrowing, thereby increasing the national debt. Most worrisome was the fact that the Mexican economy was still not producing jobs at a rate fast enough to absorb all the Mexicans entering the workforce.

To soften political opposition, López Portillo sponsored a program of reforms. Two innovations seemed particularly far reaching: first, the rules for registration of political parties were made easier, so much so that the Communist Party gained official recognition, and second, opposition parties were guaranteed a total of at least 100 seats in an expanded, 400-member Chamber of Deputies. Such alterations seemed unlikely to lead to a fundamental change in the locus of power, but they at least provided an outlet—within the system—for the opposition. As his successor, he selected Miguel de la Madrid, a Harvard-trained technocrat and cabinet minister who won a predictable victory in the elections of July 1982.

Before de la Madrid could take office on December 1, however, the Mexican economy was shaken by a much larger financial crisis. Mexico had run out of dollars with which to make payments on its foreign debt—now over $80 billion. Near panic ensued in Washington, New York, Frankfurt, and London, where it was feared that other Latin American debtors might follow Mexico's example and declare a de facto default. If that were the case, U.S., European, and Japanese banks would face huge losses, posing a formidable threat to world financial markets. The causes of the crisis were obvious. The price of Mexico's prime export (oil) had nosedived, interest rates had spiraled upward, and rich Mexicans had transferred billions of dollars out of the country. The U.S. government, the International Monetary Fund (IMF), and the commercial banks rushed a "rescue" loan package to Mexico. These new loans enabled Mexico to continue paying interest but did not allow for amortization.

The rescue had its price: Mexico had to adopt an IMF-approved austerity plan. A key goal was to reduce the inflationary public deficit, which was at a dangerously high 15 percent of the GDP. This meant phasing out government subsidies on food and public utilities. Mexico also had to reduce its tariff barriers, thereby stimulating greater industrial efficiency and thus greater competitiveness in world export markets.

President de la Madrid dutifully followed the IMF prescription, but at the price of inducing a deep recession. By 1985, real wages had fallen by 40 percent from their 1982 level; living standards fell even further as subsidies for such staples as corn tortillas were ended. In September 1985, a severe earthquake in Mexico City compounded the economic disaster. The 1985–86 drop in oil prices depressed export earnings, further weakening the economy.

Amid these difficulties, de la Madrid and his advisers decided to adopt a dramatic shift in economic policy, a new emphasis that came to be characterized as "neoliberalism"(see Chapter 12). There were two main pillars to the program. One was to reduce and recast the economic role of the state. This was to be done through continued cuts in public spending and through a program of "privatization" of state-owned companies. Of the 1115 publicly owned companies that his government inherited in late 1982, de la Madrid managed to sell off nearly 100 and to close down 279 by late 1986.

The second component of the new policy was commercial liberalization and "opening up" of the economy. This was most dramatically demonstrated by Mexico's accession to the General Agreement on Tariffs and Trade (GATT) in

---

Mexico: Vital Statistics, 2007

Population (millions)	105.3
GDP (billions of $U.S.)	893.4
GNP/capita ($U.S.)	8340
Poverty rate (% in 2006)	31.4
Life expectancy (years)	74

SOURCES: World Bank and Economic Commission for Latin America and the Caribbean.

September 1986, which meant a long-term commitment to the reduction of barriers to imports from abroad. Mexico promptly began lowering and phasing out its tariffs and promoting its exports, especially nonpetroleum exports. For all practical intents and purposes, these changes amounted to a near-complete abandonment of the postwar policies of import-substitution.

By early 1988, the de la Madrid government could see little prospect for relief. Inflation had accelerated to an annual rate of 143 percent, the public-sector deficit was approaching 19 percent of the GDP, and the domestic capital market had been shaken by a 75 percent drop in the Mexican stock market. Yet another U.S.-engineered capital infusion came in December 1987. In a complex scheme, Mexico would buy U.S. bonds to post as collateral against commercial bank loans. The move offered no prospect for large-scale relief from the debt, which had clearly become unpayable.

Despite these agreements, there would be continuing friction with the United States. After Ronald Reagan won the U.S. presidency in 1982, the de la Madrid government cosponsored a new proposal to settle the raging conflicts in Central America through multilateral negotiation. Known as the "Contadora" initiative (named for the site of the first meeting), the plan called for regional peace on the basis of political democracy and economic cooperation. The idea quickly gained support from the United Nations but encountered bitter opposition from hard-line Reaganites—who objected to its de facto recognition of Nicaragua's revolutionary government and to its restrictions on U.S. intervention. The Contadora vision expired when, under intense pressure from Washington, pro-American governments in Costa Rica, Honduras, and El Salvador expressed their opposition. Even so, Mexico had once again asserted its autonomy.

An additional ongoing cause for bilateral tension was the U.S. policy toward Mexicans working (legally and illegally) in the United States. The Simpson-Rodino Act, passed in 1986, laid down tough penalties for employers who hired "undocumented aliens." The prospect of its implementation sent shudders through northern and central Mexico, whose younger generations had long seen jobs in the United States (usually temporary) as their main hope for a decent life. Within a few years, the law appeared to have had only a minimal impact on actual migration flows, but Mexicans remained wary.

The debt crisis and economic stagnation in the late 1980s intensified social inequality and popular pressures. Investment plummeted, unemployment increased, and per capita income declined by more than 9 percent during the 1980s. In contrast to the Southern Cone countries in the 1960s and 1970s, however, Mexico did not resort to pervasive, large-scale authoritarian repression. Key attributes of the Mexican political system—its restricted competition, its control of working-class movements, its autonomy from private interests, and its tactical flexibility—help explain why Mexico managed to avoid declaring open warfare on its citizens.

Aware of their sagging credibility, PRI leaders made the process of choosing the official nominee for president more visible (if not more genuinely open) than the ritual had ever been. De la Madrid's eventual choice was another U.S.-trained economist, Carlos Salinas de Gortari, only thirty-nine years old, who as the incumbent budget and planning minister had authored the highly unpopular austerity policies of the 1980s.

The election of 1988 brought surprises—and suggestive portents of meaningful change. For the first time in its history, the PRI faced serious opposition from both the right and the left (as Cuauhtémoc Cárdenas, son of the revered ex-president, led a breakaway faction from the PRI itself). Organized labor also showed its displeasure with the PRI candidate. Salinas de Gortari won with a bare 50.3 percent majority, according to official returns, and in claiming victory he declared an end to an era of "what was practically[!] one-party rule." Opponents nonetheless accused the regime of electoral fraud. The youthful Salinas took office in December 1988 under exceedingly difficult conditions. Would he be up to the challenge?

The first task for Salinas was to demonstrate political authority. He began by naming a cabinet dominated by his personal associates, instead of mending political fences. In January 1989 he masterminded a spectacular raid on the headquarters of the independent-minded and financially corrupt head of the oil workers' union, who was promptly placed under arrest (for illegal possession of firearms). Shortly thereafter he dismissed the long-standing chief of the large and powerful teachers' union. Later he fired the naval secretary from his cabinet post, an unusual move in view of the delicate balance of civil-military relations in Mexico.

As promised during his campaign, Salinas de Gortari promoted a modest political opening. He commanded PRI officials to recognize a gubernatorial triumph for the PAN in the important state of Baja California (just south of the California border). He oversaw reforms of the electoral system and of the internal workings of the PRI. But there were limits to this strategy. The PRI claimed unrealistic victories in key elections in the state of México, near Mexico City, an area that had shown itself to be a left-wing opposition stronghold in the presidential election of 1988. The government also harassed and intimidated Cuauhtémoc Cárdenas and his followers, who found it extremely difficult to organize their forces into a coherent and durable political party. The opening, such as it was, was biased toward the right (and the PAN); it did not include the left.

Indeed, for the first time in memory, the question of human rights appeared on the national agenda. Critics called attention to a number of abuses committed by Mexico's national police force in alleged pursuit of drug dealers. They reported the assassination or "disappearance" of at least sixty pro-Cárdenas sympathizers in 1990 alone. They expressed outrage at the murder of a prominent human-rights activist. To assuage the criticism, Salinas appointed a National Commission on Human Rights, led by former university rector Jorge Carpizo, but did not give it genuine authority.

It was in the economic arena that Salinas sought his most lasting achievements. In hopes of completing Mexico's structural adjustments, he continued and extended the neoliberal strategy initiated under de la Madrid. Salinas and his team kept lowering trade barriers. They aggressively promoted the privatization of state-owned industries, even putting up for sale such sacred cows as the telephone company and the banking industry (nationalized by López Portillo in 1982). With the support of the U.S. government, Salinas negotiated a new debt-restructuring agreement that promised to reduce the net outflow of funds by $2 billion a year until the mid-1990s. The government also sought to assist local development by establishing a "program for national solidarity" to provide seed money for self-help projects throughout the country. Perhaps in response to these measures, the national economy showed signs of picking up: annual inflation moved down to the 20–30 percent range, while annual growth rates for the GDP rose to 3.1 percent for 1989 and 3.9 percent for 1990.

North American Free Trade

The crowning achievement of the Salinas *sexenio* was the North American Free Trade Agreement (NAFTA). Unable to attract large-scale investment from Europe or Japan, the Salinas administration announced its intent to negotiate a free-trade compact with the United States. The proposal entailed a total repudiation of the protectionist strategies of import-substituting industrialization, and it discarded the national tradition of keeping a suspicious distance from the "Colossus of the North." Small-scale industrialists and grain farmers expressed fear that they might be destroyed by U.S. competition, and some intellectuals mourned the imminent demise of the nation's economic sovereignty and cultural pride. Salinas persisted nonetheless.

Unveiled in August 1992, the NAFTA accord envisioned the creation of a three-nation partnership (including Canada as well as Mexico and the United States) that would forge one of the largest trading blocs in the world—with a population of 370 million and combined economic production of approximately $6 trillion. It would promote the free flow of goods among the member countries by eliminating duties, tariffs, and trade barriers over a period of fifteen years. Sixty-five percent of U.S. goods gained duty-free status immediately or within five years; half of U.S. farm goods exported to Mexico immediately became duty-free. There were special exceptions for certain "highly sensitive" products in agriculture, typically one of the sectors most resistant to economic integration; phaseouts on tariffs for corn and dry beans in Mexico and orange juice and sugar in the United States would extend to the year 2009. Tariffs on all automobiles within North America would be phased out over ten years, but rules of origin stipulated that local content would have to be at least 62.5 percent for vehicles to qualify. Not surprisingly, Asian governments regarded this clause as a thinly disguised effort to exclude their industries and products from the North American market.

NAFTA opened Mexico to U.S. investments in various ways. Under the treaty, U.S. banks and securities firms could establish branch offices in Mexico, and U.S. citizens could invest in Mexico's banking and insurance industries. While Mexico continued to prohibit foreign ownership of oil fields, in accordance with its constitution, U.S. firms became eligible to compete for contracts with Petróleos

Mexicanos (PEMEX) and operate, in general, under the same provisions as Mexican companies. One item was most conspicuous by its absence: beyond a narrowly written provision for the movement of corporate executives and selected professionals, the treaty made no reference at all to the large-scale migration of labor.

NAFTA precipitated strenuous debate within the United States. In the heat of the 1992 presidential campaign, Democratic candidate Bill Clinton pledged to support NAFTA on condition that there be effective safeguards for environmental protection and workers' rights; by September 1993 the governments reached "supplemental" or side agreements on labor and the environment. As the U.S. Congress prepared to vote on ratification, Texas billionaire (and erstwhile presidential hopeful) Ross Perot led the charge against the treaty, claiming that NAFTA would entice business to seek low-wage Mexican labor and thus lose jobs for millions of American workers. Proponents insisted that NAFTA would stimulate U.S. exports, achieve economies of scale, and enhance U.S. competitiveness. Disregarding vociferous opposition from unionized labor, a historic bastion of support for Democrats, Clinton lobbied tirelessly on behalf of the treaty. And after Perot stumbled badly during a memorable television debate with Vice President Al Gore, the House of Representatives finally approved the NAFTA accord by 234–200; the Senate followed with a vote of 61–38.

In final form, the NAFTA accord had several outstanding characteristics. One was its implicit commitment to regional economic integration. Despite its title, NAFTA was not primarily concerned with "free trade." By 1990 tariff and even nontariff barriers to U.S.-Mexican commerce were already low. NAFTA was primarily concerned with investment. By obtaining preferential access to U.S. markets and a formal "seal of approval" through NAFTA, Mexico was hoping to attract sizable flows of direct foreign investment—from Japan and Europe as well as from the United States. By obtaining untrammeled access to low-wage (but highly skilled) Mexican labor, the United States was hoping to create an export platform for manufactured goods and thus improve its competitive position in the global economy. It was for these reasons that the NAFTA treaty contained extensive chapters about investment, competition, telecommunications, and financial services. Implicitly, NAFTA envisioned a substantially more profound form of integration than its label acknowledged.

Second, NAFTA made explicit provision for environmental protection. As originally negotiated, NAFTA made only passing reference to environmental concerns. In keeping with his campaign pledge, however, President Clinton oversaw negotiations on a supplementary provision for environmental protection, and under a separate agreement, the U.S.-Mexican border received special attention under a bilateral Integrated Environmental Plan. While some observers raised doubts about the practical significance of these agreements, the mere fact of their negotiation made one point clear: trade and environment had become inextricably intertwined.

Yet another distinguishing characteristic of NAFTA was its underlying political rationale. The United States was seeking several goals. One was the preservation of stability on its southern border. The idea was that NAFTA would stimulate economic growth in Mexico, easing social pressure and sustaining the political regime. A second goal was to assure the United States of increasing access to petroleum from Mexico, one of the five leading sources of U.S. imports. A third purpose was for the United States to obtain an important bargaining chip in its trade negotiations with Europe, Japan, and the General Agreement on Tariffs and Trade. And fourth, the United States wanted to consolidate diplomatic support from Mexico on foreign policy in general. As demonstrated by disagreements over Central America during the 1980s, this had long been a source of bilateral tension. But with NAFTA in place, Mexico became unlikely to express serious disagreement with the United States on major issues of international diplomacy.

For its part Mexico was seeking, first and foremost, preservation of its social peace. The hope was that NAFTA would attract investment, stimulate employment, provide meaningful opportunity for the 1 million persons entering the job market every year—and thus reduce social tension. Second, NAFTA offered Salinas an opportunity to institutionalize his economic reforms, insulating them from the historic vagaries of presidential succession by inscribing them in an international treaty. Third, Mexico was seeking international benediction for its not-quite-democratic political regime. This was especially important because, in comparison with Argentina, Chile, Brazil, and other countries undergoing processes of democratization, Mexico no longer looked like a paragon of political civility. Finally, Mexico believed that NAFTA would provide the country with diplomatic leverage vis-à-vis the rest of Latin America and, by extension, the Third World as a whole. Association with Canada and the United States would link Mexico with advanced industrial democracies and leaders of the First World. Consequently Mexico could serve as a "bridge" between the developing world and the developed world as a representative and interlocutor for aspiring peoples of the South.

Whatever its political motivation, NAFTA appeared to achieve the economic goal of expanding commerce. Two-way trade between Mexico and the United States climbed from $83 billion in 1993 to $108 billion in 1995 and more than $200 billion by 2000. By this time the United States was exporting more to Mexico than to China, Korea, and Singapore combined, and Mexico became, after Canada, the second largest trading partner of the United States (it was later displaced by China). Contrary to widespread (and exaggerated) expectation, however, NAFTA could not provide a cure for all of Mexico's problems.

THE CONTEMPORARY SCENE (1994–PRESENT)

All the optimism resulting from the NAFTA accord promptly came under assault. On January 1, 1994—the day that NAFTA went into effect—a guerrilla movement in the poverty-stricken state of Chiapas rose up to denounce centuries-old grievances, the *salinista* economic model, and the undemocratic character of the political regime. With colorful and able leadership, the Zapatista National Liberation Army

(EZLN) captured national and international attention during the course of highly publicized negotiations with governmental authorities. Despite a variety of governmental responses, from military pressure to political negotiation, the Zapatista movement would remain a thorn in the side of the regime.

Two months later, as public attention turned toward presidential succession, an assassin's bullet struck down Luis Donaldo Colosio, Salinas' handpicked successor and the candidate of the PRI. Salinas hastily chose another nominee, the forty-two-year-old Ernesto Zedillo Ponce de León, who scurried to develop a credible campaign for the upcoming August election. These developments inflicted a devastating blow to Mexico's international image. Mexico could no longer be seen as an up-and-coming country on the brink of joining the First World; it looked, instead, like a Third World society threatening to come apart at the seams.

Earnest and intelligent, Zedillo was a technocrat par excellence. A Ph.D. in economics from Yale University, Zedillo had spent most of his career in the central bank and the planning ministry. As a result, he had very few contacts with career politicians or officials in the "political" ministries of the federal government. Despite a lackluster campaign, Zedillo won the August 1994 elections with 48.8 percent of the vote (compared with 26.0 percent for the rightist PAN and only 16.6 percent for Cuauhtémoc Cárdenas' left-wing Party of the Democratic Revolution, PRD), thus becoming the fifth man in a row to reach the presidency without ever holding prior elective office.

Inaugurated in December 1994, Zedillo faced crisis right away. Fearful of the overvaluation of the peso, investors withdrew more than $10 billion from Mexico within a week. In response, the Zedillo administration had to devalue the peso, which eventually lost more than half its value against the U.S. dollar, and the government was coming close to insolvency. Early in 1995 the Clinton administration put together a multilateral package of nearly $50 billion, including $20 billion from the U.S. government. One major goal of this measure was to head off a potential default on $30 billion in *tesobonos* (short-term bonds issued by the Mexican treasury, payable in dollars), which would have inflicted major damage on U.S. pension funds, mutual funds, and other institutional investors. Another was to sustain the credibility of economic reform and the viability of NAFTA itself.

The financial crisis provoked a political crisis as well. As criticism mounted against Salinas' insistence on maintaining an unrealistic exchange rate throughout 1994, the ex-president publicly criticized Zedillo and his economic cabinet for mishandling the December devaluation. Zedillo reacted by sending Salinas into de facto exile in the United States, then authorizing the arrest of the former president's older brother on charges of corruption. The detention by U.S. authorities of an assistant attorney general under Salinas led to further denunciations of corruption, family intrigue, and official involvement in the assassination of a high-level PRI leader in September 1994. As Carlos Salinas became a figure of widespread revulsion, serious fissures threatened to split apart the Mexican political elite.

The public promptly showed its disapproval. For the first time in decades, rumors began circulating that an elected PRI president might not be able to finish his term. One poll in early 1995 showed that nearly half the respondents thought a military coup was possible. In municipalities and states, from Jalisco to Querétaro and Nuevo León, opposition candidates began winning public office. And in 1997, for the first time in its history, the PRI lost control of the national Chamber of Deputies.

The apparent decline of the PRI led to restiveness within the party's rank-and-file and its traditional bosses, pejoratively known as "dinosaurs" or *dinosaurios*. Chafing under the decades-long dominance of technocrats or *técnicos* like Salinas and Zedillo, the party's national assembly ruled that its next presidential candidate would be required to have held elected office (a stipulation that would have disqualified every president since 1970). President Zedillo publicly proclaimed that he would not himself designate his successor through the time-honored *dedazo*, so the PRI designed a new primary system for the 2000 election and gave responsibility for its management to one of the party's most venerable political figures. By mid-1999 there were four candidates for the party's nomination, none of whom could be called a technocrat. As one analyst and former congressman proclaimed, perhaps wishfully, "This is the end of government by technocracy, thank goodness."

Dawn of a New Era

The presidential election of 2000 marked a watershed in Mexican politics. A hotly contested campaign involved three major candidates: Francisco Labastida of the PRI, Cuauhtémoc Cárdenas of the PRD, and a newcomer to the scene—Vicente Fox of the conservative PAN. Tall, rugged, *macho* to the core, Fox was a private businessman and rancher. He became CEO of Coca-Cola of Mexico in the late 1970s and entered politics only in 1988, when he joined the PAN and won election as a congressional representative. He subsequently served as governor of the small state of Guanajuato. From that unlikely background, in his late fifties, he launched his quest for the presidency.

A charismatic campaigner, Fox pledged an honest government. He denounced the PRI as hopelessly corrupt and obsolete. Vague on specifics, Fox asserted that it was time for a change—and that he would lead Mexico into a new, modern, and democratic era. In contrast Labastida seemed to personify the PRI's most traditional elements, while President Ernesto Zedillo insisted that the election would have to be clean.

Fox won the presidency by a plurality, with 42.5 percent of the vote; Labastida received 36 percent and Cárdenas took 17 percent. Mexico was jubilant, as though it had surprised itself. According to one observer, this was a triumph of "modern" Mexico over "traditional" Mexico—and his challenge would be to reconcile the two. Taking office in December 2000, Fox enjoyed approval ratings around 85 percent. His political honeymoon would be unusually long—but it would not last forever.

Despite the strength of his popular support, Fox had to deal with a recalcitrant legislature—a novelty in Mexican politics. The PRI held pluralities in both houses of Congress; the PAN had only 46 seats in the Senate (out of 128) and 207 seats in the House of Representatives (out of 500). Moreover, Fox had troubled relations with the *panista* delegation, whose members did not see him as a party loyalist— but as an outsider who had hijacked the presidential nomination. As a result, Fox found it impossible to gain congressional approval for his most important initia- tives—tax reform, privatization, and resolution of the crisis in Chiapas. Things got only worse after the midterm elections of 2003, when the PAN received only 32 percent of the popular vote and lost a number of important seats. One skeptical observer claimed that, as a result, Fox would be a "political corpse" until the end of his term in 2006.

Economic development presented Fox with another dilemma. As a pro- American businessman, Fox had touted the virtues of NAFTA during his presidential campaign. During the first half of his presidency, however, eco- nomic performance was absolutely anemic: a decline in the GDP of –0.3 percent in 2001, barely positive growth of 0.9 percent in 2002, a rate of 1.4 percent in 2003. The principal drag on the Mexican economy was, of course, the ongoing slowdown in the United States (to which Mexico sent nearly 90 percent of its exports). People pointedly asked: Where are the benefits of NAFTA? Their discontent became all the more intense when it became clear that Mexico was losing jobs and market share to mainland China, itself embarked on rapid expansion.

Mexico's relationship with the United States took unexpected turns. Assuming office almost simultaneously, Vicente Fox and George W. Bush promptly estab- lished a strong and positive personal connection. Fox persuaded Bush to look into the possibility of immigration reform—an amnesty for resident illegals in the United States plus a large-scale guest-worker program, steps that would "deepen" NAFTA along the lines of the European Union. And in late summer 2001, during a visit to Washington, Fox challenged Bush to enact such reforms before the end of the calendar year. As observers praised the Mexican president's boldness, it appeared that he would get his way. Then came the terrorist attacks of September 11, 2001, and expansive immigration reform became utterly unthinkable. Tension flared between the two governments (and the two presidents) in early 2003 when Mexico, temporarily chairing the UN Security Council, failed to support the U.S. invasion of Iraq. It was not until January 2004 that Bush unveiled a modest guest- worker proposal that had little chance of congressional approval during an election year. For all this time, Vicente Fox was left holding the bag.

Popular disenchantment with the Fox administration helped to fuel a new challenge to Mexico's fledgling democracy: the rise of a political left, which bolstered a strong presidential bid in 2006 by the PRD's Andrés Manuel López Obrador (a.k.a. AMLO). Presenting himself as a candidate of workers, peasants, and the poor, AMLO sharply criticized NAFTA, Fox, and pro-American policies. Despite double-digit leads in preelection polls, López Obrador ran a remarkably

A Silent Invasion?

Immigration from Mexico has provoked virulent debates in the United States. Most opponents denounce the phenomenon on cultural or economic grounds—as a challenge to long-standing American values, or as a threat to job-seeking workers. In response, proponents maintain that the Mexican presence enriches American culture and provides much-needed labor for the U.S. economy.

The intensity of the controversy tends to revolve around numbers. How many migrants are there? Is there some sort of "silent invasion" at work?

It has been virtually impossible to measure the size of the undocumented Mexican population with great precision. Skilled demographers have managed to make responsible estimates, though, and here are some findings for the year 2002:

- There were 9.8 million Mexican immigrants (legal and illegal) in the United States—equivalent to 9 percent of the entire population born in Mexico;
- Of these 9.8 million immigrants, 5.3 million were undocumented—equivalent to less than 2 percent of the U.S. population.
- Approximately 57 percent of all undocumented migrants in the United States (9.3 million) came from Mexico; the rest of Latin America, mainly Central America, accounted for nearly 25 percent.

Starting in the early 1990s, migration from Mexico revealed three suggestive long-term trends. First, undocumented migrants included not only working-age males, as in previous eras, but also entire families with women and children. Second, as law enforcement tightened at the U.S. border, the migrants began staying stateside for longer periods of time. Third, Mexican migrants were finding work all over the United States, from the Northwest to the Southeast, not just in traditional areas (e.g., California and Texas). For these reasons, proposals for U.S. "immigration reform" needed to deal not only with prospective border crossings in the future, but also with an already-resident undocumented population.

All in all, this pattern doesn't look very much like an "invasion"—in the sense of a deliberate and coordinated occupation of territory for strategic purposes. It represents, instead, an accumulation of millions of decisions by individuals and families. That said, it still poses delicate challenges for public policy.

Data from Jeffrey S. Passel, "Mexican Immigration to the US: The Latest Estimates" (Washington, D.C.: Migration Policy Institute, 2004).

lackluster campaign. The eventual winner by a hair's-breadth margin was the youthful Felipe Calderón, a lifelong member of the conservative PAN and a former minister of energy. Calderón garnered 35.9 percent of the vote, compared with AMLO's 35.3 percent (the PRI's Roberto Madrazo won only 22.3 percent). As these results suggest, Mexico was becoming polarized—a society divided between rich and poor, right and left, north and south, more and less developed. It would not be an easy place to govern.

As Calderón settled into office, three challenges loomed large. One concerned the extension or "deepening" of Mexico's political democracy. Free and fair presidential elections could not by themselves assure democratization in state, municipal, and local arenas. In fact, there persisted a significant number of authoritarian strongholds—bastions of hierarchical tradition under domineering *jefes* (bosses), usually linked to the old-time PRI. The result was a "checkerboard" pattern of democratic and nondemocratic localities that created confusion, inconsistency, and inefficiency throughout the political system. Adding to this problem was the chronic weakness of Mexico's judicial branch. Courts were regarded as powerless and corrupt, thus undermining the constitutional ideal of a separation of powers, and the law was not applied fairly or evenly. The police frequently acted arbitrarily, human rights were often abused, and dissent was sometimes suppressed. As a result, Mexico had what political analysts have called an incomplete or "illiberal" democracy—a system combining free and fair elections (at the national level) with systematic restrictions on the civil liberties of ordinary citizens. The process of democratization in Mexico represented a major achievement— above all, on the part of its people—but there was still a long way to go.

A second major challenge, connected to the first, involved conflict with criminal organizations—specifically, drug trafficking cartels. Mexico was serving as the transit point for nearly 90 percent of the cocaine heading from Colombia toward the U.S. market (as well as one-third of all the marijuana and an increasing share of methamphetamines). Annual earnings from the drug trade were enormous, somewhere between $8 billion and $24 billion, which not only yielded handsome profits but also enabled pervasive corruption. This commerce was controlled by four dominant organizations—based in Culiacán (Sinaloa), Tijuana (Baja California), Ciudad Juárez (Chihuahua), and Matamoros (Tamaulipas). All of these groups had extensive marketing operations within the territorial United States. Indeed, the Sinaloa cartel created retail outlets in such faraway locations as Oregon, Florida, and Massachusetts, while the Gulf cartel established a major distribution center in the city of Atlanta. And in their local domains within Mexico, the drug cartels exercised supreme authority: they were states within the state. They were powerful, efficient, creative, ruthless—and prone to use violence.

Seeking to enhance national authority, Calderón made an early decision to take on the drug lords of Mexico. He augmented (and cleaned up) the federal police, enlisted the services of the army, and, in effect, declared war on the cartels. The result was a bloodbath. Cartels fought furiously with the police, with the army, and among themselves. During 2007 more than 2500 people were killed, many of them innocent bystanders; during 2008 the death toll rose to more than 6000. The U.S. government under President George W. Bush pledged to support Calderón's campaign with $1.4 billion in military hardware, and tentatively agreed to reduce the cross-border sale of high-powered firearms to Mexico. As of early 2009, however, there was still no end in sight. So long as American consumers continued to demand illicit drugs, especially cocaine, the commerce would no doubt continue. Calderón's best hope was that the price of conducting business in Mexico would become so high that traffickers would take their business elsewhere. (In theory, that might solve Mexico's problem with the cartels; it would not solve the U.S. problem of illicit drug abuse.)

Economic development posed a third major challenge. Despite continuous growth from 2003 through 2008, the Mexican economy was struggling. Nearly one-third of the population still lived in grinding poverty. And in view of the global recession of 2008–9, the short-term outlook was troubling. Mexico sent 80 percent of its exports to the United States, but American consumers weren't buying. The price of Mexican oil was declining. Meanwhile, contractions in the U.S. job market were persuading migrant workers to go back home, which meant a sharp reduction in remittances (which had grown to more than $20 billion per year) and a likely increase in Mexico's own level of unemployment. As a result, Mexico's projected growth rate for 2009 had fallen to right around zero. This outcome merely confirmed an age-old pattern: as the U.S. economy slows, the Mexican economy takes an even bigger hit.

As President Felipe Calderón was well aware, Mexico's relationship to the United States was a mixed blessing for his country. That knowledge did not make his job any easier.

4

Central America and the Caribbean
Within the U.S. Orbit

There can be peril in proximity to the United States. Along with Mexico, nations of Central America and islands of the Caribbean have shared this stark reality. Through trade, investment, invasion, and diplomacy, the United States exerted extraordinary influence over trends and events in this area throughout the twentieth century. The use (and abuse) of this power not only yields insight into the behavior of the United States. It also enriches our understanding of ways that Latin Americans have interpreted the motives and actions of their giant neighbor to the north. Analysis of Central America and the Caribbean provides important perspective on the challenges facing the region as a whole and on the complexity of inter-American affairs.

Islands of the Caribbean Sea tend to be small. Topographies vary from the flat plains of Barbados to the rugged coasts of Martinique and Guadeloupe. A few of the islands, like Cuba and Jamaica, have rolling hills and substantial mountain ranges. The climate is mild, rainfall is abundant, and soil is fertile. Similarly, the modern-day states of Central America line the western edge of the Caribbean basin. From Guatemala to Panama, the isthmus exhibits sharp contrasts: a spectacular mountain range, studded by volcanoes of 10,000 feet or more; some arid zones; and verdant jungles along the coasts. There are lakes in the mountainous areas but no major navigable rivers. Nor do the coasts have sufficient deep-sea harbors. As in the rest of the Caribbean basin, nature can bring calamity through violent earthquakes, torrential rains, and devastating storms.

WORLD POWERS, THE UNITED STATES, AND THE GREATER CARIBBEAN

Control of the Caribbean Sea has for centuries commanded the attention of major world powers. Together with the Gulf of Mexico, it contained sea lanes of great strategic importance. During the colonial era, the Caribbean provided routes of access to Spain's most highly prized New World dominions (as well as routes for Spanish

Map 4 Central America and the Caribbean

treasure fleets). The islands furnished ideal climates for the production of sugar, one of the most lucrative crops of the era. As European powers jockeyed for economic and geopolitical advantage in the Americas, the Caribbean became the principal theater of conflict—as one historian has noted, much like the Mediterranean Sea.

The sixteenth-century discovery of precious minerals in Mexico and Peru distracted Spanish attention from the Caribbean, which became little more than a gateway to the then-prosperous mainland. Hispaniola, Cuba, and Puerto Rico served merely as supply stations and military garrisons for royal fleets loaded with silver and gold. Meanwhile, the Spanish crown proved unable to sustain its commercial and political monopoly. The area was simply too large, settlements and fortresses too thinly dispersed, and the economic stakes too high. Indeed, the Caribbean Sea offered an inviting target for mercenary privateers and buccaneers. Spain's leading rivals, especially England, encouraged and sometimes outfitted these pirates; Francis Drake, John Hawkins, and Henry Morgan all became knights of the English realm.

Other European powers established settlements as well. The English seized Jamaica in 1655. The French took the western half of Hispaniola in 1659 and named it Saint-Domingue (present-day Haiti). Having occupied northeastern Brazil from 1630 to 1654, the Dutch moved onto a number of islands off the coast of Venezuela. Little by little, Spain ceded or accepted de facto loss of some of its colonial claims. Caribbean holdings became pawns in European wars, handed back and forth between winners and losers like the proceeds in a poker game.

By the early nineteenth century, Great Britain emerged as Europe's preeminent military, economic, and political power. Its principal objective in the Americas was economic—to promote Britain's commercial interests, which had relied on contraband trade throughout the eighteenth century. The basis for this activity would be strong economic institutions: the best available in shipping, banking, insurance, and investment capital. In effect, the British were seeking to replace the former Iberian colonial infrastructure linking Latin America to the world economy. Yet for the most part, the English sought economic gain without the burden of direct political rule. It was an "informal imperialism," whereby Europe's chief investor and trader avoided the expensive link of territorial control—with its potential military entanglements.

What of the United States? As the young republic undertook its quest for geopolitical status, domination of the Caribbean became a matter of national security—but the nation's ambition was much greater than its power. In fact, the United States was unable to prevent the city of Washington (and the White House) from being devastated by the English in the War of 1812. It was not a major power at this time.

The United States attempted to assert its authority with the "Monroe Doctrine" in 1823. Originally aimed at czarist Russia's potential encroachments on the American Northwest, the doctrine became better known for its challenge to Europe's conservative Holy Alliance, apparently planning to help Spain reconquer its former colonies. President James Monroe firmly declared that "the American continents, by the free and independent condition which they have assumed and maintained, are henceforth not to be considered as subject for colonization by any European powers." Further strictures warned the Europeans against using indirect means to extend their political power in the New World. As later put in a popular slogan, the basic message was clear: "America for the Americans."

In fact the message evoked indifference and scorn in continental Europe, mild concern in Britain, and considerable sympathy in Latin America. Within the United States the Monroe Doctrine, jingoistic and assertive, became a cornerstone for U.S. policy toward Latin America. Yet the nation lacked both the will and the capacity to enforce the declaration: it was preoccupied with continental expansion, including a victorious war against Mexico, and with struggles over slavery, including a frightful civil war.

It was not until the late nineteenth century that the United States was ready to take action in the Caribbean—which resembled a "European lake." With the exception of Hispaniola (shared by Haiti and the Dominican Republic), every single island was a European colony. Spain still held possession of Cuba and Puerto Rico; Britain held Jamaica, part of the Virgin Islands, Grenada, and several of the Leeward Islands (plus the mainland dominions of British Honduras and British Guiana); France held Martinique, Guadeloupe, and French Guiana; the Dutch held several islands plus Dutch Guiana (present-day Suriname) on the northern fringe of South America. These European outposts presented unwelcome limits on the exercise of U.S. power.

This fact helps explain U.S. intervention in Cuba's war for independence from Spain in 1898. The idealistic desire to expel Spain from the hemisphere no doubt played a role in the U.S. decision. After all, Spain appeared to represent the most reactionary elements of European society. A colonial monarchy, Spain stood for everything the United States claimed to oppose, and it represented a continuing violation of the Monroe Doctrine. Popular acceptance of the "black legend" (exaggerated accounts by British historian-publicists about Spanish atrocities in the Americas) further contributed to this conviction.

But the idea behind the intervention was not only to liberate Cuba; it was also to assert American power. (As will be explained in Chapter 5, policymakers in Washington had long assumed that Cuba would someday become part of the United States.) In a similar vein, U.S. officials became deeply concerned about European efforts to collect debt payments from countries around the Caribbean basin by force of arms; this gave rise to "dollar diplomacy," through which the United States assumed responsibility for the debt payments—so long as Europe would keep its gunboats home. Completion of the Panama Canal only strengthened U.S. determination to convert the Caribbean into an "American lake." From Washington's standpoint, the stakes were multiple—commercial, economic, political, military—and unnervingly high. And as we shall see, this strategy led to a consistent pattern of U.S. military interventions and/or clandestine subterfuge.

The outbreak of the Cold War in the 1940s added a new dimension to U.S. security concerns: the threat of international communism—not only in the hemisphere but also in America's "backyard." The anticommunist rationale was internally consistent and well articulated (which does not mean that it was accurate). The United States had no choice, so the reasoning went, but to fight back against the Soviet Union and its client powers, which were dedicated to the overthrow not only of capitalism but of all the Western democracies. The Third World would be a favorite Soviet target, argued Cold War theorists, and would be subverted by communist parties or their fellow travelers. The most drastic challenges by the early 1950s had been in Europe (the Berlin Blockade, the Greek Civil War, the French and Italian elections) and in Asia (the Korean War, the fall of Nationalist China, and the Indo-Chinese civil war). Was Latin America to be immune? Could the Caribbean become a beachhead for the communist cause? Operating under this logic, American governments took repeated actions within the region to (a) repress leftist tendencies, (b) support anticommunist regimes, and (c) overthrow socialist and left-of-center governments.

American hegemony would extend well beyond the Cold War. One impetus for a continued military presence, and even military intervention, stemmed from the U.S. "war on drugs." Another concern focused on illegal migration. And after the attacks of September 11, 2001, the Caribbean came under the umbrella of "homeland security" and the global war on terror. Small, impoverished, and relatively weak, nations of the area could not escape the shadow of the Colossus of the North.

FROM COLONIES TO NATIONHOOD

Columbus landed on a sizable island in December 1492 and christened it *La Española* (or Hispaniola in English). His arrival signaled the inexorable doom of the area's native population, estimated at 750,000 persons, divided among three separate groups: Ciboney or Guanahuatebey, Taino Arawak, and Carib (from which the region gets its name). Unable to develop significant trade, the Spaniards chose to exploit the island as a source of land and labor through the *encomienda* system. Semifeudal institutions were imposed upon the native society. Indians were forced to work in mines and fields. Harsh labor conditions and physical contact with Spaniards led to their decimation: disease and debilitation took a staggering toll. Realizing what fate held in store, many fled to the mountains in search of safety and freedom. As in New France and New England, the native population fell victim to virtual elimination.

It was in the Caribbean where Spanish clerics first protested against abuse of the natives. In 1511 Antonio de Montesinos shocked a congregation in the island colony of Santo Domingo by denouncing maltreatment of the Indian population. Soon afterward Bartolomé de las Casas began his fervent campaign to protect the Indians from adventurers and conquerors. In response to these pleas, the crown ultimately agreed to regulate the treatment of the native population. But to protect the American natives, Las Casas also made a fateful suggestion: that Spain import African slaves as a source of necessary labor.

Spaniards first reached Central America in 1501. In contrast to Mexico and Peru, it was not the site of a centralized Indian empire. Indigenous peoples lived in stable, autonomous communities and engaged in trade with one another. After 500 B.C.E. a relatively advanced civilization appeared in the highlands of Guatemala and El Salvador, and it was greatly influenced by Olmec culture from the Veracruz-Tabasco coast of Mexico. Nahuatl settlements later followed, and classic Mayan culture appeared in the lowlands of northern Guatemala. The period from 600 to 900 C.E. marked the apex of the Old Maya Empire, as it was formerly called, though it did not constitute a highly organized political unit.

The diversity of native cultures meant that Spaniards penetrated Central America in stages, not all at once, and each conquest required the establishment of a new government. The result was decentralization. Municipalities assumed day-to-day authority, and town councils *(ayuntamientos)* became the most important governing bodies. Nominally under the control of distant viceroys, Spanish residents of the isthmus functioned under separate royal orders for all intents and purposes. Attempting to assert authority, the Spanish crown established the Kingdom of Guatemala (as part of the vice-royalty of New Spain) in the mid-sixteenth century. As in the Caribbean and Mexico, the church followed closely on the heels of conquest. Secular and regular clergy, especially Franciscans and Dominicans, took active part in missionary efforts.

Economic activity was modest. Mining was from the beginning a small-scale operation. The first major export was cacao, though Venezuela soon preempted this market. Indigo then took over as the leading export, and there was a bustling contraband trade in tobacco. In the 1660s the English established a foothold at the mouth of the Belize River (later British Honduras or Belize), which they used as a base for commerce in dyewood and mahogany and for buccaneering raids. But for the most part, Central America was not a source of great wealth, and it received little attention from the Spanish crown.

The social structure was controlled by a two-part elite. One element consisted of Spanish-born bureaucrats whose political base was the imperial court *(audiencia)* in Guatemala. The other consisted of locally born landholders whose strength resided in town councils. At the bottom was the labor force, comprising Indians and African slaves. There also emerged a stratum of people of mixed racial backgrounds, known as *ladinos* in Central America, who worked as wage laborers or small farmers in the countryside and as artisans, merchants, and peddlers in the towns. Near the end of the colonial era, approximately 4 percent of the region's population was white (either Spanish or creole), about 65 percent was Indian, and 31 percent was *ladino* (including those of African descent).

During the eighteenth century the Bourbon monarchy attempted to reassert royal control of Spanish America, a move that everywhere reduced the political autonomy of the landed creole class. In Central America a continuing decline in cacao production and a precipitous drop in the indigo trade between the 1790s and the 1810s led to further discontent within the creole ranks. These factors heightened long-standing differences between the imperial bureaucracy and the local aristocracy, between the capital and the provinces.

Independence in the Caribbean

What is now Haiti, on the western side of the island of Hispaniola, was once one of the most prosperous overseas possessions of France. The island's original inhabitants were almost entirely replaced by African slaves imported to work on sugar estates. During the French Revolution, Haiti's residents, including landowners of mixed African and European descent, were granted full citizenship, a move that white estate owners resented. Resulting conflicts led to a wave of rebellions. This time the slaves wanted not only personal freedom but national independence as well.

Under the leadership of Pierre Dominique Toussaint L'Ouverture, the blacks of Haiti revolted in 1791 and in 1804 declared national sovereignty. This was to be the second free nation in the Americas and the first independent black country in the world. Although Toussaint led the rebellion, he was seized and sent to France, where he eventually died in an obscure dungeon. It was one of his lieutenants, Jean Jacques Dessalines, who proclaimed the nation free from colonial rule.

The wars broke up and destroyed the large sugar estates. Land was at first worked collectively under a system called the *corvée*, but individual aspirations in the postindependence period led to the distribution of parcels to freeholders. Thus the legacy of large oligarchic landowners, so prevalent elsewhere in Latin America, did not take root in independent Haiti. Instead, a large number of small holdings replaced the sugar estates, and production decreased drastically. Independence gave power to the blacks, who still form about 90 percent of the population, a fact that light-skinned mulattoes have resented all along. Indeed, the mulattoes became a prosperous minority, clinging to an ideal of French civilization and speaking French on a regular basis. The majority black population, by contrast, spoke a native language, Haitian, and found spiritual inspiration in *vodun*, an eclectic blend of Dahomian religions and Catholicism. A kind of caste system divided the mulattoes from the blacks, and conflict between the two elements formed a persisting theme in Haitian history.

These events had complicated spillover effects throughout Hispaniola. Since the late seventeenth century, colonial authority over the island had been divided between France, with Saint-Domingue (later renamed Haiti), and Spain, with Santo Domingo. This pattern began to unravel in 1795, when Spain ceded Santo Domingo to France in the Peace of Basel (thus settling one of Europe's endless wars). This gave France titular possession of the entire island. When Haiti achieved independence in 1804, however, the eastern part remained under French authority. And when Napoleon invaded Spain in 1808, the creoles of Santo Domingo rose up in protest against France—and, as loyal subjects of the crown, they restored Spanish rule over their colony. Powers came and powers went: this incipient phase of Dominican independence resembled a game of musical chairs.

Plots and counterplots ensued for the next dozen years. As insurgent military campaigns gained momentum in Mexico and South America, local leaders of Santo Domingo in 1821 declared the independence of what they decided to call "Spanish Haiti." Within a matter of months, armed forces from Haiti invaded the country, seized power, and imposed a military government. As on their side of the island, Haitian authorities took radical steps—abolishing slavery, nationalizing property, and reducing the role of the church. The Haitian occupation lasted for twenty-two years, when local patriots finally ousted the invaders. This made 1844 the second date of Dominican independence—this time from Haiti, not from a European power.

Haitian forces mounted near-continuous invasions against their neighbor throughout the 1840s and 1850s. Out of exasperation and fear, one enterprising Dominican president hit upon the ideal solution: he returned his country to Spain, which resumed colonial rule from 1861 to 1865. This action provoked bitter protest in Haiti, apprehensive about Spanish power, and in the United States, outraged by such a flagrant violation of the Monroe Doctrine. Shortly after Spain was driven out, another national leader pursued yet another solution: annexation to the United States. Surely, this would protect the struggling nation from further intrusions by Haiti or anyone else. U.S. president Ulysses S. Grant strongly supported the plan, thinking it might provide a homeland for American slaves freed by the Civil War, but the proposal failed to obtain congressional approval.

The Dominican Republic thus lapsed into independence almost by default. Its citizens suffered a series of self-seeking and vainglorious rulers. Most prominent among them was Ulises Heureaux, a dictator who ruled from 1882 to 1899 in ways comparable to those of Mexico's Porfirio Díaz. Political intrigue and economic disarray thereafter plagued the nation, which would eventually find itself under U.S. military occupation by 1916. Authentic sovereignty looked like a mirage.

Independence for Central America
Just as the fate of the Dominican Republic was so strongly affected by Haiti, Central America's path to independence was conditioned by events in Mexico (and/or the Viceroyalty of New Spain, to which Central America belonged). After the Napoleonic invasion of Spain in 1808, pro-colonial authorities at first managed to maintain control of Central America by forging an alliance with *ladinos* and Indians against the upstart creoles. In 1820 Spain's adoption of a liberal constitution sent shock waves throughout the area, and in mid-1821 Agustín de Iturbide's declaration of the Plan de Iguala in Mexico forced the issue. Partly fearing "liberation" by Mexican troops, the socially conservative landowners of Central America decided to break with now-radical Spain; in January 1822 they proclaimed annexation of the isthmus to imperial Mexico. This lasted for only one year, and Iturbide's abdication led to independence. Chiapas remained with Mexico. The other states, from Costa Rica to Guatemala (excluding Panama), became the United Provinces of Central America. Despite discord and disagreement, Central America managed to separate itself from Spain—and from Mexico—in a relatively peaceful fashion.

As happened elsewhere, the Central American political elite divided into two factions: Liberals and Conservatives. The Liberals advocated the continuation of reforms started by the Bourbon monarchy. They called for restrictions on clerical power, the abolition of slavery, the reduction of taxes, and the promotion of economic development. They drew their support from emerging professional classes, white and *ladino,* and from upper-middle sectors excluded from the circles of the landed creole aristocracy. Led by creole landowners, the Conservatives stood for order, moderation, and stability. They upheld Hispanic institutions, especially the church, and they expressed suspicion of progressive reform.

Violence erupted in the 1820s, and the Liberals at first appeared to have the upper hand. Conservatives rebounded in the 1830s under the leadership of José Rafael Carrera, a *ladino* swineherd with no formal education. In mid-1837 he defined the goals of his movement as the reinstatement of traditional judicial procedures, the restoration of religious orders and ecclesiastical privilege, amnesty for all his supporters in exile—and obedience to his authority. Carrera remained as the dominant figure in Central American political life until his death in 1865. Roman Catholicism became the official state religion, priests regained protection of the ecclesiastical *fuero,* and education was turned over to the church. The government abandoned the goal of assimilating Indian masses and decided instead to protect indigenous communities, much as the Spanish crown had done, a policy that helped prolong the segregation that has persisted to this day.

Liberals began a resurgence after Carrera's death. Believing in notions of progress and development, they sought to integrate their countries with the rest of the world, to acquire the trappings of civilization, and to promote material improvement. In outlook they shared the views of Mexico's *científicos,* and in politics they followed the example of Porfirio Díaz—establishing what came to be known as "republican dictatorships." They centralized authority, rigged elections, and kept themselves in power for extended periods of time. They drew domestic support from the landed aristocracy and from some middle-sector elements. They forged close alliances with foreign interests—British, German, North American. They also modernized the police and military establishments, which they routinely used to intimidate the opposition.

This pattern produced significant social alterations. Where Conservative-Liberal distinctions were clearest (Guatemala and Costa Rica), they led to the near-total eclipse of the Conservative families. Where partisan lines were blurred (Honduras, El Salvador), some dynasties managed to hang on. Nicaragua proved to be an exception, as Conservative families had managed to consolidate their position in advance. Generally speaking, Liberal ascendancy opened opportunities to middle-sector professionals and *ladinos* and led to the formation of new elites.

In addition, Liberal domination stripped the church of power and prestige. The church's economic role was diminished and its legal privileges were abolished. As one historian would later write, "The major role the clergy had played in rural Central America became minor. This was one of the most important changes ever to take place in Central America." The demise of the church left an institutional vacuum. It would eventually be filled, at least in part, by a new kind of Roman Catholic Church in the late twentieth century.

OVERVIEW: ECONOMIC GROWTH AND SOCIAL CHANGE

Economic developments in Central America and the Caribbean produced a common denominator. With few exceptions, such as Costa Rica, countries of the region forged "plantation societies." As a result, they shared a cluster of defining characteristics:

- Extensive production of export cash crops on large-scale *latifundios* (a.k.a. haciendas, *fincas,* estates, or plantations)
- Mobilization (and control) of rural labor for harvesting and related tasks
- Concentration of land ownership in very few hands
- Inadequate emphasis on subsistence farming, usually carried out on tiny *minifundios*
- Formation of economic and social "enclaves" where local elites and foreign owners could live and work in relative isolation from the host society at large

Plantation societies were highly unequal, juxtaposing luxury and poverty. They survived in small countries which lacked the population and resources to undertake industrial development. They were underdeveloped. They were economically vulnerable to overseas changes in market conditions. But because of their institutional rigidity, they were resistant to change. Beneath superficial appearances of harmony, they could give rise to volatile discontent.

The Caribbean: Sugar (and More Sugar)

The principal crop in the Caribbean was sugar. One of the early expeditions from Spain brought sugarcane cuttings from the Canary Islands, an act that would alter the course of history. And after the Dutch brought new technologies from the Brazilian Northeast to the Caribbean in the mid-seventeenth century, the production of sugarcane exploded. It became virtually the only crop on British islands, especially Barbados and Jamaica, and it was the dominant crop in French areas, including Martinique and Saint-Domingue (i.e, Haiti). Together, colonial holdings in the Caribbean accounted for 80 to 90 percent of all the sugar consumed in eighteenth-century Europe. By the 1740s, Jamaica and Saint-Domingue were the world's largest producers of sugar.

As production increased, the need for labor became all the more apparent. African enslavement appeared to provide a solution. Thus began the tragic history of forced migration from the western coast of Africa. Of the 10 to 15 million people who were sent to the New World as slaves, approximately 5 to 7 million found their way to the Caribbean—where they would work on sugar plantations, alter the racial composition of the area, and, ultimately, help to establish commercial links with nineteenth-century Europe and the United States.

The loosely organized societies of the sixteenth century, dominated by whites and small-household units, gave way to a strictly organized and hierarchical society of masters and slaves by the seventeenth century. Production was firmly controlled by the mother countries. With the exception of England, each European country formed its own trading company; in addition to the *casa de contratación* of Spain, there were the Dutch West Indies Company and the French *Compagnie des Isles d'Amérique.*

A primary consequence of these developments was the creation of a rigid system of racial stratification. Virtually everywhere a three-tiered pyramid existed: whites at the top, browns in the middle, and blacks at the bottom. As whites returned to Europe and Indians disappeared, the African heritage became dominant. This pattern would have long-run effects on race relations in the region and would sharply distinguish the Caribbean from mainland areas, such as Mexico and Peru, with large and persisting indigenous populations.

Another result was the transformation of once-diversified systems of production into single-product economies, emphasizing sugar for export. Most consumption needs had to be imported—from other islands, from the mainland, or from Spain itself. Only on the smaller islands, such as Grenada, were other products (in this case, coffee) more important than sugar. Since most of the original population had died and Spanish settlers did not like to work with their hands, the demand for slaves continued through the eighteenth century.

Central America: Vital Statistics, 2007

	PANAMA	NICARAGUA	EL SALVADOR	GUATEMALA
Population (millions)	3.3	5.6	6.9	13.3
GDP (current $U.S. billions)	19.7	5.7	20.2	33.4
GNP/capita ($U.S.)	5510	980	2850	2440
Poverty rate (% in 2006)	29.9	61.9	47.5	54.8
Life expectancy (years)	75	72	72	70

The Caribbean: Vital Statistics, 2007

	DOMINICAN REPUBLIC	HAITI	PUERTO RICO
Population (millions)	9.8	9.6	3.9
GDP (current $U.S. billions)	36.7	6.1	67.9
GNP/capita ($U.S. dollars)	3550	560	10,950
Poverty rate (% in 2006)	44.5	—	—
Life expectancy (years)	72	60	78

SOURCES: World Bank and Economic Commission for Latin America and the Caribbean.

European demand for sugar permitted many of the settlers to make large fortunes, which they used to build great manorial houses and to purchase acceptance into the political and social life of the mother country. Yet French and British colonists never felt at ease on the islands. Most longed to return home, and, in fact, some went back to positions of power and prominence. If there appeared a plantation aristocracy in some parts of the Caribbean, it was not a deeply rooted one.

Spanish colonists initiated sugar production in Santo Domingo in the early sixteenth century, when they also began importing African slaves. Production grew steadily over the years and expanded in the eighteenth century. The Dominican sugar industry received a substantial boost in the mid-nineteenth century as a result of three factors: civil strife in Cuba, which led some prominent planters to transfer their operations to the Dominican Republic; warfare in Europe, which wrought devastation on the continental sugar beet industry; and the U.S. Civil War, which reduced sugarcane production in Louisiana and further reduced the competition. In the early 1880s a market crash led to a temporary decline in the harvest; it also resulted in sharp concentration of ownership because only the largest mills were able to survive.

As production recovered, labor for the backbreaking work on plantations was imported directly from neighboring Haiti. Continuation of this trend would provoke social and racial tension within Dominican society. Relations between the two countries had never been very good; the degrading treatment of Haitian workers in the Dominican Republic only made things worse. Anti-Haitian sentiment often took the ugly form of racial prejudice.

As in Cuba, American investors began showing interest in Dominican sugar around the turn of the century. U.S. military intervention from 1916 to 1924 sealed this bilateral relationship. By the end of the occupation, two American conglomerates owned eleven out of the twenty-one *ingenios* (mills) in the country—and five of the others were owned by U.S. citizens. Almost all Dominican sugar exports were sold on the U.S. market. As shown in Figure 4.1, production climbed strongly

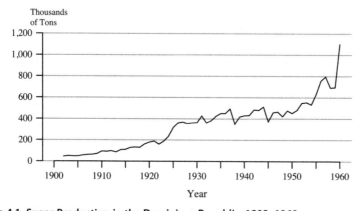

Figure 4.1 Sugar Production in the Dominican Republic, 1902–1960
SOURCE: Michael R. Hall, *Sugar and Power in the Dominican Republic: Eisenhower, Kennedy, and the Trujillos* (Westport Greenwood Press, 2000).

Table 4.1 Caribbean Trade with the United States, 1920–2000 (as % of total)

	1920		1950		2000	
	EXPORTS	IMPORTS	EXPORTS	IMPORTS	EXPORTS	IMPORTS
Haiti	14	81	58	72	86	62
Dominican Republic	79	42	38	73	87	59

Sources: James W. Wilkie, *Statistics and National Policy* (Los Angeles: UCLA Latin American Center, 1974); Economist Intelligence Unit, Country Reports, 2003.

through the 1920s, held steady from the 1930s through the 1940s, then soared upward in the late 1950s. After Cuba, the Dominican Republic was the second-largest producer of sugar in the Caribbean. Hardly any of the profits were reinvested in the local society. This was an enclave economy par excellence.

For Haiti as well as the Dominican Republic, reliance on the American market accentuated over time. As shown in Table 4.1, the U.S. share of Haitian exports climbed from 14 percent in 1920 to 58 percent in 1950 and 86 percent by 2000; similarly, the U.S. share of Dominican exports rose from 79 percent in 1920 to 87 percent by 2000. (Postwar Europe consumed a very large share of Dominican sugar production in the late 1940s and early 1950s, accounting for the low proportion of U.S. exports in that era.) Ever since the early 1960s, the Dominican Republic has held the largest single allocation of the U.S. sugar import quota. The United States was also the largest single source of imports in both countries, although the European Union was making headway as the twentieth century came to an end.

Central America: Coffee and Bananas

While sugar was the undisputed "king" in the Caribbean, two export products came to dominate economic life in Central America: coffee and bananas. Differences in production led to variations in social structures, but the cultivation of these crops created plantation societies nonetheless.

Costa Rica began serious coffee production in the 1830s, shipping exports first to Chile and later to Europe. Guatemala promptly followed suit, and by 1870 coffee was the country's leading export, a position it has held ever since. El Salvador, Nicaragua, and Honduras joined the coffee trade in the 1870s and 1880s. Central American coffee exports have not risen to enormous volumes—never accounting for more than 15 percent of the world supply—but they have always been of high quality.

Coffee had important social consequences. Since it was grown in the cool highlands, along the mountain slopes, it did not necessarily require large-scale usurpation of land from lowland peasants. There were substantial takeovers in Guatemala and El Salvador, though less dramatic than what occurred in Porfirian Mexico. In Honduras, Nicaragua, and Costa Rica, dislocations were less common.

Also many coffee plantations were modest in size, and they were usually owned by Central Americans. Foreign investors came to play an important part in coffee production in Nicaragua, and Germans acquired substantial amounts of coffee-growing land in Guatemala. But in general, coffee production remained in Central American hands.

Though Liberal leaders sought to encourage immigration, Central America never received the kind of massive, working-class influx that went to South America and the United States. Labor for coffee cultivation instead came from the mostly Indian and *mestizo* peasants. In time they fell into two groups: *colonos,* who lived on the plantations and leased small plots of land for subsistence cultivation, and *jornaleros,* day laborers who worked for wages while living at home and retaining control of small plots of land. In either case they retained close contact with the earth and retained outlooks of traditional peasants, rather than forging class consciousness as a rural proletariat.

Although coffee production dominated the agricultural sector in the nineteenth century, the banana trade would eventually become emblematic of Central American culture. It had an unlikely start. In 1870 a New England sea captain named Lorenzo Baker began shipments from Jamaica to the East Coast of the United States, and years later he found a partner to form the Boston Fruit Company. In the meantime, another investment group began shipping bananas to New Orleans and created the Tropical Trading and Transport Company. In 1899 the two companies merged to form a singular enterprise: the United Fruit Company (UFCO). Here began a remarkable chapter in the history of U.S. investment, penetration, and control in Central America.

UFCO, or *la frutera* (the fruitery), as Central Americans called it, established a virtual monopoly on the production and distribution of bananas. Through government concessions and other means, the company acquired vast tracts of land in the hot, humid, sparsely settled Caribbean lowlands. It dominated transportation networks and owned a major corporation, International Railways of Central America. It built docks and port facilities, and created the Tropical Radio and Telegraph Company. *La frutera* possessed a large number of ships, widely known as the "great white fleet," and it exerted enormous influence on marketing in the United States. UFCO tolerated and even encouraged small-scale competition, but it was never seriously challenged in the decades after World War I.

The banana trade created plantation societies and enclave economies par excellence. UFCO supervisors and managers came from the United States, most notably from the South, and black workers were imported from Jamaica and the West Indies. One result was to alter the racial composition of the eastern lowland population. Another was to create harshly enforced racial divisions within *la frutera* itself.

The industry became a giant foreign corporation. Some banana lands remained in local hands, but UFCO possessed control of technology, loans, and access to the U.S. market. Because of natural threats from hurricanes and plant disease, UFCO sought to keep substantial amounts of land in reserve. These could usually be obtained only by government concession, a fact which required the company to enter local politics. The picture is clear: UFCO provided relatively scant stimulus for Central America's economic development, but became directly involved in local matters of state.

Coffee and bananas dominated the Central American economy after the turn of the century, accounting for around 75 percent of the region's exports up through the 1930s and 67 percent as late as 1960. As a result, the economic fortunes of Central America became extremely dependent on the vagaries of the international market. When coffee or banana prices were down, earnings were down, and there was little room for flexible response—since coffee and banana plantations could not be easily or quickly converted to producing basic foodstuffs (assuming that the owners wanted to do so, which was hardly the case). It is worth noting, too, that coffee consistently formed a larger share of exports than bananas, and UFCO could not control the coffee market. In strict economic terms, only Costa Rica, Honduras, and Panama were "banana republics." Guatemala, El Salvador, and Nicaragua were mainly coffee countries.

As with Caribbean sugar, the coffee-banana strategy led to heavy reliance on trade with a single partner: the United States. In the late nineteenth and early twentieth centuries, Central America had a flourishing trade with Europe—Germany, in fact, was the biggest coffee customer. But after World War I the United States asserted its supremacy. From the 1920s through the 1950s, as Table 4.2 demonstrates, the United States purchased 60–90 percent of the region's exports and provided a similar share of imports. The North American predominance in international transactions faded to 40–60 percent by 2000 for most countries, but the United States still had considerable commercial leverage over nations of the isthmus.

Within these broad analytical contexts, geopolitical and economic, we now turn to the historical development of selected countries. In Central America, we focus on Panama, Nicaragua, El Salvador, and Guatemala; in the Caribbean, we deal with the Dominican Republic, Haiti, and Puerto Rico. (We cover Cuba in Chapter 5.) Many

Table 4.2 Central American Trade with the United States, 1920–2000 (as % of total)

	1920		1950		2000	
	EXPORTS	**IMPORTS**	**EXPORTS**	**IMPORTS**	**EXPORTS**	**IMPORTS**
Costa Rica	71	52	70	67	52	53
El Salvador	56	79	86	67	65	50
Guatemala	67	61	88	79	57	35
Honduras	87	85	77	74	39	46
Nicaragua	78	73	54	72	38	25
Panama	93	73	80	69	45	33

Sources: James W. Wilkie, *Statistics and National Policy* (Los Angeles: UCLA Latin American Center, 1974); Economist Intelligence Unit, Country Reports, 2003.

of these nations emerged as prototypical plantation and/or enclave societies; at one time or another, all felt the heavy hand of American power.

POLITICS AND POLICY: PANAMA

As the United States began flexing its muscles on the international scene, the most conspicuous sign of its expansionist zeal came from efforts to construct a canal between the Atlantic and Pacific oceans. Plans for an interoceanic canal through Central America went back as far as the seventeenth century. In 1878 the government of Colombia authorized a French consortium to dig a route through its northwestern-most province, in what is now known as Panama. U.S. engineers tended to favor Nicaragua, and a North American firm received a contract to start excavations in that country. Competition came to an end with the financial Panic of 1893, when both groups ran out of money and quit.

Turn-of-the-twentieth-century America was nonetheless determined to enhance its position on the world stage. And in such magisterial books as *The Influence of Sea Power upon History* (1890), the historian-publicist Alfred Thayer Mahan forcefully argued that naval power was the key to international influence, a doctrine requiring a two-ocean navy for the United States. After Theodore Roosevelt became president in 1901, it was clear that Washington would make a move.

As will be explained in Chapter 7, Colombia was enduring a domestic political struggle that culminated in the "War of the Thousand Days" (1899–1903). As the fighting was nearing its end, Washington dispatched troops to quell disorder in the province of Panama. This resulted in a diplomatic crisis which eventually produced the Hay-Herrán Treaty, an agreement permitting the United States to build a canal through Panama. The U.S. Congress eagerly approved the document—but the Colombian legislature, unwilling to compromise national sovereignty, refused to go along.

The next step was insurrection. With Roosevelt's full knowledge, a French engineer named Philippe Bunau-Varilla started laying plans for a separatist rebellion in Panama. As the uprising began, U.S. ships prevented Colombian troops from crossing the isthmus to Panama City. The revolt was a success.

Within days, Washington extended recognition to the newly sovereign government of Panama and received Bunau-Varilla (still a French citizen) as its official representative. U.S. secretary of state John Hay and Bunau-Varilla hastily signed a treaty giving the United States control of a ten-mile-wide canal zone "in perpetuity...as if it were sovereign." A pliant Panamanian legislature soon approved the document. Bunau-Varilla and administration lobbyists then turned their attention to the U.S. Senate, where pro-Nicaragua sentiment was still fairly strong. On the morning of the decisive vote, Bunau-Varilla placed on each senator's desk a Nicaraguan postage stamp depicting a volcanic eruption, and the silent message took hold. The Senate approved the measure by a 66–14 margin, and the die was cast.

A masterpiece of engineering, the Panama Canal opened in 1914 and immediately became a major international waterway. The Canal Zone became a de facto U.S. colony, an area of legal privilege and country-club prosperity that stood in conspicuous contrast to local society. Outside the Zone, Panama developed the characteristics that typified Central America as a whole: dependence on agricultural exports (especially bananas), reliance on the U.S. market, and domestic control by a tightly knit landed oligarchy. This situation could not last forever.

It was not until the 1950s that a military president of Panama, Colonel José Antonio Remón, began renegotiation of the 1903 treaty. Three years later his efforts resulted in an agreement that increased the annuity payable to Panama, curtailed economic privileges for U.S. citizens, and sought to equalize wage rates for North Americans and Panamanians. But the question of sovereignty was left untouched. It came up in 1956, after Egypt's seizure of the Suez Canal. When President Ricardo Arias bitterly protested Panama's exclusion from a conference on the Suez crisis, Secretary of State John Foster Dulles frostily replied that the United States had "rights of sovereignty over the Panama Canal . . . to the entire exclusion of the Republic of Panama of any such sovereign rights, power, or authority."

Tensions rose and fell in subsequent years. The dynamics changed after a controversial election in 1968, when Panama's National Guard seized power and formed a ruling junta under Brigadier General Omar Torrijos Herrera. This marked a clear assertion by the National Guard of hegemony in politics. It led to the emergence of Torrijos as the nation's strongman. And it yielded continuity in leadership, as Torrijos patiently pursued negotiations with the Nixon, Ford, and Carter administrations in the United States.

The United States finally accepted a treaty in the 1970s that provided for complete Panamanian sovereignty over the canal by 1999. Ronald Reagan and other American conservatives vigorously denounced the agreement as a sellout, but Democratic president Jimmy Carter eventually obtained Senate approval. Intellectuals and statesmen throughout the hemisphere applauded the move. However briefly, U.S.–Latin American relations took a positive turn.

Presidential elections produced both continuity and change. In May 1999, a lackluster campaign featured leading contenders from two prominent families—Martín Torrijos, the son of Omar Torrijos, and Mireya Moscoso, the widow of another former president. In somewhat of a surprise, Moscoso triumphed with 45 percent of the votes, compared with 38 percent for Torrijos and 17 percent for a third-place candidate. (This made Moscoso the first woman president in the history of Panama and only the second woman anywhere in Latin America to become president by direct election.)

Moscoso's most immediate challenge would concern the Panama Canal, scheduled to transfer from the United States to Panama at the end of 1999. As she proclaimed in her victory speech, "We are going to show that we can run the canal as well as the Americans did." And while there was little doubt about Panama's technical ability to manage the waterway itself, there arose concern

Operation Just Cause

Underlying friction between Panama and the United States resurfaced in the 1980s. Strongman Omar Torrijos died in an airplane crash and was succeeded by General Manuel Antonio Noriega, widely reputed to be involved in drug-related corruption. (He had also been a part-time agent for the Central Intelligence Agency [CIA].) Panamanian nationalism flared when the Noriega government refused to renew the bilateral agreement for operation of the "School of the Americas," a U.S.-financed and -directed training program for the Latin American military.

Anti-American feeling surged again in 1988, when President George H. W. Bush imposed an economic boycott in an effort to oust Noriega as part of the "war on drugs." The following year, Noriega annulled elections apparently won by Guillermo Endara, leader of an oppositionist "civic crusade" against the dictatorship, and the United States tightened the screws. In December 1989 the Bush administration launched "Operation Just Cause" with more than 20,000 U.S. troops and extensive aerial bombing. The invasion force overwhelmed Panamanian resistance and captured Noriega himself—taking him to Miami, where he would stand trial for alleged complicity in drug trafficking. U.S. officials reported that only twenty-three American servicemen had lost their lives, but there would be continuing controversy over the death toll for Panamanians (estimates ranged from several hundred to several thousand). Economic damages from the invasion may have been as high as $2 billion.

Many Panamanians initially greeted American troops with enthusiasm but soon became disenchanted. As a result of the sanctions and the invasion, the gross national product shrank by 22 percent between 1988 and early 1991. Popular support for the new president, installed by the United States, declined from 73 percent in mid-1989 to 17 percent in March 1991. An opposition party accused the hapless president of links with money-laundering schemes, the very charge that the United States had used to justify its invasion in the first place.

about its capacity to maintain support facilities. Additional apprehensions focused on security, especially after the breakdown in 1998 of negotiations for the possible creation of a U.S.-led antinarcotics center in Panama (which would have required a U.S. military presence). Such fears became all the more intense after the September 11, 2001, attacks on New York and Washington, because the Panama Canal seemed to provide an inviting target for further terrorist assaults.

A decisive victory of the populist Martín Torrijos in the presidential election of 2004 did little to assuage these concerns. Following policies similar to those of his father, Torrijos supported the cause of independence for Puerto Rico and extended a hand to Cuba. At the same time, his administration initiated a Panama Canal expansion project to double the canal's capacity and allow more traffic. An abrupt shift in political direction occurred in 2009, as economic anxieties led voters to elect conservative multimillionaire Ricardo Martinelli as president. Whatever change this might portend, one fact remained crystal-clear: Panama's economy remains tightly intertwined with that of the United States.

POLITICS AND POLICY: NICARAGUA

For much of its history, Nicaragua has been a pawn of outside powers, especially the United States. During the nineteenth century it received unceasing attention from avaricious adventurers, many of whom sought to build a canal, and it endured the brief but ignominious presence of William Walker. The pattern would continue into the twentieth century.

Washington developed a strong dislike for José Santos Zelaya, the dictator who had staunchly resisted foreign control in negotiations over a canal route. In 1909 Zelaya ordered the execution of two North American adventurers. Secretary

The William Walker Affair

Geographic and economic considerations had long stimulated interest in the idea of an interoceanic route through Central America. Having failed to discover a system of lakes and rivers connecting the Pacific Ocean and the Caribbean Sea, planners and visionaries pondered the possibility of an isthmian canal. Because of its extensive lakes and the San Juan River, Nicaragua seemed a natural site for the canal project, and in late 1849 Cornelius Vanderbilt and his associates secured a concession from a Liberal government. Intrigue rapidly thickened. Costa Rica claimed jurisdiction over the proposed terminus at the eastern end of the route for the canal. Hoping to block their U.S. rivals, the British supported Costa Rica. By 1853 Conservatives had gained power in Nicaragua, and, without conceding territorial rights, they chose to take sides with the British.

Frustrated Liberals turned to the United States for help. What they got was William Walker, the glib and intellectually gifted son of an austere, frontier-funda-mentalist family from Tennessee. As a young man, Walker studied medicine in the United States and Europe, then took up law in New Orleans. Under a contract with the Liberals, Walker hired a small army and invaded Nicaragua in 1855. He seized one of Vanderbilt's passenger vessels, won a quick victory, named himself head of the armed forces, and settled in as the country's authoritative ruler.

The U.S. government took a permissive view of these developments, openly tolerating intervention by a North American citizen in the affairs of another state. Walker staffed his forces with veterans from the 1846–48 war with Mexico, accepted support from Vanderbilt's business competitors, and invited migrants from the U.S. South—who brought slavery along. Opposition mounted from the British and from Conservatives in other states, however, and Walker was driven from power in 1857. He tried to return and met his death in 1860.

Thus ended the "National War," an event with long-lasting implications. It discredited both the Liberals and the United States and helps explain why the Conservatives stayed in power much longer in Nicaragua than in other parts of nineteenth-century Central America.

of State Philander C. Knox denounced Zelaya as "a blot on the history of his country" and expelled Nicaragua's ambassador from the United States. Subsequent U.S. support for an anti-Zelaya revolt helped force the president to resign.

Financial chaos ensued. European creditors began demanding payment on their debts. In desperation, the new president, Conservative Adolfo Díaz, asked the United States to send military aid to protect North American economic interests from the threat of civil war within Nicaragua and to "extend its protection to all the inhabitants of the republic." President William Howard Taft promptly dispatched the marines. A plan for fiscal recovery obtained a guarantee from a New York banking conglomerate, which received control of the national bank and the railway system as security on its investment. Politically and economically, Nicaragua became a full-fledged protectorate of the United States. This condition lasted until 1933.

In the mid-1920s a dispute arose over presidential succession. The United States imposed the trusty Adolfo Díaz and agreed to supervise upcoming elections. As a result of this compromise, a Liberal named Juan Bautista Sacasa became president in 1932 and called for the withdrawal of U.S. troops. The New York bankers had already recovered their investment, and Franklin Delano Roosevelt was about to proclaim the Good Neighbor policy. In 1933 the marines left Nicaragua.

But one Liberal activist, Augusto César Sandino, refused to abide by these agreements. A fervent patriot, a nationalist, and a social moderate, Sandino had waged a guerrilla campaign against U.S. intervention and Nicaraguan collaborationists. As he gained a widespread popular following, the United States worried about the presence of leftists among his supporters—and deployed U.S. Marines to join in the campaign against him. After the departure of American forces, Sandino agreed to meet with Sacasa in order to discuss terms for peace. After leaving the presidential palace, Sandino and his two military aides were seized by uniformed officers and executed. A genuine national hero, Sandino now became a martyr as well.

The National Guard thereafter became the dominant force in Nicaraguan politics. At its head was General Anastasio ("Tacho") Somoza García, a ruthless tyrant who had given the order to execute Sandino. He eventually unseated Sacasa and took over the presidency in 1937. Amassing an enormous fortune for himself and his family, Somoza promoted the nation's economic growth, formed alliances with the landed elite, and assiduously cultivated support from the U.S. government. He was shot by an assassin in 1956 and rushed to a hospital in the American-controlled Panama Canal Zone. Ever grateful for Somoza's rabid anticommunism, U.S. president Dwight D. Eisenhower sent his personal surgeon to try to save the dictator's life. Somoza nonetheless succumbed.

The family enterprise endured. The elder son, Luis Somoza Debayle, won rigged elections for president in 1957. A trusted family associate, René Schick, assumed office in 1963. Power then passed to the younger son, Anastasio Somoza Debayle, a West Point graduate and, like his father, head of the National Guard. Self-seeking and corrupt, Somoza clamped an iron rule on the country, but eventually offended thoughtful Nicaraguans by his excesses. Particularly unsettling were rumors that he extracted massive profits from the reconstruction of Managua after a devastating earthquake in 1972.

The complete absence of representative institutions meant that effective opposition to Somoza could take only one form: armed resistance. In the 1960s a guerrilla movement emerged. Taking their name from Augusto César Sandino, divergent forces combined their efforts to form the Sandinista National Liberation Front. After years of bitter struggle, the Somoza regime suddenly collapsed in 1979.

As in post-1959 Cuba, Washington now confronted a thoroughly unwelcome development: the triumph of a leftist revolutionary movement. Given the logic of the Cold War, this was a threatening—and potentially unacceptable—turn of events.

The Sandinistas proclaimed two broad policy goals. One called for implementation of an "independent and nonaligned" foreign policy, which meant no more submission to the United States. The other envisioned the creation of a "mixed economy" in order to achieve balanced development and socioeconomic justice. They also attacked such fundamental problems as illiteracy, health care, and access to education. Their economic task was paradoxically eased by the magnitude of the Somoza family fortune, which included about 20 percent of the country's cultivable land. This made it possible to nationalize these holdings and undertake agrarian reform without provoking diehard opposition from an entrenched landed aristocracy.

The new government at first received encouraging signs of international assistance. They solicited help from the United States, under President Jimmy Carter, who initially responded with a $75 million aid program. Far more substantial support came from Western Europe—especially western Germany, France, and Spain. The Soviet Union extolled the revolution and intensified (virtually nonexistent) commercial ties, but offered little hard-currency assistance. In the meantime, the Sandinistas welcomed approximately 2500 Cubans (the count was carefully monitored by the CIA and State Department)—doctors, nurses, schoolteachers, sanitary engineers—to help raise basic living standards. Cuban military, police, and intelligence personnel also arrived to protect the regime against what the Sandinistas (and Cubans) were convinced would be antirevolutionary attacks from within and without.

Euphoria did not last long. In the United States, the Republican Party electoral platform of 1980 formally deplored "the Marxist Sandinista takeover of Nicaragua," and the Reagan administration thereafter launched a campaign to undermine the Sandinista government—imposing a trade embargo, authorizing clandestine CIA attacks, and resorting to psychological warfare. Perhaps more important, the U.S. government supported and funded a counterrevolutionary exile army (known as the "Contras") commanded in large part by former Somoza army officers. Although the Contras met with limited military success, they forced the Sandinista government to spend half of its total budget on defense. Partly as a result of these factors, the economy went into a serious tailspin. Output declined by 4 percent in 1987 and 8 percent in 1988, when inflation reached the unthinkable level of 33,000 percent!

In this context, elections took place in 1990. With Daniel Ortega as their candidate, the Sandinistas confidently anticipated victory. At the head of an opposition coalition (UNO from its Spanish initials) was Violeta Barrios de Chamorro, the widow of a distinguished journalist who had been assassinated by *somocista* henchmen in 1978. To the surprise of most analysts, UNO captured 54.7 percent of the vote, against 40.8 percent for the Sandinistas. At the urging of Jimmy Carter (present as an international observer), Ortega made a gracious concession speech.

Chamorro proclaimed an end to the fighting and, at her inauguration, announced an "unconditional amnesty" for political crimes and an end to the military draft. She was nonetheless unable to consolidate her political base. Assisted by over $860 million in direct foreign aid and more than $200 million in debt write-offs, Chamorro's economic team managed to bring down inflation, but overall growth remained sluggish. Unemployment rose from 12 percent in 1990 to 22 percent in 1993 (with underemployment affecting another 28 percent). Now known as *recontras,* former Contras engaged in occasional skirmishes with demobilized Sandinistas, known as *recompas,* but the two sides accepted a peace agreement in April 1994. Sporadic clashes nonetheless continued, as the national government proved unable to maintain law and order in the countryside.

The late 1990s drew attention to political issues. A series of constitutional reforms in February 1995 reduced the presidential term from six to five years, placed a ban on immediate reelection, and—in an effort to thwart long-standing traditions of nepotism—prohibited the president from being succeeded by a close family relative. Barely meeting these conditions, the 1996 election went to Arnoldo Alemán Lacayo of the right-wing *Alianza Liberal.* The following year, Alemán took steps to advance the painful process of national reconciliation, reaching a final agreement with the *recontras* and coming to terms with Sandinistas over property confiscated during the 1980s. In early 1998 the International Monetary Fund approved a second major loan for structural adjustment of the economy. Things seemed to be looking up.

Then came Hurricane Mitch in October 1998, pouring torrential rains down on Nicaragua and leaving a staggering toll: nearly 3000 dead, about 1500 missing or injured, and at least $1 billion in damages. Aside from the economic and human costs, Mitch inflicted political damage as well. Alemán failed to call a national emergency, bungled international relief efforts, and displayed an awesome level of overall incompetence. In the meantime the Sandinistas were faring little better, since party chieftain Daniel Ortega was publicly accused by his stepdaughter of child abuse.

Amid a swirl of rumors, the two besieged leaders, Alemán and Ortega, reached a political compact in January 2000. Their transparent goal was to secure the dominance of Nicaraguan politics by their respective parties. They called for constitutional reforms that would permit reelection, which Alemán favored, and establish a single-round system of elections, which the Sandinistas supported. The election of November 2001 went to Enrique Bolaños Geyer, the candidate of Alemán's Partido Liberal Constitucionalista (formerly Alianza Liberal). Shortly after taking office, Bolaños broke with Alemán, who was placed under house arrest on charges of corruption—and later transferred to prison. With only modest support in the legislature, however, Bolaños was finding it difficult to lead. Seeking international approval, he backed the U.S. position on Iraq in early 2003 and eagerly signed on to a U.S.–Central American free trade treaty later in the year.

The Sandinistas mounted an impressive comeback in 2006, as Daniel Ortega won the presidency (under the terms of the pact with Alemán) with 38 percent of the vote. Two years later the Sandinistas won 94 out of the 146 municipal elections. The country nonetheless was highly polarized. The poorest nation in Central America, Nicaragua continued to face a precarious future.

POLITICS AND POLICY: EL SALVADOR

El Salvador, Nicaragua's neighbor to the north, faced similar periods of turmoil. As in other countries of Central America, oligarchic control eventually took hold during the nineteenth century. A series of legal decrees paved the way for the usurpation and consolidation of land by a tiny aristocracy—*las catorce*, a notorious clique of "fourteen" families (which have meanwhile expanded in number and size). Coffee became the leading export crop, commerce flourished, and from 1907 to 1931 political power rested in the hands of the patriarchal Meléndez clan.

Peasants did not accept this situation passively. Angered by the loss of land, they staged four separate revolts between 1870 and 1900. The movements were crushed, but they carried a message: like the *zapatistas* of Mexico, the *campesinos* of El Salvador were willing to fight for their rights.

In May 1930 a popular throng of 80,000 held a demonstration in downtown San Salvador against deteriorating wages and living conditions. The next year an idealistic landowner and admirer of the British Labour Party, Arturo Araujo, won the presidential election with the support of students, peasants, and workers. Somewhat naively, he announced that the Salvadoran Communist Party would be permitted to take part in municipal elections in December 1931. Exasperated by this prospect, the armed forces dismissed him from office and imposed a right-wing general, Maximiliano Hernández Martínez.

Peasants broke out in rebellion. In late January 1932, as a chain of volcanoes erupted in Guatemala and northwest El Salvador, bands of Indians with machetes made their way out of the ravines and tangled hillsides down into townships. Led by Agustín Farabundo Martí, a dedicated communist who had fought alongside Sandino in Nicaragua, the peasants murdered some landlords and plunged the country into a state of revolt.

Hernández Martínez responded with ferocity. Military units moved on the rebels, and the conflict took on the appearance of a racial war, as Indians—or anyone resembling Indians—suffered from the government attack. Between 10,000 and 20,000 Salvadorans lost their lives.

The events of 1932 sent several messages. Peasants learned to distrust city-bred revolutionaries who might lead them to destruction. Indians began to seek safety by casting off indigenous habits and clothes. On the political level, leftists concluded that they could still cultivate followings in rural areas, especially in the absence of a reformist alternative. The right drew harsh lessons of its own: the way to deal with popular agitation was by repression, and the way to maintain security was through military rule. With the consent and blessing of *las catorce,* army officers held the reins of government until the 1970s.

A reformist challenge finally came from José Napoleón Duarte, who founded the Christian Democratic Party (PDC). As mayor of San Salvador (1964–70), the dynamic and articulate Duarte built up a strong following among the intellectuals, professionals, and other urban middle-sector groups. The PDC bore a commit-ment to peaceful reform through electoral means. Though Duarte may have won the presidential election of 1972, the recalcitrant military turned power over to one of its own, Colonel Arturo Armando Molina. Duarte himself was imprisoned, tortured, and exiled—but he did not take to the hills.

Conditions worsened for the peasants. Coffee exports were thriving, but the poor were suffering. About 80 percent of the people lived in the countryside, and by 1975 about 40 percent of the peasants had no land at all—compared to only 12 percent in 1960. Increasingly unable to gain access to the soil, the *campesinos* of El Salvador were getting ready to rebel.

Reform-oriented options vanished during the 1970s. The electoral road was proving to be a dead end. The 1977 election was tightly controlled by the military and resulted in the presidency of General Carlos Humberto Romero, who pro-ceeded to legalize repression through "law to defend and guarantee public order." For an alternative means of public expression, many dissidents turned to "popular organizations," apolitical groups that sought nonviolent routes to change. Sometimes organized by exiles like Duarte, they found support and stimulus from a revitalized institution: the Roman Catholic Church.

The reawakening of the church proved to be one of the most decisive devel-opments of the time. The trend went back to two events: the Second Ecumenical Council of the early 1960s (Vatican II) and a conference of Latin American bishops at Medellín, Colombia, in 1968. Serving as a platform for "liberation theology," the Medellín conference denounced capitalism and communism as equal affronts to human dignity and placed the blame for hunger and misery on the rich and powerful. To redress these inequalities, the bishops called for more education, increased social awareness, and the creation of *comunidades de base,* small grass-roots groups of Catholics.

These events had a profound impact on the ecclesiastical hierarchy in El Salvador, then under Archbishop Oscar Arnulfo Romero. As repression mounted, the church eventually acknowledged, in Romero's own words, "the case for insurrection . . . when all recourses to peaceful means have been exhausted." No one was immune to violence: in 1980 the archbishop himself was shot dead in the cathedral of San Salvador. So much for political reform through theological salvation.

Despite the formation of a coalition government, things took a turn for the worse. Denouncing all dissidents as "communists," right-wing officers and para-military "death squads" intensified repression. Killings continued at the astonishing rate of 1000 per month. The cabinet resigned in protest, but the minister of defense—General José Guillermo García—clung to his government post. The liberal wing of the Christian Democratic Party defected from the coalition. Now appearing undeniably conservative, the beleaguered Duarte took over as head of the government and announced a plan for land reform.

The opposition then moved underground. The most important organization was the Farabundo Martí National Liberation Front (FMLN)—named for the leader of the 1932 uprising. In late 1980 four American women—three nuns and a lay worker—met with brutal deaths. The Carter administration vigorously protested this abuse of human rights, and Duarte promised an investigation. In early 1981 the Reagan administration, more concerned with Cold War anti-communism than with social change or human rights, softened the U.S. demands. By mid-1982 a few low-ranking members of the National Guard were implicated in the crime, but there would be no serious prosecution. With tacit support from the U.S. government, thus the regime survived international furor.

Hopes were high in Washington that Duarte, a Notre Dame graduate and a favorite of U.S. policymakers, would realize the reformist programs designed to undercut support for the Marxist-Leninist guerrillas. In fact, Duarte was less effective in San Salvador than in Washington. FMLN fighters were highly disciplined and deeply entrenched in zones they had controlled for years. Duarte's government did redistribute significant chunks of farmland, but he could not displace the oligarchy that had made El Salvador's gap between the rich and poor among the worst in the Third World.

U.S. public opinion became a major factor. As of early 1983, the Reagan administration was supplying the Salvadoran regime with $205 million in economic aid and $26 million in military assistance, with higher requests pending in Congress. Growing opposition to the U.S. aid came from congressional liberals and religious groups, especially the Catholic Church, still incensed over the 1980 killing of the four American Catholic women. The intensity of U.S. opposition feeling could be seen in the bumper stickers that read "El Salvador is Vietnam in Spanish."

The battle continued in the Salvadoran countryside. FMLN guerrillas made periodic raids. Aided by U.S. military "trainers" (not called "advisers," to avoid association with Vietnam), government forces conducted sweeping search-and-destroy missions. Villagers and peasants grew fearful of both sides. A decade of continuous fighting resulted in stalemate. It also led to the loss of 75,000 lives.

Presidential elections in March 1989 led to a decisive triumph for Alfredo Cristiani of the conservative ARENA party with 53 percent of the vote. Many

U.S. policy in Central America prompted a great deal of public controversy and debate in the 1980s. Top, cartoonist Tony Auth satirizes President Reagan's position and the hesitancy of the U.S. Congress in voicing opposition; bottom, Steve Benson dramatizes the left-wing threat to U.S. interests. (Reprinted with permission of Universal Press. All rights reserved.)

observers believed that Cristiani, an athletic playboy without political experience, would be merely a puppet for right-wing forces. Months after his election, six Jesuit priests were brutally murdered, apparently by a military-sponsored death squad. Cristiani solemnly declared that his government would capture and prosecute the assassins, but little was accomplished. Once again, a rightist regime was paying scant attention to human rights.

Even so, Cristiani agreed to negotiate with the FMLN under the supervision of the United Nations. In early 1992 the government and the FMLN signed a historic agreement for peace and reform. The FMLN agreed to lay down arms in exchange for wide-ranging reforms in political and military structures, including a reduction in the role and size of the armed forces and a purge of flagrant human-rights abusers. By December 1992 the movement disarmed its guerrilla forces and became a legal political party, and the FMLN established itself as the country's second-largest political force.

Subsequent elections resulted in three straight victories for right-wing ARENA candidates: Armando Calderón Sol in 1994, Francisco Flores Pérez in 1999, and Antonio (Tony) Saca in 2004. Not until 2009 did the unthinkable occur: Mauricio Funes of the FMLN won the presidency with 51.3 percent of the votes (and no major charges of fraud!). Even as a new day dawned, the ARENA faithful continued to lament the dangers of communist takeover. Echoes of the Cold War continued to reverberate throughout this tiny and beautiful land.

POLITICS AND POLICY: GUATEMALA

Guatemala has a long history of strongman rule. After Rafael Carrera died in 1865, Justo Rufino Barrios established a twelve-year dictatorship (1873–85), and Manuel Estrada Cabrera followed with a twenty-two-year, iron-fisted regime (1898–1920), the longest uninterrupted one-man rule in Central America. In 1931 General Jorge Ubico seized power and immediately launched a campaign to crush the fledgling Communist Party. Instead of relying on coffee planters alone, Ubico built a tentative base among agrarian workers by abolishing debt slavery. A national police force maintained law and order. As Ubico himself once said, "I have no friends, only domesticated enemies."

A wave of strikes and protests led Ubico to resign in July 1944. He was replaced by a military triumvirate, and this in turn was ousted by a group of junior officers. Thus erupted the October Revolution of 1944, an event that signaled the beginning of a decade-long transformation.

In 1945 Guatemalans elected as president Juan José Arévalo Bermejo, an idealistic university professor who proclaimed a belief in "spiritual socialism." Arévalo oversaw the promulgation of a progressive new constitution in 1945, modeled in part on the Mexican charter of 1917, and he encouraged workers and peasants to organize. Industrial wages rose by 80 percent between 1945 and 1950. Arévalo pushed education and other reforms as well. But the going was not easy: during his five-year term in office, Arévalo weathered no less than twenty-two military revolts.

In 1950 Arévalo turned the presidency over to Colonel Jacobo Arbenz Guzmán, the minister of defense, who led a center-left coalition in the elections of that year. A central figure in the October Revolution of 1944, Arbenz developed profound social concerns—partly at the insistence of his wife, María Vilanova, a wealthy daughter of the Salvadoran elite. Arbenz accepted communist support, both during and after the election, but he was a reformer at heart. At his inauguration he spelled out his hopes for the country's future:

> Our government proposes to begin the march toward the economic development of Guatemala, and proposes three fundamental objectives: to convert our country from a dependent nation with a semi-colonial economy to an economically independent country; to convert Guatemala from a backward country with a predominantly feudal economy into a modern capitalist state; and to make this transformation in a way that will raise the standard of living of the great mass of our people to the highest level.

To achieve these goals, Arbenz said, Guatemala would need to strengthen the local private sector, "in whose hands rests the fundamental economic activity of the country." Foreign capital would be welcome so long as it respected Guatemalan law and "strictly abstains from intervening in the nation's social and political life." Finally, the president declared, Guatemala would embark on a program of agrarian reform.

Arbenz set quickly to work. He authorized construction of a public port on the Atlantic coast and the building of an east–west highway. He convinced the legislature to approve an income tax—a watered-down version of a mild proposal, to be sure, but the first in Guatemalan history. He pushed for expanded public works and the exploitation of energy resources, including petroleum.

The centerpiece of the Arbenz agenda was agrarian reform. Enacted in June 1952, the bill empowered the government to expropriate only uncultivated portions of large plantations. All lands taken were to be paid for in twenty-five-year bonds bearing a 3 percent interest rate, and the valuation of land was to be determined according to its taxable worth as of May 1952. During its eighteen months of operation, the agrarian reform distributed 1.5 million acres to some 100,000 families. The expropriations included 1700 acres belonging to Arbenz himself, who had become a landowner through the dowry of his wife.

Almost immediately, Arbenz and the agrarian reform ran into a serious obstacle: implacable opposition from the United Fruit Company and from the U.S. government. *La frutera* had obvious reasons for resisting the reform. The company held enormous tracts of land in Guatemala, 85 percent of which was unused—or, as the company maintained, held in reserve against natural catastrophes. And in arranging tax payments, UFCO consistently undervalued its holdings. (On the basis of tax declarations, the Guatemalan government in 1953 offered UFCO $627,572 in bonds in compensation for a seized portion of property;

on behalf of the company, the U.S. State Department countered with a demand for $15,854,849!)

Washington was deeply involved. Secretary of State John Foster Dulles and his brother, CIA Director Allen Dulles, for example, both came from a New York law firm with close links to United Fruit. The company's Washington lobbyist was Thomas Corcoran, a prominent lawyer who was on close terms with President Eisenhower's trusted aide and undersecretary of state, General Walter Bedell Smith, himself once interested in a management position with UFCO. More important than personal ties, however, was the anticommunist doctrine developed in Washington.

U.S. policymakers were pushing a hard anticommunist line in relations with Latin America. The Rio Pact of 1947 had laid the groundwork for collective action, or so the United States hoped, against communist advances in Latin America, whether from within or without. In early 1953 John Foster Dulles was clearly worried about Latin America, where, he said, conditions "are somewhat comparable to conditions as they were in China in the mid-thirties when the communist movement was getting started. . . . Well, if we don't look out, we will wake up some morning and read in the newspapers that there happened in South America the same kind of thing that happened in China in 1949." The test would come in Guatemala.

UFCO publicists and the Dulles brothers accused the Arbenz regime of being "soft" on communism and branded it a threat to the United States and to the free world at large. They cultivated fears that defeat in Guatemala might lead to a Soviet takeover of the Panama Canal. They warned that if Guatemala fell, then the rest of Central America might go as well (in keeping with the so-called domino theory). But the principal issue was agrarian reform. Such writers as Daniel James of *The New Leader* warned that communists would use the program as a stepping-stone to gain control of Guatemala. Whatever his intentions, the United States insisted, Arbenz was just a "stooge" for the Russians.

In August 1953 the United States decided to act. John Foster Dulles led a campaign in the Organization of American States (OAS) to brand Guatemala as the agent of an extra-hemispheric power (the Soviet Union) and therefore subject to OAS collective action under the Rio Treaty of 1947. Although Latin American leaders resisted this interpretation, Arbenz clearly realized that U.S. intervention was likely. His government cracked down on domestic opposition and turned to East Europe for small arms, which were en route by May 1954. Meanwhile the Eisenhower administration was demanding, in increasingly blunt language, compensation for U.S. property in Guatemala, meaning, of course, United Fruit.

Having failed to get OAS sponsorship for intervention, the U.S. government opted for covert action. The CIA organized an exile invasion under an obscure renegade Guatemalan colonel, Carlos Castillo Armas. A rebel column of a few hundred men was assembled across the border in neighboring Honduras. They were equipped and directed by the CIA, which set up and operated a rebel radio station and provided a few World War II fighter planes to strafe Guatemala City. Under attack by these planes, and convinced that a large army was approaching the capital, Arbenz lost his nerve and gave up. The Castillo Armas rebels rolled into the capital virtually unopposed.

The new government purged communists and radical nationalists, reversed the expropriation of United Fruit lands, and dutifully signed a mutual defense pact with the United States in 1955. Mission accomplished: an errant Central American republic had been brought back into line by a cheap and efficient CIA operation.

The United States was strongly denounced by Latin American nationalists for its intervention in Guatemala, and to this day the episode remains a symbol of cynical U.S. action. Even so, the fate of the Arbenz regime would serve as a warning to nationalist leaders who contemplated challenging U.S. corporations.

The 1954 coup marked a turning point in Guatemalan history. It virtually eliminated the forces of the political center (as represented by Arévalo and Arbenz). So the country had only a left and a right, and the right was in control. Coffee planters, other landowners, and foreign investors and their subsidiaries regained their power under the protection of right-wing military regimes. Individual rulers came and went, but this alignment persisted until the 1990s. The more the leaders changed, the more the system stayed the same.

POLITICS AND POLICY: THE DOMINICAN REPUBLIC

Washington's overthrow of the Arbenz government was an ominous sign for those who feared expanding U.S. intervention in Latin America. It offered yet another crude example of unwelcome meddling in regional affairs. Yet the pattern would continue.

The strategic position of Hispaniola made the island important to the United States, committed by the early nineteenth century to keeping European powers from intervening in the hemisphere. Anarchy and chaos had prompted the United States to intervene at various times. From 1916 to 1924, U.S. Marines occupied the Dominican Republic (as well as neighboring Haiti). A National Guard was created to fight guerrilla bands. Among the most brilliant disciples of the American occupation force was Rafael Leonidas Trujillo, an ambitious soldier who would eventually become one of the most ruthless dictators in the hemisphere.

Thanks to the stimulus of World War I, which boosted prices for exports, economic conditions improved in the Dominican Republic during the American occupation. U.S. troops strengthened the country's infrastructure, upgrading the educational system and imposing control on public finances. Critics nonetheless began to complain about the "dumping" of inferior U.S.-made products on the local market and about the general disdain the invaders displayed for local citizens.

An agreement between the United States and Dominican leaders in 1922 led to the formation of a provisional government. Two years later, elections gave power to Horacio Vázquez, a respected politician of long standing. Yet in 1929, Vázquez made the error that has plagued so many leaders in Latin America's history: he tried to revise the constitution so he could run for office again.

A rebellion erupted, and Trujillo presented himself as a candidate in the 1930 elections. Wielding his power base (the National Guard), he made clear that he would win at any cost and claimed victory with 95 percent of the vote. He quickly began banishing political opponents from the scene. The future belonged to Trujillo.

As with so many dictators, Trujillo exploited the country's resources in order to amass his own personal wealth. During the 1950s the average annual growth rate was 8 percent, an impressive performance by any standard, but benefits failed to reach the general population. Much of the nation's income was stashed in foreign bank accounts, while peasants and workers remained woefully poor. Paradoxically, economic prosperity heightened contradictions between Trujillo and his coterie of sycophantic supporters: the more he took for himself, the more discontented his collaborators became. The most egregious offense involved his personal takeover of the sugar industry: by 1957 Trujillo controlled more than 70 percent of the nation's production. In 1961 his former friends and cronies, not his enemies, staged a coup and masterminded his assassination.

Free and fair elections in 1962 led to the triumph of Juan Bosch, a former journalist and social reformer who sought to confiscate and redistribute Trujillo's landownings as part of a program of agrarian reform. His efforts at improving the lot of the masses aroused discomfort among the traditional elites, who saw his innovations as dangerously "communistic." A military coup ousted Bosch in 1963. A countermovement then sought to reinstate him as president. The resulting conflict led to a civil war between the armed forces and the pro-Bosch "constitutionalists," mainly workers and students.

As the struggle intensified, the United States under Lyndon B. Johnson grew fearful of "another Cuba" and took over the country in April 1965. The invading force consisted of 22,000 marines, a contingent whose size amazed even American officials on the scene.

To justify its action, the U.S. government tried to engage the participation of other countries from Latin America through the OAS. Favorable responses came only from Paraguay and Brazil, both under right-wing military rulers. The Johnson administration's attempt to form an "inter-American peacekeeping force" not only failed to legitimize the intervention, but also discredited the OAS as a whole and contributed to the subsequent debilitation of that institution.

The U.S. intervention led to the formation of an interim government and, eventually, to elections in June 1966. Victory went to Joaquín Balaguer, an ex-Trujillo official and favorite of the United States. With full blessing from Washington, the Balaguer government implemented a number of important developmental programs. Housing was built, land was distributed, and education was strengthened and improved. Austerity programs reduced severe problems with the balance of payments, and, to assist with these and other challenges, aid from the United States climbed to more than $132 million for 1968. Agricultural production rebounded and foreign investment responded. Economic growth was substantial.

The Dominican armed forces underwent moderate reform, and its most recalcitrant elements were dispatched abroad, often on fictitious diplomatic missions. Despite poverty and deprivation, the transition toward democracy continued. Elections survived minor threats in 1970 and in 1978, when the armed forces threatened to annul the results, but on both occasions the outcome was eventually allowed to stand. Balaguer's opponents won the elections of 1978 and 1982, but he bounced back to win three subsequent times—in 1986, 1990, and 1994.

After Balaguer finally retired from public life, partisan squabbling came to characterize the political process. The elections of 1996 resulted in triumph for Leonel Fernández Reyna, an able and charismatic politician who nonetheless faced opposition majorities in both houses of the legislature—which gleefully paralyzed executive policy initiatives. Elections in 2000 led to victory for Hipólito Mejía, who presided over the collapse of one of the country's largest banks, a scandal that discredited most of the political class. Despite resistance from within his own party, Mejía insisted on running for reelection in May 2004. After a highly charged campaign, he lost by a wide margin to Fernández Reyna, who was reelected president in 2008. Despite spurts of economic growth, the nation still faced significant social and economic problems.

POLITICS AND POLICY: HAITI

Like other island nations of the Caribbean, Haiti fell under the long shadow of the United States in the twentieth century. As the second republic in the Americas, independent Haiti faced many challenges. Political life was plagued by instability. From 1804 to 1867 Haiti had only ten chief executives. From 1867 to 1915 there were sixteen presidents, with an average term of only three years. And from 1911 to 1915 Haiti faced one of its most chaotic periods, during which time six presidents met violent deaths.

Confronting World War I and equipped with "dollar diplomacy," the United States occupied Haiti in 1915 and stayed until 1934. This was a full-scale military occupation. U.S. authorities abolished the army and replaced it with a national police force. A cadre of American technicians and bureaucrats took over the financial administration of the country, ensuring prompt payment of all foreign debt obligations (especially those owed to the United States). New public works were initiated and old ones were repaired, but the majority of the population regarded the foreigners with smoldering resentment.

One reason for this feeling was dismay over the loss of sovereignty. As an occupying force, the United States took over general administration but, in particular, the management of the customs houses. As a matter of fact, American financial experts would remain in Haiti until 1941—seven years after the departure of the military garrisons. Another reason was the marked preference of U.S. officials for the mulattoes, whom they brought to power in a variety of ways—including the superficial election and reelection of Sténio Vincent as president during the 1930s.

Racist depiction of Haiti as a naive, inept black child formed and reflected U.S. attitudes about military intervention. Occasioned by the political and economic crisis of 1915, this cartoon expressed the helplessness of Haiti—through the caption "I'm in for something now!"—and Uncle Sam's determination to take charge. (Hanny, *St. Joseph News-Press*, 1915. Courtesy of the St. Joseph NewsPress/Gazette.)

In time the black population, backed by the Haitian Guard (as the police force was known), ousted another mulatto president and installed Dumarsais Estimé in 1946. He replaced mulatto officials with blacks and undertook a series of reforms designed to benefit both urban workers and agricultural producers. He discharged the country's debt to the United States and signed an agreement with the Export-Import Bank for the development of the Artibonite Valley. In 1950 Estimé tried to amend the constitution so he could remain in power, and for this he was deposed by the army and sent into exile.

Control passed to Colonel Paul E. Magloire, a black leader who was influential within the army and popular among the nation's masses. At his inauguration he promised to safeguard the rights guaranteed by the constitution, to continue irrigation projects and other public works, and to promote public education. In the international arena Magloire sought good relations with the United States, while the increase in export prices brought on by the Korean War helped to stimulate economic growth. Resented by ambitious rivals, he was overthrown in a coup in 1956.

After months of uncertainty, there emerged the figure of François Duvalier, who had himself elected president in September 1957. Soon after seizing power, Duvalier set out to bend the nation to his will. The army, the police, and the security forces became accountable to him alone. He created a special police force, which came to be known as the *Tontons Macoutes,* the most dreaded repressive force in the country. Through sheer terror he rid himself of his opponents and maneuvered elections to become president for life *(président à vie).* As necessary, he mobilized large crowds with insistent propagation of the official slogan: *Dieu, Duvalier, et le frapeu, un et indivisible*—God, Duvalier, and flag, one and indivisible.

A proponent of *noirisme,* a movement that looked to Africa for inspiration, Duvalier expelled mulattoes from the national bureaucracy. He gained influence over the masses by cannily associating himself with the figure of Baron Samedi, the earthly keeper of the *vodun* tombs. He created a sort of latter-day court, whose favorites gained riches through the dispensation of state favors. To institutionalize a system of kickbacks, Duvalier even set up an umbrella organization, the Movement for National Renovation, which collected contributions from business and high government employees for the ostensible purpose of building public facilities. Needless to say, the money was never used for such ends.

Until his death in 1971, Duvalier took the side of the United States in most international arenas, including the United Nations and the OAS. On occasion pro-U.S. votes would lead to increased aid or loans for his corrupt regime. For the most part, American governments tolerated Duvalier as a distasteful but useful if unpleasant ally in the Cold War.

As death neared, Duvalier persuaded the National Assembly to lower the minimum age for president from forty to eighteen and proceeded to install his son as his successor and *président à vie.* Young Jean-Claude Duvalier, or "Baby Doc" as he was sometimes known, inherited a bitterly impoverished country. Though he may have been less brutal than his father, he retained a parasitical group of favorites—a "kleptocracy" of sorts. Government became a means of self-enrichment. Popular discontent and internecine struggles finally led to his demise in February 1986, when he boarded a U.S. Air Force plane and departed for France.

Political recovery was tentative. For decades the opposition had been suppressed, labor unions controlled, and the media corrupted. When Baby Doc left the country, there were cries for liberty and calls for *dechoukaj,* an "uprooting" of the Duvalier regime: tombs and statues fell, policemen felt popular wrath, and erstwhile collaborators fled the country. Elections in 1987 resulted in a bloodbath, as paramilitary forces assaulted voters and opposition candidates. A subsequent ballot resulted in the controversial election of Leslie Manigat, a well-known social scientist who lasted in office for less than a year. Yet another coup led to the ascendancy of General Prosper Avril, an ambitious young military officer who revived the Tontons Macoutes and imposed a new wave of repression. To many observers it appeared that Haiti was suffering from "Duvalier without Duvalier."

Authentic change began in 1990. Protest demonstrations and a general strike persuaded Avril to leave the country. Under a woman interim president, Ertha Pascal-Trouillot, open elections took place in December 1990. Emerging with two-thirds of the vote was Jean-Bertrand Aristide, a Roman Catholic priest who espoused liberation theology and advocated far-reaching political and social change. In January 1991 disgruntled "Duvalierists" attempted a military coup to prevent the "communist" Aristide from taking office: the effort failed but left 74 dead and 150 injured. Later in the year, unruly elements within the military ousted him from office. The United States and other nations promptly condemned the coup, and the OAS slapped an embargo on trade with Haiti, but diplomatic negotiations for a peaceful solution to the crisis dragged on for years.

As Haitians sought to escape the oppression imposed by the new military regime of General Raoul Cédras, it was the prospect of a large-scale flood of immigrants that gave shape to U.S. policy. The Coast Guard started picking up thousands of Haitians who were attempting to reach U.S. shores on homemade rafts and took them to an encampment at the U.S. naval station at Guantánamo (in Cuba). In May 1992 President George H. W. Bush ordered the Coast Guard to return all Haitian rafters to their homeland without any screening to determine eligibility for political asylum. Democratic presidential candidate Bill Clinton denounced the Bush policy as "a callous response to a terrible human tragedy," but then consented to its continuation after his election as president. By early 1994 leaders of the African American community mounted sharp criticism of Washington's inaction, and Clinton reversed himself by announcing that U.S. authorities would process rafters at sea and grant asylum to victims of political repression. This led to yet another wave of rafters.

Despite public skepticism, Clinton began to contemplate the use of military force. In mid-September he denounced the Cédras government as "the most violent regime in our hemisphere" and stressed the dangers of inaction: "As long as Cédras rules, Haitians will continue to seek sanctuary in our nation. . . . Three hundred thousand more Haitians, 5 percent of their entire population, are in hiding in their own country. If we don't act, they could be the next wave of refugees at our door. We will continue to face the threat of a mass exodus of refugees and its constant threat to stability in our region and control of our borders."

As tension mounted, Clinton dispatched a high-level delegation under former president Jimmy Carter for a last-ditch effort at negotiation. At the final minute, as U.S. troops were already en route for an invasion of Haiti, Carter reached an agreement with the Cédras government. Clinton canceled the invasion but instead imposed an occupation; in less than a week there were more than 15,000 American troops on the ground. Aristide returned to office in mid-October, and the U.S. occupation gave way to an international peacekeeping force in early 1995.

Under intense international observation (and quasi-military occupation), elections took place in an orderly fashion. Aristide resisted the temptation to succeed himself, and René Preval, one of his former associates and ex–prime minister, took office in February 1996. Governing was something else again. Aided and abetted by the international community, Preval sought to impose pro-market economic reforms. Aristide suddenly moved into the opposition, refurbished his populist credentials, and assumed the leadership of the Lavalas Party. Strikes, demonstrations, and violence mounted.

The political stalemate continued through the presidential election of November 2000, which Jean-Bertrand Aristide won by an overwhelming—but contested—majority. In protest against electoral irregularities in parliamentary contests, the oppositionist Convergence Démocratique refused to recognize the legislative victory of Aristide's Lavalas Party. Aristide nonetheless took office in February 2001. Once a hero to Haiti's poor and underprivileged, Aristide seemed ever more distant from his people—and ever more inclined to impose his will through autocratic means. Street protests resumed, and violence continued to plague the political process.

The economy was faring no better. By 2000 the growth rate had declined to less than 1 percent. In both 2001 and 2002 economic output contracted by 21 percent. Three-quarters of the population was living in abject poverty. Less than half the adult population was able to read and write. Unemployment was running around 60 percent.

Matters came to a head in early 2004. While Aristide retained a substantial amount of popular support, opponents claimed that he had become autocratic, intolerant, and corrupt. Dissident gangs clashed with pro-Aristide groups known as *chimères*. Under the leadership of Guy Philippe, a former officer in the long-discredited Haitian army, armed rebels advanced through provincial cities and soon approached the capital of Port-au-Prince. Appeals by the besieged government for help from the international community, especially the United States, were to no avail. Faced with the prospect of large-scale civil war, Aristide resigned and left the country. Critics chided U.S. president George W. Bush and Secretary of State Colin Powell for failing to support a democratically elected government in the Americas.

Together with detachments from Canada and France, U.S. Marines moved in to establish a modicum of order. In 2006 René Preval was elected president with over 50 percent of the vote. After several unsuccessful attempts to appoint a prime minister, the president designated Michèle Pierre-Louis, the director of an internationally recognized educational foundation. Off to a shaky start, the government faced endemic poverty, unemployment, and social unrest. Haiti remained in desperate condition.

POLITICS AND POLICY: PUERTO RICO

As we have seen, U.S. administrations—Republican and Democrat alike—asserted their right to interfere directly in the domestic affairs of countries in Central America and the Caribbean for the sake of "national interests." One island nation, however, remained under permanent American control.

Puerto Rico became part of the United States as a result of the Spanish-American War. In July 1898, in retaliation for the sinking of the U.S. vessel *Maine* in Cuba, American troops disembarked in Puerto Rico, initiating the country's first act of European-style colonial expansion. The island thus became the pawn in a war between Cuban patriots and Spanish garrisons. It had not expected military occupation.

Quite the contrary. Spain had already agreed to grant Puerto Rico autonomy and to devise some sort of "home rule" for the island. The U.S. invasion changed all of this. Suddenly, Puerto Rico became a crucial factor in U.S. global strategy—not only because of its potential for investment and commerce, but also because of its geopolitical role in consolidating U.S. naval power. But there remains a basic question: Why did the United States take Puerto Rico as a colony while helping Cuba achieve independence?

The difference may well reside in the histories of the two islands. There was a long-standing armed insurrectionary movement against Spain in Cuba, an island which would have been much more difficult to occupy. Puerto Rico, however, was on the way to a negotiated settlement and could present less resistance to outside forces. Puerto Rico thus became caught in a complex struggle between major powers and Cuba's insurgents.

Puerto Rico bore clear signs of Spanish domination. During the colonial period, the island had served as an important military garrison and commercial center, a role that intensified as the slave trade reached its peak in the 1700s. Sugar production became the predominant agricultural enterprise. There were also small farmers, *jíbaros,* rugged individualists who cultivated staple crops and helped maintain a diversified economy. Because of this, the slave population always remained a minority.

After the arrival of the marines, Puerto Rico developed a peculiar relationship with the United States. After 1898 residents of the island had no clear legal status of any kind. In 1917 they were granted citizenship in the United States. In 1947, nearly half a century after the invasion, Puerto Rico was permitted to attempt self-government. In 1952 the island was granted "commonwealth" status within the United States. This remains an ambiguous situation: Puerto Rico is neither a nation nor colony nor a state, but something else again.

To develop the island, to demonstrate the virtues of free-world capitalism, and to provide an inspiration for Latin America, the United States collaborated with dynamic governor Luis Muñoz Marín to undertake "Operation Bootstrap" during the 1950s and 1960s. Under this plan, the U.S. federal government would encourage investments in Puerto Rico through a series of tax holidays and other allowances. Bootstrap wrought tremendous changes in the social and economic life of Puerto Rico. Sugar estates and small farms were replaced by factories; as industrialization thrived, citizens joined the ranks of the laboring class. But the overseas investments did not provide enough jobs to absorb the growth in the working-age population, and the result was massive unemployment.

One consequence was to accelerate the flow of migrants to the U.S. mainland, where 40 percent of Puerto Ricans came to reside. Fully one-half of the migrant population settled in New York City. In a sense, this trend formed two Puerto Ricos: one on the island and one on the mainland. There has been considerable movement and communication back and forth, but social tensions and cultural differences separate the two communities. In demonstration of this fact, Puerto Rican residents of New York are sometimes known as "Nuyo-ricans."

Political life on the island has been active and orderly. The chief executive is the governor, who is elected every four years. The dominant issue has been the island's relationship with the United States. In a 1967 plebiscite on this question, 60 percent favored the continuation and improvement of the commonwealth status, and 38 percent came out in favor of statehood. Those who favored complete independence chose to boycott the plebiscite, but this faction has been vocal and visible (in 1950, in fact, a pro-independence group made an attempt on the life of U.S. president Harry S. Truman).

The pro-statehood forces, represented by the New Progressive Party (PNP), won gubernatorial elections in 1968, 1976, and 1980. Under the leadership of Luis Ferré and Carlos Romero Barceló, this group subscribed to the belief that full statehood would provide working-class Puerto Ricans with increased access to federal welfare programs, stimulate economic growth, and remove the stigma of "second-class citizenship" associated with commonwealth status. Popular support for this movement came especially from urban areas.

The pro-commonwealth party, or Popular Democratic Party (PDP), won the elections of 1972, 1984, and 1988. Its most prominent leader was Rafael Hernández Colón, who called for a greater degree of meaningful autonomy within the commonwealth relationship. As governor, Hernández Colón actively promoted worldwide economic relations for the island and played an active role in the development of the "twin plant" concept—dividing the production process into separate parts, with initial phases to be done in some other area of the Caribbean and final assembly in Puerto Rico.

Concern steadily mounted over economic issues, and, largely as a result of a U.S. recession, Puerto Rico faced a downturn in the early 1990s. Amid this atmosphere the 1992 gubernatorial election went to the PNP's Pedro Rosselló, who vowed to press for statehood. His first act in office was to sign a bill giving English equal status with Spanish as an official language. And in November 1993, fulfilling a campaign promise, Rosselló held a new plebiscite on the island's status. To the surprise of many observers, the pro-commonwealth position won with 48.4 percent of the vote; statehood obtained 46.2 percent; the pro-independence stance got only 4.4 percent. Five years later— on December 13, 1998, exactly 100 years and one day after Spain officially ceded Puerto Rico to the United States—yet another plebiscite yielded a similar result: 46.5 percent for statehood, 2.5 percent for independence, 0.4

percent for "free association" or commonwealth status, and 50.2 percent for "none of the above." The status quo won out again.

Elections of 2000 brought the pro-commonwealth PDP back to power under Sila María Calderón, the first woman ever to serve as governor. As mayor of San Salvador and then as governor, Calderón focused on urban redevelopment, prosecution of government corruption, and an end to U.S. Navy bombing exercises on the offshore island of Vieques. Her successor, Aníbal Salvador Acevedo Vilá, also of the PDP, governed under a cloud of alleged electoral fraud. In 2008 he lost a reelection bid to Luis Fortuño, a pro-statehood candidate of the PNP and card-carrying member of the U.S. Republican Party. His election gave every indication that Puerto Rico would continue its strange and ambiguous relationship with the United States in the foreseeable future.

5

~~

Cuba

Key Colony, Socialist State

Cuba has a history of beating odds. Coveted for centuries by major powers, the nation found a way to assert its independence and identity. Influenced (and often dominated) by the power and proximity of the United States, it became a bastion of anti-American sentiment. Shaped for generations by the forces of international capitalism, it produced a genuine social revolution—one that spawned admiration, adulation, and fear and loathing in many parts of the world. Contrary to the confident predictions of critical observers, Cuba's socialist experiment managed to outlast the end of the Cold War, the demise of the Soviet Union, the widespread discrediting of Marxist ideology—and the unyielding hostility of the U.S. government. One of the smaller countries in the Western Hemisphere, an isolated island in a dangerous sea, Cuba has come to play a thoroughly outsized role on the stage of global geopolitics. How did these things happen?

Geography offers one basic clue. Cuba's historical development has been deeply affected by its strategic location in the Caribbean basin. Columbus discovered the island on his first voyage (1492), and it soon became a staging ground for Spanish expeditions to the Mexican and Central American mainland. Its commercial and political importance grew with the expansion of royal fleets between Spain and its American colonies.

FROM COLONY TO NATIONHOOD

The indigenous population scarcely survived the first century of the Spanish colonization. Here, as elsewhere in Latin America, the European conquerors turned to black Africa for their labor supply. As a result, Cuba became a multiracial society: by the twentieth century, according to one estimate, the population was 40 percent black, 30 percent white, and 30 percent mixed (including Asian and Indian).

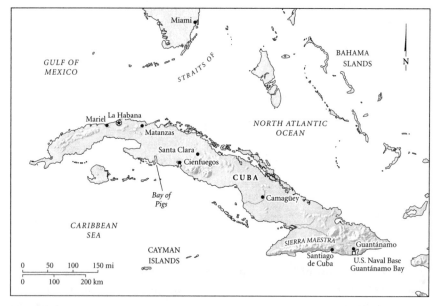

Map 5 Cuba

Cuba's economy languished under the rigid mercantilist policies of the Spanish crown until the Bourbon reforms of Charles III (1759–88) provided the stimuli that led to growth. The nineteenth century saw a brief coffee boom give way to the cultivation of tobacco, which became a major crop by midcentury—a position it still holds, as Cuban cigars *(puros)* continue to be regarded as among the finest in the world.

But the most important source of wealth was another product: cane sugar. Emphasis on sugar began in the eighteenth century, and by 1860 Cuba was producing nearly a third (500,000 tons) of the world's entire sugar supply. The human power to fuel this boom continued to come from the nightmarish slave trade, which delivered more than 600,000 Africans in chains to Cuba between 1800 and 1865. Slavery itself lasted until 1886, longer than anywhere else in the Americas save Brazil.

Cuba's economic development has thus been typical of tropical America: a monocultural, slave-based, export-oriented "plantation"society.

As a crown jewel of the Spanish empire, Cuba remained a colony throughout the nineteenth century. Even so, Spain's effective control of "the pearl of the Antilles" was steadily declining over time. It took ten years of bitter warfare to crush an early independence movement (1868–78). And by the 1880s, Cuba's trade and investment were almost exclusively with the United States. The U.S. economic interest in Cuba led to numerous offers to purchase the island country. The Spaniards invariably refused, although some prominent Cubans strongly favored annexation by the United States. Meanwhile, Cuba was drawn ever closer into the U.S. orbit.

A handful of Cuban nationalist fled into exile and plotted a new rebellion against Spain. The most famous was José Martí, an eloquent revolutionary poet-lawyer. A revolt for independence broke out in 1895. Cuba was soon engulfed in another savage war, which dragged on for three years. The Spaniards resorted to brutal methods, such as the use of concentration camps, to liquidate the guerrilla-style patriots.

Given its huge economic stake in Cuba, the United States was unlikely to stay on the sidelines. The U.S. public was excited by sensationalist press accounts of Spanish brutality, and business and religious leaders demanded U.S. recognition of the rebels. The expansionist urge in the United States was fed both by those who stood to gain economically and by those who preached of a U.S. mission to rescue the Cubans from Spanish misrule.

Although President McKinley resisted pressure to intervene, events overtook him. In April 1898 the USS *Maine* mysteriously exploded in Havana harbor. The blast, which has never been satisfactorily explained, swept away the last vestiges of antiwar sentiment, and Congress promptly declared war on Spain. The ill-equipped Spaniards went down to humiliating defeat. They had little choice but to grant Cuba independence in December 1898.

Dubious Independence

Cuba began her new status under U.S. military occupation, hardly favorable for a healthy sense of national identity. The U.S. authorities immediately disbanded the rebel army, thus removing the only potential source of armed opposition to

---

The Bronze Titan

The most famous Afro-Cuban of the nineteenth century was Antonio Maceo, the military genius of Cuba's two wars for independence (1868–78 and 1895–98). Born of a Venezuelan mulatto émigré and a free Afro-Cuban, Maceo entered the rebel army as a private in 1868 and reached general only five years later. Having established military leadership among the rebels (despite racist sniping from his white comrades), Maceo led highly successful guerrilla operations in the 1895–98 war. His soldiers were mostly Afro-Cuban, and Maceo himself had been an outspoken advocate of abolition, thereby arousing white fears that he wanted to establish a "black republic." Even Winston Churchill, then a young volunteer with the Spanish forces, repeated that prediction in a magazine article.

Maceo was killed in 1896 by Spanish troops who caught him in an ambush. He has entered Cuban history as an exemplary patriot and soldier. He had faith that Cuba would create a rightful place for Afro-Cubans. He also opposed U.S. entry into the 1895 war, arguing "I should not want our neighbor to shed their blood for our cause. We can do that for ourselves."

American rule. The occupation was a textbook example of what was regarded as "enlightened" intervention. The North Americans built badly needed schools, roads, sewers, and telegraph lines. But it was all in the service of integrating the now "civilized" Cubans within the U.S. sphere of influence.

U.S. government leaders saw these economic, moral, and political responsibilities all going hand in hand. The Cubans were allowed, even encouraged, to choose a constitutional convention, which produced a charter in 1901. But the U.S. government harbored doubts about the new country's ability to govern itself, so Washington forced the Cubans, under protest, to incorporate a provision (the "Platt Amendment") which gave the United States the right to intervene in domestic politics at will. This stipulation made Cuba an American protectorate.

Around this time, the United States also leased rights "in perpetuity" for installation of a naval base at Guantánamo Bay. In other words, the U.S. government acquired a permanent foothold on Cuban national soil. This agreement would have unforeseen consequences more than a century later, as Guantánamo came to be used as a detention center for suspects in the U.S.-directed "war on global terror."

Cuba's first president, Tomás Estrada Palma (1902–6), favored outright annexation by the United States. He was typical of much of the Cuban elite, which saw little future for an independent Cuba. Their willingness to embrace Yankee encroachment aroused the fury of those few Cuban nationalists who kept alive the flame of José Martí's dream of a Cuba free from Yankee dominance.

Estrada Palma won a second term by electoral fraud. The ensuing revolt, led by the defeated Liberals, brought a second U.S. military occupation (1906–9). The United States imposed an interim president, Charles Magoon, who oversaw a new election. Fraud recurred, however, triggering another U.S. military intervention in 1917. All these interventions presented opportunities for U.S. economic interests to deepen their hold over the Cuban economy.

OVERVIEW: ECONOMIC GROWTH AND SOCIAL CHANGE

During Cuba's years as a protectorate, it underwent a great sugar boom. Cuba emerged as one of the world's most efficient sugar producers, helped by the modern vacuum methods of refining. As output increased, sugar came to dominate Cuba's economy and, eventually, to have a lasting effect on the class structure and social relationships.

By the early twentieth century, as shown in Figure 5.1, Cuba was producing several million tons of sugarcane per year—nearly one-quarter of the world supply around World War I, about 10 percent of the total during the Depression years, and close to 20 percent just after World War II. Throughout this entire period, sugar exports earned approximately 80 percent of the island's foreign exchange. Such dependence on a single product obviously placed the Cuban economy in an extremely vulnerable position. If the harvest was poor or demand was low or prices were down, the Cuban economy would suffer. Sharp declines in production during the 1930s and 1950s illustrate some of the dangers of this situation.

Another feature of the sugar boom was concentration of ownership, especially in the hands of American investors. After the 1870s, the new technology, particularly railways, stimulated a rapid reduction in the number of sugar mills (from 1190 in 1877 to only 207 in 1899). The independent growers, whose small- and medium-sized farms had produced most of the cane before the 1870s, now sold out in growing numbers to the big sugar companies. By 1912 large firms controlled more than 10 percent of all land in Cuba. By 1925 the number of sugar mills had dropped to only 184, and they controlled 17.7 percent of Cuban land.

This concentration of mill and land ownership was a natural result of the manner in which the sugar boom had proceeded. Under the shield of the protectorate, U.S. investors poured capital into the building of modern mills *(centrales)* and the consolidation of cane-growing lands. American-owned mills produced only 15 percent of Cuba's sugar in 1906, but by 1928 their share reached about 75 percent; by 1950 it stood at 47 percent.

The technology of sugar production affected labor as well as ownership and management. Cultivation came to require a large-scale workforce. Cane needs to be replanted only periodically, at intervals of five to twenty-five years. Therefore the principal need for labor is for the harvest, or *zafra*, mostly spent on the arduous cutting of cane with machetes. The rest of the year was known in Cuba as the "dead season" of widespread unemployment and underemployment.

But workers had nowhere to go. Because of the enormous plantations, they could not lease or purchase small-scale plots of land for their own use. Managers

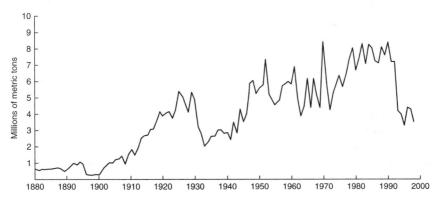

Figure 5.1 Sugar Production in Cuba, 1880–1998

SOURCES: Manuel Monreno Fraginals, *El ingenio: complejo economico social cubano del azúcar* (La Habana: Editorial de Ciencias Sociales,1978), III; Arthur MacEwan. *Revolution and Economic Development in Cuba* (New York: St. Martin's Press, 1981); Oscar A. Echevarria, "Cuba and the International Sugar Market," Proceedings of the Fifth Annual Meeting of the Association for the Study of the Cuban Economy, August 10–12, 1995; G. B. Hagelberg and José Álvarez, "Historical Overview of Cuba's Cost of Sugar Production: Implications for the Future," Institute of Food and Agricultural Sciences, University of Florida (2005); James W. Wilkie, ed., *Statistical Abstract of Latin America 37* (Los Angeles: UCLA, 2001).

wanted to keep them near the mills, available for work, and for this they devised several tactics. One was to purchase a steady share of cane from independent growers nearby who would share the problems of labor with them. Another was to let workers go into debt, so they would remain under obligation to the ownership. A third was to encourage the formation of modest urban settlements, called *bateyes*, that would create working-class communities.

As a result, Cuba witnessed the appearance of a rural proletariat, a social group that differed greatly from a classic peasantry. Workers in the sugar mills and in the *zafras* were laborers, not farmers. They were concerned more about wages and working conditions than about the acquisition of land.

Moreover, the rural laborers had intimate contact with the working class in the cities. They often migrated to urban areas, living in the kind of slums that have come to characterize many of Latin America's largest metropolises: known as *colonias populares* in Mexico and *favelas* in Brazil, they acquired in Cuba the suitable name of *llega y pon* ("come and settle"). And their residents were blighted by poverty and deprivation. Only 40 percent of urban lower-class dwellings had inside toilets, only 40 percent had refrigeration of any kind, and as many as a dozen people lived in a single room.

Contact and communication between urban and rural elements of the Cuban working class would eventually have a decisive effect on the course of the country's history because they permitted the sort of unified, classwide social movement that has been found so rarely in Latin America. It is worth noting, too, that the church played only a minor role in Cuban society, and trade unions had a sporadic and precarious existence. In other words, the outlook and behavior of the Cuban laboring classes were not conditioned or controlled by existing institutions. Workers would, in time, be available for mobilization.

Meanwhile, the United States built up more and more control over the Cuban economy. Not only did American capital take over major ownership of plantations and mills, the United States became by far the largest customer for Cuba's sugar exports—usually purchasing 75 or 80 percent of the total. Through it all, Cuba was dependent upon U.S. decisions for the fate of its major industry. And U.S. sugar import policy was invariably a topic of prolonged debate in Washington.

Newly independent Cuba had originally signed a reciprocal trade treaty in 1903 which gave Cuban sugar a 20 percent reduction from the existing U.S. tariffs. In return, Cuba reduced its tariffs on American goods by 20 to 40 percent. For the next thirty years, U.S.-Cuban trade relations grew ever closer, as the Cuban economy was for all intents and purposes integrated into the U.S. economy.

U.S. investors in Cuba might well have smiled over their good fortune. The end of World War I had brought a widespread food shortage, and all exporters, Cuba included, found themselves cashing in on near-panic buying conditions for commodities. A crash then came in 1920. Prices suddenly plummeted, and the value of the sugar crop declined to little more than one-quarter of the postwar level. The ensuing crisis had a devastating effect on the economy, hitting especially those rural workers whose existence was precarious even in the best of times.

A steam-driven engine hauls wagons of sugar cane to the mill in the early 1900s. (Courtesy of the Library of Congress.)

With the collapse of the world economy in 1929–30, Cuba soon suffered for its (somewhat involuntary) dependence on one trading partner. The U.S. Congress, under pressure from the domestic sugarbeet producers, passed the Smoot-Hawley tariff in 1930, burdening Cuban sugar with new duties. This merely increased the pressure on the staggering Cuban sugar economy, which contracted severely. The only bright spot came with Franklin Roosevelt's assumption of power in Washington in 1933. Roosevelt and the Democratic Congress brought lower tariffs. In 1934 Congress mandated fixed quotas among domestic and foreign suppliers of the U.S. sugar market. Cuba's quota was 28 percent, a share that endured, with modifications, until 1960. This provision gave Cuba a privileged access to the U.S. market. It also tied Cuba to the will of the U.S. Congress, which could change the legislation at any time. It symbolized all the vulnerability which independence had brought Cuba in the era of American dominance.

In sum, the reliance on sugar produced mixed blessings for Cuba's economy and society. It brought considerable prosperity to the island, especially in good *zafra* years, but it also created a volatile social structure, one in which rural and urban elements of a long-deprived working class maintained communication with each other. The top of the social pyramid was occupied not by resident landlords, as in classic haciendas, but by foreign entrepreneurs or Cuban owners who often lived in Havana or New York: the upper class was absentee. There was a sizable middle class, at least by Latin American standards, but it was an amorphous stratum that lacked cohesion and self-consciousness. As sociologist Maurice Zeitlin once observed, this combination of factors was bound to have its effect: "Large-scale enterprise in the countryside and the intermingling of industrial and

---

Cuba: Vital Statistics, 2007

Population (millions)	11.3
Literacy (age 15 and over) (%)	99.8
Unemployment (%)	1.9
GNP/per capita, in purchasing power* ($U.S.)	9500
Life expectancy (years)	78

*This figure is adjusted for estimated "purchasing power" in the local economy. The actual dollar figure would be closer to $3500.

SOURCE: World Bank and Country Profile and Demographics. Data on gross domestic product and poverty levels are not available.

---

argricultural workers in the sugar centrals permeated the country largely with capitalist, nationalistic, secular, anti-traditional values and norms of conduct. In this sense, the country was *prepared* for development—the only thing lacking being the revolution itself."

POLITICS AND POLICY: PATTERNS OF CHANGE

Cuban governments in the 1920s and 1930s were among the most corrupt and brutal of the republic's history. Gerardo Machado gained the presidency by election in 1925 and soon used his executive powers to make himself forever unbeatable at the ballot box. Machado's repressive measures and the growth of nationalist opposition, especially among students and urban labor, brought out the uglier realities of the U.S. protectorate. When the global Depression hit, Cuba's export-oriented economy suffered badly. The bottom dropped out of world sugar prices yet again, and the Cuban economy contracted even further. Total income plummeted, and unemployment mushroomed.

Economic distress provoked political conflict. Opposition to Machado included a coalition of students, labor leaders, middle-class reformers, and disgruntled politicians, held together by a common hatred for the dictator and a common aspiration for a more honest and more just Cuba. Armed plots abounded. Machado's police and military bore down with more repressive measures. The United States, so attentive to some other kinds of deviations from democracy in Cuba, stood by passively.

Franklin Roosevelt's election victory brought an activist to the White House. While Washington assumed a more critical stance toward Machado, the Cubans took matters into their own hands. A successful general strike in August 1933 helped prod the army toward undercutting the dictator, who fled Havana. Now opinion began to polarize sharply. The young radicals dominant in the provisional government joined with army enlisted men, led by Sergeant Fulgencio Batista. This alliance took over the government, alarming Roosevelt's high-level envoy, Sumner Welles. The new civilian leader was Ramón Grau San Martín, a doctor-professor and long-time hero to the student left, with whom he had invariably sided. "Soviets" were formed, followed by occupations of factories and farms. The new government proclaimed a socialist revolution.

Washington became deeply worried over the sharp leftward turn by its protectorate. U.S. Navy ships took up stations off the Cuban coast; old-style intervention seemed near. But a new strongman, eager to follow the Cuban formula for finding power and wealth, was already on stage. On signal from the United States, Batista easily ousted Grau and the radicals. A front-man president acceptable to Washington was soon arranged, and the radicals, the nationalists, and the reformers watched with bitterness as Cuban politics returned to business as usual. U.S. hegemony was so certain that Washington had no trouble agreeing to abrogate the Platt Amendment in 1934. The U.S. naval base at Guantánamo was not affected.

For the next twenty-five years, Cuban politics was dominated by Fulgencio Batista. Between 1934 and 1940, Batista ran his country through puppet presidents. He ruled directly from 1940 to 1944, then went back to a behind-the-scenes role as the onetime radical Grau San Martín returned to the presidency (1944–48). There was little left of Grau the idealist, and the spectacle of his descent into the nether world of Cuban political corruption merely deepened the disgust and moral fury burning in the radicals and nationalists. Grau's successor, another Batista front man, was Carlos Prío Socorrás (1948–52). Batista himself retook the presidential reins in a coup and henceforth ruled with dictatorial powers (1952–59).

Death at the Microphone

Cuba of the 1940s and 1950s had no better-known radio personality than the volatile Eddie Chibás. His Sunday evening program was "must" listening for millions of Havana residents, especially the middle classes who resented the cynical machinations of the political establishment. Chibás was a die-hard leader of the opposition "Orthodox" political party, and he poured forth endless invective against the corruption and hypocrisy of Cuban politics.

In July 1951 he launched wild corruption charges against the education minister of President Carlos Prío. When challenged, Chibás failed to produce the promised proof. Instead he went on the air with a passionate self-defense, crying out to his fellow citizens: "Comrades of Ortodoxia, forward! Sweep away the thieves in the government!" A pistol shot then rang out. Eddie had shot himself in the stomach. Evidently he had meant only to wound himself with a dramatic gesture that would galvanize his listeners. Unfortunately, however, he had gone off the air just before pulling the trigger. Chibás died ten days later. His own party could not agree on a successor and went into rapid decline. The stage was set for the final act of Batista's long rule.

In reality, Cuban society and politics saw little change between 1934 and 1959. The futility of the electoral system was repeatedly demonstrated, as the perennial strongman (yesterday Machado, today Batista) worked his will. The honest opposition scrapped and struggled in vain. What had happened to the revolutionary fervor of 1933? Where was the coalition that had so frightened Washington? It had gone the way of all Cuban nationalist movements—rendered impotent by the unbeatable alliance of the Cuban elites, their political and military handmaidens, and Uncle Sam. If one had asked most Cubans in 1959 whether their little island had any chance of true independence, how many would have dared say yes? Very few. Most educated Cubans undoubtedly thought that the best their country could hope for was to win a few advantages at the margin. What else could one hope? A startling answer soon came forth.

In the meantime, America's power and presence exercised a dominating influence. Thousands of North Americans lived in Cuba, chiefly in Havana. They enjoyed pride of place, mingling with members of the Cuban elite, along with wealthy expatriates at the Havana Country Club, the Havana Yacht Club, the Miramar Yacht Club, and other exclusive social establishments. Many more Americans visited the island as tourists. Gambling and gangsterism became synonymous with the U.S. presence as Batista welcomed mobsters like Meyer Lansky and Santos Trafficante Jr. The gangsters in turn shared their earnings with the dictator and his henchmen. Prostitution spread to cater to North American sun-and-sex tourists.

U.S. films and music filled Cuban cinema and radio as young Cubans rushed to learn the latest dances and catch the most recent performances of John Wayne and Marilyn Monroe. English words were incorporated into Cuban Spanish: *jonrón* (home run) and *doble plei* (double play) illustrate not only the popularity of baseball on the island (introduced in the 1860s) but also the growth of a more recent phenomenon, "Spanglish."

By the 1950s, a North American–style consumer culture had taken hold in Havana and the larger provincial cities. Cuban elites bought U.S. automobiles and went on lavish shopping trips to Miami and New York, bringing the latest fashions and consumer durables. While their social betters lived in the style of the North American rich, middle-income Cubans struggled within a dependent economy to obtain the U.S. consumer goods demanded by their precarious social position.

Fidel Castro and the Batista Regime

Born in 1927, Fidel Castro was the son of a successful Spanish immigrant, and he represented an old Cuban tradition—the heir of a *peninsular* who had "made America," as the Spaniards put it in the sixteenth century. But this immigrant's son was not interested in enjoying the comfortable life his background and training might have promised. He wanted to make a different America.

Fidel had followed the classic path—primary and secondary education with the Jesuits, then a law degree. He plunged into the turbulent world of student politics.

He proved to be strong-minded, articulate, and ambitious. Passionately nationalist, he steered clear of the communists, who were the best organized of the student groups.

Soon after graduation, Fidel began traveling in Latin America, meeting other radical nationalists and learning about other political realities. His most dramatic experience came in Bogotá in 1948, when the colossal urban riot of the *bogotazo* turned the city upside down for two days. The triggering event had been the assassination of a young and progressive politician named Jorge Eliécer Gaitán. The populace rose as one and took over a city whose authorities had abdicated in terror. Fidel was swept up into the wave of popular outrage and, in the process, acquired a glimpse of the possibilities of popular mobilization.

Fidel Castro's first assault on Batista's state came straight out of the tradition of romantic Latin American revolutionaries. It was an attack on the 26th of July 1953, against the provincial army barracks at Moncada in the southeastern city of Santiago. Fidel led a band of 165 youths who stormed the garrison. The government reaction was swift and ruthless. The police began slaughtering suspects. Fidel and his brother Raúl were captured, tried, and sentenced to fifteen years in prison. During the trial Fidel gave a long, impassioned, rambling speech ("History Will Absolve Me"), little noticed at the time but later to become a sacred text of the revolution.

The Castro brothers were lucky. They stayed in prison only eleven months before Batista granted amnesty in an attempt to court public opinion and to improve his political image. Given his freedom, Fidel immediately fled to Mexico to begin organizing a new revolutionary force.

In 1956 Fidel set out with a new band of revolutionaries in the *Granma*, an ancient yacht. With him once again was his brother Raúl, more politically radical than Fidel. Also aboard was Ernesto ("Che") Guevara, a twenty-seven-year-old Argentine physician who had personally witnessed the CIA-conducted overthrow of radically anti-American Guatemalan president Jacobo Arbenz in 1954. After a harrowing voyage, Fidel and his fellow survivors fled into the Sierra Maestra in eastern Cuba. From this forsaken outpost, Fidel rebuilt his rebel band and renewed his war against Batista.

Fidel and his top lieutenants knew that a key to toppling Batista would be the erosion of the dictator's foreign support, especially from the United States. Fidel's contacts found the perfect vehicle: Herbert Matthews, a veteran foreign correspondent of the *New York Times*. Matthews was smuggled up to Fidel's mountain hideout and from there wrote a series of stories which exploded on the front page of the most prestigious newspaper in the United States. Matthews' dramatic dispatches portrayed Fidel as an idealistic reformer and gave the rebels international status overnight. Suddenly Batista was on the defensive in world public opinion. He was in that most dangerous of realms—seen to be both brutal and impotent.

As their ranks increased, Fidel's youthful followers encountered the harsh and difficult world of Cuba's peasantry. The rebels took a strong interest in these people's fate. It was the first principle of the guerrilla: retain the sympathy of the local residents, not only for supplies but also so they will not betray you to the authorities.

The rebel band was still, however, primarily middle class. A few peasants joined the rebels, but they never came in large numbers, and they never held positions of leadership. This is hardly surprising. Most revolutions in history have been led by a counterelite. This is not to say that participation and support from peasants was unimportant. But the Fidelista phenomenon was middle class in origin and leadership. Its later directions were another matter.

Guerrilla warfare is a lonely and dangerous business. Month after month through 1957, the rebels managed the essential—to survive. But they failed to score seriously against the enemy.

Early 1958 brought some encouraging signs. In February the Cuban bishops issued a pastoral letter calling for a government of national unity. In March the U.S. government, under pressure for supplying arms to the repressive Batista regime, placed an embargo on arms shipments to both sides. This move amounted to a partial withdrawal of legitimacy for the established government. After a general strike failed in April 1958, Fidel decided to become more aggressive. Batista's army launched a "liquidation campaign" that resulted in disaster. By August the army had withdrawn from the mountains, defeated by their own poor leadership and faulty training and by superior intelligence and dedication on the rebel side.

Through the rest of 1958, a savage guerrilla war raged on. There were never any set battles. It was a war of hit-and-run, with bombings, sabotage, and harassment. Batista's response was counterterror. Since he could seldom catch the guerrillas, he sent his thugs against the students and the middle class suspected of having links to the 26th of July Movement. In so doing, Batista was rapidly enlarging the support for Fidel. Ironically, the repression ended up attracting new recruits to the rebel cause.

Support for Batista began to evaporate. As dictator his greatest card to play had always been his ability to keep order. Now even that was disappearing. Batista and his army were unprepared for the kind of underground that could elude their network of regular informants. Torture and execution only sparked popular outrage.

By late 1958 Batista had no desire to fight a losing cause to the end. He could see that his power was shrinking daily. His army and police had become both hated and derided. He had lost the all-important support from Washington. And the country had become so convinced of his fall that the economy was increasingly disrupted as businessmen and bankers waited for the inevitable. Suddenly, on New Year's Eve, he called his aides together, designated a successor president, and took off with a planeload of relatives for the Dominican Republic. The way was now clear for Fidel's triumphal entry into Havana.

THE CUBAN REVOLUTION

Euphoria is the only word to describe the country's mood in the early days of 1959. Fidel had achieved genuine heroic status. The question now occupying the minds of the middle class, workers, peasants, foreign investors, the U.S. embassy, and other observers was, What kind of revolution would this be?

Fidel entered a political vacuum. The civil war had not only discredited Batista; it had besmirched the entire political class, all of its members, to greater or lesser degree, compromised by the dictator. The momentum now lay with the guerrillas in the green fatigue uniforms. The rebel army was to remain the key political institution thereafter.

Fidel's greatest asset, aside from his own formidable leadership gifts, was the desperate desire for change among his fellow Cubans. The most underprivileged, the rural poor, had never counted for anything in the electoral system. Working classes in the cities and towns had precious little more weight.

The most restless and most important social sector was the middle class, which was ready to receive a new political message. Its members were first of all disgusted by the old political cadre. Second, they were moved by appeals for greater social justice. Third, they longed for a more independent Cuba. That meant a Cuba freer of the United States. Yet any assertion of Cuban national dignity was bound to collide with the Yankee presence.

1959 was a year of drama for the Revolution. The first major political crisis arose over what to do with the captured Batista officials who had been responsible for the worst of the repression. The revolutionaries resorted to arbitrary procedures in trying their victims, appealing to sentiments of "ordinary justice" to legitimize their executions. Within six months, about 550 were put to death, following trial by various revolutionary courts. These executions, punctuated by cries of *paredón!* (to the wall!), worried moderates in Cuba and their sympathizers abroad, especially in the United States.

In April 1959 Fidel set out for New York, where he was to visit the UN headquarters. He managed to project the image of a nationalist reformer, strongly opposed to foreign intervention, but also not a communist. He was careful to maintain only distant contact with the U.S. government while skillfully cultivating elite centers of opinion with, for example, a triumphant appearance in Harvard Stadium.

Fidel returned to Cuba to carry out his most radical measure to date: the Agrarian Reform Law of May 17, 1959. The law eliminated the giant estates, expropriating farmlands over 1000 acres, with compensation to be paid in Cuban currency bonds. No foreigners would henceforth be allowed to own agricultural land. The expropriated lands would be turned over to small private holders and cooperatives. A National Institute of Agrarian Reform (INRA) was created to implement these far-reaching measures. Critics in Cuba and abroad, especially in the United States, began to raise the alarm. Was this not the first step to communism? Hadn't Fidel appointed a communist as the operating head of INRA?

Political polarization heightened throughout the year. Fidel announced the discovery of a plot against the Revolution. Noncommunists among the supporters of Batista's overthrow became increasingly alarmed. A former president of the Senate attacked the agrarian reform and called for the elections which Fidel had promised. The commander of the air force resigned in protest over alleged communist influence in the military. In July Fidel staged what was to become a recurrent drama: he resigned the premiership in the midst of what he described as conspiracies against the Revolution. There followed massive rallies, where the carefully primed multitudes called for Fidel to return to the premiership. He bowed to their will and, in so doing, announced a lengthy moratorium on elections.

There was now brewing a case that would for many become a hallmark of the Revolution's radicalization. Major Hubert Matos, one of Fidel's oldest political allies and a longtime revolutionary, chose to break with the Fidelista line. He resigned from the armed forces and issued a letter attacking the growth of communist influence. Fidel's response was swift. He jailed Matos and mobilized a huge propaganda campaign against him as a traitor to the Revolution. For the next decade and a half, Matos, locked away in prison, remained for the Fidelista regime the supreme symbol of revolutionary deviationism. For many foreign observers, Matos remained the quintessential victim of Stalinist-style repression.

The year 1960 proved to be even more decisive for the course of the Cuban Revolution. Four basic trends took hold: (1) the nationalization of the economy, (2) a sharp swing to the Soviet bloc, (3) the establishment of an authoritarian regime, and (4) the launching of an egalitarian socioeconomic policy.

It was inevitable that any Cuban government attempting to reassert Cuban control over its economy would collide with the United States. The first major clash came over oil. When Fidel had discovered that he could buy crude oil cheaper from the Russians than from Venezuela, he ordered the U.S.-owned oil refineries located in Cuba to process the Russian crude. Although an old law obligated them to comply, they refused. Fidel promptly confiscated the U.S. oil companies. Partially in retaliation, President Eisenhower suspended the Cuban sugar quota in the United States.

The Cuban government now followed by seizing virtually all the rest of U.S. property. That included electricity and telephone companies (another prime irritant to the nationalists), sugar mills, and nickel mines. Washington reacted by embargoing all trade to Cuba, except medicines and foodstuffs. This embargo would later be tightened in 1962—and remain in place for decades to come.

The swing to the Soviet bloc was neither a cause nor an effect of the clash with the United States; it was part and parcel of the same process. Initially it was a question of how far the Soviets might be willing to commit themselves in Cuba. The Russians proved bolder than almost anyone expected. In February 1960, well before the full economic break with the United States, the Soviets signed a trade agreement with Cuba, granting $100 million credit to buy equipment and promising to purchase 4 million tons of sugar in each of the coming four years. Fidel was now developing an alternative source of technology and equipment, and the Soviets were getting ready to integrate Cuba as a "socialist" ally in the Third World.

Revolutionary Cuba's state was emerging in a piecemeal, ad hoc fashion. Fidel began by proclaiming his commitment to the 1940 constitution, which

Batista had repudiated by his coup of 1952. The problem was a classic one: how to carry out fundamental economic and social change when existing government institutions were set up to maintain the status quo. Fidel resolved this dilemma with authoritarian efficiency, asserting revolutionary control over key institutions of the "bourgeois" social order—the media, courts, unions, universities, and schools.

Though the old legal system remained in place, there was never any attempt to elect a new legislature. The 26th of July Movement could hardly provide an institutional base. It had never developed into a tightly knit organization, and it was far from a political party. From the start, Fidel relied on the most responsive and popular institution at hand: the revolutionary army.

Late in 1960 the government created an important new institution: Committees for the Defense of the Revolution (CDRs). Locally based citizens' groups, they were organized primarily for civil defense. The constant threat of invasion necessitated such a measure. Since the Revolution also had enemies at home, the CDRs also had the task of monitoring the population for counterrevolutionary opinions or behavior.

The Revolution set out to create new institutions in place of the old. Fidel seemed to be everywhere. Mobilization was the inexorable theme: mobilization against invaders, mobilization against social and economic problems at home. To achieve this goal, a huge militia was created: by the end of 1960 it totaled 500,000 out of a total population of 6.7 million. And none could doubt the identity of the commander-in-chief.

The only political party to survive the revolutionary transition was the Cuban Communist Party. Never a member, Fidel had carefully avoided any personal identification with the party. But he made it clear that anticommunism would be considered counterrevolutionary. He also entrusted party members with such programs as agrarian reform.

What most Cubans cared about was not political structure but how the Revolution would change their lives. On this score, Fidel and his guerrilla companions kept their eyes fixed on the poor, especially in the countryside. The revolutionaries were determined to attack the legacy of the corrupt, capitalist Cuba: illiteracy, disease, malnutrition, and dilapidated housing. A yearlong crusade cut illiteracy rates in half (Cuba's illiteracy rate was already low by Latin American standards), and illiteracy has virtually disappeared since then. Sensing the direction of the Revolution, the rich (and many from the middle class) began to flee, and the government acquired a windfall: the refugees' abandoned assets—homes, offices, farms—that the state could now distribute.

The number of defectors steadily grew. Most attacked the guerrillas for betraying the hope of rapid elections. Instead, they charged, Fidel and his clique were leading Cuba toward communist totalitarianism. Most probably were sincere. Others also thought it the best tactic to arouse the United States.

FRAMING U.S. POLICIES

The Cuban Revolution was utterly unacceptable to the United States. After all, U.S. policymakers had long claimed to have a "special relationship" with Cuba—which, in effect, meant control of the island's destiny. As John Quincy Adams put it so famously in 1823, "There are laws of political as well as physical gravitation; and if an apple severed by the tempest from its native tree cannot choose but fall to the ground, Cuba, forcibly disjoined from its own unnatural connection with Spain, and incapable of self-support, can gravitate only towards the North American Union, which by the same law of nature cannot cast her off from her bosom." (In the end, racial prejudice prevented outright annexation of the island—how could the United States absorb such a substantial black population?) But the basic consensus was clear: one way or the other, as either a state or a protectorate, Cuba rightfully belonged to the United States.

In this spirit, Republicans and Democrats vociferously denounced Fidel Castro's upstart regime. The notion that this small-sized plantation society could challenge Wall Street's investments and Washington's authority was deemed to be absolutely galling. It challenged conventional wisdom about the benevolence of U.S. power, about the solidarity of the Western Hemisphere, and about the forces of historical change. Given the dynamics of the Cold War, something had to be done.

The U.S. government developed antirevolutionary policies in stages over time. As Fidel and his followers were still fighting in the mountains, the Eisenhower administration began searching for an alternative—preservation of the status quo under another pro-American autocrat, under the formula of "*Batistianismo without Batista.*" The dictator's sudden departure at the end of 1958 brought that option to an end.

After the triumph of the Revolution, Castro's nationalization of American-owned enterprises offered grounds for governmental overthrow (as in Guatemala in 1954). While diplomatic hostilities intensified, U.S. political leaders decried what they saw as the leftward drift of this onetime protectorate, only ninety miles off the Florida coast, into the orbit of the Soviet Union. Washington could simply not abide a "communist beachhead" within the Western Hemisphere. This was the thinking that prompted the Eisenhower administration to sever diplomatic relations with Cuba in January 1961, and to accelerate planning for an effort to overthrow the Castro government.

The most obvious strategy for Washington was to support an exile invasion of Cuba. That was how José Martí had returned to the island back in 1895, and it was the standard strategy in Caribbean-exile politics. In July 1960, the CIA convinced President Eisenhower to approve the training of an invasion force.

The "toughness" of U.S. policy toward revolutionary Cuba became an issue in the 1960 presidential campaign, which featured Eisenhower's vice president, Richard Nixon, and the relatively unknown senator from Massachusetts, John Fitzgerald Kennedy. In their first televised debate, Kennedy took a more aggressive stance toward Cuba than Nixon—who knew of the invasion plan, but was unable to acknowledge it in public.

It was Kennedy, the ostensibly tougher candidate, who won the presidency and inherited the "Cuban problem." Eisenhower broke diplomatic relations in January 1961, in response to Fidel's demand that the United States drastically reduce its embassy in Havana. In April, Kennedy found himself pressured to approve an exile invasion of Cuba. Wanting to do his anticommunist duty, but fearful of the possible effect on world opinion, the new president demanded that there be no identifiable U.S. involvement. It proved to be an ironic and fateful concern.

The Bay of Pigs

As rumors mounted, an invasion force headed for Cuba in April 1961. The operation proved a misadventure from the beginning. After strenuous debate, President Kennedy reduced the exile-piloted air cover and vetoed the use of any U.S. planes. The invaders foundered in an ill-chosen bit of southern coast, on the Bay of Pigs. The hoped-for uprisings, which would supposedly paralyze the Cuban defenders, never materialized. The Cuban defenses proved more than adequate. The invasion brigades were quickly captured. They never had a chance to adopt their fallback procedure—head for the mountains and mount a guerrilla operation.

The Bay of Pigs could not have been a greater triumph for Fidel and the revolutionaries. The United States had finally shown its intentions to be what Fidel had always said they were: a desire to turn the clock back in Cuba. Although the CIA had tried to screen out the more unsavory ex-Batista types, the invaders included more than a few who had served the dictator. Fidel and his supporters seized on those names to prove that the United States wanted to restore the discredited tyrant.

The Missile Crisis

The failed invasion marked a watershed in U.S.-Cuban relations. Washington's most obvious strategy had failed. What options were left for the United States?

The issue now shifted to the level of the superpowers. In 1960 Nikita Khrushchev had rattled Soviet missiles in defense of Cuban socialism. The Soviets thereafter decided they must back up their threat by putting missiles in Cuba itself, and by October 1962 they were installing intermediate-range rocket bases in Cuba. This was an unprecedented challenge to the balance of military power. The United States demanded that the Soviets withdraw their missiles from Cuba, under sanction of a naval quarantine on all Soviet military shipments to Cuba. The world seemed to balance on the edge of nuclear war. After a fateful interval, Khrushchev complied. The missiles were withdrawn.

The superpower confrontation in the Caribbean had fateful implications for Cuba. First, Fidel himself was not consulted at any stage. The result was to make Cuba, in Latin American eyes, into a Soviet satellite in essential security matters. Second, the Soviets withdrew their missiles only because Washington (secretly) promised it would not invade Cuba. The Soviets had forced the United States to allow the socialist experiment in Cuba to proceed.

The Hardening of U.S. Policy

The survival of Cuba's revolutionary government not only intensified U.S. hostility. It also affected Washington's policy toward Latin America as a whole. The central premise became: no more Cubas. No more socialist experiments, no Soviet puppets, no anti-American ideologies. In the context of the Cold War, the United States could not and would not permit any such forms of political deviation. This conviction provided the underpinning for subsequent overt or covert U.S. interventions in Brazil (1964), the Dominican Republic (1965), Chile (1973), Grenada (1983), and Central America (the 1980s). In the eyes of Washington, Cuba became an object lesson for the hemisphere.

As for Cuba, the U.S. goal was simple—bringing down the regime. Toward this end, American policymakers pursued a variety of tactics—removal of Fidel Castro, support for refugees and dissidents, and strangulation of the Cuban economy. These policies remained in place for decades to come.

The first strategy was rather primitive: assassinate Castro. At the behest of the White House, the CIA orchestrated multiple schemes and attempts. Such plots included an exploding cigar, a fungal-infected diving suit, and a gangland-style shooting. (American Mafia bosses had lost control of profitable businesses in Havana as a result of the Revolution, so they were as eager as the politicians to remove Castro from the scene.) According to one of Fidel's former security guards, in fact, the CIA took direct or indirect part in 638 assassination efforts against him over the years! As Castro is reported to have said, "If surviving assassination attempts were an Olympic event, I would win the gold medal."

The reasoning behind these attempts was as flawed as the execution. The predominant assumption was that Cuba's revolutionary movement was Fidel's personal creation: through the force of his character—untrustworthy, ruthless, and megalomaniacal—he had taken his country away from its proper historical path. Eliminate him and everything would change. What this logic failed to acknowledge, however, were the factors behind the revolution: inequality, frustration, long-simmering resentment of U.S. domination, and popular support for programs of radical change. This approach also got the U.S. government into the distasteful business of attempting to assassinate foreign heads of state, a tactic that was later declared unlawful by an act of Congress.

The second broad strategy was to embrace Fidel's opponents. From the time of Batista's departure in late 1958, the United States welcomed Cuban exiles and refugees with open arms. And they came by the thousands, settling for the most part in the Miami area—where they formed a vibrant and successful community, eventually transforming what had been a sleepy beachside resort into a multilingual "capital of Latin America." The U.S. government hailed all dissidents as freedom fighters (remember, the Bay of Pigs operation was carried out by anti-Castro Cubans) and proclaimed that their exodus provided unmistakable proof of the superiority of capitalism over communism. For practical intents and purposes, Washington regarded the anti-Fidelista community in Miami as a government in exile.

This long-term reliance on Cuban dissidents would have fateful implications. One was to give the Cuban American community in Miami inordinate influence over U.S. policy toward the Castro regime. As their numbers grew and prosperity swelled, the exiles formed a powerful political force within the state of Florida. And through a right-wing organization known as the Cuban American National Foundation, their leaders bitterly—and effectively—opposed any relaxation of hostilities toward the revolutionary government. To a considerable extent, Cuban Americans in Miami managed to tie the hands of elected politicians in Washington.

An additional consequence was entirely unintentional: the U.S. policy enabled Castro to export his opposition. Over time, Fidel's most vociferous critics were obliged (or encouraged) to leave the country. As a result, the most resourceful center of dissidence was nowhere to be found within Cuba; it was in Miami. Ironically, this process provided Castro with a political safety valve. It also allowed him to taint his opponents as unprincipled traitors of the fatherland, as opportunistic *gusanos* (worms) rather than loyal *cubanos*. Words were important weapons in the struggles over Cuban destiny.

U.S.-Cuban relations took an unexpected turn in 1980. After anti-Castro dissidents stormed the Peruvian embassy in hopes of gaining political asylum, the Cuban government retaliated (against Peru) by withdrawing its security guard around the diplomatic compound. Word suddenly spread that the embassy was unguarded, and within twenty-four hours 10,800 Cubans rushed onto the embassy grounds. The Castro government announced that they would all be allowed to emigrate, along with anyone else who cared to inform authorities. The total exodus eventually climbed to 125,000 people (including criminals and deadbeats). Departing from the port of Mariel, most went via small craft provided by the Cuban American community in what became known as the "Mariel boatlift." After that, the Castro government prohibited unauthorized emigration from Cuba to the United States.

The third and final pillar of U.S. policy toward Cuba was an economic embargo. In late 1960 President Eisenhower imposed a partial trade embargo on Cuba, excluding food and medicine. The Foreign Assistance Act of 1961 prohibited aid to Cuba and authorized the president to impose "a total embargo upon all trade" with Cuba, which John Kennedy did in response to Castro's expropriations of U.S.-owned properties (notably, those belonging to the United Fruit Company and International Telephone and Telegraph). This took place in February 1962—months before the missile crisis of that year.

The embargo has remained in place ever since. In 1992 it was codified into law for the stated purpose of "bringing democracy to the Cuban people." In 1996 Congress passed the Helms-Burton Act, further restricting U.S. citizens from doing business in or with Cuba, and in 1999 President Bill Clinton amplified the embargo by prohibiting foreign subsidiaries of U.S.-owned corporations from conducting trade with Cuba. In large part, continuation and extension of the embargo reflected the electoral power of the Cuban American community in the all-important state of Florida. The result was perpetuation of the most enduring trade embargo in modern history.

The idea behind this policy appears to be that strangulation of the Cuban economy would generate widespread discontent that would result in a popular uprising against the Castro regime, which would lead to its eventual downfall. As of early 2009, after nearly half a century, nothing of the kind had taken place. One reason, mentioned earlier, was that the most resourceful opposition to Castro was not in Cuba but in Florida: the exile leadership was absentee. Moreover, the embargo (or *bloqueo,* as it is known in Spanish, i.e., the "blockade") had enabled Castro and his colleagues to blame any and all economic setbacks and downturns on the U.S. government and its embargo. American policy thus became a useful scapegoat for the Cuban leadership.

POLICY EXPERIMENTATION AND REGIME CONSOLIDATION

After defeating the Bay of Pigs invasion in 1961, the revolutionaries could concentrate on the economic tasks facing the new Cuba. The central fact was that the Cuban economy revolved around exporting sugar, especially to the United States. The revolutionaries were determined to change that humiliating dependence. The chief architect was Ernesto "Che" Guevara, the Argentine physician-guerrilla who was the most creative theoretician among the revolutionaries. Guevara drew up a Four-Year Plan which called for agricultural diversification (a de-emphasis on sugar) and industrialization (the manufacture of light consumer goods). Cuba launched this ambitious plan amid great fanfare.

By 1962 the results had already proved disappointing. In part, Guevara and his youthful planners were reaping the whirlwind of the shortsighted policies of 1959–60. Sugar production had taken a plunge. In 1961 the Cubans had produced 6.8 million tons of sugar, the second highest harvest in Cuban history. This output merely disguised the deliberate neglect the government was showing to sugar. In 1962 the harvest dropped to 4.8 million tons and in 1963 it was only 3.8 million tons, the smallest since 1945. The fall was disastrous for export earnings.

The industrialization drive was also going badly. Cuba lacked the raw materials and expertise to rush into industrialization. Since 1960 the United States had enforced an economic embargo against Cuba, pressuring all U.S. firms (and their Latin American and European subsidiaries) to cease trade with Cuba. This embargo forced Cuba to depend largely on the Soviets and the Eastern bloc for equipment. Direction was to come from highly centralized planning bureaucracies, modeled after Soviet and Czech patterns. The effort was ineffective and expensive. Even the Russians seemed uneasy about underwriting a socialist utopia in the Caribbean.

In mid-1963 the Soviets put their foot down. The Cubans must slow down the industrialization drive and improve their planning. They must recognize Cuba's comparative advantage: sugar. Che Guevara resigned, confessing his errors. Fidel, ever on the initiative, now embraced sugar, which he had so recently spurned. In 1963 he announced that in 1970 (later labeled the "Year of the Decisive Endeavor") Cuba would break all records for sugar production: it would harvest 10 million tons. Like other plantation societies, Cuba thus fell into the trap of reliance on a single export crop.

Debate continued over strategies for economic development and political consolidation. Still active in the regime, Che Guevara argued for an "idealistic" strategy, a Maoist approach that would totally eliminate the market and material incentives. The economy would be fully collectivized and directed by a centralized planning authority. A radical break with the capitalist past would require a "new man," a Cuban who would work for moral rewards (decorations, public praise) and thus reflect a new, higher level of political consciousness. Here the Cuban leaders were going through the familiar dilemma of communist regimes: how to reconcile Marxist idealism with a pragmatic economic policy.

Guevara's idealists further argued that the construction of socialism at home required the aggressive promotion of revolution abroad. They wanted to prove that a guerrilla strategy could work throughout Latin America and perhaps the entire Third World.

Guevara's main opponent in this debate was Carlos Rafael Rodríguez, an economist and longtime Communist Party member. Rodríguez took a practical approach. He favored a more measured use of central planning, partial reliance on market mechanisms, and autonomy left to the individual enterprises. He thought state firms should have to account for their expenses and earnings. In short, Rodríguez and his allies proposed a more conventional path, relying on material incentives instead of only moral ones. They favored also a strong party and a "flexible" policy toward Latin America. This meant a willingness to deal with regimes that Guevara saw only as targets for revolutionary opposition.

While the arguments went on, Cuba was returning to sugar. Economic production was nonetheless disappointing. The year 1964 yielded a 9 percent growth rate for most of the economy, but that was primarily a catch-up from the declines of 1961–63. In 1965 the figure slipped to 1.5 percent, less than the rate of population growth, and in 1966 became negative again (–3.7 percent). Indecision in basic policymaking was not building a dynamic socialism.

At this point Fidel brought the debate to an end by endorsing Che Guevara's idealism. Cuba would make a gigantic collective effort accompanied by moral incentives. This immediately increased Fidel's own power, since he himself took charge of the now strengthened central planning apparatus. He and his trusted lieutenants plunged into the minutiae of economic management. The atmosphere recalled the early romantic days of the Revolution—endless rhetoric, euphoric dreams, celebration of the selfless "new man."

Fidel Castro addresses a rally in the early 1960s; the doves, frequently used as a political symbol, represent the idea of a society at peace. (Center for Cuban Studies, New York.)

Along with this idealistic mobilization at home went a stepped-up commitment to revolution abroad. Cuba sought out guerrilla movements across Latin America, offering arms, training, and expertise. Che Guevara spearheaded the drive. Always a heroic figure, Che became the nemesis of the CIA and the Latin American military. Unfortunately for Che, however, he chose the *altiplano* (highlands) of Bolivia to start the spread of his "many Vietnams" in South America and there met death in 1967 at the hands of U.S.-trained Bolivian Ranger troops.

By 1968 Fidel was pulling back from the Guevarist line. There had already been signs that Che did not get full support from Havana during his ill-fated campaign in Bolivia. By supporting the Soviet invasion of Czechoslovakia in 1968, Fidel signaled a return to Soviet orthodoxy. He then began to downplay the export of revolution.

On the domestic front, however, Guevarist policies continued intact. The spring of 1968 saw a "revolutionary offensive." The remainder of the private sector was nationalized, consumption was subordinated to investment, and Cubans were exhorted to give their all to reach the omnipresent target of 10 million tons of sugar in 1970.

The magic year came, and all of Cuba was mobilized to cut cane. Everything was sacrificed to release labor for the cane fields. Sensing that the target was distant, the authorities left some of the 1969 harvest in the fields, hoping to improve the 1970 figure. It was no use—the *zafra* reached only 8.5 million tons. It was a prodigious total, the largest in Cuban history, but it still fell short of its much-touted goal. So much propaganda, so many promises. It was a mortal blow for the "voluntaristic" philosophy of Che. The psychological toll was enormous. But Fidel, ever resourceful, was about to change policies again.

Consolidating the Regime

The failure of the 10-million-ton effort made Fidel's about-face easier. Everyone could see that the "idealistic" model had failed. On July 26, 1970 Fidel confessed all. In a marathon speech ("Let the Shame Be Welcome"), Castro took on his own shoulders the responsibility for the quixotic crusade for the super-harvest. He offered to resign, but the crowds cried no. The economic failure was obliterated by revolutionary theater.

Cuban policy now turned more pragmatic. First, there were to be new management and planning systems and more use of "profits" as a basis for decision making. Second, the private sector was to be given a greater role in both agriculture and services. Third, wages and salaries would now be linked to output, with premiums for needed skills. Finally, there was to be greater economic interaction with the West.

This more conventional economic policy was accompanied by a similar shift in institutional policy. The Communist Party was now strengthened; the unions and other mass organizations were reorganized and given a greater role. This move toward greater "orthodoxy" (i.e., closer resemblance to Soviet practice) affected culture as well. Central controls over education and the mass media were tightened.

In early 1971 Fidel launched furious attacks on "former friends" of the Revolution who had charged that Fidel's personalistic regime was leading Cuba toward economic defeat. In addition, Fidel cracked down on the Cuban artistic scene by arresting the internationally known writer Heberto Padilla. Apparently under coercion, Padilla was forced to confess crimes against the Revolution. He later repeated his mea culpa before a writers' conference, which set the tone for a tougher standard of political loyalty now expected of all artists in revolutionary Cuba. Use of the police to enforce political conformity brought back unpleasant memories of recent dictators.

Part and parcel of this policy shift was an increasing approximation of Soviet models of economic and political decision making. It had been under way for several years, but the shift in domestic policy now made Cuba's overall stance more consistent. Radical experimentation was over. The inevitable logic of Cuba's enormous economic and military dependence on the Soviets was being played out. Fidel was now a reliable ally of the USSR in the Third World. The Cuban Revolution was approaching the Soviet model more closely than ever before.

Cuba thus settled into an extreme economic dependence on the USSR, one that bore much resemblance to her onetime dependence on the United States.

Although the exact total was difficult to calculate, it probably equaled about one-quarter of the Cuban gross national product (GNP). The integration of trade with the Eastern bloc was close to what it had once been with the United States. Had Cuba merely traded one brand of dependency for another? Yet the ties to the Soviet Union did not produce the direct ownership which had created such a nationalist backlash against U.S. economic penetration before 1959.

What were the consequences of this new dependency? We know that Fidel had echoed the Soviet-line denunciation of the Solidarity movement in Poland and praised the Soviet intervention in Afghanistan. Cuba sent more than 30,000 troops and social service personnel to support a Marxist regime in Angola. Some observers suggested that Cuba had produced a new hybrid regime of "state capitalism." In one key respect, Fidel's regime had shown little change. He constantly promised more meaningful public participation, but actual rule remained top down and the final voice was always his. Ironically, applying Marxist dogma in the Caribbean had produced Latin America's most durable *caudillo*. The profound social revolution in Cuba had been possible only because of Soviet military protection and economic aid. It remains unclear whether Cubans had more bargaining power with Moscow than they once had with Washington, since Soviet-Cuban relations occurred in far greater secrecy than had relations with the United States. The Cubans, who often acted against Soviet wishes, achieved brilliant military victories over the South African army in Africa and, as a result, won much praise in the Third World.

The Revolution brought many changes to Cuba. Socialist Cuba's greatest triumphs have been in serving basic human needs. Illiteracy has been wiped out, and a comprehensive school system has been created. Its teaching content is, not surprisingly, highly ideological, designed to inculcate the new socialist values. Basic health care, especially preventive care, has been extended to the lower sectors. Medical training has been geared to public health. Food distribution, always one of the most shocking reflections of social inequality, has been guaranteed by rationing. The result is that life expectancy rose from sixty-three years in 1960 to seventy-eight in 2007, and the infant mortality rate fell by more than two-thirds in the same period.

Race relations underwent major improvements as well. In Cuba, as elsewhere, the legacy of slavery had been extensive racial prejudice. Whites occupied the topmost social rungs, mulattoes were in the middle, and blacks were at the bottom. Given the determination to rectify social injustice, Fidelista policies enabled Cuba's blacks to acquire education and advance in careers on the basis of merit. Afro-Cubans climbed to notably high ranks within the armed forces. Because of these improvements, the black community in Cuba remained as one of Fidel's most loyal bastions of political support.

The role of women has been another area of significant change. The tradition of *machismo* has proved a major obstacle to the feminist movement. To take a striking example, by mid-1980 only 19 percent of the Communist Party members and applicants for membership were women. Nonetheless, the Federation of

Cuban Women (Federación de Mujeres Cubanas, or FMC) has gone a long way toward changing opinion and behavior. The number of women in higher education and professional schools (especially medicine, where female students now outnumber males) has increased sharply. The FMC was instrumental in getting adopted in 1975 an egalitarian family code which obligated husbands to do half of all family chores. Any viewer of the Cuban film *Portrait of Teresa* knows that this and other feminist goals will not be easily reached in Cuba. Despite the perceptible change in Cuban attitudes, married women, especially those with children, have found it difficult to enter the full-time labor force. One reason is the cost and inconvenience of child care.

Housing was the other basic need that had been so unequally distributed before 1959. Here the revolutionaries had trouble making rapid progress. It was easy enough to expropriate the residences of the wealthy and give them to special groups (like students). But new construction was slower and more expensive. In the short run, investment in new housing was not seen as a top priority.

Ironically enough, one of Cuba's greatest economic failures was in agriculture. In the early years of the Revolution, that was understandable. The guerrillas were eager to repudiate Cuba's longtime bondage to a single export crop. Even after the turn toward economic realism in 1963, food production lagged. According to a United Nations study, Cuba's agricultural performance for 1961–76 was tied with that of Chile for the worst in Latin America. After 1976 farm output grew at a healthy rate, but by the end of the 1990s, there were desperate food shortages.

Although Cuba reached the 1990s without the signs of mass discontent that doomed communism in East Europe, the strain had started to show. In May 1987 the deputy chief of the Cuban air force and a hero of the Bay of Pigs climbed into a plane and defected to Florida. In June 1989 a heavier blow fell. The army's most respected leader, General Arnaldo Ochoa Sánchez, architect of brilliant battlefield victories over South African forces when Cuba fought to consolidate the communist regime in Angola, was tried and executed, along with three other high officers. The charges were drug running and embezzlement. Many asked how officers who had enjoyed Fidel's closest confidence could have organized such a vast conspiracy without the knowledge of a leader who possessed a legendary appetite for administrative detail. Or was this a way of eliminating a potential rival for ultimate power?

A key to the Revolution's survival would be the ability to institutionalize the revolutionary process. The basic challenge was to transform leadership from a tiny elite of guerrilla veterans and party faithful to a growing base of loyal supporters. The most obvious means was to broaden the base of the Communist Party. In 1975 this process began. Under the banner of "popular participation," grassroots elections for regional assemblies were held. Yet by the mid-1990s Cubans were still complaining about a highly centralized, bureaucratized, inefficient state apparatus.

THE CONTEMPORARY SCENE (1990–PRESENT)

After 1990 Cuba underwent a painful reality check as the foreign underpinning of its economy vanished. The collapse of the USSR and of Comecon (the foreign trade authority for the USSR and Eastern Europe) brutally exposed Cuba's economic vulnerability. By 1992 all Russian economic and military aid was gone. Oil shipments fell 86 percent from 1989 to 1992, while food imports dropped 42 percent in almost the same period. Vital equipment, such as buses, once supplied by Eastern Europe, now languished for lack of replacement parts. General economic activity fell by at least 29 percent between 1989 and 1993. Cuba suffered an economic blow greater than any (including the Great Depression) experienced in Latin America in the twentieth century.

Dissolution of the Soviet bloc imposed enormous strains upon the island. It brought a sudden end to Moscow's economic subsidies and, more important, to commercial links with Comecon. Cuba thus faced what analysts called a "double embargo"—one reflecting the longtime policy of the United States, the other resulting from the implosion of the USSR. The demise of the USSR also brought an end to thirty years of Soviet support for Cuba's political sovereignty. Ominous warnings from the Cuban American community in Miami about plans to "retake" the island by force acquired a new sense of plausibility. Isolated by Washington and abandoned by Moscow, Cuba found itself in an extremely vulnerable position.

Fidelista leadership forged a double-edged response. One part was to hunker down: to assert the integrity of the Cuban Revolution, to stress the importance of national unity, and to maintain a commitment to socialist ideals. As a matter of fact, Cuba was virtually the only former member of the Soviet bloc that retained a one-party communist system. The other part involved modest political reforms. Direct elections for the national legislature (Asamblea Nacional del Poder Popular) were introduced in 1992. Procedures for selecting local and provincial representatives were thereafter opened up as well. Restrictions on religious organizations were relaxed, and, in the aftermath of a visit by Pope John Paul II in 1998, the Roman Catholic Church assumed a significant role in national life. In these and other ways, Cuba's leadership made significant efforts to strengthen the legitimacy of the regime.

Tolerance of dissent remained a delicate issue. The regime carefully permitted the existence of a "legal" opposition and allowed writers, artists, and athletes to cultivate international links and travel abroad. Yet it also imposed harsh penalties on the "illegal" opposition that echoed U.S. government demands for "regime change," which, in effect, meant overthrow of the political system. It has been estimated that Cuba holds between 100 and 1000 political prisoners.

A major crisis emerged in 2006, when Fidel Castro underwent an emergency operation for gastrointestinal complications. Could the Revolution survive without its "maximum leader," the only president that it had ever had? Fidel responded by "temporarily" stepping down and handing over power to his deputy and younger brother Raúl. Fidel also assigned key responsibilities to

The Saga of Elián González

Cuba's economic crisis of the early 1990s prompted a large number of Cubans to sail to the Florida coast on improvised vessels or homemade rafts (*balsas*). The crossings led to many deaths and created an immediate humanitarian crisis. In response, the two governments reached an agreement under which Cubans intercepted at sea are sent back to Cuba, while those who make it to American soil are permitted to remain in the United States. This came to be known as the "wet-foot, dry-foot" policy.

This imperfect but workable arrangement came under severe pressure in a highly publicized case involving child custody, political maneuvering, and national pride. In November 1999 a little boy named Elián González, his mother, her boyfriend, and others left Cuba in an aluminum boat. The engine failed amid rough seas, the vessel sank, and most passengers died. The boy and two survivors floated in an inner tube until they were rescued by fishermen and turned over to the U.S. Coast Guard. This was a clear case of "wet-foot" apprehension.

The Immigration and Naturalization Service (INS) temporarily released Elián to his paternal great-uncle, Lázaro González. The boy's father, Juan Miguel González, had in the meantime notified Lázaro by telephone from Cuba that the mother and his son were missing. Backed by Cuban American leaders, however, Lázaro claimed that the boy should stay in the United States—rather than go back to Cuba.

Wrangling followed under the glare of intensive media coverage. Elián's father and both grandmothers came from Cuba to plead for his return. The U.S.-based relatives countered by seeking legal asylum for the boy. A federal judge denied the petition. Miami-Dade County authorities vowed to resist official efforts at repatriation. Elián went to Disney World one day, and met with political figures the next.

Seeking to enforce the court ruling, Attorney General Janet Reno ordered the return of Elián to his father by no later than April 13, 2000. Defiant Miami relatives kept the boy in a house surrounded by protesters and police. A week after the deadline, Reno authorized a raid by SWAT-equipped officers of the U.S. Border Patrol. Onlookers protested and a chaotic melee ensued. Crowds jammed a ten-block area of Miami's Little Havana district, police were deployed in riot gear, and tear gas filled the air.

An obviously happy Elián was reunited with his father but had to remain in the United States while the Miami relatives exhausted their legal options. A circuit court eventually ruled that the relatives lacked the legal standing to seek asylum on his behalf. In June 2000, nearly a half year after the saga began, the U.S. Supreme Court let the circuit court decision stand. Later that same day, Elián González and his father finally returned to Cuba.

Throughout the case, elected U.S. officials from both political parties were attacked for getting involved in what some people regarded as a private family matter. Wrote a columnist in the *Washington Post*: "Elián and Juan Miguel González, son and father. The former is an innocent child, the latter a man whose boy was taken from him. Elián has behaved like a typical 6-year-old, Juan Miguel like a typical father. And most of the politicians like typical fools."

other aspiring leaders, including such young figures as Carlos Lage and Felipe Pérez Roque. And then in February 2008—days before the National Assembly was due to elect the president—Fidel announced that he would not accept another term, and Raúl was duly elected. Although Raúl lacks Fidel's charisma and popular appeal, he expresses a realistic and pragmatic sense of national needs. More to the point, Cuba's political institutions managed to survive a major challenge.

On the positive side, the Soviet departure facilitated the reopening of Cuba's diplomatic relations with nations of the Americas, most of which were either democratic or embarked on paths of democratization. Three nations of the hemisphere—Canada, Mexico, and Venezuela—became especially prominent partners in trade and investment. (It did not escape international notice that Canada and Mexico were founding NAFTA members.) As Hugo Chávez intensified efforts to forge "twenty-first-century socialism," Venezuela began providing Cuba with low-cost oil and abundant foreign exchange in return for the service of thousands of teachers and doctors. Largely as a result of the Chavista subsidies, in fact, Cuba began to register very high rates of growth.

Figure 5.2 offers a broad summation of Cuba's overall economic performance since 1990. The gross domestic product (GDP) dropped sharply at first, plunging to −15 percent in 1993. Thereafter came a decade-long modest recovery, with consistent and positive rates of growth (sometimes over 5 percent). And with strong support from Venezuela, Cuba enjoyed a brief "boom" in 2005–7, as the growth rate exceeded 12 percent in 2006. One way or another, Cuba was managing to navigate its way through this era of uncertainty.

Notwithstanding the end of the Cold War, the United States continued its strident opposition to the Cuban regime. After the Soviet threat disappeared, Washington focused its wrath on the persistence of one-party rule. In October 2003 the George W. Bush administration went so far as to create a shadow

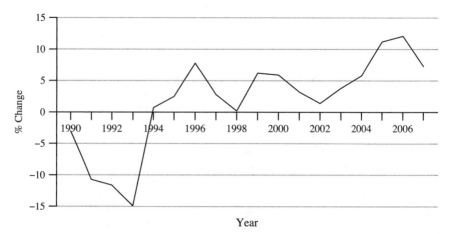

Figure 5.2 Cuba: Annual Percentage Change in GDP, 1990–2007

SOURCE: CEPALSTAT: Latin America and the Caribbean Statistics (http://www.eclac.org/estadisticas/bases/).

government, a so-called Commission for the Assistance of a Free Cuba (CAFC) that was intended to "help prepare the U.S. government to provide effective assistance to a free Cuba" and to step up the enforcement of sanctions. The following year led to a tightening of restrictions on travel and remittances. And in 2007, the CAFC reiterated persistent U.S. official demands for "regime change" in Cuba as a precondition for relaxation of sanctions.

The U.S. embargo remained firmly in place under Bush, but not without increasing controversy. For the seventeenth straight year, the UN General Assembly adopted in October 2008 a nonbinding measure urging termination of the embargo—by a vote of 185-3-2 (Israel and the Pacific island state of Palau sided with the United States in opposition, while Micronesia and the Marshall Islands abstained). American business interests also expressed mounting frustration with the embargo, since it prevented U.S. companies from seizing potentially lucrative opportunities for trade and investment in Cuba—and left the field clear for European and other competitors. Time was running out for Cold War leftover policies.

It was in this atmosphere of uncertainty that Cubans marked the fiftieth anniversary of the Revolution on January 1, 2009. Apart from obligatory displays of posters and flags, the event gave rise to little fanfare. An ailing Fidel did not take part. Plans for an ambitious celebration were toned down in light of major damage from three hurricanes. Raúl Castro led the main gathering in the eastern city of Santiago, praising the regime's survival "despite the unhealthy and vindictive hatred of the powerful neighbor." Effervescent Cuban citizens hugged and kissed and drank on New Year's Day, while children ran and played in the streets. One observer, a reflective middle-aged man, expressed faith in change of leadership— not only in Cuba but also in the United States, with the inauguration of Barack Obama as the U.S. president. "We are hoping and counting on things getting better," he said. Only time would tell if he was right.

6

The Andes
Soldiers, Oligarchs, and Indians

The Andes Mountains define the terms of life in much of South America. With summits approaching 23,000 feet above sea level and with deep interior valleys, this imposing *cordillera* (from the Spanish word for "rope") stretches 4400 miles along the north-south length of the continent. To the west, its snow-capped peaks tower over narrow coastal areas; to the east, they slope through verdant jungles and expansive plains toward the vast Amazon basin. For human settlements, the rugged terrain of the Andes has had a divisive effect: conditions in the highland *sierra* are worlds apart from lowland areas, and communication between the regions has been slow and difficult. This basic reality has led to social, economic, and political fragmentations within all nations embraced by this majestic feat of nature.

We focus here on countries of the central Andes—Bolivia, Peru, and Ecuador.* In precolonial times, these areas were home to large and settled Indian societies under the rule of the Incan empire, centered in the ancient city of Cuzco. Even today, native-speaking Indians make up significant shares of the national populations: about 62 percent in Bolivia, 38 percent in Peru, and 25 percent in Ecuador. Indians live (and have lived) mainly in the highlands, often in tightly knit traditional communities, perpetuating folkways that go back to Inca days. Such facts raise tantalizing questions about the contemporary welfare and status of indigenous peoples. How have Indian communities fared in modern Latin America? Have they done better in some places than others? What might explain the differences?

Racial and ethnic diversity has created complex and fascinating societies within the Andes. Mixed-blood *mestizos* everywhere form the largest single demographic element. Descendants of African slaves make up about 5 percent of the population of Peru and 10 percent in Ecuador. Perceived labor shortages in the nineteenth century brought hundreds of thousands of Chinese laborers to Peru.

---

*We use the term "Central Andes" in a loose sense. Technically speaking, the "central" Andes extend from northern Chile through Bolivia and Peru into southern Ecuador, while the *cordillera* in northern Ecuador is generally considered to belong to the "northern" Andes.

Thereafter, Japanese and Lebanese immigrants further enriched Peruvian society. Indeed, Japanese Peruvians have played a prominent role in recent Peruvian politics, as have those of Lebanese descent in Ecuador.

FROM COLONY TO NATIONHOOD

The Viceroyalty of Peru provided staggering amounts of income for imperial Spain. During the sixteenth century, the mines of Potosí in Upper Peru (what is now Bolivia) produced no less than two-thirds of the world's known output of silver; the city of Potosí, initially created as a highland outpost, was larger than contemporary London. Rich veins were later found in the *sierra* of what is now Peru, further stoking the quest for precious metals. In contrast, colonial Ecuador (under the *audiencia* of Quito) never became a mining center. Instead, it relied on Indian labor for textile production and local agriculture in the highland regions.

Map 6 The Central Andes

The eighteenth century plunged the viceroyalty into a prolonged economic crisis. Bourbon free trade policies led to the displacement of Ecuadorian textiles by inexpensive cloths from Europe; they also eliminated Peru's legal monopoly on commerce with Upper Peru and Chile, as goods could now come overland from Buenos Aires. Silver production went into a slump. Administrative reorganizations further weakened Lima's importance, while the creation of the Viceroyalty of New Granada (present-day Ecuador, Colombia, Panama, and Venezuela) fostered a sense of regional autonomy among local creole elites.

Paradoxically, these negative trends did not produce a widespread independence movement in Peru. Rather, Lima's intellectuals argued for concessions within the colonial framework and for policies that would restore the privileges and prosperity of the pre-Bourbon era. As independence movements were sweeping through the rest of Spanish America, Peru remained a loyalist stronghold of the crown.

Napoleon's invasion of Spain in 1808 and his assumption of monarchical powers sent shock waves through the empire. In the absence of the king, local juntas in Spain resisted the French takeover. In the Viceroyalty of New Granada, the creole-dominated town council (cabildo) of Santafé de Bogotá threw its support to the junta at Seville. In 1809 creole elites in Quito challenged royal power and established their own junta; angered by the viceroy's repressive reaction, creoles promptly began plotting against the Spanish regime. Early in 1810, elites in Caracas and elsewhere removed their colonial governors. Almost everywhere, these movements avowed their loyalty to Ferdinand VII, the Spanish king. Eventually, they would openly assert their independence.

In 1812, Spanish forces inflicted a crushing defeat in Venezuela on pro-independence troops under Simón Bolívar. By mid-1816 all of the more populous regions of New Granada were back under royalist control. Brutal repression during this Spanish "reconquest" merely served to strengthen the insurgents' determination to gain complete independence. Aided by arms and troops from Great Britain, patriots regained the initiative and Bolívar returned to the fray. After the defeat of royalist forces at Boyacá in 1819, insurgent forces took control of most of New Granada.

During the course of his military campaign, Bolívar led a movement to unite Venezuela and Colombia. The Republic of Colombia was proclaimed in 1819. Ecuador joined in 1822. (Much later, this composite state was called "Gran Colombia," or Greater Colombia, to distinguish it from present-day Colombia.) From its inception, the new republic faced two challenges: warding off continuing threats from Spanish forces, and laying the foundations for political order.

Meanwhile, José de San Martín led his troops over the southern Andes from Argentina to Chile. Late in 1820, he reached the coast of Peru. Several months later the Spaniards evacuated Lima, and on July 28, 1821 San Martín proclaimed the independence of Peru. Recognized as the "protector" by the local populace, he made plans to establish a monarchy and commissioned an agent to search for a suitable European prince. This brought opposition from liberals, who wanted a republican form of government, and the project disappeared after San Martín's fateful meeting with Bolívar in late 1822 and subsequent withdrawal from the scene. Bolívar won a decisive victory over imperial forces at the battle of Junín in 1823, and in December 1824 Antonio José Sucre delivered the coup de grâce at Ayacucho. Royalist troops thereafter surrendered, ending Spanish rule in South America.

To foster continental unity, Bolívar proposed a confederation of Peru with Upper Peru and Gran Colombia—under his leadership, of course. In the meantime, creole leaders in Upper Peru decided to establish an independent state. They named it after Bolívar, and invited him to compose its constitution and rule as president. Thus was the state of Bolivia founded. The Liberator proposed an extremely strong executive power—a president for life who, in nominating his vice president, could name his successor.

Smitten by his own creativity, the Liberator regarded his Bolivian constitution as the ideal solution for all of Spanish America and sought to impose it on Gran Colombia. Critics dismissed it as a prescription for monarchy in republican dress. As disagreements mounted, two rival factions emerged: pro-centralist supporters of Bolívar and pro-federalist dissidents who expressed alarm over his authoritarian tendencies. By 1830 Bolívar's health was in rapid decline, and he died in December of that year.

Gran Colombia thus broke apart. It was riven by conflicts between the clergy and university-educated liberal politicians, between the military and those same politicians, between the central government in Bogotá and elites in Venezuela and Ecuador, and between Bolívar and his rivals. By 1831 the confederation fell into its constituent parts—Venezuela, Ecuador, and Colombia. In the meantime, Bolivia and Peru retained their separate claims to national sovereignty. Less than a decade after independence, Spain's former viceroyalty in South America had broken up into nine different republics.

OVERVIEW: ECONOMIC GROWTH AND SOCIAL CHANGE

Cycles of export-led growth have characterized the Andean economies. The rhythms of expansion and decline in exports have varied from country to country, but patterns have been consistent. International trade in agricultural products or natural resources led to growth in specific sectors and enriched those in control of production and commerce. Declines in world prices (often brought by competition from other countries) provoked periodic crises in national economies. As other products proved profitable on the world market, different regions came to prominence. Individual and family wealth rose and fell with upturns and downswings in the export sector. Unable to share these profits, vast sectors of the population remained marginal and poor.

Peru: From Guano to Minerals

Nature bestowed an unusual bonanza on postindependence Peru. For centuries the coldness of the country's offshore waters had attracted large numbers of fish. The fish in turn attracted birds, which left their droppings on islands near the coast.

Atmospheric dryness aided the preservation and calcification of these deposits, known as guano, which had a high concentration of nitrogen. And guano, as the Incas had known, turned out to be a first-class fertilizer.

From 1841 until the 1890s, guano exports fueled the Peruvian economy and created the appearance of prosperity. Since the islands were public property, not private land, national policymakers faced a thorny question: How to take advantage of this virtual monopoly? The answer was a "consignment" system. The government leased out (usually exclusive) exploitation rights to a merchant house or partnership. In return it obtained a fixed share of total sales, rather than a tax on profits. The merchants (usually foreign) received the remaining percentage of sales plus reimbursement for costs. On its face, the strategy involved a mutually beneficial partnership between a liberal state and private enterprise.

But the consignment system placed the state in constant conflict with the merchant houses. The government wanted to sell the guano for as high a price as possible. This could mean holding back on shipments to keep prices up. Merchants were more interested in the total sales volume because they had time-specific contracts; from their standpoint, it was often more profitable to sell large amounts of guano at moderate prices than to sell small amounts at high prices. As a result, state authorities and their consignees constantly bickered.

By the early 1860s, the Peruvian government was earning 80 percent of its revenues from guano. At the same time, about half the government's receipts on guano were destined for payments on loans from English bondholders. The guano boom therefore provided little stimulus for long-run economic development: as historian Fredrick Pike has observed, "The greater the windfall gains became, the less self-sustaining the economy grew." Deposits neared exhaustion by the late 1880s. The "guano age" thus came to an end.

From the 1890s to the 1930s, the Peruvian economy experienced a series of booms (or boomlets) in export products. Prominent among them:

- A rubber boom in the Amazon rainforest. Hard-driving entrepreneurs like Julio C. Arana amassed huge fortunes, and by the turn of the century the city of Iquitos had grown to about 20,000 inhabitants. But then Peru, like Brazil, was eventually pushed out of the market by the more efficiently grown plantation rubber from the Far East.
- Sugar production in the coastal lowlands. This was a profitable operation that required substantial capital investments. Machinery for the modern mills was expensive, and it took large amounts of land to feed sufficient cane to the mills. In contrast to the Caribbean (see Chapter 4), Peruvian production was a year-round activity and required a permanent labor force. Afro-Peruvians, immigrants from China and Japan, and Indians from the *sierra* all came to work in coastal plantations under coercive conditions. Sugar output and exports grew rapidly through the 1920s, though the market collapsed at the end of the decade.

- Cotton, also grown along the coast. Some cotton farmers were small-scale peasants, although the most common labor was sharecropping (*yanaconaje*). Peruvian nationals were the largest investors, as foreign capitalists were reluctant to engage in nonmarket relations of production. By 1930 cotton accounted for 18 percent of Peruvian exports.
- Wool from the Andean highlands, always a secondary export product. Traditional peasants produced the highest-grade variety from the alpaca; sheep wool came from large-scale haciendas. The collapse of the market in the 1920s brought on a recession, especially for sheep raisers.

Meanwhile the once-dominant sector of the Peruvian economy, mining, underwent a shift from precious metals, such as silver and gold, to industrial metals. Copper gained special importance. Large-scale U.S. investment arrived in 1901, with the purchase of a complex at Cerro de Pasco, and production quickly accelerated. Ownership fell almost completely under the control of foreigners, especially from the United States, while migrant *serranos* provided the workers.

Petroleum extraction also expanded in these years, especially during World War I. Coastal fields contained notably high-grade deposits, and U.S. capitalists took active part from the start. In 1913 the International Petroleum Company (IPC), a Canadian-registered subsidiary of Standard Oil, gained access to major fields. By 1930 oil made up about 30 percent of total Peruvian exports.

The Great Depression and World War II altered the structure of international markets and prompted a modest reorientation of the economy. In contrast to their counterparts in Mexico (and Argentina and Brazil, as we shall see), however, Peruvian policymakers did not attempt to embark on a sustained program of import-substitution industrialization. When opportunity beckoned in the later 1940s, they reverted instead to a tried-and-true strategy: export-led growth in cooperation with foreign investment.

Sugar production expanded in the 1960s, as Peru received a share of the U.S. market quota that was taken away from revolutionary Cuba. Cotton production more than doubled between the 1940s and the 1960s, then declined in the face of competition from synthetic fabrics. Copper retained its position as the leading mineral export, although iron ore became important as well. Fishmeal exports underwent a brief surge from the 1950s to the 1970s, later declining as a result of changing ocean currents.

In sum, the Peruvian economy underwent three long cycles of export-led growth. Figure 6.1, showing the volume and value of exports, illustrates the general pattern. The first phase, corresponding to the guano age, stretched from the 1830s through the 1870s. After a period of oscillation, the economy recovered in the 1890s and began a period of expansion that lasted until the Great Depression in the 1930s. The conclusion of World War II reopened international markets and precipitated a third cycle of growth that continued to the mid-1970s, when world prices for agricultural and other commodities went into decline once again.

Silver refining at Cerro de Pasco in the early 1900s featured large-scale technology. (Courtesy of the Library of Congress.)

Figure 6.1 serves to illustrate key features of Peru's economic development. First, the country remained highly dependent on exports as a stimulus to growth. Second, Peru was extremely vulnerable to price swings in the international market and thus to forces beyond its control. Third, twentieth-century Peru created an economy with very few productive links between the capital-intensive "modern" sector, mainly on the coast, and the labor-intensive "traditional" sector, mainly in

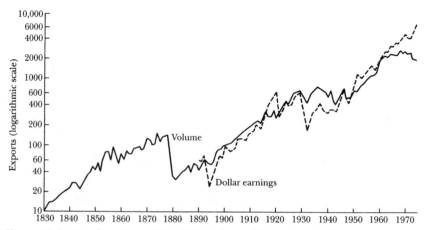

Figure 6.1 Exports from Peru, 1830–1975: Indices of Volume and Dollar Value (1990 = 100)

SOURCE: Rosemary Thorp and Geoffery Bertram, *Peru 1890–1977: Growth and Policy in an Open Economy* (New York: Columbia University Press, 1978), p. 5.

the highlands. And fourth, Peru forged a highly unequal pattern of income distribution. By the 1980s the top 20 percent of the population received 51 percent of the income, while the lowest 20 percent got only 5 percent. (Decades later, the figures were about the same.)

During the late 1970s and 1980s, the most profitable Peruvian export crop was illicit—coca leaves, used for the production of cocaine (in hidden laboratories in Colombia). Cultivated mainly in the Upper Huallaga Valley, the coca leaf harvest came to 200,000 metric tons in the year 1990, equivalent to two-thirds of world production. By this time coca leaf production engaged perhaps 10 percent of the nation's agricultural labor force and 200,000 workers at all stages of production, with a total economic impact of about $1 billion. While this was a major activity, it did not create multimillionaires among the highland *campesinos*. Farmgate prices for coca leaf were actually rather modest; large-scale profits in the drug trade came through wholesale and retail sales in overseas markets, especially Europe and the United States. As the century came to an end, government policies and plant diseases combined to reduce the Peruvian harvest. The slack would be taken up by other countries.

Bolivia: Silver, Tin, and Gas

Bolivia has long been renowned for its mining. During the colonial era, the principal product was silver; by the twentieth century, tin became the leading export. In fact these two minerals tend to appear alongside one another, and a good deal of tin was jettisoned as useless by Spanish imperial overlords. As the Industrial Revolution accelerated in nineteenth-century Europe and North America, how- ever, world demand for tin increased; and with the construction of suitable rail- road lines during the 1890s, the prospects for profitable exploitation became abundantly clear.

Local entrepreneurs seized upon the opportunity. The most prominent was Simón Patiño, a *mestizo* of modest background who started out as a mining apprentice. By 1924 he owned one-half of the nation's production, controlled the European refining of Bolivian tin, and was becoming one of the world's richest men. While Patiño spent much of his life in Europe, the other leading entrepre- neurs, Carlos Aramayo and Mauricio Hochschild, resided primarily in Bolivia.

These three families controlled about 80 percent of Bolivian tin. They formed a close-knit group: along with their retainers, they were nicknamed *la rosca*—"the screw," in a pointed metaphor. Because taxes and fees from tin production formed an important source of national revenue, the mining barons wielded considerable influence over governmental policy. Unlike the silver magnates of the nineteenth century, however, the tin-mine owners did not intervene directly in politics. They relied instead on pressure group tactics, which proved to be highly effective.

Bolivia quickly became one of the world's leading sources of tin. Production climbed from an annual average of nearly 15,000 metric tons in 1900–1909 to 39,000 in the 1940s. The peak individual year was 1929, with an output of more than 47,000 metric tons; by that time Bolivia plus three other countries accounted for 80 percent of the world's tin. As a result of this transformation, La Paz eclipsed Potosí as the financial and service center for the nation's mining sector.

Yet the tin boom led to social tensions and to frequent strikes. Highland Indian peasants provided most of the labor, moving from traditional rural communities into rough-and-ready mining camps. They lived and worked in atrocious conditions. They labored at altitudes of 3000–4000 feet above sea level, descending every day into deep and precarious mine shafts. Illness and injury were commonplace. Women labored alongside the men, bearing equal risks and dangers. "We eat the mines," explained one female worker, "and the mines eat us."

The Great Depression had an especially devastating impact on Bolivia, causing tin prices to plummet from $917 a ton in 1927 to $385 a ton in 1932. In comparison with its leading competitors, Bolivia had the lowest-grade ore and the highest transportation costs and would therefore find it harder to recover. World War II brought a boost in tin prices, but a postwar slump left the nation's economy weak.

And while *la rosca* survived the 1930s and 1940s, its vast holdings were expropriated by the government as a result of Bolivia's Revolution of 1952 (described later). Management of the tin industry passed to the *Corporación Minera de Bolivia* (a.k.a. Comibol), a state-run entity that was controlled in large part by organized labor. As the second-largest tin enterprise in the world, Comibol took fifteen years to bring production back to pre-1952 levels. Even so, tin accounted for more than half of Bolivian exports in 1968. During the 1990s, Bolivia regained its status as the world's fourth-largest source of tin, with most exports heading for Europe and the United States.

Outside of Comibol, small- and medium-size operations continued to seek other metals, such as silver, zinc, antimony, lead, and tungsten. A short-lived "gold rush" in the late 1980s attracted hundreds of cooperatives and thousands of individual prospectors; it was estimated, in fact, that contraband sales were equivalent to 80 percent of legal gold exports. Bolivia's historic mining fever remained alive and well.

Explorations for petroleum began as early as 1916. These operations were nationalized in 1937 under the control of the state-run *Yacimientos Petrolíferos Fiscales de Bolivia* (YPFB)—one year before Mexico's nationalization of oil in 1938. Bolivian production peaked in the early 1970s but declined thereafter. YPFB was privatized in 1996.

More important was the "associated natural gas" typically found in conjunction with petroleum. As proven reserves became significant, Bolivia negotiated the construction of a pipeline to Argentina in 1972. A later agreement with Brazil led to construction of a second pipeline in the 1990s all the way to São Paulo, at a total cost of $2.2 billion. As a result of subsequent discoveries, Bolivia's estimated reserves of natural gas increased exponentially between 1997 and 2003. In 2004 natural gas accounted for 29 percent of all exports. By this time Bolivia was known to possess the second-largest reserves in all of South America. In keeping with the then-prevailing emphasis on privatization, exploitation of the newly discovered reserves was granted to an international consortium of companies from Brazil (Petrobras), Spain (Repsol), and France (Total).

Inevitably, the natural gas bonanza sparked intense political controversy. The location of the reserves, in the department of Santa Cruz and surrounding southeastern areas, provided a harsh reminder of social and economic cleavages between the highlands and the lowlands. Antigovernment critics denounced a wide range of official decisions: the pricing agreements with Argentina and Brazil, the leasing agreements with foreign companies, and tax collections by central authorities. Venting regional frustration with the political preeminence of La Paz, leaders in Santa Cruz mounted insistent campaigns for vaguely defined goals of regional "autonomy."

Generally speaking, the story of Bolivian mining reveals two important differences from the Peruvian experience. First was the predominant role of national investors, rather than foreign companies, most notably in tin production. Second was the economic role of the state. Whereas Peru relied almost exclusively on private enterprise, the government came to perform dominant roles in Bolivia's extractive industries. Through Comibol, YPFB, and other forms of regulation, the state proved to be a major economic actor in Bolivia. As we shall see, the end of this story was nowhere in sight.

As in Peru, coca production had a long and complex history in Bolivia. Originally grown for traditional consumption by highland *campesinos,* coca leaf contributed more than 6 percent of GDP by the late 1980s. Production took place in two principal areas: the Yungas, a high-mountain area with uneven terrain, where it accounted for 35 percent of agricultural production (mainly for local consumption); and the lowland Chapare, where it amounted to more than 90 percent of agricultural output (mainly for export abroad). Ever since the early 1950s, coca leaf growers (known as *cocaleros*) were recognized as a legitimate group of farmers. In the 1980s the *cocaleros* joined a *campesino*-labor alliance organized under the nation's peak labor syndicate. While the international drug trade was illicit, the harvesting of coca leaves was not.

Ecuador: From Cacao to Petroleum

The stimulus for Ecuador's contemporary economic development has come mainly from the coast, rather than the *sierra*. In contrast to Bolivia and Peru, high-altitude mining never took root in this country. Largely as a result, Ecuador played a minor role in Spain's imperial designs.

Independence left the nation with a rural economy of only half a million inhabitants. Labor relations took the form of peonage and sharecropping. Activity focused on cash crops and inexpensive raw materials for the world market. Vulnerable to changing market demands and price fluctuations, Ecuador's economy was subject to uncertainty and instability. These conditions changed little during the remainder of the nineteenth century.

Starting in the 1880s, Ecuador's first commercial boom involved the export of cacao. (The international market expanded greatly at this time, partly because milk chocolate became an item of mass consumption in the United States.) By 1904, Ecuador was the world's largest producer of cacao, accounting for 15–20 percent of world output. Indians and *mestizos* left the highlands to work as wage laborers in the cacao plantations. Grown under natural shade on lowland plantations near the coast, Ecuadorian cacao became famous for the exceptionally high quality of its aromatic "fine" beans.

The coast became the center of the nation's economic activity. Guayaquil dominated banking, commercial, and export-import affairs. Cacao producers built alliances with wealthy merchants who could provide access to international markets and imported goods. Although cacao amounted to 60–70 percent of all Ecuadorian exports, generating labor and income, it provided little stimulus for the national economy as a whole. Instead of promoting infrastructural development, the plantations relied on rivers for transportation and communication. Moreover, the owners preferred to use their profits to purchase imports from abroad, rather than investing in the local economy. As with other commodities in Latin America, cacao production led to the creation of an "enclave" economy.

Around 1915 the cacao bonanza began to falter in the face of competition from West Africa and Brazil, and, more importantly, the appearance of a dreaded plant disease known as the "witch's broom." By the 1930s Ecuador was producing only 7 percent of the world harvest. The industry enjoyed a partial revival in the 1950s as a result of government-sponsored replanting efforts. By 1958 Ecuador was the world's sixth-largest exporter, although its grades were not of the same quality as before, and production was taken over by small-scale planters. Exports remained significant, but not on the scale of earlier years.

Ecuador's second major export boom involved the production of bananas. Because of the dangers of plant disease and the cycles of soil exhaustion, large-scale banana cultivation turned out to be a seminomadic enterprise, as producers were constantly seeking new areas for cultivation. These conditions restricted the industry to large companies with sufficient resources to spread out production over a number of countries. United Fruit was far and away the largest entity, and in 1934—right in the middle of the Great Depression!—UFCO established operations along the Ecuadorian coast, particularly in the coastal areas surrounding Guayaquil. The climate, sun, and soil of this tropical area would amply justify the company's choice of location.

A post–World War II surge in world demand for bananas led to a steep takeoff in production. The government helped by building roads connecting inland growers to the coastal ports; to a much greater degree than cacao, the banana boom fostered national development. By 1960 Ecuador provided 30 percent of total world output, and bananas represented 60 percent of all Ecuadorian exports. The economy grew at a rapid pace, and tariffs increased government revenues. Notwithstanding foreign investment's early role, the actual production of bananas eventually moved into Ecuadorian hands. Workers invaded UFCO lands in 1962, and a series of strikes and mishaps convinced the company to cede direct owner-ship of the plantations to local investors. (UFCO might also have learned some lessons from its experience in Guatemala, described in Chapter 4.) But this did not mean that UFCO disappeared. On the contrary, it remained in control of marketing and distribution. This way the company could avoid the risks of labor agitation and/or plant disease, but still earn profits from overseas sales.

Oil provided the foundation for Ecuador's third export boom. The discovery of petroleum fields in the eastern Amazon region in the late 1960s transformed the country into a world producer of oil and brought large increases in government revenue. The year 1972 saw completion of the trans-Ecuadorian pipeline, extending from the Oriente region to the port city of Esmeraldas. In addition, substantial deposits of natural gas were found in the Gulf of Guayaquil in the 1970s. Largely because of petroleum exports, Ecuador's net foreign exchange earnings climbed from $43 million in 1971 to over $350 million in 1974.

Augmented by OPEC-led increases in international prices, the petroleum boom promoted unprecedented economic growth. Real GDP increased by an average of more than 9 percent per year from 1970 to 1977 (compared with 6 percent for the 1960s). Ecuador became the second-largest petroleum exporter in South America, after Venezuela, and in 2007 crude and refined petroleum products accounted for 58 percent of the nation's total export earnings. At the same time, the oil boom caused severe environmental damage to the Oriente region and posed serious health hazards for the local indigenous population. And as in other nations, petroleum-led development led to massive increases in imports and in foreign debt. As Mexico discovered (Chapter 3), oil was not a magic panacea.

Social Transformations

These processes of economic change led to fundamental alterations in the social structure of the central Andes. Patterns were broadly similar across the three countries, but there were significant variations as well.

At the top was a capitalist elite, though it was by no means monolithic. This was a cosmopolitan group, shrewd and well educated, with its center of action in major cities (Lima, La Paz, Guayaquil). This cadre took a flexible, pragmatic approach to matters at hand, often collaborating with foreign investors and frequently permitting newly rich investors and military officers to join its social circles. In Peru and Ecuador this segment was headquartered along the Pacific coast; in Bolivia, its center of action alternated between La Paz and Santa Cruz.

The *serrano* oligarchy was in general more traditional, in attitudes and insularity. In Ecuador and Peru the provincial *patrón* was bound to the land and maintained an intimate (though hierarchical) relationship with the working *peón*. Over time, however, the preeminence of highland *hacendados* came under intense pressure. In Bolivia, the Revolution of 1952 (described later) led to large-scale land reform and liberated *campesinos* from the oligarchic stranglehold; in Peru, a gradual erosion of elite authority was hastened by the agrarian project of a military government in 1968–75. Many *peones* left the haciendas, looking for jobs either in coastal sugar or cotton plantations or in mountain mining camps. As if in admission of defeat, some frustrated landlords simply turned their lands over to pasture.

Beneath the elite there were people of moderate income, members of middle sectors if not a middle class (in the sense of a cohesive, self-aware social class that emerged in nineteenth-century Europe). Most of these heads of household lived in urban areas, had high school or university-level education, and held white-collar jobs. Large enterprises employed engineers, computer programmers, and technicians. Many aspiring professionals found positions in government—including the military. Bureaucracy, as well as commerce, became the ultimate middle-sector occupation. In Ecuador, most middle-class citizens resided in Guayaquil and Quito; in Bolivia, they emerged in La Paz, Cochabamba, and Santa Cruz; and in Peru, Lima remained the most powerful magnet for ambitious would-be professionals.

And the lower classes, perhaps 80 percent of the Andean population, remained socially heterogeneous. They included the rural proletariat on the sugar and banana plantations, tenant farmers and hired hands in the coffee and cotton fields, and peasants and subsistence farmers in the *sierra*. They were wage earners on fishing boats, miners in the mountains, and organized workers in the cities. They included domestic servants in Quito and Bogotá, coca leaf growers in Peru and Bolivia, and residents of suburban squatter settlements in Lima and La Paz. As native speakers of Aymara and Quechua, many remained on the fringes of national society. This was an expansive stratum, divided along three dimensions: between workers and peasants, between coast and *sierra*, between non-Indian and Indian. Network and family lines often bridged these divisions, however, and the effects of migration reduced once-major geographic gaps.

The exodus from rural to urban areas occurred later in the Andes than in other parts of Latin America, but it has intensified over the past forty years. Over 70 percent of the population of Peru now lives in cities. Approximately 76 percent of the citizens of Ecuador reside in towns or cities, as do 63 percent of the people of Bolivia. Accelerated movement from the countryside to cities has created new social problems—slums, crime, and visible poverty.

The Central Andes: Vital Statistics, 2007

	BOLIVIA	PERU	ECUADOR
Population (millions)	9.5	27.9	13.3
GDP (current $U.S. billions)	13.1	109.1	44.2
GNP/capita ($U.S.)	1260	3450	3080
Poverty rate (% in 2006)	63.9	44.5	39.9
Life expectancy (years)	65	71	75

SOURCES: World Bank and Economic Commission for Latin America and the Caribbean.

Inequality and poverty have been persistent and widespread. During the 1980s, the incomes of more than half of the populations fell below the poverty line. Although those figures have dropped slightly, the absolute number of people living in poverty has increased. Social and economic hierarchies continue to prevail. The persistence of these neocolonial legacies poses intractable questions about the Andean region as a whole. How did political actors address national problems in the aftermath of independence? What were the ways in which indigenous people fought for greater access to land and a better livelihood? What have been the effects of the export-driven models of development? How have political and social movements transformed these countries?

POLITICS AND POLICY: PERU

Peruvian politics in the postindependence era presented a paradoxical scene. Having defeated Spain through the help of outsiders, Peru found it difficult to assert autonomy from neighboring states. The economy was exceedingly weak. Fighting had ravaged landed estates along the coast and in the *sierra*. Commerce remained in depression. The mines were in disrepair. The country's leaders desperately needed money in order to build the new nation, but the treasury was nearly empty. From the 1820s onward, the government began to accumulate a series of foreign debts (mainly to British lenders) that would later prove to be ruinous.

Nor did conditions improve for the Indians, who composed about 70 percent of the total population of approximately 1.5 million. Politicians replaced the traditional tribute, formally abolished with the expulsion of Spain, with the *contribución de indígenas,* a head tax (a flat tax on everyone, regardless of income). Since nineteenth-century liberalism regarded Indians as individuals, not communities, they no longer enjoyed their previous legal protections. Some sought refuge as peones on estates or as workers in mines. Others tried to pass as *mestizos* and find employment in cities and towns.

By 1845, as the guano trade was expanding, Peru came under the rule of Ramón Castilla, its strongest nineteenth-century leader. A military officer, Castilla sought to modernize the country. He organized the first national budget and promoted public works, including the construction of a railroad connecting Lima with the port city of Callao. During a second term in office, Castilla abolished the *contribución de indígenas* and emancipated black slaves. To make up for lost labor, Peru imported 100,000 Chinese coolies and Polynesians as indentured workers from the mid-1850s to the mid-1870s. A builder of institutions, Castilla also encouraged military professionalization and public education.

The nation's spiraling debt posed insoluble problems for subsequent presidents. Under José Balta (1868–72), the government turned over the foreign debt to the Parisian firm of Adolfo Dreyfus; in exchange, Dreyfus took over the management of guano consignments. The deal might have made economic sense; for many Peruvians, however, it represented an unacceptable forfeiture of the national patrimony. Partly for this reason, President Manuel Pardo (1872–76) responded to

---

The War of the Pacific

As nitrate production expanded in the 1870s, Chilean mine owners coveted the rich reserves owned by Bolivia and Peru. In 1879, Chilean investors refused to pay new taxes on Bolivian nitrate reserves. In retaliation, Bolivian president Hilarión Daza (1876–79) ordered the seizure of Chilean-owned nitrate operations in Antofagasta, Bolivia. Chile sent in troops to occupy the region. After some hesitation, the Peruvian government decided to honor an 1873 alliance with Bolivia and join the war.

Thus began the War of the Pacific (1879–83), pitting Peru and Bolivia against Chile. Chile won a stunning military victory and occupied Lima. In the ensuing peace treaty, Bolivia lost its province on the coast. Chile gained outright control of the nitrate-rich Peruvian province of Tarapacá, including the city of Iquique; and it was to keep control of Tacna and Arica for ten years, their subsequent fate to be decided by a plebiscite.

The War of the Pacific had far-reaching effects on all three countries. For Chile, it ushered in a nitrate boom and boosted national confidence. For Bolivia, it denied access to the sea. For Peru, it was a humiliating defeat, which discredited the politicians and accelerated the decline of the economy. It was a failure for Bolivia and Peru in every conceivable way.

---

this sentiment by nationalizing the country's nitrate fields. Alas, that gesture would come undone in the War of the Pacific.

In the wake of this calamitous defeat, Peru managed to produce a new class of civilian leaders who resembled the *científicos* in Mexico. Highly educated, neopositivistic by training, and liberal by outlook, they comprised a curious breed: for lack of a better phrase, they might be classified as aristocratic technocrats. Their initial spokesman was Nicolás de Piérola, who, as a brash young treasury minister, had negotiated the controversial Dreyfus contract of 1869. After forming the Democratic Party, Piérola became president in 1895. Eager to reinvigorate export-led expansion, he moved to strengthen Peru's credit rating. He tightened tax legislation and increased duties on commerce, which led to a doubling of government income during his four-year term. He also established a ministry of development to assist local entrepreneurs and facilitate governmental participation in economic growth.

After Piérola stepped down, Peruvian politics entered an era of "bossism" known as *gamonalismo*. Effective competition for power was restricted to the upper-class elite. Elections took place but ballots were not secret, so landowners could herd their workers and peones to the polls and monitor their votes. *Hacendados* from the *sierra* had themselves elected to the national Congress, where they customarily supported the president—in exchange for unchecked local power. Meantime, the coastal elite, consolidating its control of economic policy, pursued the path of export-led growth.

As the twentieth century opened, an urban working class began to assert its interests through collective action, including serious protests against inflation in 1911. In this context, Guillermo Billinghurst, a naïve and erratic populist, triumphed in the 1912 elections. A proponent of enlightened capitalism, Billinghurst demonstrated his sympathy with the workers by supporting public housing, an eight-hour day, and collective bargaining. When he encouraged street demonstrations in support of his policies, however, the elite closed ranks against him. A coup deposed him in 1914.

Power reverted to civilian technocrats under José Pardo, a moderate reformer. In January 1919, as labor protests erupted in Buenos Aires, Santiago, and São Paulo, workers in Lima-Callao proclaimed a three-day general strike. With support from university students, they demanded lower food prices, an eight-hour day, and enactment of other legislation. A hesitant Pardo eventually called out the army to disperse the workers, and in the wake of the violence, he acceded in part to their demands.

In the midst of resulting confusion, Augusto B. Leguía won the 1919 election. Eager for absolute rule, he staged a coup prior to his own inauguration and seized the national palace, sent Pardo off to exile, dissolved the legislature, and ensconced himself in power. Thus began Leguía's dictatorship, a watershed remembered throughout Peru as the *oncenio,* or eleven-year rule. A pliant constitutional assembly devised a charter that legitimized Leguía's authority and prescribed a strong state role in the economy. To construct the "new fatherland," Leguía undertook a vigorous program of public works and promoted foreign investment. He also moved aggressively to silence his critics, dismissing dissident professors from university chairs and turning against students, among them a young leader by the name of Víctor Raúl Haya de la Torre.

In foreign affairs, Leguía settled in 1927 a long-standing boundary dispute with Colombia. Two years later, in 1929, he reached an agreement with Chile: the northern province of Tacna would go to Peru, and Arica would remain under Chile's control. The War of the Pacific, so catastrophic for Peru, finally reached the end of its diplomatic coda. Within this carefully constructed political environment, Leguía had no trouble getting reelected in 1924 and 1929. He seemed invincible.

Flirting with Policy Alternatives

As in other parts of Latin America, the Great Depression prompted military intervention. In August 1930 a young army officer, Luis M. Sánchez Cerro, became head of an interim junta. A man of modest background, he brought a distinctive touch to the executive office, seeking to build a populist coalition between disgruntled upper-class elements and the working masses. In 1931 he became a formal candidate in upcoming elections. His principal opponent was Víctor Raúl Haya de la Torre, the erstwhile student agitator and now leader of the Alianza Popular Revolucionaria Americana (American Revolutionary Alliance Party, APRA), an organization that would become the most durable political party in the nation's history.

¡SOLO EL APRISM(
SALVARA AL PERU

OTE PO?
HAYA DE LA TORRE

An *Aprista* election poster expresses both the party's outlook and the intensity of the 1931 campaign; the slogans say "Only *Aprismo* will save Peru . . . vote for Haya de la Torre." (Private collection.)

The 1931 campaign proved to a fateful event. Sánchez Cerro called for agrarian reform, rural extension programs, and assimilation of the Indians. Haya de la Torre countered by stressing the evils of imperialism and the injustice of social inequities. It was an intense campaign, marked by violence and mutual accusations. Although APRA received ample support, Sánchez Cerro emerged as the victor.

Polarization ensued. In 1932 a fanatical young *aprista* tried to assassinate Sánchez Cerro. APRA partisans organized an insurrection in the provincial city of Trujillo, which led to the arrival of a heavily armed military column. As panicky *apristas* fled the premises, they executed army officers, policemen, and other hostages. When the government troops discovered this atrocity, they summarily executed at least a thousand local residents suspected of supporting the insurgents. This set the tone for APRA-army relations thereafter and convinced many officers that they must never let APRA come to power. This determination gained strength the following year, when another *aprista* gunman succeeded in killing Sánchez Cerro.

Beset by crisis, Congress elected General Oscar R. Benavides to serve out the remainder of the presidential term. As Benavides took office, Peru entered a transitional phase that held out the possibility of reducing the country's dependence on international markets and investments. Exports started to recover. Foreign capital beat a steady retreat. Local entrepreneurs, sometimes with government help, gained partial control of some mineral resources. Petroleum output went up. Industrial capacity was modest but growing. It appeared that Peru was now in a position to redirect its economy.

Benavides attempted to seize the opportunity. In 1934 his administration began the state-directed development of petroleum. Trade doubled from 1933 to 1936, while the national currency (the *sol*) remained stable. The government actively promoted public works and social projects, including road construction, working-class housing, and a compulsory social security system. Benavides also supported an agricultural bank to give credit to cotton planters and other land-owners, thus reducing the role of foreign merchant houses.

The presidency then passed to moderate civilians, Manuel Prado and José Luis Bustamante y Rivero, both of whom governed with *aprista* support. In tandem, they furthered the modest reorientation of the Peruvian economy away from excessive reliance on international markets. They increased government spending and established controls on imports and foreign exchange. They launched a scheme for a state-controlled iron and steel plant. They sought to diversify agriculture and challenged the coastal sugar barons, requiring them to meet domestic-market quotas before exporting to overseas markets. Amid public controversy, Bustamante approved a contract giving IPC permission to search for oil in the Sechura Desert. Taking advantage of a nationalist outcry over this decision, the coastal elite engineered a military coup against the government in 1948.

Once in office, General Manuel A. Odría promptly restored the country's traditional export-led growth model. Orthodox economic policies encouraged foreign investment and restricted governmental intervention. Odría consolidated his position by winning the 1950 elections—there was no opposition—and proceeded to tighten his hold on power. Much in the manner of Argentina's Juan Perón, he courted working-class masses, lavished funds on ostentatious public works, and developed a personalistic following. With the aid of his wife, María Delgado de Odría, he mobilized women in support of the regime, extending suffrage to females in 1955. He harassed and imprisoned opponents, especially *apristas*. As civilian oligarchs expressed apprehension over his capricious form of rule, Odría finally consented to free elections in 1956.

The leading contenders were former president Manuel Prado, supported by APRA, and a political newcomer named Fernando Belaúnde Terry, candidate of the National Front of Democratic Youth. Belaúnde, a University of Texas–trained architect, articulated the hopes and frustrations of the educated middle sectors. After winning the election, Prado brought in a period of political liberalization, permitting trade-union organization and allowing communists as well as *apristas* to operate freely. He proclaimed a program for "shelter and land" *(techo y tierra)* in the name of the peasants, but did little about it.

The next presidential election, in 1962, offered a clear picture of political forces. Candidates included Haya de la Torre, able at last to run on the *aprista* platform; Belaúnde, representing a new organization called Acción Popular; and the always hopeful Odría. Haya won the most votes, with 33 percent of the total, but the military annulled the results in order to forestall a possible *aprista* presidency. Elections the following year produced a more acceptable result: victory for Belaúnde. (The rules of this electoral game thus became clear: *apristas* could run, but they were not allowed to win.)

Belaúnde revealed himself to be an appealing, charismatic politician. An avid proponent of U.S. president John F. Kennedy's Alliance for Progress, he proposed construction of a trans-Amazon highway, invoked the memories of Incan power, and urged fellow citizens to aspire to national greatness again. On a more practical level, he sought to increase the role of the state, expand social services, encourage manufacturing, and undertake agrarian reform. After a hostile Congress emasculated his land reform bill, however, peasants in the sierra reacted angrily by invading haciendas and taking over lands. As conflict raged throughout the *sierra,* a Cuban-style guerrilla movement began using violent tactics in order to spark a countrywide revolution. In spite (or because) of his reformist leanings, Belaúnde responded with force. In a vicious campaign, the army killed and jailed thousands of highland peasants. The repression formed a traumatic experience for both the *campesinos* and the soldiers.

One of Belaúnde's other promises was to resolve a long-lasting dispute with the IPC. He faced a no-win situation. After five years of protracted negotiations, marked by constant hostility from the U.S. authorities, IPC gained access to new fields in the Amazon, and the Peruvian government agreed to sell crude oil to IPC at a fixed price for refining at the company's complex. Opponents accused Belaúnde of selling out national interests. As criticism swelled, Belaúnde's optimistic vision of a united and prosperous Peru proved illusory. Military officers once again sent their tanks to the presidential palace.

The Military Revolution

The 1968 coup paved the way for one of Latin America's most ambitious military governments. Led by General Juan Velasco Alvarado, the junta declared its intention to bring far-reaching changes in the structure of Peruvian society. What Peru needed, the officers proclaimed, was a new economic order, "neither capitalist nor communist," a system that would abolish prevailing inequities and create the material foundations for harmony, justice, and dignity.

Three qualities set this regime apart from other episodes of military rule. One was its social and political autonomy. The Peruvian armed forces acted alone, rather than in collusion with civilian power groups. Second, the leaders of the regime adopted the outlook and premises of the "dependency" school of analysis, seeking to end what they called "the subordination of the Peruvian economy to foreign centers of decision." Third, largely because of its experience with antiguerrilla campaigns in the *sierra*, the Peruvian military exuded genuine sympathy with the plight of the long-oppressed peasantry. The result was a revolutionary military regime.

A key to the government's program was agrarian reform. In mid-1969 the Velasco regime announced the most sweeping land reform program in Latin America since the Cuban Revolution. All large estates, regardless of productivity, were subject to expropriation. The highly mechanized sugar plantations of the coast came under the administration of worker-run cooperatives. By the mid-1970s, three-quarters of the country's productive land was under cooperative management of one sort or another. Many of the huge estates that had dominated the Peruvian agrarian sector disappeared.

To consolidate its reforms, the Velasco regime created the National System for Support of Social Mobilization (*Sistema Nacional en Apoyo de la Movilización Social,* or SINAMOS). Sometimes written as two words—*sin amos,* "without masters"—it was to serve as the integrating institution for peasant and working-class groups. It linked the regime with the masses, identified the government with its constituent groups, and promoted a harmonious set of leader-follower relationships. This desire to organize and mobilize the peasantry became one of the government's hallmarks.

A second priority was the sprawling squatter shantytowns around Lima and other cities. Military officers organized the settlements, renamed "young towns" *(pueblos jóvenes),* and enlisted the aid of the church in their efforts. Part of the solution was simple enough: the granting of property titles to the migrant occupants. Another tactic was bringing the *pueblos jóvenes* under the umbrella structure of SINAMOS and thus promote stability. By 1974 the majority of urban squatters had been reorganized from above into state-chartered *pueblos jóvenes.*

This top-down pattern of organization and mobilization revealed a crucial feature of the Velasco regime. It was not attempting to construct a socialist society, as did Fidel Castro in Cuba. Nor was it seeking to exclude and repress already organized working-class movements, as would military governments in Chile, Brazil, and Argentina. Instead, the Peruvian regime was intent on integrating marginal urban and rural masses into the national society in order to lay the groundwork for industrialization and autonomous development. In this sense the Peruvian regime emerged as a quintessential corporate state, reminiscent of the Cárdenas government in Mexico (1934–40).

In addition, the regime took aggressive measures to reduce the role of foreign capital. Soon after the coup, the regime announced the nationalization of IPC and the establishment of the state-supported *Petroperú.* In time the government took over other prominent foreign-owned firms: ITT (1969), Chase Manhattan Bank (1970), Cerro de Pasco (1974), and Marcona Mining (1975)—the latter two replaced by *Minoperú.* These actions met with predictable hostility from the United States, but in February 1974 the two governments reached an accord. Peru paid $150 million as full settlement of all outstanding claims and the Nixon administration withdrew its opposition against international loans to Peru.

Despite its populist stance, the Velasco government met with considerable resistance at home. Preexisting labor unions, such as the *aprista*-dominated organizations among sugar workers, resented the inroads on their terrain. Peasants often found the top-down institutions unresponsive to their demands and began to stage protests. Traditional elites voiced their horror at the regime's policies. In response, the generals seized control of newspapers and television and radio stations, while six other dailies in Lima came under pro-government management. This compounded the government's problem, as intellectuals and journalists denounced restrictions on freedom of speech.

Economic conditions added to governmental woes. Export earnings declined, petroleum explorations yielded no new oil deposits, and world prices for sugar and copper dropped. The balance of payments deteriorated, the foreign debt swelled, and inflation struck. Workers began to demonstrate their discontent. As these problems first loomed on the horizon, Velasco himself succumbed to ill health. In August 1975 Peru's joint chiefs replaced him with General Francisco Morales Bermúdez. Under pressure from the IMF, the government imposed an extremely harsh economic austerity program that reduced the real income of the urban working class by 40 percent. Further, Morales Bermúdez unveiled plans to convene a constitutional assembly in 1978 and hold general elections in 1980. The officers were getting out.

In retrospect, the Velasco regime failed to gain solid support from any social class or grouping and, thereby, establish institutional foundations for its authority. By reaching into so many areas of Peruvian society, the military government succeeded in alienating almost everyone. No group felt safe from intervention or control; no stratum offered its unconditional adherence. Ironically, the feature which had given Peru's revolutionary military government so much freedom of action—its autonomy—also led to its eventual demise.

Struggles of Civilian Governments

For the 1980 general elections the top two parties were APRA, whose ticket was now led by Armando Villanueva (Haya de la Torre having died), and Acción Popular, still under Fernando Belaúnde Terry. After an arduous campaign, Belaúnde captured a commanding plurality with 42 percent of the vote. Chastened by his earlier experience with far-reaching reform, the statesman-like Belaúnde now espoused centrist policies: reducing the role of the state, strengthening private enterprise, and encouraging foreign investment. His economic team had close ties to international banking circles, and its pro-free-market orientation helped to renegotiate the foreign debt and attract foreign capital. An unusual surge of optimism spread throughout much of Peru.

Insurmountable problems then arose. By far the most serious was the debt crisis triggered by Mexico's near-default in 1982, a shock that was greatly amplified by the 1981–83 world recession. After modest growth in 1982, the Peruvian economy contracted by 12 percent in 1983. This was a crushing blow.

Economic uncertainty and social injustice provided a fertile environment for revolutionary activity. Around 1980 a movement known as *Sendero Luminoso*

("Shining Path") emerged in the impoverished highland province of Ayacucho. Combining ideological indoctrination with physical intimidation, these guerrillas burst onto the scene by assassinating village leaders who resisted their call to smash authority and establish an egalitarian utopia. Mounting *Sendero* violence forced Belaúnde to authorize a military offensive, which left its own legacy of repression and helped Sendero spread its influence. Around 1984 another group, the *Movimiento Revolucionario Túpac Amaru* (MRTA), also began high-profile operations. More in the classic mold of revolutionary movements, the MRTA hailed the Cuban Revolution and used kidnapping and ransom—rather than violence—to attract attention and to accumulate resources. As guerrilla activity intensified, Peru fell into a state of near civil war.

Despite these problems, Belaúnde managed to serve out his term in office, and in 1985 the electorate chose as his successor Alan García, a thirty-six-year-old newcomer from APRA. With his party in control of Congress, García moved swiftly on the economic front. He increased real wages, slashed taxes, reduced interest rates, froze prices, and devalued the *sol*. The net effect was greater demand, which the García team hoped would activate Peru's dormant industrial capacity. The government announced investment programs for agricultural development in the long-neglected highlands and, in defiance of the international community, proclaimed a default on Peru's external debt. This was an enormous gamble.

It did not pay off. García's "heterodox" economic policies produced a short-lived economic boom soon followed by collapse. A mushrooming trade deficit rapidly exhausted foreign exchange reserves. International credit and investment withdrew in the face of the debt default. Violent strikes paralyzed many areas of economic activity. An economic "shock" program in 1988 proved disastrous, and massive unemployment drove millions of Peruvians into the illegal or "informal" economy. Amid skyrocketing hyperinflation, the gross domestic product plunged more than 30 percent in three years. The country was teetering on the verge of collapse.

As the 1990 elections approached, a new savior seemed ready to rescue Peru from its doldrums—the internationally acclaimed novelist Mario Vargas Llosa. A series of gaffes and miscalculations by Vargas Llosa gradually squandered his lead, however, and he eventually lost to Alberto Fujimori, a little-known agrarian economist born of Japanese immigrant parents. A quintessentially antiestablishment candidate, Fujimori used Cambio 90, an ad hoc organization rather than a political party, to build electoral support. Projecting himself as a man of the people, Fujimori vowed to improve their economic plight.

It did not take long for him to break these promises. Instead of a populist program, Fujimori's technocrats launched a radical restructuring program. They slashed tariffs, welcomed foreign investment, and undermined the role of organized labor. These measures controlled hyperinflation, and Peru resumed payments on the foreign debt. With moral and financial encouragement from Japan, where Fujimori cultivated special ties because of his personal ancestry, Peru resumed a path of strong (if not steady) economic growth.

Fujimori's Limited Democracy

Annoyed by dissidence and eager to maintain the offensive, Fujimori suddenly shut down the Congress in April 1992 and announced a sweeping reorganization of the judiciary. In effect he struck down his own government in what became known as an *auto-golpe,* or "auto-coup," made possible because of solid military backing. Peru thus became the first South American country of the 1990s to slip back toward authoritarianism.

Behind this striking development, as both cause and consequence, was a progressive weakening of Peru's traditional institutions. Political parties (especially APRA) lost credibility because of their patent incompetence and occasional corruption. Labor unions retained little influence. Universities lost vigor and vitality. Against this vacuum Fujimori built his own power base in the armed forces and the intelligence services. He also clamped down on the press, as state-owned media became blatantly pro-government and official intimidation pressured many other journalists into self-censorship.

Conspicuous success followed the *auto-golpe.* Government forces arrested the top leader of the MRTA. A few months later, Abimael Guzmán, the founder and maximum leader of Sendero Luminoso, was captured, imprisoned, and theatrically put on display for the press. More arrests of high-level Sendero leaders followed, and the movement started to disintegrate. Many Peruvians applauded Fujimori's decisive leadership. Riding this tide of popularity, Fujimori won the 1995 election with 64 percent of the vote.

As the 1990s came to a close, Fujimori laid the groundwork for yet another presidential term. In 1998 the Supreme Court ruled that Fujimori would be legally entitled to run once again, since it would be his first reelection under the constitution of 1993. Even so, the long-embattled opposition was showing signs of life. Dissatisfaction with Fujimori was growing over Peru's economic performance, which was not helping workers or the lower middle classes, and over the president's high-handed abuse of power. Fujimori continued to cultivate support, however, particularly among long-neglected peasants and among middle-class women. As the election drew near, a Fujimori victory appeared to be a foregone conclusion.

Suddenly there emerged an upstart candidate, Alejandro Toledo, a U.S.-educated economist whose come-from-nowhere campaign was reminiscent of Fujimori's own meteoric rise in 1990. By winning more than 40 percent of the vote in the April 2000 contest, Toledo denied a majority to the president and forced a second ballot. Then, with little warning, Toledo withdrew from the race in protest against what he claimed would be electoral fraud. Fujimori resolutely prepared to take office, but then a bombshell struck: a tape was released to the public showing Vladimiro Montesinos, Fujimori's top adviser and intelligence official, bribing an opposition congressman to join the Fujimori coalition. The public outcry was deafening. Montesinos and Fujimori were hopelessly exposed. Late in November 2000, while on a visit to East Asia, Fujimori resigned from the presidency and sought asylum in Japan. His carefully controlled democracy came to an unexpected end.

The Contemporary Scene (2000–present)

A caretaker government oversaw free and fair elections in 2001. In a second-round runoff (against former president Alan García), Alejandro Toledo emerged as a clear winner with 54 percent of the votes. Electoral democracy was back, but governing was difficult. One reason was the congenital weakness of the party system in Peru, characterized by numerous parties with fickle followings. Toledo's own party, Perú Posible, was internally divided by constant bickering and held only 40 percent of the seats in Congress. To secure passage of legislation, Toledo therefore had to forge ad hoc alliances with a bewildering array of opposition parties.

Economics posed another problem. Like other politicians, Toledo found it impossible to live up to his campaign promises about employment, growth, and safety nets for the poor. He saw little alternative to free-market economics. In 2002 Toledo went ahead with the privatization of two electricity companies, which provoked three days of violent protest. The government then backed down and reversed its decision. This sent a fatal sign of political weakness. Capitulation to protest would become a hallmark of this government.

There were personal issues as well. After prolonged denials, Toledo acknowledged that he had an illegitimate daughter. As is so often the case, the problem lay not in the truth—but in the attempted cover-ups. His wife, a Belgian-born anthropologist named Elaine Karp, also annoyed many Peruvians, especially members of the elite, because of her outspoken comments about the persistence of social injustice. Predictably enough, she was both praised and denounced as "the Hillary Clinton" of Peru.

The 2006 elections pitted the indefatigable Alan García against Ollanta Humala, a left-leaning nationalist and army colonel who had led an unsuccessful military uprising against Fujimori in October 2000. (The Congress pardoned him after Fujimori's downfall.) Humala outpolled García in the first round with 31 percent to 24 percent. During the runoff campaign, Venezuelan president Hugo Chávez proclaimed his support for Humala, which provoked a ferocious backlash against the idea of foreign—especially *chavista*—intrusion in national affairs (see Chapter 8). For his part, García insisted (without any sense of irony!) that he alone possessed the stature to negotiate successfully with international economic organizations. In the end, García won 53 percent of the popular vote, although exit polls suggested that he was seen mainly as "the lesser of two evils." A resounding mandate this was not.

POLITICS AND POLICY: BOLIVIA

Although some radical creoles and *mestizos* clamored for independence in 1809, elite society in Upper Peru was hesitant to align with rebel forces. In their repeated attempts to invade the highland areas, insurgent armies sought support from local Indians with promises to terminate forced labor, abolish taxes, and redistribute land. Such overtures intensified creole fears that independence from Spain might upset a well-established social and economic hierarchy. For the next sixteen years, civil war enveloped the region.

As in Peru, the economy of the newly founded republic was in shambles. Thousands of mines had been flooded. Owners lacked the capital to renew production, while the collapse of the forced labor system *(mita)* created a scarcity of workers. Agricultural production stagnated as well. Indigenous communities retained age-old traditions, living on community land and producing only for local markets. At least 80 percent of the inhabitants spoke Quechua or Aymara as a main language. Formerly one of the wealthiest regions of the Spanish empire, Bolivia was suffering from profound economic malaise.

As the nation's first president, José Antonio Sucre (1825–28) attempted to construct a liberal state and reinvigorate prosperity. With declining revenues from silver production and a standing army that consumed almost one-half of governmental expenditures, his administration decided to replace the recently abolished Indian tribute with a head tax on the indigenous population. Between 1835 and 1865, this *contribución de indígenas* provided a constant revenue stream that covered 40 percent of state expenses. Sucre also weakened the church by confiscating its properties. His successor, Andrés de Santa Cruz (1829–39), sought to achieve one of Bolívar's goals by establishing a confederation with Peru. Threatened by this potentially powerful alliance, Chile declared war on this would-be confederation. Although Santa Cruz won some initial victories, the Chilean army soundly defeated Bolivia and Peru. He went into exile in 1839.

Political instability ensued over the next three decades. In contrast to his predecessors, Manuel Isador Belzú (1848–55) was the first president to appeal directly to lower-class urban *mestizos* (especially artisans) and peasants. He encouraged domestic production by raising tariffs on imported cloths. He closed foreign warehouses and declared that only Bolivians could engage in internal trade. To increase state revenues, he established a state monopoly on the export of *chinchona* bark (used for quinine, an antifever agent employed especially against malaria). He also voluntarily retired from office, the first president to do so since Sucre.

Another prominent president, Mariano Melgarejo (1864–71), oversaw legislation in 1866 that gave the state the power to confiscate all Indian community land. Those who worked individual plots had to register title to their land within sixty days and pay a sum of 25 to 100 pesos. If they failed to do so, the state would put their land up for public auction. Many Indians did not have the cash to pay the required fees. Others lost their land through fraud. The beneficiaries of this dubious statute included wealthy landholders who enlarged their haciendas, medium-sized landowners who purchased more property, merchants with available capital, and urban investors who used the land as a source of income or as collateral for minor mining investments. In response to this legislation, a series of indigenous rebellions broke out. Although Melgarejo brutally crushed these uprisings, he was subsequently forced to reverse some of the land confiscations.

In foreign affairs, Melgarejo entered into dubious international agreements. Opponents charged that they favored only the personal financial interests of the president, rather than Bolivia. In 1866, he signed a treaty that recognized Chilean territorial claims to the nitrate-rich Mejilones region of the Atacama Desert. In 1868, he ceded 40,000 square miles to Brazil in the Amazonian region. Melgarejo arranged free trade agreements with Chile and Peru that hurt the Bolivian economy, and gave up guano extraction rights along the Pacific coast. He was finally overthrown in 1870, when an alliance of creole oppositional leaders and altiplano Indians forced him to flee the country.

As noted earlier, the War of the Pacific had utterly disastrous consequences for Bolivia. It also led to the displacement of the military *caudillos* who had dominated politics since independence. Organized through the Conservative Party, oligarchic mining interests swiftly moved into this vacuum. They continued free trade policies, improved transportation, and developed the eastern lowland frontier region through state land sales to speculators and settlers. Government subsidies and international financing provided the necessary capital to construct railway lines that could move minerals to the Pacific port of Antofagasta, Chile (formerly Bolivia). An upturn in silver production and new road construction expanded internal markets. Moreover, Bolivia took advantage of the international rubber boom by encouraging exports from its Amazonian territory of Acre.

Indian lands remained a troublesome issue. Conservatives repeated the commonplace arguments that Indian community land should be broken up into individually owned plots, and governments continued the initiatives begun by Melgarejo a decade before. Many Indians were forced to sell the land they had worked. With landless Indians in their employ, hacienda owners increased both their holdings and production. Indians once again rebelled against these measures. In 1899 under the leadership of Zárare Willka, and with support from the Liberal Party, indigenous communities of the altiplano defeated a Conservative-led national army. Willka then turned against his allies, massacred a detachment of Liberal soldiers, and declared a race war on all whites. Horrified by this development, Liberals and Conservatives quickly joined forces and defeated the rebels.

As a collapse in international silver prices weakened the Conservatives, demands by the Liberals to move the national capital from Sucre to La Paz intensified conflict between the two parties. In 1900 Liberals wrested political control of the country from the silver oligarchy. At the same time, tin mining was emerging as Bolivia's major export. Some silver barons quickly adapted to the new export mineral, while others saw their fortunes decline. It was not long before a new and close-knit mining oligarchy took hold—*la rosca,* under the patriarchal leadership of Simon I. Patiño.

Despite the importance of mining, the vast majority of the Indian population remained in agriculture. Liberal Party promises to stop land usurpation did not prevent the transfer of property to non-Indians. By the 1920s Indians retained only one-third of the land of the highlands, while *hacendados* controlled the other two-thirds. Indigenous frustrations about the loss of access to land would spark new rebellions in the 1940s and 1950s.

The increasingly autocratic rule of Liberal Party politicians provoked a split in their ranks and the formation of the dissident Republican Union that came to power from 1920 to 1934. By breaking up a two-party monopoly, Republican rule opened the system to multiparty groupings. Although the sale of Indian community lands virtually ceased under Republican administrations, the government continued to put down indigenous rebellions, such as the 1927 Chayanta uprising, one of the largest Indian revolts in the twentieth century, by brute force. The Chayanta insurrection against owners of large haciendas began in southern Bolivia and quickly spread to nine provinces, involving over 10,000 rebels. Historian Eric D. Langer has noted that "although the revolt was suppressed, it effectively halted the expansion of the hacienda onto Indian community lands and prompted the government to replace corrupt local officials."

In Bolivia, as elsewhere, the Great Depression had a decisive impact on politics. In this particular case, the economic crisis helped lead the government into an expensive war.

The Chaco War (1932–35)

Border skirmishes between Bolivian and Paraguayan forces over the Chaco region in the eastern Bolivian lowlands had broken out in the 1920s. The discovery of oil in the Andean foothills in 1928 raised the possibility that further exploration might find reserves in the lowlands to the east. In 1932, Bolivian president Daniel Salamanca (1931–34) ordered troops to occupy a Paraguayan garrison, and war broke out between the two countries.

Opponents claimed that the conflict was a cynical effort to distract attention away from the country's economic crisis. Bolivian soldiers from the highlands were poorly supplied and did not easily adapt to the tropical lowland climate. The army's conventional fighting strategy also proved ineffective against the guerrilla tactics of the less numerous but more seasoned Paraguayan forces. Thousands of soldiers on both sides died in the war, mostly due to diseases such as malaria. Bolivia lost 65,000 young men, a significant number in a total population of only 2 million. In the peace treaty, Bolivia lost the Chaco Boreal region (which ended up not containing oil reserves), but retained territories that in fact held a rich supply of oil and natural gas.

The Chaco war had long-term implications. First, the conscription of highland Indians into the Bolivian army hastened the integration of traditional communities into the national society. No longer isolated in remote villages, indigenous soldiers acquired a new sense of perspective (and grievance). Second, the military defeat discredited the traditional parties and provoked a widespread desire for change.

Youthful generals responded to this clamor by seizing power and implementing populist reforms that led them to be called "military socialists." David Toro (1936–38) established a Ministry of Labor and nationalized Standard Oil of Bolivia, which had controlled the nation's oil production. The constitution of 1938 granted the government a more active role in the economy. Even so, it retained literacy requirements that restricted political participation to the small Hispanicized upper and middle classes. As a result, less than 50,000 people were eligible to vote in national elections.

Leftwing and labor forces nonetheless entered the political stage and formed three separate parties—the Party of the Revolutionary Left, the Trotskyist Revolutionary Workers Party, and in 1940, the National Revolutionary Movement (MNR), which appealed to moderate, middle-class nationalists. All three platforms called for nationalization of the tin mines. Under the leadership of Juan Lechín, a militant Trotskyist, tin miners formed the Federation of Bolivian Mine Workers. In 1945 over 1,000 Quechua- and Aymara-speaking leaders gathered at the first National Indian Congress in La Paz. As historian Herbert Klein has noted, Bolivia had "changed from being one of the least mobilized societies in Latin America, in terms of radical ideology and union organization, into one of the most advanced."

In the late 1940s, peasant revolts flared up throughout the countryside. The miners' union, the Revolutionary Workers Party, and the MNR backed these struggles and began to forge a broad political alliance. A drop in tin prices after World War II forced mine owners to cut wages, provoking greater labor militancy. A massacre of striking workers in the Catavi mines by army troops in 1947 deepened hostility toward the central government. Inflation and economic stagnation further intensified popular discontent. In 1949, the MNR under the leadership of Hernán Siles Zuazo organized a civilian armed revolt against the army that united miners and middle-class supporters. Although the uprising failed, the MNR led an armed labor strike the next year among factory workers in La Paz. The government required artillery and airplanes to crush the labor revolt.

The MNR then turned to an electoral strategy in its pursuit of power. In the 1951 presidential elections, MNR leader Víctor Paz Estenssoro ran on a ticket with Siles Zuazo and garnered 53 percent of the vote. Using Cold War anticommunist rhetoric, the military refused to let the MNR take office and annulled the elections. The MNR again rose up in revolt, seizing weapons from armories and distributing guns to the public. Radicalized workers, peasants, and the middle class defeated the army and the MNR seized power. Thus began the Bolivian Revolution, the first successful massive and popular revolt in Latin America since the Mexican Revolution of 1910.

The Revolution of 1952

Paz Estenssoro, the new president, had graduated from the National University with a degree in economics. He volunteered in the Chaco War against Paraguay and then joined a group of young Turks that supported the "socialist military." In power he built the MNR into a broad coalition that ranged from the Communist Party to the middle class. He gave three cabinet posts to the tin miners and carried out his campaign promises: nationalization of the mines, across-the-board wage hikes, and government subsidies for basic sectors of the economy.

The Bolivian Revolution of 1952, like the Mexican Revolution, had a profound effect on the country. The new government dropped all electoral literacy require- ments and enfranchised hundreds of thousands of Indians. The voting population increased fivefold. By nationalizing the mines (with compensation to the owners) and setting up a state-owned mining giant (Comibol), the government gained effective control over refining plants outside of Bolivia and could essentially dictate the price of tin. The miners' federation also formed an all-powerful *Confederación Obrera Boliviana* (Bolivian Labor Federation, COB) that pushed for better wages, working conditions, and overall policy.

Furthermore, Paz Estenssoro purged military officers who favored the tradi- tional elites and reduced the size of the army. The miners' militias became the most important armed force in the country. Throughout the highland countryside, peasants began taking over medium and large estates by force of arms and forming peasant unions under the guidance of the COB. The MNR intervened in this process and implemented comprehensive agrarian reform. After obtaining land, the peasants tended to become more conservative and less involved in national politics, although they continued to provide a loyal political base for the MNR.

While land reform took place in the highlands, large estates remained intact in the eastern lowlands. U.S. aid and capital poured into this region to finance commercial agriculture. Unable to shift the course of the Bolivian Revolution in the highlands, Washington policymakers attempted to build their influence in the country's most dynamic economic area. A regional boom drew highland peasants, and the city of Santa Cruz became a power center for large-scale landowners.

Siles Zuazo succeeded Paz Estenssoro in the 1956 elections, capturing 83 percent of the vote. The son of a former president, he represented the more moderate wing of the MNR. During his administration, the MNR split into diverse factions along personal lines over policy implementation. As inflation soared, Siles Zuazo decided to stabilize the economy through an austerity program under the auspices of the U.S. government and the International Monetary Fund (IMF). In the midst of Cold War polarization, he also realigned foreign policy in support of the United States. At the same time, the right-wing Falange Socialist Party mobi- lized discontented sectors of the elites and the middle class in an unsuccessful attempt to topple the MNR government.

Unable to block the radical reforms of the Bolivian Revolution, the Eisenhower and later the Kennedy administrations chose to offer economic and military aid to the country as an alternative means of establishing influence. The U.S. government also consolidated support in the armed forces by providing officer training in the United States and counterinsurgency instruction in Bolivia. (In contrast to Guatemala, where the Arbenz reforms had directly chal- lenged American economic interests, the MNR programs of nationalization and redistribution focused exclusively on Bolivian-held properties. This greatly reduced the incentive for decisive U.S. intervention.)

When Paz Estenssoro returned to the presidency in 1960 with Juan Lechín as his running mate, tin prices had flattened and the government had few disposable resources to meet economic problems. Impatient with the slow pace of reforms, opposed to the government's move to disarm the workers' militias and strengthen the military, and resistant to a constitutional amendment that would have allowed Paz Estenssoro to run for reelection, Lechín resigned from his post as vice president and split the MNR coalition. Siles Zuazo also broke with the MNR over Paz Estenssoro's maneuvers to run for reelection. Having lost support from the left wing of his party, Paz Estenssoro attempted to shore up his popularity by selecting General René Barrientos, the charismatic commander of the Bolivian Air Force and a longtime MNR supporter, as his running mate in the 1964 election.

Over time, the military had become resentful of the erosion of its prestige and power. Three months after the election, vice president Barrientos and Alfredo Ovando, commander of the army, ousted Paz Estenssoro and declared themselves co-presidents. Eager to claim another ally in the Cold War, Washington immediately backed the new government. For the next dozen years, the military dominated the political life of the country.

Military Rule and Popular Resistance

A native Quechua speaker, Barrientos saw his own political fortunes on the rise. In 1966 he resigned from his interim position and campaigned for the presidency, developing a conservative populist base among rural Indians, peasants, and the middle class. As president, he promoted pro-market and anticommunist measures, breaking strikes that ended in the massacre of workers. He also oversaw the counter-insurgency campaign led by U.S.-trained Bolivian Rangers that in 1967 successfully tracked down and executed Argentine Cuban revolutionary Ernesto "Che" Guevara, who had attempted to establish a guerrilla base in the Andean foothills.

Barrientos' sudden death in a helicopter crash in 1969 opened disputes within the army corps until Juan José Torres came to power in 1971. A radical nationalist, Torres turned to the left, convoked an Assembly of the People, and signed a contract with the Soviet Union to build a new tin smelter. Given the imperatives of the Cold War, Torres was overthrown within a matter of months.

Bolivia's new leader was General Hugo Banzer (1971–78), a native of Santa Cruz who went on to become the longest-surviving military dictator in the nation's history. In the midst of favorable economic conditions, Banzer ruled from the right with a conservative wing of the MNR and the semi-fascist Falange Socialist Party. Tin prices soared, and the country's relatively small oil reserves provided significant foreign earnings after the OPEC-inspired oil crisis of 1974. Moreover, the long-term effects of Bolivia's radical land reform and infrastructure development expanded markets and increased agricultural production. The export of sugar and later cotton from the Santa Cruz region strengthened commercial agriculture. Banzer also sought closer economic ties with Brazil and Argentina, especially in the hydrocarbon sector. At the same time he governed with a heavy hand, banning left-wing parties, suspending the COB, and closing down universities.

After Jimmy Carter assumed the U.S. presidency in 1977, the Banzer government came under pressure to enact a democratic transition. When it seemed likely that his handpicked successor would lose to Siles Zuazo, however, Banzer annulled the election results. Exasperated by his stubbornness, army officers summarily removed him from office.

Over the next two years, a string of civilian and military governments alternated in power, as Paz Estenssoro and Siles Zuazo vied for the presidency. New political forces emerged, including the radical Movement of the Revolutionary Left (MIR) and the right-wing National Democratic Action, headed by Hugo Banzer. Amid this political chaos, General Luis García Meza (1980–81) seized power. When the international press revealed that key figures in his government were involved in the cocaine trade, Meza quickly lost credibility. Soaring inflation and broad-based popular protests against his rule led to his ouster in 1981. The next year, Bolivia returned to free and fair elections.

The Contemporary Scene (1980s–present)

Once again, the older generation of politicians disputed presidential power. Because it was widely considered that Siles Zuazo had won the 1979 elections, the Congress elected him president in 1982. He faced a catastrophic economic crisis. The bottom dropped out of the world tin market, and in 1985 hyperinflation reached an annual rate of 60,000—the fourth-highest level in world history. Frustrated by his inability to govern, Siles Zuazo stepped down early and elections were called.

Not surprisingly, Paz Estenssoro emerged as the winner. Gone, however, was the program that once favored state control over the major sectors of the economy. Paz Estenssoro tossed aside all of the nationalist and radical programmatic points of the MNR. Building an alliance with former dictator Hugo Banzer, Paz Estenssoro proposed a neoliberal New Economic Plan. Following orthodox monetary policies, he cut government expenses, freed public-sector prices, and increased revenue collection. When inflation dropped to double digits, he moved to dismantle the state mining agency and open the county to unrestricted free trade. Hit hard by the economic crisis, miners offered resistance but to no avail. Many who lost their jobs moved to other regions and eventually became small-scale coca growers.

Succeeding presidents followed Paz Estenssoro's neoliberal policies. Jaime Paz Zamora (1989–93) of the MIR built a curious coalition with right-wing Hugo Banzer and further broke the power of the labor movement. His successor, Gonzalo Sánchez de Lozada (1993–97), ran on a ticket with Víctor Hugo Cárdenas, a leader of the Tupac Katari Revolutionary Liberation Movement. Although he continued orthodox monetary policies, his nod to indigenous movements strengthened their claims to greater political participation. Among Sánchez de Lozada's reforms was a capitalization program enabling joint ventures between private capital and state-owned industries. At the same time, he declared Bolivia to be a pluricultural state, decentralized municipal governance (strengthening indigenous communities), and permitted indigenous languages to be taught in schools. In response to U.S. pressures about drug trafficking, Sánchez de Lozada also set up a voluntary cocaine eradication program that reportedly reduced production by one-third.

A newly minted "democratic" Hugo Banzer returned to power in 1997 and continued free-market and privatization policies. He embraced a U.S.-sponsored 100 percent cocaine eradication program, known as Plan Dignidad, that poured millions of dollars into the country for counternarcotics efforts. Banzer also encouraged the sale of state-owned resources to the private sector. An agreement with the Bechtel Corporation that privatized the water supply system in Cochabamba met with popular resistance when the company tripled its rates; in the face of significant mobilization, the government rescinded the contract. Resigning from office early for health reasons, Banzer was succeeded by his vice president.

In 2002 Sanchéz de Lozada regained the presidency with a minimal plurality in a multiparty contest. His chief opponent was Evo Morales, a leader of the coca growers' union running on the ticket of the Movement toward Socialism (MAS). (The Spanish word acronym MAS means "more.") Morales surprised political observers by coming in a strong second. This was but a prelude of things to come.

Sánchez de Lozada inherited an economy in sharp decline and a swelling fiscal deficit. In early 2003, radical oppositionists formed the People's High Command to challenge his policies. Evo Morales of the coca growers' union led this initiative. Now an emerging leader of indigenous and popular social movements, Morales and the People's High Command launched a series of protests against government measures. Their demands ranged from long-held local grievances to opposition to coca eradication policies. Protesters blocked roads, and cities and towns across the country came to a standstill. In October 2003 Sanchéz de Lozada dispatched security forces to open the way for fuel trucks en route to La Paz; soldiers opened fire on the demonstrators, killing scores of unarmed citizens. The president stepped down and boarded a commercial flight to the United States.

A New Course for Bolivia?

Elections took place in late 2005. Once again, Evo Morales ran for the office, and this time he swept to power with 54 percent of the votes. Turnout reached an all-time high, with 85 percent of eligible voters participating. An Aymara Indian from the highlands of Orinoco, Oruro, Morales had moved with his extended family to the Cochabamba Valley to find work as small farmers producing fruits and coca leaves. He got involved in the *cocalero* union, rising to national leadership and becoming an outspoken opponent of the government's cocaine eradication policies.

His victory evoked a return to the ideals of the 1952 revolution—land reform and the nationalization of industries and natural resources. Morales, however, broadened its scope to include real participation of the Indian population in local and national governance. To signal this shift, Morales organized a special inauguration ceremony following Aymara rituals prior to the official event. He represented himself as the first full-blooded indigenous president who was dedicated to overturning Bolivia's centuries-old social hierarchy. After centuries of oppression, this was a stunning culmination and display of newly found Indian power.

Soon after taking office, Morales took over Bolivian hydrocarbon assets and negotiated new contracts more favorable to Bolivia with Petrobras, Brazil's

Evo Morales dons a poncho presented by the Mapuche Indians of Chile during a political rally; as a democratically elected president, Morales has become a figurehead for indigenous movements throughout Latin America. (Getty Images/AFP.)

state-owned oil company, which imported two-thirds of Bolivia's natural gas. He also oversaw a decisive turn in foreign policy, aligning himself squarely with the iconic Fidel Castro and the firebrand Hugo Chávez. Gratefully accepting economic aid from oil-rich Venezuela, Morales became a key member of the leftist political movement known throughout Latin America as the "pink tide" (see Chapter 12). And as an ardent nationalist, he distanced himself from the United States. The George W. Bush administration in Washington took great umbrage over this development, but was unable—or unwilling—to devote the resources to opposing it.

The Morales administration also presided over the writing of a new constitution. In an early 2009 referendum with a 90 percent turnout, 61 percent of voters approved the new national charter. It acknowledged Bolivia as a unitary, plurinational, secular state, and it declared that natural resources were the exclusive patrimony of the Bolivian people and should be administered by the state. In a separate referendum, 81 percent endorsed a restriction on private land possession to 12,400 acres, thus opening the door to additional redistribution of large landholdings.

The Morales government encountered significant opposition, especially from agribusiness interests in Santa Cruz that used demands for regional autonomy and threats of secession as rallying cries. A recall effort against Morales in 2007 failed,

Why Bolivia and Not Peru?

The political success of the indigenous population in Bolivia offers a striking contrast to the relative quiescence of pro-Indian movements in Peru. Indigenous peoples constitute more than 60 percent of the Bolivian population, of course, compared with less than 40 percent in Peru, but that is not the only reason. From the Chaco War through the Revolution of 1952, major events in Bolivian history have mobilized resources and heightened consciousness among the nation's Indians.

But the differences do not stop there. According to political scientist Donna Lee Van Cott, factors internal to Peru offer important elements of explanation:

> The lag [in Peru] is attributable to the dominance of Marxist and Maoist ideologies in the majority-indigenous highlands; the negative connotations attached to indigenous ethnicity there; the partial success of the land reform of the 1970s; a legal system that has traditionally treated highland and lowland Indians separately, making joint action more difficult; the policy of the Shining Path during the 1980s and early 1990s to assassinate rival leaders of subaltern groups; the policy of the Alberto Fujimori government to label as terrorist any oppositional political activity; and heavy migration to the cities during the 1980s and 1990s, which removed Indians from areas that were traditional indigenous territories. Since the recuperation and defense of indigenous territories is the centerpiece of indigenous mobilization in neighboring countries, the dislocation of much of Peru's indigenous population deprives the Peruvian movement of a powerful organizing theme.

SOURCE: Donna Lee Van Cott, "Turning Crisis into Opportunity: Achievements of Excluded Groups in the Andes," in Paul W. Drake and Eric Hershberg, eds., *State and Society in Conflict: Comparative Perspectives on Andean Crises* (Pittsburgh: University of Pittsburgh Press, 2006), p. 162.

when 67 percent of the electorate voted to keep him in office. An underlying anti-highland Indian prejudice was lurking within the movement against Morales. Following a visit to Santa Cruz in 2007, Rodolfo Stavenhagen, the UN Special Rapporteur on Human Rights of Indigenous Peoples, observed that the political climate had given rise to "manifestations of racism more suited to a colonial society than a modern democratic state."

Morales' multiple electoral victories revealed his broad popular support, especially among the indigenous population. They also reflected the ongoing willingness of popular movements to push for a social and economic restructuring of the country. The new constitution permits the reelection of the president. Short of significant political turmoil, Morales seems likely to remain in power until 2014. During a celebration after the ratification of the new constitution, Morales proclaimed, "They can drag me from the palace. They can kill me. Mission accomplished for the re-founding of the new united Bolivia."

POLITICS AND POLICY: ECUADOR

Ecuador has endured ongoing political volatility for the last two centuries. Between 1830 and the present, only twenty presidents have completed constitutional terms in office. The nation has had twenty-one different constitutions since independence. During the twentieth century alone, the military seized political power on no less than thirteen occasions. Political institutions have remained weak and democratic governance fragile.

Caudillos, Conservatives, and Liberals

With the achievement of independence, Ecuador joined Colombia and Venezuela in Bolívar's Gran Colombia project. Bolívar in turn appointed Juan José Flores, a Venezuelan commander in the Wars of Independence, as governor of Ecuador. Although Flores was of humble origins, he quickly married into the local creole elite of Quito to gain acceptance.

After Ecuador broke away from Gran Colombia in 1830, Flores became president of the new republic. When congressional opponent Vicente Rocafuerte rose up against him, he jailed his adversary and then struck a deal. Flores would fulfill his term and Rocafuerte could then assume office. Flores continued to rule behind the scenes as the head of the army. When Rocafuerte's term expired, Flores returned to the presidency and then forced the ratification of a new constitution that enabled him to serve another eight years. As elsewhere in nineteenth-century Latin America, these early events established a pattern of *caudillo* politics. In Ecuador, however, the pattern became a tradition.

In the meantime, Liberals and Conservatives vied for control of the state. The Liberal Party tended to draw its support from the business classes of Guayaquil, while the Conservatives relied on the landowners of Quito. Both factions used military strength to impose their political will. General José María Urvina, a Liberal, seized power in a coup d'état in 1851. Urvina quickly signed a decree freeing the nation's remaining slaves. Ratified as president in a controlled election, he remained in office until 1856. His successor, General Francisco Robles, also a Liberal, ended Indian tribute requirements. These measures built sympathy for Liberals among the lower classes, but Liberals soon lost control of the government in a series of interregional battles among rival *caudillos* in 1859 (known as "the terrible year").

Conservative leader Gabriel García Moreno joined with other military forces to put down the regional rebellions, restored order, and came to power in 1860. A devout Catholic, Moreno governed the country with an iron fist for the next decade and a half, either as president or as power broker. He oversaw a new constitution in 1861 that made Roman Catholicism the official state religion, and another charter in 1869 that linked citizenship to the Catholic faith. Although Moreno remains a controversial figure in Ecuadorian history, even his detractors admit that he helped improve the educational system by expanding primary schools, establishing technical institutions, and improving universities with the help of Jesuit instructors. He also strengthened the country's infrastructure, building roads between the highlands and the coastal region and initiating a railroad line linking Quito with Guayaquil.

Cacao, Prosperity, and Turmoil

As Liberals and Conservatives battled for control of the presidency, a boom in cacao exports brought increasing economic prosperity for the merchants and landowners along the coast. Lacking political power, this *arriviste* oligarchy financed a military coup in 1895 by longtime Liberal leader Eloy Alfaro. Coastal elites remained in command of the state for the following three decades.

Once in power, the Liberals carried out two major reforms. First, they separated the Catholic Church from the state, legalized divorce, and established civil marriage. This meant that the state would now administer education and social welfare programs, services that the church previously had provided. Second, the Liberals relied on revenues drawn from tariffs on imports to finance public works, education, and government-run welfare services. These costly programs depended increasingly on loans from the banking sector, as customhouse revenues were insufficient to fund the burgeoning budget of an activist state. The government found itself deeper in debt.

In the 1920s, Ecuador lost its market share of the cacao trade due to plant disease and rising competition. Declining revenues made it increasingly difficult to sustain the nation's political model and discredited Liberal politicians. Once again the military moved to center stage, and a group of young officers seized power in a bloodless coup.

This *golpe de estado* of 1925 marked a significant shift in the role of the armed forces. Up to this point, military rule had been linked to personal ambitions; all of the country's most important leaders from 1830 to 1916 were military officers. In a country with weak governmental institutions and sharp regional differences, military might had become the privileged means to power. Yet the armed forces did not have a strong institutional identity. In the early twentieth century, however, reforms within the military were creating a more professional officer corps—drawn less from the upper class and more from the middle sectors of society. Coming mainly from the highlands, these new soldiers saw the Liberals as having mortgaged the country to coastal banking interests.

The League of Young Officers that took control of the government in 1925 did so in the name of the nation and not on behalf of any single individual. Still, old patterns of governance died hard. Power soon shifted to Isidro Ayora, who quickly assumed dictatorial powers and undertook a reform of the country's financial system. Ayora appointed a team of foreign economic advisers, headed by Edwin W. Kemmerer of Princeton University, to suggest ways to improve the nation's fiscal and banking systems. Ayora established a Central Bank and restructured budgeting, taxation, and custom collection. These reforms brought significant new revenues to the central government and reduced the financial role of the Guayaquil elites.

In addition, the military oversaw the passage of a new 1929 constitution that granted suffrage to women—the first in Latin America!—and included progressive social measures for the working classes. It also granted more power to the legislature. This latter provision, designed to limit arbitrary presidential rule, ended up weakening the executive branch's ability to govern as the country faced the Great Depression.

In the wake of the worldwide crisis, an abrupt drop in the international demand for cacao and other export products devastated the Ecuadorian economy. Disillusioned with Ayora's leadership, the military soon ousted him from power. Warring political factions and parties battled for control of the government, and a string of military and civilian figures temporarily held executive power. Liberal candidate Juan de Dios Martínez won election to the presidency in 1932, but partisan opposition paralyzed his would-be government. The challenge to Martínez was led by José María Velasco Ibarra, the charismatic president of the Chamber of Deputies, who insisted that he personally retained no presidential aspirations. Popular mobilizations forced Martínez to resign; less than a year later, Velasco Ibarra won a resounding electoral bid for the presidency. Eleven months later, after he attempted to close Congress, jail his opposition, and seize dictatorial powers, the military removed him from office. This was the first of five times that Velasco Ibarra would occupy the presidency over the next three and a half decades.

In 1941, Ecuador and Peru engaged in a war over disputed territories in the Amazon River basin that would have devastating results for Ecuador. The peace treaty recognized Peru's territorial claims and deprived Ecuador of access to the Amazon River and, as a result, of an outlet to the Atlantic Ocean. The defeat provoked an outburst of nationalism that coalesced in the Democratic Alliance led by Velasco Ibarra. The president resigned in the wake of an uprising in Guayaquil, and Velasco Ibarra came to power on the wings of a populist promise to contain the "corrupt Liberal oligarchy" responsible for the loss of the war.

Although Velasco Ibarra promised social justice for the lower classes, he did little in practice. As inflation increased and foreign exchange reserves dwindled, he too lost popular support. Once again, the military stepped in and removed him from office. After another year of partisan disputation, the U.S.-educated Galo Plaza Lasso defeated his Conservative opponent and led a coalition of independent Liberals and socialists into power.

Bananas and Dictators

In the 1950s bananas became the new export product that offered sufficient economic stability to ensure political tranquility and democratic transitions of power for another dozen years. Traditional parties lost their electoral appeal, and new political formations sought support from the middle and lower classes.

Velasco Ibarra's term in office from 1952 to 1956 exemplified this new political strategy. His program of massive public works projects, from roads and bridges to schools and electrical plants, won him widespread popular support. In fact, he rode to power for the fourth time in 1960 garnering the largest vote in his entire career. Unfortunately for Velasco Ibarra, earnings from banana exports temporarily declined. Facing capital flight and economic crisis, Velasco Ibarra responded slowly and clumsily. He soon lost popularity. A general strike led by the national labor federation clamored for wage protections and an end to his government. Although the army successfully repressed the work stoppage, soon thereafter it stepped in and ousted Velasco Ibarra.

The new incumbent was Carlos Julio Arosemena Monroy, Velasco Ibarra's vice president. At this juncture, the Cuban Revolution and Cold War politics determined the shape of national politics. Arosemena Monroy proffered an independent foreign policy and, like his counterparts in Mexico, refused to break diplomatic relations with Cuba. Conservative forces pushed for his removal, and in 1963, the military deposed him.

As in 1925, the army remained in the presidential palace for an extended period. More autonomous and professional than before, the military junta initiated a series of structural reforms supported with U.S. government aid through the Alliance for Progress. They changed the tax system to increase revenue and control the budget deficit. They decreed a modest land reform and eliminated the *huasipungo* labor system that tied Indian peasants to the land as sharecroppers. Since the economy remained stagnant, the junta raised revenues by increasing import duties. The Quito and Guayaquil chambers of commerce countered this proposal with a general strike, signaling that the economic elites would not allow the military to contravene their commercial interests. A renewed effort the following year brought similar protests.

Quite abruptly, the military left office in 1965. Frustrated by the inability to make even mild reforms, and fearful of a decline in the public image of the military, the officers simply relinquished power. In the process, neither the military nor the economic elites mobilized popular support for political reforms or for plans to oust the generals. Citizens remained on the sidelines. A provisional government ruled for twenty months.

Once again, Velasco Ibarra came to power in the 1968 elections, and as in the past, he faced revenue shortfalls that could not finance the public programs he promised in his electoral campaign. Facing a belligerent Congress, he gained support from the military for his move to assume dictatorial powers "to save the country from total ruin." He closed universities, exiled opponents, and restructured government operations to ensure more fiscal efficiency.

Although widely regarded as a "populist," Velasco Ibarra relied less on popular mobilization than on empty promises. He built no base within the working class, as Perón and Vargas had done in Argentina and Brazil. Nor did he solidify his movement through a nationalist, anti-imperialist discourse as had Haya de la Torre in Peru. Having weathered repeated political storms, he relied more on his longevity as a political figure than on his achievement of concrete results.

The military grew distrustful of Velasco Ibarra, especially as newly discovered oil reserves presented new possibilities of government mismanagement. In 1972 the military ousted him from office for the final time. The armed forces, however, did not simply move in, exchange politicians, and retreat from the presidential palace. This time they remained in power for seven years.

The defining feature of this period came from the discovery of petroleum deposits in Ecuador's Amazon region. General Guillermo Rodríguez Lara, who

The Curse of Oil?

Oil currently represents more than 50 percent of Ecuador's exports. It finances a third of the national budget. Yet some observers view the rich deposits of Amazonian oil as a curse. What might have led them to such a conclusion?

In 1964, the U.S.-based company Texaco began searching for oil in the northwestern Amazonian region of Ecuador. After mapping the area and doing sample drilling, the company marked off an eighty-mile swatch of rainforest and signed an agreement with the government. Texaco struck oil in 1967. It built a pipeline across the Andes and began full-scale production in 1972. Oil extraction brought hefty profits to the company and significant revenues for the government.

Yet there was a problem: How to dispose of waste? Side products of the drilling process, these noxious materials included toxic water and mud, carrying high levels of carcinogens and heavy metals. The company's solution was to dump them in large, unlined clay pits. Environmentalists charge that, over the course of twenty years, at least 12 billion gallons of this waste have leaked into the aqua firm. They also assert that Texaco handled toxic waste in ways that violated U.S. law. The company retorted that it undertook cleanup activities in the early 1990s, when it pulled out of Ecuador, and denied any link between their operations and reported health problems in the area.

When Texaco left Ecuador in 1992, it handed over drilling to Petroecuador, the state-owned oil company. The next year Ecuadorian and U.S. lawyers filed a class-action lawsuit against Texaco in a New York federal court on behalf of 30,000 Amazon residents, known as Los Afectados—the Affected Ones. The attorneys charged that the groundwater was contaminated from the leaky open pits, causing high rates of cancer, skin disease, and other health problems among those living in the region. In 2001 a U.S. judge ruled that the case should be tried in Ecuador. That same year, Chevron bought out Texaco. The second-largest oil company in the United States became the new plaintiff in a multibillion-dollar lawsuit.

Do the benefits of oil revenues outweigh potential harm to residents and the environment? David Poritz of Esperanza International, Inc., a nongovernmental organization that has been involved in the lawsuit, sees this case as a potential watershed: "If justice is brought to the people of Ecuadorian Amazon, it could serve as an example in other parts of the world for those fighting against the negative impact of resource extraction."

---

headed the military government when it took power in 1972, initially proposed to rationalize government operations to better benefit from the country's new windfall revenues. He employed nationalist rhetoric and to a certain extent modeled his rule after the military regime of Juan Velasco Alvarado in Peru. Rodríguez Lara created new government entities to operate the oil industry, nationalized failing enterprises, and set up state-owned financial institutions.

Navy captain Gustavo Jarrín Ampudia, the new minister of natural resources and an ardent nationalist, pushed for a renegotiation of contracts with foreign oil companies. Ecuador joined the Organization of Petroleum Exporting Countries

(OPEC) and hosted a meeting in Quito. When Jarrín became OPEC president, he proposed that the Ecuadorian state should acquire a 51 percent interest in the Texaco-Gulf consortium. Jarrín's hard-line stance toward foreign oil companies provoked a negative reaction from the U.S. government, which threatened to cut off military aid unless Jarrín resigned. The government dismissed him soon thereafter.

By 1975, sectors of the military and civilian leadership backed a coup to remove Rodríguez Lara from power. Although this effort initially failed, he resigned the next year, and a triumvirate of service commanders slowly eased the country once again to democratic rule.

The Contemporary Scene (1979–present)

As one scholar has noted, Ecuador's post-1979 generation of politicians "supported the modernization of the political system through the expansion of the electorate, issue-oriented campaigning, and the development of modern political parties." Reform measures proposed by President Jaime Roldós Aguilera (1979–81) and his successor, Osvaldo Hurtado (1981–84), to invest petroleum revenues in infrastructure, education, and rural development were nonetheless thwarted by warring factions within Congress. An economic downturn following a drop in oil prices increased the difficulties of harnessing petroleum revenue for economic and social reforms.

Throughout the 1980s and into the mid-1990s, presidents swung back and forth between the right and the left. It seemed as if the political system had broken down. Abdalá Bucaram, the grandson of Lebanese immigrants and a member of a Guayaquil political clan, came to power in 1996; six months later, the Congress dismissed him on the unusual ground of "mental incapacity." An interim president, a vice president, and the interim president (again) quickly followed. Jamil Mahuad, an Arab Christian of Lebanese descent, took office in 1998, but demonstrations forced him to resign. Then Lucio Gutiérrez, a member of the short-lived junta that ousted Mahuad, won the 2002 elections on a platform to increase social spending; once in office, he reversed his promises and implemented austerity measures in order to obtain a new loan from the IMF. Opposition forces from the left and the right joined in an attempt to impeach him on corruption charges, and subsequent street demonstrations led Congress to remove him from office.

Indigenous movements played shifting roles in these developments. In the absence of a transformative historical event (such as the Bolivian Revolution of 1952), Ecuador's Indian communities were dispersed and fragmented between the coast, the *sierra,* and the Amazon. Organizational efforts over the years had been made by such diverse (and opposing) groupings as the Communist Party, the Catholic Church, and evangelical Protestants. It was not until 1986 that ethnic-based federations coalesced in the Confederation of Indigenous Nationalities of Ecuador (CONAIE), which mounted major efforts on behalf of Indian rights in 1990 and 1994. By the late 1990s CONAIE represented 80 percent of the country's indigenous population, and in 1998 it led the popular demonstrations that forced

Abdalá Bucaram from the presidency. But CONAIE in particular and the pro-Indian movement in general lost coherence and strength after participating in the Lucio Gutiérrez government, an experience that proved to be extremely divisive. And as a result, CONAIE played only a minor role in the civil uprising that ousted Gutiérrez in 2005.

Finally, in 2006, Rafael Correa, a young U.S.-trained economist and former finance minister, won a runoff election, seemingly stopping the presidential revolving door. As a declared Christian leftist and a proponent of "twenty-first century socialism," Correa terminated ongoing negotiations for a free trade agreement with the United States, criticized America's imperial pretensions, and denounced the Bush administration's role in world affairs. Together with Evo Morales of Bolivia, he became a prominent and highly articulate member of the left-leaning "pink tide" in Latin America.

Like most of his predecessors, Correa relied on strong personal and presidential power. A new constitution in 2008 permitted a two-term presidency and increased executive power. In the electoral contest of early 2009, Correa won a decisive victory. He repudiated Ecuador's national debt, calling it immoral and tainted by bribery, and promised to use oil revenues for poverty alleviation. As international prices for petroleum remained at modest levels, it was unclear if Ecuador's earnest chief executive would be able to fulfill that solemn pledge.

7

Colombia

Civility and Violence

Colombia is a land of paradox. The intrepid navigator for whom it is named, Christopher Columbus, never once set foot upon the nation's present territory. Although Colombian leaders sought to promote unity among the independent republics of Spanish America in the early nineteenth century, their own country would later suffer from dismemberment and fragmentation. Although political elites thereafter cultivated an ethic of civility, or *convivencia*, the nation plunged into eras of extraordinary violence. Although Colombia is now widely judged to be the longest-surviving democracy in Latin America, it has the longest-lasting guerrilla movement in the entire region. And while it has long been neglected by world powers, especially the United States, Colombia has suddenly risen to the forefront of the inter-American agenda.

FROM COLONY TO NATIONHOOD

As in the case of the central Andean nations, geography has played a major role in shaping Colombian development. The equator crosses the southern part of the country. As elsewhere in the tropics, temperatures vary with altitude and are relatively constant; rainfall is abundant. The Andes in Colombia form not a single mountain range, as in Peru, but three separate *cordilleras* that branch off from each other just north of the border with Ecuador and run more-or-less parallel in a north-northeasterly direction. This rugged terrain has made land transportation especially difficult. From colonial times to the present, this topography has divided the country into three major regions: the East, the West, and the Caribbean coast. Under Spanish rule the East became the seat of political power, with the capital of the Viceroyalty of New Granada located in the city of Santafé de Bogotá (now known more commonly as Bogotá). Gold mining provided economic power to the West and spurred the growth of such municipalities as Popayán in the central valley and Medellín in the province of Antioquia. Along the Caribbean coast the dominant city was Cartagena, which became the hub of

Map 7 Colombia

legal commerce with the outside world and, not surprisingly, of a thriving contra-band trade.

Also in contrast to Peru, Colombia's indigenous population did not form a cohesive and centrally organized empire in precolonial times. Instead, three linguistic families predominated—the Chibcha, the Carib, and the Arawak. Around the Caribbean, the most impressive civilization was that of the Chibcha-speaking Tairona, who constructed engineering works in stone—including temples, roads, stairways, bridges, and irrigation and drainage works. Around the gold-bearing region of Antioquia, a cultural matrix embraced as many as 1 million inhabitants—divided into many tribal groups, speaking different dialects, chronically at war with one another. Farther to the south, Chibcha-speaking highland groups were mostly docile farmers; they stoutly resisted domination by outsiders, however, including agents of the Incan empire. The eastern highlands were controlled by the Muiscas—more commonly known as Chibchas—with a total population between 800,000 and 1.2 million, but without any great urban centers. Along with the Tairona, the Muiscas had the most hierarchically organized and territorially extensive social systems by the time the Spaniards arrived.

The European conquest of Colombia was incremental and uneven. The eastern *cordillera* was conquered by Spaniards who were making their way down from the Caribbean coast. Western Colombia fell to *conquistadores* who were coming northward from Peru and Ecuador and southward from Cartagena; partly for this reason, much of western Colombia never came under the effective jurisdiction of colonial authorities in Santafé de Bogotá. Along the central *cordillera*, indigenous groups offered ferocious resistance to would-be Spanish conquerors. The Tairona around the Caribbean also put up a strong fight. In the coastal lowland areas, however, the arrival of the Europeans—and their diseases, particularly malaria and yellow fever—led to demographic catastrophe.

As a result of these geographic and historical differences, the three regions developed distinctive racial and cultural profiles. The rapid decline of indigenous populations on the Caribbean coast and in gold-mining regions of the West led to their replacement by a largely African labor force. In the eastern highlands, by contrast, indigenes survived in greater numbers, and few African slaves were introduced. In the East, social relations were formalistic and hierarchical; along the Caribbean coast and in parts of the West, there existed more ease and informality between the dominant classes and a spirited Afro-Colombian labor force.

Ultimately, and perhaps inevitably, the population of Colombia became predominantly mixed-race—*mestizo,* mulatto, or some combination thereof. According to a national census of 1912, just over one-third of the country's inhabitants (34.4 percent) were classified as "white," 10 percent were black, only 6.3 percent were Indian, and 49.2 percent—nearly one-half of the total—were recorded as "mixed." Here and throughout Latin America, miscegenation played a central role in the formation of society.

Independence and Its Aftermath

New Granada played a central role in the continental struggles for liberation from Spain. Local elites firmly rejected Napoleon's assumption of power in the wake of his 1808 invasion of the Iberian Peninsula. Although they initially supported restoration of the Spanish monarchy, creoles eventually came out in favor of national independence. And as events unfolded, the demands of a drawn-out military campaign led them to mobilize popular masses in support of their cause. By joining the independence movement, lower-status groups—widely disdained by the elite as the *populacho*—added a social-class dimension to the anti-Spanish turbulence. Women here played a conspicuous role. During an upheaval in Santafé in 1810, as the viceroy's wife was being led to the women's prison, an observer noted that "the vile rabble of women" lined the route to the jail, broke through the protective cordon, tore off the good lady's clothes, and showered her with curses. "The insolences that they were saying," said the startled observer, "were enough to make one cover his ears." Fearing that they might lose control of the masses, local leaders soon attempted to restrain such popular excess.

While creole elites remained supreme, the Wars of Independence brought significant social change to New Granada. Military exploits fostered upward social mobility, and many Afro-Colombian slaves obtained their freedom in compensation for their service in the patriot cause. The *populacho* revealed itself as both a political asset and a potential source of danger. Ever so slightly, women found means of expression in the public arena. The church lost some of its power but retained substantial moral authority.

In the political arena, Simón Bolívar's attempt to create a composite state of "Gran Colombia" produced a constitutional charter in 1821 that combined a centralist form of government with progressive social measures. It proclaimed an end to the Inquisition, established freedom of the press, and sought to incorporate blacks and Indians as eventual citizens. A "law of free birth" stipulated that children of slaves should be free, while another clause indicated that Indians should be called "indigenes" and have the right to hold public office.

As recounted in Chapter 6, Gran Colombia was doomed from the start. Its component parts—Venezuela, Ecuador, Colombia—each went their separate ways. As historians Frank Safford and Marco Palacios have noted, "The collapse of greater Colombia was inevitable." What would happen next?

CREATING POLITICAL PARTIES

During the 1830s, Colombia resumed its path as a sovereign liberal republic. Yet another constitutional convention proclaimed the need for reconciliation and installed Francisco Paula de Santander as president. In comparison with other postindependence governments of Spanish America, Colombia enjoyed one distinct advantage: the demobilization of the patriot army and the departure of Venezuelan forces meant that, as a corporate group, the remaining military would have less weight in Colombian politics than would its counterparts in Mexico, Peru, or Venezuela.

The aftermath of Bolívar's short-lived Gran Colombia produced a truly remarkable development: the emergence of the political parties, Liberal and Conservative, that would dominate the nation's political life from the 1830s to the present. What determined the formation of these parties?

At least in part, the parties emerged as a sequel to the conflict between pro-federalist Santanderistas and pro-centralist Bolivarians. A conflict known as the "War of the Supremos" hardened lines of disagreement. Strident opposition drove many moderates into the arms of the Bolivarians and the clergy, where, as so-called *ministeriales,* they became supporters of the administration. In 1848, these pro-government forces founded the Conservative Party. Pro-federalist Santanderistas retained the label of Liberals.

The sharpest source of disagreement between Liberals and Conservatives focused on the church. Liberals thought the church was too strong and that its influence tended to restrain economic productivity and public enlightenment. Conservatives, in contrast, saw the church as an indispensable foundation of social order and cohesion and contrasted their commitment to religion, harmony, and morality with what they regarded as the irreligious anarchism of radical Liberals. A second issue concerned the relationship between the central state and provincial authorities, but here the divisions were less clear. Most Liberals espoused federalism, but some feared a weakening of central control. And most Conservatives supported centralism, but some (especially in Antioquia) regarded federalism as a refuge from liberal excess.

Partisan conflict thus defined the shape of Colombian politics. Yet it was neither peaceful nor predictable. The struggle between Liberals and Conservatives led to frequent outbursts of violence, to periodic civil wars, and to the concomitant elevation of military officers to the presidential office. It led to a pendulum-like alternation of Liberals or Conservatives in power, rather than to compromise or coalitions. And it led to chronic instability—partly as a result of fissures and contradictions within the two parties and partly as a consequence of the tendency for individuals to switch sides.

The *ministeriales* held power through most of the 1840s, then the Liberals came to power with the election of General Hilario López in 1848–49. With the urging of "radical" Liberals, the López administration abolished slavery outright, expelled the Jesuit order (perceived as the vanguard of the most aggressive church position), and declared an end to the ecclesiastical *fuero* (which assured trials for priests in ecclesiastical rather than civil courts).

After the election of José María Obando in 1852, Liberals in Congress adopted a highly secularized new constitution that called for separation of church and state, legalization of civil marriage and divorce, abolition of the death penalty, drastic reduction in the standing army, and direct election of provincial governors rather than their appointment by the president. Obando deplored these developments: without presidential control of the church and of provincial governors, he believed, it would be impossible to govern. In 1854 Obando thus acquiesced in the over-throw of his own government. There ensued another civil war, this one marked by deep class antagonisms—between an elitist coalition of Conservatives and Liberals on the one hand and an alliance of military soldiers and popular classes on the other. In December 1854 the Conservative–Liberal alliance achieved a decisive victory.

Conservatives triumphed in the subsequent election of 1856, winning the presidency (under Mariano Ospina Rodríguez) and majorities in both houses of Congress. Two basic policy initiatives of the Liberals nonetheless survived. One was the continuous scaling down of the national army. The other was the redis-tribution of power from the central to the provincial governments: a new constitution of 1858 went so far as to rename the country the "Granadine Confederation."

After another devastating civil war (1859–63), the Liberals assumed command of national politics during the 1860s and 1870s. The most prominent figure of this era was Tomás Cipriano de Mosquera—formerly a centralist, now a federalist, forever a mercurial and ruthless opportunist. As victor in the civil war, Mosquera drastically attacked the church—asserting civilian control, expelling the Jesuits (again), and declaring state control of unused church properties. While the Liberals shared Mosquera's dislike of church support for the Conservative Party, many believed he went too far.

Fearful of Mosquera's impetuousness, the Liberals adopted a constitution in 1863 that limited presidential terms to only two years and prohibited reelection. Their intent was to discourage civil wars by making the presidency less of a prize. But the constitution also made the national government too weak to provide effective governance or to establish economic policy. And while nationwide wars were avoided, conflict—and violence—often erupted at the state level instead. Contemporaries often described the result as "organized anarchy."

Rafael Núñez and the Politics of Regeneration

Ironically, the Liberals' preeminence led to their downfall. During the 1879 election campaign, moderate Liberals gave their support to Rafael Núñez, an intellectual and diplomat who had attracted attention by warning that Colombia stood on the brink of "fundamental regeneration or catastrophe." After a two-year term in 1880–82 he returned to the presidency in 1884, this time with avid support from the Conservatives, and he would remain in office until his death in 1894.

It was during this decade that Núñez implemented his program for national regeneration. What the country needed, in his view, was a "scientific peace" (a conception that would be echoed by contemporaries in Mexico and elsewhere). For Colombia, this meant a centralist constitution that would enshrine Catholicism as a core element of social cohesion. Núñez' basic criticisms focused on a political culture characterized by intolerance and violence. Adopting premises from the philosophical positivism that pervaded much of Latin America at the time, Núñez concluded that popular religiosity could be an instrument of social cohesion, so he forcefully rejected the anticlericalism of earlier Liberalism.

This vision led to the adoption of still another constitution in 1886—one that would last until 1991. "In the name of God, supreme source of all authority," the charter emphasized the role of Catholicism but also called for religious toleration. It centralized power and strengthened the presidency: terms were lengthened to six years (later amended to four), and chief executives were endowed with a variety of special powers. Key to the system was the alliance of church and state, formalized in a concordat of 1887 and an additional covenant in 1892, which granted the church control over texts used in public schools. Elections during this era lacked substance but nonetheless marked the rhythm of public life, ritualizing disputes within the government party.

By the end of the 1890s, Colombia was in a commercial depression. Increasingly resentful of the Conservative monopoly on power, a group of Liberals rebelled in October 1899. The central government reacted by granting departmental governors the authority to decree forced loans and expropriations, which were levied on affluent Liberals and in areas occupied by the "authors, accomplices, supporters and sympathizers" of the uprising. Known as the War of the Thousand Days, the struggle lasted three years. Conservatives eventually triumphed, but at an astronomical cost.

THE LOSS OF PANAMA

The War of the Thousand Days consumed the energies and resources of the Colombian government and paved the way for a pivotal and traumatic event: the loss of Panama.

Panama had belonged to the viceroyalties of Peru and New Granada ever since the Spanish conquest and, after independence, to the Colombian nation. Because of its physical location—separated from the main body of the republic by impenetrable jungles and accessible only by sea—Panama always had a special status within the federation of Colombia. (At one point the National Congress even declared Panama to be a "sovereign federal state.") And because of its potential to link the Atlantic and Pacific oceans, Panama was of great interest to the world's most powerful nations.

As an incipient world economic power, the United States asserted its claims with ever-increasing intensity. Under the Mallarino-Bidlack Treaty of 1846–48, the United States presumed to guarantee the neutrality of the isthmus and freedom of transit across it. The California gold rush of 1849 heightened U.S. interest and soon led to the construction of a U.S.-financed railway. As American passengers rushed across the isthmus, a dispute with native Panamanians led to a riot and the death of fifteen U.S. citizens in 1856. In response, Washington demanded an indemnity of $400,000, the creation of self-governing municipalities at terminal points of the railway, a sovereign cession ten miles wide on each side of the railway, and the use of two islands by the U.S. Navy.

Such extravagant demands provoked strong reactions from Colombians. Many called for heroic resistance. Others succumbed to a sense of helplessness. The Liberals were perhaps the most confused: they had long regarded the United States as a political model—and now the United States was acting with imperial haughtiness, issuing an unreasonable ultimatum. A Conservative secretary of foreign relations suggested that Colombia goad the Yankees into seizing Panama and then collect an indemnity from Washington. Mariano Ospina, soon to be president, briefly imagined that Great Britain or France might intervene on Colombia's behalf; when that hope vanished, he thought of annexing not only Panama but all of New Granada to the United States.

The dispute was eventually settled for a modest indemnity, but Colombians would thereafter view the United States with suspicion. During the 1840s and

1850s, they noted, the United States was taking land from Mexico and filibustering in Nicaragua. Expressing a generalized sentiment, José María Vargas Vila would write of "the unruly and brutal north that despises us." And interestingly enough, Rafael Núñez' regeneration would inspire a conservative nationalist current with antiliberal and anti-Yankee tones. Following the papal encyclical *De Rerum Novarum* (1891), Colombia's conservative nationalism exuded an anticapitalist flavor as well.

In 1879 the Colombian government granted a contract for construction of a canal to Ferdinand de Lessups, a French engineer and entrepreneur, already famous for his creation of the Suez Canal. De Lessups began construction in 1882 but ran into numerous delays. A third extension of his contract came in 1900, just as the War of the Thousand Days reached the isthmus.

Meanwhile the U.S. government, now under Teddy Roosevelt, decided to build the canal. It acquired rights from the New French Company and signed a treaty with Colombia in 1903. The Colombian Senate rejected the treaty on the ground that it violated national sovereignty. There followed a conspiracy of diverse interests that ended with a declaration of Panamanian independence, under the vigilant protection of the U.S. Navy, and recognition of the new republic by the United States in November 1903. As Roosevelt reportedly declared with pride, "I took Panama!"

Negotiations thereafter focused on U.S. compensation to Colombia. A treaty in 1914 initially offered an indemnity of $25 million, payable in five installments, together with a statement of "sincere regret" on the part of Washington. American politicians denounced the pact as "blackmail," and the Senate withheld ratification. Years later, the treaty was rewritten, the "regrets" were excised, and the first of five annual payments of $5 million was made in 1922.

OVERVIEW: ECONOMIC GROWTH AND SOCIAL CHANGE

The Colombian economy was conspicuously underdeveloped during most of the nineteenth century. Part of the problem came from political instability, which hindered long-term planning and investments. Equally important was the country's formidable terrain, which presented serious obstacles to commerce among the three major zones—Caribbean, East, and West. Overland transportation was dangerous and prohibitively expensive (around 1850 it cost no more to move freight from Liverpool across the Atlantic and then up the Magdalena River by steamboat to the interior port of Honda than for it to travel by mule down the mountain from Bogotá, less than 100 miles away). As a result of the geographic dispersion of the population, consumer markets were modest in size.

During and after the colonial period, the only substantial and reliable export was gold, which remained important into the early twentieth century. From the 1850s to the 1880s, Colombia exported significant amounts of tobacco and Chinchona bark (the source of quinine). Bananas also became important in the Santa Marta region of the Caribbean coast, where the U.S.-based United Fruit

Company not only owned a large plantation but also controlled shipping and exports.

But the most durable development, the one that laid the eventual foundations of Colombia's economic development, was the cultivation and exportation of coffee. By the late 1880s, coffee became the country's leading export. By 1906 it accounted for more than 37 percent of the nation's export earnings, a figure that climbed to 70 percent in the 1920s and as high as 80 percent in the 1950s. As a result of coffee exports, Colombia became fully integrated into the world market. There could be no doubt about it: coffee was king.

By the 1930s coffee in Colombia was produced mainly by small- and medium-sized cultivators. In other areas—notably Brazil, El Salvador, and Guatemala—coffee flourished on large-scale estates. Given the requirements for intensive manual labor in cultivating coffee trees, however, coffee production did not yield significant economies of scale, so small-scale farmers could remain competitive. In Colombia, it would eventually be asserted that the survival of a substantial stratum of small coffee cultivators would help provide a middle-class base for the consolidation of political democracy.

Furthermore, coffee production spurred the development of transportation networks, when it became necessary to ship freight from the highlands to rivers (and then to the coast and abroad). Unlike Argentina (see Chapter 9), Colombia made little progress on railway construction during the late nineteenth century. As coffee cultivation expanded, so did the railway system; as of 1930, however, the two largest cities, Bogotá and Medellín, were not yet linked directly by rail. Thereafter, the government began stressing the construction of highways instead of railways. (During the 1930s and 1940s, highways and railways each carried about one-third of all freight; by the 1990s, the highways carried 80 percent and the railways only 3 percent.) In view of Colombia's challenging topography, airways also became a central part of the nation's transportation network. With only some exaggeration, it has been said that Colombia leaped directly from the mule to the airplane.

By far the dominant overseas market, the United States was consuming more than 90 percent of Colombian coffee exports in the 1920s and 1940s. Despite this connection, Europe remained the source of social and cultural prestige for the country's elites. Suspicion of the Colossus of the North continued to pervade Colombian society.

During the 1920s, the coffee bonanza in Colombia led to rapid growth and an expanding creditworthiness that came to be known as "the dance of the millions," as New York bankers offered sizable loans. Contributing factors to this bullish optimism and its financial bubble were steadily expanding exports of bananas and petroleum, both produced in U.S.-dominated enclaves, and receipt of the $25 million Panama indemnity. Much of Colombia's burgeoning debt was incurred not by the national government but by municipalities and local governments.

Then the Great Depression struck. Even so, the socioeconomic and political effects of the Depression were less severe in Colombia than in many other countries of Latin America. The country's recovery was greatly assisted by the Brazilian policy of "valorization" (see Chapter 11) which reduced the world's coffee supply through the destruction of 78 million sacks of coffee between 1931 and 1940 (the equivalent of two full years of world production!). Also helpful to recovery were the rising international demand for gold, the adoption of exchange controls, and the devaluation of the Colombian peso. Besides, exports accounted for less than one-quarter of Colombia's gross national product, so the impact of declining export prices was relatively limited.

Fluctuations in international coffee prices tended to respond to variations in the world's supply, rather than to consumer preferences. (Consumers could be counted on: by the twentieth century, coffee had become a basic product, not a luxury, something that people just had to have—even if their incomes declined.) Periodic but unpredictable freezes in Brazil could bring sudden reductions in production, causing prices to rise—stimulating growers in Colombia and else-where to plant more bushes, which would come to maturity in four or five years and thus create an eventual overproduction that would drive prices down-ward again. Moreover, coffee could be cultivated not only in Latin America but in many parts of the world, which introduced threats of competition; in fact, Colombia's share of world production never quite reached 20 percent, a situation that made it vulnerable to developments in other coffee-producing areas. Partly in response to this uncertainty, coffee-exporting and -importing countries reached an International Coffee Agreement in 1969 that was designed to stabilize prices.

After a period of relative retrenchment from the 1940s to the mid-1970s, Colombian coffee production regained its expansive mode as larger-scale produ-cers managed to increase productivity and profit margins. Cancellation of the International Coffee Agreement in 1989 brought increased exposure to price fluctuations, but the risk seemed manageable for the ensuing decade—if not forever. Through the 1990s, coffee exports picked up from other parts of the developing world—including southern Africa and from such unlikely locations as Vietnam, which became the world's second-largest coffee producer in 2002.

As Colombia's economy diversified, coffee's importance declined. As shown in Figure 7.1, coffee dropped from more than 80 percent of the total exports in the 1950s to around 20 percent for most of the 1990s and to less than 10 percent by the end of the decade. In the early 1950s, coffee accounted for more than 10 percent of the country's GDP; by the 1990s, it was down to only 2 percent.

At least in part, the relative decline in coffee was compensated by the growth of nontraditional exports—cut flowers, bananas (again), shoes, tobacco, and processed food. A surge in petroleum production in the mid-1980s also contrib-uted to export earnings.

But the largest export, even before the 1980s, was illicit drugs, especially cocaine. One estimate holds that drug trafficking brought $36 billion into Colombia between 1980 and 1995. That was equivalent to more than 5.3 percent of GDP, oversha-dowing contributions from both coffee (4.5 percent) and petroleum (1.9 percent). The absolute volume of trafficking increased steadily from the 1980s to the 1990s.

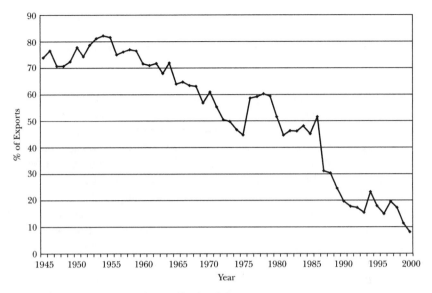

Figure 7.1 Coffee as a Percentage of Colombian Exports, 1945–2000
SOURCES: Departamento Nacional de Planeación and Banco Central, República de Colombia.

This development has had far-reaching impacts—on Colombian society, its economy, and its relationship with the United States. Among other things, the unregulated inflow of dollars introduced enormous uncertainty into economic policymaking. It also helped sustain the value of the Colombian peso (during the early 1990s, dollar-peso exchange rates on the black market were usually lower than the official rates!). The surge of dollars encouraged imports that, in turn, threatened domestic industry. There is some evidence, as well, that windfall earnings from petroleum and drugs discouraged active investment in other potentially productive areas, a phenomenon known as "Dutch disease."

As Colombia's economy underwent change, so did its society. The population expanded from just 2 million in 1850 to 4 million in 1900 and more than 42 million in 2000. Its mobility and dispersion were as important as its size. The Colombian population has never been concentrated around a single location. Around the mid-nineteenth century, most people lived in the highlands—not in large cities, but in a congeries of middle-or small-size towns. Then began a steady movement of people from the cool highlands to the warmer zones of the mountain slopes and valleys and to the Caribbean lowlands, a trend that some historians regard as the most important social phenomenon of the hundred-year period from 1850 to 1950.

Urbanization followed, but later than in Argentina or Chile. By the late 1930s, less than 30 percent of the Colombian population resided in cities; by the end of the century, around 70 percent did. The process of urbanization reached its maximum velocity in the 1950s—but it was fragmented and divergent, not concentrated or centralized. In sharp contrast to Argentina and Chile, dominated respectively by

Buenos Aires and Santiago, Colombia has four large regional capitals: Bogotá, Medellín, Cali, and Barranquilla.

Like other countries of Latin America, Colombia developed a substantial middle class—but one that is less distinctly urban than in the Southern Cone. As shown by the history of coffee production, the middle class in Colombia has a sizable rural component. Moreover, its urban elements are spread out among diverse cities in different (and often competitive) regions, so they are not especially cohesive.

Furthermore, economic change gave rise to a working class. Initially, the working class was concentrated not so much in manufacturing as in foreign-dominated enclaves, such as oil fields and banana plantations, and in the transportation sector, especially railways and river navigation. After the turn of the century many workers in these areas became markedly radical, nationalist and anti-imperialist in ideology, sometimes with socialist overtones or inspiration. In the cities, labor unions were created, controlled, or co-opted by one of three entities: political parties (usually Liberal, sometimes Conservative), the church, or the communist left. Indeed, the political left (Liberal, Socialist, or Communist) came to dominate an important segment of the union movement through the creation in the late 1930s of the Confederación de Trabajadores de Colombia (CTC). The process of unionization was nonetheless slow: out of 4 million workers in the 1940s, only 90,000 (2.25 percent) were unionized. By the mid-1960s, union membership climbed to 700,000, approximately 13.4 percent of the labor force, but this proportion has declined in recent years. At present, the rate of union membership is among the lowest in Latin America.

When all is said and done, Colombia's reliance on export promotion failed to create a truly prosperous society. To be sure, the Colombian economy grew slightly faster than the average for Latin America during the course of the twentieth century. In 1950 the country's GDP per capita ranked tenth in Latin America, and by 1995 it was eighth. But by 2002 Colombia's per capita income was $1,830, still far below comparable levels in Argentina, Chile, or Mexico. According to worldwide standards, Colombia now falls in the "lower-middle" income category. This was progress—but on the installment plan.

Colombia: Vital Statistics, 2007

Population (millions)	46.1
GDP (current $U.S. billions)	172.0
GNP/capita ($U.S.)	3250
Poverty rate (% in 2006)	46.8
Life expectancy (years)	73

SOURCES: World Bank and Economic Commission for Latin America and the Caribbean.

Inequality and poverty have been persistent and widespread. During the 1970s and 1980s, the incomes of nearly 60 percent of the population fell below the poverty line; by the 1990s the figure had dropped slightly to 55 percent, although the absolute number of people living in poverty had increased. By the late 1940s, as well, less than 1 percent of the people were earning one-third of the national income. In Colombia, as elsewhere, such patent injustice necessarily impacted politics. In particular, inequalities of land distribution would lead peasants to take direct action themselves.

POLITICS AND POLICIES: PATTERNS OF CHANGE

The War of the Thousand Days and the catastrophic loss of Panama marked a major turning point in Colombia's national life. For a time, at least, political elites interacted through rituals of *convivencia,* the genteel rules of parliamentary debate. Civil war was delegitimized as a form of competition. New political actors appeared—such as labor unions—and social and political rights were broadened. And thanks to coffee exports, Colombia would at last find its niche within the world market.

Fresh from their triumph in the War of the Thousand Days, the Conservatives retained control of the army, the ballot box, and institutional power. General Rafael Reyes became president in 1904 and proceeded to rule with an iron hand. When Congress failed to cooperate, he dissolved it, jailed some members, and exiled others. Reyes declared martial law and assumed dictatorial powers. Even so, he managed to reorganize the nation's finances, restore Colombia's credit in world markets, accelerate the construction of railways and highways, and stimulate coffee production. In such ways, his rule resembled not only that of his predecessor Rafael Núñez, but also that of Porfirio Díaz in Mexico. Yet opposition swelled when Reyes attempted to conclude a treaty under which the United States would pay $2.5 million in return for Colombia's formal recognition of the independence of Panama. This appeared to set an unduly low price on Colombian sovereignty! Confronted by popular fury, he resigned from office in 1909.

Although Conservatives continued their control of power, the pace of social change was quickening. Labor agitation led to a decade of "heroic unionism," which peaked in the late 1920s. Tensions came to a head in the town of Ciénaga in 1928, when a union guided by the Revolutionary Socialist Party (a precursor of the Communist Party) declared a strike and 25,000 workers, particularly those at the U.S.-owned United Fruit plantations, stopped cutting bananas. The American manager dispatched an urgent message to the Colombian president, Miguel Abadía Méndez, describing "an extremely grave and dangerous situation." Abadía Méndez responded by deploying army units in order to maintain "public order." The ensuing confrontation led to what has come to be known as "the massacre of the banana plantations," a central event in the collective memory of Colombians— and recounted, albeit with purposeful exaggeration, by Gabriel García Márquez in *One Hundred Years of Solitude.* (The tragedy did not, however, convince United Fruit to leave Colombia. That occurred only in the 1940s, after an outbreak of sigatoka disease devastated the banana plantations it controlled.)

The entire period from 1885 to 1930 is often called one of "Conservative hegemony," but it was more complex than that. The Catholic hierarchy indeed had a strong political role and was considered part of the government under the constitution of 1886, especially with the Conservatives in power. Yet the church did not spread its activities evenly across the country. In ethnic terms, the church focused more on *mestizo* populations and less on blacks and mulattoes. The conservative province of Antioquia had an especially close connection to the church. Social change nonetheless posed a threat to tradition. In 1925 the rector of a church-run school offered a lament about elite youths and "the changeability of their spirit, the yearning for diversions, the futility caused by the cinema ... the rebelliousness that each day progresses more in the mass of undisciplined students, thanks to the socially destructive press." Secularization was spreading through society.

Conservative rule was weakened by the onset of the Great Depression, and a schism within the party made it possible for a moderate Liberal, Enrique Olaya Herrera, to become president. This inaugurated a fifteen-year period known as the "Liberal republic." This era would witness considerable expansion in the role and strength of Colombia's national government. On a less positive note, it would increase the politicization of policymaking processes and thus intensify partisan rivalries.

Midway through his term, Olaya formulated a visionary proposal for agrarian reform. A task force under his direction suggested a reform based on principles of socialist-inspired French law and on the agrarian principles of the Mexican Revolution and the Spanish Republic. It established a presumption of state ownership of "all uncultivated land"—and a corollary principle that public lands could be obtained only by individuals who were working on them. The final statute approved by the legislature was much more conservative, however, privileging the security of title of landowners over the allocation of land to peasants. In effect, the agrarian law of 1936 resolved conflicts by methods in use since the 1920s—that is, through the private or government division of large estates that were besieged by *colonos* and by the adjudication of public lands on a case-by-case basis. Very little, if any, good land was redistributed in fact. As a result, conflicts over landownership and colonization would continue for the next half century.

Succeeding Olaya in the presidency was the charismatic Alfonso López Pumarejo, who proclaimed the initiation of a *revolución en marcha* during his 1934–38 term. A strong supporter of unionization, he became the supreme arbiter of worker-management conflicts. Directly confronting the paternalist control of labor unions by industrialists in Medellín and other cities, he actively encouraged strikes by coffee harvesters and their quest for unionization. In 1936 López also oversaw the extension of the vote to all adult males, a step that moved Colombia down the road toward mass-based politics.

Eduardo Santos (1938–42), a social moderate, took strong stands on economic policy. To promote industrial development—specifically, import-substitution industrialization (ISI), a recipe followed elsewhere in Latin America—he created the Instituto de Fomento Industrial. His administration thus backed the construction of a steelworks in Medellín (1942), a rubber factory near Bogotá

(1942), a shipyard in Barranquilla (1943), and a steel plant in Boyacá. Santos also promoted low-cost housing and the development of infrastructure, including aqueducts and sewers. All such programs strengthened the authority and expanded the reach of the national state.

From the 1940s to the 1970s, Colombia thus adopted a pragmatic economic policy that combined elements of both protectionism and free trade. Downturns in the international coffee market accentuated support for some degree of ISI, even as the reliance on exports stressed the need for free trade (especially in Colombia's major markets!). Meanwhile, Washington chose Colombia as a favorite recipient of economic assistance under the Alliance for Progress, launched in 1961. Initially heralded as a "showcase" of the Alliance, Colombia got off to a fast start, but the collaboration with the United States soon soured. Corruption, mismanagement, and partisan politics marred the Colombian effort, while Washington's mounting preoccupation with other parts of the world—particularly the war in Vietnam—led to virtual abandonment of the Alliance. During the 1980s there emerged in Colombia a new commitment to the dogmas of free trade, according to many observers, a position that appeared to be justified by the debt crisis of that era, the subsequent globalization of markets, the expectations created by growing income from petroleum exports, and the impact of drug trafficking.

Gaitán, Reaction, and La Violencia

Politics was relatively peaceful during the transition from Conservative hegemony to the Liberal republic and through much of the 1930s and into the 1940s. Elections became free and fair, elites interacted with mutual respect, and there was evidence of social progress. This tranquil interlude would not last for long.

The initial challenge came from within—in the person of Jorge Eliécer Gaitán, a maverick Liberal who cultivated a mass following among the disadvantaged sectors of society. Based largely in the cities, his movement bore a resemblance to populist movements in Argentina, Brazil, Chile, and other countries of Latin America, although it lacked significant support from Colombian industrialists. Himself an outsider, Gaitán vigorously attacked the nation's "oligarchy" and championed the empowerment of ordinary people. Constructing his public image with care, he provided free legal defense to destitute criminal defendants. Calling for a "moral restoration" (as had Rafael Núñez a half century before), Gaitán spoke of the division of Colombian society into "the political country" and "the national country." For Gaitán, the "national country" represented all those who were excluded by the oligarchy from the "political country"—not only working people but also industrialists, agriculturalists, and members of the middle class.

Gaitán represented a threat—not only to the Conservatives, who held the presidency under Mariano Ospina Pérez (1946–50), but also to leaders of his own Liberal Party. Gaitán did not come from the elite. He denounced the oligarchy's ethos of civility as a charade for the perpetuation of power. He mobilized the masses. An electrifying speaker, he could command extraordinary loyalty—to

Mobilizing Masses, Empowering People

Rhetoric has always been an important source of political power, especially in Latin America. Artfully and thoughtfully, Jorge Eliécer Gaitán appealed to his followers with a series of carefully crafted slogans. As analyzed by historian Herbert Braun, Gaitán's phrases often held multiple meanings:

> Gaitán's slogan *"El pueblo es superior a sus dirigentes"* ("The pueblo is superior to its leaders") . . . was the most far-reaching of all his slogans, for it pointed to an overturning of the social order. Gaitán threatened the leaders with what they most feared, an ochlocracy [rule by the rabble], and he offered his followers a democracy. . . .
>
> Yet another masterfully crafted slogan—*"Yo no soy un hombre, soy un pueblo"* ("I am not a man, I am a pueblo")—reunited the two worlds that Gaitán had separated and reversed. He represented a new order with himself as head of the *país nacional*. The slogan contradicted the traditional distinction between private and public life. Gaitán was claiming to be an entirely public figure for reasons that were precisely the opposite of those of the *convivialistas:* they separated themselves from the pueblo; he was giving himself over to it. For his followers the slogan meant that their leader, a distinguished man with the character to challenge the convivialistas, was returning to the pueblo from which he had come.
>
> Gaitán's other major slogan, *"Por la restauración moral y democrática de la república"* ("Toward the moral and democratic restoration of the nation"), succinctly captured the elusive ideal of a return to a social order that the *convivialistas* had betrayed. It must have produced an intense feeling of racial isolation in the white elite, which saw any restoration, any return to the past, that was not led by them, as a return to the indigenous, pre-Hispanic origins of the nation.
>
> Even Gaitán's simple call to arms—*"A la carga"*—contained a meaning that is not readily apparent. The word *carga* also signifies a physical burden, a heavy weight to be carried. Every time Gaitán called the *pueblo* to action at the end of his orations, he was eliciting images of the daily world of labor. Gaitán ended most of his speeches by repeating these slogans. As the crowds grew accustomed to the ritual, he would call out, *"Pueblo,"* and the crowds responded: *"¡A la carga!" "¡Pueblo!" "¡Por la restauración moral y democrática de la república!" "¡Pueblo!" "¡A la victoria!" "¡Pueblo!" "¡Contra la oligarquía!"*

From Herbert Braun, *The Assassination of Gaitán: Public Life and Urban Violence in Colombia* (Madison: University of Wisconsin Press, 1985), pp. 102–3.

himself, not to the system or its leaders or even its institutions. To Colombia's traditionalists, Gaitán was an upstart—dangerous and unpredictable.

On April 9, 1948, Gaitán was shot by an unknown assailant in the center of Bogotá. His assassination prompted massive riots throughout the city, the so-called *bogotazo*. At first the uprising horrified and unified the traditional political elites. Once Gaitán became a martyr, however, the elites opted to destroy his

Angry crowds react violently to Gaitán's assassination by attacking symbols of traditional authority in the *bogotazo*.

legacy—by inciting partisan hostilities. This was a painful and defining moment in Colombian political life. The assassination of Gaitán closed the way to centrist and reformist solutions for decades to come. *Convivencia* was gone.

Gaitán's murder thus led to a grisly acceleration in political violence, an era known simply as *La Violencia*. It stretched from 1946 to 1964, with its most destructive period in 1948–53. Unbelievably, it resulted in as many as 200,000 deaths. Its fundamental cause was virulent partisanship, intensified by the Gaitán assassination and by the ethos of the Cold War. In part, it emerged from long-standing vendettas between rival family clans that had little to do with ideology. And from the mid-1950s to the mid-1960s it took the form of "Mafia" violence, as marauding groups sought economic gain instead of political power (by threatening coffee workers at harvest time, they could bring landowners to their knees). Concentrated in specific regions of the country, including the coffee belts, *La Violencia* nonetheless inflicted trauma on the national society at large.

In protest against what they regarded as the Conservative abuse of power, the Liberals abstained from the presidential election of 1949. This gave President Ospina an excuse to close Congress, pack the high courts with party loyalists, and declare a state of siege. Aided by the police, Conservative mobs sacked and burned the buildings of two of the most important and respected Liberal newspapers, *El Tiempo* and *El Espectador*. Thrown on the defensive, the Liberals formed guerrilla units. Violence and counterviolence mounted. Approximately 50,000 people were killed in 1950 alone.

With Liberals abstaining from the election, Conservative candidate Laureano Gómez assumed the presidency in 1950. An open admirer of Salazar's Portugal and Franco's Spain, Gómez sought to establish an ultraconservative order based on economic industrialization under state guidance, control (and repression) of labor unions, and electoral demobilization, to which Liberals unwittingly contributed by abstaining from elections. Eager to stimulate development, Gómez also promoted the expansion of the country's infrastructure—electrification, transportation, and communications.

Yet Gómez ran afoul of the military. When he attempted to remove General Gustavo Rojas Pinilla as commander of the armed forces in 1953, Rojas responded with a coup d'état. One of his first acts was to offer an amnesty to guerrillas, mostly Liberals, thus bringing the first phase of *La Violencia* to an end (as was mentioned earlier, a second phase would stretch to 1964). Inspired by the example of Juan Perón in Argentina, Rojas attempted to form his own political base, the Movimiento de Acción Nacional, and his own political party, the Third Force—which both major parties perceived as a threat. Also like Perón, Rojas sought to advance the position of women, incorporating women into the police force, appointing the first woman governor and the first woman cabinet minister in the history of the country, and promoting suffrage and full political rights for women in general. Moreover, he attempted to curry support among industrial workers.

As an economic crisis gripped the country, Colombia's traditional elites turned against him. In 1956 a coalition of Liberals and Conservatives formed an alliance to oust Rojas from power. Stiff opposition mounted from the church and from industrialists, merchants, and bankers, who managed to mount a general strike. In 1957 a frustrated Rojas resigned from office in favor of a military junta that oversaw a peaceful transition to a constitutional government.

These developments serve to highlight two distinctive characteristics of Colombia's twentieth-century politics. One was modest experience with military intervention. The Rojas Pinilla dictatorship was unquestionably authoritarian—but it was relatively mild and brief, more populist than conservative in ideological orientation. Unlike countries of the Southern Cone, Colombia never had to endure a "bureaucratic-authoritarian" regime or a state-sponsored "dirty war" against alleged subversives. In subsequent years, the Colombian military would exert significant influence on the political process and acquire a considerable degree of institutional autonomy. But it would not overthrow elected civilian governments.

Second, Colombia's transition to electoral democracy in the late 1950s was conspicuously uneventful. There was no wave of political assassinations, no bloodshed in the streets, no external war. Essentially, the return to democracy resulted from an amicable bargain among traditional elites. The process was remarkably smooth. In retrospect, it may have been too smooth.

The National Front

Emerging from the anti-Rojas coalition of 1956–57, the National Front resulted from a formal pact between the majorities of both the Liberal and Conservative parties. Under the terms of the agreement, the presidency would alternate between Liberals and Conservatives, and all positions in the three branches of government, throughout the country, would be distributed evenly between the two parties. In effect it created an automatic mechanism that would remove uncertainty from electoral politics. Endorsed by nearly 95 percent of the participants in a national plebiscite in late 1957, the compact was scheduled to last until 1974. In 1968 the two parties reached a supplementary pact called the *desmonte* (or "dismantling"), which confirmed an understanding that there would be an "equitable" representation of the two parties in the national cabinet after the expiration of the Front in 1974.

The National Front had several goals. One key purpose was to bring an end to the still-continuing *Violencia* by freezing the current distribution of political assets. A second was to restore constitutional democracy and the ethos of civility or *convivencia*. A third, of course, was to ensure that politicians of both parties would have access to power. As they learned during the Rojas Pinilla dictatorship, any share of power would be much more pleasing than none.

With access to office guaranteed, political competition during the National Front took place not so much between the parties as within the parties. This led to the trivialization of political discussion and a plethora of factional infighting. And by definition, the Front denied political representation to those who did not support the traditional parties. So it ended partisan fighting between the Liberals and the Conservatives; by excluding all others, however, it provoked new forms of anti-system violence.

Nor did the National Front lead to a visionary social policy. One of the most important issues for Colombia was agrarian reform. Legislation adopted under the Liberal Alberto Lleras Camargo (1958–62) was disregarded by Conservative Guillermo León Valencia (1962–66). It was resuscitated by another Liberal, Carlos Lleras Restrepo (1966–70), who encouraged peasant mobilizations. Later, under another Conservative, the government suspended land distribution in 1972, and the leaders of both parties agreed to abandon the entire project. In its place, the Liberals proposed an income tax on land—which would presumably encourage the sale of lands—but that proposal was blocked by the Conservatives in the late 1970s. Such a prolonged partisan stalemate provoked discontent throughout the countryside.

As might have been expected, this situation gave rise to armed revolutionary movements representing political elements that were excluded from the National Front. First to appear was the Ejército de Liberación Nacional (ELN, or National Liberation Army), created in 1962 by university students who denounced the "parliamentary cretinism" of the Communist Party and, by extension, traditional elites and the National Front as a whole. Initially focused on urban areas, the ELN extended its operations in the late 1960s to the countryside, where it met with a decisive military defeat in 1973. As distress mounted among *campesinos*, the ELN would later regroup, and by the 1980s it began launching systematic and repeated attacks on oil pipelines owned by U.S. companies.

The Fuerzas Armadas Revolucionarias de Colombia (FARC, or Revolutionary Armed Forces of Colombia) emerged in 1966. The FARC had its roots in communist-led peasant agitation dating back to the 1920s, and, unlike the ELN, it had a largely agrarian focus. From experience in these struggles, the FARC's preeminent leader, Manuel Marulanda, had acquired the nickname of "Tirofijo" ("Sureshot"). In reaction to attacks from government forces, the FARC developed mobile guerrilla units for offensive action. In the 1980s FARC leadership broke with the Communist Party and became an independent revolutionary organization with its own military and political doctrines. The FARC also formed tactical alliances with narco-traffickers, and by the 1990s it was the most powerful guerrilla movement in Colombia.

In the meantime, Gustavo Rojas Pinilla had returned to the political stage in the 1960s and established an opposition party, Acción Nacional Popular (or ANAPO). Starting out with less than 4 percent of the vote in 1962, ANAPO soon became a potent electoral force—thus threatening the National Front, whose basic premise was a Liberal-Conservative duopoly on power. Espousing a credo of "socialism on Christian bases in the Colombian manner," Rojas Pinilla directed his appeal to the country's urban masses. A nationalist, he sought to impose restrictions on foreign investment; a social conservative, he endorsed a ban on birth control. In some ways Rojas bore an uncanny resemblance to Jorge Gaitán, who had so effectively mobilized the working class and urban poor during the 1940s.

As a result of ANAPO's rise, the National Front lost credibility in the election of 1970. Many people thought Rojas Pinilla won the most votes. On election night the government cancelled the transmission of results, however, and the next day it announced the victory of the official candidate, the Conservative Misael Pastrana. The official tally awarded ANAPO 35 percent, still a respectable showing. President Carlos Lleras Restrepo, an otherwise distinguished statesman, confirmed this outcome and promptly imposed a curfew in the nation's major cities. Initially hailed as a triumph for democracy, the National Front came to an ignominious end.

The disputed election of 1970 spawned yet another guerrilla movement, the April 19th movement (or M-19, named for the date of the election). A radical splinter group from ANAPO, urban in origin and focus, M-19 was initially influenced by the (temporary) success of Montoneros in Argentina and Tupamaros in Uruguay. It mounted some spectacular operations. In a monumentally symbolic attack, M-19 chagrined the Colombian military by snatching the sword of Simón Bolívar. In 1980 its adherents seized the embassy of the Dominican Republic, holding diplomats and others hostage. And in November 1985, M-19 guerrillas seized the Palace of Justice, prompting an all-out assault by the military; the resultant pitched battle led to the deaths of twelve justices of the

Supreme Court, all forty-one guerrillas involved, and many lawyers and innocent citizens. (Over the door of the Palace of Justice, through which army tanks rolled to mow down the rebels, are written the words "Colombians, arms have given you independence. Laws will give you freedom." This lofty rhetoric was overshadowed by harsh reality.) Thereafter viewed in a negative light, M-19 eventually chose to abandon armed struggle in order to participate in civilian politics.

In the 1974 election—the first without guarantees for the two parties—the Liberals overwhelmed the Conservatives. Alfonso López Michelsen (the son of Alfonso López Pumarejo) became president after forging an alliance with a notorious machine politician, Julio César Turbay, a move that disillusioned many citizens. The Liberals dominated both houses of Congress by a ratio of nearly 2:1. Undivided government did little to improve the policy process, however, and many citizens became alienated from national politics. Disillusion spread even further as Turbay, master of the Liberal machine, won the party's nomination and became president in 1978.

Colombia was hit by the debt crisis during the administration of Belisario Betancur, a Conservative (1982–86). In contrast to Argentina and especially Mexico, Colombia had kept public borrowing to modest levels, but private debts incurred by manufacturing enterprises created an acute industrial crisis. To assist with debt scheduling, the International Monetary Fund followed its usual policy of economic orthodoxy by demanding a drastic reduction in public expenditures, which required a freeze on public-sector wages and cuts in education and housing for the poor, and devaluation of the peso, which had the effect of protecting domestic manufacturers from foreign competition.

The presidential baton then passed to Virgilio Barco (1986–90), a Liberal who brought the *desmonte* to a close by abandoning the concept of a bipartisan cabinet. Barco began to dismantle the tariff protection of domestic industry, a process that would be completed in the early 1990s. Even so, guerrilla groups and drug cartels were gaining strength, and political violence continued to mount. In August 1989, the assassination of Liberal presidential candidate Luis Carlos Galán, ordered by drug traffickers, sent shock waves throughout Colombian society. In an effort to address these challenges, Barco made his most significant decision: to hold a plebiscite that would pave the way for a constitutional convention.

THE CONTEMPORARY SCENE (1990–PRESENT)

In response to popular demand, Liberal Party president César Gaviria (1990–94) oversaw the election of a constitutional assembly in December 1990. A special feature of this process was an offer of amnesty to guerrilla movements—an invitation that was promptly accepted by the M-19 movement, which became a significant force within the assembly itself. The delegates held sessions until mid-1991, at which time they approved a new charter. It sought to strengthen key institutions, protect civil rights, open channels for citizen participation in politics, and regulate the relationship between the executive and legislative branches. Indeed, it was hoped that the new constitution would work miracles, establishing peace and promoting national reconciliation. Offering a controversial judgment, political scientist Fernando Cepeda Ulloa declared: "It would not be an exaggeration to state that the new 1991 constitution left Colombia well endowed as far as the potential for democratic governance was concerned."

Despite its virtues, the new constitution created its share of problems. By establishing processes of executive and legislative appointments for the majority of positions on the top administrative court, it tended to politicize the country's already tottering judicial branch. By mandating the transfer of nearly one-half of national revenues to municipalities and provincial departments, it brought about a fiscal crisis for the central state. By encouraging the formation of multiple parties, it contributed to the fragmentation of political forces. And by establishing a vice presidency and runoff elections for the presidency, it not only undermined the dominance of the Liberal Party—but also weakened the nation's long-standing party system.

One positive trend was increased enfranchisement for women. By 2002, women held 12 percent of the seats in the lower House and 13 percent in the Senate—just about the same proportions as those in the United States. Equally significant, women held nearly one-fifth of the cabinet positions. (Indeed, a woman would serve as minister of defense.) Unlike some other Latin American countries, Colombia did not establish a "quota law" for female representation in parties' electoral slates, but it eventually took the unusual step of requiring that women make up 30 percent of senior decision makers in the public sector.

Despite the new constitution, Colombia would face the prospect of disintegration throughout the 1990s. Outlaw organizations posed serious and mounting threats to state authority. One source of danger came from narco-trafficking gangs that made enormous profits from the export of cocaine, principally to the United States. Especially prone to violence was the Medellín cartel, under the ruthless leadership of Pablo Escobar, who finally met his death in a shoot-out in late 1993. The U.S. government was deeply involved in the hunt for Escobar, dispatching technical assistance and a military sniper team. And all the while, Washington insisted that the cause of illicit drug trafficking came from production in South America, rather than consumption within the United States.

After Escobar's demise, a cartel from the city of Cali came to the fore, less violent, more subtle, and focused more on profits than on the elimination of enemies. When this group was disbanded and broken up as a result of top-level arrests, drug trafficking continued—now in the hands of dozens of smaller cartels, less centralized, less visible, and more difficult to trace. Colombia thus confronted a simple fact: as long as there was strong demand for illicit drugs in foreign markets, especially the United States, there would be supply.

As drug cartels were rising and falling, Colombia shifted its position in the production of cocaine—made from coca leaves grown only in South America. Traditionally, Colombian traffickers relied on Bolivia and Peru for their raw product, purchasing coca leaves (or coca paste) and transforming it into powdered cocaine in clandestine laboratories. In effect, this arrangement gave Colombian traffickers a virtual monopoly on world cocaine supplies. Shipping their goods to overseas markets

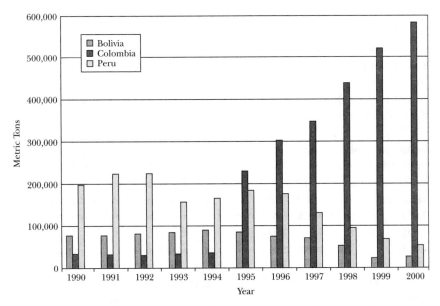

Figure 7.2 Coca Leaf Production: Colombia and Other Countries, 1990–2000
Note: Estimates of coca and cocaine yield figures for Colombia were revised upward in 1999, beginning with data for 1995.
SOURCE: U.S. Office of National Drug Control Strategy, *National Drug Control Strategy* (Washington, D.C.: The White House, 2003), Data Supplement, Table 46.

(principally the United States and Europe), they could acquire massive profits. During the 1990s, however, production declined sharply in Bolivia and Peru—for a variety of reasons, including governmental repression—and Colombian *campesinos* picked up the slack. As is revealed in Figure 7.2, Colombia became the world's leading source of coca leaf by the mid-1990s and would continue its ascendancy, producing nearly 600,000 estimated metric tons in 2000. By 2003, Colombia was thought to produce three-quarters of the cocaine consumed in the United States.

Drug cartels undermined the authority of the Colombian government in several ways. First, they employed violence and intimidation. Especially under Escobar, the Medellín cartel waged virtual war against the government in the late 1980s and early 1990s; in particular, they were reacting against an official decision to extradite drug traffickers for trial in the United States. To emphasize their point, they assassinated scores of judges, prosecutors, law enforcement agents, and political figures. Medellín operatives went so far as to blow up an Avianca airliner that was thought to be carrying police informants. Four out of six presidential candidates in the 1990 election process were shot to death. Second, narco-traffickers compromised government authorities through the extensive and effective use of bribery. Third, they won public support by presenting themselves in Robin Hood roles—sponsoring soccer teams, building playgrounds, supporting charities, and the like. Fourth, the drug lords displayed a brazen sense of impunity. The weakness of the judicial system and police corruption became especially conspicuous. At one point Pablo Escobar, for example, had submitted to detention only after lengthy negotiations with authorities; he then continued to conduct day-to-day business in a special and luxurious prison of his own design, from which he later walked away. In its confrontations with drug traffickers, the government seemed powerless.

The second threat came from guerrilla groups, which gained strength through the 1980s and 1990s. The FARC acquired economic leverage through its alliances with narco-traffickers, and it moved directly into the cultivation of coca, marijuana, and opium poppies. According to official estimates, the FARC expanded from 3600 insurgents in 1986 to about 7000 in 1995 and as many as 15,000 (or even 20,000) by 2000. During the same period, the ELN grew from only 800 insurgents in the mid-1980s to 5000 by 2000. In sharp contrast to other countries of Latin America, where revolutionary movements had all but disappeared, Colombia continued to face serious challenges from armed insurgencies.

Relationships between drug cartels and guerrilla groups were mercurial and changeable. Alliances were tactical, instrumental, and often extortionate. In exchange for a "tax" on drug profits, for instance, guerrilla groups sometimes furnished military protection for traffickers and coca-growing *campesinos*. By the late 1990s, too, it appeared that the FARC was actively involved in the cultivation of coca leaf. To this extent guerrillas and traffickers shared common interests. At the same time, conflict and tensions persisted. M-19 and other guerrilla groups attempted to extract ransom from drug traffickers by kidnapping relatives of cartel members; in furious response, the cartels unleashed a vicious campaign of "death to kidnappers" (*muerte a secuestra-dores*). On their part, nouveau riche drug traffickers sometimes used their vast profits to purchase rural estates—thus joining the landed oligarchy against which agrarian rebels had taken up arms in the first place. Guerrillas and traffickers fought one another just as often as they forged alliances.

Directly and indirectly, these developments led to the emergence of still another threat: armed "paramilitary" units that presented themselves as self-defense groups. If the government could not protect its citizens, according to maximum leader Carlos Castaño, the people would have to fend for themselves. In fact the paramilitary groups functioned as self-appointed vigilante units that unleashed violent attacks for a broad variety of motives—economic, political, and personal. With a vaguely right-wing ideology, paramilitary units tended to offer their services to prominent landlords, wealthy businessmen, and, at times, opportunistic drug traffickers. By 2000 they were said to have 4500–5000 members. Evidence showed that paramilitary units had close ties to the Colombian armed forces and that their ranks included soldiers, policemen, and even ex-guerrillas.

Triangular conflicts among drug cartels, guerrillas, and paramilitaries inflicted frightful levels of violence on Colombian society. From the 1950s through the end of the 1970s, homicide rates in Colombia averaged around 30 per 100,000 citizens—the highest in Latin America, but still within range of other violent countries (including Brazil, Mexico, Nicaragua, and Panama). Then levels in Colombia began to escalate: by 1990 the rate had climbed to 86 per 100,000, and by 1995 it was 95 per 100,000.

Assaults, kidnappings, and assassinations mounted steadily throughout the late 1990s. Violence had returned to the land of *La Violencia*. The traffic in drugs was clearly a major provocation as Medellín became the nation's murder capital.

Colombian governments struggled to meet these multiple challenges, but with little visible success. Glimmers of hope appeared under César Gaviria, a Liberal, who oversaw the constitutional process of 1991 and the disarming of M-19 (it was troubling, though, that neither the FARC nor the ELN accepted the government's offer of amnesty). An effective leader, Gaviria undertook what he called a "peaceful revolution," more popularly known in Colombia as *el revolcón* (literally, the upset, tumble, or turnover). In addition to promoting peace, he accelerated the process of economic opening, creating a new ministry for foreign trade, reducing tariffs, and encouraging foreign investment. At the end of his term, he was elected secretary-general of the Organization of American States, in which post he would serve with distinction.

The Liberal Party won the elections of 1994 but only after a second-round runoff, when Ernesto Samper defeated Conservative Andrés Pastrana by just 2 percentage points (50.3 percent to 48.2 percent). Almost as soon as he took office, Samper's presidency fell under the cloud of scandal—specifically, accusations that he had accepted over $6 million in campaign funds from the Cali drug cartel. Under pressure, Samper conceded that campaign operatives had accepted drug money, but he denied any personal knowledge of these transactions. In what became known as "the trial of the century"—the first time a sitting president was subject to possible impeachment—the Colombian Congress undertook an investigation. In June 1996 the legislature voted to discontinue its inquiry (implicitly absolving Samper) by a margin of 111–43. Suspicious of a cover-up, skeptics noted that the president's own party dominated the Congress and that two dozen members of Congress were themselves facing charges of corruption. As a result, the Samper administration became virtually powerless—while public confidence in the nation's political system plummeted to all-time lows.

Assuming a moralistic stance, the United States responded to these developments by "decertifying" Colombia for inadequate efforts in the fight against drugs. In particular, Washington was unhappy with Samper's refusal to extradite captured drug kingpins to the United States. And in July 1996, shortly after the congressional vote in his favor, the Clinton administration revoked Samper's visa for travel to the United States.

With the Liberals discredited, the Conservatives finally won the presidential election of 1998. This time Andrés Pastrana selected a provincial governor associated with the M-19 as vice presidential candidate and, in a second-round runoff, defeated the Liberal candidate by 49 percent to 46 percent. Yet the Liberals did well in legislative races, so Pastrana took office without a working majority in either chamber of congress. Colombians thus encountered the realities of a divided government.

In search of peace and reconciliation, Pastana adopted a fresh approach toward the guerrillas, creating a demilitarized zone (DMZ) by withdrawing army units from the southwestern part of the country and opening negotiations with the FARC. Talks dragged on for years and then broke down in 2001–2. In September 2001 the FARC murdered the wife of the attorney general, herself a well-known public figure who had served as the minister of culture, and blocked efforts to resume negotiations. Full-scale hostilities resumed when Pastrana ordered military units to retake the DMZ, and guerrillas stepped up activities in urban as well as rural areas.

Observing these developments with mounting alarm, the United States finally agreed to provide the Pastrana administration with a $1.3 billion aid package in support of "Plan Colombia," initially designed as a multifaceted strategy to facilitate peace, revive economic development, combat drug trafficking, and strengthen the democratic pillars of Colombian society (the estimated price tag: $7.5 billion). Yet the Clinton administration earmarked almost all its aid for military hardware, rather than regional development or crop substitution, and stipulated that it should be used only for antidrug efforts—not for counterinsurgency. Critics of the plan voiced warnings about the dangers of getting involved in a Vietnam-like "quagmire," raised concerns about the potential for violations of human rights, and expressed skepticism about the plausibility of separating antidrug operations from antiguerrilla campaigns.

The terrorist attacks against the United States on September 11, 2001, suddenly altered this entire context. U.S. policymakers became less queasy about the use and risks of military force. Terrorists everywhere became a source of danger. As talks broke down with the FARC and ELN, President Pastrana denounced the insurgent groups as "terrorists." For different but related reasons, both the United States and Colombia adopted implacable stands.

In this atmosphere the election of 2002 went to Álvaro Uribe, a dissident Liberal who vowed to crush guerrilla movements with unyielding force. (His own father had been assassinated by FARC guerrillas.) A former mayor of Medellín and governor of Antioquia, Uribe took 53 percent of the vote as Liberals won majorities in both houses of Congress. His get-tough attitude got off to an uneven start when guerrilla violence surrounding his inauguration prompted him to declare a ninety-day state of emergency. As president, Uribe confronted two major challenges: managing the apparently intractable internal conflict while upholding civil liberties and improving the human-rights records of the military and the police, and consolidating the country's finances amid poverty and unemployment (which had climbed to more than 15 percent).

The Bush administration offered strong support to Uribe. Washington resisted the temptation to extend its own antiterrorism war to Colombia—despite impassioned entreaties from some quarters—but continued military aid. In 2002 the U.S. Congress authorized the use of American counternarcotics assistance for counterinsurgency operations, thus erasing the line that had been drawn under Clinton. For 2003 U.S. aid came to approximately $573 million. Of this amount, about $100 million was intended to protect an oil pipeline operated by Occidental Petroleum, the target of more than a thousand guerrilla attacks since its opening in the mid-1980s.

Uribe retained substantial popularity, if polls can be believed, with a 64 percent approval rating in mid-2003. Like others before him, however, he discovered that there were limits to his power. Congressional support remained fragile. Opposition parties achieved important footholds in local elections, taking office in such prominent cities as Bogotá, Cali, and Medellín. Voters rejected a complex proposal for constitutional reform. Eventually, though, Uribe managed to secure approval for a constitutional amendment permitting reelection. In May 2006 he triumphed in a landslide, with 62 percent of the vote. At the same time, legislative elections produced a pro-Uribe majority and heralded the imminent demise of Liberal-Conservative traditional party dominance. Something new was in the air.

The Kidnapping of Ingrid Betancourt

One of the most highly publicized confrontations between the FARC and the Colombian government involved the case of Ingrid Betancourt.

A woman of aristocratic bearing and French-Colombian citizenship, Betancourt ran for the presidency on behalf of the Green Oxygen (*Oxígeno Verde*) party. One of her signature campaign gambits was to distribute Viagra pills to startled Colombian men and proceed to explain that the country needed a comparable boost of energy. She consistently denounced the FARC's strategy of seizing prominent hostages and demanded a halt to this practice: *No más secuestros,* she declared more than once, "No more kidnappings."

On February 23, 2002, en route to a meeting with guerrilla leaders, Betancourt's entourage ran into a FARC checkpoint and she was taken hostage. According to one of her captors, the kidnapping was not planned beforehand. Her name still appeared on the presidential ballot and she received a token vote. Because of her international profile, nongovernmental organizations in the European Union and around the world rallied to her support.

Years of agonizing uncertainty followed. The newly elected administration of Álvaro Uribe was reluctant to exchange guerrilla prisoners for the FARC's hostages. (Having launched its own "global war on terror," the Bush administration in Washington supported this hard line.) Betancourt's family members rejected an armed rescue attempt as too dangerous. The governments of France and Venezuela offered to mediate some form of humanitarian exchange. Rumors indicated that Betancourt's health was failing.

On July 2, 2008, six and a half years after the kidnapping, Colombian security forces succeeded in rescuing Betancourt and fourteen other hostages (three Americans, eleven Colombians). Code-named "Operation Jaque" (Spanish for "check," as in checkmate), this was a daring and carefully planned maneuver.

Freed from captivity, Betancourt became the object of enthusiastic international acclaim. She met with Pope Benedict XVI and received the French Legion of Honor and the Concord Prince of Asturias Award. President Michelle Bachelet of Chile announced her intention to nominate Betancourt for the Nobel Peace Prize. Addressing herself to the FARC leadership at a rally in France in July 2008, Betancourt issued an eloquent appeal: "See this Colombia ... and understand that it is time to stop the bloodshed. It is time to drop those weapons and exchange them for roses, substitute them with tolerance, respect, and as brothers and sisters that we are, find a way so that we can all live together in the world, live together in Colombia."

Colombia thus confronted an enduring dilemma: how to meet serious challenges from antisystem forces while sustaining its commitment to electoral democracy and capitalist economics. This was made all the more difficult by what observers regarded as the country's "crisis of governability." National politics revealed unresolved tension between the lure of the future and the pull of the past. At the same time, a new generation of politicians was coming to the fore—more parochial than national in outlook, more opportunistic than pragmatic or patriotic. In a society that was accustomed to moderate leadership, governance became erratic and uneven.

It would be an exaggeration to classify Colombia as a "failed state." But it is a gravely weakened state. As historian John Coatsworth has said, Colombia remains "a shaky archipelago of modern cities surrounded by an ocean of neglect." The outcome of this nation's search for social comity and governmental capacity will have serious consequences not only for Colombia but also for the Western Hemisphere.

8

~~~

Venezuela
The Perils of Prosperity

Venezuela is a land of surprises. Instead of finding the mythical El Dorado, European explorers encountered native huts on stilts in a large lake and christened the area "little Venice"—a name that has stuck ever since. Despite visionary leadership and ideological zeal, the Wars of Independence from Spain led to little alteration of the colonial order. Departing from long-term reliance on traditional agriculture, twentieth-century Venezuela embarked on a free-wheeling petroleum bonanza, a decision that would change the face of the country. When neighboring nations were succumbing to brutal military repression, Venezuela was proudly upholding a political democracy. And in a sharp reversal of roles, Venezuela has most recently been moving toward populist authoritarianism—just as other countries in the region have been holding free and fair elections. Indeed, Venezuela has somehow seemed different from the rest of Latin America—a nation apart, distinctive in orientation, out of step with continental trends, an "exception" to dominant patterns and trends. Is this really the case?

The tale of Venezuela begins with geography. Located on the northern tier of South America, it embraces a remarkably diverse topography—mountains, valleys, coastline, rivers, deserts, and jungles. Along the western border with Colombia, a spur of the Andes splits east and west to form the gigantic basin for Lake Maracaibo. In the central part of the country, a lesser mountain range runs parallel to the Caribbean coast; it was in this temperate zone that settlers founded the capital city of Caracas, safely protected from pirates, with La Güaira serving as its port. The eastward coast of Venezuela moves into the majestic Orinoco Delta, spanning some 250 miles on the ocean side, a low-lying humid zone with a rainy climate—not an inviting site for settlement, but an efficient route to the interior. East of the Andes and south of the Orinoco there stretch vast and extensive plains, known as *llanos*, reaching all the way to the Guyana highlands. South of these *llanos* lies a sizable portion of the Amazon jungle, an area that crosses the country's border with Brazil.

Map 8 Venezuela

FROM COLONY TO NATIONHOOD

Columbus made landfall on the Caribbean coast in 1498, on his third voyage, believing that he had reached India. Venezuela did not offer a tempting site for conquest. There was no mythical kingdom, no prosperous civilization sitting atop a mountain of gold. Early explorers instead encountered a large number of indigenous groups, each with its own language. In contrast to Mexico and Peru, where the *conquistadores* struck at major urban centers, the Spaniards took control of Venezuela at a gradual, tentative, and erratic pace—expeditions were small, resistance was determined, and native communities were scattered and diverse.

There were no great fortunes to be made. Pearl beds around Isla Margarita led to a short-lived boom, but the real wealth of colonial Venezuela came from livestock and agriculture, especially cacao. As the indigenous population of the Caribbean declined, slaving raids for Indians set the tone of Spanish-Indian relations. And after smallpox decimated the native population, additional slaves were imported from Africa.

From the sixteenth to the early eighteenth century, Venezuela developed as an outpost for Spain's empire in America. Its principal roles were to produce food-stuffs for the larger and more important colony of New Spain (Mexico) and to bolster the southern flank of imperial defenses in the Caribbean. Founded in 1567 and governed by capable municipal elites, Caracas eventually became the central hub of political and economic life. A site of higher learning, the Real y Pontífica Universidad de Caracas, was established in 1725. Given the crown's relative inattention to the region, missionary orders picked up the slack: Franciscans, Capuchins, Dominicans, Jesuits, and Augustinians all became key actors in the formation of colonial society.

As in other parts of the Americas, the Spanish crown's attempts to improve and centralize imperial administration helped lay the basis for independence. Bourbon reforms in the late eighteenth century enhanced the already-dominant position of Caracas and created a nascent sense of unity. Prominent among these were the establishment of colony-wide intendancy (1776), a single captaincy-general (1777), an *audiencia* (1786), a merchant-farmer *consulado* (1793), and finally an archbishopric (1804)—all headquar-tered in the city of Caracas. The more important Venezuela became, the more likely it was to break away.

Not surprisingly, it was the newly empowered Caracas elite that led the charge for independence. Upon news of the Napoleonic invasion, the *caraqueño* cabildo proclaimed its support for Ferdinand VII—and, for good measure, abolished the slave trade as well. A declaration of independence in 1811 led to the inauguration of a hapless *patria boba* ("republic of the dunces") that was promptly overthrown by Spanish forces. Simón Bolívar entered the fray in 1813, took temporary control of Caracas and in the face of defeat fled to exile (where he wrote the memorable "letter from Jamaica," an exposition of his political philosophy). The indefatigable Bolívar returned to action in 1816, led successful military campaigns, issued a proclamation on freedom of the slaves, and was elected president of Venezuela by a congress of notables in 1819. After crossing the Andes later that year, he became president of the newly formed republic of Gran Colombia (including Ecuador, Venezuela, and Colombia).

The decade of the 1820s gave political shape to continental independence. In 1824 Bolívar and Antonio José Sucre secured the independence of Peru with decisive military victories. In the meantime, José Antonio Páez—a rough-hewn warrior from the *llanos*—was chafing under Bolívar's domineering leadership and launched a separatist movement. Five years later, his continued agitation resulted in Venezuela's formal secession from the Gran Colombia and in sovereign independence. National liberation thus came at the expense of one of Bolívar's fondest dreams.

Throughout the hard-fought independence wars, Venezuela suffered frightful levels of physical and economic devastation. In the face of Spanish military might, insurgent elites needed all the help they could get. To attract support from blacks, liberation leaders proclaimed an end to slavery; to engage mulattoes *(pardos)* and mixed-bloods as well, they pronounced their opposition to official ethnic labeling. Yet these were timid steps, and they did not precipitate a major social transformation. In the judgment of historian John Lombardi:

> If great changes were to have come to Spanish America in the upheaval of independence they should have happened in the land of Bolívar, where institutions were recently formed and relatively weak, where the power and wealth of the local aristocracy appeared much less than in viceregal capitals, where the racial tensions of a *pardo* society appeared very high, and where the disorder and destruction of a decade of civil war provided an excellent opportunity for radical change. That republican Venezuela managed to preserve intact many colonial forms and most colonial structures is eloquent testimony to the strength of the Spanish-American social and economic system, one carefully created and adjusted to local requirements for three hundred years.

Essentially, the neocolonial social structure of Venezuela would remain in place for the following 100 years. It was not until the 1920s that major change would come.

Coffee and Caudillos

With the onset of independence, Venezuela succumbed to political rule by *caudillos*—military chieftains, official or unofficial, in command of personal armies dedicated to the advancement of their leader and to judicious shares of the spoils from combat. The essential ingredients for success were military prowess and control of the capital city.

At stake were the terms of Venezuela's relationship to newly available markets in Europe and, later on, the United States. Which regions would take charge? Which interests would benefit the most? Would it be coffee planters of the Andes, cacao farmers along the central mountain range, or ranchers of the *llanos?* Caracas, of course, formed the pivotal link between the hinterland and the overseas markets.

Within this context, José Antonio Páez, a tough-minded *llanero* of rudimentary education, dominated Venezuelan politics from 1830 to 1848. His principal achievement was to promote the transition from a cacao-oriented colonial economy to a coffee-producing international economy. In exchange for generous loans from European merchant houses to the local planter class, the Páez administration adopted a free trade model of development which included two vital conditions—security of property and sanctity of contracts. The scheme worked well enough throughout the 1830s.

A drop in coffee prices in the 1840s brought underlying tensions into the open. Invoking the sanctity of contracts, the money lenders demanded payments on their loans; with earnings in decline, the planters could not keep up with their obligations.

Disagreements between Conservatives and Liberals were at this point more instrumental than ideological. Since the Catholic Church had never acquired the power during the colonial period that it had in Mexico or Peru, the church-state relationship posed a less inflammatory issue in nineteenth-century Venezuela. More prominent differences concerned the relative strength of central versus local government, but even that question often became blurred by personalistic struggles between rival *caudillos*.

Economic interests also shaped political allegiances. The Conservatives, under Páez, were tied to the moneylenders and foreign agents; the Liberals, led by Antonio Leocadio Guzmán, represented the debt-ridden planters. After several years of discord and confusion, the Monagas brothers, José Tadeo and José Gregorio, imposed a period of Liberal domination—replete with laws for debt relief and a repeal of the sanctity of contracts. They abolished slavery and passed a mining code affirming the traditional Spanish rule that subsoil rights belonged to the nation. To symbolize national progress, the Monagas brothers oversaw installation of a telegraph line between Caracas and its coastal port at La Güaira. The economy continued to founder, however, as Liberal officials scrambled to rescue the agricultural elite from the debt-mongers. Easy credit and uncertain profits created a volatile mixture.

Intensification of regional and economic conflicts erupted in full-scale civil strife in 1858. The septuagenarian Páez returned to establish a dictatorship from 1861 to 1863, at which point his Conservatives lost the war to a faction calling themselves Federalists. Installed as vice president in 1864, the ultimate leader of the Federalists would prove to be Antonio Guzmán Blanco—the son of Antonio Leocadio Guzmán, former spokesman of the Liberals. True to *caudillo* traditions, Guzmán Blanco would lead an uprising against his president and seize power in 1870.

An unusual figure, Guzmán Blanco belonged to both of Venezuela's worlds, archaic and modern. Fond of being known as "The Illustrious American" *(el americano ilustre)*, he set about three related tasks: establishing public order, revitalizing international trade, and improving governmental efficiency. A reformer of sorts, Guzmán Blanco openly challenged the traditional monopolies of the church: he made education free and compulsory, closed religious seminaries and convents, awarded responsibility for religious studies to the national university, and established civil marriage. Intent on self-enrichment as well as economic development, he cultivated foreign loans as both a personal and national resource. During the 1870s and 1880s Guzmán Blanco had himself reelected as necessary, claiming victory by "acclamation" for his third and final term. Yet popular reaction mounted against his use of repression. He departed on a trip to Europe in August 1887 and, learning of the discontent back home, he resigned the presidency in 1888.

GUNBOATS AND DIPLOMACY

Subsequent years marked Venezuela's entry onto the stage of global politics. It was not an auspicious debut. Two prominent events would confirm a time-honored maxim of international relations: big powers do what they want, small countries do what they must.

The first episode concerned a boundary dispute in the mid-1890s between Venezuela and British Guiana, which England had acquired from Holland by treaty in 1814. In 1835 the British claimed a western boundary that effectively expanded its territory by 30,000 square miles; Venezuela insisted on the delineations in place at the time of independence from Spain. When gold was discovered, Britain further extended its claim by an additional 33,000 square miles. But the most critical issue was neither land nor minerals; it was control over the Orinoco Delta.

Earnestly invoking the Monroe Doctrine, Venezuela appealed for help to U.S. president Grover Cleveland. The United States had two interests in the dispute: maintaining its access to the Orinoco, and curtailing British influence within the Western Hemisphere. In 1895 the U.S. Congress announced its opposition to the British claims, and Secretary of State Richard Olney dispatched an unusually blunt message to London:

> Today the United States is practically sovereign on this continent, and its fiat is law upon the subjects to which it confines its interposition. Why? It is not because of the friendship or good will felt for it. It is not simply by reason of its high character as a civilized state, nor because wisdom and justice and equity are the invariable characteristics of the dealings of the United States. It is because, in addition to all other grounds, its infinite resources combined with its isolated position render it master of the situation and practically invulnerable as against any or all other powers.

Even while scoffing at the Monroe Doctrine, Britain's foreign minister accepted Olney's proposal for arbitration. A boundary commission was initially formed with two American jurists, two British, and one Russian; after a vigorous protest, Venezuela was allowed to have one representative on the board. Four years later, the commission rendered a decision that confirmed the 1835 boundary.

For the United States, this outcome represented a major step in its long-term campaign to assert hegemony over the Americas. For Britain, it represented a tactical retreat—and a willingness to recognize U.S. dominion in the hemisphere. For Venezuela, it was a bitter pill to swallow. And for Latin America as a whole, Olney's intemperate message offered a transparent declaration of U.S. arrogance and condescension.

The second episode occurred during the dictatorship of General Cipriano Castro, who governed with an iron hand from 1899 to 1908. The most memorable development of his tenure would illustrate the dangers of defaulting on debts.

Confronted by an economic downturn, near-constant regional uprisings, and budget deficits resulting from his personal excesses, Castro declared a moratorium in 1902 on debt payments to Venezuela's European creditors. In a furious response, Britain, Germany, and Italy dispatched warships to blockade the Venezuelan coast and, thereafter, to bombard the country's ports. A distinguished Argentine diplomat, Luis María Drago, passionately urged the United States to declare its opposition to the use of military force for the collection of debts. President Teddy Roosevelt demurred but initiated negotiations that resulted in the Washington Protocol of 1903, an agreement obliging Venezuela to allot 30 percent of its customs duties toward payment of the European claims.

Surveying the situation a year later, Roosevelt laid a cornerstone of U.S. policy toward the region. "Any country whose people conduct themselves well," he began,

> can count upon our hearty friendship. If a nation shows that it knows how to act with reasonable efficiency and decency in social and political matters, if it keeps order to pay its obligations, it need fear no interference from the United States. Chronic wrong-doing, or an impotence which results in a general loosening of the ties of society, may in America, as elsewhere, ultimately require intervention by some civilized nation, and in the western hemisphere the adherence of the United States to the Monroe Doctrine may force the United States, however reluctantly, in flagrant cases of such wrong-doing or impotence, to the exercise of an international police power.

Known as the "Roosevelt Corollary" to the Monroe Doctrine, the statement contained a dual purpose. First, it warned Latin America of U.S. readiness to exercise an "international police power" whenever necessary. Second, it warned Europe to keep its gunboats out of the Americas, now proclaimed by Roosevelt to be an exclusive U.S. sphere of influence. Once again, Venezuela was finding itself to be merely a pawn in big-power politics.

In the wake of this humiliation, Castro decided to curry the favor of foreign interests. To take advantage of lucrative asphalt deposits, a new mining law in 1905 allowed the government to grant concessions to private companies for up to fifty years. (Essentially, these concessions were identical to the "consignments" that nineteenth-century Peruvian governments had granted for exploitation of guano deposits.) In 1906 Castro persuaded pliant legislators to agree that the asphalt concessions would not require congressional approval; they could be granted merely by the flourish of the presidential pen. As chief executive, Castro thus put himself in a position to make huge amounts of money. Because of his egregious corruption and mismanagement, he was ousted from office in 1908. The presidency thereafter passed to Juan Vicente Gómez—who would hold the reins of power until 1935.

The Generation of 1928

Student protest has often played a major role in national politics throughout Latin America. Perhaps the most significant sign of this trend in Venezuela began during "Student Week" at the Universidad Central in 1928, when a young firebrand named Jóvito Villalba and two other students were arrested for speaking out against the Gómez dictatorship. As crowds of students gathered in support of their fellows, more were carted off to jail. This led to a large-scale popular demonstration that was met by violent police retaliation. Some protestors were killed, many went to prison, and others escaped into exile.

Among the youthful refugees were three future presidents: Rómulo Betancourt, Rafael Caldera, and Raúl Leoni. Clearly, this episode proved to be a formative experience—not only for this generation, but for the nation as a whole.

Gómez ruled with skill and ruthless competence. His technique for resolving political problems was to remove whoever appeared to be responsible—through admonition, imprisonment, torture, exile, or assassination. Placed in charge of key activities, the military became his praetorian guard. A secret police agency searched out and hounded dissidents. Peace eventually settled over Venezuela. Ironically, Venezuela's most powerful *caudillo* brought the age of *caudillismo* to an end.

OVERVIEW: ECONOMIC GROWTH AND SOCIAL CHANGE

Petroleum was in the meantime asserting its importance at the global level. Oil was becoming an essential ingredient for industrial development and military strength. Under Juan Vicente Gómez and shadows of World War I, Venezuela entered its petroleum age. Nothing would ever be the same again.

In keeping with Cipriano Castro's mining laws, the Gómez regime offered concessions to private investors. Under this system, the government awarded permits for exploration and extraction within a designated area for a specified period of time; in return, the concessionaires would pay an annual fixed fee that was analogous to "rent." For Venezuela, windfalls from oil concessions thus incurred little cost or sense of obligation. "To reap the riches of petroleum," as one analyst has said, "the government had only to provide scraps of official paper granting rights to drill on relatively worthless agricultural land, or even better, the empty bed of Lake Maracaibo." Petroleum profits were freebies.

The parade of concessions began in 1914, when the Caribbean Petroleum Company, a subsidiary of Royal Dutch/Shell, began commercial production. As the economic stakes became increasingly apparent, a subsequent law made clear that concessionaires would have rights to *exploration* of designated parcels, not outright ownership. Translation: concessions were not equivalent to sales. Three major companies got in on the ground floor: Royal Dutch/Shell, Gulf, and Pan American (soon to be purchased by Standard Oil of Indiana).

A few years later, Gómez invited representatives of the foreign oil firms to draft a new law on concessions. As a result, a 1922 law increased the size of allowable parcels and lengthened the periods of exploitation (just what the companies wanted). With only minimal adjustments, this law would remain in force for more than twenty years.

Production accelerated rapidly. By 1926 petroleum became the country's chief export, surpassing coffee in value. By 1929 Venezuela was the largest oil exporter in the world, second only to the United States in total output. And as shown in Figure 8.1, output increased throughout the 1930s—the worldwide era of the Great Depression—and climbed up steeply from the 1940s to the early 1970s (when Venezuela deliberately reduced production as part of a strategy to elevate prices). An oil bonanza was under way, and it would remake the nation.

One effect of this development was the creation of a "petro-state," a political system that became utterly dependent upon—and shaped by—the emphasis on oil. Venezuela had an extremely weak state at the time the concessions began. There was no civil service, no central bank, and no independent judiciary. *Caudillismo* had created a legacy of personalistic rule, presidential power, and predatory politics.

The concessions under Gómez represented crass but shrewd bargains. The foreign companies could expand their control of the international market, diversify sources of production, and punish uncooperative governments in countries with oil deposits (especially Mexico and Russia, the sites

Figure 8.1 Petroleum Production in Venezuela, 1918–2007

SOURCES: US Department of Energy, Energy Information Administration, *Annual Energy Review 2007* (http://www.eia.doe.gov/emeu/aer/); Jorge Salazar-Carrillo, *Oil in the Economic Development of Venezuela* (New York: Praeger, 1976); Edwin Lieuwen, *Petroleum in Venezuela: A History* (New York: Russell & Russell, 1967).

of social revolutions during the decade of the 1910s). For his part, Gómez could prolong his hold on power and increase his personal wealth. As testament to his effectiveness, the dictator would die from natural causes in 1935 while still in office.

The legislative centerpiece of this evolving system, the Petroleum Law of 1922, had several important effects. First, it shifted power from private property to the state; only the government possessed the authority to negotiate with foreign companies. Second, it strengthened the (already dominant) role of the president, as the chief dispenser of concessions. And third, it encouraged rulers to maximize income however they could and to use it however they wanted—which very often took the form of lavish public works. Oil concessions worked to the advantage of political incumbents.

Production took place in the steamy areas around Lake Maracaibo, remote from bureaucratic and political power centers in Caracas. Foreign companies paid fixed rents (plus necessary bribes) to the national government and raised their profits to the maximum possible extent. They brought in their own machinery, their own technicians, and their own geologists. To be sure, the international firms employed local workers—in isolated camps where company stores could charge outlandish prices for basic goods. Much as banana plantations did in Central America, the concessions to petroleum companies formed economic enclaves within Venezuela.

The oil bonanza had downsides as well. Perhaps most important, it led to the decline of agriculture and of the once-prominent landlord class. With the collapse of coffee and cacao exports during the Depression, non-oil interests faded from the scene. And since oil earnings tended to bolster the strength of Venezuela's currency, the *bolívar,* the result was to encourage imports and to discourage exports (which became increasingly expensive in terms of other currencies). Within a generation, Venezuela—once one of the most prosperous agricultural producers in South America—could no longer feed its people and would start importing foodstuffs from abroad.

Together with the promise of employment, the de-emphasis on agriculture intensified processes of internal migration, as peons and *campesinos* searched for work in public works programs and/or the oil fields. Urbanization came much later to Venezuela than to many other countries of Latin America, but it accelerated sharply over time. By 1950 over 30 percent of the Venezuelan population lived in settlements of 20,000 or more inhabitants; by 1975 that proportion would rise to nearly 64 percent (with 46 percent living in cites of 100,000 or more). In the meantime, Caracas, always the dominant metropolis, grew to have more than 2 million inhabitants.

The class structure evolved in unusual ways. The emphasis on oil tended to postpone industrialization: since everything could be imported, there was little reason to initiate domestic manufacturing. As a result, urbanization in Venezuela did not endow the industrial working class with substantial levels of power. Instead it stimulated the formation of a commercial and professional sector, a new and dominant class with close ties to the oil sector. As Terry Lynn Karl has put it, Venezuela witnessed between 1920 and 1935 the paradoxical emergence of urban middle classes together (and to a lesser extent) with working classes "who were vested both in the performance of the oil sector and in a potentially adversarial relationship with it." In other words, these groups stood to benefit from the overall development resulting from the petroleum bonanza, but they would eventually come to resent the privileges accruing to well-connected elites. It was these burgeoning middle sectors, the *capas medias*, that would eventually call for economic intervention by the state in order to rectify injustice and inequality.

Demands for a stronger and more autonomous state intensified during World War II. And in 1943, the Venezuelan government undertook a radical change in petroleum policy, shifting its revenue base from leases on concessions to income taxes on earnings. The principle was clear: the higher the company profits, the greater the state revenues. This was the first significant sign of a governmental challenge to the multinational firms. (As a means of defending its interests, Venezuela would later encourage other petroleum-exporting countries—Saudi Arabia, Kuwait, and Iraq—to adopt this basic policy. A common front would benefit all.)

The bonanza continued through the 1940s and 1950s as a result of international factors: pent-up demand in the post–World War II period, a political crisis in Iran (one of the world's major producers), and a temporary closing of the Suez Canal (which cut off Europe's supplies from the Middle East). Venezuela stepped into this situation and profited handsomely. Increasing state revenues tended to benefit cities, especially Caracas, often resulting in monumental public works projects.

During this same period, a commitment to strong state intervention gained increasing momentum. The driving idea was that revenues from oil should be used to stimulate non-oil activities. A widespread slogan neatly captured the concept: *sembrar el petróleo* ("to sow the petroleum"). Given its never-ending (and low-cost) resources, the state expanded its roles in geometric progression. And while the state became adept at dealing with foreign companies, it did not have truly effective reach into Venezuelan society. The resultant gap between jurisdiction and authority produced what one observer has called "a hollow strength."

By the 1960s and 1970s, Venezuela looked very different from most of Latin America. It was the richest country in the region. Its principal export was petroleum, not coffee or sugar or bananas. It conducted successful negotiations with powerful multinational companies. It confronted a hopeful future. It seemed to have left its past behind. In the words of Juan Pablo Pérez Alonzo, the country's outspoken oil czar: "Of course we *are* different. We look more like Saudi Arabia than Brazil. We are *Venezuela Saudita*." Oil not only altered the course of history; it even affected national identity.

Venezuela: Vital Statistics, 2007	
Population (millions)	27.5
GDP (current $U.S. billions)	228.07
GNP/capita ($U.S.)	7320
Internet users (per 100 people)	20.8
Life expectancy (years)	74
Poverty rate (%)	28.5

SOURCES: World Bank and Economic Commission for Latin America and the Caribbean.

POLITICS AND POLICY: PATTERNS OF CHANGE

In the wake of the Gómez regime, two factors emerged as dominant forces in national politics. One was the armed forces; the other consisted of political parties. Complex interaction between these two institutions would give shape to Venezuelan politics for decades to come. The relationship between them varied from conflict to cooperation to extended periods of truce, but it was always subject to change and renegotiation.

Military officers moved into power upon Gómez's death. First to govern was Eleazar López Contreras (1936–41), followed by General Isaias Medina Angarita (1941–45). Given their innate sense of discipline, both made strenuous efforts to maintain law and order. And given their sense of patriotic duty, they sought to take full advantage of Venezuela's privileged position as an exporter of oil. It was the Medina Angarita regime, after all, that changed the terms of foreign exploitation from long-term concessions to taxes on income.

At the same time, dissident forces were gathering. The "generation of 1928," back from exile under the leadership of Rómulo Betancourt, cultivated support among nascent labor unions and established the Partido Democrático Nacional. Temporarily outlawed by López Contreras, the party reemerged in 1941 under the name of Acción Democrática (AD). In 1943 the government responded by forming a party of its own. In 1945 a constitutional reform retained indirect election of the president but established a direct popular vote for congressional deputies, while lifting a long-standing prohibition on communist activities. Grudging though it was, tolerance was giving way to change.

Yet the opposition grew impatient, and in October 1945 a group of young military officers joined with AD leaders to oust the Medina Angarita regime. Under Betancourt, a governmental council exiled Medina Angarita and López Contreras, suspended constitutional guarantees, created a ministry of labor, and recalibrated the oil company earnings tax in order to assure a fifty-fifty split in profits (with half for the government). In this heady atmosphere two new parties emerged as well: the Comité de Organización Política Electoral Independiente, a right-of-center Christian Democratic organization known as COPEI; and the Unión Republicana Democrática (URD) of Jóvito Villalba, a member of the generation of 1928 who decided to form his own personal vehicle.

A presidential election in 1947 gave victory to Rómulo Gallegos, a well-known intellectual and AD candidate. His term in office was marked by utopian schemes, ideological rigidity, and political naïveté. Having assisted in the coup that brought AD to power, military officers resented their subsequent exclusion from key policy decisions. Eventually they demanded that Gallegos include COPEI in the government and banish Betancourt into exile (partly because of his prominence in AD, partly because of rumors that he had lent Venezuelan support to Gaitán and the *bogotazo* in Colombia). When Gallegos refused to capitulate, the military deposed him in November 1948. The three-year period of party rule, the *trienio,* thus came to an ignominious end.

The armed forces wielded power with a vengeance. Clashes with students and workers led to the dissolution of oil-industry labor unions, the suspension of classes at the national university, and the outlawing of the Communist Party. In 1952 the regime declared elections null and void—to avert an opposition victory—and installed one of its members, Marcos Pérez Jiménez, as provisional president.

There followed a thoroughly unsavory dictatorship. Proclaiming a "New National Ideal," Pérez Jiménez sought to consolidate power through a combination of massive public works, extensive political repression, and allegiance to the United States in the Cold War. In 1954 the Eisenhower administration rewarded his loyalty with the Legion of Merit at an ostentatious ceremony in Caracas. In the name of anticommunism, Pérez Jiménez jailed outspoken dissidents and attempted to obliterate AD. But when he sought to prolong his time in office through a rigged election in 1958, the military drew the line: the air force led a popular rebellion that sent him into exile. What would happen next?

Punto Fijo Democracy

Opposition leaders had learned the lessons of the *trienio.* In a series of meetings before and after the coup, they reached agreement on explicit rules of the political game. The basic principle was inclusion: all major interest groups must benefit from petroleum-based prosperity. In other words, all major contending forces agreed to forego their capacity to harm each other by extending guarantees not to threaten each other's vital interests. Appeasement became the order of the day.

One specific agreement focused on the military. In return for a commitment to political neutrality, the armed forces would receive substantial improvements in salaries and equipment, a pledge of amnesty, and public recognition for their patriotic services. Younger officers agreed to these terms as means to enhance the professional standing of the military and erase the stigma of association with dictatorship.

In the Pact of Punto Fijo, party leaders agreed to respect the electoral process and, more important, to share power according to voting results. The spirit of a "prolonged political truce" would govern the distribution of cabinet posts, state jobs, and governmental contracts. The resulting spoils system would ensure the political survival of all signatories. Noteworthy here was the exclusion of the Partido Comunista Venezelano (PCV), the communist party of Venezuela.

In the economic realm, a "minimum program of government" obliged the parties to economic moderation: although the economic role of the state would expand, democratic governments would avoid drastic nationalizations and expropriations and support the principles of private enterprise. In effect, the nation's capitalists exchanged the right to rule for the right to make money.

In spite (or because) of its reformist thrust, the political pact also included adherence to the U.S. cause in the Cold War. This proved highly controversial. Leftist groups had taken prominent part in the opposition to Pérez Jiménez, often at great sacrifice, while Eisenhower's support for the dictator had left a bitter aftertaste. When Vice President Richard Nixon visited Caracas in May 1958, shortly after the coup, angry crowds disrupted his arrival and nearly overturned his limousine. Safely back in Washington, Nixon denounced the agitation as "Communist-planned, Communist-led, and Communist-controlled." One U.S. senator concurred that the demonstration represented "100 percent Russian penetration," while another averred that it revealed a "world-wide pattern of Communist stimulus." Even so, anti-American sentiment was widespread in the Venezuela of that era.

Late 1958 ushered in an era of democratic politics. As the newly elected president, Rómulo Betancourt of AD undertook a series of gradual reforms in keeping with the Pact of Punto Fijo. The minister of mines and hydrocarbons, Juan Pablo Pérez Alonzo, established a state-run corporation to deal with foreign companies. Equally important, the Betancourt government played a key role in forming OPEC. Pérez Alonzo had long insisted on the need for cooperation among oil-producing countries. The opportunity for action came in 1960, in the guise of two hostile developments: a unilateral cut in world prices by the major corporations, and the imposition of a mandatory quota on Venezuelan imports by the Eisenhower administration (presumably in order to assure overland access to oil from Canada and Mexico in the event of war, but actually in order to protect domestic producers). In response, Pérez Alonzo helped arrange an urgent meeting in Baghdad. At this gathering, representatives of five countries—Iran, Iraq, Kuwait, Saudi Arabia, and Venezuela—agreed to promote their mutual interests by establishing a producers' cartel known by its initials as OPEC. At the time, it was not at all clear whether and how this new entity would be able to influence world markets; it would do so with a vengeance in the 1970s. Even so, the organization's founding showed that Venezuela was prepared to assert a proactive role in the international arena and that, through the shared involvement with petroleum, it was developing unusually strong bonds with nations of the Middle East.

On the domestic front, the Betancourt administration passed in 1960 an agrarian reform law calling for expropriation with compensation. Painfully aware of their declining influence, landowners happily accepted the government's generous terms: lords and peasants were both able to benefit.

Peace was nonetheless fragile. Members of the Venezuelan Communist Party and radical elements within AD objected to Betancourt's moderate style and joined guerrilla movements. The discovery of a weapons cache in 1963 exposed their ties to the Castro government. Venezuela promptly severed diplomatic relations with Cuba and cracked down on the revolutionaries. The AD thus defined its position as a party of the anticommunist left.

As a left-of-center reformer, Betancourt became a prominent figure in hemispheric affairs. His antagonism toward both the revolutionary left and the authoritarian right gave him unique international credentials. Aside from Fidel Castro's unsuccessful meddling, Betancourt survived an assassination attempt in 1962 orchestrated by the Dominican Republic's Rafael Trujillo, who objected to his principled stance against dictatorial rule in the Americas. Betancourt also developed an excellent relationship with U.S. president John F. Kennedy, who sought his advice during the Cuban missile crisis of October 1962. In every way, he personified the lofty ideals of JFK's Alliance for Progress. With his trademark pipe and heavily-rimmed glasses, Rómulo Betancourt came to be hailed as "the father of Venezuelan democracy."

Subsequent elections led to the victory of Raúl Leoni (AD) and Rafael Caldera (COPEI), as the two major parties continued to monopolize control of national office. Leftist agitation nonetheless persisted—more as an irritant than as a major threat, but a revealing sign of discontent. A group called the Movimiento al Socialismo (MAS) formed in 1971, and two years later the Caldera administration lifted an eleven-year suspension against the Movimiento de la Izquierda Revolucionaria (MIR). The general idea, of course, was to co-opt these elements and bring them into the institutionalized political game.

The year 1974 brought the inauguration of Carlos Andrés Pérez (AD), a flamboyant left-of-center candidate who captured 49 percent of the presidential vote. Widely known by his initials, CAP distanced himself from the Cold War policies of Kissinger and Nixon. He restored diplomatic relations with Cuba and firmly opposed the anticommunist dictatorships in Chile and Nicaragua. Emerging as a hemispheric statesman, he helped facilitate the Carter administration's negotiations over the Panama Canal and, together with the president of Mexico, cofounded an organization for economic and scientific cooperation among countries of Latin America. (To consolidate his progressive credentials, CAP would become vice president of the Socialist International after the end of his term.)

And as OPEC cut back on production in order to raise world prices for oil, Venezuela suddenly received a $10 billion windfall. In 1975 CAP raised the income tax on oil companies from 63.5 to 70 percent. A subsequent law nationalized the petroleum industry and created a state-run company, later known as PdVSA, which would take direct part in petroleum production. Anything and everything seemed possible. As CAP repeatedly exclaimed, "We are going to change the world!" It was the equivalent of El Dorado—or so it seemed at the time.

The following decade proved relatively tranquil. The Pact of Punto Fijo remained in place, oil income was substantial, and the economy performed fairly well. Presidents Luis Herrera Campins (COPEI) and Jaime Lusinchi (AD) led moderate and competent administrations, although accusations of corruption were starting to mount. A surprise devaluation of the *bolívar* in 1983 temporarily reduced popular confidence in the AD-COPEI government, but the system still survived. Despite disagreement with Ronald Reagan's policy toward Central America (described in Chapter 4), the bilateral relationship with the United States remained on a mostly even keel. By the late 1980s, Venezuela appeared to offer an enviable political model for other Latin American countries: it was a stable and prosperous democracy with a two-party system (or two and a half parties, according to some analysts). What more could anyone want?

The wheels began to come off when Carlos Andrés Pérez made a triumphant return to the presidency in 1989. Suddenly reversing course, CAP imposed a program of stringent neoliberal economic reforms that included privatization of state-owned companies, liberalization of trade, and deregulation of economic activity—along with sharp increases in the price of gasoline and public transportation, including bus fares. Enraged citizens of Caracas took to the streets in spontaneous protest, and a beleaguered CAP called on the military to restore order. Army tanks rolled down major thoroughfares, skirmishes broke out, and looting became widespread. The government later acknowledged a death toll of 287; independent observers put the total at nearly 2000. Either way, the *caracazo* was a time of tragedy, despair, and disillusionment.

A few years later, the unthinkable occurred: elements of the armed forces tried to seize power by force. In February 1992 a group of paratroopers mounted an unsuccessful coup under the leadership of a young colonel named Hugo Chávez. As demonstrations continued throughout the year, another attempted *golpe*

The Devil's Excrement

One of the most telling analyses of Venezuela's oil bonanza came from none other than Juan Pablo Pérez Alfonzo (1903–1979)—two-time cabinet minister, author of the fifty-fifty formula, and OPEC's founding father. Writing in the 1970s, Pérez Alfonzo warned his fellow citizens about overexploitation of the country's oil reserves, reckless government spending, insufficient attention to non-oil economic development, and—above all—the false illusion of prosperity. "Ten years from now, twenty years from now, you will see: oil will bring us ruin. . . . Oil is the devil's excrement."

followed in November 1992. CAP managed to serve out his term, but with little satisfaction. In 1993 he was impeached on charges of embezzling more than $17 million.

The Punto Fijo system was running out of steam. Middle-class citizens expressed mounting outrage over the blatant self-enrichment of leading politicians, including Lusinchi and CAP. Organized workers became aware that they were not receiving a fair share of benefits from the petroleum windfall. And recent migrants to the cities, underemployed and underpaid, began demanding social services and economic opportunities.

As cause and effect of this exhaustion of the Punto Fijo arrangement, citizens were turning away from the traditional parties—and from elections in general. Since CAP's embrace of neoliberal economic policies, in fact, there seemed to be no substantive differences between AD and COPEI. Why vote if there was no meaningful choice? As shown in Figure 8.2, voter turnout dropped from a peak of 96 percent in 1973 (a remarkably high level) to 88 percent in 1978 and 1983, 82 percent in 1988, and 60 percent in the 1990s. In the meantime, the combined vote for AD plus COPEI would plunge from around 90 percent in the presidential elections of 1978–88 to 45 percent in 1993 to merely 11 percent in 1998.

As though to underscore these trends, Rafael Caldera—COPEI president in 1969–74—returned to win the election of 1993, but this time as an independent candidate! Unwittingly, his triumph revealed two fundamental weaknesses in the Punto Fijo system. One was the refusal of the "founding generation" to make room for new, young, fresh faces. Another was the increasing irrelevance of the traditional parties.

Social conditions were worsening as well. As a result of chronic inflation, the purchasing power of average salaries had fallen to only one-third of what it had been in the late 1970s. During the course of the 1990s the poverty rate would

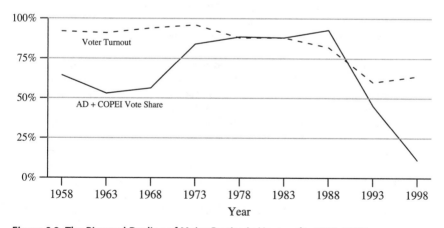

Figure 8.2 The Rise and Decline of Major Parties in Venezuela, 1958–1998

SOURCE: Jennifer McCoy and David J. Myers (eds.), *The Unraveling of Representative Democracy in Venezuela* (Baltimore: Johns Hopkins University Press, 2006).

double, approaching 60 percent by the end of the decade. An amorphous "informal sector" was spreading through the cities, as poor people sought to make ends meet by working on the streets. Meantime the elite remained above it all, cloistered in country club security, as Venezuela retained one of the highest levels of economic inequality in the world. The situation called for drastic measures.

THE CONTEMPORARY SCENE (1998–PRESENT)

The collapse of Venezuela's two-party system left an enormous vacuum in the nation's politics. Into this breach stepped Hugo Chávez, leader of a failed coup attempt in 1992.

Pardoned after a two-year stint in prison, the unrepentant Chávez emerged as a national hero with a messianic commitment to his own personal destiny. Brash, outspoken, unconventional and down-to-earth, the ex-paratrooper succeeded in building powerful grassroots support among groups that had been neglected by the Pact of Punto Fijo—most notably, the middle classes and the urban poor.

Who Is This Guy?

Hugo Chávez defies straightforward classification. Supporters regard him as a patriot, a protector, a savior, and a revolutionary; detractors denounce him as a dictator, an opportunist, a populist, and—ironically—a revolutionary. Who is this person? Where did he get his ideas?

Born in 1954, Chávez grew up in the poverty-stricken hamlet of Sabaneta on the *llanos* of Barinas. As a young man, he dreamt of becoming a professional baseball player. Through informal tutorials with the father of some boyhood friends, he also received a rudimentary introduction to Marxist teachings and Venezuelan history.

At the age of seventeen, he entered the nation's military academy in the faraway city of Caracas. While there he developed a strong interest in the leftist military regimes then present under Omar Torrijos in Panama and, especially, under Juan Velasco Alvarado in Peru. "With Torrijos," Chavez later recalled, "I became a Torrijist. With Velasco, I became a Velasquist. And with Pinochet (in Chile), I became an anti-Pinochetist."

After graduation from the academy, Chávez established links with recalcitrant military colleagues and with dedicated members of the Venezuelan left. He began living a double life: as a disciplined soldier, and as a conspirator against the government. As a military officer, Chávez disdained what he considered to be the corrupt and foppish political elite; as a person born to poverty, he bitterly resented the country's economic oligarchy. His nationalism and anti-Americanism intensified (to the point where he even rejected baseball as a U.S. import). And he nurtured grand ambitions. "Before 2000 I'm

---

going to be a general," he boasted to his friends, "and I'm going to do something major in this country."

In a scornful response to Black Friday of 1983, Chávez and young fellow officers took a solemn oath, quoting from Bolívar: "I will not let my soul repose, nor my arm rest until my eyes have seen broken the chains that oppress us and our people by the order of the powerful." The group thus formed the Ejército Bolivariano Revolucionario (Bolivarian Revolutionary Army) and waited for the opportunity to strike. They believed the time had come in 1992, during the second presidency of Carlos Andrés Pérez, although events would prove them wrong.

It was not until the mid-1990s that Chávez and his cohorts decided to pursue the electoral route to political power. During the inauguration ceremonies after his election as president in 1998, Chávez stopped to embrace a former coconspirator and quietly whispered to him, "We did it, brother. After all those years, the revolution can finally begin."

SOURCE: Cristina Marcano and Alberto Barrera Tyszka, *Hugo Chávez* (New York: Random House, 2007).

Preparing for the election of 1998, Chávez founded a new political party called the *Movimiento Quinta República* or "Fifth Republic Movement," known by the Spanish-language acronym MVR (the *V* should be read as a Roman numeral). Presenting himself as a latter-day Bolívar, the charismatic forty-four-year-old mounted a whirlwind campaign. He claimed that AD, COPEI, and other long-standing parties were obsolete and out of touch. He denounced the economic and business elite as a "rancid oligarchy." He insisted that there could be only one explanation for poverty in a nation as oil-rich as Venezuela: corruption, corruption, and still more corruption. It was time for radical change, he argued, and he was the person to bring it about. Heeding his message, the people rewarded him with 56.2 percent of the vote—a remarkably substantial mandate.

Two related factors combined to produce this result. One was the incompetence and irrelevance of the opposition. As Chávez's own campaign manager acknowledged, "The victory had more to do with his adversaries' political errors than the quality of our own electoral campaign, which was relatively disorganized. . . . The elections were won more because of what the opposition didn't achieve than because of what *chavismo* actually achieved." According to the respected newspaper *El Nacional,* the other key stemmed from "the tremendous levels of frustration that have turned the majority against the old political leadership. It is absolutely clear that the entire country has chosen an option that is different from that which the traditional ruling class was trying to impose." The time for change had come.

The first phase of Chavista rule brought mixed results. On one hand, Chávez hastened to consolidate political power. He called elections for a constituent assembly to write a new constitution. Once the convention was seated, progovernment delegates used their majority to dismantle the Supreme Court, disband the elected legislature, and anoint themselves to serve in place of congress. Overriding the opposition, they approved a constitution that permitted reelection of the president, enhanced (already-strong) executive powers, and created a unicameral legislature (thus weakening checks and balances against presidential authority). Insofar as possible, Chávez and his followers determined to destroy Venezuela's long-standing political institutions—parties, legislatures, courts—for the sake of revolutionary transformation. From 1999 forward, the cards were stacked in favor of the government and against the opposition. As an indication of this situation, Chávez went on to win the presidential election of 2000 with 59.8 percent of the vote.

On the other hand, Chávez faced serious economic difficulties. Oil prices were low and petroleum earnings were hovering at modest levels. Leery of the president's incendiary rhetoric, the business class—foreign and domestic—refrained from making new investments. During Chávez's first year in office, 1999, Venezuela's gross domestic product contracted by more than 5 percent.

The solution was straightforward: to rectify economic injustice, Chávez would have to gain control of the petroleum industry. This meant taking charge of PdVSA, the state-sponsored enterprise that had become "an empire within the empire." Admired abroad for their managerial skill, PdVSA executives were seen by Chavistas as members of a global (and alien) capitalist elite, while the oil workers formed a well-paid and privileged aristocracy of organized labor. Early in 2002 Chávez fired the company's president and tried to take over the board of directors. In retaliation, oil workers went out on strike. Most lost their jobs as a result.

Tensions came to a head in April 2002. After a week of marches and countermarches, opposition leaders demanded Chávez's resignation. The president responded by closing down five private television stations and denouncing demonstrators as "subversives" and "traitors." As he spoke, violence escalated outside the presidential palace. Gunmen opened fire on the crowds, killing at least fourteen people. Military leaders thereupon arrested Chávez on the charge that he ordered thugs to open fire on unarmed demonstrators. As would-be president Pedro Carmona issued a series of draconian decrees, abrogating the constitution of 1999 and dissolving the legislature, Chavista loyalists mobilized hundred of thousands of supporters to demand the return of their hero. Within forty-eight hours, Chávez was released from captivity and restored to power.

The struggle over petroleum continued. With unemployment around 20 percent and inflation nearing 30 percent, a general strike hobbled the economy in late 2002. Chávez took advantage of a subsequent PdVSA strike to fire more than 17,000 workers, replace the board of directors, and restructure the organization. It seemed at the time like a pyrrhic victory: the president had won the political battle, but economic output plummeted by 13 percent for the year.

Conflicts with Uncle Sam

Under President Clinton, American officials had expressed concern about Chavez's politics but adopted a wait-and-see attitude. "Watch what Chávez does," was the advice of the U.S. ambassador, "not what he says." Under President George W. Bush, in contrast, the administration took a hard-line stance. In the words of Henry J. Hyde (R-Illinois), the alliance of Chávez with other left-leaning rulers in the hemisphere formed an "axis of evil in the Americas." After 9/11, Bush officials were outraged by Chávez's condemnation of U.S. military actions in Afghanistan as "the massacre of innocents. Terrorism cannot be fought with terrorism."

The 2002 coup brought an irreversible downturn in Venezuela's relationship with the United States. Chávez became utterly convinced that the Bush administration had aided and abetted the *golpe* of 2002. There is no question that U.S. officials were in communication with the plotters or that they applauded the result. They might well have given a green light to the plan. According to presidential spokesman Ari Fleischer, Chávez had brought events upon himself; the overthrow was not a coup, but "a change in government."

From that point onward, Chávez became an implacable foe of the United States under George W. Bush. He forged an early alliance with Fidel Castro's Cuba. He successfully spearheaded opposition to U.S. plans for a Free Trade Area of the Americas, proposing instead a scheme of his own—the *Alternativa Bolivariana para las Américas* (ALBA). He pledged strong support for Evo Morales of Bolivia and other left-leaning presidents throughout Latin America, claiming de facto leadership of a "pink tide" that was surging in the Americas (see Chapter 13). He launched a Banco del Sur (Bank of the South) for developing nations as an alternative to the World Bank, and forged links with MERCOSUR as well. He lampooned President Bush as "the devil" in a speech before the General Assembly of the United Nations.

This conspicuously undiplomatic minuet took place within a decidedly pragmatic context. The fundamental fact was (and remains) that Venezuela and the United States were inextricably tied to one another by their mutual dependence on petroleum. Three-quarters of Venezuela's oil exports went to the United States; Venezuela accounted for roughly 12 percent of U.S. oil imports. Venezuela had 78 billion barrels of conventional crude oil reserves, while the United States had only 22 billion. Despite occasional threats that Venezuela would stop shipments—or that the United States would halt purchases—these were empty rhetorical gestures. Political hostility had economic limits.

Yet the tension extended well beyond the bilateral and regional arenas. Apart from its occasional pyrotechnics, Chavista foreign policy had three related goals: challenging the hegemony of the United States, discrediting the economic prescriptions of the Washington consensus, and unifying the developing world— often referred to as "the South." With the approval of an aging Fidel Castro, Chávez became the leader of a revitalized movement of "nonaligned" nations. With the aid of his minister of energy and mines (a former communist rebel!), he helped resuscitate OPEC. He vigorously denounced U.S. policies in Afghanistan, Iraq, and the Middle East. He conducted intensive diplomacy throughout the Arab world, building on Venezuela's long-standing association with that region, and he courted solidarity with both Russia and the People's Republic of China. And as an

art of this campaign, he subjected the unpopular George W. Bush to
ss ridicule.

The Limits of Participatory Democracy

After gaining control of petroleum, Chávez proceeded to tighten his hold on the nation's political process. With growing intensity (but not much clarity), he proclaimed his commitment to building "socialism for the twenty-first century." While he described his political formula as a new kind of democracy—"participatory democracy"—his actions acquired increasingly authoritarian overtones. Despite well-meaning advice from Lula of Brazil and other sympathizers, Chávez demonstrated little real awareness of the need for a loyal opposition. Flaunting the powers of the presidency, he routinely expressed contempt for dissidents while his followers harassed, denounced, and bullied outspoken critics of the government.

One of the most striking parts of this equation was, in fact, the chronic weakness of the opposition. Official intimidation was only partly to blame. Anti-Chavista elements in Venezuela were dispersed, disorganized, and leaderless. They came from various quarters—the business elite, the media, the church, and parts of the intellectual community—but they lacked a common agenda. The collapse of AD and COPEI left them without a legitimate political party. Many were also tainted by association with the 2002 coup attempt. As a result, the opposition could take only a negative stance: it was anti-Chávez, but not pro-anything. One of its most fateful decisions was to boycott the legislative elections of December 2005— which merely guaranteed Chavista unanimity. In this way, the opposition unintentionally silenced itself.

Under Chavista rule, politics in Venezuela became polarized, personalized, and centralized. With the partial exception of the military, national institutions— especially the legislature and the courts—were notoriously weak. There was no doubt that Chávez enjoyed considerable popular support, winning the presidential election of 2006 with 63 percent of the vote. By this time the social base of his electoral success assumed clear-cut form: near-unanimous support from the lower classes, especially the underemployed that lived in shantytowns near major cities; partial (but diminishing) support among the middle classes, increasingly opposed to his authoritarian tendencies; and near-total opposition from the upper class. And through his triumphs at the polls, Chávez was fostering a tyranny of the majority.

Especially telling were persisting efforts to prolong his stay in power. In keeping with many other Latin American charters, the Venezuelan constitution of 1999—the one that Chávez himself oversaw and imposed—called for a limit of two consecutive terms. Unhappy with this restriction, the president called for a popular referendum in 2007 that would remove the limits on reelection. It was defeated by a narrow margin of 51 to 49 percent. Chávez temporarily accepted this result under international pressure (and, it was said, under pressure from the armed forces). Just over a year later, he submitted a new proposal to lift the ban on

Raising his fist in a characteristic gesture, Chávez addresses a partisan crowd in his hometown of Sabaneta during the 2006 presidential campaign.

reelection (not only on the presidency, but also on all elected offices) and won approval in a referendum by 54 percent. As of this writing, there was no foreseeable limit to his length of rule.

A Decade in Power

Domestic politics and international markets have enabled Chávez to pursue his dream of "socialism for the twenty-first century" with considerable effect. One key factor was a steady rise of oil prices, which climbed from just over $10 per barrel in the late 1990s to $59 per barrel in 2005 and $147 per barrel in mid-2008. As a result, the value of Venezuelan oil exports increased from just over $10 billion in 1998 to more than $50 billion in 2007—an increase of nearly five times!

Not all this money was wisely spent. Large amounts went into Chavista foreign policy schemes, military procurement, wasteful projects—and, it is said, into the pockets of government loyalists. Blatant corruption became a central topic in Venezuelan gossip. As political scientist Francisco Rodríguez wrote in 2006, "There is little or no evidence that Chávez is finally sharing Venezuela's oil wealth with the poor. Most existing statistics do not show significant improvement in either the well-being or the share of resources directed at Venezuela's most disadvantaged citizens."

Other experts have disputed such assertions. They observe, for instance, that the Chávez government devoted substantial funding to social programs, so-called missions on behalf of the poor, especially in the fields of health and education. According to official statistics of the Venezuelan government, as analyzed by a Washington D.C.–based research group, these expenditures had discernibly positive effects:

- Real social spending per capita (adjusted for inflation) more than tripled between 1998 and 2006.
- The poverty rate declined from 59.4 percent in 1999 to 30.2 percent in 2006, while "extreme" poverty went down from 21.7 percent to 9.9 percent.
- Income inequality was reduced (although vexing measurement issues underlie this claim).
- Infant mortality fell by more than one-third between 1998 and 2006.
- Substantial gains were made in health care and education, especially access to higher education.
- Over the course of the decade, the number of social security beneficiaries more than doubled.

After the first quarter of 2003, when the government took control of PdVSA, the economy grew at an average annual rate of 13.5 percent. Much of this growth took place in the private non-oil sector.

If the underlying data are accurate, this would look like quite a respectable performance. Yet any such analysis raises fundamental questions of cause and effect: Did these developments take place as a consequence of governmental policy? As the result, instead, of rising petroleum prices? Or in response to other factors?

In retrospect, it appeared that Hugo Chávez drew his political strength from a variety of sources: (1) the increasing income from petroleum, (2) his charismatic appeal to popular masses, (3) the organizational weakness of the opposition, and (4) his resistance to U.S. hegemony and, especially, his ability to exploit widespread distaste for President Bush. Those factors sustained his grip on power for the decade from 1998 through 2008.

But things could also change. As a result of the global economic meltdown of 2008–9, the price of oil dropped precipitously from $147 per barrel to only $37 per barrel. Consequently the Venezuelan economy was projected to contract in 2009, a downturn that could impose significant constraints on Chavista foreign policy. And as a result of partisan realignment, the political campaign of 2008 led to the installation of Barack Obama as president of the United States. A chastened Chávez announced that he would be more than willing to meet with Obama "on equal and respectful terms." Whether an extended one-on-one encounter would ever come to pass was a topic of widespread speculation.

On balance, Hugo Chávez cut a distinctive historical figure. In his aspirations, he often compared himself to Simón Bolívar and claimed to be the Liberator's modern-day heir. In action, however, the former paratrooper bore an even greater resemblance to such erstwhile rulers as Antonio Guzmán Blanco, Juan Vicente Gómez, and—it must be said—Cipriano Castro. In this sense, he was a nineteenth-century *caudillo* in twenty-first-century guise. With the ascent of Hugo Chávez, Venezuela came face-to-face not only with its future, but also with its past.

9

Argentina
Progress and Stalemate

Argentina began the twentieth century as the richest country in Latin America, with a standard of living comparable to that of Europe. Together with a powerful wave of immigration from Europe, robust exports of beef and wheat laid the foundation for dynamic economic growth. In the wake of World War II, Juan Domingo Perón reshaped the country's political map, and in the 1970s a brutal military dictatorship unleashed a campaign of violent repression that shocked international public opinion. Even as the nation returned to democracy, it struggled with economic uncertainty and political strife. By the start of the twenty-first century, after a disastrous history of economic crisis and political foment, Argentina's relative standard of living had undergone precipitous decline in global terms. What are the roots of these problems? What can account for such paralyzing discord in such a highly educated and well-endowed society?

FROM COLONY TO NATIONHOOD

Present-day Argentina started as a backwater in the Spanish American colonial empire. Unlike Mexico or Peru, the region of the Río de la Plata had no settled native population. The Indians were few in number and nomadic, so the Spaniards had no ready large-scale labor source. The area's greatest resource was its fertile land—among the richest in the world. A further asset was the location of Buenos Aires, which was well situated to become a great port. Yet no dynamic economy emerged in the colonial era.

For most of the colonial era, Argentina was included within the Viceroyalty of Peru, and its economic development was closely linked to the northward shipment of cotton, rice, wheat, and leather goods. The coastal region around Buenos Aires was less active. Its greatest industry was smuggling. Only in 1776 did Buenos Aires assume importance, when it was made the seat of a new viceroyalty. Power then began to shift from the northwest to the southern coast, as Buenos Aires became the entry port for European imports.

Map 9 Argentina

The Wars of Independence shook the Viceroyalty of the Río de la Plata, but without the property damage that hit Mexico (and Uruguay). Anti-Spanish sentiment in La Plata united the local elite and produced what became an enduring myth of military prowess, as General José de San Martín defeated the troops loyal to the Spanish crown. With independence achieved in the 1820s, the landowning aristocracy viewed its realm with satisfaction. Most important, Buenos Aires and the interior to the north and west grew steadily farther apart.

Struggles for Supremacy

In the decades after independence, competing regional groups battled over the direction of national development. One faction was made up of the "unitarians," mainly from the province (and city) of Buenos Aires. They wanted to nationalize the port city of Buenos Aires: strip it of its autonomy, then use it as a base for reducing provincial barriers to trade, and thereby open the entire country to international commerce.

The second group was the "federalists," who were from the interior. They agreed on the need to nationalize the city of Buenos Aires because they wanted the city's customs receipts distributed to all the provinces. At the same time, they wanted to maintain provincial autonomy, especially the ability to levy interprovincial tariffs and thus protect local industries.

The third group was also called the "federalists," but they were of a very different kind: they were from the province of Buenos Aires and opposed nationalization of the port city of Buenos Aires, since that would mean the loss of their province's existing monopoly over the city's customs revenues. They also wanted free trade. In effect, the third group was advocating the status quo.

The conflict among these three groups lasted through the 1830s and 1840s. The issue was eventually decided by one of Latin America's famous dictators: Juan Manuel de Rosas, a politically ambitious cattle rancher from the province of Buenos Aires, who won the governorship of his province in 1829. But his ambitions did not stop there. He wanted to rule all of Argentina, and pursued his goal with policies favoring the *estancieros* (ranch owners), thus furthering the consolidation of a landed aristocracy. As an ardent Buenos Aires federalist, Rosas was determined to subdue rival *caudillos*. He extended the power of the province of Buenos Aires over the country, in effect building up a nation on the principle of federalism. At the same time, Rosas built a powerful government machine, with an enforcement squad *(Mazorca)* that terrorized all who dared oppose him, even if only because they failed to wear the official color of red.

Rosas's eventual undoing was his effort to apply the same dictatorial tactics that had worked so handsomely in domestic politics to Argentina's foreign policy. Unfortunately for Rosas, he succeeded in arousing a powerful opposition alliance that included Brazil and Uruguay, as well as the Argentine General Justo José de Urquiza, who commanded a force that deposed Rosas in 1852 and forced him into immediate exile. Despite his ignominious fall, Rosas had succeeded in creating a united Argentina out of the disparate provinces. From the moment of his defeat,

Argentine nationalists adopted him as an Argentine patriot who pursued national development against the alien forces seeking to subvert Argentina's rise to full nationhood. In this respect, Rosas resembles Chile's Diego Portales and Mexico's Agustín de Iturbide, who also became strong-arm autocratic rulers in the decade after independence.

During the Rosas era many Argentine intellectuals, such as Domingo Sarmiento and Esteban Echeverría, fled the repressive regime. Sarmiento described Rosas as the man "who applied the knife of the gaucho to the culture of Buenos Aires and destroyed the work of centuries—of civilization, law and liberty." These intellectuals dreamed of capturing control of Argentina and steering it onto the course of liberal representative government. With the fall of Rosas they got their chance.

Justo José de Urquiza, a federalist from the interior, promptly rose to power. He began by calling a constitutional convention, which promulgated a constitution in 1853, closely following the U.S. example. It was to be a federal system, with the president chosen by an electoral college. And the federal congress was to have two houses, with the Chamber of Deputies elected by direct vote and the Senate elected by provincial legislatures.

The controversy over the status of the city of Buenos Aires was far from settled, however. Protesting the nationalization of the city in the new constitution, the province of Buenos Aires refused to join the new confederation. Defeated in a brief civil war in 1859, the province rose in revolt two years later, led by Bartolomé Mitre, and captured control of the confederation.

For the next two decades the liberals continued in power. In 1862 Mitre was inaugurated as president, and he launched a new drive to unify Argentina. He was followed in the presidency by Domingo Sarmiento, author of *Facundo* (1845), the most famous literary attack on the *caudillo*-style gauchos. Sarmiento believed ardently in North American–style public education and urged Argentines to follow the U.S. model. The drawn-out Paraguayan War (1865–70) intervened, in which tiny Paraguay held off Argentina, Brazil, and Uruguay for five years, as it tried (unsuccessfully) to monopolize access to the all-important Paraná River basin.

The third liberal president was Nicolás Avellaneda. In his term (1874–80), Argentina undertook its last major territorial conquest—the "Indian wars." The provinces to the south and west of Buenos Aires had long been plagued by Indian raids. Now an army force under the command of General Julio Roca subdued or exterminated the indigenous bands—the "Conquest of the Desert."

By now, the liberals had enjoyed power long enough to lay the basis for their country's rapid integration into the world economy. The symbolism of the new leadership could hardly have been better: the Indian-fighter presiding over the Europeanization of a South American republic.

The political elite had few doubts about its mission. Like their counterparts in Brazil and Mexico, the Argentine politicians and intellectuals saw themselves as applying the true principles of both economic and political liberalism. Quoting the pseudoscience of Herbert Spencer, they argued that if an aristocracy ruled Argentina, it was the result of natural selection. With the Indian and the gaucho safely subdued, the elite confidently looked forward to enriching itself, and, by liberal logic, thereby enriching their country.

OVERVIEW: ECONOMIC GROWTH AND SOCIAL CHANGE

Argentina achieved notable economic growth in the 1880–1914 era. This success was based on supplying agricultural goods to the North Atlantic industrial world, since Argentina had a comparative advantage in producing meat and grain. Two technological advances had made it practical to ship foodstuffs the many thousands of miles from Buenos Aires to London and Antwerp. One was the steam vessel, with its faster and far more certain pace than the sailing ship. The other was a process for chilling meat, which kept the products fresh for sale in European markets.

Argentina's pampas were among the most fertile lands in the world. But Argentina lacked capital and labor. England, Argentina's principal customer, sent the needed capital in the form of investment in railroads, docks, packing houses, and public utilities. English firms also handled shipping, insurance, and banking. This inflow of capital was exactly what the Argentine political elite saw as essential for their country's development.

The solution for the other missing factor, labor, also came from Europe, although not from Britain. The badly needed workers streamed into Argentina from southern Europe, especially Italy. Between 1857 and 1930, Argentina received a net immigration (immigrants minus emigrants) of 3.5 million, meaning that about 60 percent of the total population increase could be attributed to immigration. Of these immigrants, about 46 percent were Italian and 32 percent were Spanish. The demographic effect of immigration on Argentina was greater than on any other major country of the Western Hemisphere. With the epic tide of immigration, the national population swelled from 1.7 million in 1869 to 7.9 million in 1914, about 30 percent of which was foreign born. (At the same time in the United States, another haven for European emigrants, only about 13 percent of the population was foreign born.) The result was to give Argentina a distinctly European quality, with a resulting tension among Argentines as to their real national identity.

This immigrant labor force offered a textbook example of the mobility of labor. There was a remarkable movement of laborers back and forth between Italy and the Argentine pampas (earning them the nickname of *golondrinas*, or "swallows"). There was a fluid movement within Argentina, too, with Buenos Aires always attracting a large share of the foreigners.

The rapid economic growth of the 1880–1914 era had profound social implications. At the outset the landed elite was on top, gauchos and wage labor on the bottom. As the economy boomed, new economic niches appeared. The Italians and Spaniards came first to the farms, as colonists, tenant farmers, and rural laborers. Other jobs then opened in the urban sector: in transport (especially the railroads), processing, and the service industries (banking, government).

Argentina's economy thus entered an era of increasing prosperity based on the exportation of meat and grain and on the importation of manufactured goods. From the 1860s to 1914, Argentina's GDP grew at an annual average rate of at least 5 percent (exact data for pre-1900 are sketchy). This is one of the highest sustained growth rates ever recorded for any country.

But the country paid a price for this success, because of its overwhelming export dependence on foodstuffs. This made the entire Argentine economy vulnerable to fluctuations in the world prices of agricultural and pastoral goods, with any dip in those prices provoking an overall economic downturn within Argentina. As shown by Figure 9.1, Argentine exports consisted almost entirely of products from farming and ranching; manufactured goods (the "other" category) were miniscule throughout the entire period from 1880 to 1960. Because of vagaries in market demand, the value of Argentine exports was extremely unstable over time: up during World War I, down in the early 1920s, then up and down again with the arrival of the Great Depression in the 1930s. A brief upward spurt after World War II was followed by sharp declines in the early 1950s and then the appearance of a short-lived steady state up to the 1960s. Thus Argentina, like other exporting countries of Latin America, came to be economically dependent on trends and decisions made outside the confines of the nation, in the industrialized center of the world-system.

Economic dependency also appeared in the Argentine banking system, which was periodically tied to the gold standard. Short-term fluctuations in trade caused sharp changes in Argentina's gold reserves, thus contracting or expanding the

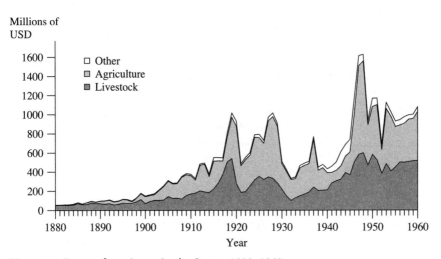

Figure 9.1 Exports from Argentina by Sector, 1880–1960

SOURCE: Orlando J. Ferreres. *Dos siglos de Economía Argentina: Historia Argentina en Cifras, 1810–2004* (Buenos Aires: Fundación Norte y Sur, 2005), pp. 594–5.

domestic money supply and making Argentina's economy a hostage to international currency movements.

Still another link to the world economy posed further long-term problems: the large role played by foreign capital and foreign businessmen. From 1900 to 1929, 35 percent of the country's total fixed investment came from foreigners. Britain was the principal source, followed by France and Germany. This high degree of foreign economic involvement later became a prime target for the economic nationalists.

Argentina's growth pattern also created inequities at home, especially among geographic regions. While prosperity blessed the pampas and Buenos Aires, parts of the interior stagnated. Only Mendoza, Tucumán, and Córdoba escaped this fate, thanks to their wine and sugar production. Throughout the nineteenth century, the interior had fought to prevent its demise at the hands of Buenos Aires. It lost, and the price of its defeat was poverty.

Of course, inequities also existed within the prosperous regions. The wealthy *estancieros* built elegant chalets, while foreign-born tenant farmers and displaced native workers scratched out a meager existence. In Buenos Aires, elegantly attired aristocrats met at their European-style clubs while workers struggled to protect their families from inflation. The Argentine boom, like so many others in capitalist countries at this time, did facilitate considerable upward mobility. But it also fostered huge income discrepancies, which were ultimately bound to create social and political tensions.

One crucial social effect of Argentina's late nineteenth- and early twentieth-century expansion was a nonevent: *the country never developed a peasantry.* The Conquest of the Desert in the 1870s virtually eliminated the Indian population, and the land was promptly distributed in large tracts appropriate for raising cattle and sowing grain. In contrast to the policy in the Great Plains of the United States, Argentina did not give its land to family farmers or individual homesteaders. Cattle ranching did not require a large-scale workforce, since barbed wire was sufficient to contain the herds; and though wheat was often grown by foreign colonists who rented land, they did not constitute an influential social group. As a result, a classic peasantry—such as those of Mexico, Chile, or northeastern Brazil—did not exist in Argentina.

This fact meant, for instance, that land reform would never become the vital and symbolic issue that it was in such countries as Mexico. It was not that land was so evenly distributed in Argentina; it was that there were no longtime rural dwellers to lay historic claim to the soil.

Further, no peasantry meant there was no power base on which to build coalitions with other social groups. Landowners could not resort to the time-tested alliance with the peasantry that frequently occurred in other countries, and urban laborers could not enlist peasants in broad-based warfare with the social system at large.

In the big cities, however, wage laborers found strength in organization. Manual workers accounted for nearly 60 percent of the population in Buenos

This difference in living conditions reflects the social inequality that accompanied Argentina's economic expansion after the 1880s. *Top,* luxurious residences of aristocratic families in Buenos Aires; *bottom,* temporary shacks for workers in the city's port area around 1910. (Courtesy of the Archivo General de la Nación, Buenos Aires.)

Aires in the early twentieth century. And about three-fifths of the working class, in turn, consisted of immigrants who retained citizenship in Italy and Spain.

The first efforts at organizing Argentine labor were influenced by European precedents. In the 1870s and 1880s, European anarchist and socialist exiles began vigorous organizing, and in 1895 Argentina's Socialist Party was founded. These Socialists were molded on the European model: a parliamentary party, clearly committed to an electoral and evolutionary strategy. As of 1900 one might have expected the Socialist Party to become a major political voice for the Argentine working class. Yet it failed to attract the immigrant workers.

The urban working class proved receptive to another message; it came from the anarchists. Their Federación Obrera Regional Argentina (FORA) caught the workers' imagination with its call for direct action. The FORA-sponsored local and general strikes worried the government, which assumed that any labor problems must be the work of foreign agitators. Congress therefore passed the Ley de Residencia ("Residence Law") in 1902, which empowered the government to deport all foreigners whose behavior "compromised national security or disturbed public order"—by participating in strikes, for example.

The anarchist campaign reached a climax in 1910, the centennial of the declaration of Argentine independence, when a great public celebration was planned to glorify Argentina's progress. As militant opponents of the liberal elite, the anarchist leaders wanted to raise their protest against the farce of the European-oriented model of progress. The protestors filled the streets and plazas, but were crushed and scattered by masses of police. The reaction against the protestors spilled over into the Congress, which approved a new law (Ley de Defensa Social, or "Social Defense Law"), making the arrest and prosecution of labor organizers even easier.

This was the death knell for Argentine anarchism, but not of urban protest. Strike activity in Buenos Aires reached another peak in 1918–19, and it would oscillate from time to time after that. In the early years of the twentieth century, organized labor emerged as a key actor in Argentine society.

Argentina: Vital Statistics, 2007

Population (millions)	39.5
GDP (current $U.S. billions)	262.3
GNP/capita ($U.S.)	6050
Poverty rate (% in 2006)	21.0
Life expectancy (years)	75

Sources: World Bank and Economic Commission for Latin America and the Caribbean.

Rhythms of Popular Culture

Argentina's national dance, the tango, traces its origins to the late nineteenth century, when Buenos Aires street toughs *(compadritos)* borrowed features of the Afro-Argentine *candomblé dance*, which they married to the milonga, a folk music originating on the pampas. In the dance halls and brothels of Buenos Aires' déclassé *barrios*, these working-class men and their partners gradually created the dance that would become the tango to music created by amateur musicians, whose improvisation on flute, guitar, harp, violin, and clarinets matched the contortions of the dancers.

By the turn of the twentieth century, the tango acquired additional refinement as professional musicians and dancers emerged. Italian immigrants added their accordions and mandolins to the instrumentation. Musicians began composing and publishing tangos for piano, ending the era of loose improvisation. The tango also acquired a wider audience as it moved into more respectable dance halls and clubs and the first true "stars" emerged—dancers, musicians, and bandleaders who have remained famous to the present day. The Argentine elite scorned the tango, however, because of its origins in the seedy neighborhoods of Buenos Aires. It was not until the 1913–14 tango craze in Europe, when a softened version swept London and Paris, that it won respectability in Argentina. The more outrageous aspects of the dance were left behind, and the music slowed as it reached the ballrooms of Buenos Aires.

Tango now entered its Golden Age at home, in cafés and cabarets, where elite men paid to dance with lower-class women. Musicians were increasingly professional, playing to huge crowds at thriving nightclubs, while silent movies appeared at city cinemas. Vocalists became ever more central to the tango, above all the world-famed Carlos Gardel.

The Golden Age was over by the early 1950s. Venues closed and tango bands shrank in size, facing competition from a new generation of folk musicians, who enjoyed increasing airtime on Argentine radio. The tango nevertheless survived. In the 1980s and 1990s, it enjoyed a resurgence of popularity in the United States and Europe, suggesting that the tango is, after jazz, the Americas' second great contribution to international music.

POLITICS AND POLICY: PATTERNS OF CHANGE

The liberal politicians were known as the "Generation of 1880" (so labeled for their emergence that year). They were themselves members of, or very close to, the landowning class that produced Argentina's riches. They managed to control the army and the elections, resorting to vote fraud when necessary. They also operated a highly effective political machine. The most important national decisions were made by *acuerdo*, an informal agreement between the president and oligarchic power brokers. In this respect the Argentine liberals ignored one key aspect of the British/U.S. example—the central role of the legislature, which in Argentina had been rendered inconsequential in this period.

At first glance this political system seems to have admirably served the agro-export interests that profited from the post-1880 expansion. But the aristocrats in control did not go unchallenged. The spreading prosperity helped feed political discontent among three groups: (1) newly prosperous landowners; (2) old aristocratic families which had failed to profit from the agro-export boom; and (3) members of the middle class doing well economically but excluded from political power.

These three groups created the Radical Party, destined to play a major role in twentieth-century Argentine politics. In 1890, just as the country entered a short but severe economic crisis, the Radicals attempted an armed revolt. An *acuerdo* ended the rebellion, but some intransigent leaders founded the Radical Civic Union (Unión Cívica Radical, or UCR) two years later. Unable to make electoral progress against the fraud routinely practiced by the ruling politicians, they resorted twice more to armed revolt. Both attempts failed. Nonetheless the Radicals, led first by Leandro Alem and then by Hipólito Yrigoyen, maintained their stubborn pursuit of political power. As for economic goals, the Radicals remained committed to the agro-export economy. They simply wanted a share in the political direction of their society.

Not all the oligarchs endorsed the government position of freezing the Radicals out of power. A more enlightened wing saw labor organizers and the working class as the real threat—not the middle classes. This group won out in 1911 when President Roque Sáenz Peña proposed an electoral reform aimed at co-opting the middle classes. Passed in 1912, the new law called for universal male suffrage, the secret ballot, and compulsory voting. The well-organized Radicals immediately capitalized on the new rules and got their longtime leader, Hipólito Yrigoyen, elected president in 1916. Was this to be a new era?

An early test came in the government's behavior toward the workers. The Radicals began with a genuine concern for the working class, partly because they hoped to win eventual votes in their struggle with the Conservatives. As labor-management conflicts arose, the Yrigoyen government followed an apparent pro-labor stance in its interventions. Labor organizers saw this as an improvement, but one that would depend on government action case by case.

A crisis came in 1918–19, however, when the entire Western world was shaken by strike waves. It was a confluence of specific grievances and generalized hostility. In Argentina, workers were aroused over the reduced buying power of their wages. Food prices rose sharply, stimulated by European demand, but wage increases lagged. Union leaders called a series of strikes in late 1918, and in early 1919 syndicalist organizers decided the time was ripe for a general strike—the syndicalist instrument for bringing down the bourgeois state.

Their idea had tragic consequences. The Yrigoyen government decided it had to act firmly. Antilabor hysteria was promoted by a newly formed ultra-rightist civilian paramilitary movement, the Argentine Patriotic League (Liga Patriótica Argentina), which effectively exploited the middle- and upper-class fear of the popular challenge. League members took to the streets to attack workers; it was class warfare with a vengeance. Hundreds of demonstrators were shot. The labor leaders were again repressed, this time by the Radicals, with the heaviest blows falling on the syndicalists and the last remnants of the anarchist leadership.

Organized labor did not disappear. Two other ideological currents began to make headway among Argentine workers: socialism and communism. The former stressed political action, betting on the Socialist Party as the hope for change in Argentine capitalism. The Communists emphasized the labor union movement instead of the ballot box, and they soon made modest progress in gaining key union positions.

The 1920s did not bring much success to labor organizers. Declines in strike activity allowed the government to ignore key questions in labor relations. By 1930 organized labor had become a relatively subdued actor on the Argentine stage.

At the other end of the political spectrum were the Conservatives, whose hopes of co-opting the Radicals had been sorely disappointed. Instead of sustaining the tradition of agreement by *acuerdo,* the Sáenz Peña electoral reform led to basic changes in the political system.

First, the electorate was steadily enlarged and elections became highly competitive. All Argentine males over eighteen years old now had the right to vote, and nearly 1 million people qualified in 1912. Winners rarely emerged with more than 60 percent of the vote. Universal male suffrage distinguished Argentina from other major Latin American countries, such as Mexico or Brazil, whose far more restricted electorates reflected lower national literacy rates and more closed political systems.

A further consequence of expanded voter participation was the increased importance of the political parties. Almost nonexistent under the Generation of 1880, after 1912 the parties became primary vehicles for the organized pursuit of power, spawning a new kind of political elite: middle-class professionals who made careers out of politics.

As innovative as the Sáenz Peña electoral reform was for its day in Latin America, it left the political system still limited. It not only excluded women but also left out at least half of the adult males because so many were still foreign citizens. Since the unnaturalized immigrants were more numerous among the working class, the reform disproportionately helped the middle class.

The practical result of all these changes was to leave the Conservatives far from power. The Radicals, building upon their popular base and using machine tactics, displayed continuing electoral supremacy: Marcelo T. de Alvear became president in 1922, Yrigoyen was reelected in 1928, and the Radicals dominated both houses of Congress. The political system came to represent an autonomous threat to the socioeconomic system, both through the hegemony of political professionals and through the accumulation of political power within an increasingly autonomous state. For Conservatives and their allies, Argentina's experiment in limited democracy was becoming distasteful and risky.

The world economic crash of 1929 hit Argentina, but not as soon or as hard as some other countries. The prices and values of beef exports held up until 1931. The wheat market was suffering badly, but mainly because of a drought; besides, farmers exerted scant political influence, partly because so many, as noted, were unnaturalized immigrants. In 1930 real wages underwent a brief decline and unemployment was starting to spread, but labor agitation remained at a moderate level. The Great Depression no doubt exacerbated the tensions in Argentina's political sphere, but it alone would not have been enough to cause a political breakdown.

The Military Turns Back the Clock

On September 6, 1930, a coalition of military officers and civilian aristocrats ousted President Yrigoyen, claiming his government was illegitimate, and set up a provisional regime. How had these soldiers come to intervene in what seemed to be a smoothly functioning constitutional order?

The liberals who came to power back in 1852 believed that a professional army was indispensable for Argentina's development. They wanted a well-trained military to crush provincial *caudillos* and to provide the order necessary for economic growth. Seeking to strengthen their armed forces, the Argentines looked to Europe for their models. In 1899 General Roca and his colleagues negotiated the visit of a German mission to train staff officers in modern military technology. That collaboration with Germany was to last forty years.

The increased professionalization of the military led to a shift in the outlook of the Argentine officer corps. By 1910 there was a change in the criteria for promotion: now it became seniority and mastery of the new technology rather than political favoritism. At the same time, there was a shift in control over promotions—from the presidency to an all-military committee made up of army division commanders and chaired by the highest-ranking general. This change enabled the military to develop a higher degree of institutional autonomy.

The increased emphasis on merit also opened military careers to aspiring sons of the middle class. Not surprisingly, this soon included sons of immigrants, especially from Italy. Successful recruits who made their way up the hierarchy forged a strong allegiance to the military as an institution. The reverse side of this loyalty was a deep suspicion of outsiders, especially politicians. By 1930 most officers concurred that the only way out of the political mess was to revise the rules of the political game.

Agreement stopped there, however. On everything else the military divided into factions. One faction, led by General Agustín P. Justo, wanted to return to the oligarchical system of the pre–Sáenz Peña reform days. These officers thought if Yrigoyen and the Radicals were removed from politics, then power would revert to the aristocrats and the specter of class struggle would disappear.

Another faction, led by General José F. Uriburu, suggested a more sweeping solution: the establishment of a semi-fascist corporate state. They saw the problem to be the very attempt to try democracy in Argentina, reflecting the antidemocratic doctrines already rampant in Europe, especially in Italy, Spain, and Portugal. They envisioned a "functional democracy," where the elected legislators would represent functional (or "corporate") interests, such as ranchers, workers, merchants, and industrialists. The theory was that a vertical structure would reintegrate the political system with the economic system, so that the political arena would once again reflect the distribution of economic power. It was also, quite obviously, a formula for stopping class-oriented politics.

Although Uriburu directed the provisional government in 1930, the Justo group eventually won out. After Justo became president in 1932 he created a pro-government coalition of parties called the Concordancia, and he replaced a number of military men in sensitive posts with well-known politicians. Clearly, Justo was hoping to form a broad, national government that would give him the authority to respond to the socioeconomic effects of the world depression.

This proved impossible. One reason was the expansion of an urban working class which made repeated demands on the government. Another was that political professionals—committed to partisan interests—refused to play by the old-fashioned rules. This became clear when Radical Party leader Roberto Ortiz, Justo's successor in 1937, stopped electoral fraud and thereby allowed the Radicals to win control of Congress.

Ortiz' health forced him to leave office in 1940. His successor, Ramón Castillo, resorted to the technique typical of embattled oligarchs when faced with elections:

Despite its historic importance, the military coup of 1930 was a relatively genteel affair—here a white flag of surrender flutters from the presidential palace (see arrow) as onlookers gather in the Plaza de Mayo. (Private collection.)

stuffing the ballot box. This cheating only dramatized the illegitimacy of the incumbent civilian government.

Military officers watched with increasing impatience. As World War II spread in Europe in the early 1940s, and the Axis—which included Germany, Italy, and Japan after 1940—seemed to be carrying the day, the Argentine military chieftains saw the need for steady, sure leadership in their own land. The obstacle as they saw it was the cabal of civilian politicians, who had continued pursuing their petty interests, and thereby rendering their country vulnerable.

Politics in Argentina was taking a unique path in Latin America. The causes were several. In contrast to Brazil, whose government had, after a long flirtation with Nazi Germany, decided to cast its lot with the United States in 1942, Argentina wanted to preserve its "neutrality." That meant it would continue to sell essential foodstuffs to besieged Britain while refusing to join the U.S.-led military effort.

Behind this rough consensus about neutrality among the Argentine elite lay the continuing military impatience with the civilian politicians. Dissident officers mounted several plots to seize power. The triumphant group was called the GOU (Grupo Obra de Unificación or Grupo de Oficiales Unidos), which justified its seizure of power in 1943 as a response to popular demand.

In fact, the ambitious officers wanted to revamp the entire political structure. They began by dissolving the Congress, that target of their oft-expressed scorn. The ascendant military, led by the first provisional president, General Arturo Rawson, grandly announced, "Now there are no political parties, but only Argentines." The military set themselves to rid Argentina of politics, as well as politicians. In 1944 they decreed the end of political parties, and they excluded from the cabinet all professional politicians, aside from a few "collaborationist" Radicals.

Another factor was at work as the military was seizing control of the political system. Class consciousness was growing among the workers. By the 1940s the urban working class was now about 90 percent literate, and it was mobile, with many of its members having recently arrived from the countryside. In contrast to the era of the great export boom (1880–1914), most urban workers were now native Argentines, not European immigrants.

As the political drama unfolded, the principal actors turned out to be the military and labor. The military had its own institutional base, but the large and growing urban working class lacked effective political representation. Why? In part, this was because the Radicals and the Socialists were geared to the electoral system as modified in 1912, when over half the adult male population remained excluded from the vote. With the partial exception of the Socialists, none of the major political parties created an authentic working-class base.

Enter Juan Perón. A man of middle-class origin, he had risen to the rank of colonel in the Argentine army. Ambitious and outgoing, nearing fifty, he had taken an active part in the GOU movement that ousted Ramón Castillo from the presidency in 1943. Perón became secretary of labor, a fairly minor post, but one that he transformed into a bastion of strength. Using both carrots and sticks, Perón courted the support of industrial workers. Partly because of this influence, he later became minister of war and vice president. When jailed by rivals among the military officers who feared his growing popularity, his supporters mobilized a massive demonstration on October 17, 1945, forcing his release. A hero to the dispossessed, he immediately entered the presidential contest of 1946.

The U.S. government unintentionally provided ammunition for Perón's campaign by accusing him of pro-fascist sympathies. The outspoken American ambassador, Spruille Braden, repeated these charges in public and claimed to support them with evidence in a so-called *Blue Book on Argentina*. Nationalists pounced on these undiplomatic interventions and asserted that citizens would now have a clear choice at the polls—"Braden or Perón." Given this option, the voters chose Perón by a solid 54 percent majority.

Even so, this episode revealed the force of changing international realities. In the wake of World War II, with the rise of U.S. power and the decline of Europe, Argentina would have to cope with the power and preeminence of the United States. A new world order had begun, and it would affect Argentina in myriad ways.

Peronism and Perón

Once installed as president, Perón proceeded to put into practice the corporatist principles of the GOU. Argentina would now be organized according to functional groups: industrialists, farmers, workers. The government would act as the final arbiter in case of conflict among groups. A Five-Year Economic Plan was issued, and a powerful new foreign trade institute (Instituto Argentino de Promoción del Intercambio, or IAPI) was given a state monopoly over the export of key agricultural crops. Argentina now began the most state-directed economic policy thus far seen in twentieth-century Latin America.

Perón was carrying out the 1930s corporatist vision of General Uriburu, but with a vital difference: Perón made urban workers his most important political ally, flanked by industrialists and the armed forces. He mobilized popular support by using resources to promote his ideology. Known as Justicialismo, this ideology promised social justice and public welfare.

Perón had campaigned for the presidency on a nationalist and populist note. "Argentina was a country of fat bulls and undernourished peons," said Perón in 1946. He promised truly Argentine solutions while channeling to the workers the rewards they had been unjustly denied. Perón continued the tactics he had been perfecting since 1943: the encouragement of strikes which the government then settled in favor of the workers. Real hourly wage rates jumped 25 percent in 1947 and 24 percent in 1948. Labor's share of the national income increased by 25 percent between 1946 and 1950. The losers were the owners of capital, especially the landowners, since the government trade monopoly (IAPI) bought most of their products at low, fixed prices.

At first this bold strategy worked well. The GDP grew by 8.6 percent in 1946 and by the even more startling rate of 12.6 percent in 1947. Even the lower rate of 5.1 percent in 1948 was still very respectable by world standards. This growth was fueled in part by Argentina's booming exports, which produced healthy trade surpluses from 1946 through 1948.

Perón also made good on his promise to reduce foreign influence in the economy. In 1948 Argentina nationalized the British-owned railways. Also nationalized was the leading telephone company (from U.S.-controlled ITT) and the French-owned dock facilities. In every case, the Argentines compensated the owners, at prices Argentine nationalists later claimed were too high. And in July 1947, Perón paid off Argentina's entire foreign debt, accompanied by a "Declaration of Economic Independence."

Eva Perón also emerged as a political power in her own right. A former radio actress from a small town in the interior, "Evita" was snubbed by the society matrons (señoras gordas) who had always monopolized the political careers of past first ladies. To establish a popular base, Evita set up her own foundation in 1948. Dispensing cash and benefits personally, she rapidly built up a fanatically loyal following. Evita's charisma complemented her husband's, and they together succeeded in building an imposing political machine, but one that was steadily choking off any open political dissent.

By 1948 it seemed clear sailing for the Peronists. Social justice was rapidly being accomplished, and the economy continued to hum. The political opposition had been demoralized and humiliated. The streets were continuously full of the faithful. It was the realization of the "New Argentina" Perón had promised.

This success proved short-lived, however, as 1949 brought the first foreign trade deficit since the war. Equally important was the sudden jump in inflation to 31 percent, double the previous year. To make matters worse, a severe drought curtailed the production of exportable goods. World prices for Argentina's exports were dropping; prices for imports, especially manufactured goods, were rising. And Peronist policies compounded the problem. IAPI, the government foreign trade institute, had set unrealistically low prices for agricultural goods to keep down food prices in the cities. But the effect was also to discourage production, thus hurting exports.

Perón reacted to the economic crisis in 1949 by appointing a new finance minister who launched an orthodox stabilization program: tight credit, reduced government expenditure, and tough limits on wage and price increases. Perón was determined to get the economy under control and resume as soon as possible his ambitious social politics.

Amending the constitution of 1853 to permit a second term, in 1951 Perón was reelected with 67 percent of the 6.9 million votes cast. He drew especially heavy support from women voters, who had gained the right to vote in 1947. A Peronist party was also founded. The government now reverted more frequently to authoritarian measures, such as the expropriation in 1951 of La Prensa, the leading opposition newspaper.

On one political front, however, Perón was defeated. In running for reelection in 1951, he wanted Evita to be his vice presidential candidate. Her political influence had grown enormously, as many workers had come to identify her as the heart of Peronism. She was brilliant at promoting this image, aided by huge (and largely unaccounted for) government funds. But the military refused to accept that a woman might, by succeeding to the presidency, become their commander-in-chief.

The military veto of Evita's candidacy foreshadowed a far greater blow. Evita fell ill and eventually could not hide the fact that she was dying of cancer. She grew hauntingly thin but fought the disease ferociously and continued her exhausting schedule. In July 1952 she finally died, depriving Perón of a political partner who had become fully as important as he.

Evita now became larger in death than she had ever been in life. The government suspended all functions for two days, and the labor union confederation, the CGT (Confederación General del Trabajo), ordered its members to observe a month's mourning. The outpouring of grief was astounding. There were immediate plans to build a mausoleum 150 feet taller than the Statue of Liberty. Dead at the age of thirty-three, Evita became a powerful myth binding together the Peronist faithful.

Ill, gaunt, and nonetheless compelling, Evita Perón waves to the crowd during a motorcade for the inauguration of her husband into his second presidential term in June 1952; she died the following month. (Corbis/Bettman/United Press International.)

The good news of 1952 was that the tough austerity plan of Finance Minister Alfredo Gómez Morales was beginning to produce results. Perón and his advisers now opted for a second Five-Year Plan, far less populist and nationalist than the policies of the late 1940s. There was a direct appeal for foreign capital, resulting in a contract with Standard Oil of California in 1954. There were also new incentives to agriculture, previously a prime target for exploitation under the cheap-food strategy. Workers were asked to accept a two-year wage freeze as a sacrifice in the name of financing much-needed investment.

In order to regain economic growth, Perón believed he had to reverse some of his nationalist and redistributionist policies. As long as the economy was expanding, it was easy to favor one social sector; with a stagnant economy, however, the workers could gain only at the direct expense of the middle or upper sectors. Class conflict threatened to tear apart Perón's carefully constructed populist coalition.

Perhaps for this reason, the Peronist political strategy became more radical. After 1949 Perón moved to win control over the army by promoting political favorites. A new program was set up to indoctrinate cadets with Peronist teachings and to dress up the lower ranks with flashy uniforms. Perón knew he had opponents within the army, and in 1951 they attempted a coup against him. He easily suppressed them, but the germ of discontent remained alive.

After Evita's death in 1952, Perón shifted his attention from the army to the labor unions, led by loyalists. As the economic policy became more orthodox, a militantly Justicialist working-class tone became evident. In 1953 a Peronist street crowd pillaged the Jockey Club, the bastion of the Argentine aristocracy.

In 1954 the Peronist radicals took on another pillar of the traditional order: the church. Divorce was legalized, and all parochial schools were placed under government control. The year 1955 brought mass demonstrations against the church, orchestrated by the Peronists. Several famous cathedrals in Buenos Aires were burned by Peronist crowds. The Vatican retaliated by excommunicating the entire governmental cabinet, including Perón. Perón vowed to mobilize his masses against the "conspirators" who menaced Argentine independence.

In fact, the Peronist government was out of control. Many officers became convinced that he was bent on destroying the country. The ugly battle with the church finally gave Perón's enemies within the military their chance. In September 1955 military conspirators presented their president with an ultimatum: resign or face civil war. Perón, so often given to extreme rhetoric, had no stomach for a bloodbath. He retreated to the refuge of a Paraguayan gunboat that took him to asylum across the Paraná River.

The Military Stewardship

Perón had not really been defeated. He had departed under duress, making no effort to mobilize his followers. Despite the sudden vacuum created by his departure, neither Perón nor Peronism was finished.

The new president was Eduardo Lonardi, a moderate general who wanted to avoid a vindictive policy, which he thought would keep the Peronists united. But the hard-line military grew impatient with his conciliatory approach. In November they deposed Lonardi and installed General Pedro Aramburu as provisional president. The anti-Peronist zealots now got their chance to purge everything Peronist. Perón's Party was outlawed, and every scrap of Peronist propaganda became contraband.

The hard-line military and the Aramburu political strategists believed that they could reshape the political system for a transition to a post-Peronist era. Former property owners hit by Peronist expropriations had their holdings restored. The government pushed the crackdown on Peronist leaders, especially in the unions. In June 1956 the Peronists struck back. A revolt of pro-Peronist military took place in several provinces, and the government responded with force. In the follow-up some forty leaders were executed. However authoritarian Perón's government, it had never resorted to such a level of official killing. Finally, all parties were now required to commit themselves to democracy. Having to establish such a "requirement" was itself dramatic proof of the fragility of Argentine democracy.

As Argentina headed into its first elections since Perón's overthrow, the political scene was confused because the anti-Peronist civilian politicians were deeply divided. The largest party was still the Radicals, the venerable party of Yrigoyen and his acolytes. But at a party convention in 1956, the Radicals (UCR) split in two. One faction was the "Popular Radicals" (UCR del Pueblo, or UCRP), led by Ricardo Balbín, the party's elder statesman who had run for president in 1951. The other was the "Intransigent Radicals" (UCRI), led by Arturo Frondizi, an economics professor. The Balbín faction was fanatically anti-Perón, while the Frondizi faction advocated flexibility in dealing with the Peronists. This paralleled a similar split of opinion within the military.

Political uncertainty reigned in elections for a constituent assembly. The two Radical factions won an almost equal number of seats in the convention, which reinstated the constitution of 1853 but was otherwise so split that it was disbanded. The military held new elections in February 1958. Unable to get the votes from the Balbín wing (UCRP) of the Radicals, Frondizi struck a deal with the Peronists, promising to restore their party to legality. His aggressively nationalist campaign won him the presidency and a majority in the national Congress. It looked as if Argentina would now have a centrist government that could take up the political and economic challenges that lay ahead. But a major cloud was hanging over Frondizi—his debt to the Peronists.

The Failure of Developmental Reformism

The new president seemed to be from the same mold as other democratic reformers then making their mark in Latin America, such as Eduardo Frei of Chile and Juscelino Kubitschek of Brazil. Like them, he decided to take major gambles.

On the economic front, Frondizi put into place an ambitious program to accelerate industrialization while also stimulating agricultural production, thereby boosting export earnings. While state intervention in the economy was to be reduced, much of the financing for new industry was to come from abroad. Almost immediately, however, Frondizi faced an acute balance of payments crisis. Since he needed to impress Argentina's foreign creditors, from whom he was seeking new investment, Frondizi decided to accept their bitter medicine: a huge devaluation, stiff controls on credit, cuts in public spending, tough wage limits, reduction of subsidies on public services, and the dismissal of redundant public employees.

The inevitable effect of these policies was a sharp shift in income away from the working class. The purchasing power of industrial workers dropped by almost 29 percent in 1959, compared with an increase of 97 percent for *ganaderos* (cattlemen)—who enjoyed the gains from higher prices but failed to increase the volume of beef exports in any commensurate degree. There were general strikes in April, May, and September of 1959 and an extended railroad strike in November of that year. An embattled Frondizi was forced to accept a compromise settlement in which labor was the effective winner. The stabilization policy also came under attack from Argentine businessmen, especially those from smaller firms, who denounced the credit restrictions and the huge increase in import prices resulting from devaluation.

As a result, Frondizi's political fortunes were foundering. Labor and the left never forgave his orthodox stabilization policy, with its cut in real wages and its embrace of foreign capital (including secret contracts with U.S. oil companies). And while the military had supported—indeed forced him to adopt—his IMF-style economic policy, the officer corps deeply distrusted his conciliatory moves toward the Peronists, whose party had regained its legal status. The climax came in the elections of March 1962. The result was a disaster for the government. The Peronists led all parties in total votes, with 35 percent. The Frondizi Radicals got 28 percent and the Balbín Radicals 22 percent, the rest going to smaller parties.

The military quickly forced the president to annul the Peronist election victories in the provinces. The Frondizi Radicals then tried for a coalition with the Balbín faction. This might seem an obvious way out, since together, the Radicals represented half the electorate. But the Balbín followers rejected the Frondizi overtures. Once again the middle-class party, the Radicals, proved unequal to the task of governing Argentina, the most middle-class country in Latin America.

Yet Frondizi refused to resign. On March 29, 1962, the army tanks rolled onto the streets and removed him. Into the presidency stepped the constitutional successor, Senate President José María Guido.

Guido served as acting president for a year and a half. The real power was held by the military. But they were still deeply divided on how to deal with the civilian politicians, which led to repeated intramilitary revolts. In particular, the military were divided over the advisability of trying to "reintegrate" the Peronist masses into the political system. Complicating this situation was the exiled Perón himself, continuously sending instructions to his lieutenants in Argentina.

The military finally decided to annul entirely the election results of 1962 and to hold a new round of elections in July 1963. This time the Balbín Radicals won the largest total, with 27 percent of the ballots. The new president was Arturo Illia, a colorless provincial physician who was to lead the second Radical attempt at governing post-Peronist Argentina. Unlike Frondizi, Illia had made no overtures to the Peronists. Nonetheless, the hardline military were ever vigilant to find any signs of softness toward Peronism or the left.

Illia was relatively fortunate in the economic situation he found. The government began very cautiously. It soon became evident, however, that the policymakers were set on expansion, granting generous wage increases and imposing price controls. These measures helped to swing Argentina into the "go" phase of the "stop and go" economic pattern (alternately stimulating and contracting the economy) it had exhibited since the war. The GNP showed small declines in 1962 and 1963, but spurted to gains of 10.4 percent in 1964 and 9.1 percent in 1965.

On the agricultural front, the Illia government suffered through a downswing in the "beef cycle," when the depleted herds were withheld for breeding. The resulting shortage irritated urban consumers—always voracious beef eaters—and reduced the production available for export. Cattlemen were angry because the government did not let prices rise to the levels indicated by market demand. Illia, like virtually every other Argentine president since 1945, found the rural sector virtually impossible to harness for the national interest.

The Peronist unions were opposed to Illia from the moment he entered office, in part because they were barred from the 1963 elections and despite Illia's initially large wage settlements. The Peronist-dominated CGT drew up a "battle plan" *(plan de lucha)*, which included strikes and workplace takeovers. In the congressional elections of March 1965, the now legalized Peronist party won 30.3 percent of the vote, against 28.9 percent for the Illia Radicals.

Perón, in his Spanish exile, was encouraged by the vote and sent his third wife, Isabel, to Argentina to negotiate directly with the feuding Peronist groups. The hard-line military grew ever more worried over the apparent Peronist comeback. The economic scene was also taking a disquieting turn. Inflation erupted anew, and the government deficit was out of control. In June 1966 the military intervened again. Illia was unceremoniously ejected from the Casa Rosada. Once again the officers had removed a Radical government unable effectively to either court or repress the Peronist masses.

The Bureaucratic-Authoritarian Solution

The military coup of 1966 marked a sharper break with the past than any coup since 1943. It was the most repressive, at least in the initial stages. Proclaiming the advent of "the Argentine Revolution," General Juan Carlos Onganía, the new president, sought to implant a new kind of regime—a bureaucratic-authoritarian state. The goal was to attack the root causes of Argentina's problems, rather than to deal with the symptoms: society must be transformed. The Onganía government shut down the recalcitrant Congress, ousted opponents from the universities, and set out to control (and purportedly "uplift") the tone of social life. Dismissing politicians from positions of authority, the military leaders forged alliances with technocrats and foreign investors, whose capital was sought to spur economic growth.

The economics minister, Adalberto Krieger Vasena, announced a wide-ranging plan. A key feature was a two-year wage freeze in 1967, which the government was able to enforce because of its authoritarian methods and its relative success in holding down price increases.

The new military government also thought it had another factor working in its favor. A significant wing of organized labor, led by CGT executive Augusto Vandor, wanted to support them, which would have the benefit of dividing labor. This tactic proved partially successful in 1967 and 1968. But in 1969 it was engulfed by an explosive labor rebellion that developed in the provincial city of Córdoba, where there had been a series of antigovernment protests and labor stoppages. During a street protest the troops opened fire, killing some tens of protestors and bystanders. A howl of protest went up in the country. The many enemies of the government's economic program, including some military who opposed the wage freeze, seized the occasion to lobby for Krieger Vasena's ouster, which finally came in June 1969. The Onganía government lasted another year, but its credibility was shattered.

It was not only the labor opposition that doomed Onganía's regime. There was also a shocking rise in political violence, including clandestine torture and execution by the military government and kidnapping and assassination by the revolutionary left. Labor policy soon came to depend on coercion, so the left now decided to reply with violence of its own. In 1970 leftist terrorists kidnapped ex-president Aramburu, who had ordered the execution of Peronist conspirators in 1956. Aramburu was later found murdered.

The Onganía government was by all standards a political failure. Although it brought off postwar Argentina's most successful economic stabilization program, it failed to create a broad-based political coalition that could make possible genuine planning for the future. This outcome left Argentina with few alternatives.

The new president was another general, Roberto Levingston, a little-known intelligence officer, who faced immediate threats from rising inflation. He pursued a moderately expansionary course, but a downswing in the beef cycle caused shortages and high prices. Never well endowed with military prestige, Levingston found himself isolated. Yet another military coup removed him and installed General Alejandro Lanusse, who had been the brains behind the ouster of Onganía eight months earlier.

Lanusse made no pretense at having an answer for the economy, deciding to ride along with growing budget deficits and mounting inflation. His real ambition was to achieve a new political accord. He opted for a relegalization of the Peronists and, in an even greater gamble, decided to allow Perón to return. Elections were announced for March 1973. Perón briefly returned to Argentina in late 1972 and lobbied intensively for his stand-in, Dr. Héctor Cámpora, as his own presidential candidate. Meanwhile, the violence continued. The guerrillas became bolder, directly striking at high-ranking military officers, as well as at prisons and barracks.

Cámpora received 49 percent of the popular vote, far ahead of Balbín's 22 percent. The president and like-minded officers began to see Perón as the only hope against the left. When Héctor Cámpora was inaugurated in May 1973, more than a few officers felt that the first step toward a solution to the leftist threat might be at hand.

Peronists Back in Power

Cámpora had left no doubt that he was only a stand-in until Perón could return and run in a new election. Nonetheless, his government launched a bold new economic policy. It was aimed at first stabilizing prices and then boosting workers' earnings back to the share of national income they had reached in the earlier Peronist era. Obviously this would require extraordinary cooperation from all interest groups. The Cámpora government managed to negotiate agreement to its proposed "Social Contract" (Pacto Social), which was formally ratified by labor and business organizations. A parallel compact with rural producers (except for the rabidly anti-Peronist cattle breeders) promised price, tax, and credit incentives in return for a promise to double farm production by 1980. Surprisingly, the new Peronist regime had constructed a coalition that included almost every interest group in Argentine society. How was it possible? In part, because both exhaustion and realism had taken hold of Argentines. Indeed, more than a few longtime anti-Peronists looked to the new Perón government as perhaps their country's last chance to solve their problems by something short of continued naked force.

Even so, the odds for success were not high. Political violence was rising steadily, as guerrilla forces rejected the new Peronist regime and tried, through kidnappings and assassinations, to destabilize the fragile political balance. A further liability was the age and health of the once-charismatic figure around whom the new social consensus had to be built: Perón was seventy-seven and in failing health.

New presidential elections were scheduled for September 1973. Perón now succeeded in a political tactic which had failed in 1951: he got his wife, Isabel, nominated for the vice presidency. They swept the election with 62 percent of the vote. Perón now began to turn against the revolutionary left, whom he had often encouraged in his comments from exile. Just as Lanusse might have hoped, Perón was proving the perfect sponsor to preside over a military and police counteroffensive against the revolutionary left.

On the economic front, 1974 brought trouble. An OPEC oil price increase hurt the balance of payments, although Argentina was importing only 16 percent of its oil. Furthermore, some non-CGT unions won new wage agreements, in violation of the Social Contract. Several CGT unions soon followed suit. Under growing pressure from union leaders, Perón agreed to large year-end bonuses for all CGT unions, thereby undermining his own anti-inflation program.

Whether Perón could have yet again worked his magic with the workers was not to be known. In July 1974 he died; the president now was Isabel. Perón had met her when she was a nightclub dancer in Panama, during his leisurely journey after his 1955 overthrow. Isabel was no Evita, as her insecurity and indecision had already made clear. She assumed office as the Peronists were bitterly squabbling. There was an immediate scramble to gain influence over the frightened woman who had succeeded to the presidential duties.

The adviser with the greatest influence was Isabel's minister of social welfare, José Lopéz Rega, an ambitious and bizarre figure well known for his militantly right-wing Peronist views. López Rega first helped convince Isabel to purge her cabinet of the more moderate ministers in October 1974, then persuaded her to crack down on the left—including left-wing Peronists. This became the direction of policy in 1975, as unions began negotiating new contracts with 100 percent wage increases or more. Isabel mounted a countercampaign, annulling the huge wage settlements, but later, after a series of massive strikes, reinstating them. López Rega resigned in frustration, and the president also lost her congressional majority as the Peronist delegation split apart.

The guerrillas continued their provocative attacks on the police and military, bringing off some dramatic assassinations. The right answered through equally violent organizations. The value of money shrank daily, almost hourly, as inflation rocketed by 335 percent in 1975. Fear of terrorists, whether of the right or left, took hold of the populace, especially the urban middle class. The president was terrified, utterly unable to wield command. Once again an elected government disappeared from the Casa Rosada.

In March 1976, in Argentina's best-predicted coup, the military placed Isabel Perón under house arrest, a year before her term was up. Why had the military waited so long? Perhaps because they did not want to take over formal responsibility for governing until the national situation had become so violent and the economy so chaotic that no one could doubt the need for military intervention.

The Military Returns

When the armed forces finally moved against Isabel, they were determined to impose a bureaucratic-authoritarian solution that would last. Under General Jorge Rafael Videla, the regime launched a vicious campaign, alternatively known as a "dirty war" or "holy war" against the opposition. The government began arresting "subversives" at will. And then there were the *desaparecidos*, those who simply "disappeared," perhaps 10,000 or 20,000 in all. These people were abducted by heavily armed men who were undoubtedly "off-duty" security men operating with the military government's knowledge. Virtually none of the abducted were ever heard from again.

We shall never know how many of the "disappeared" were totally innocent and how many actively supported the guerrilla movements. Thousands of Argentines were no doubt involved in one way or another. From bank robberies and ransomings, the guerrillas built a war chest of at least $150 million, and they proved highly adept at paramilitary strikes.

The generals decided to pursue an all-out offensive without any legal constraints. The "disappeared" were victims in a tactic consciously designed to terrorize the country. In the end the generals won, but at a terrible price. Once proud Argentina became an international pariah, along with Chile and South Africa, and its people, by habit articulate and argumentative, suffered the ignominy of silence and intimidation.

What had the guerrillas wanted? With minor disagreements over emphasis, they sought the violent overthrow of the government and the installation of a revolutionary socialist regime along Marxist-Leninist lines. Predominantly middle class and deeply alienated by the merry-go-round of Argentine politics, they were caught up in a passionate rebellion against a socioeconomic structure that was, ironically, one of the most "modern" in Latin America. Once locked in battle, there was no exit for the guerrillas. It was a war to the death.

The war showed that a well-equipped and determined government can, barring any major split among the society's ruling elites, defeat a guerrilla movement. A key factor was the tacit (and often explicit) support of the middle class for the antiguerrilla campaign. The Argentine middle class was proportionately the largest in Latin America, and therefore a crucial actor in the political drama. It had

---

The Mothers of the Plaza

The Argentine military junta that seized power in 1976 left an appalling record of torture and repression. The least hint of opposition could result in "disappearance." The only protesters who managed to defy the generals were a small group of older mothers who met spontaneously every Thursday to march around the Plaza de Mayo in downtown Buenos Aires prominently displaying the names and pictures of their missing children. Hesitant at first, they courageously stood their ground when police and military harassed them with threats and intimidation. By some miracle the women were allowed to continue. Were these men, normally so ready to brutalize any suspect, now afraid to attack mothers, the supreme symbol of the values they claimed to be defending?

Their demands were simple. They wanted an accounting of what had happened to their loved ones. They had no illusions. Most knew their sons and daughters had been executed. They wanted confirmation and the chance to bury their lost progeny. They rarely got that satisfaction. Yet they continued marching for years, a somber reminder of the terrible price that Argentina has paid for the demented fanaticism of its military.

watched with dismay the decay of order under Isabel Perón, and most of it supported, at least initially, the coup of 1976.

That fateful takeover was intended as a coup to end all coups. Videla and his colleagues proclaimed that their goal was not merely to terminate the chaos of the Peronist years, but also to restructure Argentine society. The junta promised to eradicate terrorism and thereby remove some potent actors from the political scene. They planned to reduce the public sector, and consequently to rearrange relationships among business, labor, and the state. They affirmed Argentina's alignment with the "Western and Christian world," and in keeping with these lofty principles, they promised to "reeducate" the populace by emphasizing "morality, uprightness, and efficiency."

In pursuit of these ideas, the military penetrated Argentine society more deeply than ever before: in addition to abolishing the General Confederation of Labor, military officers took over other institutions, such as sports and charitable organizations.

In 1978 the generals got a heaven-sent propaganda opportunity when Argentina hosted the World Cup soccer matches and won the cup, to the ecstatic cheers of the home crowd and the obvious pleasure of the generals. For a few weeks at least, ordinary Argentines could take pride in their country. But the euphoria was soon dissipated by the realities of Argentina's plight.

Among the gravest worries was the economy. Economics Minister José Martínez de Hoz, an outspoken representative of the "neoliberal" view, immediately imposed a stabilization program. Labor faced declining real wages, while businessmen found credit increasingly hard to obtain. Martínez de Hoz also moved to privatize a number of state enterprises, while slashing tariffs on almost all industrial goods.

These policies succeeded in bringing inflation down to 88 percent in 1980 and in achieving a surplus on the balance of payments for four successive years (1976–79). By 1981, however, the picture had darkened. Inflation again exceeded 100 percent, industry operated at only half capacity, and real income was less than in 1970.

Despite these economic troubles, the armed forces demonstrated notable coherence and unity. This was an institutional regime, not a one-man show, and Videla turned the presidency over to General Roberto Viola in March 1981. Viola lacked the stamina needed in the pressured position and passed the presidency in early 1982 to General Leopoldo Galtieri, the commander-in-chief of the army.

In March Galtieri chose to stake his government's fate on the Falkland Islands controlled by the British but long claimed by the Argentines, who called them the Malvinas Islands. The military thought the British would not defend the desolate islands—8000 miles away from Britain, populated by only 1800 inhabitants and 600,000 sheep. So on April 2, 1982, a large Argentine force invaded the islands and quickly overwhelmed the badly outgunned royal marine garrison.

But the British denounced the invasion and mobilized a major task force. In late May, the British landed thousands of troops onto Falklands/Malvinas beachheads. All but three other Latin American countries backed Argentina in an Organization of American States vote condemning Britain as the aggressor.

Why had the Galtieri government decided to invade? Clearly the Argentine economy was on the rocks again. Only days before the April 2 invasion there had been the largest antigovernment demonstration since the military seized power in 1976. Galtieri and his fellow officers undoubtedly saw the lure of a quick military victory in the Falklands/Malvinas as a boost to the government's sagging popularity. Furthermore, Galtieri felt certain that he would have at least the tacit support of the Reagan administration, with which the Argentine generals had developed a warm relationship.

In the short run, Galtieri was right about the Argentine reaction, although wrong about the United States. The invasion brought an outpouring of patriotic sentiment in Argentina. In part that was due to government-controlled reporting that told of nothing but Argentine victories. But the Argentine public soon suffered a rude return to reality. The better trained and more experienced British troops laid effective siege to the 7500 Argentine troops holed up in the Malvinas capital, Port Stanley. After brief consultation with Buenos Aires and sporadic resistance, the Argentine commander surrendered—the only sensible option, given the poor morale, condition, and positioning of his troops. Yet the sudden surrender hit Buenos Aires hard. Britain, supposedly enfeebled and unable to defend these distant islands, had decisively defeated numerically superior Argentine forces. Only the Argentine Air Force emerged as having had both the skill and the courage to fight effectively.

THE CONTEMPORARY SCENE (1983–PRESENT)

The Galtieri-led junta had made a mortal error as a military government: it began a military adventure that it failed to win. Patriotic fervor turned into ugly demonstrations outside the Casa Rosada. Galtieri came under intense fire from his fellow officers. He resigned as military unity began to unravel, and passed the presidential baton to an obscure retired general, Reynaldo Bignone. Upon assuming office in July 1982, Bignone repeated Argentina's claim to the Falklands/Malvinas. He promised an election in 1983 and a return to civilian government by 1984.

The Argentine economy went from bad to worse in 1982. Inflation shot up to 200 percent, workers lost about one-quarter of their real income, and the country went into de facto default on its private foreign debt.

To virtually everyone's surprise, Radical Party leader Raúl Alfonsín won 52 percent of the vote in the presidential election of 1983. The Radicals also gained majority control of the Chamber of Deputies. Alfonsín had been a courageous battler for human rights during military rule. Also, his party was the only non-Peronist group capable of forming a viable government.

The new regime faced formidable problems. First was the commitment to prosecute the military personnel and police who had killed or "disappeared" more than 10,000 suspects. The public revulsion against the perpetrators was deep and had helped give Alfonsín his vote. Argentina, would be the first country to try its own military for domestic crimes.

The second problem was the economy. Inflation had reached 400 percent in 1983, and Argentina could not service its huge foreign debt. Alfonsín also faced the ever-present struggle for income among competing classes and sectors, with the huge labor unions bloodied but unvanquished by military repression.

The third problem was finding a viable political base. Could the Radicals, a minority party since 1945, retain the majority Alfonsín had won? If not, was an effective coalition feasible?

Alfonsín struggled valiantly with all these challenges. Prosecuting the torturers proved almost a no-win situation. A presidentially appointed commission documented the death or disappearance of 8906 Argentines. The government charged the nine military commanders-in-chief for crimes ranging from murder to rape. Five were convicted and given prison terms, while three of the four acquitted were later tried by military justice and sentenced to prison. But how far down should the prosecutions go? A 1987 military revolt protesting further prosecutions forced Congress to exempt all officers below the rank of general. Even the ongoing prosecutions bogged down, spurring human rights advocates to denounce the failure to pursue the hundreds of other cases. Alfonsín supporters replied that no other Latin American government had ever dared to prosecute its officers for crimes committed during a military government.

Meeting payments on the massive $50 billion foreign debt was an immediate economic problem for the Alfonsín government. Alfonsín had to seek new loans, but the price was an IMF-designed austerity policy at home. Inflation roared up to 627 percent in 1984 and approached 700 percent in 1985. With its back against the wall, the Alfonsín government unveiled a wage-price freeze. Inflation dropped to less than 100 percent, but a recession and a sharp fall in real wages also occurred. Only makeshift measures allowed the government to avoid defaulting on the foreign debt.

Then the wage-price freeze unraveled. By early 1989 prices were rising at more than 30 percent a *month;* they would reach more than 100 percent a month by midyear. The gross domestic product shrank by 3 percent in 1988 and 6 percent in 1989 (overall, per capita income for Argentines declined by nearly 25 percent during the 1980s).

Peronists seized the opportunity. In the presidential elections of May 1989, the party's candidate, Carlos Saúl Menem, governor of the interior province of La Rioja, took 47 percent of the popular vote—and a clear majority in the electoral college—winning handily over the Radical candidate Eduardo Angeloz. This marked a potential watershed in Argentine politics: it was the first time that an opposition party had triumphed in a presidential election in over seventy years. If the country could take these steps, some analysts reasoned, Argentina might have a realistic chance of achieving genuine democracy.

It would not be easy. The economic crisis intensified. Argentina, the proverbial breadbasket of the continent, suffered the humiliation of food riots. A stunned President Alfonsín declared a state of siege, then announced that he would resign from office six months ahead of schedule.

Argentina's persistent financial crises stemmed from its failure to adjust to changing world realities. From 1946 to 1956, Perón had imposed an inward-looking nationalist economic policy. This experiment failed to create self-sustaining growth, although urban workers' income had certainly improved. Unfortunately, the years after 1955 brought a succession of contradictory policies. Neither the liberals, with their anti-Peronist obsession, nor the nationalists, with their hostility to the market and to foreign trade, ever controlled policy for more than a few years at a time. Instead, the economy was pulled back and forth in anticipation that whoever was in opposition would soon gain power and change course again.

This pattern seemed to have ended with the election of Carlos Menem. His prospects seemed favorable because as a Peronist he could presumably retain the nationalists' loyalty, while also following a Washington-endorsed neoliberal restructuring. But Menem had his hands full. Inflation was running at 150 percent per month. The country was nearly $4 billion in arrears in payments on the external debt. Menem installed a new economics minister who imposed a strict austerity program. In January 1990 he shocked the public by transferring interest-bearing bank certificates into ten-year bonds—in effect, confiscating the savings of the middle class. These hard-nosed policies eventually provoked a recession that brought an end to hyperinflation.

Violating cherished principles of Peronism, Menem and his ministers embarked on a program to "privatize" state-owned companies by selling them off to private investors. In 1990 the government auctioned off Entel, the national telephone company, and the national airlines, Aerolíneas Argentinas. Menem also announced his intent to proceed with the privatization of electricity, coal and natural gas, subways, and shipping. Neoliberal economic doctrine seemed to be triumphant.

In early 1991 Menem named as the new economics minister Domingo Cavallo, a firm believer in strict market-oriented reforms. Cavallo extended the privatization campaign and centered his program on a "convertibility law"—which restricted public expenditures to revenues and, most important, established a one-to-one exchange rate between the Argentine peso and the U.S. dollar. Adherence to this exchange rate became the "anchor" for economic confidence, neutralizing the Argentines' well-founded fears of hyperinflation. As a result, inflation declined from 4900 percent in 1989 to 4 percent in 1994.

But there were negative features as well. One was overvaluation of the peso, leading to a trade deficit of more than $6 billion in 1994. Another was impoverishment of the middle class. According to one study, nearly half the country's middle class slipped down into the lower class during the early 1990s. In the meantime, open unemployment increased from 6.5 percent in 1991 to 12.2 percent in 1994. These were the typical fruits of a "hard money" policy that was enthusiastically endorsed by the IMF and the World Bank.

Not surprisingly, the Menem initiatives caused disruption and discord within the labor movement. It seemed ironic to many, and grievous to some, that a Peronist government was breaking strikes by organized labor and confronting protests from the working class. Similarly, Menem offered a round of pardons in favor of former leaders of the military government. There would be no continuing sentences or prosecutions for human-rights offenses committed in the dirty war.

In 1994 the administration gained congressional approval for a constitutional amendnent that would reduce presidential terms from six to four years, but permit one reelection; reduce the president's authority to rule through emergency decree; and create the post of cabinet chief, who would be subject to removal by majority vote in Congress. Proponents insisted that the reforms would improve govern-mental accountability. Opponents, including many Radicals, regarded the reform as a maneuver by Menem to perpetuate himself in power.

Menem promptly declared himself a candidate for the presidential elections of May 1995. Despite continuing rumors of high-level corruption and widespread resentment of the president's authoritarian style, Menem won 49.8 percent of the vote. Divided, demoralized, and represented by a lackluster candidate, the once-proud UCR earned only 17.1 percent.

In the international arena, Argentina promoted the continued development of MERCOSUR (the "Common Market of the South"), a four-partner association that included Argentina, Brazil, Uruguay, and Paraguay. Established in 1991, the scheme envisioned creation of a free trade zone that would eventually evolve into a full-fledged "common market" along the lines of the European Union. Despite occasional tension among the members, the volume of trade and investment within MERCOSUR grew rapidly throughout the 1990s. Its apparent success bolstered Argentina's claims to leadership in South America, although Brazil would claim this mantle as well.

Until the late 1990s, Menem's commitment to the neoliberal model had brought unprecedented economic growth and stability. Inflation had been brought under control (less than 1 percent in 1996 and 1997), while privatization had been extended to virtually all state-owned industries and utilities. The GDP grew an average of 5 percent per year for the middle years of the decade. The "dollarization" of the economy proceeded to a point where dollars were a normal means of exchange for most transactions (by 1999 there was talk of abandoning the peso altogether). The decade's liberalization had a darker side as well. Unemployment and high living costs combined to weigh on the lower sectors of society, and corruption affected the lives of Argentines of all classes.

Even though Argentines were tired of public malfeasance, they were wary of disturbing the existing political order, which had hinged on Menem and his party since 1989. In preparation for congressional elections in 1997, however, opposition groups banded together under the label of the Alliance for Work, Justice, and Education. Careful to reassure nervous voters, Alliance candidates declared their support for the neoliberal model while using the issues of unemployment and corruption to criticize Peronist candidates. The results were surprising: opposition candidates together garnered 46 percent of the vote and more than half the seats in the lower chamber. While the Peronists still held an absolute majority in the Senate, the dissident coalition emerged as a potential threat to Peronist dominance.

In office, the Alliance congressmen, as promised, supported Menem's economic policies while criticizing corruption in government. The process of turning the electoral coalition into a viable opposition and a contender for national power also began. Menem toyed with the idea of trying for a third term, but the negative polling results soon discouraged him. By mid-1999, the Alliance presidential candidate, Fernando de la Rúa, faced a divided Peronist camp led by Buenos Aires provincial governor Eduardo Duhalde,

---

The Ten-Year Honeymoon

Argentina's relations with the United States became unusually warm during the decade of the 1990s. This represented a major departure for a nation that had historically considered itself as a cultural equal and political rival to the Colossus of the North. How and why did this occur?

The shift began with the election of Carlos Saúl Menem, a Peronist, in late 1989. Surveying the impending post–Cold War world, the new administration came to the conclusion that Argentina's national interests would be best served by close alignment with the United States.

By mid-1990 Argentina declared its acceptance of the neoliberal principles of the Washington consensus, especially in regard to free trade and stability of the currency. In December of that year, Guido di Tella, Menem's urbane foreign minister, offered the tongue-in-cheek observation that his country would be seeking *relaciones carnales* ("carnal relations") with the United States.

There followed an astonishing turnabout in foreign policy. In short order, Argentina abandoned the Movement of Nonaligned Nations, took active part in the U.S.-led Gulf War of 1991 (for which President George H. W. Bush sent Menem a note of warm appreciation), terminated its nuclear collaboration with Iran, joined every phase of the Haiti operation in and after 1994, proposed the deployment of UN "White Helmets" for peacekeeping and humanitarian purposes, and dispatched peacekeeping missions to Central America, Kosovo, Bosnia, and other distant locales. (The peacekeeping operations served domestic purposes too: they gave Argentina's armed forces an opportunity to repair their tattered public image, while keeping them out of the country and out of political mischief.)

In early 1998 President Bill Clinton rewarded these efforts, especially the peacekeeping missions, by designating Argentina as a "major non-NATO ally." This rather strange-sounding status was created by the U.S. Congress in 1989 for countries that had close strategic working relationships with American military forces but were not members of NATO. Initial designees were Australia, Egypt, Israel, Japan, and South Korea.

For Argentina, the principal benefit was symbolic. It entailed membership in a privileged club. It granted legitimacy to the nation as a whole. It also implied

primacy in Latin America—more particularly in South America, and most specifically in comparison with arch-rival Brazil.

Normalcy returned after Menem left office. His immediate successor, Fernando
de la Rúa, decided to reemphasize alliances with MERCOSUR partners, including
Brazil. And in recent years, Argentina has aligned itself with Hugo Chávez and the
left-of-center "pink tide" surging through Latin America. Like all honeymoons, this
rapprochement with Washington could not last forever.

a bitter political enemy of Menem. It was de la Rúa who prevailed in the
election.

The new president now had to pay for the economic policies of his predecessors. The prosperity soon faded. It turned out that the fixed exchange rate, which
was intended to be an "anchor," could not be maintained by mere rhetoric. The
actual value of the peso began to slip. Since the peso rate was unconditionally
guaranteed (at 1:1 for the dollar) by the Central Bank, the scene was set for a
massive run on the bank's dollar reserves. Cavallo, with Menem behind him,
vehemently refused to devalue, which was the obvious short-term remedy.
A massive flight of capital, both Argentine and foreign, resulted. Panic swept the
financial markets. Suddenly Argentina faced the ultimate: default on its international debts. Earlier the IMF had bailed out Argentina. Not this time. The land of
the pampas was Latin America's first nation since 1945 to collapse into total
foreign default.

The domestic consequences were horrendous. The economy fell into its
deepest decline since the 1930s. In 2001 GDP per capita fell 12 percent, as 24
percent of bank deposits fled the country. Argentine incomes shrank alarmingly,
as unemployment leapt toward 20 percent and savings were wiped out (dollar
accounts were frozen). Riots and looting ensued in major cities; public order
collapsed. Foreign trade slumped, further reducing the supply of foreign exchange.
In the days of easy money, the foreign debt had soared to $141 billion. Measured
as a percentage of export earnings, that debt was the highest of all major countries.
Especially distressing was the drop in Argentina's trade in MERCOSUR because of
the advantage that Brazil had gotten from its 1999 devaluation. Argentina, once
the wealthiest land in Latin America, was now a showcase of economic and
political bankruptcy.

The country was on its own. The IMF, initially sympathetic to Cavallo's
orthodox policies, grew disenchanted with Argentina's swelling public sector
deficits. The newly inaugurated George W. Bush administration in Washington
was even less sympathetic. It dismissed Argentina as a self-made disaster of only
secondary importance. Reconstruction would have to come from within.

The key to further recovery lay with the political leadership. Following a phase
of intense political confusion, the 2003 presidential election was crucial. The

winner was Néstor Kirchner, a minor Peronist ex-governor. Despite his modest credentials, Kirchner promptly earned popular support by asserting independence from the Peronist machine and condemning the military's human-rights abuses of the past by overturning amnesty laws for military officers. But his principal task would be to negotiate reentry into the international financial community.

As president, Kirchner restructured Argentina's $178 billion debt with a deep discount on most bonds, paid off loans to the IMF (although not to many private U.S. and European holders of Argentine bonds), and renationalized some previously privatized enterprises. He emphasized the nation's social problems and devoted additional energy and resources to developing closer economic and political ties with other countries of Latin America, in part by strengthening MERCOSUR. He picked up support in midterm congressional balloting but decided not to run for reelection, instead backing his wife, then senator Cristina Fernández de Kirchner. In October 2007, as a boom in agricultural exports elevated economic growth rates, she won a landslide victory at the polls. She thus became the first Argentine woman directly elected to the presidency, and the second to serve as president.

In office, Fernández de Kirchner employed some of the militant nationalist rhetoric of the Peronist movement, and advocated a larger role for the state in management of the economy. She proposed that private pension funds be redirected to the government social security system. In 2008 she attempted to raise the export tax on agricultural commodities, including soybeans, an initiative that engendered a massive (and effective) backlash from Argentina's rural sector. Unable to solve the country's economic problems in the midst of world recession, she saw her public support drop sharply.

The presidencies of Néstor Kirchner and Cristina Fernández de Kirchner demonstrate the persisting popular appeal of Peronist nationalism, with its reliance on governmental intervention and its attention to the plight of the poor and working class. But the state of the economy reveals serious vulnerability. Argentina continues to struggle to find a balance between its reliance on export agriculture and its need to develop a vibrant source of national growth. A return to prosperity remains, for now, a still elusive promise.

10

~

CHILE
Repression and Democracy

Chile made a much-delayed entrance onto the world stage. It was for centuries an object of benign neglect. As a colony, it received scant attention from the Spanish crown. Small, remote, and lacking in precious minerals, it was a rough-and-tumble outpost of the empire—a "frontier society" in every sense of the term. Independence brought little fundamental change, although the discovery of industrial minerals led to the country's eventual insertion in the world economy. It was not until the mid-twentieth century that Chile acquired prominence as the site of contradictory political experiments: populism, reformism, socialism, and authoritarianism. When the subsequent restoration of democracy went hand-in-hand with impressive economic growth, Chile became a first-class poster child for the neoliberal conventional wisdom of the 1990s. The nation's record of struggles, setbacks, and achievements thus acquired special meaning through a process of extrapolation: Chile became important not only for its own sake, but also as a test case for what might happen elsewhere. Within Latin America, Chile gained stature as an example, a warning, a public-policy laboratory—and, notwithstanding its diminutive size, a continental leader.

FROM COLONY TO NATIONHOOD

What we now call Chile was one of the most inaccessible realms within the Spanish empire. It was hemmed in by barren deserts (in the north), the Andean cordillera, and treacherous seas around Cape Horn (to the south). In time the region's central valley became valued for its agricultural production. The Spaniards encountered a strong-minded indigenous population, but many perished under the onslaught of diseases brought by the Europeans. A relatively homogeneous population, *mestizo*, emerged from the colonial era, although few of the "European" inhabitants wished to admit the extent to which their Spanish forebearers had mixed with indigenous partners.

Map 10   Chile

When Napoleon invaded Spain, the colonists in Chile reacted much as their counterparts elsewhere, showing strong loyalty to the crown. As the French control of Spain dragged on after the conquest in 1808, the Chileans seemed headed for independence, but the royalist forces regained the initiative and by the end of 1814 won control of Chile. It was against this royalist "reconquest" that Bernardo O'Higgins helped lead a revolutionary army from Mendoza. The rebels won Chilean independence from the Spaniards in 1818. As the new republic's supreme director, O'Higgins proved a decisive but autocratic leader. The constitutional congress he had promised was rigged, however, and in 1823 the discontented Chilean aristocrats forced him to resign.

The following years saw political instability, as Liberals and Conservatives struggled for control. The latter won in 1830, beginning the three decades of the "Conservative Republic." The key figure was Diego Portales, who became the strongman of the regime, although never president in name. A Constituent Assembly produced a constitution in 1833. It created a strong central government, with economic power in the hands of the landowners. Portales ruled unchallenged because the government controlled the electoral machinery and the landowners were happy to let Portales exercise power (including repression when deemed necessary) for their benefit.

Portales' undoing was a war with Peru (1836–39), which provoked a military rebellion at home and brought the dictator's assassination. Chile then went on to defeat the Peruvians. Chile's principal war hero was General Manuel Bulnes, who served as president for a decade after 1841, overseeing an era of ferment and creativity.

The 1850s brought another decade of fruitful consolidation for the new nation. The status of the church proved a key political question. One wing of the landowning elite wanted greater state control over the church, especially in education and finances. Their opponents defended the church's privileges. When the normally anticlerical Liberal Party softened its stance in the late 1850s, dissident Liberals founded the Radical Party, an organization that would come to play an enduring role in the political life of the nation.

OVERVIEW: ECONOMIC GROWTH AND SOCIAL CHANGE

For Chile, as for many Latin American countries, the nineteenth century marked a period of far-reaching economic and social transformation. During the colonial era, Chile played a relatively minor role in the Spanish American economy. Land in the fertile central valley was concentrated in the hands of a small number of powerful landlords. Their vast estates produced agricultural goods, especially fruit and grain, some bound for such cities as Santiago or Valparaíso, but most destined for export to Lima and other urban markets in Peru. Maritime trade along the west coast of South America thus connected Chile to the centers of the Spanish empire.

The Wars for Independence interrupted this coastal trade, and Chilean agriculture promptly entered a period of relative stagnation. The situation was

Though mining became the most dynamic sector of the Chilean economy, agriculture continued to play a significant role; here sacks of beans are loaded for export at the port of Valparaíso sometime after 1900. (Courtesy of the Library of Congress.)

further affected by protectionist policies in Peru. In the 1840s, the California gold rush provided a temporary stimulus for a boom in agricultural exports. But thereafter they leveled off and then declined again. Completion of the U.S. transcontinental railroad helped to take away the California market, although export to England continued. With its advantageous location and fertile pampas, however, Argentina had better access to Europe. Agricultural production and commerce in Chile continued, of course, but they did not become the leading forces for economic growth.

It was mining, initially of nitrates (used for fertilizer and explosives), that became the country's leading export sector. This development was made possible by the acquisition of northern territory from Peru as a result of the War of the Pacific (see Chapter 6). Foreign investors (especially British) quickly rushed in, and Europeans owned about two-thirds of the nitrate fields by 1884. But Chilean investors retained a hold in this area, reaping over half the total earnings by 1920. Eventually, however, the nitrate market declined. An increase in exports during World War I was followed by a cutback in the early 1920s, then a brief recovery, then a steep and final reduction in the 1930s. Synthetic nitrates took over after that.

The nineteenth-century growth of Chilean mining—in silver, copper, and nitrates—led to important changes in the country's social structure. One was the appearance of new elements within the elite, consisting of mine owners in the north and merchants from the growing towns and cities. Yet these elements did not truly rival the traditional landowners. For in Chile, more than in most Latin American countries, the landowning elite did not remain isolated and apart from the manufacturing and mining elites. There was, instead, a kind of merger, often achieved through family ties, so landowners frequently had relatives in upper levels of the other sectors if they did not take part themselves. Brothers, cousins, and brothers-in-law provided important links, and these connections tended to minimize conflict between the city and the countryside.

There also appeared a working class, first unionized in the nitrate fields of the north. Chile's economic development in the late nineteenth and early twentieth centuries did not require the massive importation of labor, however, and this fact points to a central feature of the country's working class: it was native born. This stands in clear contrast to Argentina, where 25 percent of the population was foreign born in 1895; for Chile the proportion was less than 3 percent. From the outset, Chilean workers had direct access to the political scene.

Copper production underwent a technological revolution just after 1900, due to the invention of a new smelting process, and this led to a major transformation in Chile. Investments required large amounts of capital, and these came from abroad. In 1904 the Braden Copper Company began exploiting the El Teniente mine near Santiago. British interests were soon taken over by the Guggenheims, and by 1920 the industry was dominated by only three companies, known from their initials as "the ABC": Andes Copper, Braden Copper, and the Chile Exploration Company–Chuquicamata. The first and third belonged to Anaconda, while Braden was a subsidiary of the Kennecott Corporation.

The Chilean copper industry thus was concentrated in a few hands, and these hands were American. It came to constitute a foreign enclave, one that would provide relatively little stimulus to the rest of the economy. The heavy reliance on capital and technology meant modest levels of employment for Chilean workers. The importation of equipment and parts did not give much business to Chilean manufacturers. And most of the profits, often large, were returned to parent companies in the United States instead of being invested in Chile. It is little wonder that resentment grew.

An additional problem came from the great instability of copper prices on the world market. Indeed, copper prices could fluctuate as much as 500 or 1000 percent within a single year. This made it extremely difficult for Chile to anticipate the dollar amount of foreign exchange earnings. Unpredictable gyrations in the world copper market could wreak havoc with the most carefully laid-out plans.

And copper came to dominate the Chilean economy (see Figure 10–1). By 1956 copper production accounted for half of all the country's exports, and taxes on the companies' profits yielded one-fifth of the government's entire revenue. As copper went, it was often said, so went Chile's economy.

In summary, these developments formed a complex social structure. The rural sector contained a traditional landowning elite, a peasantry tied by labor obligations to the estate where they lived, and a small but mobile workforce that provided wage labor for the large commercial estates. There was a mining and industrial elite, many of whose members had kinship ties to the landed aristocracy. There

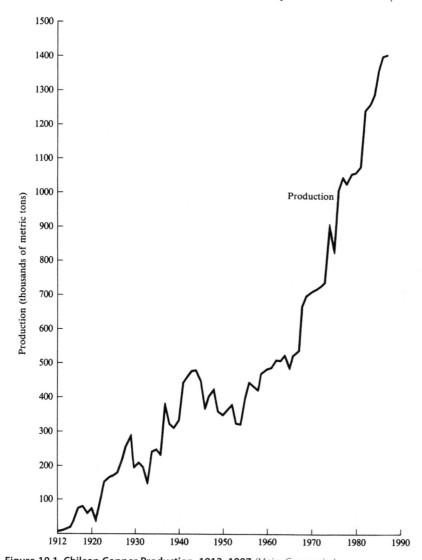

Figure 10.1 Chilean Copper Production, 1912–1987 *(Major Companies)*

SOURCES: Markos Mamalakis and Clark W. Reynolds, *Essays on the Chilean Economy* (Homewood, Ill.: Richard D. Irwin, 1965), pp. 371–72; Ricardo Ffrench-Davis, "La importancia del cobre en la economía chilena," in Ffrench-Davis and Ernesto Tironi, eds., *El cobre en el desarrollo nacional* (Santiago: Universidad Católica de Chile, 1974), Cuadros 2, 7; Manual Lasaga, *The Copper Industry in the Chilean Economy: An Econometric Analysis* (Lexington, Mass.: D. C. Heath, 1981), p. 10; International Monetary Fund, *International Financial Statistics*, various years.

were middle classes as well, and a growing, native-born, urban working class. Foreign investors were conspicuous from independence onward, but by the twentieth century their presence was epitomized by the preeminence of U.S. copper companies.

Chile: Vital Statistics, 2007

Population (millions)	16.6
GDP (current $U.S. billions)	163.9
GNP per capita ($U.S.)	8350
Poverty rate (% in 2006)	13.7
Life expectancy	78

Sources: World Bank and Economic Commission for Latin America and the Caribbean.

At least Chile has not had to face one problem that has beset so many other countries of Latin America: excessive population growth. Indeed, Chile has consistently had one of the lowest annual rates of population growth in the hemisphere: in 1900–1910 it was just 1.2 percent, and in 1970–80 it was only 2.1 percent (compared to 2.8 percent for Latin America as a whole).

As cause or effect of this situation, women in Chile have enjoyed more opportunities than in many other countries. Females entered the workforce with relative ease, and by 1970, for instance, nearly 16 percent of Chile's employed females held professional or technical jobs (higher than the U.S. rate of 14.7 percent). Social customs also reflected fairly open and egalitarian standards in the relative treatment of the sexes.

POLITICS AND POLICY: PATTERNS OF CHANGE

As nineteenth-century Chile began to consolidate its place in the international economy, political crisis ensued. A civil war in 1859 had convinced the elite it was a time for quiet consolidation. They got it from José Joaquín Pérez, who began a ten-year presidential term.

The two most important political issues of this era were the constitution and the status of the church. On the second issue, the Liberals continued their campaign for equality of religion, while the Conservatives fought to protect the state-favored position of the Catholic Church. Slowly the Liberals won concessions, as non-Catholics received the right to have churches and religious schools. In effect, this was a modest opening of the elite, making it more pluralistic.

As for the constitution, the elite was struggling with how to achieve effective government while avoiding despotism. In 1871 the constitution was amended to prohibit presidents from serving two consecutive terms. In 1874 further changes made government ministers more accountable to Congress, thereby strengthening the legislative powers. This diminution of the power of the church and president led to labeling the years between 1861 and 1891 the "Liberal Republic."

The mid-1870s brought a severe economic depression. They also brought Chile's most famous foreign conflict: the War of the Pacific (1879–83), when Chile fought both Peru and Bolivia. The ostensible issue was the treatment of Chilean investors in the desert territories governed by Peru. After extended fighting, the Chileans won an overwhelming military triumph. As victors, the Chileans took control of the mineral-rich coastal strip that had belonged to Bolivia and Peru. This conclusion had two important effects: to increase the self-confidence of the Chileans and to arouse deep resentment among the Peruvians and Bolivians. It also led to Chile's nitrate boom.

The 1880s saw much activity on the church-state issue. The Liberal reformers made new gains. Civil registration of marriage, birth, and death was made compulsory, further eroding church control over daily life. In these same years, the Congress extended the vote to all literate males over twenty-five, eliminating the previous income test.

The second half of the 1880s brought the presidency of José Balmaceda (1886–91), the most controversial leader of late nineteenth-century Chile. Conflict over food policy arose when Chilean cattle raisers proposed a tariff on Argentine beef, which would have meant less meat and higher prices for Chileans. They were countered by the new middle-class-led Democratic Party (founded 1887), which helped mobilize Santiago's artisans, small merchants, and skilled workers against the tariff. The opposition carried the day. Balmaceda convinced the bill's proponents to withdraw it.

This early triumph of the Democratic Party signaled the start of an important trend. It was a direct appeal on economic grounds to the middle and lower sectors of the cities. Seeking a broad electorate, the Democrats argued for laws that would help workers, while they also presented classic liberal demands for compulsory free education and democratic procedures in electing governments. The party's articulation of mass demands showed how far Chile had already come on the road toward modern politics.

The fate of Balmaceda's presidency was sealed by civil war. To this day Chileans argue passionately over the war, its causes, and its meaning. The president wanted to increase government intervention in the economy. In order to pay for the building of new railways, roads, and urban infrastructure (water and sanitation), Balmaceda needed growing tax revenues from the nitrate industry in the northern province of Tarapacá. Foreign investors firmly resisted, and stiff opposition emerged in Congress. In fact, Balmaceda's boldness masked a deeper constitutional struggle, that of legislative versus presidential authority. Congress had been fighting to establish its supremacy in the constitutional structure, while Balmaceda was determined to impose his will. The result was instability.

In 1890 the Congress failed to produce a budget, whereupon the president ruled that the previous year's appropriations would apply. Balmaceda had earlier ventured into an area which had always proved sensitive: the choice of a presidential successor, whom he tried to nominate on his own authority. The Congress passed a law voiding any such nomination, which Balmaceda then refused to sign.

Congressional opposition was now ready to seek a remedy by force of arms. The mining region in the north proved a rebel stronghold, where the mine owners were happy to support a force that promised to unseat the president who threatened to savage their economic interests. The resulting combat produced the bloodiest battles in Chilean history, with Balmaceda's forces going down in defeat. The president took refuge in the Argentine embassy, where he committed suicide one day after his presidential term ended. In less than a month a new president was elected: Jorge Montt. One of the key issues of the war—the status of foreign investors—had been settled. Nationalization was out, but the parliamentary victors continued pressuring the European investors. Nationalistic sentiment had penetrated all sectors of the Chilean elite.

Balmaceda's fall at the hands of the congressional rebels changed Chile's constitutional structure. The strong presidency gave way to parliamentary dominance, but it proved impossible for ministries and governments to last very long. This instability was reinforced by the fragmentation of the party system, which expanded to include five major parties by 1900.

Political control remained in the hands of an oligarchy representing primarily agricultural interests. Occasionally they were challenged by urban groups, such as merchants. The workers, although not yet organized into political parties, were already beginning to make their weight felt. The issue that aroused them was rising prices. In 1905 workers staged a series of protests that led to direct confrontation with armed members of the oligarchy, and a miners' strike in 1907 in the northern city of Iquique similarly erupted into violence and bloodshed. Workers became even more militant after 1910. The leading organizers were the anarcho-syndicalists, indefatigable activists who excelled in organizing small firms. Centered in Santiago, the anarcho-syndicalist unions won significant improvements in wages and working conditions.

These unions did not, however, represent a basic threat to the political system. As for working conditions and fringe benefits, the employers could undercut much of the militancy by granting social welfare benefits. The Congress did exactly this, legislating workmen's compensation in 1916, employer's liability in 1917, and a retirement system for railway workers in 1919.

After a slowdown in strike activity and a loss in bargaining power, organized labor began to revive in 1917. Economic recovery strengthened labor's hand, as World War I had greatly stimulated the demand for nitrates. By 1918 the growth of labor strength led Congress to pass a *ley de residencia*, designed to facilitate the deportation of aliens who were active labor organizers. Since immigration from Europe had been minimal in Chile, however, the deportation strategy proved to be irrelevant.

The year 1919 marked the peak of labor mobilization, as union leaders called huge rallies to protest the high prices of wartime inflation. A mammoth demonstration came in August, with 100,000 participants marching past the presidential palace. The next month a general strike in Santiago failed, however, and worker morale was shaken. Thereafter, the rate of strikes declined.

Surprisingly enough, the government response to strikers had been moderate since the labor upsurge began in 1917. In December an executive edict made the government a mediator in stalemated labor conflicts. Although rejected by anarchist and syndicalist leaders, it was heavily used, often for labor's benefit, in 1918 and 1919. That pattern continued into 1920, in part because the government was worried about the presidential elections scheduled for June.

Chile, like Argentina, had opened the door to middle-sector political participation, a process far less advanced in Brazil. The number of working-class voters, although still small, had begun to attract the attention of Chilean bourgeois politicians, especially in Santiago. Their support could be crucial, especially when the vote was divided among many parties, as in Chile. The political leader who saw this most clearly was Arturo Alessandri, who campaigned for the presidency by making a passionate appeal to urban voters, including workers. Alessandri represented an "enlightened" middle-sector view. He proposed to legitimize unions, but also put them into an intricate legal framework determined by the government.

Alessandri won the 1920 election, by a narrow margin. With this democratic exercise past, the outgoing president Juan Luis Sanfuentes felt free in his few remaining days to answer the labor challenge. Workers were harassed by paramilitary street activists recruited from right-wing middle- and upper-class families. Virtually all anarcho-syndicalist and other leaders who did not choose exile or go underground were arrested and imprisoned. The leaderless workers were further demoralized by a wave of lockouts, as employers revoked many of the concessions made between 1917 and 1920.

There was hope that the antilabor policy would change when Alessandri assumed office. For the first half of 1921, the Alessandri government intervened in a number of strikes, favoring workers in their mediation. But conflict mounted, and Alessandri drew attacks from all sides—from the right for being too soft on labor and from the left for winking at aggressive employer tactics. In July 1921 Alessandri finally opted for the employers and reverted to systematic repression of labor.

While organized labor was struggling against adverse economic and political conditions, Alessandri pushed his proposals for a labor code and social welfare package, introduced in Congress in 1921. Conservatives balked at these ideas, since they preferred the status quo—where unions had no legal status. Some Conservatives also feared that Liberals might pick up new voters among urban workers. The impasse between Liberal president and Conservative Congress continued until 1924. Then the military intervened.

From Instability to Popular Front

A military junta took partial control of the government in early September 1924, and three days later issued a manifesto listing legislative demands, with Congress dutifully approving every one. Most important was an elaborate labor code that subjected unions to close government supervision.

This social advance was *not* the product of a political process in which workers played a direct role. Rather, it was a preemptive move by the government to head off further mobilization by workers' organizations. In Chile this apparently progressive step resulted from the pressure of a government cadre that had much to fear from worker mobilization—the military officer corps.

Alessandri, in the meantime, was losing ground in his struggle with the army and took a leave from office for a trip to Italy. He was recalled after a second military coup in early 1925. At this point, ironically, the officers now in control felt they needed both Alessandri and urban labor support to bolster their legitimacy. The new military government intervened frequently in strikes, usually on the side of the workers. It seemed that organized labor might be on the verge of gaining power. Fear spread among the elite, which could see its power slipping away.

The revolution was not at hand. Alessandri returned from his leave in March 1925 and within months ordered government troops to crack down on nitrate workers. Soon thereafter, the embattled Alessandri resigned. Unrest and instability prevailed.

Colonel Carlos Ibáñez emerged as the strongman from this atmosphere of turmoil. In May 1927 he was formally elected president by the Congress, and he proceeded to consolidate a dictatorship that lasted until 1931. Chileans, having prided themselves on their relative democracy, were shocked. The general-president jailed opponents, especially labor leaders, and suspended civil liberties.

The government now greatly enlarged its role in the economy. That meant speeding the construction of railways, roads, and power facilities. Not surprisingly, Ibáñez also stepped up spending for the military. Much of the financing came from abroad—loans and especially U.S. investment in mining. The world economic expansion of the 1920s made it all possible.

The Wall Street crash of 1929 abruptly ended that era, in Chile as elsewhere. Mineral exports fell disastrously and foreign financing dried up. Desperate attempts to create a national cartel for nitrate sales abroad failed. Protests against the government grew. An ever-widening spectrum of the society, now including professional persons as well as workers, joined attacks on the dictator. Ibáñez finally gave in. In July 1931 he resigned, joining the ranks of the other South American heads of government who had the misfortune to be governing when the Great Depression hit.

For the next year Chile lacked a stable government. The interim regimes included a thirteen-day interlude of a "Socialist Republic" in which Colonel Marmaduke Grove became the best-known figure. Another presidential election was finally held. The winner was a familiar face: Arturo Alessandri.

The once-fiery Alessandri was now more interested in order than change. In 1936, when a wave of strikes broke out, Alessandri took tough measures. He proclaimed a state of siege, closed Congress, and sent labor leaders into exile.

In economic policy the Alessandri presidency was quite successful. An ultra-orthodox finance minister, Gustavo Ross, drastically reduced public-sector spending and dismantled some of the key government agencies that Ibáñez had created. Thanks to recovery of world demand for Chilean exports, especially minerals, the foreign trade balance improved dramatically. The official unemployment figure, at 262,000 in 1932, dropped to less than 16,000 by 1937. Inflation remained a problem, however, as wage increases seldom kept pace with price increases.

Chile approached the presidential election of 1939 with apprehension. In 1935 the world communist movement, dominated by the Soviet-directed Comintern, had called for a coalition strategy in battling fascism, in effect encouraging communist parties to seek alliances with parties of the left and center. In 1936 the Communists and Radicals in Chile joined forces in a "Popular Front," which by 1938 came to include a broad spectrum of parties: Radicals, Socialists, Communists, Democrats, plus a new Confederation of Chilean Workers. After the left-leaning Marmaduke Grove withdrew his candidacy, the nomination went to Pedro Aguirre Cerda, a wealthy Radical known for his reformist ideas on the agrarian question.

The incumbent political alliance nominated Alessandri's finance minister, Gustavo Ross, who presented an inflexible and backward-looking image. The campaign was bitterly fought, and Aguirre Cerda won by the narrowest of margins—a mere 4000 out of 241,000 votes cast.

Despite its narrowness, or perhaps because of it, this election set the political context for years to come. Centrist voters had tipped the balance by opting for the left. At the same time, however, they were voting for a moderate reformist, so the outcome seemed ambiguous. What sort of a mandate would the resulting government have?

The Popular Front government soon suffered the strains inherent in such a heterogeneous coalition. The Radicals were the dominant element and the least radical in ideology. They focused on economic development, not social welfare. The Communists and Socialists were natural antagonists because many Socialists were ex-Communists who had refused to knuckle under to party discipline. Both the Communists and Socialists tried to mobilize rural workers, thereby alarming the powerful landowners—and placing themselves in competition with each other.

Yet the policies of the Popular Front were anything but menacing. Economic policy concentrated on an expanded economic role for the national government. In 1939 a new state corporation was created: CORFO (Corporación de Fomento), which was to stimulate economic development by strategic investments in both the public and private sectors. Moreover, Congress was controlled by the right-wing opposition, which was able to impose effective limits on executive power.

The Popular Front lost even its titular leadership when poor health forced President Aguirre Cerda to resign in 1941. The following president was another Radical, Juan Antonio Ríos (1942–46), who struggled to keep Chile neutral during World War II. Under U.S. pressure to join the Allies, he feared a reaction from the

German colony in the south of Chile. He also feared possible Japanese attack on Chile's long, undefended coastline. In January 1943 Chile finally broke relations with the Axis.

The succeeding president, Gabriel González Videla (1946–52), was once again a Radical. He accepted Communist support, but this modest throwback to the Popular Front did not last long. A call for a general strike in 1946 provoked strong police measures, and riots ensued. A full-scale social conflict loomed. The government declared a state of siege and suspended civil liberties. Strikes continued into 1947.

González had by now purged the Communists from his cabinet. The strikes gave the right its chance to mount an offensive. The rightists had been alarmed by the steady rise in the Communist vote, which came to 18 percent in the municipal elections of 1947 (up from 12 percent in the congressional elections of 1941). The Chilean government now decided to move against the left, and in this it had plenty of support from abroad. In these early years of the Cold War, the U.S. government was launching a major campaign in Latin America to isolate the left, especially the communist parties, and the U.S. embassy strongly encouraged the Chilean conservatives. The left fought back by attacking the González government and the United States. The climax came in 1948: by an act of Congress, where the left was greatly outnumbered, the Communist Party was outlawed, and its members were banned from running for office or holding official posts. A witch-hunt followed. Together with the rightists, the centrist Radicals had again shown how they were prepared to use "legal" means to eliminate their most dangerous adversaries from the political game. For the left, the Popular Front became an object lesson, and they vented their anger on González Videla.

The Era of Party Politics

The final demise of the Popular Front ushered in a period of intense political competition based on party organizations. During this period, the Chilean political system displayed several identifying characteristics.

First, elections were extremely competitive. There were many different parties, so it was rare for any one of them to receive more than one-quarter of the total vote. This fact accounted for a second feature: in search of governing majorities, the parties had to take part in coalitions. Alliances were fragile, however, and political leaders were constantly in quest of new arrangements and intent on mending fences. Underlying this was an increased tendency toward ideological polarization.

Third, the system was highly democratic. In contrast to Argentina, where trade unions had uneasy relationships with political parties, the Chilean labor movement was closely identified with various parties, mainly on the left, so it did not form a separate power center. Measured as a percentage of registered voters, electoral participation was high (around 80 percent, compared to 50–60 percent in the United States), and registration grew rapidly in the early 1960s. And election results were accepted by almost all Chileans as binding.

The 1952 presidential election brought back another figure from the past: General Carlos Ibáñez. Now in his mid-seventies, the former dictator proclaimed himself the only answer to Chile's many problems. This *caudillo* put himself forward as a true nationalist, but his appeal was really aimed at the right and center, who were once again worried about the left. Socialists and Communists formed another electoral alliance, although the latter were hobbled by their illegality. The election results were indicative of the path Chile was to follow for decades: a deeply divided vote with no candidate or party getting a clear majority. Ibáñez took office with a plurality of 47 percent.

Ibáñez claimed to be the apolitical man able to solve all the political problems, but not surprisingly he failed to deliver on these promises. His prime economic problem was inflation, which had hit Chile earlier and harder than most of Latin America. Because he faced a major deficit in the balance of payments, Ibáñez had to look abroad for help. The logical source was the International Monetary Fund (IMF). Unfortunately for the Chileans, it was not simply a matter of arranging a foreign loan. In effect it meant the IMF must oversee the borrowing country's economic policies. As a result, the IMF came to be seen by most Chileans (and by most other Latin Americans) as an extension of U.S. economic and political power.

Ibáñez was thus caught in the typical policy dilemma produced by inflation. His government had to act because it was running out of foreign exchange. Yet the sources of foreign financing offered their help only on the condition that they have a veto over basic policymaking. Ibáñez knew that the left would be in full cry against him if he acceded to the IMF terms. He decided to take the gamble.

His government soon paid the price. The initial measures were for austerity. Early targets were public utilities and transportation, which invariably charged very low rates in times of rapid inflation, since managers hesitated to pass rising costs on to customers and thus spark popular protests. An increase in bus fares provoked a furious response. Riots began in Santiago and spread to other cities. Given the strength of labor and the leftist parties, Chile was a difficult place for anti-inflation policies. In the end Ibáñez proved to be a tired old general with a modest political base and even lesser ideas.

The 1958 election produced a new president with a familiar name: Jorge Alessandri, the son of Arturo. Although considering himself an independent, Jorge had run as the leader of the right, on a combined Conservative-Liberal ticket. His opponents were Salvador Allende, a medical doctor and longtime politician who represented the Socialist-Communist alliance (FRAP), and Eduardo Frei, an ambitious young idealist who headed the Christian Democrats (PDC), a relatively new party on the national scene. Alessandri won a plurality of the vote (31.6 percent), as against 28.9 percent for Allende and 20.7 percent for Frei, with the remaining 18.8 percent split between the Radical candidate and a maverick priest. A vote for president then took place in Congress, as required by the constitution when no candidate won an absolute majority, and Alessandri's plurality was readily confirmed. Once again, the Chilean electorate had shown itself to be deeply divided.

The new president was an authentic representative of conservative political and economic thought in Chile. He strongly believed in free enterprise economics, including monetary orthodoxy and an open door to foreign investment. His government attacked the serious inflation with an orthodox IMF-style stabilization policy: budget cutting, devaluation (to a fixed exchange rate), and an appeal for new foreign investment.

Alessandri's stabilization efforts were undercut by a bitter battle over copper policies. The government tried to convince the U.S. copper companies to increase their investment. The idea was to get more of the processing of the copper to be done in Chile. This would increase the economic returns to Chile, as well as make Chile more self-sufficient in marketing the final product. But Chilean nationalists were incensed: they wanted to expropriate the companies, not just encourage their investment. Government policy carried the day—but copper company investments did not increase, and Chile did no better at exploiting its only major asset in international trade.

Alessandri hoped that his orthodox policies could make progress against the mounting social problems being created by Chile's slow and uneven economic growth. Large-scale public works projects were launched, financed mainly by foreign funds. A principal source was the United States, where worry over the threat of pro-communist revolution had led to hurried formulation of a major economic assistance program known as the Alliance for Progress. Alessandri even dared to tackle the agrarian question, long a forbidden subject in his political ranks. Although the law passed in 1962 was thought by all on the left to be ludicrously inadequate, in fact it did furnish the basis for an aggressive expropriation program.

Not surprisingly, none of the Alessandri policies did much toward solving the grave socioeconomic problems facing Chile. The steady exodus of the rural poor to the cities, especially Santiago, continued. There they were ill-housed, ill-fed, and ill-educated. Furthermore, there was little work. These "marginals" were the tragic underside of capitalist urbanization in a developing country.

Alessandri would have liked to govern a tranquil land. Events soon ruled out that dream. In the early 1960s the Chilean political scene began to change significantly. There was first the great growth of the electorate. Just over 500,000 in 1938, by 1963 it had reached 2,500,000—a fivefold expansion in twenty-five years. Second, a realignment of political forces had occurred. There were now four main groupings: (1) the right, including the Conservative and Liberal parties; (2) the centrist Radicals, long the masters of opportunism; (3) the Marxist left, composed primarily of the Communists and Socialists; and (4) the Christian Democrats, located in the center, a reform-oriented party now building its electoral following. In the 1963 municipal elections, each of these four won roughly equal percentages of the vote. The biggest net gainers were the Christian Democrats, who were attracting votes from both the left and the right.

The 1964 presidential election loomed as a crucial one for both Chile and Latin America. The left once again ran Salvador Allende. FRAP's strident criticisms of capitalism seemed all the more relevant, now that a classically conservative government had so recently failed. Concerned about the rising strength of the left, Liberals and Conservatives quickly decided that their only salvation lay in an alliance with the Christian Democrats. When the rightist parties decided to endorse the PDC candidate, Eduardo Frei, the Christian Democrats gained an enormous boost. It was made out of the fear that the FRAP might win a plurality victory, as almost happened in 1958. The rightists decided this despite their misgivings about the PDC's reformist ideas, which many conservatives saw as dangerously close to the formulas of the left.

The PDC campaign was designed to convince the electorate that Frei could bring a "Revolution in Liberty." In fact, however, the Christian Democrats were promising reforms, not revolution. The reforms added up to a more efficient capitalist economy, to be achieved by such measures as agrarian reform (through the expropriation of underused land), increased public housing, and greater control over the U.S. copper companies (through Chilean acquisition of part ownership).

Frei and the PDC wasted no time in branding FRAP as an extension of Moscow. Cleverly written campaign cartoons and radio jingles played on fears of "another Cuba" in Chile. The U.S. government, as well as West European Christian Democrats, also took a strong interest in this contest between reformism and Marxism. The Central Intelligence Agency would later admit to contributing more than 50 percent of Frei's campaign expenses.

It may have been a case of overkill. Frei won the election more handily than anyone had expected, with 56 percent of the vote. Allende got 39 percent, well over his share in 1958. The difference, of course, was that this time it was a two-way race. The triumph belonged to Frei, but the Revolution in Liberty owed its birth far more to the absence of a rightist candidate than to any sudden change of mind by Chilean voters.

Frei's government began with high expectations. First priority was given to economic policy. One of the hottest issues was copper. Here, as elsewhere, the Frei strategists sought a middle way. Outright nationalization (with compensation) would be too expensive, they reasoned, since Chile would have to come up with enormous dollar payments. Simply encouraging the U.S. companies to increase their investment under the old terms was equally unacceptable, since it would be a backward step on the path toward greater national control. Their solution was centrist: the Chilean government would buy into part ownership of the companies, with the proceeds to be reinvested by the companies in expanded facilities, especially for processing. The goal was to double copper production by 1970. If successful, Frei's plan for "Chileanization" would increase both national control and export earnings.

The proposal was savagely attacked by the left, which branded it a sellout. With congressional support from Christian Democrats, Frei reached agreements with Anaconda and Kennecott, the two leading companies, but copper production increased by only 10 percent over the ensuing five years. Export earnings doubled, but that was because of a rise in the world price of copper, not because of output. Furthermore, a big share of those higher earnings went to the companies because of technicalities in the new contracts. Frei had won a hollow victory.

The agrarian sector was another key policy area. Chile had long suffered under one of Latin America's most archaic rural structures, with the marginalized rural masses daily becoming more desperate. The Christian Democrats pushed through a land reform act in 1967 which was another compromise. Elaborate provisions were made for land to be distributed to 100,000 peasants by 1970. The program went more slowly than hoped, and by the end of Frei's term there were only 28,000 new farm ownerships, a number whose significance was obscured by the high expectations the Christian Democrats had aroused.

The United States continued to take a strong interest in the fortunes of the Frei government. It had all the marks of the kind of reformist regime that the Alliance for Progress was designed to support. The United States, as well as the multilateral agencies, such as the Inter-American Development Bank and the World Bank, gave Chile extensive financing.

In the political sphere, the Christian Democrats attempted to deliver on their promise of a new kind of popular participation. Rejecting the massive state role that the solutions of the left would inevitably bring, they pushed for a new kind of grassroots political activity. In practice it meant a mixture of communitarianism, self-help, and cooperatives. Above all, it meant heading off the left, which had, through its unions and party structures (both communist and socialist), gotten a head start in organizing at the mass level. The net effect was a dogfight to win elections throughout the society: in unions, student associations, cooperatives, bar associations, and every kind of professional group. Politics was penetrating more and more deeply into Chilean society.

Time was running out on the Revolution in Liberty. The reformist gains had been substantial, if measured by past Chilean standards, but they were no longer enough. Because the constitution forbade consecutive reelection of the president, the Christian Democrats had to find a new candidate. Frei had been an over-shadowing figure, but not without detractors within the party. In fact, progressive Christian Democrats had veered sharply in the direction of radical change.

The 1970 presidential election in some ways resembled 1964. But this time the right decided to run its own candidate, Jorge Alessandri, the magic name in twentieth-century Chilean politics. The divided Christian Democrats nominated Radomiro Tomic, whose leftist stand precluded any possible electoral alliance with the right. The Communists and Socialists, now united under the rubric of Unidad Popular (UP or Popular Unity), once again chose Allende. The UP relentlessly attacked the Christian Democrats' record under Frei, charging a sellout to imperialism and domestic oligarchs. Alessandri offered an old-fashioned conservative recipe. Tomic sounded remarkably like Allende. He favored radical change, including complete nationalization of the copper companies.

When the votes were counted, Allende had won a plurality, but it was far from a decisive result. His vote total was 36.3 percent. Alessandri got 34.9 percent, and

Tomic only 27.8 percent. The left was jubilant, but their more sober leaders were aware of the fragility of Allende's mandate.

The White House Reacts

The results of Chile's election aroused intense displeasure in Washington, D.C. An outraged President Richard M. Nixon took the news as a personal affront, smashing his fist into his hand and repeatedly denouncing "That S.O.B., that S.O.B.," then adding for clarity's sake that he was referring to "that son of a bitch Allende." Meantime national security adviser Henry Kissinger perceived a dire threat to American interests and darkly proclaimed, "I don't see why we need to stand by and watch a country go Communist due to the irresponsibility of its own people." Something would have to be done.

What could account for such a strong reaction? The first concern was geopolitics. Within the context of the Cold War, then at its height, a socialist triumph in Chile—or anywhere else in the Third World—would constitute a victory for international communism. This was not only undesirable; within the Western hemisphere it was unacceptable, since it had taken place within America's "backyard." This would tarnish the U.S. image as a superpower and, presumably, weaken its position in the global arena.

A second concern focused on ripple effects. One of the fundamental tenets of U.S. policy during the Cold War was the "domino theory," which held that one country's fall to communism would lead to the fall of neighboring countries. It was therefore essential to hold the line. In Kissinger's view, a socialist government in Chile would greatly increase the likelihood of communist takeovers in Argentina, Peru, and Bolivia.

A third concern was somewhat more subtle. Events in Chile suddenly presented the United States with what seemed like an impossible prospect: the installation of a socialist government through a free and fair election. This contradicted a fundamental line of Cold War thought—the association of socialist ideology with brutal tyranny. Within U.S. policy circles, it was widely assumed that socialism (or communism) could come to power only through revolutionary violence (as in Cuba), and that it could remain in power only through repressive dictatorship (as in the USSR). Chile refuted this idea. Its citizens had voted for an avowed socialist through the exercise of democratic choice, in what came to be known as *la via chilena* ("the Chilean way"). Such an example would legitimize Marxist movements as democratic forces and broaden the path toward leftist and anti-American politics around the world.

Finally, Allende's socialist orientation posed a threat to American economic interests. Prominent U.S. corporations—such as Ralston Purina, Ford, and ITT (International Telephone and Telegraph)—had major investments in Chile. Corporate executives understandably opposed any program of nationalization or government expropriation, and in any case they would insist upon satisfactory compensation.

In a word, Chile was dangerous. Nixon and Kissinger promptly formed a so-called Forty Committee to design policies to prevent Allende's coming to power. One idea was to reinstate Eduardo Frei as president. According to this plan, the Chilean Congress would snub Allende and cast its vote instead for runner-up Alessandri, who would then call for new elections—which Frei would be allowed to win. In keeping with long-standing tradition, however, the Congress ratified the results of the popular election and elected Allende as president.

A second idea was to promote a military coup, either before or after Allende's inauguration. A key obstacle came from top-rank Chilean officers, who tended to uphold the nation's democratic traditions. A U.S.-approved plot to kidnap the army commander-in-chief (a strong supporter of the constitution) failed only when he fought off his assailants and was murdered instead. Nonetheless, the U.S. Central Intelligence Agency relentlessly pressed the military option. According to one CIA cable, "It is firm and continuing policy that Allende be overthrown by a coup. We are continuing to generate maximum pressure toward this end utilizing every appropriate resource."

Once Allende was in office, the Nixon administration took steps to impose an "invisible blockade" against the Chilean economy. This policy went into effect before the nationalization of such major U.S. companies as ITT and Ford, but its legal foundation was strengthened by the Allende government's refusal (and\or inability) to reach agreements on suitable compensation. U.S. government measures included a shutdown of all economic assistance to Chile, opposition to international credits (from the World Bank and the Inter-American Development Bank), discouragement of private investment, and disruption of the world copper market. In Nixon's memorable phrase, the intent was to make the Chilean economy "scream."

Working mainly through the CIA, the Nixon-Kissinger team attempted to exert direct influence on Chilean politics. The U.S. government provided substantial support for the anti-Allende media, most notably the conservative newspaper *El Mercurio,* and for opposition parties in local and legislative elections. CIA funding also supported strikes, lockouts, and other actions designed to destabilize Allende's government. (It was not until the year 2000 that the CIA officially confirmed its activities in Chile, finally acknowledging the disbursement of $6.5 million "for Chilean political parties, media and private sector organization opposed to the Allende regime.") This included, of course, constant efforts to provoke a military coup.

Socialism via Democracy?

Allende's three-year presidency was rich in significance, for both the history of Chile and that of Latin America, although the nature of that significance is still bitterly argued. The president and his advisers decided that despite the narrowness of their election victory, they would seek radical change—but by legal means. Was such a course of action possible? Could socialism be introduced in a genteel fashion?

Allende's initial economic strategy was similar to that of Perón in 1946 and Castro in 1959: freeze prices and raise wages. The result was an immediate boom in consumer buying. This caused a significant short-term redistribution of income. Merchants' inventories were quickly depleted, while producers put a hold on all orders until they could see how long price controls would last. Here Allende pursued an essentially populist strategy in order to expand his political support.

Allende's other economic policies flowed from campaign promises. Top priority went to the complete nationalization of the copper companies. Most significant, the congressional vote on this issue was unanimous. That spoke volumes about the growth of nationalist sentiment in Chile and the perceived failure of Frei's Chileanization policy. Later, the Allende government argued that no compensation was due the companies because of what the president charged were their previous illegally high profits. That aggressive stand furnished U.S. government hard-liners with "proof" that Chile had declared war on private property in the hemisphere.

The UP government also extended state control into many other economic sectors. Coal and steel were nationalized, along with 60 percent of the private banks. As the "transition to socialism" continued, more and more firms and businesses were nationalized, with Allende's hand often forced by workers who occupied management offices and refused to leave until expropriation was announced. Foreign firms were a favorite target, including such well-known names as ITT and Ford.

In the rural sector the Allende government moved with speed. The expropriations came faster than the government's ability to ensure the services (credit, access to supplies, equipment) needed by the new small owners. Furthermore, the government was increasingly outflanked by peasants, often organized by leftist radicals, who seized land on their own. Landowners hired armed guards, tried to fight back legally, or simply fled the country. The long-standing agrarian problem was being met by radical means.

In its overall management of the economy, the Allende government took an early chance. Facing a majority opposition in the Congress, Allende's political strategists decided to go for a constitutional amendment that would create an assembly of the people in place of the Congress. The populist policies of 1970–71 (freezing prices, raising wages) were intended partly to build support for the amendment. It was a risk because the populist measures were bound to be inflationary. A great deal was riding on the gamble to win increased constitutional power because the Congress could block so much of the program Allende sought to carry out.

Not surprisingly, Congress rejected the amendment in 1972. At that point, Allende and his advisers decided to pause in order to consolidate their political gains. They planned eventually to submit the amendment to a popular plebiscite— thereby bypassing the opposition-dominated Congress. The proper moment never came; at least they could never identify it. As 1972 continued, the government was preoccupied by the enormous dislocations hitting the economy. First, there were the distortions resulting from the attempt to enforce price controls. Second, there was extensive sabotage or deliberate diversion by producers, landowners, and merchants who wanted either the UP experiment to fail or wanted to make quick profits, or both. Finally, there was the inefficiency of an inexperienced government trying to take over and run huge sectors of the economy. New and often untrained bureaucrats, frequently appointed for political rather than technical qualifications, could hardly master tasks that still bedevil their counterparts in tightly controlled societies.

The Chilean economy was falling into a shambles. Monetary authorities were pumping out money to cover huge budget deficits, thereby provoking inflation. An overvalued exchange rate was encouraging imports, while low world copper prices depressed export earnings. Foreign credits and investments had virtually disappeared. Partly under the pressure of the Nixon administration's "invisible blockade," Chile's gross national product declined by 0.8 percent in 1972 and by nearly 5 percent in 1973.

But how could the transition to a socialist economy be smooth? In Cuba (see Chapter 5), there certainly was dislocation in the early years, and Chile faced much greater obstacles. Allende did not have the power Fidel enjoyed in Cuba. Chile was still a pluralist democracy. The opposition still controlled the Congress. The economy was still open to international blackmail.

Added to these inherent difficulties was the intransigence of the opposition. At no time, one should remember, did the Allende government get over half the vote. Allende became president in 1970 with a smaller percentage of the vote than he had received when he lost in 1964 (36.3 percent, compared with 38.9 percent). In the local elections of April 1971, the UP parties received 49.7 percent, their high point. Subsequent months saw furious battles in every political arena—elections in unions, student groups, and professional associations.

The UP itself was weakened by splits within its own ranks. The far left, led by the MIR (the Movimiento de la Izquierda Revolucionaria, or Movement of the Revolutionary Left), pressed for more radical action. They wanted faster nationalizations, tough police action against the opposition, and rule by decree. The moderates within the UP, including the Communists, urged caution, arguing that precipitous action would play into the hands of the rightists who could manipulate the military and the middle class.

By mid-1972 the political climate had become superheated. Massive street mobilizations by both pro- and anti-Allende forces became routine. In August shopkeepers staged a one-day boycott to protest government economic policies. In October a series of protests began to sweep the country. These eruptions showed that widespread sectors of the Chilean public were willing to confront the government in the streets. They were determined not to go down without a fight.

The government had its own mass support. The UP could on command turn out several hundred thousand disciplined marchers. Their ranks included the many Chileans who had already begun to experience significant changes— higher real wages, subsidized fresh milk, a role in administering their community or workplace. They also responded to the new nationalism—the takeover of the copper companies, the tough line toward all foreign firms, the highly publicized welcome to Fidel Castro when he came to Chile in 1971.

March 1973 brought another political test. At stake was the composition of Congress. The opposition hoped to gain a two-thirds majority and thereby be able to impeach Allende. When the votes were counted, the government had done better than even it had dared to predict: UP got 43 percent, reducing the opposition's majority from 32 to 30 (out of 50) in the Senate and from 93 to 87 (out of 150) in the lower house. UP leaders jubilantly pointed to the increase in the leftist vote over 1970, noting that no previous Chilean president had ever been able to increase his support in a midterm congressional election. The opposition pointed to its 56 percent vote as equivalent to Frei's landslide victory in 1964.

The election returns could be used to buttress almost any political position. One thing was certain: the opposition had not gotten the big electoral boost it had sought. Allende may have lacked an absolute majority, but he had rock-hard support among the workers and an increasing number of rural laborers.

There had never been a shortage of plots to overthrow the elected Marxist government. The rightist Patria y Libertad (Fatherland and Liberty) had already been engaged in terrorist attacks against government officials and vital economic installations. By 1973, however, more and more of the middle class had come to think there was no democratic solution to the crisis.

In April a strike of copper workers began, giving the opposition ideal grounds to claim multiclass resistance to Allende. In July the truck owners struck, triggering a wave of strikes by middle-class associations, such as lawyers, physicians, and architects. The pro-Allende mass labor organizations staged huge counterprotests. Chile was in the grip of a feverish political battle. Terrorist incidents became frequent. Few thought the situation could remain peaceful until 1976, when the next president would be elected.

Allende knew this. He had long since rejected his far left's advice to resort to extralegal means, and he knew the Christian Democrats were the only political force that was strong enough and possibly willing to reach an agreement that might preserve the country's democratic system. Allende negotiated with Frei and his fellow leaders, but after extended deliberation they refused. They did not want to be drawn into joint responsibility for a collapsing government; equally important, they suspected they had much to gain from further discrediting of UP. They may even have anticipated that a military coup would restore them to power.

Allende concluded that he had to increase military participation in his government. Although it might give short-term stability, it might also open the way to military intrigue and to opposition charges of politicizing the armed forces. Allende sensed the danger and in August attempted to shuffle his army commanders. It was too late.

By early September the military conspiracy to depose the UP government was in high gear. Strikes and counterdemonstrations had further slowed an economy already hit by hyperinflation and capital flight. General Carlos Prats, army

The presidential palace located in central Santiago burst into flames under rocket attacks by the Chilean armed forces during the coup of September 11, 1973. (Corbis\Bettman\United Press International.)

commander-in-chief and minister of defense, proclaimed his support for Chile's constitutional democracy. Unfortunately for Allende and the UP, Prats' military prestige was slipping badly. Outvoted at a generals' council in late August, he resigned both his army and cabinet posts. His successor as army chief was General Augusto Pinochet.

The military now lost little time. On September 11, 1973, a well-coordinated coup began. Early that morning the Special Services *carabineros,* long thought to best embody Chile's tradition of nonpolitical police, were still guarding the presidential palace against possible attack. Ominously, they pulled out when informed that their commander had joined the unfolding coup. At 6 A.M. Allende decided to go immediately to La Moneda, the landmark presidential palace in the heart of Santiago.

The rest of the morning saw frenzied activity at the palace, as the defenses were prepared. Allende began receiving offers of safe exit to exile, but he chose to stand and fight. Just before noon, air force Hawker Hunters attacked the palace with rocket fire. As army troops prepared to storm the palace, Allende committed suicide.

Opposition to the coup was scattered, but the repression was rapid and brutal. We shall never know how many died—at least 2000. It was the most violent military intervention in twentieth-century South American history. The

Weaving Opposition

During the darkest days of the Pinochet dictatorship, when political opposition or even appeals to human rights were impossible, if not suicidal, ordinary Chilean women challenged the dictatorship and spoke out against human rights violations in innovative ways. Like the mothers of the Plaza de Mayo in Argentina, Chilean women were able to organize protests with a degree of impunity unthinkable for others, so long as they acted in their accepted gender roles as mothers, wives, sisters, and grandmothers, Catholic protectors of their families.

One interesting way in which these women were able to express their grief and appeal to human rights was through sewing *arpilleras*, traditional Chilean tapestries. In messages combining the personal and the political, women depicted their lost children, or better times, or even scenes of human rights violations and antiregime protests. The Catholic Church helped in the production and distribution of the *arpilleras*, setting up workshops and providing materials to weavers, as well as selling the tapestries.

The role of the *arpilleras* in allowing Chilean women to express loss and protest the human rights violations was only one of the ways in which the tapestries functioned. Sewing these visual testimonies of grief served as a kind of therapy for women whose suffering continued as they contemplated the fate of their disappeared loved ones. The sale of *arpilleras* also provided income in extremely scarce times, as Pinochet's neoliberal policies made life ever harder for poor and middle-income communities. But their most important function was to provide an avenue for protest in a society in which "de-politicization" was enforced by gun and bayonet.

"transition to socialism" that so many on the left thought to be irreversible was coming to a screeching halt.

Allende's downfall resulted largely from the interplay between social classes and political parties. The left drew its support mainly from the urban working class. It met opposition from a cohesive upper class united by family ties and objective interest, and this unified elite was able to gain the allegiance of middle-sector groups and, most important of all, militant lower-middle-class activists, such as storekeepers and truckers. Between 1970 and 1973, the worker-based Allende movement was unable to form an enduring coalition with the other strata in Chilean society. That explains its inability to win a clear majority at the polls, hence its ultimate vulnerability.

This is not to discount the effects of opposition from the United States, which worked steadily at "destabilizing" (that is, overthrowing) the Allende regime. But U.S. intervention was not the deciding factor in the government's downfall. The Allende administration had a mountain of troubles of its own. Nonetheless, the United States once again placed itself squarely on the side of counterrevolutionaries.

The Pinochet Regime

The new military government promptly set out to impose an authoritarian regime on Chile. Proclaiming its goal as "national reconstruction," the junta set about to destroy—not merely reform—the country's political system. Congress was dissolved, the constitution suspended, and parties declared illegal or placed "in recess": there was to be no more political bickering. The junta further imposed a state of siege, called a 9 o'clock curfew, and set strict limits on the media.

The armed forces sought to revamp long-standing relationships between state and society. One critical component of this plan was the unity of the military, led by army general Augusto Pinochet. Another was the disarray of civilian society, which made it possible for the regime to dismantle (or at least repress) such intermediate institutions as political parties and labor unions and to establish direct authority. Political activity in its traditional sense stopped. In January 1974 General Pinochet announced that the military would remain in power for no less than five years.

Through clever political maneuvering, Pinochet achieved supreme authority, and what had at first been a thoroughly institutionalized military regime became highly personalized—as Pinochet alone commanded power. A plebiscite in 1978 produced the widespread appearance of support for Pinochet's "defense of the dignity of Chile." Another plebiscite in 1980 approved a constitution that confirmed Pinochet's hold on his office until 1990.

In the meantime, a group of civilian technocrats introduced far-reaching changes in economic policy. These economists believed strongly in the efficiency and fairness of market competition. What had restricted Chile's growth, they reasoned, was government intervention in the economy. To put the laws of supply and demand back to work, they set out to reduce the role of the state and also to cut back inflation. The ultimate goal, Pinochet once said, was "to make Chile not a nation of proletarians, but a nation of entrepreneurs."

The regime's programs had a clear effect on inflation, which was running at an annual rate of around 500 percent at the time of the coup. By 1976 it was down to 180 percent, by 1978 it was around 30–35 percent, and by 1982 it was down to 10 percent. From 1983 to 1987, inflation fluctuated between 20 and 31 percent. This was a far better performance than that of Argentina, Brazil, or Mexico, and here the junta could justifiably claim success. They could make a similar claim for growth, which averaged over 7 percent from 1976 through 1981. But it was achieved at the cost of lower real wages and declining social services.

The University of Chicago–trained technocrats' goal was to open Chile to the world economy, drastically reducing tariff protection, government subsidies, and the size of the public sector. In late 1973 the state owned nearly 500 firms. The junta returned about half to their original owners and opened bids for many of the rest. The lack of true competition made for low sale prices, benefiting local business conglomerates and multinational corporations, such as ITT.

Economic policymakers also reduced barriers to imports on the ground that quotas and tariffs protected inefficient industries. The result was that many local firms lost out to multinational corporations. The Chilean business community, which strongly supported the coup in 1973, was badly affected. Ironically, Chile was attempting to create a free-market economy with assistance largely drawn from international organizations and other governments, not private banks and companies.

The financial crash of 1982, triggered by Mexico's de facto default on its foreign debt, hit Chile harder than the rest of Latin America. The gross domestic product plunged 10 percent that year, as unemployment (including those on government make-work programs) rose to include a third of the labor force by mid-1983. Pinochet installed a new set of conservative technocrats, who launched an even more radical economic restructuring. They stimulated investment, greatly increased exports, and sharply reduced unemployment. But wages remained chronically low, and the systematic privatization of social services left many poor Chileans without the essentials of life.

On the political front, the Pinochet regime never hesitated to use repression, especially at any hint of labor unrest or popular protest. Its brutal tactics earned widespread condemnation, as critics denounced repeated and persistent violations of human rights. In September 1976 a car bomb in Washington, D.C., killed Orlando Letelier, a former Allende ambassador to the United States and at the time of the bombing an effective lobbyist against U.S. government aid to the Pinochet government. The assassins' link with Chilean intelligence was clear, but Chile contemptuously rebuffed the Carter government's attempt to extradite the accused members of the Chilean military. The election of Ronald Reagan came as a great relief to the Pinochet government, which soon found Washington seeking closer relations.

Around 1985 the Reagan administration suddenly began to distance itself from Pinochet. By this time Chile's aging (and patently undemocratic) dictator was becoming something of a political embarrassment to the United States, especially at a time when President Reagan was loudly denouncing human rights abuses within the Soviet Union's "evil empire." Moreover, U.S. policymakers began to fear that Pinochet's repressive rule was encouraging the development of a radical opposition—a guerrilla movement that might seize power through armed violence, as had occurred so long ago in Cuba. Whatever the reason, the Reagan administration was backing away from its initial honeymoon with Pinochet.

In 1988 Pinochet took a dramatic gamble and lost. Reacting to international pressure to liberalize and feeling confident in a recovering economy, the general risked another plebiscite on his one-man rule. The opposition now united in a fourteen-party alliance, called the "Concertación," and mounted a highly effective television campaign (aided briefly by U.S. media consultants) for the "no," which triumphed by a decisive 55 to 43 percent. The die was now cast for a return to elected government.

After a tense interval, Pinochet accepted the result, knowing that the constitution ensured his continuation as army commander-in-chief until 1998. The next step was the 1989 presidential election, won by the longtime Christian Democratic leader (and implacable Allende foe) Patricio Aylwin, supported by a coalition of seventeen center and center-left parties. The extreme left failed to win a single congressional seat, as the once-powerful Communist Party dissolved into a bitter fight between reformists and hard-line Marxist-Leninists.

THE CONTEMPORARY SCENE (1990–PRESENT)

Aylwin assumed power in 1990, committed to the restoration of Chile's democratic institutions, investigation of past human rights abuses, and rapid improvement in the living conditions of the poor. His heavily technocratic cabinet was also committed to maintaining the essentials of Latin America's leading economic success story (at least by orthodox standards): relative price stability, booming exports (buoyed by high copper prices), record foreign investment, impressive foreign debt reduction, and significant progress in privatizing much of a once highly inefficient public sector.

Chile's newly restored democracy faced formidable obstacles: an ever-alert army still headed by an unrepentant Pinochet (although he was now tarnished by family financial scandals), a pro-military judiciary, a rightist-dominated Senate, sporadic terrorism from the left and the right, and the explosive issue of what to do about past human rights abuses—with its potential to ignite civilian-military conflict.

The governing coalition (the Concertación) held together for another presidential election in 1993. Once again the Christian Democrats furnished the president. He was Eduardo Frei, the son of Chile's president from 1964 to 1970, who won 58 percent of the vote. The uncharismatic Frei, whose name was his greatest asset, promised "growth with equity." The once-powerful Communist Party continued to be thoroughly marginalized, while the Socialist Party remained loyal to the coalition. Most important, there was general acceptance of the rules of the democratic game.

Chile's most notable accomplishment continued to be its noninflationary rapid growth. During the first eight years of Concertación coalition government (1990–98), Chile's GDP grew 6.7 percent per year, the highest in Latin America and one of the highest in the world. The foreign debt was significantly reduced, and new foreign capital was readily attracted. Privatization had gone virtually to the maximum. Especially impressive were high savings and investment rates, which laid solid foundations for continued productivity.

The distribution of this growth, however, was less impressive. Although statistics showed that the number of Chileans living in poverty decreased over the course of the 1990s, absolute levels of poverty remained high and disparities in income continued to grow, making Chile one of the most unequal societies in the region.

On the international front, Chile in the early 1990s staked its hopes on winning membership in NAFTA. When it became clear that the Clinton administration could not obtain congressional "fast track" authorization to negotiate Chile's entry into NAFTA, the Concertación government opted instead for associate membership in MERCOSUR.

In March 1998, General Pinochet finally stepped down after twenty-five years as army chief. The general did not, however, retreat from public life. Instead, he became a senator-for-life, joining a handful of other nonelected senators, further strengthening the hard-line right's ability to veto government legislation.

While Pinochet's assumption of his Senate seat sparked protest from the left, that gesture was soon overshadowed by developments abroad. On October 16, 1998, while visiting London, the former dictator was arrested by British police at the request of a Spanish magistrate wanting to prosecute him for human rights abuses of Spanish citizens during his seventeen-year rule. In Chile, the human rights community, the political left, and some members of the ruling Concertación applauded the arrest, while the military and the right denounced it as the work of an "international socialist campaign."

Faced with potential destabilization at home if Pinochet were extradited to Spain, President Frei maintained that the former general enjoyed diplomatic immunity because of his status in the Senate—and insisted that the whole proceeding amounted to a violation of Chilean sovereignty. In the end, the British government finally decided to let Pinochet return home on the ground that he was not mentally fit to undergo a complex and lengthy trial.

By coincidence or not, Pinochet arrived in Santiago just a few days before the inauguration of Ricardo Lagos, the Concertación candidate who narrowly defeated right-wing opponent Joaquín Lavín in a runoff election in January 2000. The victory of Lagos, a socialist, appeared to herald an era of reconciliation. But underlying his triumph were social fissures and fragmentation, continuing tensions in civil–military relations, and persisting struggles over the larger political and economic legacies of the Pinochet era.

Subsequent events revealed steady efforts to repeal the Pinochet legacy in Chile. A series of constitutional reforms in 2005 sought to reduce the primacy of the executive branch and bolster democratic institutions by reducing the presidential term from six to four years, abolishing unelected seats in the Senate, strengthening the role of the legislature, and diluting the political importance of the military. Elections in 2005–6 led to the victory of Michelle Bachelet, the candidate of the governing coalition, a socialist, and the daughter of a pro-constitutionalist military general who had been tortured and killed by the Pinochet regime. The Concertación now faced a serious challenge from the right, whose candidate won 47 percent of the vote in the second round of elections.

By this time the political atmosphere in Chile was moving away from polarization in the direction of accommodation, pragmatism, and consensus. All major parties agreed on the need to continue liberal economic policies. Key forces on the Chilean right were intent on divorcing themselves from Pinochet, while the left had secured a prominent place in the nation's political system. There were controversies, of course: Bachelet saw her popularity decline as a result of student strikes, botched policies, and accusations of corruption. But these were run-of-the-mill political disputes, not disputations over the nature of the system. As of 2009, the prospects for Chilean democracy looked extremely solid.

11

~~~

Brazil

The Awakening Giant

Brazilians and foreigners alike have long considered Brazil "the land of the future." With an area of more than 3 million square miles, Brazil occupies nearly half of South America. Its land mass ranges from the semiarid northeast, plagued by recurrent droughts, to the rich forests and fertile plateaus of the center and the south. The country abounds in natural resources, including iron and other industrial minerals. In recent years Brazil has discovered vast areas of undersea oil deposits in offshore fields within its zone of sovereign jurisdiction. Its population is creeping toward 200 million. Although Brazil relied heavily on export agriculture for much of its history, a combination of recent developments—industrialization, modernization, and political stability—has made the nation into an important regional and potential world power. Perhaps because of this anticipation, citizens tend to have an optimistic, ebullient outlook on life. As they like to say, "God is a Brazilian."

FROM COLONY TO NATIONHOOD

Brazil's relatively nonviolent acquisition of independence from Portugal in 1822 left the country with an auspicious start. The lack of large-scale conflict meant that physical and economic destruction was minimal, especially in comparison to the devastation wrought in the Río de la Plata region, in Venezuela, and in central Mexico. Nor did Brazil have to cope with the problems of demobilizing a massive military apparatus in the postwar period. And most important, the transition of the Portuguese monarchy to Brazil provided a coherent political structure endowed with the authority of time-tested tradition. There were struggles, to be sure, but Brazil did not face the same kind of instability that other Latin Americans faced at the outset of independence.

The economy was mainly agricultural, and sugar was by far the largest commercial crop. By 1822 the population included about 4 million inhabitants, more than half of whom were slaves of African birth or descent. The social order

Map 11 Brazil

consisted principally of two tiers. Landowning aristocrats and subservient farmers controlled agricultural production, while African slaves and their descendants worked the land. This dichotomy would come to be aptly and sympathetically described by Gilberto Freyre in his classic book, *The Masters and the Slaves*. There were some merchants and lawyers and other professionals, mainly in the cities and especially in Rio de Janeiro, but society was dominated by the forces of the countryside.

Dom Pedro I (1822–1831)

In nineteenth-century Brazil, many basic social issues were bound up with the fate of the crown. Most obvious was the consolidation of Brazil's independence. Related issues involved the centralization or decentralization of authority and executive versus legislative power. These questions had to be faced immediately after independence because both the elite and the emperor wanted to write a Brazilian constitution.

Dom Pedro I became the first emperor of a newly independent Brazil in 1822, when the Brazilian aristocracy forced a break with Portugal. A year earlier Pedro's father, Dom João VI, had left Brazil to resume the throne in Portugal, but only after advising his son to remain in Brazil (to which the royal family had become very attached), even if it meant creating a separate monarchy. Dom Pedro I called for a constituent assembly, and the resulting elections in 1823 revealed several political divisions. Most basic was the split between a Brazilian faction and a pro-Portuguese faction, the latter consisting of those who had opposed Brazilian independence and wanted to resubordinate Rio de Janeiro to Lisbon. Its leaders were primarily Portuguese-born, mostly military officers, bureaucrats, and merchants. The Brazilian faction was led by José Bonifácio Andrada e Silva, a São Paulo landowner who was the leading spokesman for Brazilian liberalism and the leading minister of Dom Pedro's government.

Despite majority support in the assembly, José Bonifácio's cabinet had to resign after three months because the emperor continually endorsed the Portuguese faction's protest over the government's anti-Portuguese measures. Heated polemics continued and street fights broke out, as an extremist faction of the Brazilian bloc called for decentralized rule and piled abuse on the crown. Amid the furious debate the emperor simply dissolved the assembly in November 1824. Shortly thereafter he unilaterally decreed a constitution for Brazil. It included many features from a draft prepared by Antonio Carlos Andrada e Silva, José Bonifácio's brother, but reserved greater powers for the Poder Moderador (the "Moderating Power"), which was to be the monarch himself. Most important was the power to dissolve the Chamber of Deputies and to appoint and dismiss ministers. Citizen voting was tied to a high minimum-property test, thereby severely limiting public participation in an imperial government that was to be highly centralized. Ironically, this unilaterally decreed constitution included passages from France's 1789 Declaration of Human Rights.

The story of this constitution demonstrated key features of the new nation of Brazil: (1) the monarch had seemingly preserved his absolutist initiative by dissolving the elected assembly and imposing his own constitution; but (2) the constitution, while favoring the crown in the division of powers, was more liberal than absolutist, more akin to the contemporary English parliamentary system than to the French; and (3) the commitment to human rights, however qualified by the real intentions of Dom Pedro and his loyalist advisers, thenceforth became a lodestar in Brazilian history, an ideal to which libertarians and reformers would continuously repair. The struggle over the new country's political structure thus ended ambiguously: a liberal charter imposed by an emperor who was thereby establishing limits on all future governments.

The absolutist aspects of events in Rio stirred concern in the Northeast, the region that had proved most receptive to the liberal ideas of abolition,

Celebrating the declaration of Brazilian independence from Portugal, this mid-nineteenth-century lithograph, *O Grito de Ipiranga*, depicts the "Cry of Ipiranga" by Prince Pedro (September 7, 1822) in allegorical style. (Miguel Maria Lisbôa, Barão de Japura. *Romances históricos, por um brasileiro*, 2nd ed. (Brussels: n. p. 1886). Author's copy.

federalism, and republicanism. Back in 1817 republican conspirators in Pernambuco province had stubbornly resisted the discipline of Rio. Dom Pedro's imposition of the constitution in 1824 provoked a new rebellion, which dramatized the fundamental issues at the heart of Brazilian politics for the rest of the empire.

The Pernambucans declared their independence anew. After gaining the support of other northeastern provinces, the rebels called for their own constituent assembly. The movement split apart on the slavery issue, however, as one leader shocked his colleagues by calling for an end to the slave trade. Most of the rebel organizers feared a mobilization of the lower orders, and not without reason. Discontent of marginal free persons, many of color, was threatening to turn the anti-Portuguese, anticentralist agitation into a social revolution.

The rebels' internal divisions in Pernambuco came as the military pressure from outside was growing. The emperor had hired English and French ships and mercenaries, and they taught the insurgents a bloody political lesson. Most of the rebel leaders were executed. There were limits to the range of permissible social protest in Brazil.

Rio's domination came only with British help, and that aid had its price. Having secured a favored foothold in the Brazilian economy since 1810, Britain now found itself underwriting the transition to Brazilian independence.

Britain could help consolidate the newly independent Rio government by facilitating diplomatic recognition from the world's principal powers. That goal was achieved by a series of 1825 agreements that Britain negotiated with Portugal and Brazil. They provided that the Portuguese king, now Dom João VI, was to recognize Brazil as a separate kingdom; that British exports to Brazil would continue to receive a preferential tariff rate; and, not least important, that Brazil would pay Portugal an indemnification of 2 million pounds sterling for damages suffered in the struggle for independence. (This was exactly the debt that Portugal owed to Britain; the negotiators kept this provision secret.)

The following year, 1826, Britain got from Brazil a treaty commitment to end the slave trade by 1830. The British wanted this commitment because they feared that slave-produced sugar from Brazil would prove cheaper in the world market than sugar from the British West Indies, where slavery had recently been abolished. Another reason was the pressure on the British government from English abolitionists. The new Brazilian government, with little enthusiasm and less genuine commitment, gave the British the clause they demanded. Further concessions were made in an 1827 trade treaty which put Brazilian exports to England at a disadvantage with exports from British colonies. Much of the Brazilian elite saw the concessions as excessive and explicable only by Dom Pedro's apparent desire to retain British goodwill toward Portugal, which desperately needed continued British economic help. Criticism would have been even more strident if the 2-million-pound payment had been made public.

In the end, Dom Pedro's loyalty to Portugal proved his undoing in Brazil. His new constitution had not ended the struggle over the division of governmental powers. In 1826 the emperor became the target of new attacks, from the "moderates" wanting more power for the legislature and revisions in the treaties with Britain, to the "extremists" demanding autonomy for the provinces. The emperor's critics dominated the expanding press with their drumfire of invective.

In this same period Dom Pedro suffered a serious reverse in foreign policy. What is modern-day Uruguay had been annexed to Portuguese America in 1821 as the "Cisplatine Province." But in 1825 local guerrillas seized power and proclaimed union with the United Provinces of the Río de la Plata (present-day Argentina). The resulting war between Brazil and the United Provinces ended in 1828 with a treaty that created an independent state, Uruguay. The British, again intermediaries in arranging the treaty, hoped for a buffer state between Argentina and Brazil. This setback to Brazilian ambitions in the Río de la Plata soon faded in significance when compared to the quagmire of the Portuguese royal succession.

When Dom João VI died, in 1826, Dom Pedro, his legal successor, had become increasingly absorbed in trying to protect his daughter's succession rights in Portugal. That made him less able to deal with the aggressively anti-absolutist political forces in Brazil. He found his position increasingly untenable, as his opponents mobilized street crowds to protest his preference for an absolutist ministry. On April 7, 1831, Dom Pedro I abdicated, departing the land whose independence he had helped to secure less than a decade earlier.

Dom Pedro's abdication was a victory for the anti-Portuguese forces and a defeat for the beleaguered absolutists. It also created a power vacuum because the emperor's son, later to become Dom Pedro II, was only five years old. His father had left him behind in order to maintain the Braganza family's claim to the Brazilian throne. Who would exercise power in his name? Would the huge and thinly settled lands of this former colony hold together? Or would Portuguese America follow the example of Spanish America, which immediately fissured into the patchwork of nations we see today?

For nine years after Dom Pedro I's abdication, a regency exercised executive power. In 1834 the constitution was amended to give increased powers to the provinces, partly in response to separatist sentiments. The most violent separatist movement was in the province of Pará in the Amazon valley; the most dangerous, because of its location in a province bordering Argentina, was the Guerra dos Farrapos in Rio Grande do Sul.

Dom Pedro II (1840–1889)

Dom Pedro II's accession to the throne in 1840 unified the divided elite, curtailed separatist challenges, and halted the drift toward social revolution. The emperor assumed the wide powers (the "Moderating Power") in the 1824 constitution. The young emperor and the politicians now settled into an era of relatively harmonious parliamentary politics.

The two decades after midcentury were the golden years of the empire. The emperor and his ministry exercised executive power, although this authority was dependent upon retaining the confidence of the lower house. Yet the legislature's ultimate power was more apparent than real, because the emperor could dissolve the Chamber at will, thereby necessitating new elections. Until the late 1860s, however, Dom Pedro II exercised his power discreetly, and the system seemed to function well.

By 1850 two distinctive political parties had emerged—both owing their origin to the Brazilian faction of the 1820s. The parties were Conservative and Liberal, although historians have long cautioned against taking these labels too seriously. In 1853 the two parties collaborated to form a "conciliation cabinet," which held power, except for the 1858–62 interval, until 1868.

The empire's most important test in foreign policy came in the Río de la Plata basin, the site of a longtime rivalry among Paraguay, Uruguay, Argentina, and Brazil. The Brazilian government became alarmed over the strength and intentions of Juan Manuel de Rosas, the autocratic ruler of Argentina, who was claiming the right to control all traffic on the Río de la Plata. This was a grave threat to Brazil, since the economics of its southern provinces relied heavily on access to the Plata river basin system.

At the same time Brazil was being drawn into a dangerous political battle in Uruguay, where Brazilians had gained a financial and commercial foothold. Brazilian troops were sent into domestic Uruguayan battles on the side of the "Colorado" faction, which prevailed. The Brazilians then turned to face Rosas.

They were encouraged by the French and British, who chafed over the tough terms Rosas had imposed for economic access to Argentina. The anti-Argentine coalition prevailed. Foreign troops, assisted by Argentine rebels (the latter representing the soon-to-be dominant liberals), defeated the Rosas forces in 1852, sending Rosas to a permanent exile in England.

But even with Brazilian support the Colorados lost control in Uruguay. Since the victorious Blancos could no longer look to Rosas for help, they turned to Francisco Solano López, the dictator of Paraguay. Argentina, now controlled by the liberals, joined Brazil in support of the Colorados in Uruguay. Solano López wanted to expand his rule by allying with the Uruguayan Blancos to conquer the Brazilian province of Rio Grande do Sul. He invaded both Argentina and Brazil in 1865, pushing them and the Colorado government of Uruguay into a military alliance.

The ensuing war lasted five years. The Paraguayan army proved to be well trained, superbly disciplined, and extraordinarily brave. The Brazilians bore the brunt of the fighting on the other side. At first they suffered humiliating reverses, but then triumphed after greatly expanding their army.

The Paraguayan War had important consequences: (1) access to the Río de la Plata river network was guaranteed; (2) the two major powers, Argentina and Brazil, cemented close relations; (3) Brazil consolidated its position in Uruguay; and (4) Paraguay was left with half (it is thought) of its population dead and the country in ruins.

The war also had a profound effect on politics within Brazil. It forced Brazil to enlarge its army, whose officers soon became important actors in Brazilian politics. It also provoked the emperor into unprecedented steps in asserting his authority. Pedro II demanded Paraguay's unconditional surrender, while the Liberals, who held a majority in the Chamber, wanted by 1868 to negotiate. He dismissed the Liberal cabinet and called for new elections. Some radical Liberals reacted angrily by forming a splinter group that in 1870 became the Republican Party. And the war threw a new light on slavery. The slaves recruited for the Brazilian army performed well in battle and were given their freedom in compensation. Their combat effectiveness must have given pause to the white officers who were later called on to hunt down fugitive slaves.

The End of the Empire

The final two decades of the empire were dominated by debate over the legitimacy of two institutions: slavery and the monarchy. Both came under scrutiny during the Paraguayan War.

Although the slave trade effectively ended in 1850, slavery was by no means dead twenty years later. The rapidly growing coffee plantations in the southeastern region demanded labor, and the planters turned to an obvious source: slaves from the economically decadent Northeast. Even if every slave in the Northeast had moved south they could not have furnished the labor needed in the coffee economy of the late 1880s.

The Realities of Slavery

Much historical writing on Brazil has emphasized the allegedly benevolent nature of its race relations. But it is worth remembering the nature of the institution that brought Africans to Brazil. In the late nineteenth century, the French wife of a Brazilian described her visit to a Brazilian plantation:

> Here it was that the miseries of slavery appeared to me in all their horror and hideousness. Negresses covered in rags, others half naked, having as covering only a handkerchief fastened behind their back and over their bosoms, which scarcely veiled their throats, and a calico skirt, through whose rents could be seen their poor, scraggy bodies; some negroes, with tawny and besotted looks, came and kneeled down on the marble slabs of the veranda. The majority carried on their shoulders the marks of scars which the lash had inflicted; several were affected with horrible maladies, such as elephantiasis, or leprosy. All this was dirty, repulsive, hideous. Fear or hate, that is what could be read on all these faces, which I never have seen smile.

From Adèle Toussaint-Samson, *A Parisian in Brazil* (Boston: James H. Earle, 1891), translated by Emma Toussaint. Edited and introduced by June E. Hahner (Wilmington, Del.: Scholarly Resources 2001), pp. 57–58.

The only solution, according to the coffee planters, was increased immigration. In 1886 the province of São Paulo launched a major effort to attract European immigrants to Brazil, but the *paulistas* found themselves unable to attract the amount of cheap labor they needed. Why? Partly because of the persistence of slavery. This led some of the elite to become abolitionist on the pragmatic grounds that immigrants could never be recruited unless Brazil's retrograde image in Europe was transformed. Abolition would be the most obvious step.

The manner in which Brazil carried out abolition was unique in the Americas. Brazilian slavery was a nationwide institution, thus preventing the kind of sectional conflict that occurred in the United States. Furthermore, Brazilian slaves had worked in virtually every job category, including many "skilled" ones. No less important, a large number of free persons of color had already established themselves economically, providing examples to the newly freed. Brazil had also escaped the extreme racist view that dismissed all persons of color as irremediably inferior. The large mixed-blood population, a few of whose members had reached prominent national positions by 1889 (such as the novelist Machado de Assis and the engineer-abolitionist André Rebouças), showed that some mobility was possible.

Abolition in Brazil was a seventeen-year process marked by three laws. The first came in 1871, which provided freedom for all children thenceforth born of slave mothers. But the masters were given the option of retaining labor rights over these children until the age of twenty-one.

It was not until the 1880s that the abolitionist movement was again able to force slavery to the center of the political arena. The abolitionists were led by urban professionals, especially lawyers. Prominent among them was Joaquim Nabuco, a Pernambucan deputy of impeccable social origins. Led by such orators as Nabuco, the abolitionists became the empire's first nationwide political movement. They raised significant sums to finance their propaganda and to buy the freedom of local slaves.

This mobilization had its impact on the parliament, which in 1885 passed the second abolitionist law. This one granted freedom to all slaves sixty or older, without compensation. Cynics pointed out that if any slaves survived to such an age, their masters would be delighted to be freed from caring for them. The new law did little to defuse the agitation of the abolitionists, some of whom began inciting slaves to flee from or rebel against the masters. By 1887 slavery was visibly disintegrating. The army, charged with catching and returning fugitive slaves, found their job more and more repugnant. In 1887 army officers formally refused to carry out this mission any longer.

By 1888 slave owners had had ample time to prepare for the transition to free labor. The final step was the "golden law," passed in May of that year, which freed all remaining slaves without compensation. The law was approved by an overwhelming vote in both houses. The political elite had managed to preserve a consensus while dealing with a volatile socioeconomic issue. This success at incremental reform helped to perpetuate the Brazilian elite's self-image as conciliatory. Remarkably enough, this image has come to be shared by many of the nonelites.

The other major drama of the late empire was the rise of republicanism. It had erupted earlier in the century, usually linked to regional demands for autonomy. The Republican Party, founded in 1871, also had a strong regionalist cast, especially in São Paulo. The birth of this party could be traced to Liberal deputies' reaction to Dom Pedro II's imposing, in 1868, a Conservative ministry in the face of a Liberal majority in the Chamber. In 1870 a group of indignant ex-Liberals founded the Republican Party.

At first the Republicans appeared harmless. Up to 1889 they had a very uneven following. It was strongest in São Paulo, Rio Grande do Sul, and Minas Gerais and weakest in the Northeast. The Republicans wanted a republic headed by a directly elected president, governed by a bicameral legislature, and organized on federalist principles. In effect the Republicans wanted to trade Brazil's English-style constitutional monarchy for a U.S.-style federal republic.

During the 1880s republicanism made great inroads among the younger generation—the university-educated sons of planters, merchants, and professional men. Often they combined republicanism with abolitionism. Both sentiments were reinforced by the teachings of the Brazilian Positivists, who believed in rationality, science, and logic. A dedicated group of Positivists penetrated faculties of higher education, especially in military colleges, and influenced intellectuals. The 1880s thus saw a convergence of movements that were eroding support for the monarchy and for slavery.

However, it was not high-minded debate that sealed the empire's fate. It was the army. In the late 1880s, recurring friction mounted between army officers and civilian politicians—often over the officers' rights to express publicly their political views. Because of the Paraguayan War, Brazil had created a much larger military than was wanted by the politicians, who provided meager financing for modernization of the army. By the 1880s there was a disproportionately high ratio of officers to troops. That led to frustration over delayed promotions among junior and middle-level officers, who became especially receptive to the abolitionist and republican sentiments that were so influential among their civilian counterparts.

The final agony of the empire came in 1889. The emperor had insisted on trying to rule with a Conservative ministry, despite its minority position in the Chamber. In June the emperor invited the Viscount of Ouro Preto to form a cabinet. He succeeded and formulated an ambitious reformist program. But it was too late. A military plot developed in November. Led by Marshall Deodoro da Fonseca, the conspirators demanded that the monarch abdicate. Dom Pedro II and his family calmly left for exile in Portugal. The republic was proclaimed the next day, November 16, 1889.

The empire had fallen with little upheaval. Although the planters had long feared that abolition would doom agricultural exports, they soon came to their senses. They now realized they could preserve their economic (and therefore political) dominance in a world without monarchs or slaves. Neither the abolition of slavery nor the overthrow of the empire in themselves brought structural change in Brazil.

OVERVIEW: ECONOMIC GROWTH AND SOCIAL CHANGE

In the mid-nineteenth century, the Brazilian economy began a fundamental transition, not tied to any legal or constitutional changes, that continued well into the twentieth century. It has also had a profound impact on Brazilian society and on relations between social classes.

Like most of Latin America, Brazil has exported a few primary products to the North Atlantic economies. But in contrast, Brazil has passed through a sequence of dependence on the exportation of different products at different points in time. The repeated pattern of boom-and-bust has made it difficult to achieve sustained growth. Since the various products have come from different regions, these cycles have created pockets of prosperity and decline.

After independence, sugar continued to be the most lucrative export, as during the eighteenth century. Produced mainly on large plantations in the Northeast, where labor came from slaves, sugar accounted for 30 percent of Brazilian exports in 1821–30. It then began a long decline, and by 1900 it contributed only 5 percent of the overall export amount.

Rubber production started in the early nineteenth century, principally in the Amazon, and steadily increased. By 1853 the port of Belém was exporting more than 2500 tons of natural rubber. Demand in the industrial world grew enormously in the wake of the discovery of the vulcanization process—which prevented rubber from getting too sticky in hot weather and brittle in the cold. A spectacular boom arrived in 1900–1913, when rubber amounted to about one-quarter of all the country's exports. Then the British capitalized on the more

In the late nineteenth century, sacks of coffee left São Paulo's plantations on mule trains and eventually reached overseas destinations. (Courtesy of the Library of Congress.)

efficient rubber plantations in the East Indies, and the world price collapsed. The rubber boom came to a sudden and permanent end.

It was coffee that provided the most durable stimulus to economic change in the postindependence era. Coffee production began to develop in the Caribbean in the early nineteenth century and then took hold in Brazil, where it enjoyed excellent natural conditions. The volume of Brazilian exports held fairly steady until the 1890s, then entered a period of spectacular growth. In 1901 Brazil exported nearly 15 million sacks of coffee (at sixty kilograms each) and produced nearly three-quarters of the total world supply. Early in the century, coffee yielded about one-half of the country's foreign exchange.

Coffee thus became a central feature of Brazilian life. When coffee prices were high, the prospects for Brazil were positive; if they were down, so was the national outlook. And the domestic consumption of coffee has long been an essential aspect of social life, as Brazilians conduct meetings and discussions over cup after cup of steaming coffee, usually taken with large quantities of sugar.

Coffee production flourished in southern-central Brazil, particularly in the state of São Paulo. It requires good land, a fair investment, and much labor. Coffee trees yield full production only after six years, and they need steady care. Berries need to be gathered, washed, and shelled. The beans inside the berries must be dried, sifted, sorted, sacked, and stored. This requires labor.

Like Argentina, Brazil turned its eyes to Europe. First the state of São Paulo and then the national government attracted millions of European immigrants, especially in the last quarter of the nineteenth century. The largest portion, perhaps a third, came from Italy, closely followed by immigrants from Portugal. But the relative size of the immigrant population never reached the level of Argentina. From 1877 to 1903, over 1.9 million people entered Brazil, an annual average of 71,000. From 1904 to 1930 another 2.1 million immigrants arrived, averaging 79,000 people a year.

Although ample labor was available in the Brazilian center and Northeast, where the number of jobs had fallen disastrously behind the increase in workers, the prophets of immigration opted for Europeans, who would presumably be better workers and more reliable future citizens. Racist notions also held that former slaves would be less productive laborers. So the Brazilian government paid the ocean passage of millions of Europeans, while millions of Brazilians in Minas Gerais, Rio de Janeiro, and the Northeast could not afford to move south. Great contributions were made by the transplanted Europeans and Japanese, but each of those jobs might have been held by a Brazilian who would have been rescued from the economically moribund regions.

Technology was harder to obtain. The Brazilians, like other populations outside the dynamic North Atlantic industrial complex, found themselves having to accept direct investment by foreign firms in order to get technology. The telegraph system, for example, arrived with British and American firms, which installed and operated their own equipment. The same held true for railroads, electric utilities, and shipping—most of the infrastructure needed to sustain the growing agro-export economy. These were highly visible investments and later became convenient targets for nationalist attacks.

Capital was also sought abroad. It came in the form of loans to Brazil on the state and national levels. In 1907, for example, the states of São Paulo, Minas Gerais, and Rio de Janeiro signed a coffee marketing agreement to be financed by foreign creditors. The state governments planned to repay the loans with the receipts from export taxes on coffee. Such commitments obligated Brazil not only to repay the loans but also to finance the remission of profits (and eventually capital) on direct investments by foreigners. The crucial question was the *terms* on which all these transactions took place. Available data suggest that the profit rate on foreign-owned railways, to take an obvious example, did not exceed rates for comparable investments in Britain.

Throughout the years between 1889 and 1930 the center of the Brazilian economy moved south and southwest. The primary push came from the "march" of coffee, as planters found it cheaper to break new ground than to recycle the plantation soils whose yields were dropping. The result was a path of abandoned plantations, stretching from Rio de Janeiro and Minas Gerais down into São Paulo and its vast interior.

The reliance on coffee entailed large-scale risks. One was overproduction. It was difficult to anticipate demand six years in advance, and therefore to plan when trees should be planted. In 1906, for example, Brazil produced 20 million sacks of coffee for a world market that could absorb only 12 or 13 million. A political question promptly arose: What should be done with the surplus?

A related uncertainty came from the rise of foreign competition. Brazil's share of the world market declined from 75 percent in 1900 to 67 percent in 1930 to only

32 percent in 1970 and 18 percent in 1978. With time the country gradually lost its near-monopoly on supply.

A third source of vulnerability came from wide fluctuations in the world price. This reflected not only the effects of competition but also changes in demand. Between 1929 and 1931, after the Great Depression struck, the price of coffee plummeted from 22.5 cents a pound to merely 8 cents. Frequent oscillations led to wide variation in Brazil's foreign-exchange earnings—and in government revenues, which came primarily from export duties.

To illustrate both the growth and the uncertainty of the Brazilian coffee sector, Figure 11.1 displays the volume of the country's coffee exports during the period from 1860 to 1985. The rise in output and commerce is clearly visible. So are the fluctuations, which mainly reflect the instability of world demand.

A final hazard derived from the small number of purchasers. In the late nineteenth and early twentieth centuries, Brazil sold between three-fifths and three-quarters of its exports to only three countries: the United States, Britain, and Germany. The United States was the largest single buyer. The reliance on two or three customers created unpredictable ties to outside economies, as Brazil discovered after the crash of 1929.

Prominent politicians and economists regarded this vulnerability as an inevitable result of Brazil's "agrarian vocation." Brazil, they argued, had no choice but to buy needed foreign finished goods with the funds earned by export and augmented by direct foreign investments or loans. Any significant attempt to industrialize, they reasoned, would produce inferior goods and jeopardize relations with foreign buyers and creditors. Furthermore, Brazil could not hope to copy the United States "because we don't have the superior aptitudes of their race," in the words of a Brazilian cabinet minister of the 1890s. Brazil must live with what God gave it: a comparative advantage in a few agricultural exports.

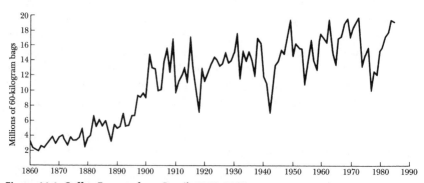

Figure 11.1 Coffee Exports from Brazil, 1860–1985

SOURCE: Werner Baer, *Industrialization and Economic Development in Brazil* (Homewood, Ill.: Richard D. Irwin, 1965), pp. 266–67; James E. Wilkie, Enrique C. Ochoa, and David E. Lorey, eds., *Statistical Abstract of Latin America, 28* (Los Angeles: UCLA Latin American Center, 1990), Table 2426.

Since the late empire, however, a handful of intellectuals and men of business began disputing this logic. They argued that Brazil should stimulate home industry. These critics had little influence on key policy areas, such as tariffs or exchange rates. Yet they did succeed in creating a "nationalist" critique that was to prove important after 1930.

Official encouragement of industrialization came forth in 1890, when a tariff revision provided mild protection for local manufacturing from foreign competition (and also lowered the duties on capital goods required for production). Engineering schools sprouted in Recife, São Paulo, Pôrto Alegre, and Bahia. By 1907 the country had about 3000 industrial establishments, most of them small, textiles and foodstuffs being the principal products. By 1920 the number of firms had grown to more than 13,000.

Brazil's industrial sector underwent large-scale expansion in the 1930s and 1940s, as the Great Depression and World War II reduced the available supply of manufactured goods from abroad (as happened elsewhere in Latin America, too). As with coffee, the center of industrial growth was in the state of São Paulo—where 15 percent of the nation's population was producing about 50 percent of the country's manufactured goods by 1940.

The upsurge continued thereafter, and Brazil moved into such heavy industries as steel and automobile production. Between 1947 and 1961 manufacturing output increased at an annual rate of 9.6 percent, compared to 4.6 percent for the agricultural sector. By 1960 industrial production amounted to more than 25 percent of the gross domestic product, and by 1975 it was up to nearly 30 percent. This diversification of the economy helped reduce Brazilian dependence on the outside world and lent credibility to claims that the country would someday join the ranks of superpowers.

These economic transformations brought far-reaching changes, such as urbanization. In 1920 about 25 percent of the population lived in urban areas, and by 2000 more than 80 percent lived in cities. But there are two unusual features in this trend. First, the tendency toward urbanization in Brazil has been *later* and *slower* than in many other Latin American countries. Second, Brazil does not have a single predominant city (like Buenos Aires or Montevideo, for instance). São Paulo and Rio de Janeiro have both become megalopolises, with millions of inhabitants and the amenities and complications of urban life, but between them they contain only about 10 percent of the national population of 192 million. Urbanization has taken place in Brazil, but the cities coexist with a large and populous countryside.

Consequently Brazil has developed an intricate social system. The upper-class elite includes landowners, frequently divided among themselves, as when *paulista* coffee planters rose up in the nineteenth century to challenge the sugar barons of the Northeast. In the course of the twentieth century, there appeared as well an industrial elite that would struggle for status and wealth, sometimes using the power of the state.

The popular masses were varied, too. There has been, and remains, a large-scale peasantry. There is a rural proletariat, in the coffee fields and elsewhere, a stratum that performs wage labor in the countryside. And in the interior there are indigenous and other groups that have little contact with national society.

An organized working class of substantial size, at least 4 million by 1970 and 6 million by 1980, emerged within Brazilian cities. Its struggles with employers and its constant manipulation by the state provide one of the central themes in late twentieth-century Brazilian life. There remains a large stratum of chronically unemployed city dwellers.

In between the upper and lower classes, middle sectors gradually appeared. They may now include as much as 30 percent of the people in some cities, though their share of the national population is less than that (perhaps 10 to 15 percent). They play important roles in commerce and the professions, and they have had a particularly intimate relationship with one major institution: the military.

Social status in Brazil is not just a function of occupation or wealth. It is also a matter of race. The massive importation of slave labor from Africa brought an additional ethnic dimension into Brazilian society, and this in turn has affected customs and attitudes.

There tends to be a strong correlation between race and social standing in Brazil: most on top are white, most blacks are on the bottom, and some mixed-bloods have won in-between positions. Some institutions, such as naval officers and the diplomatic corps, long remained white. But in Brazil race is not defined purely by physical features. It is a social concept, open to interpretation. To be "black" one has to be totally black (in contrast to the United States, where partly black in ethnic origin means black), so that people of mixed racial backgrounds in Brazil have some opportunity for upward mobility.

This is not to say that Brazil constitutes a racial paradise. Prejudice and bias have existed. For the last century the Brazilian elite has placed its faith in *branqueamento* ("bleaching"), with the unequivocally racist intention of purging Brazil of black blood. The overall correlation between status and race

---

Brazil: Vital Statistics, 2007

Population (millions)	191.6
GDP (current $U.S. billions)	1314.2
GNP/capita ($U.S.)	5910
Poverty rate (% in 2006)	33.3
Life expectancy (years)	72

Sources: World Bank and Economic Commission for Latin America and the Caribbean.

continues to exist, despite the denial of well-to-do Brazilians. Statistical studies by Brazilian demographers and sociologists have shown significant differences in income by race (controlling for all other factors). The conclusion is that race is a separate and significant variable in the Brazilian socioeconomic system. But mobility exists, marriage across color lines is common, and attitudes are more open than has been true in North American history. Nonetheless, sufficient racial discrimination exists to have provoked the federal and some state governments to adopt affirmative action programs in the early years of the new century.

Racial differentiation in Brazil has posed one obstacle to the formation of durable coalitions across social strata. Another obstacle is the size of Brazil. Distance (and poor communications) made it for a long time implausible to imagine an alliance between urban workers of São Paulo, for example, and the landless peasants in the Northeast. Such divisions enabled Brazil to attempt political solutions that would have been immediately impossible in more densely populated and integrated countries such as Cuba.

POLITICS AND POLICY: PATTERNS OF CHANGE

Although the military overthrew the empire, civilian politicians shaped the new republic. A constituent assembly was elected and produced a new constitution in 1891. It was a virtual copy of the U.S. Constitution. Brazil became a federation of twenty states, and the Brazilian president was to be elected directly and empowered to intervene in the states in case of threatened separation, foreign invasion, or conflict with other states. Suffrage was restricted to literate adult male citizens. This resulted in fewer than 3.5 percent of the population voting in any presidential election before 1930 and only 5.7 percent in 1930.

The First Republic (1889–1930)
After electing Deodoro da Fonseca president and another officer, Floriano Peixoto, vice president, the assembly rapidly collided with Deodoro over his financial policy and his interventions in the new state governments. In November 1891, plagued by ill health, Deodoro resigned, passing power to Floriano Peixoto, the so-called Iron Marshal. Floriano soon encountered a rash of revolts. In Rio Grande do Sul, the revolt was part of the deadly conflict between local factions; in Rio de Janeiro, it was a naval revolt led by monarchist officers. Both rebellions were crushed, as the new republic used censorship, martial law, and executions. When Prudente de Morais of São Paulo was elected in 1894 as the first civilian president, the new regime had gained stability. But it meant recognizing the legitimacy of the entrenched oligarchical regime in each state.

Who were those oligarchs? In every state a tightly organized political machine emerged. In states such as São Paulo and Minas Gerais, where the Republican Party had been strong before 1889, the "historic Republicans" controlled the state governments. In Bahia and the Northeast, which had few Republicans before 1889, power went to those politicians who most quickly established credentials as newborn Republicans. The resulting power structure was a "politics of the governors" at the national level and the "rule of the colonels" *(coronelismo)* at the local level. The colonels were rural bosses who could produce bloc votes in any election. In return, they obtained control over state and national funds in their area of influence. At the state level the political leaders used their deals with the colonels to bargain on the national level.

The chief prize was the presidency. As might be expected, the states enjoyed very unequal influence in this process. São Paulo and Minas Gerais were the most important, with Rio Grande do Sul able to tip the balance when the two larger states were at odds. Bahia, Rio de Janeiro, and Pernambuco were second-level states, often serving as power bases for dissident presidential nominees.

The constitutional decentralization allowed several states to gain virtual autonomy over their own development. Between 1890 and 1920, the state of São Paulo more than tripled its population. It had contracted a foreign debt larger than the national government and was accounting for 30 to 40 percent of Brazil's national output. Able to impose its own taxes on interstate commerce, it had achieved a remarkable self-sufficiency. Only a loose federal structure could have allowed São Paulo's extraordinary burst of economic development ("the locomotive pulling the twenty empty boxcars," said *paulista* chauvinists), later to propel Brazil's rise to world prominence in the mid-twentieth century.

Brazil's relatively smooth-running political machine ran into trouble soon after World War I. The political system created by the Republicans in the 1890s had not survived long in its original form. The first major crisis grew out of preparations for the 1910 elections. The "official" choice for president was Governor João Pinheiro of Minas Gerais, who died unexpectedly in 1908. The crisis deepened when the incumbent president, Afonso Pena, died in 1909, eighteen months before the end of his term. A bitter struggle ensued, with Marshal Hermes da Fonseca, son of the republic's first chief executive, becoming the "official" candidate. He won, but for the first time there was a significant opposition movement. It supported Rui Barbosa, the liberal crusader from Bahia.

During Hermes da Fonseca's presidency (1910–14), many of the smaller states experienced bitter battles within the political elite—usually between the incumbent machine and dissenters. These battles made it impossible to return to the smoothly functioning "politics of the governors," not least of all because President Hermes usually sent federal troops to the dissidents' aid. Formally, at least, the system continued functioning until October 1930. The "official" presidential nominees were invariably elected, and the federal Congress remained under the control of the state machines.

Yet the political culture of the Old Republic had become a target for criticism from every quarter. Prominent among the critics was a new generation of the elite, born with the republic. Most were educated as lawyers. They denounced as corrupt the way the politicians were running the republic. Most traced this to the republic's founders, whom they accused of having imposed on Brazil a liberalism for which it was utterly unprepared. Necessary changes could be found only after a careful analysis of where Brazil stood—economically, socially, politically, and intellectually. In a word, Brazilian problems need Brazilian diagnoses and Brazilian solutions. They described themselves as "Brazilians who think like Brazilians: American, Latin, and tropical." Leaders of this group included Oliveira Vianna, sociologist and lawyer; Alceu Amoroso Lima, literary critic and essayist; and Gilberto Amado, essayist and politician. Their mentor was Alberto Tôrres, a restless Republican of the older generation.

Criticism from intellectuals was paralleled by a mutinous mood among younger army officers. There was a series of barracks revolts in 1922 and 1924, led by lieutenants *(tenentes)*. The 1924 revolts, which began in São Paulo and Pôrto Alegre, were the most serious. But the rebel officers fled and held out for two and a half years as guerrillas on a 25,000 kilometer march through the interior of Brazil. It was dubbed the "Prestes Column," after Luís Carlos Prestes, a rebel lieutenant who was later to lead Brazil's Communist Party for more than thirty years.

The rebels' formal manifestos were vague, emphasizing the need for fair elections, along with attention to the nation's social needs. A more immediate complaint focused on professional concerns—anachronistic training, obsolete weapons, and poor prospects for promotion. This frustration was reminiscent of the late empire, when army officers had both professional and intellectual reasons for supporting a coup against the crown.

Another powerful political current of the 1920s was the Democratic Party, founded in São Paulo in 1926. Its leaders, typified by coffee baron Antonio Prado, agreed that the Old Republic was a fraud. Many of the party's votes came from the urban professionals, disgusted at seeing their votes canceled out by rural voters mobilized by the federal government's machine. They wanted what the European middle classes had won in the nineteenth century: political power through an electoral system. It was no accident that this current of "liberal constitutionalism" made its strongest showing in São Paulo, the center of the fastest economic growth and urbanization. It was the voice of "modern" Brazil speaking out against the disproportionate influence of their country's "backward" regions.

Economic development in the late nineteenth century had created a working class in three or four major cities. Workers' first organization came in "mutual-aid societies." They were superseded in the early 1900s by anarchist and anarcho-syndicalist organizers who were far more militant. In the decade after 1910, the anarchist and anarcho-syndicalist unions staged a variety of strikes, including several attempted general strikes. They met heavy repression. The Spanish- or Italian-born leaders were deported, while Brazilian leaders were jailed, beaten, and harassed. By 1921 the organized urban movement was a shambles.

In subsequent years, social welfare laws were passed, as a tardy carrot to accompany the omnipresent stick. But Brazilian workers had many fewer organizing rights and welfare provisions than, for example, Chilean workers in the same era. One reason was the continuous labor surplus in Brazil. In the face of such numbers, Brazilian workers found it hard to organize.

One result was the decline of anarchist and anarcho-syndicalist leadership and their replacement, in many cases, by communists, whose Brazilian party was founded in 1922. The communist presence furnished a new target for the authoritarians among civilians and military. By 1930 urban labor, although growing steadily in economic importance, was a political orphan. Meanwhile, employers saw no reason to change the autocratic manner in which they had long dealt with their workers.

Getúlio Vargas and the Estado Novo

The world economic crash of 1929 hit Brazil, like the rest of the Americas, very hard. The coffee exporters suffered a huge drop in foreign exchange earnings. Despite the crisis, President Washington Luís clung to a hard-money policy. In effect that meant guaranteeing convertibility of the Brazilian currency *(mil reis)* into gold or British sterling. The gold and sterling reserves were quickly exhausted, forcing the government to suspend convertibility of the *mil reis.* The government was left in a deepening balance-of-payments crisis, and the coffee growers were stuck with an unsellable harvest.

Given coffee's great importance to the Brazilian economy, one might have expected the government to rush in with help. Instead, it tried to please foreign creditors by maintaining convertibility. Such were the principles preached by the foreign bankers and economists. At a critical moment, the Brazilian government decided to stick with an economic policy which had no support from Brazilian society.

In addition to public distress about the economic situation, Washington Luís's own actions helped seal his downfall. His term coming to an end, he overrode the "politics of the governors" by endorsing as the "official" presidential candidate for the 1930 election a politician from São Paulo. Since Washington Luís was himself a *paulista,* this selection stimulated rising resentment from aspiring leaders in other states, who wanted their own turn in power. Getúlio Vargas, from the southern-most state of Rio Grande do Sul, mounted a campaign against the "official" candidate but was defeated. The result provoked widespread complaints about ballot stuffing by disgruntled politicians and their allies. Feelings ran so high that several state militias joined together in a march toward the national capital. Outnumbered by the joint forces now approaching Rio, the federal military decided to depose the sitting president (still Washington Luís) rather than risk an armed confrontation. They then passed power to Vargas, who had kept in close touch with the conspirators but was too cautious (some would say wily) to lead an overthrow attempt until success was completely assured.

The coup of October 1930 did not constitute a "revolution." The top military commanders simply unseated one chief executive and installed another. The cabinet invoked revolutionary power in order to take the ad hoc steps they thought necessary. Yet 1930 is a watershed in modern Brazilian history, even if it was not comparable to the Mexican Revolution of 1910–20.

When Getúlio Vargas moved into the presidential palace in November 1930, few guessed how important a leader he would become. He was there only because a conflict within the national political elite was turning into armed warfare. It never reached a climax only because the military intervened. After the senior commanders had deposed Washington Luís, some officers wanted to retain power themselves, but after only four days in power the three commanders transferred power to Vargas. Since there was no legislature, the president governed by decree. Meanwhile, important shifts were occurring among the nation's political forces.

First, Vargas moved swiftly to replace the governors in all the states except one, Minas Gerais. The replacements, or "interventors," reported directly to the president. Such activism from the central government often threw the state machines off balance and gave benefit to the dissenting factions, many of which had supported Vargas in the 1930 election. As in the Hermes da Fonseca presidency, political rivalries within states were being settled by decisions in Rio.

A second major development was a realignment of political forces in São Paulo. Vargas' interventor (João Alberto) had proved inept and tactless in handling the touchy *paulistas*. Their heightened sense of state loyalty and their fury at João Alberto united São Paulo against Vargas. Its leaders demanded that Vargas fulfill his promise to call a constituent assembly that would write a new constitution. In 1932 the *paulista* frustration finally erupted into an armed rebellion. The state militia fought federal forces to a standstill for four months in the Constitutionalist Revolution. The rebels had to surrender because they were trapped by the federal forces' encirclement of São Paulo City. The *paulistas* had further discredited the cause of decentralized government and strengthened the hand of the centralizers in Rio de Janeiro.

A third significant political development was the disintegration of the *tenente* movement. These young military officers had never achieved a cohesive organization. Some accompanied Vargas into power in 1930. Others founded the October 3rd Club to focus effort on achieving radical social changes, but their movement was isolated and vulnerable. Before long, police raided the club premises and the group disintegrated.

Meanwhile, Vargas was strengthening his own network of political allies and collaborators. His success became obvious during the constituent assembly of 1933–34. In the new constitution state autonomy was reduced: states could no longer tax goods shipped interstate. Yet it continued the bicameral legislature, which was to be directly elected, as was to be the president (except the first). Some nationalist measures appeared for the first time, placing restrictions on foreign ownership of land and on aliens' participation in professional occupations. The modest nature of these constitutional changes simply confirmed that the revolution of 1930 had grown out of elite infighting. The constituent assembly's most important act was to elect Vargas as the first president with a four-year term under the new constitution.

In 1934 Brazil entered one of the most agitated periods in its political history. Attention focused on two nationally based and highly ideological movements, both committed to mass mobilization. One was Integralism, a fast-growing rightist movement with affinities to European fascist parties. Founded in late 1932 and led by Plínio Salgado, the Integralists claimed a rapidly growing membership by 1935.

Brazilian Women Get the Vote

Brazil, like the rest of Latin America, began the twentieth century with women denied the vote. The few women who protested such discrimination were contemptuously dismissed by the male politicians who ran the government. The woman who organized their suffragette victory was Bertha Lutz, who was born in 1894 in São Paulo. Her father was Swiss-Brazilian and her mother was English, but Bertha proved to be thoroughly Brazilian.

She founded her first women's rights organization in 1920, which two years later became the Brazilian Federation of Feminine Progress. The Revolution of 1930 shook the political establishment, and the Lutz-led suffrage movement convinced the framers of the new civil code of 1932 to enfranchise women. Lutz subsequently served in Congress, pushing tirelessly for legislation to protect women's legal status and social rights. In addition to her intense activities in favor of women's rights in Brazil and abroad, Lutz was an accomplished botanist and expert in herpetology. She will be remembered as the preeminent advocate for women's rights in twentieth-century Brazil.

Their dogma was Christian, nationalist, and traditionalist. Their style was paramilitary: uniformed ranks, highly disciplined street demonstrations, colorful green shirts, and aggressive rhetoric. They were essentially middle class and drew support from military officers, especially in the navy. Unknown to the public, the Integralists were financed in part by the Italian embassy.

At the other end of the spectrum was a popular front movement, the National Liberation Alliance (Aliança Libertadora Nacional, or ALN), launched in 1935. Ostensibly a coalition of socialists, communists, and miscellaneous radicals, it was in fact run by the Brazilian Communist Party, which was carrying out a Latin American strategy formulated in Moscow. The first stage of the strategy in Brazil would be mobilization on conventional lines: rallies, local offices, and fund-raising efforts to forge a broad coalition on the left in opposition to the new Vargas government, the Integralists, and the Liberal Constitutionalists.

By mid-1935 Brazilian politics had reached a fevered pitch. The Integralists and the ALN were feeding off each other, as street brawls and terrorism increased. Brazil's major cities began to resemble the Nazi-Communist battles in Berlin of 1932–33. But the ALN was far more vulnerable than the Integralists. In July 1935 the government moved against the ALN, with troops raiding offices and jailing leaders.

The communists now moved to the second stage of their strategy: a revolutionary uprising. It was to be triggered by a barracks revolt, led by party members or sympathizers among officers in the army. The insurrection began in November 1935 in the northeastern state capital of Natal, spreading within days to Recife and Rio. From the rebel standpoint, it was a disaster. Although the Natal rebels controlled the city for several days, their comrades in Recife and Rio, who lacked the advantage of surprise, were contained in their garrisons and quickly forced to surrender.

Vargas and the military now had a perfect opportunity to revoke normal constitutional guarantees. The Congress rapidly voted it. The federal government imposed a crackdown on the entire left—with arrests, torture, and summary trials. The Integralists were elated. With their chief rival eliminated, they began to smell power. What could be more logical than for Vargas to turn to the only cohesive nationwide movement on the right?

It took two years for that illusion to be destroyed. Plínio Salgado and his collaborators were becoming more and more convinced that they would reach power by the 1938 presidential election, if not by other means. But Vargas had other ideas. On November 10, 1937, he took to the radio and read the text of yet another constitution to a nation that had just witnessed yet another military intervention. That morning the Congress had been dissolved, its premises occupied by soldiers. Brazil thus entered the Estado Novo, a legal hybrid combining elements of Salazar's Portugal and Mussolini's Italy. All the democratic hopes were gone. Brazil had succumbed to its own brand of authoritarianism.

Brazil's lurch into dictatorship in 1937 certainly fit the era. But was there more than a superficial similarity between Brazil's Estado Novo and European fascism? Where, for example, was the mass mobilization so typical of Hitler's Germany and Mussolini's Italy? Were the Integralists to play that role? Many—both inside and outside Integralist ranks—certainly thought so.

The Integralists in 1937 debated not whether they should enter government, but *on what terms*. Salgado, their leader, rejected Vargas' tentative offer of a cabinet post. Salgado thought he could hold out for more. In fact, Vargas and the military were playing their own game.

By early 1938 the greenshirts had become very frustrated. Soon after the coup, the government had banned all paramilitary organizations. The obvious target was the Integralists, some of whom decided to take matters into their own hands. In February they organized an armed assault on the presidential residence. There was a shoot-out and a standoff during the early morning hours at the palace gates. The battle ended at dawn, when army units arrested the remaining Integralist besiegers. The government cracked down and the Integralist movement in effect disappeared, as Salgado fled into exile.

Vargas could now survey a political scene that no longer offered any organized opposition. In the coup Vargas had appointed himself to another presidential term, to last until the elections, scheduled for 1943. Few took that commitment seriously, given the ease with which Vargas had aborted the election that was to have been held in 1938. That skepticism was well founded. When 1943 arrived, Vargas announced that the wartime emergency precluded elections. He remained president until October 1945.

What was the significance of Vargas' authoritarian rule from 1937 to 1945? First, Vargas and his political and technocratic collaborators got a free hand in maneuvering to maximize Brazil's advantage in a capitalist world-system moving toward war. At stake were two central and related questions about Brazil's international role. Who could best help the Brazilians to modernize and equip their armed forces? And who could offer the most favorable conditions in foreign trade?

Before the coup of 1937, Nazi Germany had offered attractive terms in both areas. Strategy and ideology were also at stake in these negotiations. The pro-German faction within Brazil, strongest in the military, was countered by a pro-U.S. faction. The latter argued that Brazil had opted for the Allies in World War I and had the most to gain by sticking with the United States. Many of the Brazilian elite therefore saw the flirtation with Nazi Germany as dangerous and short-sighted.

Meanwhile, the U.S. military and State Department were sparing no effort to pull Brazil back into the U.S.-dominated hemispheric orbit. They succeeded, but only after strenuous U.S. effort and German failure to offer the armaments Brazil wanted. From then onward Brazil became a vital cog in the Allied war machine, furnishing essential raw materials (like quartz and natural rubber) and air and naval bases that became critical in the "Battle of the Atlantic." Brazil even sent a combat division to Italy in 1944, where it fought alongside the U.S. Fifth Army.

Vargas had dealt shrewdly with the United States. In return for its raw materials and bases, Brazil got the construction of a network of air and naval installations along the northern and northeastern Atlantic coast. The United States also promised to help finance construction of Brazil's first large-scale steel mill, at Volta Redonda near Rio de Janeiro. It was the first time an American government committed public funds to industrialization in the "developing world."

The Estado Novo furnished a centralized apparatus through which Vargas and his aides could pursue economic development and organizational change. The federal government assumed an aggressive role in the economy, organizing and strengthening marketing cartels (in cocoa, coffee, sugar, and tea), and creating new state enterprises, such as the National Motor Factory (to produce trucks and airplane engines). Vargas also overhauled the federal bureaucracy, creating a merit-oriented system to replace a patronage-ridden structure. Finally, one of the most important measures was a new labor code (1943), which spelled out rules of industrial relations that were to last until the 1990s. Only one union was permitted in each plant—under the scrutiny of the labor ministry, which controlled union finances and elections. Unions were in effect tied to the government, but the union leaders who "cooperated" could profit person-ally. This semicorporatist labor union structure was paralleled by a semicorporatist structure among the employers. These arrangements gave the federal executive a mechanism for controlling the economy. But Brazil of the early 1940s was *not* a modern, industrialized, urbanized society. Outside of a few key cities, the corporatist structure left untouched most of the country, which was a vast, disconnected rural expanse.

The Estado Novo also had its darker side. The security forces had a virtual free hand. Torture was routine, against not only suspected "subversives" but also foreign agents (German businessmen were especially vulnerable). Censorship covered all the media, with a government news agency (Departamento de Imprensa e Propaganda, or DIP) furnishing the "official" version of the news. There were resemblances to Germany and Italy, but the Brazilians stopped well short of those extremes.

Brazil's economic history from 1930 to 1945 is not easy to capsulize. Coffee continued to be the primary foreign exchange earner, although helped during wartime by the boom in other raw materials shipped to the United States. Industrial growth continued in São Paulo and, to a lesser extent, in Rio. The war cut off trade with Europe, with most shifting to the United States.

Vargas had in 1943 promised elections, for which he would be ineligible. As the war continued, Vargas knew that a wave of democratic opinion was building, and he anticipated events by adopting a new, populist stance after 1943. The urban working class was now the object of government attention through such media as the nightly nationalist radio broadcast ("The Hour of Brazil"), and moves were made toward creating a Labor Party. Vargas was trying to create a new electoral image—something he had been able to neglect earlier in the Estado Novo.

Events moved rapidly in 1945. Vargas hoped to play down the contrast between the defeat of fascism in Europe and continued authoritarianism at home. In May 1945, with victory over the Axis a foregone conclusion, Vargas' government issued a tough antimonopoly decree aimed at restricting the role of foreign firms in the Brazilian economy. It was part of the turn toward populism begun in 1943. The U.S. government put Vargas on its list of Latin American presidents who had to go. There were plenty of Brazilians who shared the U.S. view. The Liberal Constitutionalists believed that foreign capital should be welcomed into Brazil. And they saw this issue as one that might help them gain the power they thought had been within their grasp in 1937.

There were other signs of Vargas' shift to the left. In early 1945 he decided to release leftist political prisoners. Most prominent was Luís Carlos Prestes, the leader of the Brazilian Communist Party who had been jailed since 1938. The relaxation of police control greatly helped the Communist Party, the best organized force on the left.

The polarization accelerated as the year went on. The anti-Vargas forces included the Liberal Constitutionalists, many military officers, and most state political bosses. On the other side were assorted populists, some labor union leaders, and the ideological left, which included socialists and communists. The confrontation climaxed in October 1945, when the army gave Vargas an ultimatum: resign or be deposed. He refused, so the military declared him deposed. Vargas then acceded and flew off to a self-imposed exile on his ranch in Rio Grande do Sul.

Samba and Carnival

Nothing is more Brazilian than the samba, the infectiously rhythmic dance and music of Afro-Brazilian origin. Samba has become synonymous with the lavish parades staged in Rio during Carnival week by the Afro-Brazilian samba "schools."

Although samba today is truly a national form of popular culture, it was not always such. In the late nineteenth century, police systematically repressed such expressions of Afro-Brazilian culture. That changed in the early twentieth century, however, as the poor black and mulatto neighborhoods in Rio de Janeiro earned popularity with their samba music. In 1935 the Getúlio Vargas government began funding samba schools as a uniquely Brazilian tourist attraction.

They succeeded, and now Rio's Carnival parade explodes each year in front of 90,000 spectators in the specially constructed "Sambadrome." Each samba school follows an elaborate theme, usually from Brazilian history. When one designer was criticized for dressing the paraders in lavish costumes, he replied, "The poor like luxuriousness. It is the intellectuals who like misery."

The Second Republic (1946–1964)

Three principal political parties emerged in 1945: the UDN (União Democrática Nacional), the PSD (Partido Social Democrático), and the PTB (Partido Trabalhista Brasileiro). The UDN was a coalition of anti-Vargas forces dominated by the Liberal Constitutionalists. The PSD was more heterogeneous; it included many political bosses and bureaucrats and some prominent industrialists. The PTB, smallest of the three, was created by Vargas in 1945, when he was still trying to shape the upcoming elections. The PTB was aimed at urban labor with a political approach supposedly modeled on the British Labour Party. These three remained Brazil's principal parties until 1964. They were often described as nonideological, personalistic, and opportunistic.

Elections for a constituent assembly had been called before Vargas' fall, and, when held in December 1945, they proved to be among the freest in Brazil's history. The newly elected president, with 55 percent of the vote, was General Eurico Dutra, a close Vargas collaborator in the Estado Novo and one of the officers in charge of the Brazilian Expeditionary Force that fought alongside the Allies in World War II. The chief opposition candidate was Air Force Brigadier Eduardo Gomes, a throwback to liberal constitutionalism. He won 35 percent of the vote. The Communist candidate received 10 percent of the vote, which greatly encouraged the left. President Dutra and his advisers began watching closely the growth of the left and its links to urban labor.

In 1946 the constituent assembly produced another constitution, one that resembled the constitution of 1934. There was decentralization and a return to the classic guarantees of individual liberty. The elections that produced the constituent assembly had highlighted some other trends. They showed that the traditional political machines could still dominate in a national vote. That was hardly surprising, since Brazil was still a mainly rural society, and electoral manipulation was easiest in the countryside. Nonetheless, the extensive Communist vote showed that new forces were at work on the urban scene.

Soon after the war, Brazil began struggling with the issue of how to finance its economic development. In wartime the objective was to maximize mobilization, but the same approach could be applied to peacetime economic development. Instead, the Dutra government (1946–51) avoided planning and returned to a reliance on coffee exports, dropping most of the measures taken by Vargas to stimulate industrialization. This policy made Brazil once again highly vulnerable to changes in the world demand for coffee.

On the political front, the Dutra regime soon decided to repress the left. The Communist Party, legalized in 1946, had shown surprising strength in São Paulo and Rio de Janeiro. Labor unions, despite the corporatist legal structure, were gaining de facto autonomy, to the worry of employers and conservative politicians. As would happen one year later in Chile, the Brazilian Congress in early 1947 voted to revoke the Communist Party's legality. Police raided its offices and seized its publications. The ministry of labor intervened in hundreds of labor unions and arrested or dismissed their officers, appointing government stooges in their place. The years 1945–47 proved to be a rerun of 1930–35: a political opening, then a burst of activism on the left, climaxed by government repression. Henceforth, the left was outlawed, and Communist Party candidates had to resort to electoral guises.

Vargas had not accepted his exit in October 1945 as the end of his career. Only two months later, he was elected senator from two states and chose to represent Rio Grande do Sul. During the Dutra presidency, Vargas worked steadily to retain national visibility and maintain his political contacts. Soon his friends and allies were urging him to run for president. He did not need much convincing.

In the presidential campaign of 1950, Vargas was supported by most of the PSD and PTB. His principal opponent was former *tenente* Juarez Távora, running under the UDN banner. Vargas conducted a shrewd campaign, attacking the Dutra regime for neglecting economic growth and for favoring the rich. Yet his position was moderate enough to appeal to the landowners in states such as Minas Gerais. Vargas won by a plurality (48.7 percent) and began his third presidency—the only one he gained by popular election.

In returning to power by popular vote, Vargas reversed the victory that his opponents, especially the Liberal Constitutionalists, had won in 1945. They exploded, some even calling for the army to block the return of the ex-dictator. But it was to no avail.

Vargas made economic policy his top priority, and he promptly assembled a team of young technocrats—engineers, economists, and planners. They formulated an eclectic strategy designed to maximize the inflow of capital and technology from both public and private sources abroad. The prospects looked favorable. In 1949 the U.S. and Brazilian governments had launched a joint study of the Brazilian economy. The commission's report in 1953 spotlighted inadequate energy and poor transportation as the prime obstacles to rapid economic development. The U.S. government indicated interest in channeling public funds for investment in these areas, and the Brazilian government created new federal agencies to handle the investment projects now in prospect.

Vargas' economic strategy also had its nationalist side. Profit remissions by foreign-owned firms were a frequent target for nationalist attack. In 1952 Vargas denounced the foreign firms and threatened new controls.

Another target for the nationalists was oil. Since the late 1930s Brazil had been working on a national oil policy. Argentina and Mexico had already opted for state monopolies. Throughout Latin America, international oil companies were regarded with strong suspicion. Brazil was no different. In 1951 Vargas proposed a mixed public-private corporation (to be called Petrobras) that would monopolize the exploration and production of oil.

The proposal touched off the most heated political debate since 1945. Nationalism proved very strong, especially among army officers. Bitter controversies arose, with state monopoly advocates questioning the patriotism of free enterprise supporters, and vice versa. In 1953 the Congress created an even stronger monopoly than proposed by Vargas. The debate had sharply polarized opinion, reducing the room for political maneuver.

Vargas had been elected in 1950 on a moderate platform, and the party lineup in Congress required him to maintain that course. But economic pressures were forcing hard choices on the government. First, Brazil's rate of inflation turned up from 11 percent in 1951 to 20 percent in 1952. Second, the foreign trade balance went into the red. Third, the U.S. president elected in 1952, Dwight Eisenhower, threw into doubt the loan commitments the Brazilians thought the United States had made for the infrastructural investments.

These reverses gave ammunition to Vargas' enemies on both the left and the right. The left charged Vargas with selling out to the imperialists. The right, on the other hand, charged that Vargas was alienating the trading partners and foreign creditors on whom Brazil had to depend. Most politically conscious Brazilians fell between these extremes. Yet economic and political pressures were making moderation more difficult, spelling danger for Vargas and his government.

In 1953 Vargas reorganized his cabinet to face the economic crisis. Inflation and the balance-of-payments deficit were related problems because Brazil had clung to an overvalued exchange rate which, combined with Brazilian inflation, had made imports cheaper and exports more expensive. An economic stabilization program was urgently needed. In the short run, that would mean falling real wages and strict controls on business credit and government spending. Such a policy was bound to be unpopular.

To lead the effort Vargas recruited Oswaldo de Aranha, his longtime political lieutenant, as minister of finance. Aranha pursued classic stabilization measures with apparent success in 1953. As 1954 approached, however, a bitter fight loomed over wage policy. Under the Estado Novo the ministry of labor fixed the minimum wage, which had not been increased for many years. Aranha's objective was to prevent an increase so large as to wreck the anti-inflation program. For this Aranha would have to deal with the minister of labor: João Goulart, a young PTB politician closely identified with the PTB left and the militant labor leadership.

By 1954 Aranha was pulling toward austerity and Goulart toward a populist, redistributionist path. Vargas had to decide the issue. In February, apparently opting for Aranha's austerity, he dismissed Goulart. The left, strengthened by its success in the fight over oil policy, now attacked Vargas for pandering to the imperialists with his stabilization program. Vargas cleared the air on May 1, 1954, when he announced a 100 percent increase in the minimum wage—higher even than Goulart had recommended.

This battle now merged into a wider political crisis. Vargas' bitterest enemies had found an issue on which they thought they could beat him: corruption. The anti-Vargas propagandists closed in on the weary president. Unbeknownst to him, the palace security chief had arranged an assassination attempt on Carlos Lacerda, a sensationalizing journalist who was leading the attack on Vargas. The bullet meant for Lacerda killed an air force officer who was a volunteer body-guard for Lacerda. The officer's death brought the military into the crisis. When their investigation pointed to the presidential palace, the senior officers demanded Vargas' resignation. Realizing he was trapped and isolated, Vargas put a bullet through his heart on August 24. He left behind an inflammatory suicide letter, blaming his demise on sinister forces, domestic and foreign, and proclaiming a highly nationalist position. By his sensational exit, Vargas exacted revenge on his tormentors. Lacerda had to flee Brazil, and the anti-Vargas factions, especially among the UDN and the military, found themselves on the defensive.

Caretaker regimes governed Brazil until the 1956 inauguration of Juscelino Kubitschek, elected to a full presidential term in 1955. He was an ebullient PSD politician and former governor of Minas Gerais with a reputation as a skillful campaigner. Although he won the presidency with only 36 percent of the vote, he quickly moved to gain broader support.

Mindful of how often the military had intervened in politics, Kubitschek mollified them with large weapons purchases. Kubitschek also had an effective PSD-PTB coalition in the Congress. The "Target Program" of economic develop-ment, plus the audacious idea of building a new capital, Brasília, in the interior, combined to generate enthusiasm which muffled the bitter political conflicts from the mid-1950s. No small part of Kubitschek's political success was due to his own talents. Kubitschek's motto had been "fifty years of progress in five," and the economic leap forward was impressive.

Yet it would have been too much to expect Kubitschek's political strategy to endure forever. The PSD-PTB alliance in Congress was coming apart, discord was growing among military officers, and the economy had once again run into inflation and balance-of-payments deficits. Kubitschek briefly tried economic stabilization in 1958–59, but scuttled it when the IMF demanded austerity mea-sures that would have prevented Brazil from reaching the president's economic "targets." Kubitschek pressed on with his economic program, and that created mammoth problems for his successor. When he left office in January 1961, no one doubted that a reckoning with foreign creditors was at hand.

The president who inherited this challenge was Jânio Quadros, one of Brazil's most talented and most flawed politicians. A whirlwind success, first as mayor of the city of São Paulo and then as governor of the state, Quadros won big in the 1960 presidential election, running with UDN endorsement. His campaign featured a broom as the symbol of his fight against corruption. That talk buoyed the Liberal Constitutionalists, who believed that at last power was near.

Quadros began by embracing a tough stabilization program. After seven months of idiosyncratic rule, however, Quadros suddenly resigned in August 1961. His reasons have never been entirely explained—apparently he expected the Congress to reject his resignation and offer him increased powers. He was wrong; the Congress promptly accepted his resignation. Quadros, the most charismatic populist politician of modern Brazil, faded into retirement. (He returned to public office as mayor of São Paulo from 1985 to 1988.)

Quadros' self-engineered demise was demoralizing for the anti-Vargas factions and other Brazilians who believed that his moralistic promises and his administrative success in São Paulo boded well for the new federal government. Worst of all from the UDN viewpoint, Quadros' departure meant that power would now pass to the elected vice president—Vargas' former labor minister, João Goulart, the epitome of populism and anathema to the conservative military.

The military was in no mood to agree to Goulart's succession to the presidency. But the "legalists" among the officers argued in favor of observing the constitution. A compromise was reached. The Congress created a parliamentary system in which Goulart was president but with a cabinet accountable to the Congress. It was an unworkable hybrid, designed solely to reduce Goulart's power. The new president assumed his diminished powers in September 1961 and promptly started a campaign to get the parliamentary innovation repealed. January 1963 brought success when a plebiscite restored the full presidential system. By then Goulart had precious little time left from the 1961–66 presidential term.

Goulart's presidency proved ill-starred from the beginning, compounded by his inexperience, weakness, and indecision. By 1963 inflation and the balance-of-payments deficit had grown even more difficult to deal with. Goulart chose his own stabilization team, headed by the brilliant intellectual-politician Santiago Dantas and the noted economist Celso Furtado. Dantas worked out a detailed plan, duly negotiated with the U.S. government and the International Monetary Fund. It called for the usual: reduction of government deficit, tough controls on wages, and painful reductions in credit. It was the same medicine that had been served up in the stabilization efforts of 1953–54, 1955–56, 1958–59, and 1961.

For Goulart, stabilization presented special problems. A tough wage policy, which always meant falling real wages, would strike at the social group to which

Goulart was most committed. Furthermore, meeting the harsh terms of foreign lenders would invite attack from the nationalists, another area of his prime support. Even if he could bring off stabilization, his term would probably end before Brazil could resume rapid growth.

Notwithstanding the gloomy prospects, Goulart endorsed the Dantas-Furtado plan. But he did not stay with it for long. In a few months Dantas quietly resigned, Furtado had already left Brasília, and any further serious stabilization effort was thereafter out of the question.

Stabilization was not Goulart's only worry. Since 1961 the Brazilian political scene had been heating up on both left and right. The military, as always, was a key factor. Some of the officers who had fought Goulart's accession to power in 1961 were still fighting. They had begun an ongoing conspiracy to overthrow Goulart. Many of the ideas and personnel of the conspiracy could be traced to the 1954 military cabal against Vargas. What steadily increased the strength of the conspirators was the increasingly radical tone of the political combatants.

The left of the political spectrum had become very crowded. A rising sense of confidence had gripped the radical nationalists, who included Catholic literacy teachers, labor union militants, Trotskyist student organizers, and artistic idealists, all spreading a revolutionary message through popular culture. By early 1964 the radical left had gained government blessing, sometimes even government financing and logistical support.

Conservatives were incensed over nationalist inroads among two groups. One was the military. Brazilian enlisted men had traditionally not been allowed to vote. The radicals began to advocate unionization of enlisted men. This scandalized the officers, who were hardly about to learn collective bargaining. Even politically centrist officers could understand that threat.

The other new area of mobilization was the countryside. In 1963 rural unionization was legalized, and competing groups, including several on the left, vied to win sponsorship of local syndicates. Yet the rural sector was an unpromising arena for the Brazilian left to test its power. There was always excess labor, and landowners traditionally ruled with an iron hand. This rural unionization campaign, combined with a few land invasions, provoked landowners to take decisive action. They pressured the pro-landowner politicians, who were numerous in a federal Congress which overrepresented rural districts.

Goulart's opponents did not have the votes to impeach him. The old PSD-PTB alliance still operated. It might not back a stabilization program, but it was also not ready to serve the anti-Goulart conspirators. The plotters saw only one way out: a military coup.

The president's military advisers had warned him about the conspiracy. Now even centrist officers were leaning toward a coup. The principal factor pushing them was the radical move to the left already under way, either by the president or by those who controlled him.

The U.S. government was taking a strong interest in Brazil's emerging political confrontation. Both the U.S. ambassador, Lincoln Gordon, and the U.S. military attaché, General Vernon Walters, were in close touch with the conspirators, both military and civilian. The United States had a contingency plan known as Operation Brother Sam to support the anti-Goulart rebels with fuel and weapons, if needed. As it happened, they were not. On March 31, speculation ended as a military revolt, surfacing first in Minas Gerais, spread across the country. Within twenty-four hours, João Goulart had fled into exile in Uruguay.

On April 1 the leader of the Congress, in Goulart's absence, declared the presidency vacant. Although his action lacked any legal foundation, the Congress acceded. Into the power vacuum moved the military conspirators and their civilian allies. Brazilian leaders once again opted for the authoritarian path to development.

In retrospect, the breakdown of Brazilian democracy bore a close connection to the interplay of social-class relations. The populist policies of Getúlio Vargas had created institutions for organizing urban workers. This posed a significant but ultimately acceptable challenge to the upper and middle classes, the latter represented largely by the military. But in 1964 Goulart presented, or appeared to present, a much more fundamental threat. By mobilizing peasants as well as workers, and by using radical rhetoric, he seemed to be creating the conditions for a *classwide* worker-peasant alliance against the socioeconomic establishment. Both the suddenness and the simultaneity of these movements startled and alarmed elites. The radicalization of Brazil's lower classes was simply not acceptable. The military exercised its long-standing veto power and went on to create a bureaucratic-authoritarian regime.

The Battle for Brazilian Souls

In no Latin American country has the competition between Protestants and Catholics been more intense than in Brazil, long known as the world's most populous Catholic country. Since 1960, aggressive Protestant evangelicals have made significant inroads among Brazilian worshipers. During the 1990s, the number of Protestants doubled, while the proportion of Catholics declined by 10 percentage points. One Protestant church has built up a media empire of ninety-four television stations.

Vatican authorities have expressed considerable alarm at these developments, and the pope has appealed to Brazil's younger generation of priests to take up the challenge and regain lost ground. A dramatic answer has come from Father Marcelo Rossi, a charismatic priest in his forties who has attracted huge crowds with his media-savvy preaching. His CDs have become runaway best-sellers, and he played the Angel Gabriel in the 2003 film *Maria: The Mother of the Son of God*. Addressing the faithful of Brazil, the priest has solemnly declared: "Many say they are Catholic but aren't, may this movie save them." The battle has been joined.

Military Rule

The conspirators of 1964 were surprised at the speed with which the Goulart government collapsed. Goulart's zigzagging and the divisiveness within the left had undercut any effective mass support. The rebels encountered little or no resistance as their troops seized command of the government.

From 1964 to 1985 Brazil was governed by a succession of authoritarian governments, each headed by a four-star general. Despite variations in structure and personnel, all were coalitions of military officers, technocratic administrators, and old-line politicians. They retained some vestiges of formal democracy, such as congressional elections, but every time the oppositional forces seemed to threaten their hold on the state, they changed the rules of the game to stay in power.

The most important group was the military. Army officers have had a long history of intervention in Brazilian politics since the empire was brought down. In 1930 the military ended the Old Republic by delivering power to Vargas, whom they kept in power by the coup of 1937, only to depose him in 1945. It was a military manifesto that led to Vargas' suicide in 1954, and it was a "preventive" coup in 1955 that ensured Kubitschek's succession to the presidency. Finally, the military led the fight against Goulart's succession to the presidency in 1961 and then conspired to bring him down in 1964. Army officers had become vital actors in Brazilian politics.

After 1945 conflicting political currents buffeted the army officer corps. The 1950s brought a polarization between nationalist and anticommunist positions. The anticommunists identified with the United States in the deepening Cold War and saw the nationalist left as a stalking-horse for pro-Castroites or communists.

Officer opinion turned decisively against the populists, of whom Goulart was a principal example. The Goulart government's inability to get control of the economy (Brazil was in near default to foreign creditors in March 1964), the mobilization of the lower sectors, and the direct threat to military hierarchy all pushed centrist military officers toward supporting a coup. By early 1964 the conspiracy was headed by General Humberto Castello Branco, the army chief of staff who had supported Goulart's succession to the presidency in 1961.

Once the military deposed Goulart, a new question faced the conspirators: the form and direction of the new government. One of the generals' first moves was to issue an extra-constitutional Institutional Act (the first of many with that title). It gave the Brazilian executive extraordinary and exclusive powers to adopt constitutional amendments, propose expenditure bills to Congress, and suppress the political rights of any citizen for ten years. With new authoritarian powers in place, different currents within the military debated the course of the new government. The hard-liners argued that Brazilian democracy had been corrupted by self-seeking and subversive politicians. The country needed a long recuperation, which would require such measures as purging legislators, suppressing direct elections, and firing civil servants. The hard-liners' economic views were less easy to discern. The moderate military composed another group. They believed a relatively brief interval of administrative and economic reorganization could return Brazil to the electoral democracy recently endangered by irresponsible politicians.

General Castello Branco (1964–67) was quickly chosen by the (purged) Congress as the new president. The immediate need was to bring inflation under control and to improve the balance of payments. Roberto Campos, a well-known economist-diplomat, was made planning minister and became the dominant figure in economic policymaking. The government reduced inflation and established surpluses in the foreign accounts. Campos' team also attempted to reorganize and update Brazil's principal economic institutions. The government overhauled the banking system (a proper central bank was finally created), institutionalized a stock market and a government securities market for the first time, revised labor regulations to make easier the discharge of employees, and simplified export regulations. Campos had long argued that capitalism had not failed in Brazil because it hadn't yet been tried. This was his chance. The short-term results were disappointing, but Castello Branco and Campos did not despair; they saw their efforts as indispensable for sound growth in the future.

The U.S. government gave its unconditional support to the new military regime. In part this stemmed from a tradition of close relations between the two countries that started at the beginning of the twentieth century. This "unwritten alliance," as it was called by some, was based on close military, economic, and political connections. Washington policymakers quickly recognized the new republic in 1889. During World War I, Brazil joined the United States in declaring war on Germany. Brazil sent troops to fight alongside the Allies in Italy during World War II. When the Cold War started, most Brazilian presidents sided with the United States. Starting in 1962, U.S. ambassador Lincoln Gordon kept in close touch with the conspirators that overthrew the Goulart government. Thus, it was no surprise that President Johnson immediately supported the new military regime. The United States authorized loans and other financial aid packages to help the fledgling economy. It stepped up the Alliance for Progress program that brought technicians, Peace Corps volunteers, and other resources into the country. The U.S. government increased training of military officers and the police apparatus. Brazil was the recipient of Washington's second-largest foreign aid program in the world. Anticommunist sentiment and the long-standing unwritten alliance closely bound the U.S. government to the authoritarian regime.

On the political front, Castello Branco confronted many challenges. In October 1965 gubernatorial elections, the government's handpicked candidates in the important states of Minas Gerais and Guanabara (greater Rio de Janeiro) lost to moderate opposition candidates. In response, Castello Branco issued Institutional Act No. 2 that abolished the old political parties and established a pro-government party (ARENA) and a new weakened opposition party (Brazilian Democratic Movement, MDB). The decree also made the elections of president, vice president, and all governors indirect.

Castello Branco faced other problems as well. A hoped-for economic upturn did not occur in 1965–66, so he was persuaded to extend his presidential term a year in the hope that the economy would improve. In fact, the country's economic problems could not be resolved even in his two and a half years in office. By this time it was becoming apparent that the military did not intend to leave power so quickly. In fact, the supposedly moderate Castello Branco institutionalized the authoritarian regime through a National Security Law, expanded powers to censor the press and the indirect election of the mayors of major cities. He also oversaw the writing of a new constitution that codified the authoritarian measures of the military regime.

The second military government of President Artur da Costa e Silva (1967–69) brought an even uglier turn. Soon after coming to office, the president stated that he hoped to preside over a liberalization, but events proved otherwise. Until 1967 the authoritarian government had shown considerable tolerance for the opposition, at least in comparison to Spanish American military governments of the 1960s and 1970s. But tolerance invited mobilization. In 1967 and 1968 the opposition, headed by students, mounted a series of protests, climaxing in mass demonstrations in Rio de Janeiro that were sparked by the police's killing of a young student. Protests quickly took on national dimensions.

The hard-line military, now opposing any compromise between democracy and a "tough" government, argued for a crackdown. In mid-1968 a series of industrial strikes spread from Minas Gerais into the industrial heartland of São Paulo. The Costa e Silva government hesitated, then reacted by strongly repressing the strikers. A pattern was set: an authoritarian government resorting to dictatorial measures to carry out its version of rapid economic development. It was a growth strategy based on repression of labor unions, avid recruiting of foreign investment, and high rewards for economic managers.

The military also decided to disband all student activist organizations. In October, the army surrounded a clandestine convention of the National Union of Students and arrested more than 700 activists and leaders. Protests in the halls of Congress against the escalating wave of repression against students and other oppositionists, as well as reports of torture, led to a showdown between President Costa e Silva and the legislative branch. When a majority of federal legislators refused to lift the congressional immunity of two of its members who had criticized the military, the government issued Institutional Act No. 5. On December 13, 1968, the ruling generals shut down Congress, suspended habeas corpus, extended the powers of the military to censor the press, and curtailed democratic rights. This marked the beginning of the most repressive years of military rule, when torture as a means to extract information from opponents of the regime and to strike fear among those who dared challenge the dictatorship became widespread.

In 1969 Brazil was hit with new levels of political violence. The militant student-based opposition had produced a guerrilla network, mainly in the cities. In September 1969, President Costa e Silva suffered a debilitating stroke. At the same time, two guerrilla organizations kidnapped the U.S. ambassador, whom they subsequently freed, in return for the government's releasing from prison fifteen political prisoners and the publishing of a revolutionary manifesto in all the media. For the next four years, Brazil experienced guerrilla warfare. A small cadre of revolutionary activists kidnapped foreign diplomats, holding them hostage to ransom other revolutionaries in prison, and attempted to set up rural guerrilla activities.

General Emílio Médici (1969–73), who succeeded Costa e Silva, oversaw a sharp growth in the economy and an upsurge in nationalism. After 1967 the Brazilian economy returned to a growth path, duplicating the record of the 1950s. From 1968 to 1974 the growth rate averaged 10 percent, and exports more than quadrupled. As though to mark the end of an era, manufactured goods replaced coffee as the country's leading export product. Outside observers talked of the "Brazilian miracle." Pride in the country also engendered support for the military regime. The nation broke out in exuberant celebrations when Brazil won the world soccer championship for the third time in 1970. The government initiated road construction in the Amazon and other major public works projects. Optimism and a booming economy strengthened Médici's rule.

From Liberalization to Redemocratization

By 1973 the guerrilla movements were vanquished. They had exhausted their human resources to achieve meager results. In fact, they had reinforced the repressive apparatus and made credible the hard-liners' argument that any political opening meant civil war.

When General Ernesto Geisel (1974–79) assumed the presidency, he repeated earlier promises for a return to democracy and the rule of law. A major obstacle was the security apparatus, which had gained great influence within the government. Their unsavory methods, including torture, had facilitated the liquidation of the revolutionary opposition, but had given them a powerful veto over liberalization.

Geisel's commitment to redemocratization came from his close personal link to the legalist tradition of Castello Branco. Geisel saw this process not as a response to pressure, but as the working out of a democratic commitment inherent in the military intervention in 1964.

The fundamental problem for Geisel, as for all the preceding military governments, was the inability to win a free popular election. This would not have mattered if the military had not taken the democratic rules so seriously. But they did, and the result was an endless series of improvisations and political manipulations to make the voting results fit their preferences. The depth of the problem was shown in October 1974 when the new government, in contrast to its predecessor, allowed relatively free congressional elections. The result was a landslide for the opposition party. The lesson was clear: if given a choice, the public, especially in the urban industrialized centers, would vote against the government.

The Geisel government faced serious economic problems as well. Brazil had few oil reserves, and the sharp hike in petroleum prices in 1974 forced the government to pay significantly higher prices for imports, which fueled inflation. By 1980 inflation was more than 100 percent, the foreign debt mounted, and industrial production sagged. Furthermore, industrial labor had bestirred itself in

São Paulo, staging a series of strikes in 1978, 1979, and 1980, led by the charismatic union leader Luiz Inácio "Lula" da Silva, against government wage policies. The church, in the person of Cardinal Arns, supported the strikers and helped dramatize the disproportionate share of the sacrifice they had borne during the "miracle."

The Brazilian military also faced tensions in its historic alliance with the United States during the administration of Jimmy Carter (1977–81). Brazil refused to sign the Nuclear Non-proliferation Treaty, which caused a rift between the two countries. Relations became worse when Brazil turned from the United States to Germany for technology to build nuclear reactors. The issue of human rights also provoked differences between Brasília and Washington. An international campaign had successfully called attention to the regime's use of torture on political prisoners and had badly damaged its image abroad. President Carter's 1978 visit to Brazil emphasized that Washington policymakers would not offer unconditional support to a regime that tortured its citizens. Although a break between the two countries did not take place, the "unwritten alliance" that had been forged at the beginning of the twentieth century weakened.

Before leaving office in 1979, Geisel lifted the ban on all exiled oppositional figures, allowing them to return to Brazil. His successor, General João Figueiredo (1979–85), signed an amnesty bill that freed most political prisioners and dropped the charges against many political dissidents. It also granted amnesty to those government officials involved in the torture of detainees. In an attempt to divide a mounting unified opposition to the dictatorship, the government abolished the two political parties and allowed new ones to be formed. It was a divide-and-conquer strategy. The government backed the PSD (Social Democratic Party). A majority of the opposition formed the PMDB (Brazilian Democratic Movement Party). Among the new parties set up was the Workers Party, led by Lula, the leader of the 1978–80 strike wave.

In 1982 Planning Minister Delfim Neto and his fellow policymakers hoped to engineer an economic recovery, an issue all the more pressing since it was to be an election year. These hopes were soon dashed by the world recession, which depressed the value of Brazilian exports. At the same time, high interest rates kept the cost of servicing the foreign debt at a crippling level. By the end of 1982, Brazil gained the dubious honor of having the largest foreign debt in the world ($87 billion) and, like Argentina and Mexico, had to suspend payments on principal. To get the essential "bridging loans" to meet immediate obligations, Brazil agreed to an IMF-architected economic plan that involved a brutal reduction of imports in order to earn a trade surplus.

In the midst of a severe economic crisis, for the first time since 1965, Brazil directly elected all its state governors in November 1982. The opposition Party of the Brazilian Democratic Movement (PMDB) won a smashing victory in the most developed states, winning the governorships of São Paulo, Rio de Janeiro, and Minas Gerais. The Workers Party made only a modest showing in its first electoral effort. The new government party, the PSD, lost control of the Chamber of Deputies, but retained control of the electoral college, which would choose the new president in 1985 through indirect balloting.

In 1983 massive mobilizations throughout the country demanded that the Congress pass a law restoring direct presidential elections. Millions took to the streets demanding *direita já* ("direct elections now"). They failed to win a congressional majority to change the law, and so the indirect presidential selection process took place in a very Brazilian way. The main opposition party (PMDB) candidate was Tancredo Neves, a skillful, old-style politician from Minas Gerais. He shrewdly began his campaign for the presidency by reassuring the military of his moderation. Meanwhile, Paulo Maluf, the government party (PSD) candidate, alienated his party by his heavy-handed campaign. Enough PSD electoral college delegates defected to elect Tancredo.

Tancredo did not live to fulfill the great hopes the public had in him. On the eve of his inauguration, he underwent emergency intestinal surgery from which he never recovered. Former senator José Sarney, the vice president elect, became president. Ironically, Brazil's first civilian president in twenty-one years was a previous PSD leader and former pillar of the military regime.

The best that could be said of the Sarney presidency was that the military remained on the sidelines and the president was committed to redemocratization. The new government implemented a stabilization program (the Cruzado Plan) that imposed a wage-price freeze and drastically reduced Brazil's inflation rate from its 1985 high of 227 percent. The initial success of the program enabled Sarney's backers to coast to a huge victory in the November 1986 elections. But stabilization did not hold. Inflation exploded again in early 1987. Sarney's popularity sank precipitously, and by the end of that year, his electoral victory had turned to ashes. The scene was now set for some new leader, capable of bringing new solutions to Brazil's pressing problems.

The new face was Fernando Collor de Mello, a young and previously unknown former governor of the poor northeastern state of Alagoas. He mounted a lavishly financed television-based campaign aimed at the more than three-quarters of Brazilian homes with TVs. His chief opponent in the 1989 campaign was the former labor union leader Luiz Inácio "Lula" da Silva. Collor won in a runoff, although Lula's percentage of the vote (47 percent) had reached a level unprecedented for the left.

By mid-1991, after fifteen months in office, Collor proved a bitter disappointment. He had begun, à la Jânio Quadros, with a highly autocratic style and a personal arrogance ill-suited to Brazilian politics.

Collor chose to bet on economic stabilization. Unfortunately, his program relied on such short-term gimmicks as the freezing of financial assets and the immediate abolition of indexation. Both proved ineffective after only a few months. By early 1991 the stabilization plan had come apart. Inflation hit an annual rate of 1585 percent, fiscal control was lost, and indexation was back. The Brazilian economy returned to its pattern of drift, discouraging foreign and domestic investors alike.

Collor had also begun an ambitious program of neoliberal reforms. It included privatization, deregulation, and opening of the economy through lower tariffs. Many of these proposals aroused strong opposition from industrialists and from nationalists in the Congress. The government's single victory in this sphere was the sale of a major state-owned steel mill, which greatly increased its profits and productivity once in private hands.

Collor failed to see any of his programs through. In little more than two years, he lost his mandate. His nemesis proved to be the specter he had campaigned against in 1989: corruption. Investigative reporters, a disgruntled presidential brother, and a congressional inquiry furnished proof that Collor was enmeshed in a vast web of bribery. Collor turned to television for his defense weapon, but his telegenic skills had worn thin. Public indignation led to a civil campaign for the president's impeachment and removal. In September 1992 the Chamber of Deputies overwhelmingly voted his impeachment, and Collor resigned only hours before the Senate approved his conviction on grounds of official malfeasance.

The vice president who succeeded him was Itamar Franco, a former senator and political nonentity whose personal honesty was his greatest recommendation. But his government, which lacked any party base, also lacked political direction. Inflation soared to an annual rate of 2490 percent in 1993. By hemispheric consensus, Brazil was regarded as the sick man of South America.

THE CONTEMPORARY SCENE (1994–PRESENT)

The government finally found an anchor when Fernando Henrique Cardoso became finance minister in late 1993. His talented technocrats launched yet another anti-inflation program. But this one, far better conceived than its predecessors, brought inflation under control.

Cardoso capitalized on this success and the resulting mood of confidence to run for president in October 1994. Overcoming his past reputation as a leftist intellectual, Cardoso, a former senator from the Brazilian Social Democratic Party (PSDB), won the endorsement of the conservative party. Without a significant right-wing candidate in the fray, Cardoso won 54 percent of the vote, easily defeating Lula, again the runner-up. Taking office in 1995, Cardoso took advantage of public confidence, buoyed by his stabilization success and Brazil's unprecedented fourth World Soccer Championship the previous year. Initially, Cardoso's luck held: the *real* remained stable, and the privatization program, notably stalled under Itamar Franco, picked up steam. The public-sector deficit remained unsolved, hardly surprising, given the nature of Cardoso's governing coalition and the built-in barriers to trimming government employees.

With the specter of hyperinflation gone, many poorer Brazilians could, for a year or two, now buy the consumer durables previously available only to the wealthy and the middle class. For much of the country, however, the familiar social problems remained: hunger, illiteracy, and ill health. In the mid-1990s, police massacres of peasant squatters dramatized the problems of landlessness, but they also helped provoke the government into an accelerated land-distribution program in Brazil. Unlike the rest of Latin America, Brazil had reserves of uncultivated state-owned land it could distribute. The government's failure to provide accompanying services (credit, transport, and the like), however, left new landowners unable to become economically viable. Despite his inability to achieve substantial growth, Cardoso retained public support through his first two years. In mid-1997 he even managed, at considerable political cost, to push through a constitutional amendment allowing him to run for reelection.

The next year, Cardoso's luck began to change. A world financial crisis, which began in Asia, hit Russia and then Brazil. Cardoso's economic managers responded by raising interest rates and increasing taxes, stubbornly battling to save the overvalued *real*. Capital flight surged as the government lost $1.6 billion in foreign exchange reserves per day during the first two weeks in September.

Such was the climate when Brazilians went to the polls in October 1998 that Cardoso, whose campaign managers did their best to divert attention from the worsening financial crisis, was reelected with 53 percent of the vote, with Lula trailing once again. Unlike 1994, however, Cardoso's victory did not reflect voter confidence, but rather a fear that there was no alternative to Cardoso's orthodox economic policies.

Following his victory, Cardoso was under heavy pressure from the International Monetary Fund to make broad cuts in public spending and new hikes in taxes and interest rates, which he dutifully did. In November, Brazil received $41.5 billion in credits from the U.S. government and international agencies. Capital flight slowed, but at the cost of economic growth (less than 1 percent in 1998). Cardoso and his finance minister, Pedro Malan, gained a reputation for following to the letter the demands of their foreign creditors, especially the IMF.

Economic crisis continued in the new year. Capital flight in early January accelerated to $6 billion. When a "controlled" devaluation of 8 percent failed, the Central Bank finally decided to float the *real*. Brazil's currency lost more than 40 percent against the dollar, although it soon stabilized at 25 percent.

The remainder of Cardoso's second term was spent desperately avoiding a default on the foreign debt. A modest push to strengthen elementary education, notoriously neglected by previous governments, was otherwise the most notable social gain. The highly fragmented party system—the result of very permissive electoral laws—made difficult the passage of controversial laws, such as tax or pension reform. Such fiscal reform was needed because Brazil's tax burden had risen to 40 percent of the GDP, one of the world's highest levels, and the public pension system was running a current annual deficit of over $20 billion.

The Cardoso economic record was mixed. A stubborn adherence to an overvalued currency had led to a speculative crisis in 1998–99, which climaxed in a 20 percent devaluation. The preceding overvaluation discouraged exports and led to the loss of half of Brazil's foreign exchange reserves. The next president would face a huge foreign debt and the threat of new speculative attacks on Brazil's currency. However, Cardoso could be justly proud that democratic procedures were scrupulously observed throughout his presidency, despite widespread skepticism about the stability of civilian government generally, further distancing Brazil from its still recent authoritarian past.

Brazil's First Working-Class President

The three principal candidates for president in the 2002 elections were José Serra, supported by the Cardoso government; Lula, of the Workers Party; and Ciro Gomes, a populist candidate from the Northeast. The campaign was marred by near panic in the financial markets. The cause was speculators' reaction to Lula's early lead in the polls. Lula was the ex-machinist and union leader who had helped found the leftist Workers Party during the military rule and who had run unsuccessfully for president three times. As the election approached in late 2002, Lula had striven in this campaign to appear moderate, gathering the backing of banking and industry leaders.

Lula won the final vote (there was a runoff against his principal opponent, Cardoso's health minister, José Serra) by an impressive margin. The millions of PT faithful who had fought for the return of democracy could at last taste victory. Brazil now had its first genuinely working-class president. The new president astounded all by choosing orthodox figures for key economic policy positions, such as the finance minister and the director of the Central Bank. International financial circles reacted warmly to Lula's moderate start. Foreign bankers upgraded Brazil's credit ranking, and the government achieved a satisfactory

Lula exerts a magnetic effect on crowds. Here he greets well-wishers during celebrations for International Women's Day (March 8, 2004). (Evaristo SA/AFP/Getty Images.)

primary budget surplus in the first two years, as required by the International Monetary Fund. Brazil exceeded its third-year target and paid off its IMF debt in full by 2005, two years ahead of schedule. The new government also continued monetary policies of the previous administration to restrain inflationary trends. Favorable export earnings of agricultural goods also strengthened the economy, as Brazil became the second largest soybean exporter in the world and ethanol production from sugarcane expanded significantly.

As part of a poverty reduction plan, the Lula government also stepped up efforts initiated under the Cardoso administration to benefit the poor. The new program, named Bolsa Família (Family Grant), gives direct transfers of small funds (about thirty-five dollars a month) to low-income families who commit to keeping their children in school and taking them to regular health checkups. It started off under-funded and burdened by poor administration and chaotic coordination with other government welfare programs, but now reaches 11 million families and more than 46 million people, a major portion of the country's low-income population.

This new program made the Lula administration extremely popular, especially among the impoverished sectors of the Northeast and other areas of the country where there remains a significant gap between the rich and the poor.

Overcoming Racial Disparities

Over the course of 350 years, slave traders brought four times as many Africans to Brazil than to the United States. Today Brazil has the largest Afro-descendant population in the Americas. Throughout the colonial and national periods, there has been considerable racial mixture; at least one-half of the population has some African ancestry.

Yet a racial hierarchy persists, and the darker one's skin, the lower one is likely to be on the socioeconomic scale. During the 1970s, a new dynamic black consciousness movement reaffirmed Brazil's African cultural roots and demanded that the society address long-standing patterns of racial inequality. In the 1980s, Governor Leonel Brizola of the state of Rio de Janeiro appointed Afro-Brazilians to important government posts. During the Cardoso administration, the federal government began to discuss measures that could overcome the palpable gaps between those of European descent and those of African or mixed racial ancestry.

In May 2003, President Lula appointed Joaquim Barbosa Gomes, a prominent Afro-Brazilian lawyer, to the Supreme Court. The highest court in the land was no longer a bastion of white political dominance. In recent years, a debate has ensued about the best ways to address entrenched vestiges of racial inequality through affirmative action programs and other initiatives to ensure more open access to higher education and employment. As Supreme Court Justice Barbosa Gomes observed about the society in which he grew up, "Racial issues were taboo. Brazilian society had a false ideology that this was a racial paradise." The nation, however, is now confronting this issue.

Greater investment in higher education also won backing by sectors of the middle class. The left wing of the PT, however, bitterly attacked Lula and his economic orthodoxy for having perpetrated a fraud on his party and the nation.

In mid-2005, Brazil was rocked by a series of revelations in Brasília about government corruption infesting the PT. An investigation into post office operations revealed that the PT congressional leadership had been systematically buying votes with cash of uncertain origin. The goal was to guarantee a congressional majority on bills for which the government lacked enough votes to win honestly. Charges pointed to members of the inner circle of Lula's government, including José Dirceu, the former student and guerrilla leader, who had moved the PT to moderate positions as the president of the party in the 1990s. Suddenly the ethical superiority of the PT was gone. Lula was now enmeshed in the seamy side of Brazilian politics, which the PT had claimed it would never enter. Radical left-wing members of the PT quit (or were expelled) and established a new party, PSol (Party of Socialism and Liberty), that attracted many PT disaffected dissidents.

Charges of corruption or misuse of power against PT leaders, however, never managed to reach Lula, who, like Ronald Reagan, has been called the "Teflon president." In the 2006 presidential elections, he stood down the challenge by Geraldo Alckmin, the ex-governor of São Paulo, and the candidate from Fernando Henrique Cardoso's party. In the first round of the presidential voting, Lula received 48.61 percent of the ballots cast. Alckmin garnered 41.6 percent, and PSol candidate Heloisa Helena received 6.8 percent. In the second round, Lula picked up 60.8 percent to Alckmin's 39.1 percent of the votes.

In his second term in office, Lula has proved himself a shrewd and pragmatic reformer, far from the revolutionary figure depicted by his detractors. He has spent much time abroad. Lula's attention to foreign affairs has reinforced Brazil's long-term aspiration to become a regional and world leader. Facing a conflict with Bolivia in early 2006 over what newly elected president Evo Morales considered "exploitative" natural gas contracts, Lula negotiated a new agreement that provided Bolivia (which supplies 50 percent of Brazil's natural gas) with much more favorable terms. The Lula administration has also successfully challenged U.S. trade policy through the World Trade Organization, arguing that government subsidies to U.S. cotton farmers violate international agreements. Lula's moderate policies (in comparison to those of Hugo Chávez) and his government's willingness to head the UN peacekeeping forces in Haiti, albeit criticized at home, reflect efforts to present Brazil as a "responsible" regional leader. Brazilian diplomats have so far unsuccessfully lobbied the leading world powers to grant the country a permanent position on the UN Security Council, but the effort has gained substantial support in recent years.

Nonetheless, Brazil remains, as it has for decades, if not centuries, a land of problems. Some are symptoms of its status as an "emerging nation," whose demographic growth has outdistanced its ability to generate the material resources that sustain a modern society. Although land redistribution has increased during the last decade, in part due to pressure by the Landless Peasants Movement, rural poverty continues to be endemic. The unequal distribution of wealth, despite some modest gains among the lower-income population, continues. Unemployment and underemployment remain high. Urban violence fueled by poverty and drug lords persists. Primary and secondary public education is underfunded. Many middle-class families send their children to private schools in order to prepare them to pass the competitive college entrance exams that will guarantee them a free education at state and federal universities.

Still, the Brazilian economy has diversified significantly. The export of agricultural products provides sound foreign earnings, as long as international prices remain high. Brazil has become a leading producer of ethanol and has developed alcohol fuel technology to replace petroleum in the transportation sector. The recent announcement of large offshore oil reserves may eliminate any future dependency on foreign imports. Major companies, such as Petrobras and Vale do Rio Doce, offer goods and services to nations throughout the whole world. Brazil is expanding its role in Africa through initiatives involving assistance in agricultural production, education, and health services. More than two decades of democratic governance have contributed to economic stability and strengthened confidence that Brazil is poised to play a more important international role. Brazil's future remains optimistic.

PART THREE

Themes and Reflections

12

Strategies for Economic Development

Ever since the independence era, Latin America has earnestly sought pathways to economic prosperity. Leaders and citizens alike have espoused a wide range of views, positive and negative, about the region's natural endowments, human resources, and creative capabilities. But they have consistently agreed upon the need for effective public policy—that is, for governmental promotion of societal improvement, structural development, and collective well-being. Toward this end, Latin American elites have undertaken a remarkable succession of large-scale economic experiments. Partly as a result, the implementation of each new "grand design" has provoked utopian expectations: Now, at last, we hold keys to the Promised Land! This has led to a relentless cycle of exaggerated hopes and crushing disappointments. It has revealed, as well, the persistence and resilience of Latin American society.

Our goal in this chapter is to describe the sequence, content, and outcome of the most prominent experiments. The discussion focuses on four main strategies or "ideologies":[*]

- economic liberalism, dominant from the 1880s through the 1920s,
- import-substitution industrialization, in vogue from the 1930s through the 1970s,
- socialism, especially significant from the 1950s through the 1980s, and
- neoliberalism, influential from the 1990s to the present.

Each of these doctrines espoused specific policies for economic well-being. They offered differing explanations of the reasons for the region's underdevelopment or "backwardness." Over the long run, they each promised to promote broad-gauged processes of "development"—not only to stimulate economic growth but also to eliminate poverty, reduce inequality, promote efficiency, and improve the

---

[*] The term *ideology* (of economic development) is used here to designate any moderately consistent body of beliefs, ideas, or propositions, tested or untested, that seeks to explain Latin America's economic plight and to indicate its cure.

conditions of everyday life. They did not succeed. But even so, there is considerable dignity in Latin America's continuing quest for all-encompassing solutions.

We here adopt a multifaceted approach. The chapter presents a combination of intellectual history, policy analysis, and sociological observation. As a follow-up, Chapter 13 explores the political dimensions of Latin America's long-term transformation over the past century and a half.

NARRATIVES OF BACKWARDNESS

Generally speaking, prescriptions for economic policy require understandings of the problems that need to be overcome—and this, in turn, demands a diagnosis of past failures, mistakes, and weaknesses. Central questions thus arose: Why was Latin America lagging so far behind Europe and the United States? What could account for the region's economic backwardness? Less offensive terminology referred instead to patterns of "underdevelopment," "delayed development," or "late industrialization"—but all these euphemisms meant pretty much the same thing.

This was an unpleasant task. Explaining failure is no fun. It is much more agreeable to construct national narratives around the notion of success. In contrast to Latin America, for example, the United States has shaped its patriotic story around political and economic achievement. From its beginning as "a city upon a hill," according to this view, the United States has provided a beacon for democracy around the world; and as a free-market economy, it has displayed the virtues of individual enterprise and the capitalist ethos. Setbacks occur, but they are fairly minor (notwithstanding the Great Depression of the 1930s and the economic collapse of 2008–9). The underlying trend is seen as steady improvement. American citizens have imbibed this optimistic tale of unending progress throughout their lives. Our national mythology represents a broad consensus.

Consider, then, the challenges faced by Latin America. In order to point the way toward a better future, analysts needed to identify the sources of past failure. One line of interpretation led to relentless litanies of self-laceration and self-condemnation. In a prominent book entitled *Nuestra inferioridad económica* (Our Economic Inferiority, 1912), the Chilean writer Francisco Encinas explained the region's backwardness as the result of weak character, habits, and values—themselves due to poor heredity and bad education. An alternative view gave way to scapegoating: the problem lies not in ourselves, but in the rest of the world. In one way or another, the region's relative underdevelopment was caused by Spain, Portugal, the United States, or the global economy as a whole.

Essentially, an acceptable narrative required some villains. Potential culprits were not hard to find. One was the Catholic Church, denounced for duping worshipers into seeking otherworldly salvation instead of worldly profits. Another was the Indian heritage and the supposed burden of indigenous traditions. Still another was the United States, accused of economic exploitation throughout the region. As the Mexican writer Daniel Cosío Villegas once observed, the list of suspects extended in many directions:

> Why is there so much wretchedness, so much poverty in this fabulous land . . . ?
> Ah, says one—it is the priests' fault; another blames it on the military; still others on the Indian; on the foreigner; on democracy; on dictatorship; on bookishness; on ignorance; or finally on divine punishment.

In the end, economic backwardness might simply be a matter of God's will. What could be more discouraging?

To their eternal credit, however, Latin Americans never gave up. Over the decades, they continued to seek new solutions to age-old problems. In the face of changing circumstances and economic crises, they made repeated attempts to come up with innovative policies. Whether or not they were successful is somewhat beside the point. The distinctive fact is that they kept on trying.

And as the record will show, Latin America presented itself as a laboratory for a remarkable range of economic experiments. This makes for fascinating history. In comparison, it is worth noting that the United States has never felt the need to shift course from its capitalist, free-market path. In contrast, Latin America has undertaken a relentless, seemingly endless search for programmatic solutions that would cure all the region's economic ills—a utopia of sorts. In its determination, the effort commands our admiration.

THE LIBERAL ERA (1880s–1920s)

It was not until a full half century after independence that Latin America embraced its first grand strategy for achieving prosperity—the doctrine of economic liberalism. This came about as the result of a timely convergence between ideology and opportunity.

Ideological inspiration for economic liberalism came mainly from Europe. In the context of intensive political change, eighteenth-century thinkers proclaimed the need to "liberate" economic activity from restrictions imposed by church and/or state. Extolling the virtues of personal freedom, they argued that the pursuit of individual self-interest would maximize productivity and therefore benefit the entire community. As Adam Smith (1723–90) declared in *The Wealth of Nations* (1776), private profit and collective welfare would come together under the guidance of the "invisible hand"—a mechanism that present-day economists define as workings of "the market." The natural interplay of supply and demand would therefore optimize outcomes for citizens and nations. Governments should not interfere unduly in this process (hence the term *laissez-faire*, or "let it work"). The key to prosperity was liberty.

Commerce played an essential role in this worldview. In an era when monarchical governments routinely placed extremely tight restrictions on trade—through licenses, quotas, and tariffs—liberal economists called for openness. Nations should be able to trade with each other on the basis of mutual interest.

In the words of David Ricardo (1772–1823), every nation should concentrate upon its "comparative advantage," exporting goods that it could produce most cheaply and importing goods that it could not. All nations stood to gain from such transactions. (The classic example involved the exchange of Portuguese wine for English cloth.) According to this logic, trade was not a zero-sum game; it could be good for everyone.

Economic opportunity came to Latin America on the heels of the Industrial Revolution. By the mid-nineteenth century, the process of industrialization in England and continental Europe was creating strong demand for agricultural commodities and raw materials. Embracing the precepts of Smith and Ricardo, Latin American leaders began to promote the exportation of foodstuffs and minerals in exchange for the importation of manufactured products from abroad. Instead of closing the region off from outside influence, as Spanish and Portuguese colonial rulers had attempted, liberal policies would exploit the "comparative advantage" of regional resource endowments through intensive interaction with the industrializing centers of the world economy. Free trade and *laissez-faire* became the catchwords of the day.

Liberalism thus became a dominant ideology throughout the region. Citing European theorists, its proponents confidently proclaimed that the international division of labor was "natural" (or decreed by divine intervention) and therefore optimal. Any deviation from its dictates would be folly—reducing trade and thereby reducing income. Attempts at protective tariffs were beaten back by politicians who argued that Latin America was not well suited, either by its resources or by its relative bargaining position, to violate the principles of free trade.

To some degree, liberal economic policies achieved their fundamental goals. The major Latin American countries underwent startling transitions from the 1880s onward. Argentina, with its vast and fertile *pampas,* became a leading exporter of agricultural and pastoral goods—wool, wheat, and beef. Brazil underwent a strong but short-lived rubber boom, and was a large-scale producer of coffee. Chile resuscitated the production of copper, an industry that had fallen into decay in the postindependence years. Cuba produced tobacco and coffee and, especially, sugar. Mexico came to export a variety of raw materials, from henequen to copper and zinc. As development progressed, investment flowed into Latin America from the industrial nations, particularly England. In return, Latin Americans purchased European textiles, machines, luxury items, and other finished goods in steadily growing quantities. In practice, liberalism was effectively promoting export-import development.

But there were contradictions too. Like many ideologies, Latin American liberalism was an import. Its principal sources lay in England and France. Unlike those countries, however, Latin America had not undergone significant industrialization by the middle of the nineteenth century. Latin America therefore lacked the social structure that had nurtured liberalism in Europe, a fact that was bound to lead to different outcomes.

Key debates about economic policy in Latin America were largely restricted to the elites, here defined as that uppermost stratum (less than 5 percent of the population) that had the power and wealth to control political decision making at local and national levels. Their commitment to liberalism was complicated by deep-seated racial prejudice. They viewed their native (and slave) populations as intellectually and morally inferior. This conviction challenged an underlying assumption of liberalism: faith in the rationality and enterprise of fellow citizens. In Brazil, politicians had spent years justifying African slavery on the grounds that it was a necessary evil for the nation's tropical, agrarian economy. Similar arguments rationalized the continuing oppression of indigenous communities throughout Spanish America. In time these preoccupations came back to haunt the liberals.

In response to these concerns, elites throughout the region envisioned European immigration as the solution to their lack of skilled labor. They particularly preferred immigrants from northern Europe, hoping that habits of self-reliance and entrepreneurship—the hallmarks of the liberals' ideal—could thus be reinforced in Latin America. Ironically, of course, the vast majority of immigrants came instead from southern Europe—Italy, Spain, and Portugal.

Adding to racist doubts was a collective inferiority complex. Up until the 1920s, Latin American elites frequently described themselves as little more than imitators of European culture. For the tropical countries, their worries about race were reinforced by concerns about climate, which European theorists constantly claimed could never support a high civilization. Environmental determinism thus reinforced racial determinism, and the combination appeared to disqualify much of the region as a stage for realization of the liberal dream.

Despite their faith in free markets, Latin America's liberals assigned crucial responsibilities to the state. Under their leadership, in fact, the liberal state took decisive steps to facilitate and sustain the region's new insertion into the evolving world economy. Especially in former centers of the Spanish empire, the state set out to destroy neofeudal remnants of colonial society—the structures of patronage and privilege that threatened to inhibit the development of capitalism. One key achievement was to reduce the economic power of the Catholic Church, particularly its hold over land, a step that opened up financial markets and enabled the emergence of profit-oriented agricultural elites. In Mexico and other countries, the granting of individual land titles within traditional Indian communities had a dual effect: one was to make high-quality land available for purchase and incorporation into commercial haciendas; another was to create a landless laboring class available for employment as *peones*. In addition, the liberal state actively courted foreign investment, especially for the development of infrastructure, and particularly for railroads. In Argentina the government actually guaranteed a minimal profit margin to a British railroad concession; in Mexico the government eventually purchased a majority share in railways, not so much for the purpose of creating a state enterprise as to rescue the indebted companies.

The liberal state assumed considerable responsibility for the labor force. Wherever workers were scarce, elites sought to import them from abroad. In the

1880s Argentina and Brazil began aggressive campaigns to encourage immigration from Europe; Chile received a smaller but substantial flow as well. Wherever workers were abundant, particularly in countries with large indigenous populations, the liberal state undertook to discipline the labor force. In Guatemala, the government supervised and enforced the seasonal migration of workers from traditional villages to coffee plantations; in El Salvador, it monitored labor relations between displaced peasants who had come to be employed by capitalist landlords. On banana plantations in other settings, the nineteenth-century state consistently opposed labor organization, broke strikes, and championed the interests of the capitalist class. In short, the Latin American state played an active role in the formation of export-import economies.

Precisely for this reason, governmental performance was inconsistent. Liberal theory offered no clear prescription for state roles. Its very activity posed a contradiction: in a strategy of *laissez-faire*, the state should have only a minimal role in matters economic. Almost by definition, there could be no long-term developmental "plan," and, not surprisingly, the nature and extent of governmental involvement varied from country to country. Policymakers tended to follow market signals and, more decisively, to carry out the wishes of economic elites rather than to pursue an overall design.

Social Transformations under Liberalism

Consolidation of the liberal model prompted fundamental changes in the region's social structure. First in sequence, if not in importance, was the modernization of the upper-class elite. Landowners and property owners were no longer content to run subsistence operations on their haciendas; instead, they sought commercial opportunities and the maximization of profits. This led to an entrepreneurial spirit that marked a significant change in the outlook and behavior of elite groups. Cattle raisers in Argentina, coffee growers in Colombia and Brazil, sugar barons in Cuba and Mexico—all were seeking efficiency and commercial success. They no longer formed a closed, semifeudal elite; they became aggressive capitalists.

Second was the appearance and growth of middle social strata. Occupationally, these consisted of merchants, lawyers, clerks, shopkeepers, and small-scale entrepreneurs who profited from the export-import economy but who did not hold upper-rank positions of ownership or leadership. Particularly important was growth and change in the commercial sector. Merchants, often foreign born, played an essential part in this transformation, as they worked to tighten connections between Latin American economies and overseas markets in Europe. Lawyers and other white-collar professionals also assumed critical roles in shaping the institutional and juridical frameworks for this new era.

Third was the emergence of a working class. In order to sustain expansion of the export economies, as mentioned earlier, elites deliberately attempted to import labor from abroad. As the Argentine Juan Bautista Alberdi once put it, "To govern is to populate"—a stance that prompted aggressive encouragement of European immigration. Starting in the 1880s, the tide of arrivals over the next three decades was so great that one historian labeled it as the nation's "alluvial era." Brazil also recruited immigrants, first from Italy and Spain and later from Japan, primarily to work in the coffee fields of São Paulo. Cuba remained a special case, since the importation of black slaves from Africa had long since determined the composition of the country's laboring class (this was also true in northeastern Brazil). Mexico presents a revealing exception to this pattern. Alone among the major countries, Mexico never sought large-scale immigration from abroad. The reason is obvious: the large population of Indian peasants within the country made it unnecessary to import new recruits for the labor force.

For a variety of reasons, laboring classes did not gain much of a foothold on political power in the early twentieth century. Immigrants in Argentina and Brazil were not entitled to vote unless they went through naturalization, so politicians could afford to ignore them. In Mexico, workers of peasant background had little chance of influencing the nation's authoritarian regime. And in Cuba and northeastern Brazil, the history of slavery left its own painful legacy.

What this meant, at least in the short run, was that Latin American elites could promote export-oriented economic expansion without having to face an effective threat of political participation by the working class. For much of this era it seemed, for many, like the best of both worlds.

To be sure, laborers began to organize themselves in the early twentieth century, first in mutual-aid societies and later in unions. Their role in vital sectors of the export-import economies—especially in transportation (railways and ports)—gave them critical potential leverage. Any labor stoppage posed an immediate threat to a country's commercial viability and therefore its capacity to trade; not surprisingly, the most militant (and effective) movements therefore involved miners, stevedores, and railroad workers. Yet the relatively primitive state of industrialization meant that most laborers worked in very small firms (with less than twenty-five employees). Only a few industries, such as textiles, fit the conventional image of huge factories with mass production techniques. A wave of strikes erupted throughout parts of the region during the decade of the 1910s, but they were all put down by force.

The halcyon days of economic liberalism in Latin America were brought to an end by the Great Depression. As economic crisis struck the United States and Europe, international demand for Latin American foodstuffs and raw materials—coffee, sugar, wheat, metals—suddenly faded. In 1930–34 the total value of Latin America's exports was 48 percent lower than in 1925–29. Lacking alternative outlets for their products, leaders of the region were in trouble.

A few countries sought to salvage their situation by securing market shares abroad. Argentina and Cuba both adopted this approach. Under a 1933 treaty, Britain promised to uphold its import quotas for Argentine beef in return for preferential tariffs on British-made goods. Using different means for a similar end, Cuba in 1934 obtained a 28 percent share of the American sugar market after intensive lobbying of the U.S. Congress. Such measures reflected consummate efforts by Latin American nations to resurrect the benefits of the liberal *economía agroimportadora.* They also illustrated the vulnerabilities that this strategy entailed.

IMPORT-SUBSTITUTION INDUSTRIALIZATION (1930s–1970s)

The collapse of the world economy in 1929 led to widespread disenchantment with liberal ideology. Latin American elites had done everything within their (very considerable) power to abide by the dictates of economic liberalism, and they now were forced to pay a heavy price. Earnings were down, and social agitation was on the rise. Frustration was everywhere mounting.

Moreover, the prestige of major powers was falling in decline. The senseless brutality of World War I cast doubt upon Europe's traditional claim to be the cradle of high-minded "civilization." Repeated U.S. military interventions in Central America and the Caribbean (more than thirty times between 1898 and 1932!) made the Colossus of the North look like an exploitative colonial overlord. The Russian Revolution raised serious questions about the supposedly inevitable triumph of liberal capitalism, while the Mexican Revolution unleashed powerful and pent-up forces of anti-imperialist and anti-Yankee sentiment.

In this context, social thought in Latin America displayed two related tendencies. One was to find fault with the outside world. The other was to search for Latin American solutions to the area's economic problems. As the Peruvian reformer Víctor Raúl Haya de la Torre proclaimed, it was time to discover what he called the "Indoamerican Way"—

> Why not build into our own reality "as it really is" the bases of a new political and economic organization which will accomplish the educational and constructive task of industrialism but will be free of its cruel aspects of human exploitation and national vassalage?

Latin America should cast aside imported ideologies and discover a path of its own.

Tentatively at first, policymakers in major countries began to embark on a program of industrialization. This was a gradual process. In the 1920s and 1930s, industrialization was generally seen as a supplement for agricultural production and not as a replacement for it. Manufacturing was a second-best option, and there was considerable skepticism about the feasibility of long-term industrial development. Elites approvingly cited Ricardo's distinction between "artificial" and "natural" industries, based on national factor endowments, and firmly withheld support from presumably artificial (manufacturing) activities throughout most of the 1930s.

In time, however, industrialization acquired a clear sense of purpose. The idea was not simply to copy the paths already traced by nineteenth-century Europe and America. Instead, Latin America's economies started producing manufactured goods that they had formerly imported from abroad (e.g., textiles, apparel, beverages, ceramics, cosmetics, and small appliances). Hence the name for this approach: "import-substitution industrialization," also known as ISI.

As political leaders promoted this strategy, they relied upon a strong and interventionist state. Proactive policies focused on means of achieving and assuring economic growth under governmental tutelage. State-supported entities provided credit to entrepreneurs, while public investments strengthened vital infrastructure (especially transportation and communication). Ministries and bureaucracies attempted to set goals and guidelines without regard for social pressure; not always successful in this regard, the technocrats in charge nonetheless prized the idea of insulation from political or popular influence. At times they also espoused modest redistributive policies. One of the distinctive characteristics of Latin American policy during this era was the focus on inward-looking development—a concern with national producers and consumers, rather than with overseas markets.

ISI in Theory

Ideological and theoretical support for ISI came from two principal sources. One was nationalism, the long-held desire for autonomy and self-determination. As intellectuals and policymakers surveyed the results of the liberal experiment, many concluded that the ideas of "comparative advantage" under a God-given "international division of labor" condemned the region to primitive agriculture, economic backwardness, and political vulnerability. Latin America could achieve true political sovereignty only on the basis of economic self-sufficiency and independence. This meant industrialization.

A second inspiration came from an initially unlikely source: a technocratic bureau of the United Nations. Created in the 1940s, the UN's Economic Commission for Latin America (ECLA, later known as ECLAC after the inclusion of the Caribbean) was charged with the systematic analysis of economic problems of the region and its individual countries. But it was more than just a technical secretariat. Under the leadership of Raúl Prébisch, a remarkably able economist from Argentina, ECLA became an aggressive participant in debates about Latin America's relationship to the world economy. In a deliberate effort to obtain distance from Washington, D.C.—and the power and presence of the U.S. government—ECLA established its headquarters in Santiago de Chile. From the start, ECLA set out to give voice to Latin American outlooks and concerns.

One of ECLA's major accomplishments was to train a generation of economists who learned, during their time in Santiago, to see their countries' problems within a continental perspective. They also got to know their counterparts in other nations and were able to compare notes on the problems and possibilities of economic policymaking. ECLA thus helped to produce, as well as to reflect, a distinctively Latin American approach to economic analysis.

During the 1950s ECLA began publishing a series of technical reports demonstrating that, over time, commercial relationships worked to the systematic disadvantage of primary-producing countries. Because the price of manufactured goods was increasing faster than the price of agricultural and mineral commodities, the developing countries of Latin America were obtaining less and less real value for their export products. Although ECLA usually refrained from explicit policy recommendations, there were three logical solutions to this dilemma. One was to establish international commodity agreements; a second, for larger countries, was to undertake industrialization; a third was to pursue economic integration among countries of the region and thus expand consumer markets.

ECLA's arguments provoked fierce responses in Latin America and, especially, in the United States. The Eisenhower administration (1953–61) saw ECLA as a beehive of deluded "statist" thought, promoting policies that would harm foreign investment and private enterprise.

In fact, the Prébisch-ECLA thesis furnished ammunition for centrist leaders throughout the region, not for radicals. Above all, ECLA gave reform-minded Latin Americans the confidence to shape their own economic strategies. ECLA thus offered a milestone in Latin America's search for self-knowledge and self-identity. This was a significant accomplishment, since Latin American analysts and politicians had long felt at a disadvantage when facing the economists, bankers, and businessmen of the industrial world.

Innately skeptical of conventional wisdom and diplomatic rhetoric, Raúl Prébisch displays restless impatience during a UN meeting in the 1940s.

ISI in Practice

A principal goal of import-substitution industrialization was economic independence. The idea was that by building its own industry, Latin America would become less dependent on Europe and the United States for manufactured goods. National economies would become more integrated and self-sufficient and, as a result, less vulnerable to the kind of shocks brought on by a worldwide depression. This aspiration often appealed to military officers, eager to uphold the sovereignty of what they called *la patria* ("the fatherland").

A second goal was job creation. Concentrated almost entirely in cities, the Latin American proletariat was by the 1930s and 1940s beginning to exert its power as a social force. In some countries, such as Chile, union movements were relatively free of arbitrary government involvement. Elsewhere, as in Mexico and Argentina and Brazil, politicians recognized labor as a potential political asset and took a direct hand in stimulating (and controlling) labor organizations. Whether perceived as ally or threat, the urban working class was seeking secure employment, and Latin American leaders saw industrialization as one way to respond.

From the late 1930s to the 1960s, at least in major countries, ISI policies met with relative success. The Depression and World War II afforded tacit protection and explicit opportunity for infant industries at home. States played key roles in taking advantage of this situation. Governments restricted foreign competition through tariffs and quotas, encouraged local investment through credits and loans, stimulated domestic demand through public-sector expenditures, and, perhaps most important, took direct part in the process through the formation of state-owned companies. As a result, larger countries of the region developed significant industrial plants. The Torcuato di Tella corporation constructed appliances and automobiles in Argentina, Volta Redonda produced steel in Brazil, and groups in Monterrey brewed high-quality beers in Mexico.

Following another ECLA prescription, nations banded together in 1960 to create a Latin American Free Trade Area (LAFTA). The intent was to create larger, integrated markets that could encourage and sustain industrial development. About twenty years later, it would be renamed the Latin American Integration Association (ALADI). Due to nationalist sentiments and competitive economies, however, neither of these experiments met with practical success.

As ISI nonetheless took hold, regional growth hovered in the 5–6 percent range from the 1950s through the 1970s. (The annual average was 5.1 percent in the 1950s, 5.4 percent in the 1960s, and 5.8 percent in the 1970s.) Prime movers behind this performance were Brazil and Mexico, each with strong gains in the manufacturing sector. Indeed, both of these countries would receive international acclaim around this time as economic "miracles"—Mexico during the 1950s and 1960s, Brazil for its spectacular growth in 1968–73. Until the mid-1970s, ISI appeared to work.

For smaller and less endowed countries of the region, however, ISI was not a feasible option. Located principally in Central America and the Caribbean, some of these countries amounted to "plantation societies" (as defined in Chapter 4). Lacking mineral and other natural resources, they built their economies around the cultivation of one or two agricultural crops for export—sugar, coffee, tobacco, bananas, cacao. Production took place on large-scale plantations that required prodigious amounts of labor, either imported from Africa under slavery or forcibly extracted from the indigenous population. Private investment came mostly from foreign sources. Landownership was highly concentrated, and the social order was sharply divided between elites at the top and peasants and workers at the bottom. Middle sectors were tiny, and local consumer markets were extremely small. From the beginnings of the colonial period, these areas shipped their products abroad—first to Spain and Portugal, then to England and continental Europe, and finally to the United States.

Within the larger countries, the social consequences of industrial development were complex. One was the formation of an entrepreneurial capitalist class. In Chile, members of this group came principally from families of the landed elite. In Mexico and Argentina, they came from more modest origins and therefore presented a potential challenge to the power of traditional ruling classes. But the basic point remains: industrialization, even of the ISI type, created a new power group in Latin American society. Its role would be much debated in the years ahead.

Ultimately, the economic trajectories of Argentina, Mexico, and (to a lesser extent) Brazil came to illustrate the weaknesses of ISI development. Typically, import-substitution industrialization produced spurts of growth in the short term but encountered limits in the medium and longer term. National markets, especially in countries with modest populations, fell subject to saturation; production processes continued to require substantial imports of capital goods; higher production costs were passed on to consumers in protected markets; and near-monopoly discouraged investment in technology. Once established under state protectionism and sheltered by tariff walls, highly subsidized and inefficient local firms were unable to compete in the international market. Moreover, the concentration of resources on industrial development tended to weaken the agricultural sector. Eventually, policymakers in Latin America would turn away from ISI in search of yet new strategies.

THE SOCIALIST ALTERNATIVE (1950s–1980s)

Neither liberalism nor ISI were providing durable solutions to the challenge of development. Both resulted in economic crisis and stagnation. Both left legacies of social inequality, favoring privileged sectors (landowners or entrepreneurs) at the expense of popular masses (peasants or workers). And both illustrated the political costs of economic vulnerability. When push came to shove, export-import strategies and industrialization drives both suffered from the vagaries of global economics and big-power politics.

Confronted by these realities, a substantial number of Latin American thinkers sought a path to radical change—and embraced the cause of socialism, or, more specifically, Marxist ideology. Many took part in revolutionary movements. For the most part, these advocates came from neither elite backgrounds nor the working class. They emerged, instead, from the region's middle classes. They were well-read, university educated, idealistic, often naïve—and committed to the goal of social justice. From their standpoint, socialist theory provided both a framework for analysis and a program for action.

As initially developed by Karl Marx (1818–83) and Friedrich Engels (1820–95), what has come to be known as "Marxist" thought embodied a series of core principles. Most fundamental was the conviction that capitalism entailed the exploitation of workers by the owners of production—a conflict that, in turn, gave rise to perpetual class struggle. Workers often accepted their plight as a result of intense ideological indoctrination, an observation which led Marx to dismiss organized religion as "the opiate of the masses." The only means of improving this situation would be through social revolution—presumably (but not necessarily) an armed upheaval from below. A revolutionary triumph would install a "dictatorship of the proletariat" that would eliminate class boundaries, implement radical change, and promote the collective welfare of the society at large.

Extending the logic of this worldview, V. I. Lenin (1870–1924) advanced the idea that imperialism represented "the highest stage of capitalism." As social-class contradictions approached the point of crisis, he argued, advanced industrial nations turned their attention toward colonial expansion in less developed parts of the world (Africa, Asia, and Latin America). Brutal economic exploitation of these colonies made it possible for capitalist nations to raise the living standards of their own workers by sufficient increments to forestall the prospect of revolution. This reasoning led Lenin to maintain, in sharp contrast to Marx, that the first true proletarian revolution would erupt not among the most advanced industrial countries, but in poverty-stricken and lesser-developed areas. (He thus saw Czarist Russia as a likely candidate.) It was through revolution, and only through revolution, that capitalism could be overthrown.

Marxist-Leninist ideology acquired substantial appeal in Latin America. Its diagnosis of class conflict applied directly to social inequities throughout the region. Its call to revolutionary action offered immediate hope to downtrodden workers and peasants. Its identification of imperialism as the culmination of capitalism offered both a coherent explanation of big-power politics and a foundation for nationalistic appeals. Moreover, Marxist internationalists and Latin American nationalists had one enemy in common: the United States, leader of the capitalist world and dominant power within the Western Hemisphere.

More important than its doctrinaire principles, however, was an underlying attraction of Marxist-Leninist thought: as an ideology of the oppressed, it struck a deep and resonant chord with the cultures of resistance that had been welling up in Latin America ever since the nineteenth century. In one form or another, socialism appeared to offer a promising pathway for Latin America.

At first, the principal vehicles for Marxist thought in Latin America were political parties. After the Russian Revolution, orthodox Communist parties appeared in a number of countries. Usually based in the cities, led by intellectuals and politicians claiming to represent the "progressive bourgeoisie," they tended to espouse "the peaceful road to power" rather than insurrectionary action. From the 1930s through the 1950s, party leaders developed close, often servile relations with the Soviet Union. By the 1960s and 1970s Communist parties had become passive observers of national politics, largely irrelevant in most nations of the region.

In contrast, socialist parties sometimes managed to play significant roles in the postwar politics of Latin America. These were leftist political groupings that, for the most part, blended Marxist analysis of class struggle with nationalist insistence on the sanctity of sovereignty; while denouncing U.S. "imperialism" they did not, however, follow Soviet dictates in the international arena. More flexible than the Communists, more attuned to local realities, socialist parties (in a variety of forms) gave substantial credibility to the political left. Their most conspicuous successes came in Guatemala, under Jacobo Arbenz, and in Chile, under Salvador Allende.

But as shown in Chapters 4 and 10, the fate of those same governments demonstrated the impossibility of the "peaceful road" toward socialism. Both were overthrown by reactionary military coups with U.S. backing. The conclusion was inescapable: no matter how free or fair the ballot, electoral politics could not offer a meaningful path to socialist transformation: Washington would always intervene.

The only option was armed revolution.

Revolutionary Movements

Revolutions are more than assaults on presidential palaces. From our perspective, we consider revolutions to be *extralegal seizures of political power, by the use or threat of force, for the purpose of bringing about structural change in the distribution of political, social, or economic power.* True revolutions are qualitatively different from barracks revolts or routine *golpes de estado,* which lead to the rotation of leaders but leave structures intact. Revolutions have far-reaching programs for socioeconomic change (usually, but not necessarily, leftist in orientation). Having attained political power, revolutionary leaders may or may not be able to carry out their social programs. There is thus such a thing as an "incomplete" or "unsuccessful" revolution.

A central idea within Marxist thought—as developed in Latin America—was faith in the power of the state. It was the state that conditioned the social order, upheld the distribution of power and benefits, and legitimized the status quo. If the state could do all these things, it could undo them as well. That is why the state was worthy of conquest. Once in control of state institutions and the "commanding heights" of the national economy, revolutionaries could bring about radical and effective societal change. Faith in the omnipotence of the state thus became a central pillar of revolutionary ideology.

From the 1950s to the 1980s, armed revolutionary movements emerged in almost every country of the region. Virtually all proclaimed Marxist ideologies, of one sort or another, though they tended to espouse nationalist and populist causes as well. They often drew inspiration from the doctrines of Mao Zedong, who challenged Marx's emphasis on the need for an industrial proletariat by claiming (and demonstrating) that revolutionary movements could originate among the rural peasantry. Their leaders and cadres were known as *guerrillas,* small-sized fighting units that attempted to wear down established authorities through a relentless and long-term series of hit-and-run assaults.

First and foremost among them was the Fidelista vanguard in Cuba, where Castro's rise to power sent shock waves throughout the hemisphere. Emboldened by the Fidelista example (and sometimes with active support from Cuba), prominent guerrilla movements sprang up in Guatemala, Venezuela, and Colombia. Other groups made brief, if unsuccessful, appearances in the Peruvian Andes. And in the Bolivian highlands, Ernesto "Che" Guevara organized an effort that was crushed in 1967. Urban guerrilla movements appeared in Argentina, Brazil, Colombia, and Uruguay, but revolutionary cadres generally made little headway in the larger and more developed countries of the region.

A second wave of guerrilla movements crested in the 1970s and 1980s, most notably in Central America. A decade-long conflict in El Salvador eventually resulted in stalemate. In Nicaragua, a youthful band of revolutionaries forced the dictatorial Anastasio Somoza out of the country and took power amid popular euphoria in 1979.

Among all these comings and goings, guerrilla movements managed to seize political power in only two cases—Cuba and Nicaragua, both "plantation societies" of modest size. The reasons are not far to seek: the success of revolutionary movements depended not only upon their own resources but also upon the social support and military strength of incumbent governments. Especially notable is the fact that the Fidelistas and the Sandinistas were both challenging corrupt dictatorships that were losing touch with their natural bastions of support—landowners, businessmen, and the United States. Throughout the Cold War as a whole, El Salvador was more the rule than Nicaragua: wherever feasible, Washington scurried to the aid of governments under siege from Marxist revolutionists.

In the face of such realities, socialism lost its ideological appeal during the 1990s. The end of the Cold War—and the collapse of the Soviet Union—served to discredit Marxist ideology. The economic strangulation of Cuba demonstrated the real-world costs of defying the United States. Perhaps most importantly, the disastrous fate of guerrilla movements throughout the region revealed the near-hopelessness of revolutionary action. As the twentieth century drew to a close, the curtain was coming down on the socialist alternative.

Liberation Theology

One of the most significant legacies of Latin American radicalism was a by-product: the emergence of "liberation theology." The doctrine represented an unlikely blend of two distinct traditions, Marxist theory and Catholic teachings. The result was a powerful and still-vibrant summons to political activism in the name of social justice.

And... Dependency Theory?

How does the theory of "dependency" fit within a discussion of Latin America's strategies for economic development?

Sideways, one might say. As it evolved over time, dependency theory proved to be more useful as a conceptual framework for historical analysis than as a prescription for public policy or social action.

Of course there were connections between theory and policy. The initial foundation for the dependency approach came from ECLA's writings about long-term deterioration in Latin America's terms of trade with advanced industrial countries. This literature suggested that global commerce unfairly favored wealthy nations at the expense of the poor, while decision-making powers were concentrated within the privileged "core" at the center of the world economic system. (For the record, it should be noted that these insights bear considerable relevance to contemporary patterns of "globalization.")

As an additional tool, social class analysis—more specifically, Marxist analysis—provided a means of detecting the differential consequences of economic development *within* Latin America. Who benefited from these dynamics? Who was left behind? For these inquiries Marxist writings offered a ready-made set of social-class categories (e.g., bourgeoisie and proletariat), a literature rich in debates and innovations, and a conviction that "class struggle" formed the ultimate basis for historical transformation. Because of this Marxist orientation, the dependency approach inevitably came to be identified with the political "left."

Within the scholarly realm, social scientists employed the dependency framework to examine variations in social-class configurations (e.g., those associated with agriculture vs. mining), to show how capitalist development in the world "periphery" intensified economic inequalities while perpetuating widespread poverty, and to speculate about the political consequences of such processes in Latin America.

But dependency theory did not yield a clear-cut set of policy prescriptions. On the contrary, it produced a plethora of proposed solutions—ranging from nationalist protection of local industry (via ISI) to regional economic integration to social revolution. All these strategies were intended to reduce economic dependency, enhance national autonomy, and promote social justice, but the means were infinitely broader than the ends.

In the long run, the dependency approach has proven to be most effective as a heuristic device. It is in that spirit that we employ it in this book.

Conventional wisdom usually depicts the Catholic Church as a bastion of conservative politics—a hierarchical institution based on reactionary principles, usually allied with elite factions in society. It is to be remembered, however, that parish priests bore intimate witness to the suffering of the poor. As they catered to their flocks, they became acutely conscious of the harsh realities of poverty, inequality, and social injustice. In time they rejected the traditional idea that, as

God's chosen people, the poor should calmly accept their plight and await salvation in Heaven. Instead, said the priests, it was time for popular action on Earth.

During the 1960s and 1970s, up-and-coming theologians managed to blend Marxist analysis of class struggle with ecclesiastical concerns about social justice and fairness—as exemplified in a papal encyclical entitled *Rerum Novarum* (1891), a sympathetic treatise about the misery of European working classes. In the view of these priests, the existence of poverty was a consequence of widespread sin—a result of avarice, selfishness, and lack of compassion. What the world needed was a path to "liberation." According to a classic treatise by Gustavo Gutiérrez, a Peruvian Jesuit, true liberation would unfold in three dimensions:

- elimination of the immediate causes of poverty and injustice,
- emancipation of the poor from "those things that limit their capacity to develop themselves freely and in dignity," and
- liberation from selfishness and sin for all believers, a more perfect relationship with God and with other human beings.

Christ was in this view not only a redeemer but also a liberator of the oppressed. The quest for social justice therefore became a solemn Christian mission. It was incumbent upon the devout to exercise "a preferential option for the poor." Political action was an act of compassion, grace, and solidarity.

This radical revision of Catholic teachings emerged mainly from Latin America. Priests and missionary nuns in the region came face-to-face not only with poverty, but also with frightful abuses of human rights under military governments. They saw the urgent need for action. In 1968 liberation theology became the dominant theme at a major conference of Latin American bishops in the Colombian city of Medellín. It was a creative and compassionate response to compelling social needs.

In sharp contrast to revolutionary theory, liberation theology did not call for conquest of the state. Instead, it espoused the empowerment of people from below—consciousness-raising, grass-roots organization, and local mobilization. In a theological sense, the governmental apparatus was regarded as beyond redemption: it was corrupt, inefficient, uncaring, an instrument of systematic oppression. Instead of taking over the state, people should create new forms of power for and by themselves. Organized in social movements, ordinary people could work to bring about meaningful improvements in their everyday lives.

Within the Catholic Church, liberation theology acquired a subversive edge. As part of the effort to raise popular consciousness, advocates encouraged parishioners to meditate upon the Bible—often in groups, or so-called base communities. This stratagem presented a frontal challenge to traditions of the church, which granted sole authority for the interpretation of God's word to the priest—and to the Pope—and not to individual worshipers. According to this view, the proper understanding of divine will was to be channeled exclusively through the ecclesiastical hierarchy (as emphasized by the notion of "papal infallibility"). There was no room for debate, doubt, or personal interpretation.

It was for these reasons that Pope John Paul II, progressive in so many ways, bitterly condemned liberation theology and excommunicated many of its leading proponents. His successor, Benedict XVI, has been even more intolerant of the liberation movement. It has presented a challenge to the power structure of the church, and that is seen as unacceptable.

NEOLIBERALISM—ONCE DOMINANT, NOW CHALLENGED (1980s–PRESENT)

In the meantime, global developments brought Latin America face-to-face with economic crisis. During the 1970s, the price of petroleum rose rapidly, largely as a result of market manipulations by the Organization of Petroleum Exporting Countries (OPEC). This increased the import bill for most countries of Latin America. It also led to petrodollar windfalls in major private banks, suddenly flush with deposits from the oil exporters. Needing to find borrowers for these new funds, bankers turned to Latin America—which had better credit ratings than other developing areas, and which also needed the money. The bankers also imagined that these customers, as sovereign states, were immune from bankruptcy. Soon the borrowed funds were going for current consumption, enabling governments—whether military or civilian—to curry short-term favor from their citizens. Thus began a wave of borrowing that greatly increased the magnitude of Latin America's foreign debt.

By the early 1980s, Latin America was finding itself in a squeeze. The borrowing countries had contracted their loans at initially modest (but variable) interest rates. As the United States and Europe adopted tight-money policies to counter crippling stagflation at home, interest rates climbed—and so did the costs of debt service. At the same time, international prices for Latin American commodities were plummeting, so debtor countries had less and less foreign exchange in their accounts. The situation was impossible.

In August 1982 Mexico declared that it could no longer meet payments on its foreign debt. A few months later Brazil, the largest borrower, followed suit. This triggered a world-wide crisis. Under the guidance of the International Monetary Fund, bankers lent additional money for "rescue" loans. This only made matters worse, as Latin America's total debt rose from U.S. $242 billion in 1980 to $431 billion by 1990.

The region's credit crisis was accompanied by a protracted economic crisis throughout the 1980s. To satisfy foreign lenders (and service the debt), country after country had to adopt an orthodox IMF-style austerity plan—slashing government expenditures and subsidies, tightening credit markets, and, wherever possible, reducing real wages. The result was stagnation. As shown in Figure 12.1, overall output for the region as a whole declined sharply in 1983–84 and showed only modest growth rates in following years. In per capita terms, in fact, Latin America's GDP fell by 8.3 percent between 1981 and 1989. Unemployment swelled and wages plummeted. In Mexico, whose conduct set a model of good behavior for other debtor countries, real wages declined by nearly 50 percent.

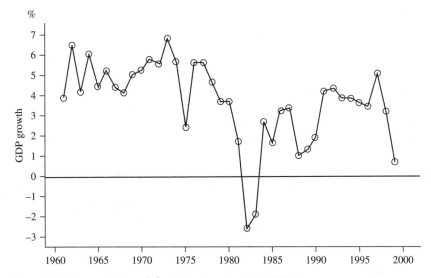

Figure 12.1 Economic Growth for Latin America, 1960–2000

SOURCE: Economic Commission for Latin America and the Caribbean (ECLAC), *Social Panorama of Latin America, 2002–2003.*

In the first stage of the crisis, from 1982 to 1985, bankers and debtors attempted to "muddle through" what they saw as problems of "liquidity" (or cash flow). This approach assured successful rescue of the banks, some of which were seriously overexposed. A second stage began in 1985, when U.S. treasury secretary James A. Baker III stressed the need for economic growth in indebted countries—thus acknowledging that those countries faced crises of solvency, not just liquidity. In 1989 Baker's successor, Nicholas Brady, announced U.S. government support for a broad portfolio of debt reduction and restructuring alternatives for countries willing to undertake market-based economic policies.

As it sought to comprehend the causes of this crisis, the international financial community eventually arrived at the conclusion that Latin America required fundamental economic reform. A principal source of the problem was held to be structural distortions arising from ISI. Of course, the debt crisis itself was largely due to factors outside of (and outside the control of) Latin America. Even so, economists and policymakers in major international institutions—from the U.S. Treasury to the World Bank and the International Monetary Fund, all headquartered in Washington, D.C.—issued a clarion call for economic restructuring in Latin America.

What came to be known as the "Washington consensus" entailed three sets of prescriptions:

- first, Latin American governments should support the private sector;
- second, they should liberalize policies on trade; and

- third, perhaps most important, they should reduce the economic role of the state (in particular, they should privatize state-owned industries).

They should exercise fiscal discipline—as commonly preached, but rarely practiced, by Washington itself. They should concentrate budgetary expenditures not on social subsidies but on long-term investments in health, education, and infrastructural investment. They should also deregulate their national economies, letting market forces operate without political or bureaucratic constraints. (Point of order: At least one prominent Latin American policymaker later denounced the "Washington consensus" label as "insulting," on the ground that "these were things we wanted to do for our countries on our own, not because of international opinion.")

In many ways, the Washington consensus called for a return to liberal export-import economic policies, much like those of the 1880s–1920s. Thus it came to be known as "neoliberalism." There were differences, of course, but both ideologies rested on the same foundation—faith in the "invisible hand" of the market.

This neoliberal vision contained one major paradox. A centerpiece of the entire program was reducing the role of the state; at the same time, implementation of these policies could be accomplished only by a powerful state. Economic reform was bound to encounter resistance from entrenched groups—sheltered entrepreneurs, unionized workers, public-sector employees. Imposition of broad, equitable, and effective tax policies, another of the Washington proposals, would generate opposition from almost everyone. It would take a strong and autonomous state to overcome such pressures. Proponents of the consensus attempted to resolve this paradox by advocating small but efficient governments—"lean and mean," in their felicitous phrasing. Even so, this lofty formulation did not squarely address fundamental questions about state participation in economic affairs.

Free Trade

As with nineteenth-century liberalism, the neoliberal consensus placed great emphasis on the role of commerce. Given the imperatives of economic globalization, nations should embrace the international division of labor and export products for which they had a "comparative advantage." Latin America should discard ISI and revert to what it did best—agriculture, mining, exploitation of natural resources.

Throughout the 1990s, economic ideology and practical considerations led the United States to advocate the adoption of "free trade" throughout the Western Hemisphere. This was to be accomplished through formal treaties, which would set schedules for the reduction of tariffs and other barriers to imports. The goals were to develop expanding markets for U.S. exports; enhance efficiency for U.S. manufacturers (mainly through access to low-cost labor); and, in a variety of ways, strengthen America's "competitiveness" in the world economy. Regional integration in the Americas would also strengthen Washington's hand in negotiations with Europe, Japan, and other economic powers of the time.

In 1990 the George Bush (senior) administration opened formal negotiations with Canada and Mexico for the creation of a North American free trade area. That same year, Bush also proposed the development of a free trade zone that would embrace the entire hemisphere, "stretching from the port of Anchorage to Tierra del Fuego."

As described in Chapter 3, the North American Free Trade Agreement went into effect in January 1994 and created one of the largest trading blocs in the world. Ultimately, NAFTA marked a turning point in U.S. economic policy and in relations with Mexico. For the first time in history, Washington was pursuing an explicit strategy of economic integration with its neighbor to the south. It was also consolidating the U.S. sphere of influence.

Yet the prospects for a hemispheric free trade zone remained remote. To initiate the process, the Clinton administration hosted a grandiose "Summit of the Americas" in Miami in December 1994. After intense behind-the-scenes negotiations, the gathering proclaimed the goal of forging a Free Trade Area of the Americas (FTAA) by the year 2005—with implementation to follow in subsequent years. Subsequent summit meetings in 1998 and 2001 paid lip service to this goal, but actual progress was painfully slow.

In the meantime, the United States embarked on a series of free trade agreements with individual countries of Latin America (and groups of smaller nations). This produced what is known as a "hub-and-spoke" formation. Under this system, a central country, or "hub," enjoys special preference in the market of each "spoke" country under a series of separate bilateral agreements. The spokes, however, do not have preferential access to each other's markets; even worse, they have to

Concerns about NAFTA prompted recollections of the Spanish conquest. (Danziger/Christian Science Monitor.)

compete among themselves for preferences within the hub market. What is good for the hub is not always so good for the spokes.

Free trade agreements (FTAs) contained a fundamental irony. As government-to-government accords, they reflected deliberate decisions by sovereign states—rather than the "invisible hand" of the market. And while they lowered barriers to trade, they did not remove them—not all of them, anyway, and not right away. Strictly speaking, the "free trade" label was and remains a misnomer. FTAs did not achieve complete freedom of trade; they represented new terms for the management of trade by states.

As of late 2009, the United States had reached free trade agreements with nine countries of the region: Mexico, Chile, the countries of Central America (and the Dominican Republic), and Peru. A treaty with Colombia was awaiting ratification by the U.S. Senate, and negotiations were continuing with Panama. At the same time, other important nations—Argentina, Brazil, Ecuador, Paraguay, Venezuela, and Bolivia, together accounting for one-half of the region's population—showed little interest in linking their economic destinies so closely with the Colossus of the North. In this sense, Latin America was being divided right down the middle. Where and how this would end were anyone's guess.

Countermoves

As the United States pursued its hub-and-spoke approach, leaders of Latin America devised an array of responses. Their efforts drew intellectual support from important developments in economic theories of international trade, which no longer rested upon classical notions of comparative advantage. As Nobel Prize–winning economist Paul Krugman noted, countries often trade with very similar partners; as a matter of fact, countries often import the same kinds of goods that they export. The reason is that companies often produce similar goods but with slight variations. As companies become more specialized and efficient at producing their goods, they increase sales, expand operations, and look for larger markets. For their part, consumers like variety, so they pick and choose their products from companies in different countries. As a result, countries end up exchanging similar products. So some Americans buy Volkswagens and some Germans buy Fords. Or, more to the point, Argentines consume delicate white wines from Chile while *chilenos* enjoy hearty reds from Argentina.

At any rate, this insight helped establish rationales for free trade agreements among countries in Latin America. In one formulation, a few nations formed hub-and-spoke arrangements. Prominent among them were Mexico, which forged FTAs with countries of Central America; Chile, which established preferential relations with other nations of South America; and Brazil, which sought to create a South American Free Trade Association (SAFTA) with itself at the center.

A second response involved sub-regional integration. The Central American Common Market was revived, the Caribbean Community (CARICOM) was reinvigorated, and the Andean Pact was reshaped and revitalized. Such projects could stimulate economic growth among the member countries and, it was hoped, strengthen their bargaining position in relation to the United States and other major powers.

The most ambitious and influential of these schemes emerged in 1991 in South America, where the "Common Market of the South" (MERCOSUR) linked the economic fortunes of Argentina, Brazil, Uruguay, and Paraguay. Member countries committed themselves to construct a "customs union" with a common external tariff, and to move onward toward a full-fledged common market in subsequent years. Especially in view of long-standing rivalries between Argentina and Brazil, MERCOSUR was a truly remarkable development. Its partners constituted nearly one-half of Latin America's GDP, more than 40 percent of its total population, and about one-third of its foreign trade.

More important than its size was its strategic orientation. In contrast to traditional free trade arrangements, MERCOSUR represented a commitment to "outward-oriented integration"—that is, from a determination to make member states more competitive in the international arena, rather than to rely completely on closed markets via import-substitution industrialization. The project also had clear political goals: the consolidation of peace and democracy throughout the Southern Cone. To reduce military tensions, Argentina and Brazil agreed to ban the development of nuclear weapons. In a sense, MERCOSUR would provide civilian democrats with regular opportunities for consultation and mutual support, thus offsetting the long-established enclaves for the armed forces of the area.

Extending the scope of its ambitions, Brazil went on to propose the formation of a South American Free Trade Association in 1994. The idea was to create a free-trade zone throughout the continent (rather than the hemisphere) by the year 2005. Public intentions were manifold: to capitalize on the experience of MERCOSUR, which was rapidly increasing intraregional trade; to avoid the "isolation" of MERCOSUR, especially from Chile and the Andean Group; and to accumulate negotiating power for dealing with the possibility of broader U.S.-led integration schemes in the Americas. Not coincidentally, SAFTA would confirm Brazil's historic claim to be the dominant power throughout South America.

By far the most direct and radical challenge to the United States came from Venezuela, where, as explained in Chapter 8, Hugo Chávez was seeking to promote "socialism for the twenty-first century." As part of an effort to boost his regional authority, Chávez launched an initiative known as the *Alternativa Bolivariana para las Américas* (ALBA), a broad alliance that would provide an "alternative" to the FTAA and, by extension, to American hegemony within the hemisphere. Rapid increases in petroleum prices provided Chávez with a massive influx of petrodollars, which allowed him to dispense all manner of economic assistance to his allies. By the year 2006, the Chavista regime had formed close relations not only with Cuba, but also with other left-of-center governments throughout the region—most notably Bolivia, Ecuador, and Nicaragua. Chávez also maintained a complex relationship with Lula of Brazil, a prominent leftist with a decidedly pragmatic streak and, in many ways, his principal rival for leadership of South America.

For different reasons, Lula and Chávez both opposed U.S. plans for the FTAA. Brazil objected to Washington's refusal to discard large-scale governmental subsidies to American agriculture; Venezuela objected to the geopolitical implications of the project as a whole. At a memorable summit meeting in Mar del Plata, Argentina, in November 2005, the two countries joined forces to dismantle the FTAA. As least for the foreseeable future, the vision of a free trade area of the Americas would have to be abandoned. What remained was a divided hemisphere with a patchwork of integration schemes.

Interim Reflections and the Crash of '08

After what seemed like interminable delays, Latin America began to reap the benefits of neoliberal policies around 2003. Faced by growing demand for commodities, countries of the region sharply increased their exports. They found avid customers not only in traditional markets, such as Europe and the United States, but also in new parts of the world, especially in China. As a result, Latin America embarked on a five-year period of continuous economic expansion, with average annual growth rates around 5 percent. These figures translated into per capita increases of 3 percent per year. This was by far the best economic performance for the region since the 1970s.

Proponents of the Washington consensus could hardly contain their glee. According to their self-confident predictions, it appeared that the unfettered interplay of market forces was unleashing economic creativity, vitality, and entrepreneurship within a globalizing world. The capitalist spirit was riding high indeed.

Yet there were warning signs as well. As prescient observers noted, Latin America's free trade expansion displayed some structural weaknesses:

- The rates of growth, while very welcome, were lower than in many other regions of the world (such as Asia and Eastern Europe).
- Levels of inequality were the highest in the world.
- While poverty rates were declining, unemployment was still high and climbing,
- Investments in infrastructure and education were inadequate, and
- The region continued to rely on traditional commodity exports, rather than on economic restructuring (as exemplified by China and India).

For all these reasons, according to these analysts, Latin America remained susceptible to external economic shocks. This vulnerability had cost the region dearly in the 1930s and the 1980s. It could happen again.

The shock arrived in late 2008, with the sudden collapse of financial markets in the United States and the world. In the waning months of the George Bush (junior) administration, the American economy plunged into a deep recession. The U.S. government rescued key financial institutions with hundreds of billions of dollars in bailouts—socializing the banking industry, in effect—while the Federal Reserve brought commercial interest rates down to nearly zero. To revive the still-sluggish economy, President Barack Obama proposed a massive program of public expenditures in early 2009 that was designed both to enhance the nation's competitiveness and to stimulate economic activity.

In terms of economic policy, these developments had far-reaching implications. They showed that "the market" was neither omniscient nor capable of self-regulation. They demonstrated the need for governmental oversight. They emphasized the importance of public investments, especially in education and infrastructure (bridges, highways, the Internet, etc.). They revealed that, in times of crisis, only the government could take decisive action. Curiously, these insights promoted a revival of interest in John Maynard Keynes (1883–1946), the British economist who argued that governments should counter the Depression of the 1930s with large-scale programs of deficit spending. The secret, according to Keynes, was not so much the amount of money the government spent, but how convincingly it signaled a revival of the economic game—and thus enticed players in the private sector to overcome their fears and start playing again.

As a corollary, these trends offered satisfaction to Latin American intellectuals and policymakers who had stoutly resisted doctrinaire imposition of the Washington consensus. Given the problems they faced, many were reluctant to remove the state from active participation in their national economies. Lo and behold, even the United States was relying on its central government to provide a pathway to recovery. State intervention would be respectable again!

Yet the near-term outlook for Latin America was far from encouraging. The U.S.-led crash of 2008 would have serious negative impacts—not because Latin Americans had invested in U.S. sub-prime loans, which they had not, but because of a sharp contraction in U.S. and European demand for Latin American products. As happened in the 1930s, overseas markets were drying up. Foreign investment was also in free-fall decline. According to one responsible prediction, economic growth for the region would decline to less than 2 percent in 2009—with no assurance that things would get better thereafter.

Under these distressing circumstances, Latin American leaders and thinkers began exploring new routes to economic development. Once again, the search for a workable strategy was under way.

13

Dynamics of Political Transformation

What have been the political correlates of Latin America's economic strategies? As shown in the previous chapter, countries of the region pursued a wide array of formulas for economic development—liberalism, industrialism, socialism, and neoliberalism. As cause and consequence of these alterations, social structures underwent change, cities burgeoned, and politics produced a bewildering assortment of experiments—revolution, reform, reaction, and democracy. Within the political realm, diversity and change have been the central and defining themes.

Comparative analysis offers an effective way to understand the underlying relationship between economic and political transformations. This chapter therefore has two goals. One is to sketch broad *similarities* in processes of political transition. Our intention is not to depict the history of any single country; rather, it is to present a composite portrait that can reveal the overall context in which individual nations have developed.

Our second goal is to identify key *differences* among the countries of the region. This allows us to pose intriguing questions. Why, for instance, were there social revolutions in Bolivia and Mexico but not in Peru? Why did such diverse countries as Argentina, Brazil, and Chile all succumb to military dictatorships at about the same time? Comparative analysis not only sharpens our perception of individual countries but also offers a key to detecting patterns of cause and effect.

To explore processes of transformation, we focus not on the rise or fall of individual presidents or of partisan administrations, but on fundamental transitions between *political systems* (a.k.a. political *regimes*). We are seeking to identify patterns of structural change over time.

For this purpose, we begin with a straightforward classification of political regimes. Under the general heading of *democracy,* we distinguish between the following:

- Oligarchic democracy, which restricted electoral competition to rival factions of the socioeconomic elite;

- Co-optative democracy, which invited rising middle classes to take part in elections;
- Liberal democracy, which combines free and fair elections with the full enjoyment of citizen rights; and
- Illiberal democracy, the most common form in recent years, which combines free and fair elections with the partial (but systematic) denial of civil liberties to citizens.

Further, we observe several types of *authoritarianism:*

- Traditional dictatorship, usually by individual military strongmen;
- One-party (or dominant-party) rule, often associated with the predominance of multi-class "populist" alliances between local entrepreneurs and organized labor;
- "Bureaucratic" authoritarianism, ruled by the military as an institution (instead of an individual officer) in collaboration with bureaucrats and technocrats from the private sector;
- Revolutionary states, intended to bring about structural change in accordance with socialist prescriptions.

As these classifications demonstrate, Latin America has experienced an unusually broad array of political regimes. The conceptual challenge is to make sense out of what might otherwise look like empirical chaos. In this spirit we offer analytical tools, not conclusive solutions.

OLIGARCHIC RULE AND TOP-DOWN REFORM (1880s–1920s)

As explained in Chapter 12, the Industrial Revolution in Europe precipitated fundamental change in the economies of nineteenth-century Latin America. Inspired by liberal theory, elites throughout the region avidly promoted the formation and consolidation of "export-import" economies. Relying on its "comparative advantage," Latin America accelerated the exportation of agricultural goods and raw materials, including minerals, and imported manufactured goods from Europe and the United States. Commerce flourished on the basis of this exchange, and foreign investment flowed from the industrial nations.

In the domestic arena, export-import development strengthened the economic power of the upper classes. At a stroke, international trade suddenly enabled traditional landowners to reap enormous profits from their ranches, farms, and fields. With so much at stake, Latin American elites—especially landowners—began to take a clear interest in national politics. No longer content to stay on their fief-like haciendas, they began to pursue political power. The era of the swashbuckling *caudillo* was coming to an end.

This upper-class quest for political authority took two basic forms. In one version, landowners and other economic elites took direct control of the government—as in Argentina and Chile. They sought to build strong, exclusive regimes, usually with military support, often proclaiming legitimacy through adherence to constitutions strongly resembling U.S. and European democratic models. In both Argentina and Chile, there was genteel competition between political parties that tended, at least in this early phase, to represent competing factions of the aristocracy. There was more agreement than disagreement about basic policy issues, and little serious opposition to the wisdom of pursuing export-oriented economic growth. Competition was restricted and voting was often a sham. One might think of such a regime as an "oligarchic democracy."

A second pattern involved the imposition of dictatorial strongmen, often military officers, to assert law and order—again, for the ultimate benefit of the economic elites. Porfirio Díaz of Mexico, who took power in 1876, is perhaps the most conspicuous example—but the pattern also appeared in Venezuela, Peru, and other countries. In contrast to oligarchic democracy, where elites exercised direct political power, here it was the indirect application of elite rule through dictators who often did not themselves come from the upper ranks of the society.

In either case, the emphasis was on stability and social control. Dissident groups were suppressed, and the struggle for power was contained within restricted circles. Indeed, a basic goal was to centralize power, stripping it from regional *caudillos* where necessary, and to create strong and dominant nation-states. In Argentina, centralism triumphed with the establishment of the city of Buenos Aires as a federal district in 1880 (much like Washington, D.C., in the United States). In Mexico, the often ruthless policies of Porfirio Díaz led to enhanced national power at the expense of local strongholds. In Brazil, the imperial government of Dom Pedro II made significant headway toward the establishment of an effective nation-state (thereby provoking a regionalist back-lash that contributed to the empire's overthrow in 1889).

A primary motivation for these centralizers was to safeguard export-import economic development. Political stability was viewed as essential to attract foreign investment, which, in turn, could stimulate economic growth. When the invest-ment came, it helped strengthen the forces of law and order. Railroads offer a classic example. Foreign investors would be reluctant to put funds into a country threatened by political disorder; but once the railroads were built, as in Mexico and Argentina, they became important instruments for consolidating central rule, since they could be (and were) used to dispatch federal troops to put down uprisings in almost any part of the nation.

Consolidation of the export-import economies led to the emergence of urban working classes. Inspired mainly by anarchist principles, insurgent labor movements rocked the capital cities of the major countries with large-scale general strikes between 1914 and 1927. Most of these actions met with violent government repres-sion, a result that would weaken organized labor for decades to come. Latin America's ruling oligarchs felt no obligation to make serious concessions to the working classes.

Co-optative Democracy

Instead, liberal elites in leading countries made assiduous efforts to gain the alle-giance of the region's rising middle classes in order to strengthen upper-class power.

The most common tactic was to promote just enough institutional reform to allow effective pursuit of political office by members and representatives of the middle classes—without incurring the risk of major policy upheaval. A voting law in Argentina opened suffrage to large sectors of the male population and permitted a middle-class party, the so-called Radical Party, to win the presidency in 1916. Changes in Chile, actually beginning in the 1890s, saw the temporary installation of de facto parliamentary rule. In Brazil, the overthrow of the monarchy in 1889 opened a period of limited electoral politics. And even in Mexico, where a large-scale revolution broke out in 1910, the generalization holds: the original goal of the movement was not to transform society but merely to acquire access to the political system for excluded fragments of the country's middle class.

Generally speaking, these reformist movements produced "co-optative democracy"—in which effective participation spread from the upper class to the middle class, to the continuing exclusion of the lower class. Although they sometimes had unintended consequences, such transitions usually reflected the attempts of ruling socioeconomic elites to co-opt the middle sectors into supporting the socioeconomic system.

One significant side effect was the formation of a cadre, in various countries, of professional politicians. Party politics created careers for ambitious young activists (mostly male) who could devote their entire adult lives to the pursuit of political power. As often as not, they represented the interests of the reigning aristocracy, but they nonetheless constituted an identifiably separate group. As prominent actors in national politics, they would often become targets for the disdainful wrath of the military establishment.

For many countries of Latin America, or at least for the elites, the reformist strategy worked fairly well. European demand for raw materials during and after World War I led to continued and sustained prosperity. The export-import model of growth appeared to offer a functional and profitable means of integrating Latin America into the global system of capitalism. Political adaptations seemed to assure the long-standing hegemony of national elites. And then disaster struck.

POPULISM AND DICTATORSHIP (1930s–1970s)

The Great Depression had catastrophic impacts on Latin America's economies. It also wrought far-reaching changes in the political arena.

One response to pressures of the time was a return to military rule. Within a year or so after the October 1929 stock market crash in New York, army officers had sought or taken power in Argentina, Brazil, Chile, Peru, Guatemala, El Salvador, and Honduras. Mexico was enduring a special constitutional crisis of its own, and Cuba succumbed to a military takeover in 1933. The underlying fear was that the economic downturn would unleash violent popular protest that could disrupt the prevailing social order. It would be an exaggeration to say that the effects of the Depression alone caused these political outcomes, but they cast considerable doubt on the viability of the export-import model of growth, helped discredit ruling political elites, engendered frustration within the lower classes, and made middle-class elements more willing to accept military intervention. From the early 1930s onward, the armed forces reasserted their traditional role as a principal actor in Latin American politics.

Practically speaking, the post-1929 wave of military coups brought the era of "oligarchic democracy" to its ignominious end. Economic development had led to significant changes in Latin American society—in particular, the emergence of middle sectors and the appearance of urban working classes. Intramural competition among factions of the traditional aristocracy could no longer make convincing claims to political legitimacy. To be sure, attempts to sustain oligarchic rule took place under the rubric of what might be thought of as "semi-democracy"—elections that were rigged from the start, so that only acceptable candidates could win. One particularly notorious episode appeared in Argentina from 1932 to 1943, a so-called "infamous decade" during which elections were settled by "patriotic fraud." For the most part, though, oligarchs made a discreet exit from the political scene.

Two additional developments had crucial implications for political change. One was the adoption of an economic policy of "import-substitution industrialization" (ISI). As explained in the preceding chapter, this strategy augmented the economic role of government. States attempted to protect national "infant industries" by erecting barriers to international trade, favored local producers in government procurements, and promoted public partnerships in state-owned "parastatal" firms. Through protection and participation, the state in Latin America was furnishing critical impetus for economic recovery.

As industry progressed in major countries, the working classes grew in strength and importance. Whether autonomous or state-directed, union movements increased rapidly throughout the 1930s, and the support (or control) of labor became crucial for the continuation of industrial expansion. Workers were needed to provide labor and profits for employers. Organized labor was emerging as a significant actor.

The political expression of these socioeconomic changes took two forms. One was the continuation of co-optative democracy, through which industrialists and workers gained (usually limited) access to power through electoral or other competition. One example was Chile, where political parties were reorganized to represent the interests of new groups and social strata. Pro-labor and pro-industrialist parties thus entered the Chilean electoral process. As long as this arrangement lasted, their participation lent valuable support to the regime.

An alternative response involved the creation of multi-class "populist" alliances. The emergence of an industrial elite and the vitalization of the labor movement made possible a new, pro-industrial coalition merging the interests of entrepreneurs and workers—in some cases, directly challenging the long-standing predominance of agricultural and landed interests. Each of these alliances was created by national leaders who exploited the power of the state for the enhancement of their personal power. In Brazil, Getúlio Vargas thus began constructing a multi-class, urban-based populist coalition in the 1930s, as would Juan Perón in

Argentina in the 1940s. Common denominators across these regimes were the capacity to mobilize working-class elements, the utilization of nationalist and anti-imperialist rhetoric (and policies) as a unifying discourse, the reliance on cults of personality, and intolerance for the domestic opposition.

Extreme versions of this populist formulation resulted in "corporatist" states, in which political institutions followed functional rather than partisan lines. This harkened back to ancient Hispanic tradition, which organized society into functional groups or "corporations"—soldiers, priests, landowners, merchants, sheepherders, etc.—all under the presumably beneficent leadership of the monarchical state. During the 1930s, contemporary inspiration came from Mussolini's Italy, which established a classic corporatist model. During the 1940s, Franco's Spain provided yet another example of this approach. Fascism, like communism, struck some responsive chords within Latin America.

To one degree or another, corporatist elements found institutional expression not only in Brazil under Vargas and in Argentina under Perón, but also in Mexico under Lázaro Cárdenas. Under his leadership, the internal structure of the ruling party—later known as the PRI—followed explicitly functional lines, with organizations or "sectors" for workers, peasants, and soldiers, and one for everyone else (known as the "popular" sector). As in Brazil and Argentina, the central purposes were to eliminate class conflict, reduce partisanship, and bolster the effective power of centralized authority.

Corporatist or not, populist regimes had two key characteristics. For one thing, they were authoritarian: they usually represented coalitions of one set of interests (e.g., industrial) against an opposing set of interests (e.g., landed) that were by definition prevented from participation, and this involved some degree of both exclusion and repression. Second, as time would tell, they represented the interests of classes (e.g., workers and industrialists) that were bound to conflict among themselves. The maintenance of such regimes therefore depended in large part on the personal influence and charisma of individual leaders—such as Vargas in Brazil and Perón in Argentina. It also meant that, with or without magnetic leadership, the regimes would be hard to sustain in times of economic adversity. Parenthetically, this also helps explain why Mexico went to such great lengths to "institutionalize" its revolutionary legacy.

Women and Politics

Traditionally, the social role of females in Latin America had long been confined to the private sphere, particularly the family. Among the lower classes, especially, women were often heads of household—because husbands (or partners) had either died or moved elsewhere. Among the upper-class elite, extended families were frequently dominated by forceful matrons, grandmotherly figures who wielded unchallenged authority over such intimate matters as marriage, place of residence, and inheritance.

Over time the boundaries of acceptable social behavior for women started to broaden. In the nineteenth century, women of culture frequently hosted literary discussions, or *tertulias,* where guests could engage in spirited discourse about novels and *belles lettres.* Some, like Clorinda Matto de Turner and Mercedes Cabello de Carbonero in Peru, became distinguished writers (a tradition first set by a seventeenth-century Mexican nun, Sor Juana Inés de la Cruz). The process of change accelerated during the twentieth century. Within middling and upper class strata, proper young women ceased to be chaperoned on all social occasions (partly because there was less at stake in the event of an inconvenient marriage). Women also entered the job market and made their mark as teachers, professors, dentists, doctors, even lawyers.

Yet the public arena was off-limits to women. Politics was traditionally viewed as an exclusively masculine domain, an arena for the interplay of high-testosterone *macho* egos. As early as the 1920s, however, women in Chile and elsewhere mobilized in order to demand the right to vote. And in time they reached their goal. As Table 13.1 indicates, Latin America's women obtained suffrage mostly in the 1930s and 1940s (and as late as 1961 in Paraguay).

Table 13.1 Female Suffrage in the Americas

COUNTRY	YEAR IN WHICH NATIONAL WOMAN SUFFRAGE WAS RECOGNIZED
United States	1920
Ecuador	1929
Brazil	1932
Uruguay	1932
Cuba	1934
El Salvador	1939
Dominican Republic	1942
Guatemala	1945
Panama	1945
<u>Argentina</u>	<u>1947</u>
Venezuela	1947
Chile	1949
Costa Rica	1949
Haiti	1950
Bolivia	1952
Mexico	1953
Honduras	1955
Nicaragua	1955
Peru	1955
Colombia	1957
Paraguay	1961

SOURCE: Elsa M. Chaney, *Supermadre: Women in Politics in Latin America* (Austin: University of Texas Press, 1979), p. 169.

It is an inconvenient fact that female suffrage in Latin America usually came from authoritarian rulers who were hoping to construct new bases of political support for one-sided or fraudulent elections. This strategy was particularly evident in the case of populist (and/or corporatist) regimes.

The pattern took root in 1929, when a military government in Ecuador imposed a constitution that included women's right to vote. Similar situations later occurred in Brazil (1932), Cuba (1934), the Dominican Republic (1942), Haiti (1950), Mexico (1953), Peru (1955), Paraguay (1961), and most of Central America. Perhaps the most well-known instance took place in Argentina (1947), where Evita Perón became one of the most powerful women in the history of the Western Hemisphere. Even so, she presented herself with self-conscious modesty:

> In this great house of the Motherland, I am just like any other woman in any other of the innumerable houses of my people. Just like all of them, I rise early thinking about my husband and my children . . . It's that I so truly feel myself the mother of my people.

Thus did Evita, willful and ambitious, evoke time-honored themes of domesticity and motherhood.

A Surge of Democracy

Latin America enjoyed substantial rates of economic growth from the 1940s through the 1960s. Allied demand for foodstuffs, minerals, and raw materials during World War II led to the recovery of traditional export sectors. And in major countries, ISI produced substantial rates of economic growth. ECLA-style writings provided inspiration and validation for continuation of import-substitution programs, while financial experts hailed the existence of an economic "miracle" in highly statist Mexico.

Within the context of post–World War II euphoria, electoral democracy began to make substantial headway. From the mid-1940s through the early 1970s, free and fair elections took place in approximately half the countries of the region—especially in South America (including Argentina, Bolivia, Brazil, Chile, Colombia, Ecuador, Peru, Uruguay, and Venezuela). These were truly "liberal" democracies, which granted citizens more or less full access to civil liberties (freedom of speech, freedom of assembly, freedom to join political parties, and so on).

Winners of presidential elections in most cases were middle-class reformers, democratic politicians who sought to modernize socioeconomic structures, give meaningful voice to lower-class sectors, and bring about significant change in the name of social justice. Eventually, these aspirations came to pose serious threats to established interests. Agrarian elites objected to land reform, industrialists opposed higher taxes (and workers' rights to organize), and, in the midst of the Cold War, the United States objected to left-of-center social programs.

Tension mounted during the 1960s and 1970s, as Latin America's postwar economic boom began to subside. As explained in Chapter 12, ISI required heavy imports of capital goods. Given the small size of national markets, entrepreneurs

An American cartoonist depicts the Latin American military as a continuing threat to democratic institutions. (Roy B. Justus, *Minneapolis Star*, 1963. Reprinted with permission of the Star and Tribune Co.)

found that local demand for manufactured goods was severely limited. Technological innovation, modest by international standards, nonetheless led to the displacement of manual labor. The internal migration of displaced *campesinos* toward major cities centers swelled the ranks of urban workers. The inevitable result was growing unemployment. This, in turn, provoked intensive reactions on the part of organized labor.

Bureaucratic-Authoritarian Regimes

As pressure intensified, ruling elites in several countries imposed highly repressive regimes, often through military coups—as in Brazil (1964), Argentina (1966), and Uruguay and Chile (both 1973). In all cases, the most important decisions were made (or were subject to veto) by the top ranks of military officers. In view of economic stagnation, the military and civilian elites believed that they had to stimulate investment. In order to accomplish this, they believed they would have to dismantle, perhaps even crush, the collective power of the working class. The more organized the working class, the more difficult this task became.

Each of these military-dominated governments assumed control over decisions concerning labor's most vital interests—wages, working conditions, fringe benefits, and the right to organize. Labor thus had to reconcile itself to measures approved by government bureaucracies. Outright strikes were virtually nonexistent in Chile and Brazil during the mid-1970s. Argentina's stronger tradition of union initiative was harder to suppress, but labor leaders there felt obliged to show prudence and restraint as well. All three military regimes took an authoritarian approach to labor relations.

Why this heavy hand? Viewed in the short term, these developments could be explained by the need to curtail runaway inflation. These regimes came to power when inflation and balance-of-payments deficits had made their economies dangerously vulnerable. International credit, both public and private, had essentially closed off. They would therefore have to launch anti-inflationary stabilization programs, which, in turn, threatened to reduce real wages for workers. Under these conditions, it was no surprise that these military governments sought strict control over organized labor.

The soldiers in power attacked civilian leadership as well. Military governments proclaimed themselves to be "anti-political." All blamed the plight of their countries on the alleged incompetence, dishonesty, corruption, or treachery of professional politicians. The rulers were particularly harsh toward politicians of the left, especially the radical left, and toward leaders of working-class movements. Few channels of political opposition were left open. Just as Chile had once been the most democratic system in the region, its military regime became the most draconian, abolishing all political parties and burning the electoral rolls.

Argentina's military government took stern measures in 1976, suspending Congress and all political parties, thereby signifying a hiatus in competitive politics. Brazil's military guardians, having come to power in an atmosphere less radicalized in Argentina and Chile, pushed to replace the old political parties (and tighten control) with two government-sanctioned new ones. In Brazil, intensified repression in the late 1960s was followed by a gradual "opening" in the late 1970s.

Regimes pursuing this path became known as "bureaucratic-authoritarian" states, and they had several distinctive characteristics. One was the granting of public office to people with highly bureaucratized careers—to members of the military, the civil service, or large business firms. A second feature was the political and economic exclusion of the working class and the control of labor movements. Third was the reduction or near-elimination of political activity, especially in the early phases of the regime: problems were defined as technical, not political, and they were met with administrative solutions rather than negotiated settlements. Fourth, and most infamous, was the widespread reliance on torture, incarceration, and assassination of opponents as instruments of intimidation and control. Particularly notorious were the "disappearances" of thousands of alleged dissidents in Chile and Argentina. Terrorism by the state became a source of power for the state, or so it seemed at the time.

Finally, bureaucratic-authoritarian governments sought to revive economic growth by consolidating ties with international economic forces—revising, once again, the terms of national dependency on the global world-system. Specifically, leaders of these regimes forged alliances with multinational corporations (vast international companies such as IBM, Philips, Dow Chemical, or Volkswagen). To establish credit and gain time, they needed to come to terms with their creditors, including U.S. and European banks and international lending agencies (such as the World Bank and the Inter-American Development Bank). Tasks of this kind were commonly delegated to the most internationalized members of the ruling coalition, frequently young economists trained at American universities—often identified by derisive nicknames, such as the "Chicago boys" in Chile.

Mexico represented a different situation. Since the state acquired effective control over working-class organizations during the 1930s and 1940s, the country was able to make a transition from semicorporatist "populist" authoritarianism toward a modified version of "bureaucratic" authoritarianism without a brutal military coup. The control of the labor force would later be tested anew during the protracted post-1982 economic crisis. And by the 1990s, even the PRI began to loosen (and eventually lose) its grip over a rapidly changing population.

THE REVOLUTIONARY PATH (1950s–1980s)

In contrast to such relatively well-endowed countries as Argentina, Brazil, and Chile, nations at the other end of the developmental spectrum presented a poignant profile of dependency and poverty. Located principally in Central America and the Caribbean, as explained in Chapter 4, most of these disadvantaged countries had less than 10 million inhabitants by 2000. Lacking mineral and other natural resources, they built their economies around one (or two) agricultural crops—sugar, coffee, tobacco, bananas, cacao. Production took place on large-scale plantations—hence the term *plantation societies*—that required prodigious amounts of labor, either imported from Africa under slavery or extracted from the indigenous population through coercion.

During the late nineteenth and early twentieth centuries, plantation societies followed essentially the same route as larger nations of the region: extending their export-import economies, achieving higher levels of efficiency, concentrating their attention on the overseas (U.S.) market. This led to an influx of foreign (mainly American) investors and to the emergence of small-scale commercial and professional elites. The socioeconomic structure of these nations was based on inequality of landholdings and exploitation of labor. The corresponding political formula was "oligarchic democracy," in which upper-echelon groups passed around the presidency among themselves, supplemented by short-term bursts of military rule, usually in times of momentary crisis.

During the 1930s these plantation societies diverged from the dominant Latin American pattern. The world depression inflicted especially pervasive damage on Central America and the Caribbean. Unlike Brazil or Argentina, the smaller nations did not have the option of import-substitution industrialization. They lacked the resources, the capital, the technology, and, most of all, the market. Because of their poverty and small size, they did not have enough consumers to support local manufacturing. Their only choice was to continue producing agricultural goods for export, mainly to the United States. While other nations were constructing industrial plants in hopes of gaining economic independence, the lower-income economies remained utterly dependent on the American market.

And while South America continued its experiments with "co-optative democracy" and mass-based populism, oligarchic democracy in these less-developed countries gave way to long-term one-man dictatorships. The list of unsavory despots included Jorge Ubico in Guatemala, Maximiliano Hernández Martínez in El Salvador, Anastasio Somoza in Nicaragua, Rafael Trujillo in the Dominican Republic, and Fulgencio Batista in Cuba. All these dictators emerged from the armed forces; all fostered primitive cults of personality; all ruled with ruthless iron hands; all enriched themselves and their families at public expense.

Social conflict intensified in the decades after World War II. Yet the principal issue in these countries did not involve an urban working class; such a thing barely existed. The main problem was land. As the plantation barons sought better efficiency and higher profits, they seized more and more lands from villages, small owners, and peasants. The result was a large, angry, and growing stratum of displaced and landless *campesinos*. As in other parts of Latin America, class conflict was intensifying, although the *nature* of the conflict was specific to plantation societies. As dispossessed peoples raised their voices in complaint, they were met with violent repression by state authorities.

The political results were predictable. One was the appearance of Marxist-oriented revolutionary movements seeking to seize power through violent means. Since institutional opportunities for social reform were nonexistent, dissidents concluded that they had no choice but to fight fire with fire. A clandestine group managed to assassinate Rafael Trujillo in the Dominican Republic, only to have their triumph hijacked by the dictator's closest henchman. In the meantime, armed guerrilla groups emerged in Guatemala, El Salvador, Nicaragua, and Cuba.

Only in Cuba and Nicaragua did Marxist revolutionary movements actually manage to take power, while guerrillas in El Salvador eventually had to settle for a truce. Everywhere else in the region, left-wing guerrilla movements suffered defeat and extermination. Clearly, the social structure of plantation societies presented a necessary (but by no means sufficient) condition for revolutionary triumph.

A principal task for revolutionary leaders in both Cuba and Nicaragua was to create strong states, not just take them over. (Indeed, they had managed to overthrow preexisting governments precisely because they were so weak.) Initially drawing much of its legitimacy from Fidel Castro's personal charisma, the Cuban state evolved in the 1970s into a powerful network of stable institutions. A Marxist constitution took effect in 1976, the Cuban Communist Party became dominant, and the military became a modern professional force. As central management became routine, the Cuban state asserted thorough command of the national economy. In Nicaragua the Sandinista directorate, never dependent on individual charisma, sought institutional legitimacy through national elections in 1984. It also established mechanisms for popular participation in governance, and assumed a major role in the economy through nationalization of Somoza-held and other properties.

Generally speaking, socialist revolutionary leaders constructed monolithic political systems. There were many reasons for this tendency, such as:

- the conviction that a powerful government was an essential prerequisite for the implementation of fundamental policy change,
- the persisting strength and truculence of the opposition,
- the threat of foreign intervention, and
- an ideological commitment to revolutionary "purity"—a partisan (and partly psychological) insistence on orthodoxy and discipline.

The idea was to establish a practical monopoly on power with or without token opposition. Cuba was more successful in this regard than Nicaragua. Whatever the causes, results were apparent: revolutionary governments tended to be authoritarian.

In keeping with utopian aspirations, revolutionary regimes sought far-reaching social change. Both Cuba and Nicaragua launched national literacy campaigns soon after taking power. The social goal was to "capacitate" workers and peasants, removing obstacles to their full participation in the national economy and thereby eliminating a primary source of long-standing inequity. The political intent was to mobilize the population and inculcate values appropriate to a revolutionary society—in other words, to forge "a new socialist man."

Land reform was another key objective. The Fidelista regime in Cuba pursued this goal in two phases: first, a "land to the tiller" program initiated in 1959, and secondly, the nationalization of all holdings over 67 acres—a step that left about 30 percent of the farm population in the private sector. The Sandinista directorate in Nicaragua focused its attention largely on former landholdings of the Somoza dynasty. By 1988 cooperatives and state farms controlled approximately 35 percent of the country's agricultural land.

Finally, the socialist governments in Cuba and Nicaragua encountered virulent hostility from the United States. As detailed in Chapter 5, the U.S. government—under Democrats as well as Republicans—made repeated (and unsuccessful) efforts to overthrow the Castro regime in Cuba. During the 1980s, the Reagan administration gave extensive political and military support to antirevolutionary contras attempting to defeat the Sandinistas. Given the logic of the Cold War, Washington regarded revolutionary movements within the hemisphere as potential inroads by the communist enemy. They could not be permitted to take power; and if they did, they could not be permitted to govern.

Partly out of fear of left-wing revolution, plantation societies in other nations fell under the heel of brutal military rule. Stoked on by the Cold War, right-wing regimes in the 1970s and 1980s embarked on massive campaigns of repression. In the name of patriotic "anti-communism," government forces in El Salvador murdered and massacred thousands of innocent citizens. And in a tacit quest for "ethnic cleansing," military rulers in Guatemala launched genocidal assaults against indigenous peoples and villages. Such dictatorships did not bear all the hallmarks of South American "bureaucratic-authoritarian" regimes—lacking, as it were, the participation of technocratic elites—but they were even more repressive. Besides, the closed nature of the military caste often lent a "bureaucratic" tone to these governments.

A RENEWAL OF DEMOCRACY (1980s–PRESENT)

Subsequent developments throughout Latin America paved the way for a remarkable and largely unexpected trend—an extensive wave of political democracy. One factor was the "debt crisis" of the 1980s, a crushing economic burden that ultimately unraveled the social coalitions which had initially supported bureaucratic-authoritarian dictatorships. Local industrialists felt threatened by multinational corporations. Under the weight of the debt crisis, too, some military leaders chose to return to the barracks—and let civilians assume responsibility for what seemed to be an "unsolvable problem."

A second factor was pressure from below. The military's relentless abuse of human rights aroused protests from intellectuals, artists, middle-sector representatives, and the international community. A prominent feature of Latin American politics throughout the 1980s and 1990s was a rise in civic participation, as ordinary citizens began to insist on their rights and demand accountability from governments. In part this resulted from the uniting of opposition forces produced by the brutality of military repression. Human rights campaigns brought to the fore a new cadre of civilian, middle-class, well-educated leaders. Once democracy took hold, there was an increasing commitment to free and fair elections.

A third factor was the conclusion of the Cold War in 1989–91. This development not only led to widespread disenchantment with the illusory ideals of Marxist ideology. It removed a principal cause of left-vs.-right polarization throughout Latin America, and greatly reduced the intensity of political conflict throughout the region. It also appeared to demonstrate the innate superiority of Western "democracy" over Soviet-style "socialism." Further, it brought an end to the anti-communist crusade that had been waged for decades by the United States. Throughout the 1990s, at least, Latin America was free to settle disputes on its own terms, rather than as part of a global struggle of titanic proportions.

A fourth and related factor was an end of ideology. As the Washington consensus spread throughout the hemisphere, public discourse became economic rather than political, pragmatic rather than utopian. After decades of intense ideological strife, political actors tacitly agreed to a truce. Neoliberal prescriptions became the watchword of the day. In the face of technocratic orthodoxy, popular traditions of vibrant and voluble debate fell silent. An air of resignation tended to replace dissent.

To illustrate the extent and timing of this political transformation, Figure 13.1 plots the incidence of democratic and semi-democratic regimes in Latin America from 1972 through 2004. The vertical axis measures the number of countries with its

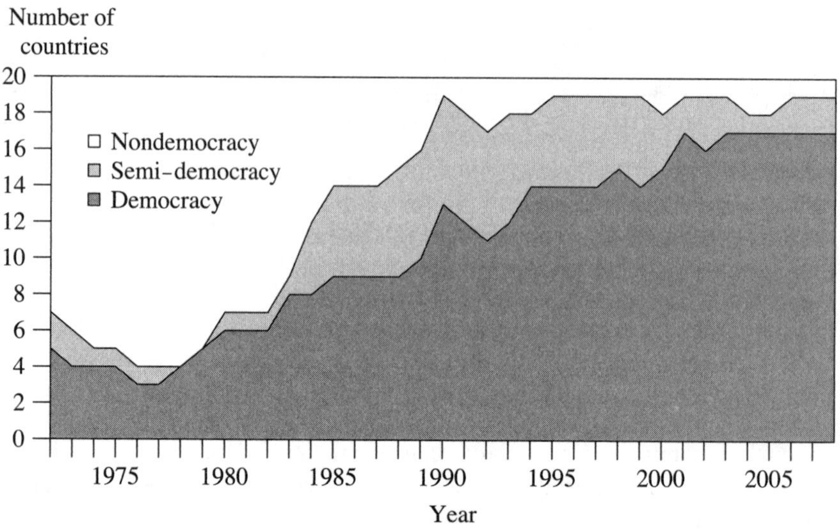

Number of
countries

Figure 13.1 The Rise of Electoral Democracy in Latin America, 1972–2008

respective regime type, and the horizontal axis measures year-by-year change over time. The "democracy" category includes countries with free and fair elections. "Semi-democracy" refers to "rigged" elections that were free but not fair: anyone could run, but only one candidate could win. The upper portion of the graph corresponds to any form of nondemocratic or authoritarian rule.

The trends reveal a long-term rise in democratic politics. In the mid-1970s, an era of stark military repression, only three countries could boast sustained records of free and fair elections: Colombia, Costa Rica, and Venezuela. What became a persistent cycle of democratization first took root in 1978 in Ecuador, Peru, and the Dominican Republic, bringing the total number of electoral democracies up to six. The 1980s witnessed the restoration of democracy throughout much of South America, with the addition by 1985 of Argentina and Uruguay and later of Brazil and Chile. The 1990s heralded the installation of essentially new democracies in Mexico, Central America, and the Caribbean. By 1998 there were fifteen electoral democracies, four semi-democracies, and only one authoritarian regime. By 2004, seventeen out of twenty countries were holding free and fair elections, the exceptions being Cuba, Haiti, and Venezuela.

Most of these democracies were limited or "incomplete." In some countries, the military still wielded considerable power from behind the scenes, and could exercise a veto over major policies. Human rights suffered continuing violations. The press was only partially free. Many crucial decisions, especially on economic policy, were made in high-handed and undemocratic fashion. After years of repression (including physical elimination) by military dictatorships, the political left was weakened and divided. Key topics, such as land reform and income redistribution, stood no chance of serious consideration. As a result, this new cycle of democratic transformation posed little fundamental threat to established interests. In contrast to the "dangerous" democracies of the 1960s, the new democracies of the 1990s were relatively "safe."

By the turn of the twenty-first century, Latin America's political spectrum encompassed a broad span. At one end was "liberal democracy," with free and fair elections and generalized respect for rights of free speech, organization, and dissent, After a long struggle with tyranny, Chile resumed its position, along with Uruguay and Costa Rica, as one of the most democratic countries of the region. At the other end were authoritarian episodes, and coups were attempted—if unsuccessfully—in Guatemala, Paraguay, and Venezuela.

In between these two extremes was "illiberal democracy," a form of incomplete democracy that combined electoral competition with pervasive constraints on citizen rights. To one degree or another, many Latin American countries—including Argentina and Brazil during the 1990s—fell into this intermediate category. Moreover, essential political institutions—legislatures, courts, regulatory agencies, and the civil service—were notoriously weak. Key questions therefore emerged: Would Latin America's fragile democracies develop the will and capacity to protect the rights of citizens? Would they acquire the strength and ability to impose the rule of law?

Empowerment of Women?

From the 1950s through the 1980s, women of Latin America became increasingly forceful. They took active part in revolutionary movements, making up one-third of the Sandinista fighting force in Nicaragua and a comparable share in El Salvador. As brutal military regimes spread throughout South America, women found ways to resist. In Brazil, they joined together in "militant motherhood" to denounce abuses of human rights and demand amnesty for political prisoners and exiles. In Argentina, the "mothers of the Plaza de Mayo" held weekly vigils demanding information on loved ones who had "disappeared." In Chile, female *arpilleras* expressed anger and grief through subversive forms of art, while other women engaged in public protests against military rule.

The trend toward democratization at first produced ambivalent effects. Eager to recoup political power, civilian men at first controlled the political process, reserving high-ranking positions for themselves and their colleagues, making only token concessions to women's demands. The pattern started shifting by the 1990s. Women now constituted significant electoral constituencies, sometimes a majority of voters. They were increasingly educated and engaged in the workforce. In solidarity, they came together to form innumerable grassroots movements and non-governmental organizations (NGOs) devoted to improving conditions for women. Feminist publications emerged in Mexico, Argentina, Chile, Brazil, and other countries.

As a result, women of Latin America gained increasing representation in positions of power. In 1990, women occupied an average of only 5 percent of the seats in upper legislative houses (or senates) and 9 percent in lower houses; by

2002, these proportions climbed to 13 and 15 percent, approximately the same level as in the United States. Laws requiring quotas for women candidates on party tickets were proving effective, especially where they were firmly enforced. By 2000, women constituted 13 percent of Latin America's cabinet ministers. They were now managing key portfolios, such as foreign relations, and in some countries they stormed the ultimate bastion of masculine authority—the ministry of defense.

Eventually, and inevitably, women became presidents. To be sure, most of the early examples—Isabel Martínez de Perón in Argentina, Violeta Barrios de Chamorro in Nicaragua, Mireya Moscoso in Panama—acquired public profiles mainly as widows of prominent men. But independent women were stepping forward as serious contenders. In 2005–6 Michelle Bachelet won the presidency in Chile. Cristina Fernández de Kirchner thereafter followed suit in Argentina (although she was the wife of the outgoing president, she had much earlier forged political credentials on her own). Legacies of *machismo* were not nearly as strong as stereotypes might suggest. By these standards, it is worth noting, Latin America was well ahead of the United States.

Economic Uncertainty and Political Disenchantment

In the economic arena, Latin America's democracies gradually began to reap rewards for imposing stringent neoliberal reforms. Inflation dropped, investment swelled, and, after a long delay, economic growth reappeared. From 2004 through 2007, the average growth rates for the region exceeded 5 percent, but then plunged again in 2008–9.

Basic problems lingered. Most new private funding came in the form of "portfolio" investments (that is, purchases of paper stocks or bonds) rather than direct investments (construction of plants or factories). Portfolio investments tend to be highly mobile and notoriously volatile, and they can leave host countries almost instantly. Despite impressive and often courageous efforts at economic reform, Latin America still remained vulnerable to the vagaries of world financial markets.

There were structural problems as well. One was the persistence of poverty. According to international standards, nearly 40 percent of the population of Latin America qualified as "poor" in the mid-1990s. A second long-term problem was inequality. Ever since data on the subject first became available in the 1950s, Latin America has displayed the most uneven distribution of income in the world—more so than Africa, South Asia, and the Middle East—and the situation was getting progressively worse. Social equity still posed a major challenge.

The persistence of these age-old problems fostered widespread disenchantment throughout the region. In response, popular frustration led to the rise of what came to be called the "new left" (a.k.a. the "pink tide"). Starting with Venezuela in 1998, the region witnessed a surge of leftist electoral triumphs—in Brazil, Argentina, Bolivia, Ecuador, and Nicaragua. Some observers believed (and many hoped) that this tide crested in 2006, with narrow losses for populist candidates in

Peru and Mexico. But in 2008, voters in Paraguay threw their support to Fernando Lugo, a former Catholic bishop and advocate of "liberation theology" whose victory ended the 62-year reign of the Colorado Party, his country's equivalent of the Mexican PRI. In early 2009, voters in El Salvador threw their support to Mauricio Funes, the candidate of a political party that grew out of the country's foremost left-wing guerrilla movement.

What was the meaning of this trend? First and foremost, the pink tide was a protest movement. It was a protest against conditions of poverty, inequality, and corruption. It was a protest against the inability (or unwillingness) of governments to promote effective social justice. It was a protest of citizens against impersonal economic forces and uncaring political leaders.

Second, it amounted to a rejection of the neoliberal policies propounded by the Washington consensus—free-market policies designed to promote free trade, foreign investment, and reductions in state power. Poor people believed that the Washington consensus favored privileged elites at the expense of suffering masses. The movement further exuded an anti-American flavor, resulting from deep-seated resentment of the George W. Bush administration's unilateral style and, more particularly, from opposition to the war in Iraq. Citizens of Latin America were casting judgment on U.S. policies around the world, not only in the Western Hemisphere, and many were losing their respect for American society.

Third, the pink tide was a broad collection of movements. It emerged from local conditions. It was not centralized. Its membership was fluid, and there was competition in its ranks. It was far from doctrinaire—ideological inspiration comes from such diverse sources as nationalism, populism, indigenous tradition, Catholicism, and, not surprisingly, diluted forms of Marxism.

It was, furthermore, a democratic trend. Its leaders came to power through free and fair elections. They represented their citizens. To be sure, Hugo Chávez of Venezuela subsequently moved in authoritarian directions, but others did not. And they were by no means all Chavistas—they might have admired Chávez's ability to yank George Bush's chain and envied his petrodollar windfalls, but they sought to emulate neither his pronouncements nor his policies. Over time, Lula of Brazil steadily distanced himself from Chávez and became his principal rival for the leadership of South America.

Ultimately, the rise of the pink tide can be understood as a reaction against the "taming" of democracy that was so apparent in the 1990s. As described earlier, post-transition democracies in Latin America posed little if any threat to established interests and elites. Policy agendas were narrow, popular sectors were disorganized, and states were lacking in resources and capabilities: in contrast to a prior generation, democracy was no longer "dangerous." After the turn of the century, however, the relentless accumulation of popular grievances and the progressive disintegration of traditional institutions created demands and opportunities for a new generation of political movements. In a dialectical sense, it was the weakness of Latin American democracy in the 1990s that paved the way for the new left in the 2000s.

EXPLORATIONS IN COMPARATIVE ANALYSIS

A second broad goal of this chapter is to explore (and explain) key differences in political conditions among countries of Latin America. Comparative analysis involves three steps: first, identifying elements shared in common by Latin American societies; second, uncovering key differences between their historical experiences; third, and most difficult, ascertaining the cause-and-effect relationship between those differences. Are there discernible patterns of economic and social development that can account for political trajectories of countries in the region? (Or, in formal terms, does variation in x really explain differences in y?)

How might this actually work? Thus far we have described *common features* of historical change for two groups of nations in Latin America—(a) larger and more advanced countries, such as Argentina and Brazil, and (b) the lower-income "plantation societies." We now turn to the challenge of identifying and explaining essential *differences* among the nations of the region. We adopt two distinct strategies:

(1) the analysis of differences in social structure and political experience *across individual countries*—an approach that would permit, for example, a comparison between Argentina and Brazil, or between Cuba and El Salvador, and

(2) exploration of *change over time* within individual countries—a focus which would allow us to trace the formation of social coalitions supporting reactionary dictatorship in Chile, for example, and/or revolutionary rule in contemporary Cuba.

Once again, our goal is to present a schematic way of thinking about such developments, rather than a definitive set of rigid judgments.

Building a Conceptual Framework

Our first task is to construct a framework for analyzing social structures. We therefore concentrate on urban and rural social-class groupings:

- the *urban upper class*, consisting primarily of industrialists, bankers, financiers, and large-scale merchants;
- the *rural upper class*, mainly landowners;
- the *urban middle class*, a heterogeneous stratum including professionals, teachers, shopkeepers, and so on;
- the *rural middle class*, not often noticed in Latin America, one that includes small farmers as well as merchants in rural areas;
- the *urban lower class*, principally an industrial working class, but a stratum that also includes the services sector and growing segments of unemployed migrants from the countryside; and
- the *rural lower class*, either an agrarian proletariat or a traditional peasantry—some of whose members may take part in the national economy, some of whom (especially in indigenous communities) may subsist on the fringes of the marketplace.

The groupings in the "lower class," often known as the "popular classes" in Latin America, represent, by far, the largest segments in society. These are poor people, undereducated and sometimes malnourished, and they have been systematically deprived of the benefits of development. Many of them participate in the rapidly emerging "informal sector," working at odd jobs outside the formal economy. (The informal sector is an unusually amorphous group, including peddlers and beggars and small-scale entrepreneurs, and for simplicity's sake, it does not receive separate consideration in this analysis.)

One additional social actor—not a class or stratum, but a critical group nonetheless—consists of the *external sector*. It includes private investors and corporations as well as international agencies (IMF, World Bank), foreign governments, and foreign military establishments. Though sometimes divided against itself, the external sector has often wielded enormous power in Latin America.

To enhance their relative position, these social actors typically compete for control of major institutions. The most crucial institution has been the *state*, which commands large-scale resources and usually claims an effective monopoly on the legitimate use of force (only a government, for example, can put a citizen in jail). One key group within the state has been the military; another consists of party politicians (when they exist); another is composed of technocrats and bureaucrats. Also important as social actors have been the Roman Catholic Church and other non-governmental organizations.

Figure 13.2 provides a general picture of these groups and institutions. It does not depict the outlines of any specific Latin American society. It is an abstract scheme, a hypothetical means of illustrating the subject of concern.

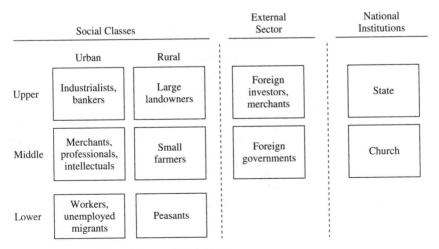

Figure 13.2 Hypothetical Array of Social Actors

To apply the framework to any historical situation, we need to pose a common set of fundamental questions. Here we thus inquire:

- What are the principal social classes? Which ones are present, and which ones are absent?
- Which social classes have the most power?
- Which groups are allied with which? On what basis?
- How powerful is the state? Is it captive to any of the social classes, or is it autonomous?
- What are the predominant factors on the international scene? What, in particular, is the position of the United States?

We next present schematic analyses of political and social transitions in selected countries. We concentrate here on the years from the 1950s through the 1990s, though the method could just as well apply to other periods in time. This is an interpretive exercise, we emphasize, not a definitive statement; it requires estimates and judgments that should provoke discussion and debate. Nonetheless, we think the approach provides strong confirmation of our basic arguments: that political outcomes in Latin America derive largely from the social class structure, that the class structure derives largely from each country's position in the world economy, and that a comparative perspective on these phenomena can help elucidate the variations and the regularities in Latin American society and politics.

Getting Down to Cases

Our first application deals with Argentina, described in Chapter 9, where the economic dominance of beef and wheat produced two major social results: the absence of a peasantry, especially in the *pampas* region, and the importation of working-class labor from Europe. In the years before Perón, the state and the foreign sector were mostly in league with landed interests, as shown in Figure 13.3. (Solid arrows represent relatively firm alliances; broken arrows represent fragile or partial coalitions.) Even the Radicals who governed with urban middle-class support in 1916–30 tended to favor the cattle-raising oligarchs.

For economic and demographic reasons, Argentina's urban working class began exerting pressure on the political system in the 1930s, but there was no possibility of a class-based alliance with a peasantry; the most likely allies, instead, were newly emergent industrialists who were ready to challenge the landowning aristocracy and its foreign connections. The preconditions thus existed for an urban, multi-class coalition of workers, industrialists, and some segments of the middle class. It took the political instinct, the populist rhetoric, and the personal charisma of Colonel Juan Perón to make this alliance a reality, and he used a corporatist state structure to institutionalize it. One reason for its initial success was that the landowners had no peasantry with which to form a common conservative front. A reason for its ultimate failure was that limited industrial growth led to class-based worker-owner conflict within the coalition itself.

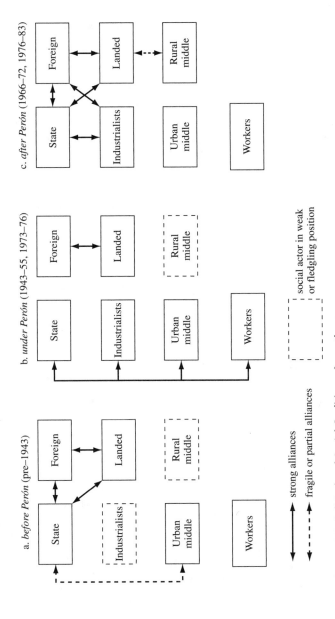

Figure 13.3 Political and Social Coalitions: Argentina

a. *before Perón* (pre–1943)

b. *under Perón* (1943–55, 1973–76)

c. *after Perón* (1966–72, 1976–83)

strong alliances

fragile or partial alliances

social actor in weak or fledgling position

Starting in 1966 and again in 1976, the military, committed to barring the Peronists from power, seized the state and attempted to impose a "bureaucratic-authoritarian" regime. The dominant alliance consisted of military officers, foreign investors, local industrialists, and landowners. Workers were repressed and forcibly excluded from power. The middle sectors played a waiting game, then found their opportunity with Alfonsín's election in 1983. Their party was, in turn, displaced by an elected Peronist president, Carlos Menem. He soon launched an orthodox stabilization program that turned Argentine class politics on its head. The Peronists, once the implacable foes of economic orthodoxy, now provided the congressional votes to put that doctrine, including wholesale privatization, into action.

Chile is quite a different case. It has contained every type of social actor, including a peasantry (and migratory rural proletariat) and a working class that, by 1900, was well organized, at least by Latin American standards. Foreign interests, especially the copper companies, collaborated with an upper class that, in contrast to Argentina, was deeply involved in finance and industry as well as land. Though political parties represented specific social groups, the state generally allowed free political competition.

So there existed elements of a powerful socialist movement (see Figure 13.4). Party politics could (and did) lead to ideological polarization. The alliance of the foreign sector with the upper class added a nationalistic dimension to antiaristocratic resentment. A broad-based coalition of workers and peasants seemed possible: hence the triumph and euphoria of the early Salvador Allende government.

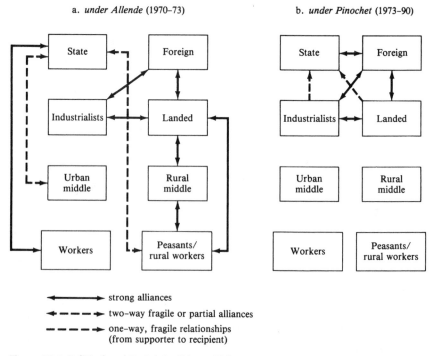

Figure 13.4 Political and Social Coalitions: Chile

Chile's socialist movement was not able, however, to expand its support much beyond its industrial working-class base. Allende supporters failed especially to convert many of the lower middle class. Urban and rural elements of the upper class, on the other hand, maintained their solidarity, partly through family connections, and landowners managed to get support from other strata in the countryside. U.S. undercover intervention further hastened the downfall of Allende's regime and thereby "saved" the Chilean conservatives.

After 1973, the Chilean military, like its counterpart in Argentina, established a bureaucratic-authoritarian system. The ruling coalition included industrialists, landowners, foreign investors, and a state that possessed extraordinary power. Staffed by generals and technocrats, especially the "Chicago boys," the Chilean government set about its course determined to prevail over any and all opposition. In the course of financial reorganization and extensive privatization, the government also increased the concentration of wealth, when a few rich clans and conglomerates bought the privatized state enterprises.

Brazil presented a similar picture. Under Vargas, the Estado Novo organized urban workers under the auspices of state control. In the early 1960s, his protégé, João Goulart, stepped up the mobilization of the workers—and also fomented (or at least permitted) the organization of peasants in the countryside. The prospect of a worker-peasant alliance antagonized both the upper class and foreign interests, depicted in Figure 13.5, and prompted the military to intervene

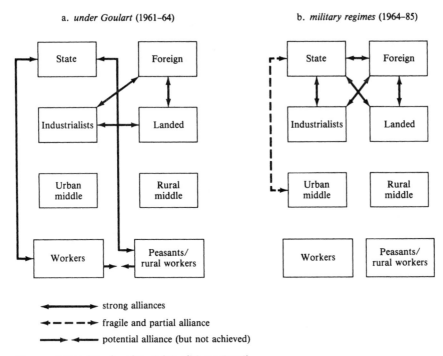

a. *under Goulart (1961–64)*   b. *military regimes (1964–85)*

⟶ strong alliances

◀ − − − ▶ fragile and partial alliance

⟶ ◀ potential alliance (but not achieved)

Figure 13.5 Political and Social Coalitions: Brazil

in 1964 and to establish a prototypical bureaucratic-authoritarian regime. Despite waves of repression that hit every social sector (although to highly differing degrees), the Brazilian government succeeded in retaining more residual middle-class support than its counterparts in Argentina or Chile, and this explains in part why the process of liberalization *(abertura)* was successful at an earlier stage there.

Mexico offers a different combination. Prior to the Revolution of 1910, the country had no indigenous industrial elite or rural middle sector; there was a nascent but unorganized working class. As shown in Figure 13.6, the ruling coalition, under the Porfiriato, included three groups: landowners, the foreign sector, and the state.

The Revolution ruptured this coalition and, through agrarian reform, weakened the rural elite. The state increased its authority and, from the 1930s onward, encouraged the formation of an industrial bourgeoisie. The postrevolutionary governments drew popular support from both workers and peasants, and under Cárdenas developed a strategy for dealing with the masses: the state would organize workers and peasants in such a way as to keep them apart. The PRI developed separate "sectors" for workers and peasants, reflecting the regime's obsession with heading off any spontaneous, class-based politics. By the

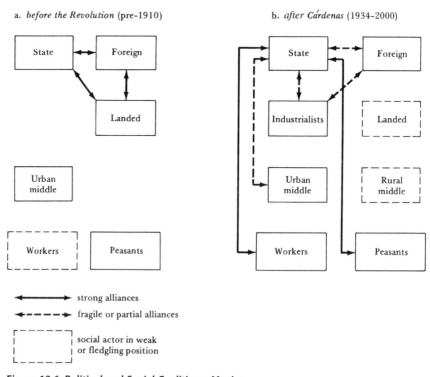

Figure 13.6 Political and Social Coalitions: Mexico

mid-1990s, however, the PRI was suffering major electoral defeats, especially on the state and local levels. Furthermore, top-level feuds were threatening to destroy the party's supposedly multi-class hegemony.

Cuba's plantation society reveals still another profile. Foreign (that is, U.S.) domination of the sugar industry meant that, for all practical purposes, there was hardly any local upper class. Workers in the mills and on plantations formed an active proletariat, as pictured in Figure 13.7, and migration strengthened ties between laborers in the cities and the countryside. Unions were weak, the army was corrupt, and the state, under Batista, was a pitiful plaything of U.S. interests.

Cuba possessed elements of a socialist movement, one that could capitalize on anti-imperialist sentiments. There was another secret to Fidel's eventual success: his movement would meet very little resistance, except for the foreign sector—whose proconsuls did not use all the resources at their disposal. Since 1959 Fidel and his lieutenants have revamped the island's social structure, eliminating vestiges of the old upper class, organizing middle- and lower-class groups in cities and the country-side, and implementing a "command" economy. It was achieved, however, only with massive Soviet support. This dependency became painfully apparent when the Soviet Union and its subsidy both disappeared in the early 1990s.

The goals of this exercise have been both methodological and substantive. Our *methodological* goal has been to demonstrate principles and techniques of

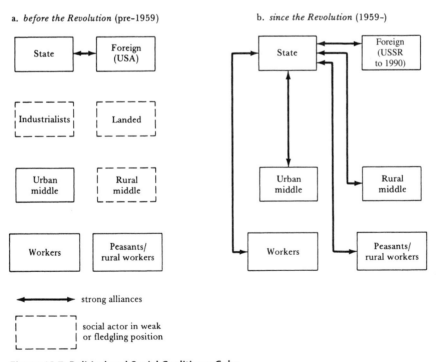

Figure 13.7 Political and Social Coalitions: Cuba

comparative analysis in such a way as to illuminate differences and similarities among countries covered in this book. Our *substantive* intent has been to support the claim that, over time, changes in social structures—and in social coalitions—can shed significant light on patterns of political change in Latin America.

We wish to emphasize that this perspective illustrates only one approach to comparative historical analysis. There are many other ways of carrying out this kind of exercise. Political scientists have focused on the importance of formal (and informal) institutions, especially electoral institutions. Gender specialists have demonstrated the utility of comparing societies according to their treatment of women and families. Sociologists and anthropologists have analyzed comparative dimensions of social movements and grassroots organizations. Practitioners of cultural studies have revealed the contours of ideology and the subtle interplay among literature, the arts, and social formations. All such perspectives can be extremely useful.

Our basic point is modest: comparative historical analysis is feasible, constructive, and enlightening. It is more art than science. At the same time, it can illuminate whatever may be "unique" about specific societies, and it can shed light on patterns of cause and effect. That conviction has established a foundation for this book.

14

Culture and Society

Richness, texture, and complexity are the hallmarks of Latin American cultural expressions. These features are deeply rooted in the region's past. The conquering Spaniards and Portuguese brought with them Iberian notions of culture and considered them to be superior to indigenous ways. Similarly, they held African religions and cultures to be inferior to their own. Throughout the colonial period, elite society looked to European literature, poetry, art, music, and theater as the standard for propriety, suitability, and creativity. This European-oriented world disdained the lower classes. At the same time, Indian societies survived and retained relative autonomy as they concurrently interacted with the Spaniards and Portuguese. Likewise, slaves maintained African traditions of religion, belief, customs, and language even as they learned to cope with their masters and their new environment.

Parallel cultures continued, yet over time mixture and hybridity intensified. The interactions among different peoples engendered new cultural forms that evolved and became distinct from their origins. Slaves and freed people of African descent created new rhythmic and musical forms and alternative ways of expressing their religious beliefs. They borrowed from indigenous and European traditions as well. Indians acculturated to Spanish ways, transforming them as they adapted. Those of European background also modified their customs and culture. Born in the Americas, they eventually saw themselves as fundamentally distinct from those arriving from Iberia.

On the eve of independence, only a small percentage of the population of Latin America was literate. Very few women had access to the written word. In the Spanish colonies, the sons of the elites and a scattering of other talented males attended universities founded in the sixteenth and seventeenth centuries (e.g., in Mexico City, Lima, Bogotá, and Guatemala), but most received education from private tutors. Brazilians had to cross the Atlantic in order to attend university in Coimbra, Portugal, or in other European cities. Only in 1808 when the Portuguese

403

royal court moved to Rio de Janeiro did the country acquire a printing press. It took another decade for universities to be established within Brazil.

Literary works, essays, and even newspapers circulated among a small segment of society, largely within urban settings. Many aspiring authors supported themselves as journalists, a tradition that would continue throughout the nineteenth and twentieth centuries. These literary venues and cultural exchanges merely reinforced a closed masculine world of intellectuals and *letrados* (men of letters) from the middle sectors or upper echelons of society, although by the mid-nineteenth century, some women participated in these circles. Thus, exemplary novels, poetry, and essays that have come to represent the classical canon of Latin American culture reflect only one segment of society and one kind of cultural production. Other forms, produced by the lower classes, remained vital to everyday life, but have been less registered and preserved.

What then has been unique about how Latin Americans have described themselves and their world through the written word, art, song, and performance? How has that changed in the twentieth and twenty-first centuries with film, radio, television, and the Internet? Moreover, how has Latin American culture been shaped by the history of a given country, region, or the continent as a whole?

FROM COLONIES TO NATIONS

In the late eighteenth century, liberal ideas derived from the European and American Enlightenment circulated in the Spanish and Portuguese empires. At times, they arrived in books and pamphlets by authors such as Voltaire, Rousseau, Jefferson, and Diderot that were smuggled into the colonies. Often they entered with the sons of the privileged few when returning from study or travel abroad. These ideas not only inspired the independence movement, but also affected architecture and literature. Architects abandoned the majestic baroque and more ornamental rococo styles when designing churches and public buildings, and constructed edifices in sharper and cleaner neoclassical styles. Inspired by the American and French revolutions, humanist thinkers penned essays and articles criticizing colonial institutions and promoting freedom and nationalism. For many, the grandeur and the potential greatness of the continent became a theme that justified a break with the old and an embrace of the new.

As the Spanish empire crumbled, patriotic poetry helped consolidate new national identities. Among the poets of the period was José Joaquín de Olmedo (1780–1847), the son of a Spanish captain and an Ecuadorian mother, who joined others in declaring the city of Guayaquil independent from Spain in 1820. His most well-known poem, *La victoria de Junín: Canto a Bolívar* (Victory at Junín: Song to Bolívar), praises the Liberator for his heroism on the battleground and legitimizes the independence movement by declaring its warriors to be the rightful heirs to the Incas.

Already a new theme had emerged. For some writers, claims to authority, legitimacy, and tradition came from the indigenous past rather than a European heritage. Patriotic poetry constructed many of its metaphors around the near-divine power of its independence leaders whose bellicose ways were deeply rooted in the colonial and pre-Conquest past. Yet they promised an enlightened future for the new nations rising out of the bloody battles for independence.

The novel offered a new form for social criticism of the old and new orders. *El periquillo sarniento* (The Mangy Parrot), written in 1816 by Mexican journalist and author José Joaquín Fernández de Lizardi (1776–1827), exemplifies this genre. Considered by many as Latin America's first novel, it is a picaresque tale of the son of a creole family from Mexico City who lives a wild and carefree life. This genre provided an opportunity for Fernández de Lizardi to paint a playful picture of his milieu and satirize all social classes during this transitional moment from colony to independence.

A number of remarkable polymaths contributed to the founding of the new nations of Latin America. Especially outstanding among them was Andrés Bello (1781–1865), a native of Caracas and a lawyer by training, who accompanied the German naturalist and explorer Alexander von Humboldt on part of his scientific expedition of South America in 1800. He also served for a short time as Simón Bolívar's tutor. After serving as a diplomat for the Venezuelan republic, he moved to Chile where he became the first rector of the University of Chile. Bello authored the 1852 Civil Code of Chile that borrowed from Napoleonic law. It was later adopted by Colombia and Ecuador. His lengthy epic poem *Silva a la agricultura de la zona tórrida (Agriculture of the Torrid Zone,* 1826), an ode to tropical products of a lush and bountiful continent, is considered a foundational work for Latin American literature. Bello represented the enthusiasm of the founding generation of the new republics that strongly desired to create a unique literature with its own cultural and intellectual traditions.

Romanticism, Indians, and Slaves

Turmoil and warring factions shaped political events from the 1820s to the 1850s in most countries as Liberals and Conservatives fought for hegemony and battling warriors laid their claims to the reins of power. Defining the nature of the nations carved out of the Spanish empire became a preoccupation of humanists and writers throughout the period. In rejecting the formalism of neoclassicism, a rising generation of intellectuals attempted to distinguish themselves from Europe. Yet in a pattern that would repeat itself throughout the nineteenth and twentieth centuries, they appropriated European trends and adapted and transformed them on American soil.

In the wake of independence, romanticism became the vehicle for defining these new countries. Enthusiastic idealism about the new nations' potential for wealth and prosperity drove this literary current. The natural riches of the land and the force of its people promised greatness. Among the first promoters of romanticism in South America was Esteban Echeverría (1805–51), an Argentine poet and writer. Having lived in Paris during the zenith of the French romantic movement, he returned to Buenos Aires intent on forging a national literature reflective of its natural surroundings and its local social reality. This did not mean turning his back on Europe, as Echeverría and many other nineteenth-century intellectuals considered the Old World to be a positive influence on the backward, primitive, and violent nature of America. His most famous work, *El matadero* (The Slaughterhouse, 1839), looks at the clashes between what he considered the reactionary and treacherous *caudillos,* such as Juan Manuel de Rosas. For Echeverría, enlightened Europeanized intellectuals were the chosen ones who could transmit the culture that was necessary to civilize the emergent nation.

In this regard, Echeverría's work stood as a precursor to that of Domingo Faustino Sarmiento (1811–88), the renowned writer, journalist, and president of Argentina, whose battles against Rosas forced him into Chilean exile. There he wrote *Facundo: Civilización e Barbarie* (Facundo: Civilization and Barbarism), that attacks Rosas for his authoritarian rule. For Sarmiento, the rural *gaucho* represented a barrier to the country's potential. Instead he favored the city where institutions of education, learning, and refinement could transform the nation's backwardness. An underlying premise of Sarmiento's work was that European immigration would solve Argentina's cultural and demographic deficiencies. Ironically, while deriding the *gaucho* for his supposed negative influences on the country, Sarmiento ended up placing this figure at the center of all discussions about the nature of the country and its people. While in Chile, Sarmiento was responsible for establishing the first school for teachers in Latin America. As president of Argentina (1868–74), he promoted the expansion of public education as the path to the country's modernization.

Not all mid-nineteenth century Argentine writers rejected the *gaucho* as a backward pull on society. In 1872, José Hernández (1834–86) penned an epic poem *Martín Fierro* that was an immediate popular success. It presents the story of a poor Argentine cowboy and his hard life on the *pampas* (grassy plains). In offering a romanticized tale of a gaucho, Hernández, who opposed Sarmiento's immigration proposals, presented this pastoral character as the "authentic" representative of Argentine people. For Hernández, the gaucho had guaranteed the country's independence and ensured its vitality. His poetic homage to the gaucho is in part a lament over the impending disappearance of this noble figure of the pampas. This tension between the rural and urban continued throughout the nineteenth and twentieth centuries. Argentine nationalists would return to the image of the gaucho as a national symbol on numerous occasions to counter what were considered the corrupting influences of the Europeanized urban world.

While residents of the Río de la Plata region debated the role of the gaucho in Argentine's future, Brazilian romanticists faced different dilemmas. The empire's political stability largely relied on the iron fist of the generals who had crushed multiple regional rebellions, including a ten-year revolt of gauchos in the country's south. For this reason, and contrary to Argentina, Brazilian gauchos were utterly disqualified from becoming a symbol of the nation as a whole.

Instead, romantic writers nostalgically turned to the figure of the Brazilian Indian. By the mid-nineteenth century, the indigenous people of Brazil had been exterminated, assimilated, or pushed into the backlands. Barely visible as a sector of society, they became an essential part of a pure and simple foundational myth of the Brazilian nation.

Two romantic writers are emblematic of what became known as the Indianist movement. One was Antônio Gonçales Dias (1823–64), who tragically died in a shipwreck before completing the epic poem *Os Timbiras* (The Timbiras, 1857). Dias believed that the Portuguese had unjustly conquered the country and wrongly decimated the indigenous population. His work laments this loss. To preserve the language of the people who had once greeted Portuguese sailors with open arms, Dias compiled a dictionary of the Tupi language in 1858. While traveling in Europe under the patronage of the imperial government with the mission of studying educational institutions, he also composed poetry that evokes his deep sense of longing for his native land. Two small passages of the poem *Canção do Exílio* (Song of Exile, 1843) are incorporated into the national anthem and express intense pride in the nature and beauty of Brazil.

José de Alencar (1829–77) was perhaps the mostly widely read author of the Indianist movement. He wrote a trilogy of novels that portray highly romanticized relations between Portuguese men and indigenous women. *Iracema* (1865), for example, is set in the northeastern state of Ceará and tells the story of the love between Martim, a white-skinned Portuguese man, and Iracema, a "honey-lipped virgin." Employing familiar romanticist tropes, Alencar creates a frustrated love affair that represents the tensions between nature and civilization. Iracema (an anagram for America) is much like the noble (and innocent) savage, who carries her lover's child but tragically dies after giving birth. Symbolically, her son is the new Brazilian nation, a mixture of Portuguese and Indian. Brazilian-born classical composer Carlos Gomes (1836–96) used this same theme in his music. His 1870s opera *Il Guarany* (The Guarani) that premiered at La Scala Theater in Milan, Italy, borrows from another volume of Alencar's indigenous trilogy. It is the only Brazilian opera that has ever won international acclaim.

Using Indians to personify the nation and portray a romantic past was possible because they were essentially invisible in nineteenth-century Brazil. Slaves from Africa were not. Their labor in the coffee plantations of São Paulo, in the sugarcane mills of Pernambuco, and in the cotton fields of Maranhão provided planters, merchants, and other members of the elite with means for accumulating significant wealth. Afro-Brazilians worked in every sector of the economy. They were considered essential for national prosperity. Because so many middle- and upper-class Brazilians owned slaves, the idea of emancipation was slow to gain support throughout society.

Nevertheless, the abolitionist movement produced a poet of great import. Antônio de Castro Alves (1847–71) wrote his first poems while a law student.

As the antislavery crusade gained momentum, he read his work aloud in public events that celebrated the emancipation of individual slaves and pushed for the end of the institution. Among his most famous poems is *O navio negreiro* (The Slave Ship, 1869) that depicts the horrific conditions facing Africans as they crossed the Atlantic, destined for hard life in Brazil.

Cuba, like Brazil, ended slavery only in the 1880s. Among the Cuban writers who used their pen to criticize the institution was Gertrudis Gómez de Avellaneda (1814–73), an upper-class woman, whose first novel *Sab* (1841), sparked a controversy in Cuba and Spain for its condemnation of slavery. Her positive portrayal of the morally superior slave Sab in comparison to his white owners, as well as her criticism of the institution of marriage, scandalized Cuban elite society. The Spanish government promptly banned the book. The next year, her novel *Dos mujeres* (Two Women) again criticized marriage and portrayed adultery in a positive light. Both themes mirrored Avellaneda's own personal, free-spirited lifestyle. She lived in Spain for most of her adult years and audaciously put herself forward as a candidate for membership in the Spanish Royal Academy, but she was barred from admittance because of her gender. Avellaneda has come to be seen as a precursor for women who would become important writers in the twentieth century.

Art took on new importance in the nineteenth century as the Spanish republics and imperial Brazil established state-financed academies. These institutions usually invited art instructors from Europe to train their students. They encouraged art with national themes and honored talented artists with prizes and trips to Europe in order to continue their studies. Artists produced epic paintings that portrayed great historic moments in the young nations' histories. Wall-sized canvases depicted independence figures mounted on horses with their swords drawn declaring independence or calling their troops to defeat the Spaniards. (See the depiction of the "Grito de Ipiranga" in Chapter 11 on Brazil.) Framing the heroes of independence were tangled bodies of soldiers of all colors, thrusting themselves into battle.

Allegorical paintings were also popular. Many drew on the Indianist literature and represented the sad tales of Indians' tragic encounters with Europeans. Landscape artists captured the majestic beauty of the Andes and the deep, dark undergrowth of the thick tropical rainforests. Still-life paintings depicted the abundance of nature's products spilling out of cornucopias. Most of these representations hung in official buildings or in the homes of the upper echelons of society. Although the market for such art was small, the state and elites provided enough demand to allow talented artists to survive. At the same time, the ongoing confrontations between Liberals and Conservatives over the separation of church and state weakened large-scale religious support of the arts. Patronage became decentralized and depended on local wealthy families to finance work usually executed by artists and architects not trained in the new national academies. Folk artists also produced colorful statues of saints as part of ongoing popular religiosity. These images were important in religious processions and in local celebrations.

A still-life painting entitled *Melon and Pineapple* by Agostino José da Mota (1821-78) portrays the bountiful natural riches of Brazil.

LITERATURE, ART, AND NEW IDEAS IN A WORLD ECONOMY

By the 1870s, political stability, increased urbanization, and the beginning of a wave of European immigration to parts of Latin America transformed the cultural landscape. Steamships and transatlantic cable brought news, people, and the latest cultural trends to Latin America and the Caribbean at an accelerated pace. The bourgeoisies that were growing wealthy from the boom cycles of export economies insisted that their major cities imitate those of Europe. With revenue increasing, they financed the renovation of their capitals, constructing beautiful Belle Époque buildings and wide avenues following contemporary European styles. By the turn of the twentieth century, Buenos Aires boasted the luxurious Teatro Colón opera house. The rubber barons and their wives of Manaus attended Italian operas at the Teatro Amazonas in the sweltering tropical heat while dressed in European frock coats and heavy velvets and silks. An internationally acclaimed pianist inaugurated the Teatro Nacional Sucre in Quito, Ecuador. The famous French stage actress Sarah Bernhardt played to packed audiences in Rio de Janeiro, São Paulo, Montevideo, Buenos Aires, and Santiago on her off-season South American tours. She declaimed in French, and her audience understood every word. French was the elite's second language and signaled worldliness, sophistication, and linkages to the Old World.

Journalists, writers, and intellectuals also looked to Europe to seek ideas about how their countries could modernize and adapt to a changing international economic order. The philosophy of positivism seemed to offer an answer. It gave those anxious to find ways to cast off colonial legacies an ideological justification for wedding their countries' economies to Europe and the United States. Developed by the French thinker Auguste Comte (1798–1857), positivism outlined the history of human development in three stages. Following superstition and metaphysics, the third and culminating stage embraced science and technology. Reason, order, and progress would open the path to evolution and prosperity. Modern roads and bridges, railroads and steamships, telegraphs and other technology improved countries' infrastructures and increased production for the export market. These advances created a sense that Latin America had the potential of "catching up" with Europe. Positivism offered a scientifically based formula for practical success.

The philosophy had its greatest impact in Brazil, Chile, and Mexico, although proponents in each country applied the ideas surrounding positivism in quite different ways. In imperial Brazil, positivism merged with republican sentiments, as figures such as Benjamin Constant of the Military Acadamy promoted the idea that the empire had become an impediment to progress and needed to be dissolved. The Brazilian positivists won support among sectors of the army, journalists, and young intellectuals. Adherents of the philosophy were influential figures leading up to and immediately after the overthrow of Emperor Pedro II in 1889. And as a result, the positivist motto, Order and Progress, even today appears on the Brazilian flag.

In Chile, positivist ideas permeated sectors of the Radical Party through Valentín Letelier (1852–1919), who was also the rector of the National University. Mexican positivism had a more lasting influence. In 1867 President Benito Juárez appointed Gabino Barreda (1818–81) to reorganize the National Preparatory School. He did so following Comte's philosophical principles. Positivist influences reached into the 1890s when a group of advisers to President Porfirio Díaz, known as the *científicos,* shaped the finances and planning of the government. They emphasized order within society as an important means of ensuring the political stability that in turn could guarantee economic progress. In doing so, the Mexican positivists aligned themselves with an authoritarian regime. They also adapted ideas that regarded Indians as inferior to Europeans. In short order, the Mexican Revolution would overturn these racist assumptions.

Realism and Naturalism

At the same time that positivism was gaining widespread influence, romanticism yielded to realism and naturalism in literary circles. Again European (especially French) trends inspired Latin American authors, as realist writers attempted to describe the "authentic" world that they inhabited. Peruvian writer Clorinda Matto de Turner (1852–1909) is considered a pioneer of realism for her portrayals of Andean society. Born in Cuzco, Peru, the former Incan capital, she became interested in colonial and Incan history and depicted the indigenous characters in her work in a positive light. Matto learned Quechua as part of her desire to understand and promote indigenous culture. In 1889 she published *Aves sin nido* (Birds without a Nest) that shows how Europeans stripped indigenous people of their rights, and how self-indulgent priests mistreated and exploited them. The novel also tells the story of a love affair between a white man and an indigenous woman.

Although this type of liaison might have been acceptable in mid-nineteenth-century Brazil, where middle and upper classes in urban centers had essentially no contact with indigenous people, social conventions were quite different in Peru. Indians and *mestizos* made up the vast majority of the population, and racist and hierarchical norms prevailed. In the context of a society where those of Indian and European descent lived side by side, proper society considered such romantic encounters as absolutely scandalous. In addition to her forward-thinking views about indigenous peoples, Matto, like Avellaneda, was a champion of greater education for women.

Naturalism emerged as an outgrowth of realism. Instead of simply describing reality in poetry or prose, naturalists tried to explain it "scientifically." Naturalism gained popularity especially among intellectuals influenced by social Darwinism. This adaption of Charles Darwin's theory of evolution considered that heredity and social environment influenced an individual's character. In many cases, an overwhelming pessimism is embedded in naturalism as social conditions and one's station in life inevitably produce grim outcomes.

A prominent representative of this literary trend, Balomero Lillo (1867–1903) grew up in the northern mining region of Chile. He was appalled by the harsh labor conditions of the mineworkers. His writing was an attempt to expose their plight to a larger public, engender sympathy, and improve their situation. In his short stories, collected in the book *Sub terra* (Underground, 1904), Lillo depicted miners trapped by their destiny and forced to live dreary lives using European machinery to provide Chilean minerals for an international market.

Adolfo Caminha (1867–97), a Brazilian naturalist, shocked the reading public in 1894 with his novel *O Bom Crioulo* (translated as The Black Man and the Cabin Boy). Caminha chose a black sailor to be the protagonist of his story, a literary choice that was uncommon at the time. He developed the tragic tale of the sailor's love for a pure and innocent blond cabin boy. Although Caminha saw the central character's homosexuality as a perverse trait, the novel remains a pioneering work for its bold subject matter.

A more immediately influential naturalist Brazilian author was Euclides da Cunha (1866–1909), a young journalist and army engineer. In 1897, he accompanied the federal army to repress the inhabitants of Canudos, a rural village in northeastern Brazil, that was led by Antonio Conselheiro, a charismatic itinerant preacher. Da Cunha documented the army's campaign in the 1902 book *Os Sertões* (published in English as *Rebellion in the Backlands*). He vividly describes the arid, harsh region and makes the naturalist argument that the backwardness of the people is environmentally determined, while the coast of Brazil is a "chain of civilizations." Peruvian novelist Mario Vargas Llosa (b. 1936) retells the story of Canudos in his beautifully written novel *La guerra del fin del mundo* (The War at the End of the World, 1984).

One literary figure towered over all other Brazilian romanticists, realists, and naturalists of the late nineteenth and early twentieth century. Joaquim Maria Machado de Assis (1839–1908) is universally considered Brazil's greatest writer and one of the most important in Latin America of all times. Born to the son of slaves and a Portuguese washerwoman, in the 1880s he began to write in a narrative manner unlike that of any of his contemporaries. His first novel in this new style is *Memórias póstumas de Brás Cubas* (The Posthumous Memories of Brás Cubas, 1881). Machado de Assis' short stories and novels combine elements of realism and surrealism along with a sharp, critical eye to the political, social, and economic dysfunctions of late nineteenth-century Brazilian society. His concise and exact style and carefully crafted studies of the psychological dimension of human interactions have rendered his work unique in Brazilian literature.

Modernism

At the end of the nineteenth century, Rubén Darío (1867–1916), a Nicaraguan poet, inaugurated a literary movement known as modernism. Enriching poetry and prose through musically constructed verse with inventive imagery and inspired symbolism, Darío catapulted to Latin American fame at age twenty-one with his collection *Azul* (Blue, 1888). A plethora of newspapers published throughout the continent at the turn of the twentieth century expanded readership for innovative cultural developments, and Darío had an immediate impact everywhere. His work was cosmopolitan in its approach to literary dialogues. It also inverted normal channels of influences between Europe and Latin America. Unlike previous literary and artistic styles, Latin American modernism originated on the American continent and then moved eastward across the Atlantic to Spain and other parts of Europe. Modernism also reflected a confidence among new generations of authors about the intrinsic value of their work in relationship to European authors. One literary critic has said, "Faced with any poem written in Spanish, one can state precisely whether it was written before or after Darío."

Another self-confident titan of the modernism movement was Cuban poet and independence leader José Martí (1853–95). His political activism led him to spend most of his life in exile, where he supported himself as a journalist. Like Darío, Martí consciously tried to innovate the Spanish language in his poetry, essays, and journalistic articles. His passionate promotion of the ideal of Cuban independence, especially his efforts to unify the Cuban émigré community, played a decisive role in gathering support for the independence cause. Unfortunately, he died in an attempted invasion of the island in 1895 before his dream could be achieved.

After U.S. and Cuban forces defeated Spain in 1898, and Theodore Roosevelt began meddling in Panama and elsewhere in Central America, Rubén Darío came to distrust Washington's intentions in the region. His collection of poems, *Cantos de vida e esperanza* (Songs of Life and Hope, 1905), expressed his deep concern that the Colossus of the North might end up dominating Latin America.

The growing influence of the United States in the Western Hemisphere alarmed other intellectuals as well. In 1900, Uruguayan essayist José Enrique Rodó

(1872–1917) wrote an essay entitled *Ariel*, inspired by Shakespeare's play *The Tempest*. In Rodó's essay, Ariel represents Latin America and Caliban represents North America. Rodó criticized what he considered to be the crass utilitarianism of a U.S. culture that emphasized specialization and materialism as the means to develop society. Rodó feared that the United States wanted to impose its culture on other parts of the world. He warned against a tendency for Latin Americans to be uncritically attracted to North America culture, wealth, and rising power. To counter this threat, he called on Latin American youth to seek inspiration in a broad classical education. Rodó's essay had a lasting effect on intellectuals throughout Latin America. It encouraged the nationalist and regionalist sentiment of those who were uneasy with the emergent power of the United States in the early twentieth century.

Although representative of a later generation of modernist writers, Chilean poet, educator, and feminist Gabriela Mistral (1889–1957) gained international appreciation for her work by being the first Latin American to receive the Nobel Prize for Literature in 1945. Recognized nationally in Chile for the collection *Sonetos de la muerte* (Sonnets of Death, 1914), she continued her poetry while working first as a primary school teacher and then as the director of Santiago's newest and most prestigious public school for girls. A second collection called *Desolación* (Desolation, 1922) won her international acclaim. That same year she left Chile to assist in the development of educational reforms taking place in Mexico under the guidance of Minister of Education José Vasconcelos. She later taught in the United States, and worked as a diplomat and cultural ambassador for Chile.

Mistral's early career as a primary school teacher started her on parallel paths as an internationally celebrated poet and educational reformer. Her experiences teaching the rudiments of literacy to young children in a small town in Chile were not unlike the careers of thousands of other lower- and middle-class women who found that the teaching profession offered possibilities of economic independence. Many became important founders and leaders in the early Latin American feminist and suffragist movements. They were joined by other women from both middle sectors and elite backgrounds in initiating a discussion about the role of women in Latin American society.

By the 1850s, these women began producing newspapers in Argentina, Brazil, Cuba, and Mexico, among other countries. These publications were dedicated to issues related to women in politics, education, and the public sphere. The movement quickly spread as debates about the emancipation of women, suffrage, their legal status, marriage, and the family attracted support from skilled workers, immigrants, government employees, and schoolteachers. Numerous congresses held around the turn of the century discussed possible paths toward greater rights. They usually became sharply divided along political lines or over divergent strategies for achieving their goals. Although women writers such as Avellaneda, Matto, and Mistral were not leaders of these movements, their published works disseminated feminist ideas and raised the social profiles of women throughout Latin America.

NATIONALISM, RADICAL POLITICS, AND TURBULENT TIMES

The first two decades of the twentieth century were times of great social upheaval around the world. International events reverberated throughout the continent: the War of 1898 in Cuba, the Mexican Revolution, World War I, the Russian Revolution, and the student reform movement of Córdoba, Argentina. In some ways, Rodó's call for an emphasis on classical education as a means of counterbalancing the rise of the United States in the region was an attempt to return to a nostalgic past. Instead, strong nationalist sentiments emerged to counter the giant to the north. They were particularly strong in Mexico where a social and political revolution upset traditional hierarchies. No longer were isolated individuals questioning the mistreatment of the indigenous population and the nation's underclasses. A new generation of Mexican intellectuals began to rethink their relationship to their country and its people. They produced new forms of art, literature, poetry, music, and theater that reflected the complexity and diversity of their nation.

Throughout Latin America, a flood of new political ideas took hold. Anarchism, socialism, and communism, in some places brought by European immigrants seeking better opportunities in the new world, seemed to offer solutions to pressing social problems. Proponents of these radical ideas encouraged mutual-aid associations, unions, strikes, and hopes of revolutionary change. The fast-paced shifts in European experimentalism also had an impact in Latin America as artists and writers adopted and adapted new trends from Europe. They included cubism, futurism, and surrealism. For these writers, modernist poetry seemed too old-fashioned, too preoccupied with aesthetics, truth, and beauty. Free verse, the subconscious, and disorderly forms of expression shaped the new poetic styles. A world war that had decimated Europe and left economic chaos and the rise of fascism in its wake polarized debate among intellectuals, as many moved radically to the left. For some, revolution seemed to offer the solution to social and economic problems.

The term *vanguardism* captured the concept of experimentation that was at the core of the cultural movements in the early twentieth century. Writers and artists saw themselves in the forefront. They wanted to take Latin American cultural production into uncharted terrains. Poets considered Rubén Darío's work overly embellished and lacking in substance. They chose to employ metaphors instead of allusion and eliminate what they considered useless words and unnecessary rhymes. They experimented with original layouts of the text of written poetry as a way of fusing it with visual arts.

Poets tested the limits of public acceptance for the themes in their work. Pablo Neruda (1904–73), a young Chilean poet, produced a collection of erotically charged love poems, *Veinte poemas de amor y una canción desesperada* (Twenty Poems of Love and a Song of Despair, 1924) that scandalized some but became his most popular book. Like many intellectuals of his generation, Neruda joined the Communist Party in the 1930s, and his poetry assumed a political and overtly Marxist content. Similarly, Nicolás Guillén (1902–89), an Afro-Cuban journalist and writer, joined the communist movement in the 1930s. Guillén's early poetry experimented with Afro-Caribbean forms and rhythms, and he became best known for *poesía negra* (black poetry).

Since the nineteenth century, Buenos Aires had been a major center of literary production, but in the 1930s it took on a new importance under the guidance of Victoria Ocampo (1890–1979), a pioneer among women writers in Argentina. Born into a wealthy nineteenth-century aristocratic family, Ocampo became a major patroness of literature and culture. In 1931 she founded the cultural review *Sur*, with the help of Eduardo Mallea (1903–82), an Argentine, and Waldo Frank (1889–1967), an American literary figure. *Sur* quickly became the best-known literary journal in Latin America. A parallel publishing house, also named Sur, was created, thanks to Ocampo's personal funding. In both enterprises she exercised a firm managerial hand, making literary quality, not ideology, her prime requirement. *Sur* became an important outlet for the translated editions of such foreign writers as André Gide, T. S. Eliot, and Albert Camus. It also offered a forum for intense literary and cultural debates in which intellectuals from all over Latin America participated.

Brazilian Modernism

Rio de Janeiro and São Paulo became other significant centers for experimentation, as a dynamic new cultural movement emerged in Brazil in the 1920s and 1930s. Known as modernism (not to be confused with the early modernist poetry movement of Spanish America), its proponents sought to rejuvenate Brazilian culture. The movement's adherents rejected what they considered to be stale, formal European cultural traditions embraced by the coffee barons that ruled high society in São Paulo, the country's most important metropolis. In 1922, during the centennial celebration of Brazilian independence, a group of young, mostly wealthy, bohemian artists and writers produced an event known as the Modern Art Week at the elegant Municipal Theater. It included art exhibits, lectures, and poetry readings. It was designed to challenge the cultural establishment that still defended nineteenth-century traditional styles. Heitor Villa Lobos (1887–1959) conducted his music at the Modern Art Week as well. Combining classical styles with popular folk music and legends, his work was an effort to compose music that conveyed unique national traditions and influences. Although the Modern Art Week was widely disdained by cultural critics of the time, many of those who participated in the event became the leading artists and writers of subsequent decades.

One important current within Brazilian modernism was known as the anthropophagic (literally, man-eating) movement. It was led by Oswald de Andrade (1890–1954). Referencing the tradition of ritual cannibalism among some Brazilian Indians during the colonial period, the movement's proponents argued that artists and writers should borrow from European and American artistic traditions. Then, after digesting these influences, they should produce their own innovative creations.

An emblematic novel of this movement is *Macunaíma* (1928), written by Mário de Andrade (1893–1945, not related to Oswald), who was an organizer of the Modern Art Week, a literary critic, and folklorist. Macunaíma, a "hero without character," is born in the Amazonian jungle but travels to São Paulo where he experiences modern urban society and then returns to the jungle. He possesses extraordinary supernatural powers, and Andrade employs literary techniques in

In 1930 this modernist painting by Emiliano de Cavalcanti (1897-1986), entitled *Five Girls of Guaratinguetá*, represented new notions of race in Brazil. (Museu de Arte de São Paulo.)

his novel that will later become known as magical realism. Borrowing freely from folk stories and traditions and using colloquial Brazilian language, the novel aspires to promote a pan-Brazilian national cultural identity.

As with literature and poetry, Brazilian art adopted very nationalist themes, focusing on ordinary people, especially those of non-European background. A new aesthetic featured people of color as positive representatives of the Brazilian nation. Tarsila do Amaral (1886–1973) was a leading painter of this trend, and her works, such as *Black Woman* (1923) and *Anthropophagy* (1929), shocked conservative bourgeois Paulista tastes.

Revolutionary Art and Literature

At the same time, Mexican artists and writers responded to the dramatic changes that had taken place in their country. By 1920, the most violent phase of the Mexican Revolution had come to an end. Álvaro Obregon had established himself in power. The task now was to carry out the reforms promised by those leaders who had survived the wars of the previous decade. As minister of education, José Vasconcelos (1882–1959) redirected the government's cultural agenda. He organized a rural education program that included 2000 new libraries throughout the country. A Department of Fine Arts had the task of preserving popular art while promoting the work of contemporary poets, writers, artists, and composers.

Vasconcelos made a major contribution to the debate about Mexican national identity through a book entitled *La raza cósmica* (The Cosmic Race, 1925). Vasconcelos argued that Latin America was producing a new "fifth race" that was an amalgamation of Europeans, Africans, Asians, and Amerindians. By today's standards, some of the characteristics that he attributes to different peoples of the world seem stereotypical and somewhat racist. Even so, he articulated the thesis that widespread *mestizaje* was a positive development for Mexico.

While Vasconcelos lauded racial mixture, other Mexican intellectuals were committed to Indianism, or indigenism. It was the central theme in the 1935 novel *El Indio* by Gregorio López y Fuentes (1895–1966). It permeated the musical works of Carlos Chávez (1899–1978), a brilliant conductor, pianist, and composer who went so far as to score his *Sinfonía India* (1935) and *Xochipili-Macuilxochitl* (1940) for pre-Columbian instruments. Emphasizing the country's indigenous history, this cultural movement became an integral part of the official political creed. As such it offered inspiration for the magnificent National Museum of Anthropology and Archeology in Mexico City.

Mexican artists entered this discussion as the Revolution unleashed a torrent of creative energy in the arts. Like Vasconcelos, many praised the indigenous and *mestizo* profile of the people. One especially prominent outlet for their work came through public murals, as a trio of gifted painters—Diego Rivera (1886–1957), David Siqueiros (1896–1974), and José Clemente Orozco (1883–1949)—sought to inform and educate the country's largely illiterate masses. "Art must no longer be the expression of individual satisfaction," they declared in a manifesto, "but should aim to become a fighting, educative tool for all." Through massive murals in such public buildings as the Agricultural School in Chapingo and the National Palace in Mexico City, they idealized the pre-Hispanic past, empathized with Mexico's masses, heaped derisive scorn on Spanish conquerors and Yankee capitalists, and elevated popular leaders like Zapata to a pantheon of heroes. Marxist in degrees but nationalist to the core, the muralists played a major role in reshaping the popular history of revolutionary Mexico.

The Mexican Revolution produced polemics and a torrent of popular novels. As early as 1915, Mariano Azuela (1873–1952) published *Los de abajo* (translated as The Underdogs), a story of characters entangled in a meaningless war: "The revolution," says one, "is like a hurricane; if you're in it, you're not a man ... you're a leaf, a dead leaf, blown by the wind." In the 1920s, Martín Luis Guzmán (1887–1976) wrote *El águila y la serpiente* (The Eagle and the Serpent), a tale of idealistic revolutionaries and venal politicians that also contained a firsthand portrayal of Pancho Villa. "When he fires, it isn't the pistol that shoots, it's the man himself. Out of his very heart comes the ball as it leaves the sinister barrel. The man and the pistol are the same thing." A generation later, Carlos Fuentes (b. 1928) presented skeptical views in two acclaimed novels, *La muerte de Artemio Cruz* (The Death of Artemio Cruz, 1962) and *La región mas transparente* (translated as Where the Air Is Clear, 1958). For these writers, the defining characteristic of the Revolution was its violence; their goal, and that of their characters, was to ascertain the purpose of it all.

Frida Kahlo: Privacy on Public View

Long in the shadow of her contemporaries, Frida Kahlo (1907–54) has emerged in recent years as one of the twentieth century's most celebrated artists. As shown in the film biography *Frida* (2002), her personal life was one of tragedy, struggle, and resistance. Stricken by polio as a child and then gravely injured in a trolley-car accident, she endured frequent illness and constant pain. In 1929 Kahlo married the already famous Diego Rivera and joined the Mexican Communist Party.

Despite her political commitment and her appreciation for the muralist tradition, Kahlo's painting was highly personal, private, and intense. Known especially for her haunting self-portraits, she combined Mexican traditions of religious folk art with European traditions of portraiture. Iconoclastic and original, she sometimes drew upon Christian images for inspiration but always in her own way, frequently challenging classic conventions of ecclesiastical representation: in Kahlo's paintings, women's bodies are as naked and bloody as those of Christ and as clothed and emotionally stoic as those of Mary. Rejecting the traditional ideal of the self-abnegating woman, Kahlo also affirmed female sexuality and sensuality. As Rivera himself acknowledged, "This is the first time in the history of art that a woman expressed herself with such utter frankness."

Beyond Mexico, young intellectuals throughout Latin America found socialist and communist movements particularly attractive after the world economy collapsed in 1929. As the demands for export commodities plummeted, countries began to feel the effect of the Great Depression. European society seemed polarized and headed toward another great war. Among the new recruits to Marxism was a Peruvian journalist named José Carlos Marátegui (1895–1930). In 1928 he published *Siete ensayos de interpretación de la realidad peruana* (Seven Interpretative Essays on Peruvian Reality), an original analysis about how a socialist revolution might take place in Latin America based on local conditions and practices. Mariátegui argued that Peru was simultaneously communal, feudal, and capitalist. He blamed the subordinate position of Indians in Andean society on the land tenure system. His solution was to reorganize landholdings so that production would be based on traditional indigenous community lands.

Rethinking Race

Not all Latin American intellectuals looked to the people of mixed racial or indigenous background as a positive representation of the nation. The *mestizo* also came in for harsh criticism. Soon after José Vasconcelos propounded his pro-*mestizo* ideas about "the cosmic race" in Mexico, Alejandro O. Deústua (1849–1945) offered in 1931 a biting critique of Peru. "Among us," he said, "the problem of the *mestizo* is much more grave than in other countries. The product of the Indian in his period of moral dissolution and the Spaniard in his era of decadence, the *mestizo* has inherited all the defects of each without being able to conserve the remains of the gentlemanly life of the conqueror. . . . The mixture has been disastrous for the national culture."

Frida Kahlo at work in her studio.

Miscegenation was for Deústua not a sign of social progress but a symptom of backwardness. Peru was condemned by the racial composition it had inherited.

Other Andean thinkers, however, found inspiration in the country's Indian heritage. Jorge Icaza (1906–78) brought attention to the exploitation of Ecuador's native population in the 1938 novel *Huasipungo* (published in English as The Villagers). Another notable case was José María Arguedas, a novelist who managed to penetrate both the indigenous and creole worlds of Peru. He was a *mestizo* who had lived in Indian communities as a child and was fully bilingual in Spanish and Quechua. In *Canto Kechwa* (1938), he argued that "the indigenous is not inferior. And the day on which the people of the highlands who still feel ashamed of the Indian discover of their own accord the great creative possibilities of their Indian spirit, on that day, confident of their own values, the *mestizo* and Indian peoples will definitely prove the equality of their own creative ability with that of the European art which now displaces and puts it to shame."

This debate about racial mixture and national culture took place in Brazil as well. Whereas much of the Peruvian population was indigenous, Brazil had the largest Afro-descendant population outside of Africa, with a significant minority of mixed racial heritage. Gilberto Freyre (1900–87) framed this discussion with the publication in 1933 of a sociological treatise entitled *Casa-Grande e Senzala* (published in English as *Masters and Slaves*). He argued that the Portuguese colonizers had created a multiracial tropical colony based on the plantation. Freyre's writings lauded the African and indigenous contributions to Brazilian culture and society. His ideas stood in sharp contrast to racist ideology still circulating in Latin America, Europe, and the United States.

Even so, critics maintained that Freyre unduly romanticized Brazil's colonial past by deemphasizing the hierarchical and the sexually coercive nature of racial mingling. They also observed that his characterization of Brazilian society, later synthesized as "racial democracy," obscured the existence of widespread hopes that European immigration would improve the nation's racial stock. In fact, this prevalent ideology of "whitening" *(branqueamento)* maintained subtle forms of discrimination against Afro-Brazilians. Moreover, Freyre's emphasis on the neatly devised triad of Africans-Indians-Europeans ignored the role of other ethnic and racial groups, such as Japanese and Syrian Lebanese immigrants. In spite (or because) of its weaknesses, Freyre's thesis nonetheless became integrated by the government of Getúlio Vargas (1930–45) into a larger nationalist discourse about the special nature of Brazil as a country that had eliminated the racial divisions and tensions plaguing the United States and permeating European fascist ideology.

At the same time that Freyre's ideas about race in Brazil received official endorsement from the Brazilian government, Aimé Césaire (1913–2008), a young Afro-descendant from the French Caribbean island of Martinique, began working on a book-length poem entitled *Cahier d'un retour au pays natal* (Notebook on a Return to My Native Land, 1939). It represented a defining moment in Caribbean culture. Césaire and other young intellectuals questioned the Eurocentric focus of traditional literature. They developed a movement called *négritude* (blackness) that turned to African roots in the construction of culture and society in the Caribbean and looked at Africa with a sense of pride. The ideas surrounding this movement had significant impact among intellectuals in Haiti and other Caribbean islands. Haitian president François Duvalier (1957–71) appropriated the ideas of the movement (called *noirisme* in Haiti) to justify marginalizing mulattoes from participation in his government. For others, it linked them more closely to Africa. *Négritude* became a prominent ideology among African students living in Europe who formed part of the generation that led the decolonization movement in Africa after World War II.

The Making of Mass Media

While essays, books, murals, poetry, paintings, and newspapers reached a limited audience, the silent film offered a new, popular cultural medium almost immediately after it was introduced in the last years of the nineteenth century. Although European and U.S. films dominated the screen at the turn of the twentieth century, Brazilian and Mexican entrepreneurs produced their own pictures that created the first national silent film stars. In the early years of film, documentaries dominated national production.

By the 1920s radio became another important new mass medium, reaching an ever-wider public with news, music, talk shows, sports, and variety shows.

Colgate-Palmolive successfully launched a Spanish version of its commercially successful soap operas in the Cuba of the 1930s. Serialized *radionovelas* became popular throughout Latin America overnight. The phonographic industry, which was largely controlled by foreign companies, worked in tandem with radio stations. They packaged and produced local musicians and singers. Through successful record promotion, distribution, and careful programming, performers could sometimes enjoy a meteoric success and become nationally known celebrities. State-owned radio stations became an important vehicle for forging a sense of patriotism and nationalism. Radio standardized the national language even as it transmitted programs that featured regional differences. (Radios remained an important means of cultural transmission well into the late twentieth century, even after television had already reached all segments of society.)

When U.S. studios began producing sound films in 1929, they quickly responded to the Latin American market with simultaneous remakes in Spanish and dubbed films featuring a galaxy of Hollywood stars. U.S. films flooded into Latin America transmitting the "American way of life" on the silver screen to audiences everywhere. Although competition from these films made it hard to develop national industries, state support in Mexico and Argentina allowed those countries to enter a golden age of film production with scripts featuring national stars, plots, and settings. Copying the Hollywood studio system, production companies established themselves in Mexico City, Buenos Aires, Rio de Janeiro, and São Paulo. Tango singers such as Carlos Gardel (1887–1935) and Mexican divas such as Dolores del Río (1905–83) became international celebrities through their film appearances. Cuba and Peru also began to produce films as well, but Mexican and Argentine cinema tended to have a greater impact on other countries in the region.

When the United States entered World War II, the government recruited Hollywood studios into the war effort. Walt Disney traveled to Latin America to develop ideas for new cartoons with Latin American–style characters as a means of promoting good relations with the country's "friendly neighbors to the south." A Hollywood studio hired Portugal-born Brazilian samba singer Carmen Miranda (1909–55) to perform in pictures as the generic "Latin bombshell." A series of movies filmed in Los Angeles but set in Latin America reproduced long-held stereotypes about the region.

Popular Culture, Theater, and Sports

Although music produced by the lower classes, generally referred to as *música popular,* had been an essential part of everyday life from the Andes to the islands of the Caribbean since the colonial period, radio and film brought these sounds to much wider, national audiences. The Afro-Cuban *rumba*, the Argentine *tango*, the sentimental and romantic *bolero*, and the Brazilian *samba* were performed in movies and transmitted over the airwaves, legitimizing what the elites had often considered "low culture."

As nationalism and anti-imperialist sentiments strengthened in Latin America, especially in the 1930s and 1940s, the "authentic" culture of the people took on additional significance. Governments promoted projects to collect and preserve indigenous and African musical traditions, and regional music received a new national prominence. At the same time, Cuban dance bands brought the cha-cha and the rumba to the United States, and the tango circulated throughout Latin America and beyond.

Modern theater came to the fore in the 1930s and 1940s. Mexican directors staged vanguard theater productions using innovative lighting and scenery and plots with political content. Argentine playwrights wrote dramas that addressed socio-cultural problems. In Brazil, Polish-emigré director Zbigniew Ziembinsky (1908–78) innovated theater with his production of *Vestido de noiva* (Wedding Dress, 1943) by Nelson Rodrigues (1912–80). The drama tells the story of a young woman's attempt to understand her failed marriage and her imminent death while in a state of coma. The ground-breaking staging that presented action on various levels—reality, memory, and hallucination—and offered a surrealistic and non-linear plot revolutionized Brazilian theater. These early works established the groundwork for an explosion in the quality and content of theater. As one expert has explained, playwrights and directors took up the challenge of bringing to Latin American theater "a new sense of its own identity, capturing the national and human spirit through believable characters who manifested the social, political, religious, and personal conflicts of individuals in modern society."

Innovative theater provided a new space for Afro-Brazilian artists to affirm their cultural heritage. In the mid-forties, Abdias do Nascimento (b. 1914), a young black intellectual, founded the Teatro Experimental do Negro (Black Experimental Theater), whose purpose was to develop new texts that focused on people of African descent. Beginning with a 1945 production of Eugene O'Neill's *Emperor Jones*, with Nascimento playing the lead character, this project broadened cultural norms by expanding the subject matter of Brazilian plays. Nascimento also promoted beauty contests to redefine hegemonic aesthetic gender standards and an art competition with the theme of the Black Christ.

By the early twentieth century, soccer had become the most popular sport in Latin America. Brought to the region by the British, the foreign economic power that dominated much of South America until the 1920s, soccer was originally played by the upper classes. The middle and lower classes quickly adopted the sport. Soccer clubs, professional players, and devoted fans strengthened the region's competitiveness worldwide. Uruguay won the World Cup in the first international competition in 1930. Latin American countries have taken first place in half of the World Championship games: Uruguay twice (1930 and 1950), Argentina twice (1978 and 1986), and Brazil five times (1958, 1962, 1970, 1994, and 2002).

Baseball is the second most popular sport, gaining Cuban adherents as early as the 1870s. Its widespread practice beyond the United States can be traced to U.S. imperial influences in the late nineteenth and early twentieth centuries. In Cuba, the Dominican Republic, Nicaragua, Panama, and Puerto Rico, occupying American troops popularized the game. In Venezuela it was played in enclave areas dominated by U.S. oil companies. As early as the 1930s, these countries began supplying talented players to the U.S. major leagues.

LATIN AMERICAN CULTURE ENTERS A WORLD MARKET

A marked increase in urbanization and the growth of the middle classes of Latin America during and after the 1940s significantly affected cultural production. Educational systems expanded, and more women attended universities. Literacy rates increased, and active reading publics grew in size. (Although television was introduced in the 1950s, it was restricted to urban and middle-class audiences until the mid-1960s when it became a mass medium.) Throughout the 1940s, 1950s, and 1960s, books and other forms of cultural production reached an ever-wider audience. The number of authors, poets, playwrights, and filmmakers increased as well. Architects built new modernist structures that borrowed from foreign trends but then created distinctive new styles. New forms of musical expression blossomed too.

Growing interest in Latin America after the Cuban Revolution produced international curiosity about the continent's authors, poets, and essayists. Latin American writers first reached a larger foreign readership through Spanish publishing houses, and soon thereafter their works appeared in English and French translations. There was a "boom" in Latin American literature. Because there is so much diversity and variety in the novels, essays, poetry, theater, and films of the period between the 1940s and the 1970s, even a brief overview cannot do justice to the plethora of innovative work produced throughout the region. Nonetheless, several merit attention here.

Already a prolific writer in the 1930s, Miguel Ángel Asturias (1899–1974), a Guatemalan poet, novelist, and diplomat, became a precursor to the "Latin American boom" in literature of the 1960s and 1970s. He combined interests in anthropology and Mayan mythology, which he integrated into his novels, with sharp political positions. Asturias was expelled from Guatemala in 1954 for his support of the reform-minded Jacobo Arbenz government that was overthrown with CIA backing. His first major work, *El Senõr Presidente* (Mr. President, 1946), was actually completed in 1933 but could not be published for more than another decade because of its scathing critique of life under a military dictatorship. A later work, *Hombres de maíz* (Men of Maize, 1949), is a defense of Mayan culture and customs. In 1967, Asturias was the second Latin American after Gabriela Mistral to receive the Nobel Prize for Literature.

Asturias' interest in indigenous America was taken up by other writers of a younger generation as well. The Peruvian author José María Arguedas (1911–69) was of mixed Spanish and Quechua descent and grew up in poverty in a village in the southern Peruvian Andes. His novel, *Los ríos profundos* (Deep Rivers, 1961), uses a mixture of Spanish and Quechua and addresses the clash between Europeanized and indigenous cultures. Similarly, Rosario Castellanos (1925–74), a Mexican poet and author, set her novels in the largely indigenous area of

Chiapas. *Oficio de tinieblas* (translated as The Book of Lamentations, 1962) reached back into the nineteenth century to tell the tale of a Tzotzil indigenous uprising. Castellanos' work reveals an identification with and deep sympathy for the indigenous people of Mexico.

Ever since the Mexican Revolution, succeeding generations of intellectuals have reflected on the roots and nature of Mexican identity and culture. In 1950 Octavio Paz (1914–98) produced a book-long collection of nine essays entitled *El laberinto de la soledad* (The Labryinth of Solitude) to address those questions. Building on the notion that individuals are inherently lonely, Paz considered that *fiestas* (public festivities) provide an opportunity to express community and allow Mexicans to cast off their usually masked self-denial. Paz also offered a sweeping analysis of Mexican history from the pre-Columbian period to the Mexican Revolution. After the massacre of hundreds of Mexican students in 1968, he republished this work with an additional essay that discussed the tragic affair. Although sympathetic to the revolutionary left in his youth, Paz moved toward more moderate positions as he grew older, criticizing the authoritarian nature of socialist regimes. For Paz, art was an important component of human existence: "There can be no society without poetry, but society can never be realized as poetry, it is never poetic. Sometimes the two terms seek to break apart. They cannot." Paz received the Nobel Prize for Literature in 1990.

Innovative Architecture

As Mexican intellectuals reflected on the impact of the past on their society, many Brazilians gazed optimistically into the future. The modern architectural style demonstrated that the country was not merely imitating Europe and the United States but creating something new. Since the early twentieth century, builders had borrowed European architectural design trends such as art nouveau and later art deco for new public buildings, private dwellings, and public monuments. Modern architecture came to Latin America through students educated abroad who returned to Brazil to design new hospitals, schools, universities, and housing projects. As one scholar has noted, "At the programmatic base of the modern movement lie the ideals of democracy, creative liberty, social equality, constructive rationality, progress, and confidence in science and the scientific method to produce a physical reality that safeguards humankind and society and reinvents the city." The energy of this movement took hold in Brazil and produced some of the most innovative modern architecture in the world.

Leaders in the Brazilian modern architectural movement included Lúcio Costa (1902–98) and Oscar Niemeyer (b. 1907), who were influenced by the 1929 and 1936 visits to Brazil of the French architect Le Corbusier (1887–1965), the father of the modern glass tower building. In the 1940s, Niemeyer designed a series of modern building projects in Belo Horizonte, including an innovative Catholic church. He did so with the enthusiastic support of Juscelino Kubitschek, the city's mayor and later the state's governor. And as president of Brazil, Kubitschek (1956–61) dedicated his administration's efforts to completing the

The glittering capital of Brasilia boasts extraordinary modernistic architecture. *Top*, headquarters of the governor of the federal district; *bottom*, the legislative palace, whose twin towers and buildings contain the separate houses of the national congress. (Courtesy of the Consulate General of Brazil, New York.)

new capital of Brasília in the country's interior. He called on architects and planners to submit their proposals to an international juried competition. Lúcio Costa's project won. The new capital took the shape of a large airplane with government buildings on a main axis leading to the presidential palace, Congress, and Supreme Court. Huge blocks of residential apartments fanned out from the center like wings on the plane. Niemeyer designed the most important buildings. The construction was innovative and bold. He used slender arches, long ramps, and large geometric shapes. Although critics claimed that the city was sterile, unfriendly to pedestrian traffic, and overly planned, it symbolized a promise that Brazil was as modern as, if not more modern than, any European or American society.

As Brasília was being built, a Franco-Brazilian film and a new musical style placed Brazil on the international map. *Black Orpheus* (1959) was set in the hillside *favelas* (slums) of Rio de Janeiro in the midst of Carnival and featured an all-black cast of characters. The winner of an Oscar for Best Foreign Film, the movie offered its audience an idyllic view of the country and race relations. It introduced the world to *bossa nova* (new style) with its cool jazz sound and its syncopated beat. Bossa nova became an immediate international success.

During the 1960s, other musical styles from Latin America moved onto the world stage as well, especially sounds from the Caribbean. Cuban salsa, Dominican *merengue,* and the Colombian *cumbia* became popular all over Latin America and moved to the United States with migrants from the Caribbean basin. Similarly, Mexican immigrants brought regional music with them, including the *canción ranchera,* which had become popular all over Latin America through Mexican films of the 1940s and 1950s.

Latin American Revolutionary Culture

At the same time that Kubitschek was inaugurating Brasília and bossa nova musicians were playing to packed auditoriums at Carnegie Hall in New York, Fidel Castro and his band of bearded revolutionaries were changing the political and cultural landscape of Latin America. A surge of artistic and literary enthusiasm followed the victory of the Cuban rebels in 1959. Early reforms won widespread popular support on the island and abroad. The new government increased the literacy rate from 76 to 96 percent in a successful 1961 campaign in which students fanned out into the countryside to teach peasants how to read. Educational opportunities expanded. Sons and daughters of the poor had access to university and technical training. Colorful wall murals and posters promoted revolutionary ideals. Schoolchildren learned new nationalistic and revolutionary songs. In the first two years of Castro's rule, cultural heterogeneity was expressed in the literary supplement *Lunes de la Revolución* (Monday of the Revolution). It provided a forum for rich debate on the relationship of culture to revolutionary change.

As the regime turned to socialism and considered outspoken critics to be enemies of the revolution, *Lunes de la Revolución* was shut down. Many of its contributors left the country. Yet revolutionary fervor that promised radical change across the continent inspired loyal internal and foreign support for the Cuban experience. The Nueva Trova (New Song) movement in the mid-1960s used politicized lyrics to praise the accomplishments of the Revolution. Cuba organized international conferences that brought authors, poets, artists, film-makers, playwrights, and musicians from throughout Latin America to the island to celebrate a revolutionary vision for the region. Cuban singers and song-writers, such as Silvio Rodríguez (b. 1945) and Pablo Milanés (b. 1943), composed revolutionary verses that circulated throughout the region as a whole.

Cuba's politically engaged music represented a larger continental trend. American (and to a lesser extent European) pop music, especially rock 'n' roll, reached ever-wider Latin American markets in the 1950s and 1960s. Many Latin American musicians adapted to these new sounds. They wrote songs and music in the same styles and found favorable reception. Others turned to local traditions to counter foreign influences. In Argentina and Chile, folklorists and musicians sought out folk sounds and instruments. Preserving songs and rhythms that seemed to be disappearing, they used their investigations to create a new musical genre, eventually known as *la nueva canción* (the new song).

Chile was at the center of this movement, and Violeta Parra (1917–67), a woman of humble origins, was one of its leaders. A supporter of the Chilean left, Parra began collecting folk music and composing her own songs that addressed the problems of poor slum dwellers, miners, and factory workers. She turned her house into a center for musicians and folk artists. She revived a tradition, known as *la peña,* a cultural center where performers could present their music. *La canción nueva chilena* became especially popular during the socialist government of Salvador Allende (1970–73) because of the songs' progressive political content. Using Andean rhythms and instruments and poetic lyrics, the music announced a national and indigenous culture in opposition to foreign, especially U.S., influences. After the military coup d'état that overthrew Allende and installed the seventeen-year dictatorship of Augusto Pinochet, musical groups such as *Quilapayún* and *Inti-Illimani* went into exile. They performed their music around the world as a means of building international opposition to the military regime. Argentine singer Mercedes Sosa (b. 1935) and U.S. folk balladeer Joan Baez (b. 1941) popularized Violeta Parra's most famous song, "Gracias a la vida" (Thanks for Life, 1966), which offered a haunting ode to human existence in the face of daunting hardships.

Brazilians made their own unique contributions to the new song movement. In reaction to rock 'n' roll and other foreign musical influences, Brazilian Popular Music, as it was known, used acoustic guitars and regional instruments to produce songs addressing national themes. Sometimes they were overtly political. Other times they drew on folk music or conveyed simple stories of everyday life.

This musical current was challenged by *tropicália* (tropicalism), an art move-ment that incorporated poetry, theater, and music into an alternative cultural outlook. Borrowing from the modernist, cannibalistic idea of *antropofagia* devel-oped in the 1920s and 1930s, its proponents insisted that artists should feel free to appropriate elements from international cultural trends and creatively transform them into national forms of expression. Tropicalismo was also a reflection of the wild and rebellious youth culture that was sweeping the world in the late 1960s. Caetano Veloso (b. 1942) and Gilberto Gil (b. 1942), the leading performers of the musical wing of this movement, were forced into exile in 1969 for a period of time, but returned soon thereafter to continue long and productive musical careers. Veloso is Brazil's most well-known artist internationally, and Gil served as minister of culture from 2002 until 2008 during the Luiz Inácio Lula da Silva government, while continuing as a songwriter and performer.

The Literary Boom

As suggested previously, the Cuban Revolution attracted worldwide attention toward all of Latin America and the Caribbean. One historian has noted, "Latin American novelists became world famous through their writing and their advocacy of political and social action, and because many of them had the good fortune to reach markets and audiences beyond Latin America through translation and travel—and sometimes through exile."

Among the first members of the "boom generation" of the 1960s was Julio Cortázar (1914–84), an Argentine who spent much of his life in France. Among his most original works was *Rayuela* (Hopscotch, 1963), which offered the reader the opportunity to read the novel's chapters in any order. Cortázar also used stream of consciousness and inner monologues in his texts. Similarly, Cuban novelist Guillermo Cabrera Infante (1929–2005), who initially supported the Cuban Revolution but went into exile in 1965, employed stream of consciousness in his experimental novels, among them *Tres tristes tigres* (translated into English as Three Trapped Tigers, 1967). Although considered among the internationally acclaimed writers of the "boom" generation, he rejected that label for himself.

Cabrera Infante became alienated from the Cuban Revolution. On the other hand, Pablo Neruda retained loyalty to the Latin American left over his long literary career that spanned five decades. His work celebrated the indigenous roots of Latin American culture and denounced U.S. multinational penetration into the region. Among his masterpieces was the book-length poem *Canto General* (General Song, 1950) that glorified the wondrous beauty of the Incan ruin of Machu Picchu. It also condemned Standard Oil's exploitation of the continent's natural resources. Neruda was a controversial choice for the Nobel Prize for Literature in 1971 because of his left-wing political views. He died twelve days after Augusto Pinochet came to power in Chile in September 1973. The new regime banned mourners from attending his funeral to avoid possible public protests against the military that had just taken over the country.

Neruda's political poetry was echoed by many journalists and novelists who saw their literary mission to awaken Latin Americans to a continental sensibility that went beyond borders and narrow nationalism. Among these essayists is Eduardo Galeano (b. 1940). In the early 1960s, he was an editor of the influential Uruguayan weekly *Marcha,* which, like the Argentine cultural magazine *Sur,* published a wide array of writers from Latin America. When the military took power in Uruguay in 1973, he fled the country for Argentina where he founded the publication *Crisis*. When the generals took power in Argentina in 1976, he fled again, this time to Spain. His most influential work was *Las venas abiertas de América Latina* (The Open Veins of Latin America, 1971), which was widely read in Latin America, Europe, and the United States.[*] Galeano offered a sweeping historical analysis of Latin America from Conquest to the present. His polemical style defended the view that first the Spaniards and Portuguese and later the British and U.S. governments exploited the people and the resources of Latin America. Like some other contemporary thinkers in Latin America, he was concerned about the continent's history. He once wrote, "I am a writer obsessed with remembering, with remembering the past of America above all and above all that of Latin America, intimate land condemned to amnesia."

Like Pablo Neruda, Brazilian writer Jorge Amado (1912–2001) joined the Communist Party in the 1930s. He spent time in prison, saw his books banned under the regime of Getúlio Vargas, and went into exile. In 1946 he was elected to the National Constituent Assembly; during the 1950s he withdrew from active political work in order to concentrate on his writing. It is largely regional in character, celebrating northeastern Brazil. His novels combined attention toward poverty and social disparities with a celebration of the African and mixed-race people of Brazil. Amado's 1943 novel *Terras do Sem Fim* (translated as The Violent Land) painted a gruesome story of the exploitation of cacao growers in Bahia who remained under the thumb of powerful landholding families. Other works were filled with picaresque and humorous depictions of memorable characters from all walks of Brazilian life. *Dona Flor e Seus Dois Maridos* (Dona Flor and Her Two Husbands, 1966), for example, recounted the comical tale of the ghostly return of a widow's carefree and womanizing husband who disrupts her new marriage to a second, more conventional spouse.

Perhaps the most internationally renowned Latin American author in the late twentieth century was Colombian journalist and author Gabriel García Márquez (b. 1927). Winner of the Nobel Prize for Literature in 1982, his most famous novel, *Cien años de soledad* (One Hundred Years of Solitude, 1967), is a modern world classic. Set in the banana-growing region of Colombia in the fictional town of Macondo, it was narrated in the style of "magical realism" in which mysterious elements invade realistic settings. Márquez once described the challenge of writing in this genre. "My most important problem was destroying the line of demarcation that separates what seems real from what seems fantastic."

Cien años de soledad is a gripping tale of fiction; a compelling allegory about the history of Colombia; and a searching exploration of life, love, passion, and personality in contemporary Latin America. Márquez drew on historical events in his work. One story in the book was based on an incident in the town of Ciénaga in

---

[*] This was the same book that Venezuela's Hugo Chávez rather intrusively presented to U.S. president Barack Obama at a meeting of hemispheric heads of state in April 2009.

1928, when a union guided by the Revolutionary Socialist Party (a precursor of the Communist Party) declared a strike and 25,000 workers, particularly those at the U.S.-owned United Fruit plantations, stopped cutting bananas. The American manager dispatched an urgent message to the Colombian president, Miguel Abadía Méndez, describing "an extremely grave and dangerous situation." Abadía Méndez responded by deploying army units in order to maintain "public order." The ensuing confrontation led to what came to be known as "the massacre of the banana plantations," a central event in the collective memory of Colombians—and recounted, albeit with purposeful exaggeration, by Gabriel García Márquez. (The tragedy did not, however, convince United Fruit to leave Colombia. That occurred only in the 1940s, after an outbreak of sigatoka disease devastated the banana plantations it controlled.) During the 1970s and 1980s, Márquez was an outspoken opponent of the Pinochet regime in Chile. He also attempted to help negotiate several unsuccessful peace accords between rebel groups and the Colombia government in the 1990s.

Literature and poetry were not the only boom industries of the 1960s and 1970s. Film and television took on new dimensions as well. In the post–World War II period, Latin American films had to compete with international cinema and the growing influence of television. As the quality of national cinema production declined overall, young intellectuals, influenced by French new wave and Italian neorealist cinematic styles, began making films designed to reflect their countries' social realities. In Brazil this movement became known as *cinema novo* (new cinema) and produced documentary-like reflections on sociopolitical themes by filmmakers such as Nelson Pereira dos Santos (b. 1928), who directed *Vidas secas* (Barren Lives, 1963), and Glauber Rocha (1939–81), whose masterpiece *Deus e o diabo na terra do sol* (released in English as *Black Gods/White Devils*, 1964) received international acclaim.

Filmmakers in other countries produced works along similar lines. Tomás Gutiérrez (1928–96) directed films about postrevolutionary Cuba. *Memorias de subdesarrollo* (Memories of Underdevelopment, 1968) examines an intellectual's ambivalence about the Revolution. The epic trilogy *Lucía* (1968), directed by Humberto Solás (1941–2008), portrays three different women in Cuban history and their relationship to revolutionary change. Argentine filmmakers Fernando Solano (1913–92) and Octavio Getino (b. 1935) directed *La hora de los hornos* (The Hour of the Furnaces, 1970) that lauds the liberation movements of Latin America, Asia, and Africa. Generally shot in black and white with innovative film techniques, these films represent the work of a generation determined to make powerful statements about Latin America's ongoing social and economic problems.

Theater underwent intense transformation in the 1960s. Playwrights and directors turned away from European and U.S. sources for inspiration and focused more on themes related to Latin America. Among the leaders of this trend was Brazilian theater director Augusto Boal (1931–2009), who developed new performance and staging styles. The musical drama *Arena conta Zumbi* (Arena Tells about Zumbi, 1965) skirted government censors by retelling the story of the seventeenth-century runaway slave community of Palmares. The play is also a metaphor about opposition to the military regime that had come to power the year before. Similarly, Colombian directors Enrique Buenaventura (1925–2003), who headed the Experimental Theater of Cali, and Santiago García (b. 1929), who led La Candelaria Theater in Bogotá, turned to innovative forms of political theater. Many theater groups moved away from the hierarchical hand of the theater director and adopted more collective processes for developing and staging productions. By 1968 theater festivals throughout Latin America created a sense of community among actors, directors, playwrights, and performers. They observed each other's work and shared ideas about how best to make theater relevant to a broader public. This is not to say that other theater genres disappeared. Middle-class audiences sought a wide variety of entertainment options, but experimental theater reflected what was new and exciting.

While theater productions were becoming more experimental, television was becoming more commercial. In its early phases, television stations had relied on local live programming similar to radio shows. By the 1960s, foreign (mostly U.S.) programming flooded the airwaves, bringing dubbed TV series and movies to an ever-widening audience. At the same time, the tradition of *radionovelas* was transferred to the new medium. *Telenovelas* became national fixations, as families gathered around television sets for favorite nighttime series. The content ranged from historical to modern dramas. Some focused on traditional romantic and family themes while others addressed social and political issues. In the 1970s and 1980s, Argentina, Brazil, Colombia, Mexico, and Venezuela began exporting their products to other parts of Latin America, to Spain and Portugal, to Spanish-language channels in the United States, and even to countries as far away as China and Russia.

Radio and television could reach an illiterate population. Comic books became a popular print medium entertainment vehicle for the semiliterate, the working class, and their children. Comic books with national themes and unique local characters achieved popularity in the 1930s and 1940s. At the same time, U.S. comic books penetrated the Latin American market. Disney cartoons and other foreign series were translated and widely disseminated. As *telenovelas* became popular, publishers produced *fotonovelas* that narrated everyday stories and reached broad audiences. Comic books also became a pedagogic vehicle in the 1970s in politicized literacy campaigns. Government agencies turned to the format as well to address social and educational issues.

DICTATORSHIP, DEMOCRACY, AND NEW SOCIAL MOVEMENTS

The authoritarian regimes that swept across South America in the 1970s and the civil strife that divided countries in Central America during the 1980s forced many of the politically engaged writers, musicians, and filmmakers, along with tens of thousands of revolutionaries and political activists, into exile. From other countries in Latin America, Europe, and to a lesser extent the United States, they wrote about their new experiences or documented the political repression taking place in their homelands. A new genre emerged, known as testimonial literature. In these works people told the story of their lives, their activism, and the repression that they had experienced.

Among the most famous (and later controversial) volumes is the first-person account of Rigoberta Menchú (b. 1959), an indigenous Guatemalan woman involved in her country's revolutionary movement in the 1970s. Her testimony *Me llamo Rigoberta Menchú y así me nació la conciencia* (published as I, Rigoberta Menchú, 1982) begins: "I'd like to stress that it's not only my life, it's also the testimony of my people.... My story is the story of all poor Guatemalans. My personal experience is the reality of a whole people." In her book, she related the ways in which the Guatemalan security forces killed members of her family for their support of revolutionary guerrillas. Her testimonial became an international success, and Menchú's activities in favor of human rights won her the Nobel Peace Prize in 1992. Subsequently, anthropologist David Stoll challenged the accuracy of the details of her story, although he acknowledged that her accounts helped to draw international focus to the brutality of the Guatemalan military.

Menchú's articulations in favor of the indigenous people of Guatemala represent a much broader and continental social phenomenon of the last several decades. Indigenous groups have forged organizations to make new claims on the state. They have demanded that natural wealth be distributed in ways more favorable to local communities. Some have insisted on cultural autonomy; others have called for indigenous languages to be an integral part of educational programs. Many organizations have focused on ensuring that lands are reserved or preserved for indigenous people. In some respects, these social articulations are a rejection of *indigenismo* in which authors spoke in the name of the Indians of their country. Pan-Indian conferences and gatherings have provided another platform for activists to reconceptualize the relationship of the indigenous population to national cultures.

Indigenous people were not the only social group articulating a critique of the social and political order. While in exile in the 1970s and 1980s, many left-wing Latin American women began to rethink normative social and cultural assumptions about gender. Some questioned the pervasive traditional gender roles on the left and the hierarchical nature of centralized political movements. Influenced by feminist ideas in Europe and the United States, many returned from exile with skills that helped build women's movements and organizations. Inspired by the United Nations First World Conference on Women held in Mexico in 1975, they joined together with activists involved in anti-dictatorial struggles and grassroots movements fighting social and economic inequality. The women's movements in different countries addressed an array of issues ranging from reproductive rights to creating new state institutions to curtail domestic violence.

Women writers became more prominent as well. Among those who gained recognition as post-boom authors are Isabel Allende (b. 1942) and Luisa

Valenzuela (b. 1938). Isabel Allende was born in Chile but moved into exile after the 1973 coup d'état. Since the 1980s, her work has reached a wide international audience. *La casa de los espíritus* (The House of Spirits, 1982), written while in exile in Venezuela, was inspired by a letter that she wrote to her dying grandfather. Her short stories and novels, influenced by magical realism, focus especially on the experience of women. Argentine novelist and short-story writer Luisa Valenzuela has employed an experimental avant-garde style to consider the impact of the Argentine dictatorship on human interactions in *Como en la Guerra* (As in War, 1977) and *Cambio de Armas* (Change of Arms, 1982). Both women represent a new consciously feminist critique of gender relations that is shared by many other authors.

Parallel to the emergence of feminist movements throughout Latin America, gay men and lesbians began to carve out a new political and social space for themselves. In 1971 several politicized groups merged to create the Frente de Liberación Homosexual de la Argentina (Argentine Homosexual Liberation Front). The wave of repression, which enveloped the country in 1975 and culminated in a military coup d'état the following year, obliterated the movement. Activists formed similar groups in Puerto Rico, Mexico, and Brazil in the mid- to late 1970s. They served both as support and as consciousness-raising groups and spaces to elaborate a new political discourse that challenged hegemonic norms about gender and sexuality. Many lesbian activists moved into the women's movement. After receiving initial resistance, they participated openly in creating an inclusionary feminist program.

The AIDS epidemic in the early 1980s both dissipated and strengthened gay political organizations, as activists developed new strategies to pressure the state to address health issues. In 1995, the International Lesbian and Gay Association held its seventeenth international conference in Rio de Janeiro, Brazil. That event encouraged new local, regional, and national organizations from Mexico to Chile. The movement's political agenda includes enacting antidiscriminatory legislation, addressing ongoing violence and gay bashing, and educating the public. Pride parades and marches have become an important means of visibility. In recent years, the annual Lesbian, Gay, Bisexual, and Transgendered parade in São Paulo, Brazil, has amassed 3 million people, making it the largest of such mobilizations in the world.

Concurrent with a politicized movement, authors writing about homosexuality have become prominent. Among them is Reinaldo Arenas (1943–1990), who clashed with the Cuban government in 1967 for his writings and openly gay lifestyle. Arenas was imprisoned for a time for having published abroad without official authorization. He finally left Cuba in 1980. His work *Antes que anochezca* (Before Night Falls, 1992) was a frank autobiography that sharply criticized the Castro regime, the Catholic Church, and U.S. culture and politics. Another well-known gay author who also fled his country was Manuel Puig (1932–90). He went into exile in 1973 as the political situation polarized in Argentina. His novel *El beso de la mujer araña* (The Kiss of the Spider Woman) told the tale of the relationship between two prisoners—a gay man and a revolutionary. It was later made into a successful Broadway musical and a prize-winning Hollywood film. Such works mark the emergence of a new generation of writers willing to publish their creative considerations about previously taboo topics.

Just as women, gays, and lesbians began to articulate new concerns about inequality and discrimination, the democratization process in many countries in the 1980s expanded opportunities for Afro-Latin Americans. New social movements such as the Movimento Negro Unificacão (Black United Movement) in Brazil presented biting critiques of ongoing social and economic gaps between Afro-Brazilians and people of European descent. Although the movement did not create a mass following, many of its ideas provoked national discussions about racial inequality, pressured the state to address historical patterns of discrimination, and created new government programs. Similar movements have developed in Peru, Ecuador, Colombia, and Mexico, where intellectuals and activists have focused attention on lingering forms of discrimination and positive African influences in these countries.

Afro-Latin American culture has enjoyed a renaissance since the 1980s. Migratory flows between the Caribbean and both Europe and the United States have increased the circulation of ideas about black identity and culture. Musical styles from salsa to the Afro-Cuban sounds of the Buena Vista Social Club have gained popularity among world music aficionados. Nongovernmental organizations, anthropologists, and ethnomusicologists have sought to record and preserve Afro-Latin American traditions.

New musical forms and cultural traditions are being created. To offer one example, Afro-Brazilian identities are being expressed in a new way through participation in *blocos Afros,* percussion groups organized to participate in Carnival festivities. These *blocos* arose in poorer Afro-Brazilian neighborhoods in the 1970s in the northeastern city of Bahia to allow residents to participate in the festival and to provide an Afro-Brazilian alternative to the *trios elétricos,* white rock bands that had come to dominate Carnival performances.

The most famous of the dozen *blocos Afros* of Salvador is Olodum, which began as a small neighborhood group and now has thousands of members in Salvador, as well as fans the world over. The group's name comes from the Yoroba word Olodumare ("God of Gods"). Olodum is widely credited with the invention of "samba-reggae," an innovative musical style in which vocal melodies characteristic of Caribbean reggae are wedded to the aggressively rhythmic drumming of Carnival street music. More recently, the group has added traditional Western instrumentation to its ensemble, but drums and voices remain at center stage. Olodum's musical repertoire has also incorporated elements of salsa, West African music, pop, candomblé chants, and African-American hip hop. As the genre "samba-reggae" suggests, the Olodum members see themselves as part of the African diaspora and as sharing musical styles with Afro-Caribbean peoples.

This connection extends to a celebration of négritude or "blackness," and of Africa and peoples of the diaspora. Olodum's director of international relations, Billy

Arquimimo, explained this by stating: "Olodum is part of the international black movement, and we want to promote self-esteem and pride." Along with this celebration of African roots, notable in a society in which Africanness is often denigrated, even by Afro-Brazilians, comes a commitment to the struggle for racial equality and a celebration of black leaders the world over. "We fight discrimination with protest songs," noted Arquimimo. "Our message is the same as Malcolm X, Marcus Garvey, Bob Marley or Martin Luther King Jr.; we're fighting for equality." While the effects of their appeals to black consciousness and racial equality are nearly impossible to gauge, they serve as powerful examples of Afro-Brazilian identity.

Films, Pop Music, and the Internet

The severe economic crises of the 1980s placed significant restraints on national film industries. Nevertheless, many of the veteran directors of the 1960s, as well as new generations of filmmakers, including many women, began producing high-quality feature films and documentaries, many with political and social content. Two films dealing directly with dramas during or immediately after the military dictatorships represented this genre. *La historia oficial* (The Official Story, 1985), directed by Luis Peunzo (b. 1946), told the story of the children of those disappeared in Argentina during the "Dirty Wars" of the 1970s and early 1980s. *O que é isso companheiro* (Four Days in September, 1997), directed by Bruno Barreto (b. 1955), recounted the 1969 kidnapping of the U.S. ambassador by urban guerrillas. Both films received international recognition.

The economic value of many of the films released over the last two decades, especially those from Mexico, Argentina, and Brazil, as well as their sophisticated scripts and outstanding acting, have made them competitive on the world market. Walter Salles (b. 1956) directed the touching film *Central do Brasil* (Central Station, 1998) about a child's search for his father in an arid, poverty-stricken region of northeastern Brazil. Veteran actor Fernanda Montenegro (b. 1929) received international praise for her leading role in the film. *Y tu mamá también* (And Your Mother Too, 2001) was a coming-of-age film of two young boys and a woman in her twenties who took a road trip with the political and social problems of contemporary Mexico as a backdrop. The film garnered many awards. *Diarios de motocicleta* (Motorcycle Diaries, 2004) continued the tradition of political themes with a romantic re-creation of Ernesto "Che" Guevara's youthful trip through Latin America before he joined the revolutionary forces that overthrew the Cuban dictatorship of Fulgencio Batista in 1959.

The underside of life in Latin America, especially pressing problems of poverty and the impact of drug trafficking, has become another prominent subject for filmmakers. The *favelas* of Rio de Janeiro provided the setting for the 2002 Brazilian crime drama *Cidade de Deus* (City of God) that tracked the lives of generations of petty crooks and drug dealers and the violence imposed upon the city's residents. The joint Colombian-American production *María llena eres de gracia* (Maria Full of Grace, 2004) also addressed the impact of drugs on poor people's lives. The film followed the ordeals of a woman who agreed to transport drugs to the United States when her family faced serious economic problems. Latin American cinematographers have also excelled at documentary filmmaking, focusing on topics ranging from immigration to environmental destruction.

Above all else, Latin American television and commercial music production have experienced significant growth over the last several decades. Although much television programming today is light entertainment for wide audiences, state-owned television and some national networks dedicate airtime to various types of culture. These include presentations of theatrical classics, historical documentaries, roundtable debates with intellectuals and authors, and programs about art. In some countries national networks have become billion-dollar conglomerates.

It is estimated that 80 to 95 percent of the populations of most countries have regular direct access to television. Viewer rates are slightly lower in rural areas and in poorer countries, but during telecasts of crucial soccer matches (especially the World Cup finals), entire countries appear to shut down as people gather with family and friends to view these all-important contests. Just as world-class soccer stars and baseball players have become export commodities to U.S. and European teams, *telenovelas* are now transmitted throughout the world, bringing multiple new images of Latin America to viewers in Miami, Mozambique, and Moscow.

Latin American pop music has penetrated international youth markets with increasing intensity since the 1970s when Bob Marley (1945–81) introduced Jamaican reggae to audiences in Europe and the United States. The performance of Jimmy Cliff (b. 1948) in the Jamaican film *The Harder They Come* (1972) created a romantic vision of gangsters and marijuana dealers in tropical Kingston. The demand for world music among discerning consumers from the north has produced a growing market for Latin sounds rooted in a diversity of national musical genres. Latino stars such as Ricky Martin (b. 1971) from Puerto Rico and Selena (1971–95, who blended Mexican *ranchera* traditions with American country, German polka, and Caribbean sounds) have offered crossover music that has reached wide audiences in Latin America and the United States.

More significantly, the Internet has revolutionized communication and culture in Latin America. Today large sectors of the middle class own computers, and cybercafés or similar businesses offer services for people to pay for Internet use by the minute. Many nongovernmental organizations have developed projects to help people from lower socioeconomic backgrounds gain access to the Internet. Locally based community programs have begun training youth to work with video cameras to produce films documenting their quotidian experiences. The cyber revolution has democratized access to culture, news, and information, and it has internationalized easy exchanges between scholars, writers, authors, and the public in general.

For all these reasons, Latin America is exerting increasing influence on the United States, the country that for so long looked down upon its southern neighbors. Cities such as New York, Chicago, and Los Angeles, not to speak of Miami, have burgeoning Spanish-speaking communities. Large concentrations of Brazilians live in and around Boston, New York, and Miami. In recent years, immigrants have moved to small towns and rural areas of the Midwest and the South. Music, dance, and cuisine are undergoing transformations. In 1992 salsa outsold ketchup for the first time in America. By 2006 the Latino population reached 43.2 million, and by 2050, it is estimated, Latinos will make up one-quarter of the U.S. population. Such change within America cannot fail to alter its beliefs about and attitudes toward Latin America.

And in the future, as in past centuries, the fate of Latin America will continue to depend on its relationship to the centers of international power. The region will remain a site of struggle, triumph, tragedy, and contradiction. Meanwhile, outsiders will continue to be startled and fascinated by what Gabriel García Márquez called "the unearthly tidings of Latin America, that boundless realm of haunted men and historic women, whose unending obstinacy blurs into legend."

Glossary

anarchism   a political philosophy which views the state as an unnecessary and harmful institution and argues that society should be organized without a centralized government, laws, police, or other authority.

anarcho-syndicalism   an ideological current within anarchism that considered workers and labor movements to be capable of revolutionary change to overthrow the capitalist state and establish workers' governance over the economy and government.

audiencia   a Spanish imperial court.

bandeirante   a backwoodsman or pioneer in colonial Brazil, often a trader of indigenous slaves.

Bourbon reforms   a series of administrative and economic measures implemented by the Spanish Crown in the eighteenth century to promote commercial and fiscal development in Spain and its colonies.

cabildo   the local town council within the Spanish empire.

campesino/a   a peasant or a rural laborer working the land.

caudillo   a charismatic military leader or strongman who takes power and rules by force with popular support.

científico   literally a "learned person," a term that refers to a circle of technocratic advisers to Mexican president Porfirio Díaz, who adhered to the philosophy of positivism as a means of promoting the modernization of the country at the start of the twentieth century.

Concertación   a center-left coalition of Chilean political parties established in 1988 that defeated the dictatorship of Augusto Pinochet in a plebiscite and governed the country thereafter.

Conservative Party   a political current that emerged in the early nineteenth century throughout Latin America that favored a strong, centralized state and support for the Catholic Church, often in confrontation with the Liberal Party.

contribución de indígenas   a head tax placed on Indians (i.e., a flat tax on everyone regardless of income).

corregidor   a magistrate or judge appointed by the Spanish Crown.

Cortes   Portuguese parliament.

criollo/creole   a person born in Latin America.

dependency theory   a set of social science theories contending that natural and agricultural resources flow from poor and underdeveloped countries of the global "periphery" to the developed countries at the "core," leaving the former impoverished and the latter richer.

ejido   communal land held by Mexican Indians; the term later referred to land distributed to peasants in the 1930s in which rural laborers gained the right to use but not own land and pass it on to their children.

enclave   a territorial unit occupied and controlled by foreigners within another country.

favela   a Brazilian slum, often associated with poor hillside communities in Rio de Janeiro, where the term originated in the early twentieth century.

foco theory   a revolutionary doctrine developed by Che Guevara, who proposed that a small group of dedicated guerrilla fighters could hold rural territory with the support of local peasants and use that base as a means to overthrow a conservative or reactionary regime.

gaucho   a cowboy who works on the grassy plains of Argentina, Uruguay, or southern Brazil.

guano   dried droppings of sea birds that accumulated on the Pacific Coast and were used as a rich nitrate fertilizer.

guerrilla movements   bands of revolutionary fighters, many inspired by the Cuban or Chinese revolutions, who attempt to take power through a relentless series of small-scale military actions (literally, "little wars" or skirmishes).

hacendado   the owner of a larger farm or estate.

hacienda   a large farm or estate.

import-substitution industrialization (ISI)   an economic policy based on the idea that a country should take active measures to reduce its foreign dependency through the replacement of imports by the local production of industrial products.

Justicialismo   an ideology promoted by Juan Perón in Argentina in the 1940s and 1950s that promoted social justice through the reliance on a strong welfare state and nationalist measures against foreign companies; in philosophical terms, it claimed to establish an appropriate balance between spiritualism and materialism, and between communism and capitalism.

ladino/a   in Central America, a person of mixed European and Indian background who is acculturated into Spanish society.

Liberal Party   a political current that developed in the nineteenth century that defended a decentralized, federated government and the elimination of special rights and privileges for the Catholic Church; it was often in confrontation with the Conservative Party.

liberation theology a set of ideas developed within the Catholic Church in the 1960s that emphasized that the Christian mission is to bring justice to the poor and oppressed through political activism.

llanos the vast tropical grassland plains of Colombia and Venezuela.

Maoism a current within Marxism based on the ideas of Mao Zedong, the Chinese political leader who believed that revolutionary change could take place through the mass involvement of peasants in rural guerrilla warfare.

Marxism a political philosophy developed in the nineteenth century by the German thinker Karl Marx, who argued that the industrial proletariat was the leading social force capable of overthrowing capitalism, establishing socialism, and later building communism.

MERCOSUR a regional trade agreement signed in 1991 among Argentina, Brazil, Paraguay, and Uruguay to eliminate tariffs and promote commerce and cooperation.

mestizaje the biological and cultural blending of indigenous and European societies.

mestizo/a a person of mixed Indian and European background.

modernismo a late nineteenth and early twentieth-century Spanish Latin American literary movement in Latin America that emphasized harmony, rhythm, and passion in its style.

Monroe Doctrine a U.S. policy introduced in 1823 asserting that any attempt by a European government to colonize or interfere in Latin America would be considered an act of aggression against the United States.

mulatto/a a person of mixed African and European heritage.

NAFTA a regional trade agreement signed in 1992 among Canada, the United States, and Mexico designed to eliminate tariffs and promote commerce.

naturalism a nineteenth-century literary current claiming that an individual's character was determined by heredity and the social environment.

négritude a literary and political movement developed in the 1930s by a group of intellectuals from French colonies emphasizing the importance of African culture and tradition in the fight against domination and colonialism.

neoliberalism a late twentieth-century policy doctrine advocating free trade, free markets, and reduction of the economic role of the state.

noirisme an ideological current that developed in Haiti in the 1930s, emphasized respect for the country's African cultural roots, and urged Haitian mulattoes to accept their African heritage; François Duvalier, who ruled Haiti from 1957 to 1971, embraced the philosophy.

obraje a textile factory.

pampas the fertile South American lowlands encompassing parts of Argentina, Uruguay, and southern Brazil.

pardo   a person of mixed African, Indian, and European ancestry; terms used mainly in Brazil, Colombia, and Venezuela.

patrón   a boss.

peninsular   a person born in Spain or Portugal.

peón   a Spanish term for a poor rural laborer

pink tide   a term referring to the wave of socialist and leftwing governments that came to power in Latin America at the end of the twentieth century and in the first decade of the twenty-first century.

positivism   a philosophy developed in the mid-nineteenth century by French sociologist Auguste Comte that outlined the history of human development in three stages, culminating in a period in which superstition and metaphysics were replaced by science and technology; its emphasis on reason, order, and progress was adopted by Latin Americans as a guide to the development and prosperity of their countries.

romanticism   an artistic, literary, and intellectual current in the nineteenth century that stressed emotion as a source of the aesthetic experience and placed value in rural and folk traditions as embodying authentic qualities and values.

realism   an artistic and literary movement of the mid- and late nineteenth century in which people were depicted as they appeared in everyday life without embellishment or interpretation.

Roosevelt Corollary   a 1904 amendment to the Monroe Doctrine by President Theodore Roosevelt asserting the right of the United States to intervene in Central America and the Caribbean to stabilize economic or political affairs.

sharecropping   a system of agriculture or agricultural production in which a landowner allows a tenant to use a parcel of land in return for a share of the crop.

socialism   a political and economic ideology contending that the state should own and control the most important sectors of the economy and redistribute wealth equitably throughout society.

Trotskyism   a political current within Marxism supporting Leon Trotsky, a Russian revolutionary who opposed Joseph Stalin; Trotskyists criticized the bureaucratic and authoritarian nature of the Soviet Union and believed that socioeconomic conditions in Latin America made a socialist revolution inevitable.

vanguardism   a literary, artistic, and intellectual movement in the early twentieth century that promoted cutting-edge and innovative styles and ideas.

viceroyalty   a subdivision of the Spanish empire in colonial Latin America headed by a representative of the Crown. There were originally two viceroyalties—New Spain, encompassing the Caribbean, Mexico, and Central America; and Peru, including Panama and Spanish South America. In the eighteenth century, the Viceroyalty of Peru was divided into three parts: New Granada (Venezuela, Colombia, Panama, and parts of Ecuador); the

Viceroyalty of La Plata (Argentina, Uruguay, Paraguay, and parts of Bolivia); and the Viceroyalty of Peru (Chile, Peru, and parts of Ecuador and Bolivia).

La Violencia   literally, "The Violence," an era of political and civil strife in Colombia between the Conservative and Liberal parties beginning in 1946 and lasting more than a decade.

Washington consensus   a term coined in 1989 to describe the neoliberal policies prescribed for Latin America by policymakers and international financial agencies in Washington, D.C., that included reliance on the free market, a diminished role of the state in the economy, and the privatization of companies under state control and ownership.

yanaconaje   sharecropping by indigenous people who have been separated from their ancestral lands and are working as rural laborers.

Guide to Website

We invite all readers to explore the website for *Modern Latin America* at www.oup.com/us/skidmore. We regard it as an integral part of the book, and not as a cosmetic "supplement" that can be safely ignored. It will be updated on a regular basis, so contents will undergo change.

For general readers and students, the website contains

- A timeline of key events,
- Analyses of major news developments,
- A list of heads of state for countries covered in the book.

On a chapter-by-chapter basis, the website provides

- Questions for review, and
- Suggestions for further reading and research.

For the region as a whole, the website also offers

- A compendium of sources for statistical data,
- A guide to internet resources, and
- A selection of primary documents.

In addition, we have created a special section for course instructors entitled "Teaching Modern Latin America." (Access to this directory will require a special password that can be easily obtained through the website itself.) This directory contains

- An essay on pedagogical challenges in teaching Latin America,
- Sample course syllabi, and
- A guide to instructional videos and films.

As we revise the website from time to time, we welcome suggestions for additions and revisions. Please click on the "suggestions" icon that appears on the home page. Our thanks in advance!

T.E.S.
P.H.S.
J.N.G.

Index